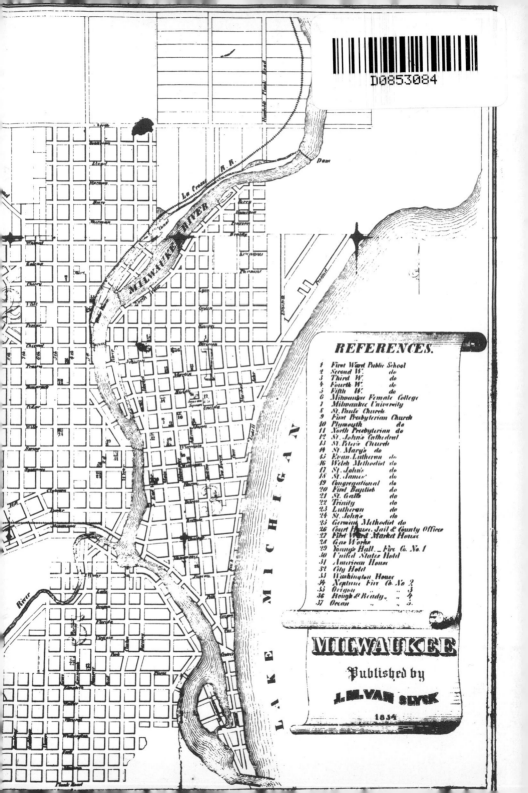

REFERENCES.

1 First Ward Public School
2 Second W.   do
3 Third W.   do
4 Fourth W.   do
5 Fifth W.   do
6 Milwaukee Female College
7 Milwaukee University
8 St. Pauls Church
9 First Presbyterian Church
10 Plymouth   do
11 North Presbyterian do
12 St. John's Cathedral
13 St. Peters Church
14 St. Mary's do
15 Evan. Lutheran do
16 Welch Methodist do
17 St. John's   do
18 St. James'   do
19 Congregational do
20 First Baptist   do
21 St. Galls   do
22 Trinity   do
23 Lutheran   do
24 St. John's   do
25 German Methodist do
26 Court House, Jail & County Offices
27 First Ward Market House
28 Gas Works
29 Youngs Hall. _ Fire Co. No 1
30 United States Hotel
31 American House
32 City Hotel
33 Washington House
34 Neptune Fire Co. No 2
35 Oregon   ,,   ,, 3
36 Rough & Ready ,, ,, 4
37 Ocean   ,,   ,, 5

MILWAUKEE

Published by

J. M. VAN SLYCK

1854

Regional History Series
of The American Jewish History Center
of The Jewish Theological Seminary of America

EDITORS

Salo Wittmayer Baron
Moshe Davis
Allan Nevins

Hebrew quotation

"And seek the peace of the city....
for in the peace thereof shall ye have peace."

ודרשו את שלום העיר
‏. . . .כי בשלומה יהיה לכם שלום.

(Jeremiah 29.7)

THE HISTORY OF
THE JEWS OF MILWAUKEE

Louis J. Swichkow *and* Lloyd P. Gartner

The Jewish Publication Society of America

5724   Philadelphia   1963

Preface

"AND SEEK THE PEACE OF THE CITY . . ."

(The Program of the American Jewish History Center)

THE AMERICAN JEWISH COMMUNITY developed primarily in cities. In the Colonial period when the Jews first immigrated in small numbers, they established themselves in Nieuw Amsterdam (before it become New York), in Newport, R. I., Savannah, Ga., Philadelphia, Pa., Charleston, S. C., Richmond, Va., and Montreal, Canada. In our time, while the estimated five and a half million Jews in the United States reside in cities and towns of varying sizes throughout the country, over four million, or some seventy-five per cent, are concentrated in twelve major American cities.

Urban life in America has brought continuing growth and change. Yet the continuity of religious, cultural and social institutions was not only maintained, but these institutions were strengthened. Despite the disintegrative effects of high mobility, impersonality in human relations, cultural assimilation, and the attenuation of traditional group ties, community solidarity prevailed; and American Jewry emerged as the largest and the most influential contemporary diaspora community. To describe and evaluate its growth in the urban setting is a central task for the historians of American Jewish life.

While there have been important advances in American Jewish historiography in the past two decades, the significance of Jewish communality in its urban and regional context has not been studied historically. Important studies on aspects of Jewish life are appearing in increasing number. General and Jewish historians are turning to American Jewish historical themes. Nevertheless, what Salo W. Baron accomplished in his comprehensive three-volume work on *The Jewish Community: Its History and Structure to the American Revolution* has not been essayed for modern American Jewish community life. Professor Baron himself pointed to the problem inherent in such an undertaking:

> ... What excuse can be offered for the neglect of scholarship in treating adequately Jewish communal life in the nineteenth and twentieth centuries, for which we have a superabundance of records? A really satisfactory solution of these difficulties will be found only when, through a large collective effort, a gigantic *corpus* of Jewish communal records covering all countries and periods is made accessible to general research. Such a *corpus* could open up, not only the vast material scattered in innumerable publications in a variety of languages, but also the enormous amount of sources still slumbering in manuscript form in the world's major libraries and archives. (*The Jewish Community* [Philadelphia, 1942], vol. III, note 12, pp. 5-6.)

An opportunity to undertake the kind of collective research envisaged by Professor Baron and others for the American Jewish community came in the following decade. In 1953, Professor Louis Finkelstein, Chancellor of the Jewish Theological Seminary of America, contemplated the creation of an American Jewish History Center, and asked me to outline a program for it. The suggested plan dealt with the need for communal and institutional histories and biographies, which might result in writing a basic history of Jews and Judaism in the United States. Materials from American as well as Jewish sources were to be gathered, in order to establish a proper scholarly basis for the interpretation of American Jewish life. As a first step it was suggested that a series of histories be prepared dealing with communities which span the country geographically and typify various phases of growth. Six diverse communities were proposed, subject to the availability of local scholars who would work with the Center and to sponsorship of the project within each community. They were Cleveland, Ohio; Milwaukee, Wisconsin; Los Angeles, California; the agricultural communities surrounding Vineland, New Jersey; Miami, Florida; and Montreal, P. Q., Canada.

The program was submitted to Professor Allan Nevins, who responded with great personal interest, and emphasized the contribution the Center could make to American history generally. He pointed to faults in existing histories of national stocks and religious groupings in the United States. In the first place, he stated, "the work has usually been done without any formulation of a careful plan, and without any comprehensive view of the field"; and secondly, "it has too often been either defensive in tone, or boastful in temper, those traits being two sides of the same quality. . . ." Professor Nevins expected that the volumes undertaken by the Center would reflect the history of the Jews as an integral part of the American people, showing how they participated and were changed by their participation in American society. After the basic plan was adopted, Professor Nevins agreed to serve as director with myself as co-director; Doctor Joseph Rapaport was appointed the first research associate. Later, Professor Baron agreed to join the Editorial Board of the projected Regional History Series.

The American Jewish History Center was created with the earnest understanding and support of Louis M. Rabinowitz, to whose memory this first volume is dedicated. Devotedly, he concerned himself with every facet of the Center's work. But the enterprise was more readily conceived than carried out. Objective and personal factors retarded progress. The much lamented passing of Louis Rabinowitz necessitated reorganization. Professor Simon Greenberg, Seminary Vice-Chancellor, and Sol Satinsky, leader in national and cultural affairs, rose to the task, giving new impetus to the Center's program. With Mr. Satinsky as chairman, a Board was formed for the Center including among its members Daniel G. Ross, Doctor Joel Geffen, Reuben Kaufman, Richard K. Manoff, Irving Neuman, William Salzman and Dore Schary. Doctor Gladys Rosen as Executive Associate, is responsible for the coordination of the Center's program.

The appearance of *The History of the Jews in Milwaukee* under the imprint of The Jewish Publication Society of America is a happy augury for the other volumes which are in varying stages of preparation. For many years, the Society has encouraged scholars to work in the field of American Jewish History and has published these works in its Schiff Library of Jewish Contributions to American Democracy. Dr. Solomon Grayzel, the Society's editor, who was intimately connected with those other works has also interested himself in the program of The American Jewish History Center.

The general aim of the Center is to combine local focus with national outlook. Thus the volume is a product of joint research and writing by Doctor Louis J. Swichkow, Rabbi of Beth El Ner Tamid Synagogue in Milwaukee and Doctor Lloyd P. Gartner, historian on the Center staff and on the faculty of the Teachers Institute-Seminary College of Jewish Studies. In this history, the reader will gain an insight into the substantive facts about the Milwaukee Jewish community and the city's impact on it, in the dual perspective of modern Jewish history and the growth of the American nation. More specifically, the student of Jewish life in America will discern several important emphases in research, chief among these being the utilization of the general American press for Jewish historiography. The basic source for Jewish history in the nineteenth century is the general press, which not only treats Jewish communal matters of the period fully but also demonstrates the relation of the Jews to the general community. Individual Jews are mentioned and Jewish business enterprise, activity and achievement are reported. For the economic, social and communal background of Jews and Jewish life, the general press is therefore even more valuable than the Jewish press of the period which is unavoidably limited in scope.

In addition, governmental materials were used in the study of housing and labor. They proved a vital resource especially for the 1890-1915 period when East-European Jews were a specifically demarcated group within their own sub-economy, neighborhood, labor unions, and other areas of American life. The papers of the Industrial Removal Office, a Jewish resettlement agency, show the extent of organized efforts of the established American Jewish community to spread Jewish immigrants throughout the country. This material has never been utilized for local history or even in

monograph studies on immigation. For example, from these records we can derive that each Jew sent by the Industrial Removal
Office to Milwaukee had a "multiplier" effect in bringing friends
and family to the city.

The distinctive character of the Jewish community in Milwaukee also emerges from the pages of this study. Like the city itself,
the Jewish community was largely influenced by German culture
and Socialism. The local economy and culture reveal the extent
of these influences. In terms of internal Jewish affairs, we note
the strength of Zionism and Yiddish culture and the relative weakness of Orthodoxy and Hebraism, essentially the result of environ-
mental forces. Finally, the genuine hospitality of the city itself is
marked; the Jews were rapidly accommodated in its midst. Even
with the unexpected advent of the first mass of East-European
immigrants to Milwaukee in 1882, the tone was set by Mayor
John M. Stowell:

> "To the People of Milwaukee:
> I learn that refugees from Russia, 350 in number, are hourly
> expected to be landed in our city. We must temporarily afford
> them sustenance and shelter until they can help themselves. . . ."

These new immigrants in time helped to shape the city's future,
as the German Jews who had preceded them had so effectively
pioneered in the building of Milwaukee. The record of the Jews
of Milwaukee has been collected in a special Louis J. Swichkow
Archive. In proper course, it will be catalogued with the archives
of the other city studies in progress and made available to scholars.
Thus a unique collection of materials from general and Jewish
sources will be created for future researchers and students in
American and Jewish history.

Through the interpretive volumes and archival collections, the
scholars associated with the American Jewish History Center may
well stimulate similar research by other scholars to explore the
distinctive development and interaction of the various religious
and ethnic communities within American cities. The cumulative
results of these stuides should eventually make possible a new and

deeper understanding of the history of the American people. Within the scope of its program, the Center hopes to find a way to interpret the impact of America on Jewish life and to indicate the significance of the American Jewish experience for the world Jewish community.

Moshe Davis

Jerusalem
Erev Pesach, 5723
April, 1963

Acknowledgments

WE WISH to express our appreciation to many individuals and institutions for their generous assistance in the preparation of this volume.

Our editors, Professors Salo W. Baron, Moshe Davis, and Allan Nevins, combined their unequalled learning with much patience and wisdom. Dr. Gladys Rosen, Executive Associate of the American Jewish History Center, was constantly efficient and thoughtful.

Our thanks are due to Mr. Max Weinschenk for his kind help in the translation of German manuscript material in the archives of Congregation Emanu-El B'ne Jeshurun; Mr. Irving G. Rhodes, who opened to us the complete files of *The Wisconsin Jewish Chronicle*, of which he is publisher; the late Isador S. Horwitz, editor and publisher of the *Milwaukee Wochenblat*, for the files of his publication; the Wisconsin State Historical Society; Mr. Peter McCormick, Coordinator of General Materials and Services of the Milwaukee Public Library, and his staff; Mr. Jack Schweers of the Milwaukee Municipal Reference Library; the American Jewish Archives of the Hebrew Union College—Jewish Institute of Religion, Cincinnati; the College of Jewish Studies, Chicago; Miss Lillian Friedman and Mr. Herman A. Mosher, for records of Congregation Emanu-El B'ne Jeshurun, as well as the other archives in its possession; and to the Home for the Aged, the Hebrew Sheltering Home, and the Milwaukee Chapter of Hadassah.

Institutions in New York City provided materials of unique value. For this we are grateful to Mr. Abraham Berger, Chief of the Jewish Division, New York Public Library, and Mr. Norman Gechlik; Mr. Ezekiel Lifschutz, Archivist of the YIVO Institute for Jewish Research; Miss Frieda Ramm, Librarian of the Council of Jewish Federations and Welfare Funds; Rabbi Isidore S. Meyer, American Jewish Historical Society; and Messrs. (now Rabbis) Sylvan D. Kamens, Daniel Leifer, Alan Lovins, and Stanley Urbas of The Jewish Theological Seminary of America. We were well served by our secretaries at the Seminary, Miss Francine Schnitzer Mrs. Aroline Rabinowitz, and Miss Hinda Rotenberg.

We are grateful to numerous persons who accorded us friendly access to records of Jewish institutions, as well as to family papers, and supplied pertinent information on Milwaukee Jewish history: Miss Rebecca B. Tenenbaum, Executive Director of the Jewish Family and Children's Service; Mr. Melvin S. Zaret, Executive Director of the Milwaukee Jewish Welfare Fund; Mr. Sidney H. Sayles, former Executive Director of the Milwaukee Jewish Council; Mrs. Ned Alpert, Dr. Louis W. Blumenthal, Bert C. Broude, Sam Dorfman, Joseph Friebert, Ben Z. Glass, Mr. and Mrs. Walter Goldsmith, Dr. Eugene C. Heifetz, Robert A. Hess, Henry Kahn, William Kay, Mrs. George Keller, Paul Lichter, Miss Ida Lisberg, Paul Moskowitz, Max Orenstein, Mrs. Louis Perchonok, John A. Post, the late Joseph Saffro, Benjamin F. Saltzstein, Amram Scheinfeld, Hyman M. Seidelman, Meyer Tarnow, I. Tuchman, Dr. Herman Weil, Ben J. Wiener, Morris Weingrod, Howard Weinshel, Aaron Weiss, David S. Wollach; and the friendly cooperation from the members of the Milwaukee Rabbinate.

Our special thanks are due to the Beth El Ner Tamid Sisterhood for their warm-hearted cooperation.

Finally, we wish to convey our gratitude to a group of friends, headed by Morris J. Okrent, who defrayed expenses connected with local research on this volume: Israel Afram, Dr. Lew R. Dubin, Harry N. Forman, Alex Himmelman, Max Kohl, Abner E. Kops, Rudy Kuper, the late Joseph Levin, Charles Lubotsky, Alvin A. Muchin, Dr. A. L. Natenshon, Jack Pessin, John A. Post, Judd Post, Louis Radin, Victor Resnick, Lionel Rosenberg, Leo Sedlet, Markus Shapiro, Michael Shapiro, A. L. Skolnik, Milton Soref, and Benjamin A. Stein.

To all of these persons, and to many others too numerous to enumerate, we are sincerely grateful.

Louis J. Swichkow
Lloyd P. Gartner

Contents

Preface: "And Seek the Peace of the City . . ."
by Moshe Davis   vii
Acknowledgments   xiii
Maps and Illustrations   xvii

PART ONE: *Pioneering Years 1844-1870*

     Prologue   3
 I From Fur Trading Post to Commercial Center   6
II Founding a Jewish Community   31

PART TWO: *Years of Growth 1870-1925*

   I Introduction: Growth in Population and Ideas   63
  II Immigration from Eastern Europe   69
 III The Native Community: Economic and Social
       Stability   93
 IV Civic Security and Public Service   128
  V Immigrant Trades and Streets   155
 VI Naturalized Judaism and Immigrant Piety (1870-
       1900)   169
 VII Religious Tradition and Communal Purpose
       (1900-1925)   200
VIII From Charity to Welfare   215

IX   The Challenge of Ideas: Zionism and Socialism
       (1890-1925)   235
 X   Education for Career and Community   257
XI   World War I: A Time of Hope and Grief   268

PART THREE: *Generation of Crises 1925-1950*

     Introduction   289
 I   Safety amid Tension   292
II   The Jewish Community Consolidates   309
III Milwaukee Jewry's Expanded Horizon   345

     Abbreviations   356
     Notes   357
     Bibliography   441
     Appendices   463
     Index   521

Maps and Illustrations

Map of Milwaukee, 1854 (*City Directory*), front end paper
View of Milwaukee, 1853 Lithograph, facing page 76

Pioneer Settlers, facing page 77

Elias Friend (1824-1890)
David Adler (1821-1905)
Max Landauer (1837-1924)
Adolph W. Rich (1843-1917)

Rabbis of Milwaukee, facing page 108

Victor Caro (1856-1912)
Charles S. Levi (1868-1939)
Samuel Hirshberg (1869-1954)
Solomon I. Scheinfeld (1860-1943), age 80

Early Synagogues, facing page 109

Temple Emanu-El, 1872
B'ne Jeshurun, 1886

Later Immigrants' Synagogues, facing page 140

Beth Israel, Fifth Street (1901)
Anshe Sfard, Sixth Street (1908)
Anshe Lubavich, N. 11 Street & Reservoir (1925)

Immigrant Life, facing page 141

>   Tenements in the Jewish district, *ca.* 1905
>   Outing of the Poale Zion Folk Shule, July 16, 1916

From Settlement to Community Center, facing page 172

>   Settlement House, Fifth Street
>   Abraham Lincoln House, Ninth Street (1911)
>   Jewish Community Center on Lake Michigan (1954)

Mrs. Kander's Golden Cook Book, facing page 173

>   Mrs. Lizzie (Simon) Kander
>   The Ninth Edition, published in 1915

Mount Sinai Hospital, facing page 204

>   Old Mount Sinai, 1904
>   Enlarged Mount Sinai, 1922
>   New Wing of Mount Sinai, 1956

Notables of the 20th Century, facing page 205

>   Charles L. Aarons
>   Joseph A. Padway
>   A. L. Saltzstein
>   Charles Friend

Conservative and Reform Judaism, facing page 236

>   Temple Emanu-El B'ne Jeshurun
>   Beth El-Ner Tamid Synagogue, 1951

Glimpses of the Cultural Scene, facing page 237

>   Peretz Hirschbein Folk Theatre
>   A Scene from "Hershele Ostropoler"
>   Beth El-Ner Tamid combined choirs in annual concert:
>   (Beth El Ner Tamid Synogogue)

A mass meeting of the Milwaukee Jewish Welfare Fund campaign, Milwaukee Auditorium, June 3, 1940, facing page 268

Against the Stream in Politics and Culture, facing page 269

Ephraim E. Lisitzky, Hebrew poet and educator
Victor L. Berger, socialist
Alter Esselin, Yiddish poet

Milwaukee Jewish Publications, facing page 300

Der Zeitgeist, January 1, 1880
Wisconsin Jewish Chronicle, 1921

Communal Buildings of the 1920's, facing page 301

Beth Israel, dedicated 1925
Jewish Home for the Aged, 1930

Map of Milwaukee, 1950 (*Municipal Reference Library*), rear end paper

PART ONE

Pioneering Years
1844 - 1870

Prologue

A GROUP of people who came off a boat in New York harbor in October, 1849, caught the eye of the editor of the New York *Jewish Chronicle*. They differed from the thousands of immigrants who were arriving every month:

> A number of highly respectable families have arrived in New York from Bohemia, to form a colony in Wisconsin. There have been for several years past many families from the same country in the neighborhood of Milwaukee; but the present party mean to establish a congregation at once, and they came provided with teachers and other necessary officers to carry their intentions into effect.[1]

Two important facts are here to be noted: first, that the Milwaukee area had already attracted "many families" of Bohemian and German Jews, and, second, that an effort at group migration was being made in 1849. This particular group soon broke up, though some members may have found co-religionists to welcome them. Earlier, in 1848 a Jewish family consisting of Bernard Heller, his wife, and their two small children had been "received royally at the depot by a former friend, Mr. B. Schram, and were taken to his house. . . ." Schram had supposed that Heller was as rich as he had been in Bohemia, and quickly cooled when he found this was untrue. Sophia Heller Goldsmith later recalled that "the first twenty-five dollars they had saved built a small frame cabin of two rooms. It was on Sixth Street near Chestnut. In the rear was a high hill on which the Indians still resided in their tents. Sister Carolina played with the papoose. We lived in that house for about two years."[2]

Other Jews were on hand or soon arrived. Henry Stern, after two years of business in America, decided to go to Milwaukee in 1850 with his partner. Taking a large stock, he relates, we

arrived on the sixth of August, 1850 and landed at the south pier, for no railroad existed at that time. We rented the first story of the building at 379 East Water Street, consisting of a room twenty-four by eighteen feet, and a smaller side room without windows, which we used as a bedroom. Beneath us and above us was Edward D. Baker's storeroom for whiskey and liquors. We boarded at the house of Mrs. Ramsom on Huron Street, and paid $1.75 per week.[3]

Such were the beginnings of Jewish settlement in Milwaukee, where the Menomonee, Kinnickinnic, and Milwaukee Rivers join each other to flow into Lake Michigan, and form a fine inland harbor.

The region that became the state of Wisconsin had a complex political history long before white men settled it. Bourbon France surrendered it to the British in 1759. After the American Revolution it became part of the Northwest Territory, and as this was broken up it was incorporated in Michigan Territory. A series of treaties with the Indians between 1829 and 1833 opened all the lands along the western shore of Lake Michigan for white settlement. They filled up so rapidly that in 1836 Wisconsin was organized as a separate territory. Settlers poured in through ports of entry at Milwaukee and Green Bay, and through the mining country in the Territory's southwest.

Meanwhile, the French-Canadian fur trader Solomon Juneau had arrived at the three rivers' junction, and founded Juneautown. The preemptive rights which he acquired to the waterfront he sold in part to two Yankee land promoters, Morgan L. Martin and Byron Kilbourn, who laid elaborate plans and invested thousands of dollars to prepare for an urban settlement. As elsewhere in the opening West, the land boom of 1833-1836 led to the collapse of 1837. Some six hungry years passed before the settlement again established itself, now permanently, as a Western city. Out of the union of Juneautown and Kilbourntown sprang the rising city of Milwaukee.[4]

From Fur Trading Post

to Commercial Center

MILWAUKEE's earliest beginnings were commercial: specifically, the American Fur Company's Indian trade. Its local agent, Solomon Juneau, had received his supplies through the Company's factors at Mackinac or Detroit. By 1836, the Company allowed Juneau to sell commodities to white immigrants.[5] Before long, however, pioneer merchants in the village were importing merchandise from Chicago and the east,[6] and there were a few grocery shops, saloons and general stores.[7] Each Milwaukee store displayed the sign of its wares: the tobacconist's wooden Indian, the fur dealer's stuffed bear, "the large teakettle," the "horse and trunk," and the "golden hoopskirt."[8]

Approaches to Milwaukee village in the 1830's were crude and undependable. There were three overland trails from Chicago north to Milwaukee. But to go west from the new town one had to travel through heavy timber land, and it took four days from Milwaukee up to Green Bay via two regularly traveled trails.[9]

While railroads were not laid until the 1850's, after unsuccessful attempts in 1836 and 1838, the construction of a harbor began in 1843 with Federal funds.[10] By 1845, vessels plying Lake Michigan daily touched the village's wharves, as did the steamers bringing immigrants and goods from Buffalo.

Merchants needed the port, while farmers built necessary roads

by private subscription to replace trails. There was a road to Fond
du Lac in 1841 and one to Muskego which drew trade away from
Racine to Milwaukee.[11] Plank roads were also built at private expense.[12]

Land business boomed after Juneau, Martin and Kilbourn had
purchased the townsite properties. The price of quarter-acre lots
shot up to an absurd $500 and $600, and Milwaukee land could be
bought in 1835 from speculators in various parts of the country.[13]
When Increase Lapham came to Milwaukee in 1836, he found its
fifty houses and 1,208 people a nucleus of intense activity. He
must have been amazed to find town lots fetching up to $5,000.[14]
Enormous rents were paid, even for permission to sell goods on
vacant lots. "Speculators went to bed at night hugging themselves
with delight over the prospect that the succeeding morning would
double their wealth."[15]

The Western land boom, of which Milwaukee was part, collapsed by the end of 1836, and the depression struck the new city
hard. By May 1837, new arrivals came penniless,[16] and lots which
had fetched $500 to $1,000 were traded for a barrel of flour to
prevent starvation.[17] Not until 1843 were the "land fever" and its
aftermath past, and new streams of immigration flowing in. By
that year, about 3,000 persons already lived in Milwaukee,[18] and
the growth of the city was set on a sounder basis.

Institutions of government grew apace. Milwaukee had rudimentary village government until its incorporation as a city on
January 31, 1846, and the first election for a Mayor and Council
took place on April 7, 1846.[19] Public services long remained
primarily an individual responsibility, with volunteers supplying
fire and police protection. Even after incorporation, neighborhood cleavages remained so pronounced that the city government
was a sort of municipal confederation that allowed each ward to
undertake improvements for itself. It was with difficulty that fire
protection was organized on city, rather than ward, lines.[20]
During the 1850's, leading businessmen still served in volunteer
fire companies and as special policemen to prevent looting during
blazes.[21] By 1870, however, regular police protection, a semi-
professional fire department and a city-wide Board of Public

Works to develop streets and sewers were supplanting voluntary effort.[22]

An Expanding City's Economy

The expanding city's economy was based at first on agricultural produce, delivered overland and shipped out on the inland seas of the Great Lakes. Despite shortage of credit and wildcat banking practices, Milwaukee's aggressive merchants succeeded in giving Chicago effective competition.[23] The wheat trade was the leading business of the city. It grew especially after railroads linked Milwaukee with its hinterland, and individual traders' purchases from individual farmers were replaced with organized buying carried on by commercial organizations.[24]

Milwaukee first traded with the hinterland for the city's own consumption. However, by the early 1840's a marketable farm produce existed. It depended on inland transportation to reach the port of Milwaukee.[25] As its village era closed in 1846, Milwaukee was exporting to the East and to Canada wheat, flour, barley, corn, lead, wool, hides, furs, and other items.[26] Warehouses opened all along its water front, and commission firms were channeling the trade. The flour milling industry was established early in Milwaukee's history, and a slaughter and packing house was built in 1852.[27] In 1857 and 1858, the first modern grain elevators were built to receive wheat in bulk, and that trade reached its peak in Milwaukee during the Civil War period. However, in the 1870's Milwaukee lost its domination of the wheat trade. Chicago's railroad route to Eastern markets was superior, and the wheat fields themselves were moved farther Northwest.[28]

Retail merchants saw opportunities in Milwaukee. Businessmen like the partners Julius Goll and Henry Stern peddled their goods through the countryside, making circuits lasting two or three weeks.[29] As the hinterland expanded during the 1850's, wholesale houses grew to do almost $17,000,000 of business in 1856.[30] By 1860, Milwaukee merchants grasped much of the Northwest's trade, especially in Iowa and northern Illinois. Milwaukee also attained a fair degree of commercial specialization, with all professions represented in its population.[31] Early manufacturing, however, was small-scale and rudimentary, limited to articles for home consumption. The production of clothing and footwear, largely for local consumption, was a relatively major industry in which Jews were very numerous. Milwaukee bricks of excellent quality began to be made as early as 1835, giving the city its name the "Cream City" because of their peculiar color.[32] Friction matches constituted the most specialized production of this period.[33] Ale was brewed as early as 1840, and the city's celebrated German lager beer first flowed in 1841.[34] The other trades and services required in a city also appeared—mechanics, bricklayers, blacksmiths, hoteliers, horse dealers, and various others.

The Civil War, which closed the Mississippi—Gulf of Mexico route to the eastern seaboard powerfully stimulated Middle Western industry. The expansion of railroads and the increasing farm population created a demand for iron products and machinery which Milwaukee's skilled and growing citizenry was to meet in the post-Civil War years.

MILWAUKEE PEOPLE

Milwaukee's population grew from 2,700 in 1842 to 9,655 in 1846; by 1850, it was 20,061. Heavy immigration, especially from Europe, caused this rapid growth. "The immigration during the present year 1848, promises to exceed that of any previous Season. From all parts of the Old, and many of the Eastern states in the New World, there is a steady and swelling current of population towards Wisconsin."[35] The years following 1848 surpassed its record.

The earliest German immigrants began to arrive in 1835. By the early 1840's, between 200 and 300 German immigrants were arriving weekly, and during the summers of 1843 and 1844 the figures reached 1,000 to 1,400.[36] Most of the Germans came from Rhenish Prussia, Bavaria, Luxemburg, Baden and Saxony, and underwent a long and fearful Atlantic voyage. As Henry Stern recalled: ". . . I had made a contract with a steerage passenger for

100 florins from Mayence by way of Rotterdam and Havre to New York . . . Our ship, the Elizabeth Hamilton, had about 300 steerage passengers, all of whom were placed in one room—with three in one berth covered with straw, and two berths together, one over the other. We all had our own bedding with us, and suffered only from the terrible odor . . . Leaving Havre on June 20, 1850, we reached New York on August 16, having had nothing to live on for the last two weeks except hardtack and rotten water. . . ."[37] Their usual route from New York ran by steamboat to Albany, to Buffalo by train, and from Buffalo to Milwaukee by steamboat and rail. Eight days were required for this journey, until the New York—Chicago railroad reduced it to four.[38]

In 1845, about one-third of its inhabitants had come from Germany, yet at that time Milwaukee was still known as a "Yankee-Yorker" village, settled primarily by people from New England and New York. The next few years imposed an enduring ethnic pattern, for in 1850 approximately 64 percent of Milwaukee's population was of foreign birth, more than a third of which was German.[39] Although the foreign-born decreased to 47 percent in 1870, natives of Germany remained at a third of the population.[40] With their children they constituted a large majority of Milwaukee's inhabitants.

Letters and articles by German-Americans, emphasizing Wisconsin's fertile soil, the presence of a German Catholic bishop, and optimistic letters from new immigrants to relatives and friends in Germany, all expressed enthusiasm and encouragement for prospective immigrants. Also, Milwaukee and the State itself were actively endeavoring to attract German settlers during the 1850's and 1860's. Another factor was the publicized sympathy of Milwaukee's German community for the revolutionary movement in Germany. This attracted "Forty-eighters" to Milwaukee in great numbers. Isaac Neustadtl, a Bohemian Jew, headed an association in Milwaukee for aiding political refugees.[41]

Next to the Germans, the Irish constituted a significant element of the population. These newcomers had also traveled long distances to Milwaukee. The depression in New England between 1839 and 1841 drove many Irish from that region, and others came from New York, Ohio, Chicago and St. Louis.[42] In time, the Irish, like the Germans, exerted wide influence in municipal and State political affairs. Other ethnic groups also found homes in Milwaukee during its village years.[43]

In 1804, years before Solomon Juneau erected his cabin, agents of Jacob Franks, an English Jew and a fur trader in Green Bay, were trading with the Milwaukee Indians.[44] Jews actually settled in the early 1840's,[45] and they first appear in the Wisconsin *Territorial Census* of 1846 (June).[46]

Among the earliest Jewish immigrants who settled in Milwaukee in 1844 were the brothers Myer, Emanuel, Gabriel, Samuel, William and Charles Shoyer; Moses Weil, Isaac Neustadtl, and Solomon Adler.[47] By 1850, at least seventy Jewish families lived in Milwaukee; by 1852, one hundred families; and by 1856, a Jewish community of about two hundred families existed. Emma Herbst, the first Jewish child born in Milwaukee, entered the world on September 16, 1849.[48]

These Jews came during the heyday of German immigration to the United States, between 1845 and 1857. Their reasons for quitting Germany were above all economic—they could not make a living under the restrictions which lay upon them, and the depression of the 1850's made matters worse. Their legal burdens grew more intolerable as German Jews became thoroughly Germanized, and bitter disillusionment set in following the suppression of the Revolution of 1848, and its aftermath. Only a tiny fraction of Jewish immigrants had actually fought in 1848, but the hope of that year and the disappointment which followed permeated the Jewish communities. The Austrian-Bohemian "On to America" movement heightened Bohemian Jewish immigration to the United States after 1848. Out of forty-seven Jewish newcomers who arrived between 1844 and 1855, twenty-four came from Germany (Bavaria, Brunswick, Baden, Prussia, Hesse, Württemberg), twenty from various parts of Bohemia, Hungary, and Austria, two from France and one from England.[49] The Wisconsin *State Census* of 1855, which listed residents by wards, shows that most known Jews had been living in the Second Ward's "German town."[50]

"German town," spreading over the Second, Sixth and Ninth wards, was a community displaying "German houses, German inscriptions over the doors or signs, German physiognomies."[51] In 1850, its residents contained a large majority of craftsmen and skilled workers who made a major contribution to the city's growth. There was no vagrancy among these early Germans, and their domestic habits were widely admired.[52]

Wisconsin's liberal suffrage encouraged foreign immigrants by giving the vote after one year's residence. Both Germans and Irish generally adhered to the Democratic Party in these years.[53] Not only could the Germans participate in public life on a par with natives, but they energetically transplanted their cultural and social life to Milwaukee. Germans formed their own debating societies, lodges, schools, and newspapers, and even German fire and military companies. They were slow to inter-marry with the natives.[54] In this generation of Milwaukee's history, the Jews formed a section of the German community.

All Milwaukeeans had festival and holiday celebrations with parties, balls, and parades. Important events were celebrated by ringing bells and kindling bonfires. The populace delighted in skating, horseracing and, during the winter, sleighing. By the end of the 1860's, organized baseball was very popular and stirred the enthusiasm of the public, including usually staid lawyers, doctors and clergymen.[56]

JEWS IN THE COMMERCIAL LIFE OF THE COMMUNITY

Jews actively participated in Milwaukee's commercial life and contributed heavily to the early commercial and industrial development of the city. They were represented among the grain dealers and were pioneer Great Lakes shippers. As elsewhere on the Western frontier, Jewish peddlers and merchants were prominent, while Jewish manufacturers clothed most of Milwaukee and its outlying districts. There were also numerous Jews among the professionals who settled in Milwaukee, and among tradesmen and craftsmen as well.

The pioneer Jewish entrepreneurs from Bavaria had acquired German and vocational education during their youth. Unwilling to remain subject to restrictions on the right to marry, settle, or practice the trades which they had learned, large families of Bavarian Jews came to America between the 1840's and 1870, generally one or two sons at a time. Their stories fell into distinct stages: country peddling; clerking in an elder brother's or near-family business (often combined with commercial studies); independent business out of town, or a subordinate partnership in the family firm; return to town as an independent entrepreneur, or in an equal partnership. The family-run business frequently expanded in order to include brothers-in-law and sons-in-law.

Many Milwaukee Jews never became entrepreneurs. Jews worked in the clothing establishments, mainly at upper levels of skill, as pattern makers and cutters. Some Jews were cigar makers, and many remained in clerical or technical positions. But independent business was the ideal of the immigrants who constituted Milwaukee Jewry during the first generation of its history, and a majority probably reached this status.

Milwaukee's first Jewish business firm was that of the Shoyer brothers. As early as April, 1845, Emanuel M. Shoyer operated as a merchant tailor. The fire which destroyed $90,000 in property and left "two whole squares in ruins," left him with a loss of $150. But he recovered quickly. By 1850, E. M. Shoyer & Co. expanded quarters and soon Emanuel, Gabriel, William, Samuel and Mayer Shoyer entered the business. After many ups and downs, their business passed into receivership in October, 1861.[56] Other clothing merchants who established themselves in these early years were H. Newhouse and Company, doing business in 1847 at 200 East Water and offering "fashionable clothing . . . coats, vests, shirts, hosiery, suspenders." Aaron Blade and Victor Simon sold ready-made clothing at 190 East Water Street.[57] Benjamin Zellner and Henry Bonns established their "U.S. Clothing House" at 106 East Water, in 1851, and enlarged it in 1856. In July, 1861, they made 500 uniforms for the Seventh Wisconsin Volunteers.[58]

One of the most successful clothing businesses was that of the Adler brothers, which lasted over eighty years. Three brothers

Adler—Solomon, David, and Jacob—were in and out of it, before the second generation entered the firm.

Solomon Adler settled in Milwaukee village in 1844 and entered the clothing trade with Jacob Steinhart in 1847. Steinhart and Adler at 120 East Water Street advertised "ready made clothing—coats, collars, vests, shirts," and continued as partners until 1851. Solomon Adler's brother David came in 1852 and opened a clothing store with $1500 which he had accumulated over five years as an immigrant baker in New York. In 1857, David Adler bought out brother Solomon, whose volume had reached between $15,000 and $30,000 per year. David then entered into a partnership with his brother, Jacob, as D. and J. Adler, and they shifted to wholesale trade. This partnership continued until 1860, when Solomon repurchased Jacob's interest. As S. Adler and Bro., the firm prospered greatly during the Civil War, with sales in one year reaching as high as $600,000. One contract was for manufacturing 12,000 Army uniforms.

After the Civil War, the Adlers retrenched. In 1870 the partnership was terminated when Solomon Adler withdrew and, after an extended trip to Germany, moved to New York City. In 1871, the firm became Adler, Mendel & Co. H. M. Mendel and Isaac D. Adler (son-in-law and son of David Adler) were admitted, and Solomon Adler remained as special partner. Sales reached $800,000 in a single year, prior to the panic of 1873.[59]

Emanuel Silverman, brother-in-law to the Adlers by marriage to their sister Peppi, also prospered in the clothing business. His $5,000 capital, accumulated as a peddler in Maine, enabled him to enter the business, and he grew big in it.[60]

The Adler firm was matched in size only by H. Friend and Brothers, founded by Henry and Elias Friend, who came from Autenhausen, Bavaria to the United States in 1840. They arrived in Milwaukee and opened their clothing store in 1847, and brother Meyer joined them in 1848. By 1853, with a retail and wholesale business and branches in Madison and Winona, they did a $50,000 business. In 1869, 400 men and women worked for H. Friend and Brothers, and the firm possessed a capital of $400,000.[61] Probably five of Milwaukee's fourteen tailors and clothiers in 1862 were Jewish.[62]

W. L. and John Hart boasted in June, 1848 that their new dry goods store had "the largest, most fashionable and varied stock of Ladies and Gentlemen's fancy dress goods ever offered before in this western country"; prices were "unprecedentedly low and for cash only, and no second price. . . ."[63] Dry goods was a family business for some early Jewish settlers such as the Macks. Herman S. Mack, a 14-year old Bavarian immigrant in 1849, clerked four years for his brothers in Milwaukee and then became their partner. The Mack brothers advertised their "superb establishment . . . brightly illuminated, there is no handsomer, or more convenient store in the West, and few superior to it anywhere." The company grew and flourished. In 1867, brothers Lewis and Max quit the city, and Herman Mack's new partner was another brother, Hugo, an immigrant of 1854.[64]

Henry Stern and his Gentile partner Julius Goll came to Milwaukee in 1850, "principally because the German immigration was directed there at that time." With $1,800 between them, they had paid $1,200 down on a $5,000 stock of dry goods, clocks, mirrors, and the like, and peddled them about the countryside by horse and wagon.[65] Goll and Stern separated in 1852, and Stern joined his brother Herman in forming H. Stern, Jr. and Brother.[66] Their $4,000 capital in 1852 reached $31,000 in 1860 and $70,000 in 1862.[67]

Alongside clothing and dry goods, such special fields as hats, caps and straw goods attracted young Jewish entrepreneurs. Henry M. Mendel, who came from Breslau to Milwaukee in 1854 at the age of fifteen, spent some years as a clerk and bookkeeper before he and Marcus Stein became successful wholesalers of hats, caps, and straw goods. This lasted until Mendel became David Adler's son-in-law and partner in 1871.[68]

Adolph W. Rich, one of the city's most interesting entrepreneurs, arrived from Hungary with his parents in October, 1853. They moved from New York to Cleveland in 1855, and to a farm in Saginaw County, Michigan, in 1857. Three years later Rich received from his father about $40 worth of goods, and started to peddle. Dissatisfied with this occupation, he worked his way to Detroit, then to Cleveland, and worked for six months on a farm at $12 per month. Eventually, he would become the patron of the Wisconsin Jewish agricultural movement. With $40 worth of spectacles, he set out as a traveling optician, arriving in Milwaukee in June, 1865. Rich hopefully put his $800 capital into an optical business with B. Gross, but failed. After paying liabilities, $450 remained.[69]

1867 was the decisive year for Rich. After another fruitless partnership,[70] he opened his own store. Women waited on women, a bold step in those days, and wares were advertised flamboyantly in the daily papers.[71] Within six years 20 employees worked in the store and 12 in the hoop skirt and corset factory.[72]

Many early Jewish settlers entered the food trades as a dependable means of livelihood. In 1848, Isaac Neustadtl and Nathan Pereles had their retail grocery on Third Street, but soon turned to other fields. Joseph Schram, a Bohemian immigrant, came from Boston to Milwaukee in 1846. He opened a grocery business in the same year and carried it on successfully for 26 years at one address.[73] G. Bremer & Co., the oldest grocery house in Milwaukee, was founded in 1850 by Joseph Bremer, a native of Gandersheim, in the Duchy of Brunswick.

Bernard Heller, Milwaukee's first sausage maker, came from Bohemia in 1848, aged 43, and cattle dealer Louis Frank, born in Bavaria in 1820, came to the United States in 1846 and founded a packing house in Milwaukee, where he arrived in 1851.[74]

On the Western frontier, where money was scarce, the money trade developed more slowly than in the East. Jews like Neustadtl, Mack, and Bremer were associated with Milwaukee's insurance companies as early as the 1850's, a measure of their wealth and position within 10 years of arrival.[75] An immigrant community also generated foreign currency exchange. Thus, Bachman and Metz advertised themselves as "Bankers and Dealers in foreign exchange and passage," as did Jacob Mahler and C. E. Wendt. Milwaukee's first Jewish lawyer, Nathan Pereles, developed an extensive investment business. One Union Army unit of 23 men confided $805 to him "for distribution and investment."[76]

Great Lakes shipping was especially important to Milwaukee in early years, and notable pioneers of Lake Superior and Lake Michigan transportation were Leopold & Austrian.[77] Both families had come to America in 1845, and settled on the Island of Mackinac. The brothers Henry, Samuel, Lewis, and Aaron Leopold traded with the Indians and also bought up the fisheries' production to salt and ship to Cleveland.[78] From 1848, Henry F. Leopold did his business at the Indian trading post of La Pointe, on Lake Superior. In 1850, he moved to Eagle River, Michigan, where with his brother Samuel and brother-in-law Julius Austrian, he founded H. F. Leopold & Bros., specializing in mining supplies. In 1866, they moved from their towns in the Lake Superior region to Milwaukee, and organized the Lake Superior Navigation Company in 1868. Their fleet linked Milwaukee with the upper Michigan region, which they had done so much to develop.[79]

The number of Jews engaged in manufacturing in the early city was limited. However, Jews achieved fair success in the tobacco industry. Nic Simon was in the trade as early as 1847.[80] Solomon Roth, another tobacconist, arrived in the United States from Württemberg in 1854, at the age of 17. He and his older brother Moses soon left Philadelphia for Milwaukee, and later brought over their mother, two sisters, and brother. After stints as a peddler, bookkeeper, and county storekeeper, Solomon Roth began to pack leaf tobacco, an important item in the agriculture of southern Wisconsin. His trade reached far out to Wyoming, where he sent the first tobacco shipment via Union Pacific Railway.[81] Other Jews followed Roth in making tobacco products.[82]

Jews were only lightly represented in the professions. There were no Jews among Milwaukee County's 136 lawyers in 1854.[83] The first Jew admitted to the bar in Milwaukee was Nathan Pereles, who had come to America from his native Bohemia in 1845, aged 21. His American beginnings resembled those of his fellow immigrants, until he began to lend money in connection with real estate transactions. Pereles presently gave up his grocery and dry goods business, read law in the office of a leading local attorney, and was admitted to the bar on September 11, 1857.[84] After twelve years in partnership, he founded his own firm in

1869.[85] Four other Milwaukee Jews followed Nathan Pereles into the law during this period.[86]

Dr. Charles C. Shoyer, the first practicing Jewish physician in Milwaukee (1851), was followed in 1862 by Dr. Louis Adler, a Bohemian trained at the University of Vienna. He had been a military physician for fifteen years before he emigrated and established a law practice in Milwaukee. In the arts, Theodore Schoenfeld, who completed his musical education at Berlin, taught music in the city for many years beginning in 1854.[87]

As early as August, 1856, when he first visited Milwaukee, Isaac Mayer Wise described the material condition of its Jews with heartfelt satisfaction:

> Milwaukee is a fine place . . . West of the Milwaukee River is the new town, increasing daily by the influx of immigration, and the building of new houses. The location of the city is charmingly beautiful, and its rapid growth is almost incredible. The German element predominates, enterprise and business show themselves in busy motions in the streets, and the constant whistling of coming and parting locomotives and steam boats.
>
> The condition of our Jewish brethren is so far a happy one, that none of them is actually poor or subsisting on charity, many of them do an extensive business in real estate, grain, cattle, provision, dry goods, clothing, groceries, etc., and there is no small number of wealthy men among the two hundred families of Israelites living there. Among the manufacturers Berliner and Brunner must be noticed, who have an extensive iron safe factory . . . every body is deeply interested in the progress and growth of the city, as everyone almost owns some real estate, . . . the Jews are respected as industrious, peaceful and law abiding citizens.[88]

Conditions in succeeding years would not have diminished his pleasure.

JEWS IN CIVIC AFFAIRS

Prior to the nineteenth century, opportunities for Jews in the meager civic life of German countries were virtually nonexistent. In Milwaukee, however, Jews participated without inhibition in local politics. In contrast to many later immigrant groups, Milwaukee's German Jews were not unconcerned spectators, but considered themselves participants and beneficiaries. The size of Milwaukee Germandom, of which they were part, offered the Jews ample political possibilities, and made their relative foreignness more an asset rather than a liability. Like liberal free-thinking Germans, and unlike conservative Catholic Germans, they frequently became Republicans. Mercantile self-interest also moved Jews into the new party. However, only one of the city's sixteen mayors between 1846 and 1870 was not a Democrat, although some conservative Democrats were elected on a coalition "People's" ticket with Whig or, subsequently, Republican votes.[89] "Regular" Democrats maintained control by their appeal to the foreign-born and their popularity with the working class.[90] Since elections were held annually, the issues of municipal government were constantly before the people.

Jewish Republican participants in local politics came from the merchants and liberal Germans. They included such men as Isaac Neustadtl, Nathan Pereles, Jacob Mahler, M. H. Schwarzenberg and Henry M. Mendel. On the other hand, Gabriel Shoyer was a "German Democrat," and Lewis S. Mack was well-known as a staunch Democrat. Major political offices were often held by commercial and professional figures in the community, and we find Jews as successful and unsuccessful candidates from their earliest years in the city.[91] Jewish aldermen included Isaac Neustadtl, one of the two city councilmen elected in the "German town" Second Ward (1852-53).[92] But in his campaigns as Republican candidate for County Treasurer in 1854 and J. P. in 1868, Neustadtl was defeated.[93] Others elected were M. Heiman, Ninth Ward (1857-58),[94] Lewis S. Mack, First Ward (1861-62), and Louis Rindskopf, Fourth Ward (1869-70).[95] Mack, a young man and a Democrat, was elected president of the Board of Aldermen at the beginning of his second year.[96] He also acted as Chairman of the County Board of Supervisors during 1861-1862.[97] The election of the Republican M. H. Schwarzenberg as Railroad Commissioner for the Ninth Ward, in 1860, moved the Milwaukee

Sentinel to hail this "result in a Ward where probably the majority are Catholics, as an evidence of the absence of religious prejudices from our elections."[98]

Members of the Jewish community were active within their parties. In the fateful election year of 1860, for example, Isaac Neustadtl served on a nominating committee for the Republican city convention. He was also a delegate to the Union Caucus of 1861. Jacob Mahler was a vice-president of the First Ward Republican Club (1860). The Fourth Ward Union Caucus chose Nathan Pereles as one of its two delegates to the County and Senatorial Convention with instructions "to vote for no man for United States Senator but those who are unconditional Union men and ready and willing to vote men and means to vigorously prosecute this war."[99] After the war, Pereles and Neustadtl represented the Sixth and First Wards respectively, at the city charter convention of 1867.[100] H. S. Mack's political reward was his appointment as Commissioner to the Paris Exposition of 1867.[101]

An adventurous politician was Baruch Schleisinger Weil (1802–1893), an Alsatian Jew who settled in Wisconsin in 1845.[102] Weil claimed that he was a successful merchant in Paris when he divorced his wife and came to America in 1843. He took up land speculation in Washington County with such success that in 1858, a depression year, Weil announced that his holdings were worth over $100,000.[103] His small town, originally named Polk, was renamed Schleisingerville.[104]

Weil's political activities ran concurrently with his land ventures. Selected to be a delegate to the State Democratic Convention in 1851, Weil was elected to the State Assembly in that year.[105] Next year, he easily won a seat in the State Senate[106] and was also chairman of the Board of Supervisors of the Town of West Bend.[107] Weil was a Democratic Presidential Elector in 1856,[108] and was re-elected to the State Senate in 1856 and 1857.[109] But his political downfall came in 1858. First, Weil's residence qualification was impugned. His fine home on Watertown Plank Road called into question his right to sit in the State Senate for a Milwaukee district.[110] Then charges were aired that he had deserted his first wife in Europe; to these, however, he effectively

gave the lie. But Weil had no answer to the Legislature committee's finding that he had accepted $25,000 in stock from the La
Crosse and Milwaukee Railroad in return for legislative favors.
If there could be a reply, it was that nearly the entire Senate
was as delinquent as he was.[111] Following this exposure, Weil
quit politics until 1870 when, at the age of 68, he returned to the
Assembly for a number of terms.[112]

Another Jew who had a checkered career in the frontier rough-
and-tumble of Wisconsin politics in the 1850's was Lion Silverman. Silverman came to Port Washington via Mansfield, Ohio,
and Milwaukee, where he had been a peddler and store-keeper.
After functioning three years as local postmaster, he was elected
as a Whig local sheriff in 1852.[113] He organized and commanded
a volunteer military company, the Washington Guards, with 43
members.[114] But Governor Leonard J. Farwell, in June, 1853,
removed Silverman from office as Sheriff, for illegally preventing the removal of public records from Port Washington to the
new county seat.[115] Notwithstanding that political reverse, he
continued to hold public office, and became a State Senator in
1858.[116]

Silverman's political career reached its climax in 1859, when
the Democrats nominated him for State Treasurer. The Democratic *News* described Silverman as "a leading businessman at Port
Washington and a hard-working democrat."[117] But not all Democrats were enthusiastic over their candidate, especially B. S.
Weil, a personal adversary. Democrats in Weil's town of
Schleisingerville accused Silverman of having spent money to
obtain his nomination. Their resolution recalled that "through a
former State Treasurer, we have seen the German name [sic]
disgraced; this must not occur a second time. . . ."[118] Silverman
ran behind his ticket throughout the State, including his own
county, and lost by 12,000 votes. If Silverman was looked upon as
a German during the campaign, the "Jewish" issue was injected
after Election Day. The Democratic Madison *Patriot* maintained
that his own party defeated Silverman because he was a Jew, a
view asserted by the defeated candidate himself. Said the *Patriot*:

. . . We believe him to be a good, an honorable, and a fair businessman. His general fitness and character were known and understood by the Convention that nominated him, but that Convention never dreamed that his reported religious antecedents would be brought in question. But in this the misfortune consisted. He was charged with being a Jew, and his Protestant and Catholic countrymen voted against him almost to a man on that account. As the Democratic creed fully tolerates all religious sentiments, no one thought of making that a test until it was too late to remedy the matter, and Mr. Silverman was brought forth to the slaughter without reserve or compunction on the part of his political and religious opponents.[119]

The Republican *Sentinel* added that "Mr. Silverman was opposed and defeated by the Sham-Democracy on account of his religious opinions. The much professing Democrats voted against him because he was a Jew! Was there ever a clearer case of prospective Know-Nothingism?"[120] But the Milwaukee *News* still insisted that Protestants and Catholics did not oppose Silverman as a Jew. Actually, Silverman was a weak "German Democrat" candidate who could not draw the German vote. After his defeat, Silverman managed a hotel at Port Washington.[121]

An immigrant of 1848 who achieved distinction as a United States diplomat in Mexico was Marcus Otterbourg of Milwaukee (1827-1893). Born in Bavaria, Otterbourg had lived in Paris and London before coming to the United States about 1850. He opened a vinegar distillery, but soon turned to politics.[122] Through his friendship with Carl Schurz, Otterbourg became a zealous Republican. His vain candidacy for Sergeant-at-Arms of the State Assembly in December, 1858 won him the *Sentinel's* endorsement as one whose success would give satisfaction to his "German fellow citizens."[123] Continuing his labors as a German journalist and orator for the Republican Party, Otterbourg became known as "a very graceful speaker" before German audiences.[124]

When Lincoln was elected, Otterbourg went to Washington as a news correspondent and, presumably, as an office seeker. The President's appointment of Otterbourg as Consul at Mexico City, on August 10, 1861, was greeted by factional opposition from a group of local German Republicans. With Isaac Neustadtl presiding, a remonstrance was adopted against his appointment as Consul to Mexico, "or to any other office in the government."[125] Otterbourg remained in Mexico City throughout the turbulent years of the Civil War and Mexico's period of French intervention, until 1867.[126] Afterwards, he and his family took up residence in New York, where he was a lawyer and politician until his death in 1893.

EQUAL RIGHTS

Enjoying full rights for the first time in their lives, the pioneer Jews of Milwaukee expressed their sensitivity to slurs upon them as a group. In 1858, when the Milwaukee *Daily News* referred to many "anxious Jews," at a police station, "so greatly excited" as witnesses and observers in a trial concerning a local row, an indignant citizen wrote to the *Sentinel*:

> . . . being withall a "Jew" myself, I should like to ask of the editor of that benighted paper, (the News,) what he means by saying a lot of "anxious Jews?" Does he wonder so much at seeing a Jew at the Police Station? (a thing which indeed so rarely occurs that the editor of the News thinks it is a treat for his readers, to inform them that for once they have found a Jew before the Police Court,) or do we live in the fifteenth century yet, to throw a stigma of hatred on the Jews? Are the "Jews" not as good a law-abiding body of citizens as the Gentiles? And why, when you try a drunken Irishman or German, does it not say, a squad of "anxious Catholics or Protestants" was found yesterday? . . . This shows too plainly that the old imported prejudices of the editor of the News have not all vanished yet. . . .[127]

Jews were militant in public protest when their character was defamed. In February, 1859, such an incident aroused the Jewish community. One litigant at a Circuit Court trial was a member "of the Mosaic persuasion," and a prominent local attorney, J. B. C. Cottrill, represented the opposing party. In addressing the jury, Cottrill proceeded "to abuse [the Jewish party] with the most insulting language, slandering him and his co-religionists." He allegedly asserted "that all Israelites, since 1800 years, made their living by stealing, lying, etc., and that what a Jew should state under oath, the jury should not believe . . . that all Jews have been branded thieves, liars, and swindlers, by all civilized nations; . . ." Simon Levy, attorney for the Jewish litigant, denounced Cottrill as "a public slanderer and liar," and called the attention of the judge, Arthur McArthur, to the insulting performance. A public meeting was promptly called for "the Israelites of this city and their friends" to vent their indignation "against the grievous offenses which lawyer J. B. C. Cottrill ventured to give to the character of the Israelites generally." The assemblage adopted resolutions declaring that:

> . . . as Jews and citizens of the United States, we feel that such conduct on the part of any attorney or any other person, is uncalled for, false, unjust, and slanderous against the whole Jewish nation, and intended to bring them into disrepute, and in all proper and suitable ways, use our best endeavors to oppose such men, and call on all respectable citizens to aid us in such honorable course . . .
>
> Resolved, that the Jews of Milwaukee will use all their efforts and influence against everyone who may attempt to depreciate their rights, on account of their Religious faith; and that they will use all legal means to maintain their rights as citizens of this glorious Republic . . .
>
> Resolved, that we shall ever hold in high estimation and respect the Honorable Arthur McArthur, for his high, dignified, and honorable course, in adverting to and condemning such conduct.[128]

Cottrill denied having made defamatory remarks but made it clear that he would continue to argue every case as he might deem essential to the interests of his clients.[129] Although he might again slander the Jews to help his case there is no record that he did.

Milwaukee Jewry also joined their fellow American Jews in the defense of Jewish rights abroad. The first case was posed by the

Swiss Treaty of 1855, which permitted the Swiss cantons to apply their restrictive or exclusionary policies against Americans who happened to be Jews. Protests were raised all over the country by Jews and Christians. Nevertheless, the treaty was ratified and went into force, and an American Jew soon fell victim to Basel Canton's discrimination. Equal rights for the Jews was supported editorially by such newspapers as the Milwaukee *Daily American*:

> If the people of England are now moving in earnest to blot out the last vestige of religious intolerance, surely the United States will not submit to any power demanding of any American citizen trading with or residing in a country that has commercial treaties with her, "what his religion is?" as the basis of citizenship or commercial relations . . .
>
> . . . it were better to notify the Swiss Confederation of the Treaty being annuled, rather than set an impolitic, dangerous and mischievous example to other nations whose antecedents towards the Israelites have been tyrannical and despotic, and who require but a Republican precedent to cloud the future of this scattered race with persecution and the imposition of further religious disabilities . . . ; the clause is a disgrace.[130]

The Jewish community of Milwaukee joined the wave of protest. They met at the B'ne Jeshurun synagogue on October 20 and 27, 1857, for the purpose of "considering the position of their brethren under the Swiss Treaty, and to elect a State Delegate to attend the convention at Baltimore, on the 28 of October, 1857." Resolutions asserted that "the said clause is unconstitutional, unjust and unworthy of our age, and therefore a disgrace to this our beloved Country."[131]

Soon after this first participation in problems affecting world Jewry, Milwaukee Jewry was drawn into the famous Mortara case of 1858. Edgar Mortara, a Jewish child in the Papal territory of Bologna, had been secretly baptized as an infant by his Catholic nurse. When she later informed the Holy Office of her act, the child was forcibly taken from his parents on the grounds that he was a "Catholic." When word of the episode reached the world, an international uproar resulted. Between October, 1858 and January, 1859, protest meetings were held in eighteen American cities. "Newspaper concern with the case was probably the broadest in any single Jewish matter between the establishment of newspapers in the first colonies and the Russian pogroms of the 1880's, or possibly the Dreyfus case."[132]

Unlike the case of the Swiss Treaty, Milwaukee opinion divided sharply; the Catholic press and others endorsed the Pope's position. The fate of Edgar Mortara became a topic of heated controversy between the Republican *Sentinel* and the Democratic *News*. The *Sentinel* carried no less than twenty-three articles dealing with it during November and December, 1858.[133] The *Sentinel* condemned the Catholic authorities, while the *News* questioned the accuracy of the reported facts. It considered the Republicans and the *Sentinel*, who were siding with the Jews, as "restless agitators." Thus the Mortara case was converted by the local press into a Protestant vs. Catholic issue for political warfare.[134]

A public indignation meeting had been planned in Milwaukee for "men of all creeds and political opinions." It was not held, however, perhaps because the Mortara case had become enmeshed in partisan politics. But Rabbi Isidor Kalisch did publicly attack "the Jesuits of the Catholic Milwaukee *Seebote*, which defended the kidnapping of the Mortara child."[135] He inquired how the Church could condemn the robbery of property yet sanction the robbery of a child from his parents.

The Civil War Years

None of the few dozen Jews who lived in Milwaukee at the time of the Mexican War served in that conflict, in which Wisconsin itself was inadequately represented. However, the state along with its Jews was fully drawn into the maelstrom of the Civil War, in which Wisconsin was a firm Union state.

When Lincoln issued his first call for troops after Fort Sumter fell, a mass meeting of Milwaukeeans in the Chamber of Commerce hall resolved to support the President. Governor Randall's call for volunteers to fill Wisconsin's army quota raised seven Companies of "American" and "German" units within two weeks.[136] Women sewed uniforms, and packed boxes of bedding, clothing, vegetables, and fruit, for shipment to the front. "Also, help was required from young girls to assist when soldiers left for the scene of war. They always had big feasts under tents, and the young girls were required to wait on them."[137] Women also organized a convalescent home on West Water Street where they cared for thousands of soldiers. On the financial side, in the Fall of 1861, a patriotic campaign floated a national loan at 7 3/10 percent interest.[138]

The first rush of volunteering was short-lived. As early as the winter of 1861-62, the community resorted to bounty offers to encourage enlistment and avoid conscription. Local businessmen paid a $50 bounty to each volunteer for the newly organized 24th Infantry.[139] The 26th Wisconsin Regiment, also of Milwaukee, was German and served with other German units in Franz Sigel's division on the Potomac. There were many Jews in this unit.

When the draft came in November, 1862, it permitted men to avoid military service by hiring substitutes, or by paying $300 in commutation money. Many joined associations which pooled the cost of commutation.[140] A typical example was Henry Stern:

> I was called three times to serve in the Army; was freed twice as being unfit for service, but the third time was pronounced fit for hospital duty. I procured a substitute whom an agent located for me for $600. I never saw him and do not even know his name.[141]

Samuel Rindskopf, of whom more later, paid the $300.[142]

Among Milwaukee soldiers who paid with their lives for the Union three were definitely Jewish: Nathan E. Neustadtl, Alexander Metzel and Jonas Goldsmith. Two others, Arnold Rosenbaum and Gustav Mahler, were probably Jews.

Nathan E. Neustadtl, an unmarried watchmaker of 24, enlisted on August 12, 1862, and was killed in the Battle of Chickamauga on September 20, 1863. His commanding officer, himself taken prisoner, answered the family's inquiry:

"Libby Prison, Richmond, Va., November 19, 1863.
To Mrs. Rosa Katz, Eagle, Wisc. Madame: . . . when I was

taken prisoner I saw [Neustadtl] lying on the field very badly wounded. The nature of his wounds were such as to leave but little hope of his recovery. It is very hard to part with one's friends, still it is a great consolation to know that they died while doing their duty. Nathan Neustadtl was a true soldier. I remain with much respect, T. S. West, Lt. Col. 24th Wis."[143]

Alexander Metzel, an unmarried "banker" of 27, enlisted for three years in August, 1862. He rose to Sergeant-Major, and saw action at Chancellorsville. At the battle of Gettysburg, Metzel was wounded on July 1 and succumbed on July 30, 1863.[144] Jonas Goldsmith, a native of Prague, aged 26, enlisted at the beginning of the War, and was killed in the Battle of Stone River, near Murfreesboro, on February 1, 1863. Eight days later, he was

"interred with appropriate ceremonies . . . in the Jewish burial ground. Sergeant Goldsmith was a nephew of Nathan Pereles and was a resident of the city when the war commenced. He . . . passed through all the campaigns in the west. The battle in which he received his death wound was the last of many in which he participated. He had a brother also in the same regiment who was killed some time ago."[145]

Arnold Rosenbaum was a victim of the Battle of Kenesaw Mountain; Gustav Mahler, who answered the first call for volunteers on April 21, 1861, died of disease at Liberty Hall, Va., in 1862.[146]

There are lighter touches to this somber record. One adventurer who had served in the Mexican War and came to Milwaukee in 1858 was Phillip Horwitz. At the age of 38 when the Civil War started, he enlisted for three months and was mustered out for disability (incurred at Williamsport, Pa.) in August, 1861. Almost immediately thereafter, he established a recruiting station to raise German volunteers for Col. Salmon's Ninth German Regiment. On August 21, 1862, he re-enlisted for three years and was commissioned Major. Four days before Horwitz left with the 26th Regiment for the Potomac, his Jewish friends presented him with a $200 horse, named General Taylor. At the formal presentation, their spokesman declared:

Some of your personal friends, among the Israelites of this city, desire to present you with a horse. They wish you to accept it as a token of their personal respect and esteem, and of their best wishes for your success and honor in the defense of your country, its constitution and government.

May this noble animal bear you only to victory . . . and when the peace shall be restored, may he bear you back, in safety, to rejoice with us, over rebellion crushed, liberty triumphant, and the people, once more, prosperous and happy. . . .

Six months later, Horwitz was again discharged "on account of disability existing before he entered the service."[147] We do not know whether he still rode General Taylor out of the Union Army.[148]

Jacob Mahler, a Milwaukeean, rose to the rank of Captain and served as Assistant Quartermaster in New Orleans throughout the War. Upon his departure in June, 1865, the New Orleans *Times* printed these words:

> . . . Captain Mahler . . . takes with him a clean record and kind regards of those of our citizens who have had business with the office under his charge.

Civil life held little attraction for Mahler. Next year he enlisted in the Prussian Army, as Quartermaster.[149]

While not a member of the armed forces, Philip Carpeles acted as an informal liaison between the enlisted men of the 8th and 11th Wisconsin Regiments, at Sulphur Springs, Mo., and their families.[150] Lion Silverman, the defeated politician of Ozaukee, actively drummed up recruits in his county.[151]

The Jewish community of Milwaukee observed the several national fasts and prayer days at its Congregation B'ne Jeshurun on Fifth Street. On June 1, the second day of *Shavuot*, 1865, the Day of National Mourning appointed by President Johnson, the services were adapted to the occasion. Rabbi Samson Falk delivered the sermon, unfortunately unrecorded, which dealt with "the life and labors of Lincoln."[152]

The 1850's had been years of extraordinary internal growth in American Jewry, and the Civil War heightened this development. It strengthened local industries, including those in which Jews were concentrated. While they were not the richest men in town at the War's end, some Jewish businessmen had prospered indeed. Of the 143 Milwaukeeans whose incomes exceeded $5,000 in 1866, ten were Jewish; of the seventy-eight who made from $5,000 to $10,000, eight were Jewish; and of the sixty-five with incomes from $10,000 and above, two were Jewish.[153]

A simpler picture of prosperous Milwaukee in 1866 is reflected in a letter of Mrs. Abraham (Maria Heller) Shakman to her daughter Lori (Elenora) and Jacques Riese, then residing in Brussels:

> . . . My Anna goes to school again now. While I was ill I could not let her go as I then had only two maids—how can one rely on them with everything? These local servants think much of themselves—almost necessarily the mistress waits on them. Wages here are very high. The cook gets two dollars a week, the second maid only twelve shillings, even less, nurse girls get six shillings as a rule. . . .[154]

In 1865, B. F. Peixotto enthusiastically viewed the advance of Milwaukee's Jewish inhabitants:

> This city of Milwaukee thirty years ago—think of it, thirty years ago only!—but a population of 600 souls. Today, it numbers a population of 75,000 inhabitants.
>
> From a few struggling shanties has sprung a city of brick and iron and stone—a marvel of beauty and a metropolis second only to Chicago in the Great North West. Its present Jewish population is estimated at 1,500—it is more likely to be greater than less, but it is certainly that number. Our people (as everyone in this great Republic) have thrived beyond measure. On every side, witnesses of their wealth and prosperity appear. Splendid storehouses, with huge stocks of goods in all lines of trade; neat and tasteful residences, and a temple—an edifice simple, plain, but so appropriate and becoming.[155]

While they were establishing themselves individually in the growing city, the Jews concerned themselves with founding a community. To these efforts we now turn.

II

Founding a Jewish Community

RELIGIOUS DIVERSITY marked Milwaukee from its earliest years. During its village era, about twelve different church organizations were born. A visitor to Milwaukee in 1845 found "1 Catholic church, 1 Episcopalian, 1 Congregationalist, 1 Presbyterian, 1 Baptist, 1 Methodist, 1 Unitarian, 4 small German congregations of different religious faiths, besides a congregation of German Rationalists who met every Lord's Day, to glorify the profound and inexplorable mysteries of a sublimated nonsense." The first congregations were small; homes, schoolhouses, or stores served as houses of worship. Most ministers were itinerant, and many were compelled to run boarding houses as a means of livelihood.[1]

Catholic mass was celebrated in Solomon Juneau's home as early as 1835. A priest was located in the village of Milwaukee by May, 1839, and the new Bishop of the new diocese of Milwaukee, John M. Henni, preached his first sermon on May 5, 1844.[2] A portion of his service was designated particularly for the German immigrant faithful.

The early Protestant churches at first depended upon traveling preachers and local lay readers. Thus, the Rev. John Clark, an itinerant Methodist missionary, first preached in Milwaukee in 1835, and officiated occasionally at classes and meetings in the homes of members. Although the Church was organized in July, 1837, the Methodists' first permanent home was not built until 1841, owing to the financial collapse of 1837-38.[3] The beginning of Milwaukee Baptism was very similar, while Congregationalists,[4] Presbyterians,[5] and Episcopalians[6] also took their place on the local scene. All these denominations were identified with the city's "Yankee-Yorker" element.

Many of Milwaukee's German settlers had come to America to avoid religious problems in their native lands. A group of Lutheran Germans organized their first church, St. Paul's, in 1845, under the auspices of the Buffalo Synod. From a schism in 1846 came Trinity Lutheran Church, which affiliated with the Missouri Synod, while Grace Church was organized under the auspices of the Wisconsin Synod of 1851.[7] The First Reformed Church of Milwaukee was founded by the Hollanders, and its first pastor arrived in 1850[8].

Radically different forms of religion appeared alongside these traditional congregations. In 1845, the Freethinker congregation, contemptuously mentioned above, was founded by Heinrich Ginal. It aimed to purge Christianity of all its miraculous traditions and to explain the life and teachings of Jesus in solely rational terms.

INTEREST IN JEWS AND JUDAISM

This religiously varied population generally viewed the Jewish residents of Milwaukee with respect and curiosity. The way in which "the Chosen people of God" maintained their ancient faith attracted the attention of non-Jews. The shut stores of the city's Jewish inhabitants impressed the editor of the *Sentinel* as he strolled past on Yom Kippur of 1856:

> Today the Hebrew population of this city . . . will close their shops and their stores; . . . And today, as we notice through our city the closed stores of the Hebrew population of Milwaukee, let no jeer or slur curl our lips, but in harmony with the spirit of our constitution, and of the Christian Religion itself, knowing that the one is founded on the other, and that each is teaching to the human race the great lesson of universal charity; let us not forget from what race sprang the people who fill their synagogues this day, but remember what they once were, how they

once trod the earth, the chosen people of God. And let us be thankful that here all are alike free in their right to worship, when and where, and in what manner they like.[9]

Not only the High Holidays, but other Jewish festivals seemed to interest the Christian community. Thus, the press explained that "with the Hebrews" the observance of Passover "is obligatory . . . and a total abstinence from malt beverages and spirits is compelled"; that the "Israelites of this city celebrated the Feast of Pentecost, in memory of the solemn proclamation of the ten commandments by the Lord on Mount Sinai"; that "some of the Israelites" celebrated the feast of Passover on the first two evenings, "owing to the uncertainty prevalent at one time with respect to fixing the time of the new moon by the Sanhedrin at Jerusalem"; and that the "Hebrew fast of Ab . . . consisted of a total abstinence from food and drink . . . reciting the past woes of Israel, and praying for her prosperity in the future." When Purim arrived, the same paper gave a detailed account of the feast day. It told the reading public that "In the synagogue the entire book of Esther was read and 'Al Anissim', a prayer of thanksgiving delivered at church and table."[10] Obviously the editor had a competent Jewish informant. Motivated by the desire to provide German Christians with news about Jews and Jewish events, the German Milwaukee *Herold* reportedly instituted a special section entitled *Reflections of a Friend of True Judaism*.[11] However, this may have been only a missionary column.

CONGREGATIONAL BEGINNINGS

Tradition tells us that on *Yom Kippur* of 1847 (5608), twelve pioneers held their first service at the home of Isaac Neustadtl, at Chestnut and Fourth Streets. In the following year, the Holy Days were celebrated in the home of Henry Newhouse, 86 Jefferson. About that time the group organized a cemetery association, and purchased one acre of land in what is now the Ninth Ward.

Interments in Milwaukee's earliest Jewish burial ground took place as early as 1848.[12] While land was probably not purchased before 1854, arrangements must already have existed in 1848 for the ultimate acquisition of that land. Twenty-two men organized the Imanu-Al Cemetery on May 1, 1850 and elected six trustees.[13] " 'Jews' Cemetery', above Fifteenth Street, between Lisbon plank road and the Fond du Lac road," was finally acquired in 1854.[14] When a unified congregation emerged in 1859, it took title to this cemetery land.[15]

The organization of the "Imanu-Al Cemetery Association" in 1848 led to the formation of Milwaukee's first Jewish congregation, "Imanu-Al." It conducted services for the Holy Days of the year 1849 (5610) in a room over Nathan Pereles' grocery, on Chestnut Street,[16] and also rented a room to hold services from time to time.

By 1850, with the considerable increase in the Jewish population of the city, the group could consider full facilities for their congregation. A few of the "most spirited," convinced that the time had arrived to erect a synagogue, subscribed a sum to buy a site, hoping that Jews elsewhere would also come to their aid. However, more cautious members preferred to renovate the premises for several hundred dollars,[17] and this attitude prevailed. A contemporary criticized the "nonchalance" which retarded the progress of this pioneer congregation, and the absence of "the vital spark to enliven and enlarge it."[18] In 1854, Imanu-Al was quartered at the corner of Fourth and Tamarack (now Kilbourn Avenue) streets, and in 1856, on Fourth between Tamarack and Prairie (now Highland Avenue) streets.[19] At the first elections held on October 17, 1853 "at the meeting house where they attend for Divine Worship," Solomon Adler was elected president and Jonas Schoenmann, secretary.[20] The congregation bought a lot for a synagogue, but did not erect a building or hold weekly services.

Dissension developed early within Imanu-Al, mainly centered about the *Minhag* (regional liturgical customs) to be followed. The adoption of a particular *Minhag* implied the predominance of immigrants from that European region, and was thus a matter of pride for each group. A great majority of the members insisted on the Polish *Minhag*, and organized Ahabath Emuno (Love of the Faith) in January, 1854, for "the promotion of a love and knowledge of our religion," and of Hebrew education for their children. To their adversaries they appeared "stabile [sic] Orthodox Jews . . . ; all they wish for, is to repeat the same *Piutim* (liturgical poems) in the same order exactly, as their fathers did." The criticism itself hints at Reform tendencies not far beneath the surface. Ahabath Emuno's first quarters were Washington Hall, on Oneida Street; then at 257 Third Street, "Upstairs"; and in 1856, at River, between Division and Knapp.[21] The congregation was incorporated on February 19, 1856, its officers being lawyer Simon Levy, president, and M. Markwell, vice-president.[22] It succeeded in erecting a small building for worship, aided by Nathan Pereles' loan of $600 on interest, and engaged a young man as minister.[23]

But secession feeds on itself and early in 1855 a *Minhag* controversy split the new congregation in its turn. For when Ahabath Emuno adopted the Polish *Minhag*, advocates of the German *Minhag* seceded and formed a third religious group, Anshe Emeth (Men of Truth). They leased the Military Hall, and two members acted as volunteer ministers.[24] With 46 members, it purchased a lot for $1,300, paid down $433, and planned to turn for aid to "brethren in New York and Cincinnati." S. Strauss was engaged as *shohet*, teacher and *hazzan*. The officers considered presenting the draft of their constitution to Isaac M. Wise for correction,[25] and secured incorporation as Congregation Anshe Emeth on March 31, 1856.[26] Since the new synagogue was not completed in time, the High Holiday services of 1856 were again held at Military Hall. Officers of the synagogue were J. M. Hart, president, M. H. Schwarzenberg, vice-president, and B. Oettinger, secretary. The women, however, maintained a single charitable society named the "Deborah Benevolent Society of Milwaukee."[27]

SYNAGOGUE GOVERNMENT

In drawing up constitutions and regulations for their synagogue, the early Jews of Milwaukee followed the traditional *Takkanot* (ordinances) used in Europe for centuries. In the United

States, synagogue regulations also were influenced by the constitutions and by-laws of American societies and institutions. Fifty members of the German Anshe Emeth signed its new constitution and by-laws, thus testifying that they would abide by them.[28] These documents conscientiously transplant specific traditions of the German synagogue, always in conformity with *halakha* (Jewish law).

Only Israelites that observed the Covenant of Abraham and had Jewish wives might become members.[29] Dues were not less than $9.00, or 75 cents a month. A member who joined another local congregation could not hold office or vote.[30] Widows or widowers could pay half the regular dues.[31]

The constitution provided for the annual election by secret ballot of officers and five trustees, who had to be residents of Milwaukee.[32] The whole Board of Trustees had to consent to spend amounts over $25.00, and funds of the congregation beyond the sum of $50.00 were to bring a return of 7 per cent. The president and vice-president were to occupy seats during all services flanking the *Aron Hakodesh*.[33] Quarterly meetings were held in February, May and August, and the annual meeting on the first Sunday after Rosh Hashanah; executive meetings were convened monthly.[34]

Salaried officials, such as the qualified *shamash, shohet* and *hazzan* were elected annually by the membership, with duties and salaries governed by written contracts.[35] Teachers were also engaged by the membership, but only the school committee, consisting of "members familiar with Jewish educational problems," could hear complaints against teachers. Should a member address teachers directly, he would be fined $5.00.[36]

The by-laws tried to settle beforehand the small matters which could stir up congregational tempests. It specified that the "ritual and order of prayers shall follow the *Minhag Frankfurt*." Conversation or disturbance during services were subject to fine. Only the *hazzan* "shall pray aloud, and only in responsive readings is praying aloud permissible." The honor of being called to the *Torah* was to "follow the order of affiliation with the congregation, in which all members shall participate." A man so honored could thereupon have complimentary benedictions ("mi sheber-akh") bestowed upon his family and no more than three others. The chairman of the executive committee assumed the onerous task of Superintendent of the cemetery. Burial for relatives of members cost not less than $5.00; burial of non-members required special application and "a down-payment of not less than $5.00 and not more than $50.00." "Persons not belonging to the Covenant of Abraham, or who refuse to be buried according to Jewish ritual" could not be buried in the congregational cemetery.[37] The superintendent of the cemetery was to prepare the body, select the grave, arrange for interment, and for services in the mourner's home.

The rabbi of the congregation could perform marriages only for those who secured a permit from the president. The fee was $3.00 to the congregation, $2.00 to the "copulant," and $1.00 to the "servant of the congregation."[38]

All this discipline was maintained by fines. An officer who shirked his duties could be fined $5.00; committee members who failed to attend meetings, members who did not honor a request to attend a funeral or to watch over the dead, or send "another honorable man to be his substitute," could be fined $1.00. Members misbehaving at the residence of a deceased member, "or are not properly dressed" (i.e. had come in work clothes) were to be fined $1.00. An array of punitive assessments for non-attendance completed the list. But fines were seldom actually inflicted.

A UNIFIED CONGREGATION

By 1856, the 200 Milwaukee Jewish families were supporting three congregations. Isaac Mayer Wise, who visited Milwaukee as a house guest of Elias and Rosa Friend,[39] was disturbed by the religious situation:

> As almost everywhere else, so also in Milwaukee you find on one side a benumbed, dead and deadening conservatism; men who . . . ruin . . . the cause for which they struggle, frightening away from their religious community the intelligent and

reflecting portion of the community, and rendering Judaism odious to the better class of society.

While at the other extreme stands frivolity and indifference, caring for gain and amusement only. . . . Between them stand the men of the earnest volition and pious desire, and attempt manfully to live in a way becoming Jews, and retain the sacred in heritage to posterity. . . .[40]

Wise was not a man to abide such conditions resignedly, and attempted "to rouse our people from the deadening lethargy." He preached on Saturday in the synagogue, and by his own account, had

. . . a larger audience, indeed, than was ever assembled in Milwaukee for the purpose of divine service.

I turned my face into a rock, and argued without fear against the existing evils . . . As severely as I attacked the impertinence and wickedness of Atheism, I also rebuked the benumbed and senseless conservatism which not only gives birth to atheism, but also tears into fractions the house of Israel . . .

Thinking as I did to have offended all the ultramen, I supposed they had heard enough preaching for the next two years, and that I would not see their faces anymore. But I was mistaken. Sunday morning, being the ninth of Ab, I preached again in the other Synagogue, and they came not only to listen, but also to act; for, after services were over, a motion was made to appoint committees from the three congregations, and make an attempt to unite them into one. In the afternoon these committees were appointed. In the evening I preached again, and before the largest crowd seen in a Synagogue in Milwaukee. My severity was not relaxed yet. I thundered with all my might against the corruptions of the place. When done, a collection was made for the benefit of Zion College, which resulted in a gift of $103.00 . . . a spirit of piety appeared to be waking.[41]

Wise learned that during the Holy Days that followed, several persons "who had never seen the inside of a synagogue in this city, closed their places of business, and attended divine services; others joined the congregation as members." His appearance was Milwaukee Jewry's first contact with the forthright, persuasive exponent of Judaism, and it left an effect. By mid-September, an

optimistic member of Anshe Emeth was convinced that the three
existing congregations would soon consolidate.[42]

Imanu-Al and Ahabath Emuno did consolidate on October 5,
1856 under the new name of B'ne Jeshurun. They agreed that
"the *Minhag* in our new Temple, when built, shall be that of *K.K.*
Bene Jeshurun, of Cincinnati, Ohio" (Wise's congregation).
Nathan Pereles was elected president of the new-born congregation,[43] which sought "Minister and Superintendent of School, at
a salary of $800, per annum."[44] After the Rev. Henry Hoch-
heimer of Baltimore declined to be Preacher of B'ne Jeshurun,[45]
the congregation elected Isidor Kalisch for a three-year term. The
new rabbi preached his "introductory sermon" on May 2, 1857,
to B'ne Jeshurun's 70 members at the synagogue on Fourth Street,
between State and Prairie.[46] The secretary could report that the
congregation was "in a flourishing condition, and peace and progress appear to be the aim of its members and officers."[47] B'ne
Jeshurun incorporated on September 20, 1858[48] and laid the cornerstone of its new synagogue on Fifth Street eight months later.[49]

Anshe Emeth's 50 members remained independent in their
synagogue on Pine Street[50] and M. Heiman came from Syracuse
in July, 1858 to be their Minister. Despite decreased membership,
the congregation planned to build a synagogue in the near future.[51]
But B'ne Jeshurun built first, and three days after the cornerstone ceremonies of B'ne Jeshurun, a majority of Anshe Emeth
voted to merge with it, members and property.[52] There was now
one synagogue in Milwaukee.

A *Sentinel* reporter viewed the new synagogue on Fifth Street
inside and out, and wrote down his impressions:

> The edifice is very plain outside, but neat and substantial,
> with the audience room raised about ten feet above the walk,
> and reached by a flight of steps in front. The decorations
> opposite the organ gallery, and above the speakers desk are
> showy and somewhat different from the Gentile idea of a
> church decoration. Three arches, [cover] almost the entire
> end wall of the room ... Under the center arch, and screening
> the vestibule or shrine where the Scrolls are kept, hangs a
> heavy crimson velvet curtain, fringed with gold, and bearing

in Hebrew characters the inscription, 'From Sarah Adler wife of Solomon Adler,' and immediately over these lines is a spread eagle with the American shield, and stars and stripes. . . .[53]

No less important to the congregation, their new synagogue was debt-free.[54]

Great preparations were made to dedicate "the new temple for the united congregations of Milwaukee," on September 16, 1859. Wise sent synagogal music to be sung at the dedication, and responded to a personal invitation by "gladly [embracing] the opportunity to speak again to his Milwaukee friends."[55] At 2:30 P.M. of the dedication day, the procession entered the crowded synagogue. Twenty-four young ladies in white bore wreathes up the aisle, followed by a number of boys, and "four old men" bearing the *Sifrey Torah*. Behind them followed the committee on arrangements and the Trustees. "As they made a circuit of the Synagogue, the choir sang *Mah Tobu*." Upon the Scroll's third circuit, the girls "at the Altar" sprinkled flowers at the feet of the Scroll bearers.[56] The Scrolls were then deposited in the Ark. Rabbi Kalisch's German sermon (by the *Sentinel* reporter's watch) "occupied an hour and five minutes." Dr. Wise then followed in English. He spoke of Mt. Moriah, which he identified with every place of divine worship.

> The mighty columns with the precious gems of this house shall be the piety, consistency and holy inspiration of Israel's sons and daughters. Why then should the hymns of your chorus be less acceptable to God than the psalms of the Levites? Why should the grave and heart touching accords of your organ be regarded slighter by our heavenly Father than the sound of the trumpets in the hands of priests of old? . . . .[57]

In good German style, the dedication of the synagogue was followed by a ball on Saturday evening, and a dinner, accompanied by toasts.[58]

Wise discounted the minority who remained dissatisfied with the unorthodox character of the new congregation:

> The union of the congregation in one is sincere and will be lasting. The few hyper-orthodox who are dissatisfied take

too much pride in the new temple which is free of debt, and feel too profoundly the benefit of union, that they should think of separation. Their number is too small to form a congregation, and so they will submit. One consideration should prompt them to go hand in hand with the reformers: Judaism can be maintained in Milwaukee in its most rational form and most attractive exterior only, and this is offered by the reform party only.[59]

Wise thus played a central role in the making of Judaism in Milwaukee. His dynamic presence, personal ties with dominant persons in the community, frequent visits, and his calls for congregational unity in Milwaukee through the columns of his *Israelite*, were largely responsible for the emergence of a moderate reformed type of Judaism in the city.[60]

SYNAGOGUE OFFICIALS

The new synagogue sought its religious leadership not of the old-style rabbinic scholar and judge, but, like congregations elsewhere in the United States and Western Europe, from a new-style rabbinic preacher and teacher. Not all preachers and teachers were actually rabbis, and there was confusion concerning their status.[61] In his *Reminiscences*, Isaac M. Wise described the *hazzan* of 1846:

> There was antipathy in America to rabbis. The *Chazan* was the Reverend. He was all that was wanted . . . the *Chazan* was reader, cantor, . . . butcher, circumciser, blower, grave-digger . . . he was a Kol-bo, an encyclopedia, accepted bread, turnips, cabbage, potatoes as a gift and peddled in case his salary was not sufficient . . . Among all the *chazzanim* who I learned to know, there was not one who had a common-school education or possessed any Hebrew learning.[62]

However, the prestige of the Protestant American minister helped to raise the meager status of his Jewish equivalent. German-Americans, in particular, manifested a dutiful submission to their religious leaders. As a man of learning, the minister's advice was constantly requested by individuals and the community, for he was apt to have read more widely and carefully than his neighbors, and often contributed to local newspapers and discussed public questions. Since ministers were few in early Wisconsin, and single congregations could not support one, the circuit-riding or traveling ministry long prevailed among practically all denominations.[63]

Isidor Kalisch, pioneer rabbi of Milwaukee, the eldest of seven children, was born on November 15, 1816 at Krotoschin, in the Duchy of Posen.[64] He studied at German universities, and contributed to German periodicals. His writings—poems and articles—were condemned as seditious and he left Germany for America in 1849. In July, 1850, he became the rabbi of the Orthodox Congregation Anshe Chesed of Cleveland. However, he soon resigned and founded Congregation Tifereth Israel (today The Temple) where he instituted a number of religious reforms.[65] Kalisch had already some reputation as a scholar.[66] In 1853, he published a German work which was translated four years later as *A Guide for Rational Inquiries into the Biblical Writings, being an Examination of the Doctrinal Difference between Judaism and Primitive Christianity, Based upon Historical Exposition of the Book of Matthew.*[67]

Isidor Kalisch next spent one year in Cincinnati when he was called to Milwaukee.[68] In his first sermon in Milwaukee, Kalisch declared that his theological position was based on historical Judaism, but that he stood opposed to the popular forms of orthodoxy. Hence, institutions which were created to give outward expression to inward Judaism must in time change and renew their forms. On the other hand, Kalisch opposed that reform which "strikes at the root of our revered faith, for which our fathers lived and died." He advocated improved worship and thorough instruction in the school and synagogue.[69]

During Kalisch's term the three congregations united and B'ne Jeshurun erected its edifice. He introduced religious innovations, wrote numerous essays on religious subjects, polemicized in the Anglo-Jewish press with both orthodox and reform elements, and wrote poems for German periodicals. He was an organizer of the True Sisters, a women's society which became one of the largest benevolent groups in Milwaukee.[70]

In August, 1858, Rabbi Kalisch sent his *Guide for Rational Inquiries into the Biblical Writings* to President James Buchanan, and wrote:

> Mr. President,
> I do myself the pleasure as a true citizen of the United States, to present you with a copy of my work, which has for its paramount aim to demolish the partition between the different denominations, and to establish truth and justice among all nations. And hence, by such Jewish opinions, which all my co-religionists also entertain, you can be assured that the Atlantic telegraph will not be misused by the millions of Jews in the old world, nor by the two hundred thousand of them in this happy land of freedom. That my work, however, displays fully the system of Judaism is proved by the most favourable opinions of the same by the press of our beloved country, as well as of France, Germany, and England, and I do not doubt a moment that you will deem it worthy of a perusal. . . .

The President replied briefly on August 30:

> Reverend Sir,
> I have received your "Guide for Rational Enquiries into the Biblical Writings," and accepted it with much pleasure, as a token of your regard. I have no doubt I shall derive both pleasure and profit from its perusal, but the pressure of public business may prevent me from doing this for some time to come.
>   Yours very respecfully,
>   James Buchanan

Probably disappointed at the President's brief reply, Kalisch wrote again on September 5, now taking Buchanan to task for using the expression "all the nations of Christendom," in his congratulatory trans-Atlantic telegraph message to Queen Victoria:

> It can be inferred that you mean either the majority of the nation, without ascribing to it a moral superiority over the

other creeds; or that useful public works are only to be held sacred by Christians, on account of their higher moral and spiritual condition . . . As you have, however, touched on a religious point in a public document, which will be perpetuated to all time, I cannot but believe it highly necessary that you should give a decided explanation of the aforementioned clause.

. . . if your expression is to be construed in a second signification, it is at variance with the spirit of the constitution, which is a revelation of universal liberty, equality, and brotherhood, without distinction of religious faith.

I respectfully request you to furnish me the information thus required, but with permission to make it publicly known.[71]

President Buchanan, nettled, replied on September 11:

My dear Sir,

I have received your favour of the 5th inst., and permit me to say that in the construction of my answer to the Queen I think you are somewhat hypercritical. Most certainly I never intended by using the expression "all the nations of Christendom", to cast any reflection upon the Jews. Such an idea never entered my mind. Both as President of the United States and as an individual, I have ever been the advocate of religious liberty, and the perfect freedom of conscience. For many of your persuasion I entertain the highest personal regard, and I should be the last man in the world, either in an official document or private letter, to use any expression derogatory to their character, or calculated to wound their feelings.

Yours very respectfully,
James Buchanan[72]

Blaming depression conditions, the congregation was compelled to forego the services of its rabbi, and Kalisch delivered his "farewell address" on April 28, 1860. The congregation expressed its high regard for Milwaukee's first rabbi, who "labored with the best and most blissful results . . . , established union and concord, and had been a faithful guide and promoter of true Judaism . . ." They decided to "subscribe for one hundred copies of the poetical work announced by him under the title *Sounds of the Orient.*[73]

Four months later, Ferdinand Leopold Sarner, formerly of Rochester,[74] entered the pulpit of B'ne Jeshurun. He officiated during the Holy days that year, but shortly afterwards left the congregation.[75] In 1863, he became the first Jewish chaplain in American history.[76]

From October, 1860 to the Spring of 1863, B'ne Jeshurun had no regular rabbi and *hazzan*. Marcus Heiman fulfilled these functions.[77] In March, 1863, Samson Falk, formerly of Albany, New York, was elected rabbi for three years. Although re-elected for three years more, with an increase of $600.00 per annum, "in acknowledgment of the strict fulfillment of his duties," Falk resigned in November, 1866.[78]

Rabbi Falk's "cultured mind . . . ," and his "finished and eloquent" speech impressed B. F. Peixotto, who worshipped in Milwaukee during the Holy Days of 1865. B'ne Jeshurun regarded Falk as "a sincere and devoted minister, an eloquent lecturer, and a hearty worker in behalf of Judaism,"[79] who continued the reform tendencies of Kalisch.[80] Falk emphasized that "since the downfall of the second Temple, Jews have ceased to be a nation. . . ." A Jew was now "a member of the primitive church, a believer in the doctrines of Judaism."[81] He emphasized that the "modern phase" of Judaism does not believe in a personal Messiah or in the restoration of the Jews to Palestine.[82]

B'ne Jeshurun offered $2,500 per annum to a proper candidate, but not until 1868 did a successor to Rabbi Falk come to B'ne Jeshurun. He was Rabbi G. M. Cohen, formerly of Cleveland. His stay in Milwaukee, however, was brief.[83] In January, 1869, the congregation was prepared to pay $3,000 for "Rabbi and Lecturer, competent to preach in the German and English languages, and superintend a Hebrew School."[84] Rabbi Elias Eppstein (1831-1906) pleased the congregation by his German sermon on Saturday morning, March 13, 1869, and his lecture in English next day, and was elected rabbi of B'ne Jeshurun for one year.[85] The new minister was the son of an Alsatian Rabbi and had received his formal secular education at Bonn; his rabbinical diploma, from Rabbi Moshe Mertzig. Before coming to Milwaukee, Eppstein had held rabbinic positions in Jackson, Michigan, and Detroit. Despite the advertised $3,000, he was re-engaged for three years in May, 1870 at a salary of only $2,000 per annum. Eppstein served Congregation B'ne Jeshurun for ten years.[86]

As in other Jewish congregations throughout the country, Milwaukee's first *hazzanim* functioned as rabbis, and *shohtim* and teachers, as well as Readers. Such was the situation in Milwaukee until B'ne Jeshurun engaged Kalisch as its first regular rabbi. Thereafter, the *hazzanim* served as Readers and teachers and in time as choir directors. Four men held these positions before 1870: a certain Alexander; S. Strauss, engaged by Congregation Anshe Emeth in 1855 as *hazzan*, *shohet*, and teacher; Raphael Lasker, performing the same duties at B'ne Jeshurun in 1856; and Marcus Heiman, appointed Minister of Anshe Emeth in July, 1858, and elected *hazzan* of B'ne Jeshurun in the following year when the congregations consolidated.[87]

In the 1860's, the lay leadership became more selective about its *hazzan*. With the arrival of Rabbi Falk in 1863, B'ne Jeshurun sought a *hazzan* who could "cooperate in divine service with choir and organ and give religious instruction at the congregational school." The same was expected in 1867, and the salary offered was $1,500 per annum.[88]

Levi M. Loevenberg described himself as "a skillful and experienced *mohel* for many years," who had performed "the operation on children of different ages in the most happy manner." He offered his services "to his brethren in faith in this city, as well as abroad, at any time."[89]

Synagogue and Community

European Jewish communities in early modern times were not much more democratic than European society. While all Jews, regardless of wealth or social standing, were equal in the eyes of Jewish law, only the richer Jews had a voice in the management of the community. They paid the highest taxes, held electoral right for themselves and their families, and chose solely from their midst the communal officers. With the decline of the community before the period of Emancipation, there developed "a kind of aristocracy which seized the reins of government." In

Germany, during the period of the Court Jews, entire communities depended on the whim of a few priviliged members.[90] There was more equality and no coercion in the American synagogue. Nostalgic recollections of religious life in the parental home and a desire for Jewish religious practice for themselves and their children, combined with the determination to preserve their identity as Jews, moved these pioneers to build houses for worship and religious training. Most of the early congregational leaders were already substantial business men, who had established a fair reputation in the general community. Some readily shifted loyalties from one synagogue to another. Thus, the lawyer Simon Levy was president of the orthodox German congregation, Anshe Emeth in 1855; president of the orthodox "Polish" congregation, Ahabath Emuno in 1856; and president of the combined moderate reform B'ne Jeshurun in 1857. M. Markwell was vice-president at Ahabath Emuno in 1856 and of B'ne Jeshurun in 1857. Similarly, M. H. Schwarzenberg, vice-president of Anshe Emeth in 1856, was vice-president of B'ne Jeshurun in 1859.[94]

Not all these leaders were motivated solely by religious ideals. Some of them, like Jonas Schoenmann, who had "once been a very diligent Bohemian young Talmudist," became estranged from Judaism, and were associated with societies of "Freemen."[92] Feelings of kinship and group solidarity still tended to keep such individuals within the fold of congregational life, particularly during the early years. Nor did all Milwaukeeans affiliate with churches and synagogues. Many, particularly exiles of 1848, together with enthusiastic champions of liberal thought, joined no church. They were members of the *Freie Gemeinde* (Free Congregation), *Verein Freie Männer* (Society of Free Men), and the Turner movement. The first two groups were anti-clericals who opposed their own free thought to the "priestcraft" of the Catholic Church, their sworn enemy. To them may be added the Sons of Hermann, such journals as Schoeffler's *Banner*, Fratny's *Volksfreund*, Schroeter's *Humanist*, and Vojta Naprstek's *Flugblätter*, all of whom assailed the Catholic clergy and the Catholic *Seebote*.[39]

Some Jews were carried along by anti-clericalism and atheism.

Isaac M. Wise derided these German atheists and their Jewish allies:

> . . . The German atheists who came to this country . . . have found their way in large numbers to Milwaukee, and there as elsewhere they attempt to corrupt the ignorant.
>
> It so happened, that some of the most ignorant Jews came to Milwaukee and became a prey of the atheists . . . I met a philosophical butcher, a superwise rag-dealer, an over-learned rum-seller, a sophistical hog-driver, an atheistical servant of a cattle dealer, and other such benighted subjects who are as ignorant as fanatic, as ridiculous as they are unhappy and forlorn . . . ; still they are but a handful among our brethren in Milwaukee.[94]

Among the leaders of the pioneer congregation were men who "joined also the society of Freemen and [the congregation's] secretary was at the same time president of a congregation of infidels!"[95]

Then there were Jews who were "ashamed to be Jews," but in free America could cease being Jews without turning Christian:

> . . . they in their immense egotism think, because they have now got some money, they are something. Yes, indeed, something they are, pitiful fools, who look like monkeys imitating the motions of somebody . . . I do not reckon the individuals of the above classes among the Jews of Milwaukee, they do not deserve this honor, I just mention them, to say that none must be mistaken to consider them Jews. There are many among them, who turned Catholics in the old country, were then Protestants, and are now Atheists . . .[96]

Jonas Schoenmann, a synagogue officer in the 1850's, broke with Jewish religious life and was buried in 1880 with no religious service. Nathan Pereles and Isaac Neustadtl, synagogue founders, spent their later years quite removed from Jewish connections. Henry Stern, leading dry goods merchant, was never interested in anything Jewish; David Blumenfeld, of Watertown, had a Christian minister officiate at the marriage of his daughter.[97]

Religious interest declined after the period of congregational beginnings, as may be seen from membership figures. Milwaukee's first synagogue, Imanu-Al, at first numbered not more than twenty families.[98] In 1857, a year after its consolidation with Ahabath Emuno, the new Congregation B'ne Jeshurun had a membership of seventy and in 1859, seventy-three. Anshe Emeth, the German orthodox congregation, counted forty-six members in 1855, fifty in 1856, and forty-two in 1858. When Anshe Emeth and B'ne Jeshurun merged in 1859, 115 of the city's 200 Jewish families held membership in Milwaukee's only synagogue. Seven years later, despite the increase in the Jewish population of the city, the number had not risen. Undoubtedly, others attended services on the Holy Days, but some neither attended those services nor contributed toward the maintenance of the congregation.[99] Even after the division of 1869, when the Reform Congregation Emanu-El was formed on the East Side, total membership was only 120, eighty in B'ne Jeshurun and forty in Emanu-El. There was thus no increase in synagogue membership between 1857 and 1870.[100]

Yet most leading Jews of the community were affiliated with the synagogue. Influential in civic and fraternal affairs and prominent in commerce, their connection with the synagogue enhanced the status of membership in a Jewish house of worship. It was the proper choice for respectable and prosperous people.

TOWARDS REFORM JUDAISM

The first Milwaukee rabbis were more eager to introduce reforms than their congregation was to accept them. From distant Philadelphia, the orthodox champion, Isaac Leeser, warned Kalisch, in September, 1857, that "an attempt to force the new creed with the new prayer book upon the people will only end in confusion, and perhaps compel Mr. K. to vacate a place which he has only just succeeded in obtaining."

The *Minhag America* prayer book arranged by Isaac Mayer Wise, who was personally so well known, was rejected[101] until 1866, when the congregation adopted it as the prayer book.[102] However, sermons, confirmations, and choirs were initiated by Kalisch with little if any opposition. Services were held at B'ne Jeshurun on Friday at 7:00 P.M. and on Saturday at 9:00 A.M.

Worshippers in the 1860's heard the sermon in their native German and only rarely in English.[103] The first confirmation ceremony in Milwaukee was introduced by Rabbi Isidor Kalisch on Shavuot, 1859, and was considered "edifying and touching."[104] A marriage was occasionally performed in the synagogue on Sunday afternoons.[105] Elements of American civic heritage also found expression in the synagogue during these years. Thus, on Saturday, July 3, 1858, in commemoration of Independence Day, Rabbi Kalisch preached an English sermon entitled "What Is Liberty?" Services on the second day of Shavuot, in June, 1865, were dedicated to the martyred Lincoln.[106]

The practice of mixed seating was instituted during Rabbi Kalisch's ministry, and the *hazzan* was accompanied by an organist and a choir of men and women. "The old men," Wise commented, "are not as stubborn as elsewhere, so as to object to choir, organ, and a divine service agreeable to modern views."[107] By 1866, however, the choir of B'ne Jeshurun consisted mainly of paid Christian singers. The Torah was read at the service "with the *Neginah* (chant) after the old style."[108]

In 1870, the services under Rabbi Eppstein were conducted in German and English, as well as Hebrew. German and English hymns or chants were sung in those languages by children and were led by the organist.[109] To accommodate all worshippers on the Holy Days, a large hall was used as "a second synagogue" in 1866.[110]

Although B'ne Jeshurun had left Orthodoxy far behind by the later 1860's, its brand of Reform Judaism was very halting. As the sole congregation, it was an arena for contests between traditionalists and proponents of completely Reform belief and practice. Another question was whether the synagogue should follow its wealthier members to the East Side.[111] The failure of B'ne Jeshurun to adopt Reform Judaism in full, to increase its capacity or to abandon its location, inspired a group of dissatisfied members to organize a Reform congregation in their East Side neighborhood. In mid-1869, 35 members announced their desire to withdraw amicably from B'ne Jeshurun to form a more liberal congregation. The division was based upon religious differences and, to some extent, social cleavage.

On August 22, 1869, B'ne Jeshurun voted that 35 members be permitted to withdraw for their announced purpose, and granted them $4,250 towards a new synagogue. On September 30, the 35 resolved "that this congregation be known as the 'Reform Congregation Emanu-El'." They also decided to model its constitution and by-laws after Temple Emanu-El of New York, and that "the discussions at all the meetings and the business of this congregation should be conducted in the English language." Steps were taken to create a charter. While renting Field's Hall for almost three years as a temporary synagogue,[112] the new congregation purchased land on Martin and Main (now Broadway) Streets for $7500 on July 17, 1870 and proceeded to erect a building.[113]

Emanu-El promptly made clear that it stood for Reform Jewish practice and ritual. A few members who found it difficult to break entirely with traditional religious practices, and held their own early Sabbath service before the regular worship, or worshipped with covered heads during the regular service, were discountenanced. Emanu-El decided to permit but one Reform service on Saturday morning, and prescribed uncovered heads during worship.[114]

EDUCATION

From the time they first raised families in Milwaukee, Jewish immigrants were concerned with providing education for their children. The pioneers of Milwaukee Judaism tried to balance general and specifically Jewish studies for their children. They were not, however, of learned stock and were content if their sons and daughters received about the same education as they had before entering a career and domestic life.

Parochial schools which offered general as well as Jewish subjects were maintained before 1860 in all larger and many smaller American Jewish communities. During the 1860's, as the tide of public school education rose, congregations abandoned their parochial schools for religious schools which met three or four afternoons a week. By 1870, English had generally replaced German as the language of instruction, and afternoon schools were replaced by Sunday schools. The Sunday schools were moralistic and catechistical in their approach, resembling the dominant form of Christian education. Their main subject, Biblical history, consisted of Bible stories told with moral didacticism. On this one day, the language of instruction was often German. The schools were hampered by a lack of trained teachers and satisfactory text books, and suffered the indifference of their pupils.[115]

Although the city's Yankees and its European immigrants were strong adherents of free schooling for all children, a generation passed before a free public school system actually existed. The East Ward had no public schoolhouse; the West Ward possessed "an old, dilapidated structure, unpainted and half unglazed, standing upon the highway. . . ." Textbooks were few, and teachers were paid little more than ordinary laborers.[116]

The public education movement gained momentum in the 1840's, and brought notable educational progress during the middle 1850's. Male teachers received an average of $500 in 1852, and $800 in 1860; female teachers' pay rose from $200 to $300.[117] A high school, opened in 1868, offered a thorough classical and scientific curriculum.[118]

Various private and parochial schools were supported by special groups, particularly German-Americans. The excellent German-English Academy, founded in 1851 and headed by the '48er Peter Engelmann, enrolled numerous Jewish children. One of its founders was Isaac Neustadtl, whose son-in-law, Henry Katz, long served as its financial secretary. Katz's wife Elizabeth was a founder of the Academy's kindergarten.[119] When the Milwaukee School Board introduced German into the public school curriculum in 1867, it drew much enrollment away from the private German schools.[120]

The foundations for two colleges, Marquette and Milwaukee-Downer, were laid during the city's formative years.[121] Business schools also appeared on the local scene, and some Milwaukee Jews laid ambitious educational plans.

Rabbi Kalisch vainly sought to establish a day school, such as prevailed in most of the larger Jewish communities during that decale.[122] A communal meeting, however, founded a school association of 80 members of the congregations, with Kalisch as superintendent. He drew up "statutes" for the "government of the school," which was to meet in the afternoon. However, it appears that such unity of action was short-lived.[123] Before B'ne Jeshurun built its new synagogue in 1859, changes were made in its plans to provide a school room in the basement.[124]

Generally, religious schools met a few hours on Saturdays, commencing at two o'clock; and on Sundays, at 9:00 A.M.[125] Religious leaders vainly urged the formation of a "Talmud Torah Society," to strengthen Jewish educational efforts. Rabbi Eppstein founded the Juvenile B'ne Jeshurun Society in 1869, consisting of pupils at the synagogue school, in an effort to encourage his Sabbath scholars. It was known as "the only juvenile society of importance in this city."[126]

WELFARE

Their first communal organization—the synagogue—served Milwaukee's Jews as the fountain-head of further activity, especially charity. From the very beginning, the Jewish group faced the problems of caring for needy Jews who turned to the synagogue, the only organized form of Jewish life. Women especially banded together for acts of kindness, and the middle 1850's was a period when women's groups began to appear in many areas throughout the United States.

Relief to the local needy was supplied through personal benevolence or by such organizations as the Milwaukee Relief Society and the Ladies' Benevolent Society, or by an association for the relief of the German poor, organized in November, 1857.[127] The needs of soldiers' families during the Civil War also called various relief societies into existence.[128] The Anshe Emeth Deborah Ladies' Hebrew Benevolent Society already existed in 1856, and the Benevolent Society of True Sisters (*Die Treue Schwestern*), organized by Rabbi Kalisch in 1857, became one of the largest benevolent organizations in Milwaukee. Both societies existed to prevent "misery and pauperism . . . support . . . the needy, the sick, the widow and fatherless."[129] The ladies paid nominal membership fees and conducted masquerade balls, strawberry festivals and other events to raise funds. Bequests were another source of income.[130]

Hebros and mutual benevolent societies relieved their own needy and sick. The most noteworthy was the Chevra Bikur Cholim (Benevolent Association), founded in 1861 and incorporated in 1868. It helped members in sickness and distress, contributed to burials, furnished aid to widows, and carried out other benevolent services. Its original twenty members held meetings in the basement of Temple Emanu-El.[131] Other charities of the old type were the ladies' Gemilas Chesed, also for aid to the poor, organized in 1862, and a Hebrew Widows' and Orphans' Association, which existed in 1863.[132] All these organizations generally had a synagogal origin or association.

The Hebrew Relief Society, not of synagogue origin, was formally organized on September 22, 1867. It gradually dominated Jewish charity in the city, and laid the basis of Milwaukee's structure of Jewish philanthropy. The object of the new Hebrew Relief Society was "to contribute to the relief and maintenance of the sick and destitute people of the Hebrew faith," and it began by disbursing $42 during its first month. The Hebrew Relief Society did not confine its scope to residents of Milwaukee or to transients. As early as 1868, it donated $20 toward the relief of Jews in Russia.[133]

Milwaukee's first charitable aid to Jews abroad came in 1859, during the Spanish-Moroccan War, when about 3,000 Jews took refuge in Gibraltar under the protection of the British flag. A Milwaukee committee raised $70 in one week of February, 1860, and sent it to Sir Moses Montefiore for the refugees' benefit. Resolutions were adopted, thanking Montefiore "especially for his noble and energetic intercession," and the Governor of Gibraltar "for the protection and support he has bestowed upon our poor Moroccan brethren."[134] In acknowledgment Montefiore wrote on March 13, 1860:

... This evidence of sympathy for our suffering brethren though so distantly located from yourselves will be warmly appreciated by the London Relief Committee, and I am but anticipating their wishes in conveying to you our grateful thanks for your benevolent assistance.

For your kind expressions to Lady Montefiore and myself, I am also indebted, and beg most sincerely to express my earnest wishes for the prosperity of your Congregation, and the welfare of its individual members.[135]

Unlike later generations, charity at home and abroad was of minor concern to Milwaukee's early Jews.

FRATERNITY AND CULTURE

Membership in Milwaukee's numerous ritualistic lodges and benevolent societies included prominent citizens alongside working people and small merchants. Affiliation provided a sense of "belonging" and security. Only later did many wealthier lodge members draw apart into their private social clubs.

Jews soon entered the mainstream of fraternal life. By the 1850's they moved in the circles of other German newcomers, where they found friendship and social contact. They were at home in such groups, especially because they shared the same language. The German element alone supported scores of lodges, such as the Sons of Hermann, Druids, Harugari, Knights of Pythias, Diamond Brothers, Sons of Freedom, Sons of Liberty, Masons, Odd Fellows, and Turnverein Milwaukee.[136] And Jews figured prominently in most of these organizations.

Three local lodges of Odd Fellows existed by 1851. In that year, its charitable benefits amounted to $4,436, of which $3,430 was expended for relief of members and $711 for burial of the dead. The Milwaukee Lodge of the Sons of Hermann was the most popular lodge of the period, listing 140 members in 1849.[137]

The Turnverein, so important in 19th century Germany, was brought to Milwaukee in 1853. It promoted the "harmonious development of the mind and body," by introducing systematic physical exercise as a regular part of education. Milwaukee became one of the main centers of the movement, with Turner Associations on the North, South and East Sides of the city.

Jews actively participated in, and in many instances officered, five Masonic lodges. Harmony Lodge, No. 142, organized in 1863, was almost entirely Jewish in membership.[138] Odd Fellows' Armenia Lodge, No. 97 (today Golden Links Lodge) was organized in 1859 by a few men, including Jacob and David Adler. The former served as Grand Treasurer for many years. Herman S. Mack, a Grand Patriarch of the Grand Encampment, represented the Grand Lodge of Wisconsin at conventions of the Grand Lodge of the United States.[138A] Influential Jews did not confine their interest to one lodge but could often be found in several lodges of the same order.

The city's Jews also wove a network of fraternal societies of their own. The mutual-aid societies which came into existence at the beginning of the modern era as an outgrowth of Jewish burial societies and other synagogue organizations were the forerunners of the Jewish lodges and fraternal orders which became important institutions in the Jewish community. The Independent Order of B'nai B'rith, the first Jewish fraternal order in the United States, was founded by German Jews in New York in 1843 as a society "based on the teachings of Judaism, [which] would banish from its deliberations all doctrinal and dogmatic discussions, and by the practice of moral and benevolent precepts bring about union and harmony" among Jews.[139] It took over the idea of a secret ritual from the Masons, for the earliest members of B'nai B'rith were also members of non-sectarian orders. By 1855, the Order had twenty lodges. German was abandoned early as the official language but lasted far longer in Milwaukee.[140]

Other organizations followed the B'nai B'rith pattern. Thus, in 1849, the Independent Order Free Sons of Israel originated among German Jews; in 1859, the German Jewish Order B'rith Abraham was organized; the Order Kesher Shel Barzel (Iron Knot) was created in 1860. Including the Order of B'nai Moshe, there were, by 1860, five national Jewish fraternal orders in the United States.[141]

Jewish fraternal activity in Milwaukee before 1870 is primarily associated with the B'nai B'rith. A lodge called *Junge Maenner Verbruederung* decided in 1861 to become the first B'nai B'rith lodge in Milwaukee.[142] As Gilead Lodge, No. 41, it was instituted on June 30, 1861, shortly after the outbreak of the Civil War. Jacob L. Miller, Grand Nassi Ab of the Order, and Isaac M. Wise came to Milwaukee to install the German lodge, which then numbered about forty members. During the Civil War years, its thirty members met in a bare room over a saloon on Market Street, "up a crooked old stairway."[143] Matters began to improve in the Fall of 1865, when it moved to better quarters, and membership soon rose to nearly eighty. The personal appearance of such distinguished personalities as Wise and Peixotto helped to attract new members.[144] Despite Gilead's opposition, a charter was granted in 1866 to the new English-language Isaac Lodge, No. 87, with about forty members.[145] There apparently was room in Milwaukee for still another B'nai B'rith lodge, for Milwaukee Lodge, No. 141, was also established.[146]

By 1870, a Jewish non-synagogal environment existed, granting material benefits, encouraging social intercourse and occupying itself generally with good works. After the Civil War years, Milwaukee's B'nai B'rith lodges dedicated themselves to raising $100,000 towards building a Hebrew Orphan Asylum in Cleveland. Milwaukee's lodges raised their share by giving a ball and a fair. The *Sentinel* hoped that "citizens, of all creeds and nationalities, will unite" at the grand ball, which took place at Music Hall on February 29, 1868.[147]

Scores of men and women industriously prepared for the Orphan's Fair held in City Hall on July 22, 1868. Homes in each ward became receiving points for contributions and gifts. The *Sentinel* commented when the fair opened:

> . . . Seldom, if ever, have we seen at a like occasion such a profusion of the very choicest flowers, embroideries, lace and white goods, furniture and all kinds of wearing apparel, as met the eyes of the lucky visitor wherever he may look. And how many are the chances to procure for a comparative small sum of money a "nice piece of honey soap," a "bottle of cologne," a "sweet cake," all offered by the very handsomest of handsome young ladies, who will "hang" on your arm for ten minutes if you will invest "ten cents" for a grab in the bag

which secures you either a piece of molasses candy . . . So go early and go often, and you will not regret it.[148]

The fair, "not like any other fair," was deemed an outstanding success, and turned over $1,644 to the Hebrew Orphan Asylum.[149] Much more modest were the cultural efforts of the B'nai B'rith lodges. In 1870, they established the Milwaukee Literary Society, to provide a reading room, a library, and monthly lectures.[150] But it did not last long.

To Milwaukee came sixty delegates for the Western District Grand Lodge convention of B'nai B'rith in 1867. They represented "the most influential and intelligent members of the District, far beyond the usual average, and showing a remarkable progress in the intellectual character of the meeting as contrasted with former ones." The Grand Lodge committee which sought a location for the planned Hebrew Orphan Asylum preferred Milwaukee, "provided that sufficient inducements in the way of a site for buildings" were offered. However, that home did not materialize.[151]

All was not business. A picnic for 1,000 men and women, including the Mayor and city officials, was held at Quentin's Park. On the second day of the convention, "at about one o'clock the Lodge, escorted by two brass bands, marched to the park, followed by a large number of carriages containing a brilliant galaxy of beauty." There was a banquet in the evening for 430 guests ending in a grand ball.[152]

CULTURAL ACTIVITY

Professional music, dramatics, and a modicum of art supplemented the amateur efforts of the village period, but remained intermittent during the first generation of cityhood. The "Forty-eighters" made their chief contributions to the city's life in the fields of music, liberal social thought and education.

Musical interest ran high among the earliest German immigrants, and Hans Balatka, a refugee from the Viennese revolution of 1848, was mainly responsible for organizing it. Through his efforts, the Milwaukee Musical Society began in 1850 with a small orchestra and chorus. Its performances on the Western frontier included the classic symphonic and operatic repertoire —Handel, Mozart, Beethoven, and the contemporary romantics. In 1864, with the erection of the Academy of Music, the Society's membership increased from 75 to 600 within a year, and by 1869, the society had given more than 185 public performances.[153]

In no cultural enterprise did Jews participate more enthusiastically than in music. The Milwaukee Musical Society was headed by Jacob Mahler, who began a long tenure as its president in 1851. His wife, formerly a soprano in the Karlsruhe court opera, performed often. Isaac Neustadtl, Lewis S. Mack and Nic Simon were managers of the society during its first decade, and Julius Bruno, one of the founders, was also active. In the 1860's Henry M. Mendel served as secretary and treasurer.[154] Common interest in music brought together Milwaukee's native Americans and German immigrants.[155]

Jews were prominent supporters of the German legitimate theatre, which was housed in the Stadt Theatre from 1868. Preceded by amateur theatricals as early as 1850, each year brought an improvement in stage production, higher literary standards and better professional acting.[156] Schiller and Grillparzer and other German classics were performed before discriminating audiences at a time when the American stage had little to show but potboilers and melodramas.

Three organizations got their vitality from the "Forty-eighters": the *Freie Gemeinde* (Free Congregation), the Society of Free Men, and the *Turnverein*. All were dedicated to liberal social thought and had numerous Jewish members.[157]

A significant cultural group was the Germania Society, organized by twelve young men in 1864 to advance German culture.[158] It paralleled the Yankee cultural sphere's Young Men's Association, organized in 1847, which maintained a lecture platform on which such men as Horace Mann, Greeley, Emerson, Lowell, and Beecher spoke.[159] By 1867, the Association counted 3,000 members and its library of 10,000 volumes was the nucleus of the Milwaukee Public Library.[160] Very few of its members would have been Jews, for the latter were predominantly in the German fold.

Other facets of cultural life were available to a limited degree. Occasionally works of art were exhibited, and transient violinists and pianists performed.[161]

Alongside B'nai B'rith social activities, the Harmonic Club was founded in 1866. Its members were the new Jewish wealthy, who desired to take their entertainment in an exclusive atmosphere.[162] Barely twenty years after the first Jews laboriously reached the wilderness town, a leisured class of rich Jews was enjoying the fruits of success in a thriving Western city.

PART TWO

Years of Growth
1870-1925

I

Introduction:

Growth in Population and Ideas

MILWAUKEE JEWRY, stable during the 1870's and 1880's, changed decisively during the first generation of the twentieth century. Between the conclusion of its pioneer period and the closing of free immigration to the United States in 1925, it expanded numerically, became a distinct cultural entity, and entered the sphere of national and world Jewish affairs. At the same time, many of the old traits persisted. The Jews, mainly merchants and professional people, along with some workers, freely took their share in the life of the city and in movements which earned national prominence for the State of Wisconsin.

From 2,000 Jews in an 1875 population of about 90,000, the Jewish population rose to about 8,000 in Milwaukee in 1900, when 285,000 people lived in the city. In 1925 about 22,000 Jews lived among some 500,000 Milwaukeeans. At least 9,000 Jews reached the city as immigrants, and often had large families, while the number of native Jews increased only slightly during this period. There were some losses owing to direct conversion to Christianity or, as more often happened, by "leakage" out of the Jewish community after a cultural and religious erosion of Jewishness. We do not know how many fell away, but the number may have reached several hundred. There were rare instances of conversion to Judaism, generally for the purpose of marrying a Jewish partner.

Nineteenth-century Milwaukee Jewry was part of the German community in America's "Deutsch Athens." All knew German, which was as integrally a part of Jewish religious life as was Yiddish among East Europeans. Jews were prominent in the German press and theatre, and taught German in the schools. Many merged with the city's German community. This ultra-Germanism was the major source of "leakage" in the nineteenth century. The new century opened a wide gulf between Germanism and Jewishness as the relentless process of assimilation insured the submersion of the German language, however slowly it was to take place. On the other hand, the anti-semitic tendencies of Imperial Germany, which affected German circles in America, do not seem to have taken root in Milwaukee. There was a second reason for the separation of Germanism and the Jewish community. The majority of Milwaukee Jewry by 1900 were immigrants from Eastern Europe, and Germanism was foreign to them and to their children. Instead, the Jews took their place as an independent ethnic group, alongside the ethnic groups which established themselves in the city: Poles, Italians, Slovaks, Greeks, Hungarians, and others.

Culturally unlike the earlier settlers, the new East European majority of Milwaukee Jewry nevertheless followed them into various branches of retail business, such as the small manufacturing of consumer goods (cigars, men's clothing), as well as the professions. The new century proved inhospitable to small business, which had to grow large to survive, and this worked in opposition to Jewish economic habits. But there was a positive side to the great trends of American employment, in the immeasurable expansion of the professions and the white collar job market. Countless sons and daughters of Jewish immigrants aspired to be doctors, dentists, lawyers, teachers, academics, accountants and civil servants. Whereas only the grandchildren of the early immigrants tended to enter these fields, the children of Russian and Polish Jews were already moving into them.

Wisconsin was one of the most exciting states in the American Union during the first twenty-five years of the century. Old-line Republicanism and Bourbon Democracy were challenged and overcome by the Progressivism of Robert M. LaFollette, and Socialism, led by Victor L. Berger, a Jew. As New York was the trial base for the urban reformism of the New Deal, so Wisconsin was the fount of midwestern agrarian and small town democracy. Milwaukee Jewry did not play the role in Wisconsin which was played by Jews in New York; neither their numbers nor the background of the Progressive program enabled them to do so. But Jewish life in Milwaukee was quickened by the vibrant politics of the time, particularly by the Social Democratic Party which rose to power with considerable Jewish support to assume control of the municipality for over thirty years.

As the vigorous political atmosphere of the city stimulated Jewish interest in politics, so the new Jewish movements stimulated Jewish life and created genuine issues in a community which saw none after the forlorn orthodox resistance to Reform. American Jewry was becoming a self-conscious body, and national organizations were sprouting up to represent its many interests. The age of insularity was ended by mass immigration, Zionism, Socialism, and the needs of European Jewry maimed by World War I.

The first generation of the twentieth century was the greatest period of Milwaukee Jewry in economic and social growth, in Jewish assertiveness, and in the seriousness of issues presented, debated, and resolved.

POPULATION GROWTH 1870-1925

The first systematic attempt to obtain definite statistics of the Jews in the United States was undertaken in 1877. A tentative report gave 189,576 as an incomplete total Jewish population, and in September, 1880 came the final figure of 230,257. In 1888, Isaac Markens estimated the country's Jewish population at 400,000; in 1897, David Sulzberger estimated it at 937,800; it was given as 1,058,135 in 1900. Wisconsin was credited with 2,559 Jews in the 1880 survey, and 10,000 in the year 1899.[1]

Early in 1873, the Milwaukee *Daily Sentinel* estimated "about 300 Jewish families in the city, which would probably equal 2,000 souls." In view of the conclusions of Rabbi Eppstein's census two years later, the *Sentinel* understated the number of families while overestimating the aggregate of persons. A better estimate might have been 360 families, representing approximately 1,800 souls.[2]

The first authentic census of the Jewish community in Milwaukee or anywhere in the United States was undertaken by Rabbi Elias Eppstein of Congregation B'ne Jeshurun, and released to the press in August, 1875.[3] It casts a penetrating light on the Jewish community of that day and on American Jewry as well. Rabbi Eppstein commented:

> The undertaking, as is always the case, was favored by some and opposed by others. By the first it was extolled above its merits, and by the latter as warmly condemned. In respect to the wishes of the latter, it should be particularly noted that the above account does not include the gentlemen and their families, as they refused to be counted in, one, on account of religious scruples, and, the other, for reasons unknown to us, and, possibly, to himself. Had they allowed their families to be enrolled, it would have added four males and four females to the number, and would have made the total of Israelitish citizens 2,074.

Reporting 417 families and 65 single persons in all, the total population of 2,068 represented 1,120 males and 948 females. A further breakdown by ages indicated the following:

Under	Males	Females
14	432	388
20	162	143
30	248	167
50	196	189
70	71	46
90	11	15
	1,120	948

Thus, we learn that the size of the average Jewish family was 4.8; children under fourteen made up almost 40% of the population; individuals under twenty years of age comprised 54% of the Jewish community. There were 514 children of school age—301 males and 213 females, of whom 404 attended the public schools, and 110, private and higher schools.

Figures on nativity revealed that 864 persons, or almost 43% of the total, were born in the United States; Germany—503; Bohemia and Austria—432; Russia—139; France—84; England—40; Roumania—4; Switzerland—2. There were one male and two females blind, one deaf and dumb and two "Inmates" of the National Home for Disabled Volunteers. There were no Jewish insane, cripples, or inmates of the Poor House.

Jewish institutions comprised two house of worship—B'ne Jeshurun and Emanu-El, together with eight benevolent associations, two literary societies, a young ladies' dramatic association, and a club.[4]

By 1895 the Jewish population had grown from 2,074 to about 7,000, in a city of some 265,000,[5] or approximately 2.6% of the inhabitants. Russian Jews, then numbering between 2,500 and 3,000, comprised about 39% of the Jewish community. Adding to these figures the two hundred Roumanian Jewish families who also arrived here, as well as individual immigrants after 1895, the total Jewish population of Milwaukee obviously reached at least 8,000 by the turn of the century. From the conclusions of a special inquiry concerning the Jews in this country carried out by the U.S. Census Office in 1890, which established 5.71 as the average Jewish family size at that time, we may assume that approximately 1,400 families constituted the Jewish community of Milwaukee in 1900.[6]

In the thirty years following 1900, Milwaukee's Jewish population multiplied about threefold, but the available estimates vary widely. In the table below, the contemporary figures which seem most nearly accurate are marked by an asterisk.

Year	Population	Source
1900	* 8,000	Authors' estimate
1903	7,000	Federated Jewish Charities, *21st Annual Report* (1922)
1905	8,000	*Jewish Encyclopedia,* s.v. United States of America
1907	*10,000	*American Jewish Yearbook*
1908	15,000	*American Israelite,* September 10, 1908
1910	[7,757]	Yiddish-speaking only; U.S. Census

Year	Population	Source
1911	10,000	Jewish Colonization Association (ICA) *Amerikanishe Shtet* (St. Petersburg, 1911)
1912	15,000	Industrial Removal Office
1917	20,000	*American Israelite*, November 22, 1917, and *American Jewish Yearbook*, 1918-1919
1917	*17,000	Authors' estimate
1922	20,000	Federated Jewish Charities, *21st Annual Report* (1922)
1923	17,000–20,000	Jewish Community survey
1925	"almost 30,000"	Federated Jewish Charities, *24th Annual Statement* (1925)
1926	"between 25,000 and 35,000"	*Jewish Community Blue Book, Supplement*, p. 11
1927	25,000	Federated Jewish Charities, *26th Annual Statement* (1927)
1929	5,000 families *25,000	Federated Jewish Charities, *28th Annual Statement* (1929)

II

Immigration from Eastern Europe

MOST OF THE CHANGES in the Jewish community, as well as its population growth, were due to the ceaseless arrival of East European immigrants alongside thousands of other newcomers from abroad. Between 1881 and 1910 at least 1,562,000 Jewish persons arrived in the United States.[1] Starting in enclaves of their own, isolated even from the settled Jewish community, the East European immigrants speedily learned American ways and the English language.[2]

Thousands of East European Jews left for America toward the end of the 1860's and the beginning of the 1870's, propelled by epidemics and famine in Lithuania in 1868—1869; the cholera epidemic in Poland in 1869; pogroms in Odessa in 1871;[3] the anti-Jewish outbreaks in Roumania, 1872; the general conscription in Russia in 1874;[4] the outbreak of the Russo-Turkish War in 1876.[5]

However, the main reasons for mass emigration were economic, and the anti-Jewish laws of Czarist Russia aggravated the problem. Despite a fivefold increase in Jewish population during the 19th century, the Jews of Russia were, with few exceptions, allowed to live only in the provinces of the Pale of Settlement. Even there, they could not live in the large cities where new industry was developing, nor on the land. Pent up in small towns and cities, they could only engage in petty trade and handicrafts, which new economic developments were undermining. Residentially restricted, politically persecuted, economically frustrated, East

69

European Jewry needed only the stimulus of pogroms and fresh decrees to convert the trickle of emigrants into a torrent. This came in 1881-1882, and again in 1891.

On March 13, 1881, Alexander II was assassinated when a dynamite bomb was hurled at him in St. Petersburg. Well-planned rumors were spread that Jews were responsible; six weeks later, on Easter Sunday, organized mob violence commenced against the Jews of Elizabethgrad, while the police stood by and watched. The pogroms spread northward, and continued intermittently for three years.

In the wake of the first pogroms came the "temporary" May Laws, on May 16, 1882, constituting "a permanent administrative pogrom" against the Jews. Jews in the Pale could no longer do business on Christian holidays, or own land or houses; they were forced out of the villages of the Pale into larger towns which were already overcrowded with tailors, innkeepers and tradesmen. As a result of all this, about 25,000 Jews left Russia for the United States during 1881—1882, and about 200,000 altogether during the 1880's.[6]

A decree of April, 1891, made the Pale of Settlement still less endurable. Among other restrictions, the Jews' urban residence was now limited to certain cities; they could not engage in agriculture, or attend universities; and they were to be dispossessed of real estate long held. Thousands of Jews were driven from Moscow and other principal cities in that year. Altogether, almost 600,000 Jews found refuge in the United States alone between 1881 and 1900. The Milwaukee public learned from their newspapers of the events of the 1890's, as they had not in 1881—1882.[7]

Jews from Western Russia and Lithuania were already in Milwaukee during the 1870's. The Old Cemetery Record Book between 1870 and 1876 names such places of origin as "Wistonitc," Kletschow, Warsaw, Cracow, Liebau, Werbalow, Funck, and Mofel Sowalk [sic], and Rabbi Eppstein's census in 1875 recorded 139 Jews who gave Russia as their birthplace. Since these newcomers constituted less than 7% of the Jewish population, and were mostly poor, the larger German-Jewish group paid them little attention.[8]

During 1881 and 1882, hundreds of those who made their way to Hamburg ultimately reached Milwaukee, after travels which lasted about six weeks.[9] Milwaukee was as remote from the problems of New York refugee relief in 1882 as New York was remote from the problems of Europe, but a few realized that some responsibility for the new immigrants would fall upon them. As early as April, 1880, local Jewish circles, encouraged by Rabbi Isaac Moses, showed interest in establishing a Milwaukee branch of the Alliance Israélite Universelle. However, Milwaukee Jewry was not ready to assume a role in world Jewish affairs, and merely took up a collection for the Alliance's Russian relief activities.[9A]

In response to American Jewish demands, the European organizations handling migration had promised to send only young, skilled workers as emigrants, and more or less tried to keep their word. But they were closer to hard realities than the Americans, who constantly complained that the rule was being broken—as it was, indeed. Besides, the European relief bodies were interested in deterring Russian Jews from settling in England, France and Germany. Thus, shiploads of Russian Jews continued to land at New York from October, 1881, throughout 1882, American Jewish protests notwithstanding.[10]

Word reached Milwaukee in October, 1881, of the imminent arrival of Russian refugees. A temporary committee, headed by Elias Friend and David Adler, was hastily formed, for "collecting money and finding shelter for prospective Russian refugees who might be sent to our city by the New York branch."[11] It addressed a circular to the city's Jews:

> Dear Sir—You are respectfully invited to attend a general meeting of the Israelites of this city for the purpose of taking under consideration a very urgent and heartrending appeal made by "The Alliance Israelite Universelle" in behalf of the unfortunate and persecuted Jews of Russia, who have recently again been the victims of religious barbarism.
>
> If you are a friend of humanity, a lover of freedom and civilization, come to this meeting, which will take place at Progress Hall (Library Building), Thursday evening, October 13th, at 7:45 P.M.[12]

Ten immigrants arrived on the morning of the meeting day. Ranging in age between 20 and 25, and described as "able-bodied and masters of trade," they encountered a friendly reception. The *Zeitgeist* found them "all nice, intelligent, and willing to work."[13]

The committee's appeal, and the presence of the refugees, stimulated about fifty "influential Israelites" to attend the meeting. The young arrivals were introduced and related their experiences and tribulations. The meeting raised $125 and constituted itself as a branch of the Alliance Israelite Universelle, known as the Immigrant Relief Society. Several neighborhood solicitation groups were appointed, and an appeal went out to Jewish communities scattered in Wisconsin. Meanwhile, jobs were procured for the refugees and for ten more who reached Milwaukee on November 16, 1881.[14]

Two weeks later, Moritz Ellinger, secretary of the New York Russian Immigrant Relief Society, who had been touring the country encouraging refugee aid, arrived in Milwaukee. He met a group of leading Jews in the afternoon, and in the evening addressed a public meeting in the Library on Grand Avenue. While insisting that he came only to bring information and not to collect funds, within ten minutes $375 was subscribed, and $1,000 within a week. The state-wide appeal brought encouraging results, as Jews of Chippewa Falls, Bloomer and Eau Claire, Wisconsin, soon turned over $101.50 to the Milwaukee committee.[15]

Three more refugee families arrived from New York between December 29 and January 3, 1882. Most of the arrivals to date had come from the neighborhood of Kiev and Odessa; a substantial number spoke English, French and German, and some brought along a few hundred dollars. Jobs had been found for many on farms outside Milwaukee. But refugees were arriving faster than it was possible to find employment or housing for them, and they were temporarily placed in boarding houses. To reduce expenses and enable the refugees to keep house for themselves, the Immigrant Relief Society rented a large house at 621 Railroad Street, "next door to St. Vincent's Infant Asylum," and 22 refugees were moved there in January, 1882. A *Sentinel* reporter found "an old-fashioned, rambling structure, a story and a half in height" inhabited by fourteen men, three women and five children (aged two months to twelve years of age) who appeared "clean-looking and neatly clad."[16]

Work had been found for some of the refugees in diverse places: one was a carpenter, another a coppersmith in railroad shops; a third was a buttonhole maker; a fourth, formerly a cigarette maker, was now a cigar maker; a fifth, a brewer at Schlitz; and a sixth, a soapmaker. Most of the refugees, however, had been farmers and merchants in Russia, and wanted commercial work from which their ignorance of English excluded them.

The Milwaukee Immigrant Relief Society decided instead to settle their clients on farms, and had $1,100 in hand to purchase land and equipment.[17] The Society arranged to settle three families in the Dakotas and eight in northern Michigan.[18] While refugees were being sent from Milwaukee, others were returning. Thus, on February 5th, five Russian immigrants who had left the Michigan pineries were quartered at the Clifton House by the Society.[19]

By April, 1882, the *Zeitgeist* reported that all refugees had found employment, were sending money to their families in Russia, and were looking forward to reunion in America. But, it noted, Russian emigrants were arriving almost every week, many of them ill and ragged.[20] Probably they were not of the organized, subsidized immigration, but had made their way on their own slight resources. Yet by May, 1882, all had found work and some had started savings accounts in local banks,[21] and the outlook was favorable.

EMERGENCY

After its first enthusiasm, the Jewish community looked apathetically upon the Russian newcomers in the Winter and Spring of 1882. Rabbi Moses complained that

> the community at large has not participated in the support of the immigrant, and except for the officers . . . no one seems to be concerned with the immigrant, and the entire burden of caring for them and providing work for them rests literally on the shoulders of three or four gentlemen. . . .[22]

The Emigrant Relief Association's efforts to become a membership association at $4.00 a year were unsuccessful.[23]

All who have been working on the project of settlement of the Russian Jewish immigrants in our community, whether it be in the capacity of raising money or finding work for the immigrant or simply caring for his needs, can testify to the complete unpopularity of this cause. . . . Those . . . who, for one reason or another, fail to respond to the cry of the needy . . . should please remain silent and refrain from decrying the fine work of the others.[24]

Late in May only seventy members were enrolled, "while 500 ought to be obtained." With few members and no funds, the "faithful co-workers tired of their heavy burden" and the group came to a dead stop.[25]

At this point, a somewhat different group took charge of the situation. They appealed once more for funds and took the unusual step of asking for donations from the non-Jewish public.[26] On June 1, 1882, it issued the following memorable broadside to the community at large:

TO THE PUBLIC: It is superfluous to attempt to recount the terrible outrages committed upon the Jewish inhabitants of Russia. . . .

The citizens of Milwaukee and vicinity well know from experience that their Jewish fellow citizens do not, as a usual thing, call upon them for assistance when it concerns their own poor and needy, but have with a will which we know is appreciated, taken care of them at their own, not inconsiderable expense. They have never called upon the public for assistance and have always been ready to aid every sectarian or non-sectarian charity that has presented itself to their consideration. When they now call attention to the fulfillment of this obvious duty, it is solely to impress upon you the urgency of the case which makes the Israelites of Milwaukee depart from a well established practice.

Thousands upon thousands of men, women and children who are driven from their homes by a merciless, fanatical mob, deprived of their all, in many instances barely escaping with their lives, after having experienced tortures which no one can describe, are trying to find refuge in this only land of liberty. They come without means, broken in spirit, discouraged, deprived of the fruits of many years of toil and labor, and ask but the privilege craved by the most humble—an existence, the permission to earn a livelihood and but slight assistance by which they can be placed in position to do so.

They are not paupers who want to live from the means and earnings of others, but are anxious and willing to work themselves. The experience of this and kindred associations has been that they *will* work, that they *are* industrious, and that like others of their race, they will be no burden to a community after the opportunity to earn a livelihood is once fairly placed in their hands.

The Jewish communities of this country have until now with alacrity taken care, almost alone, of many thousands; but the funds are becoming exhausted, the tax placed on them being very burdensome. Such has been the experience of Milwaukee Israelites, and relying upon the kind spirit, the charitable disposition, the neighborly good feeling of their fellow citizens of other creeds, they call upon them for financial assistance. The well-known probity of those Israelites, already in your midst, their honesty of purpose, cannot but be guarantee to the public that means so contributed will be expended only upon subjects worthy of such charitable consideration.

The committee hopes that this appeal to the people of Milwaukee will not be in vain, and that the occasion which obliges us to resort to such an unusual course will be one soon to be classed amongst the past and buried in oblivion with similar occurrences during the dark periods of former centuries.

Those who may be disposed to support this cause with contributions of money, are kindly requested to address communications to Mr. David Adler, president Russian Relief Association, Milwaukee.

THE COMMITTEE
Milwaukee, June 1, 1882.[27]

A freshened spirit seemed to fill the few activists as Christian citizens donated over $400 within a few weeks, prompting the *Zeitgeist* to expect that "those Israelites who have not yet given anything, or only very little, will now follow the example of those

Christian philanthropists." A theatre performance in May in Schlitz
Park brought some financial assistance; the Ladies' Sewing Society donated $100; during June $200 came from the Hebrew
Emigrant Aid Society of New York. L. B. Schram and B. M. Weil
were sent to a meeting in New York on June 4th, to consider
future plans for assistance to Russian immigrants.[28] During 1882,
the Hebrew Emigrant Aid Society in New York had dispatched
22 men, 2 women and 17 children to Milwaukee with its funds.[29]
But the critical test was at hand.

On June 27, 1882, the Hebrew Emigrant Relief Society of New
York telegraphed Louis B. Schram, secretary of the Milwaukee
Russian Relief Association: "Montreal Committee telegraphs Mr.
Yates that 350 refugees from England pass through there tonight
booked for Milwaukee."[30] The Jewish community was dumb-
founded. Relief funds were low and the organization was unpre-
pared for such news. "It has come to us like a whirlwind," wrote
the *Zeitgeist*. "The Mansion House Committee (in London) has
sent us nearly 250 persons without any previous announcement,
thus placing the poor refugees, as well as the local committee, into
a pitiful position. Words are insufficient to describe such a disgraceful action."[31]

Schram received the telegram on June 28. Next morning at
his law office, John Black, John R. Goodrich, E. P. Matthews, and
County Poor Superintendent Walthers joined with Philip Carpeles, Elias Friend, and B. M. Weil to prepare shelter for the immigrants until they could be returned "or otherwise disposed of."
A second committee was to ascertain where and when the refugees would arrive; and a third group was to solicit aid from the
public The meeting was adjourned until 2 P.M.[32]

At noon, Mayor John M. Stowell issued the following proclamation to the Cream City's 115,000 inhabitants:

MAYOR'S OFFICE
MILWAUKEE, JUNE 29, 1882

To the People of Milwaukee:
  I learn that refugees from Russia, 350 in number, are hourly
expected to be landed in our city. These people have been

VIEW OF MILWAUKEE, 1853 Lithograph (*Municipal Reference Library*)

Elias Friend (1824-1890)   David Adler (1821-1905)

PIONEER SETTLERS (*Wisconsin Jewish Chronicle*)

Max Landauer (1837-1924)   Adolph W. Rich (1843-1917)

driven from a despotic government by the most cruel atrocities known in the history of man. They are in God's image and entitled to room and life on God's earth. We must temporarily afford them sustenance and shelter until they can help themselves. The little band of noble workers who have been furnishing succor to the comparatively few that have arrived hitherto, are utterly unable to provide for such a number as are at our doors. I called upon all who are in any degree able to be ready to respond to the appeal which must, in some form, be made to their charity immediately on their arrival. Due notice will be given either through the press or by personal application, as soon as measures are definitely decided upon for their relief. Probably a depository will be designated where contributions of money, food, and perhaps clothing may be sent. I earnestly hope that our national holiday may be a glad day to these poor people.

JOHN M. STOWELL, Mayor.[33]

Stowell had barely signed the proclamation and Schram's group had not returned from lunch when word came from the railway depot that "three full carloads of refugees" had pulled in from Chicago. Instead of the expected 350, the group numbered 218, of whom 150 were men and the remainder were women and children; 25 were under twenty years of age. All were immediately taken in charge and sent to temporary quarters in the Leedom building at 197 and 199 Broadway, and the new barn of the Milwaukee Street Railway Company on West Water Street; others went to McGeoch's building, on Second between Grand Avenue and Wells Street. Youths and unmarried men were lodged in a room of the Jewett and Sherman Spice Mills.[34]

The flabbergasted relief organization called a general citizens' meeting to devise means of providing for the "moneyless and friendless." They could not refrain from bitter recriminations at the European authorities, and gave the impression that they were throwing up their hands:

The citizens of Milwaukee are informed of the arrival here from England of 350 Russian emigrants sent by the Mansion House Committee, without warning or intimation of any kind. The Emigrant relief association has provided for these people temporary shelter and food to meet their immediate and most pressing wants, but they are helpless and unable to do more. The citizens of Milwaukee must undertake the charge of these unfortunates, thrown upon our mercy by the inconsiderate, unconscionable action of the Mansion House Committee. We invite every public-spirited and charitable citizen of the city to be present at a meeting to be held at the Academy of Music this afternoon, June 30, at 4 o'clock P.M., in order to devise means to meet this emergency. THE RUSSIAN EMIGRANT RELIEF SOCIETY AND MANY OTHER CITIZENS.[35]

The arrival of 218 persons at one time was without parallel in the city's annals; it meant one refugee for each thirteen or fourteen Jews.

The local relief society instructed its president to cablegram to London:

Sending refugees without notice is an outrage upon humanity. All citizens without distinction denounce the act. No more will be allowed to land.

David Adler
President Milwaukee Russian Relief Society[36]

A second dispatch went to New York:

Milwaukee, June 30—Hebrew Russian Aid Society, N. Y.
Two hundred and twenty-five refugees arrived yesterday. No money or person here to provide for them. We are done and refuse to countenance England's shameful abuse of America's generous charity toward Europe's paupers. Our connection with you and the alliance is severed and our society dissolved.

David Adler
President[37]

At the same time, the secretary also wrote:

June 30, 1882
If you send many more Russians to Milwaukee, whether it be to this Society or "to whom it may concern," they will be shipped back to you without permitting them to leave the depot.

Louis B. Schram[38]

Elias Friend, Lewis Silber and B. M. Weil were to confer the next morning with the Mayor and the Board of Supervisors concerning temporary lodging for "the destitute and sick." At the noon session of the Chamber of Commerce on June 30, President Freeman officially called the attention of members to the needs of the refugees.[39]

One day after the refugees arrived there was a public meeting at the Academy of Music. Although not as well attended as was hoped, it was a noteworthy gathering in the history of the community. Following David Adler's opening remarks, Mayor Stowell, who presided, expressed the conviction that it would not be prudent to send the exiles back as had been suggested by some. The Rev. H. T. Rose, speaking next, emphasized that it was not only a duty of Jews, but of Christians, to relieve the pressing wants of the refugees. Other speakers included L. B. Schram, Charles L. Colby, former governor William E. Smith, and Drs. Marden (Health Commissioner) and Martin, the latter concerning the sanitary conditions of the newcomers. To provide for their immediate wants, a public committee with Mayor John M. Stowell as chairman and W. E. Smith, C. L. Colby, T. H. Rose and W. P. McLaren as members, was appointed.[40] The assemblage resolved:

Whereas, Between 200 and 300 Russian refugees have been forwarded from Russia to Milwaukee and are now in our midst, in poor and destitute circumstances,
Resolved, That it is the duty of the citizens of Milwaukee, without distinction of race or nationality, to provide for their immediate wants.[41]

The 218 unexpected refugees became equally a civic and a Jewish charity. The Jewish and non-Jewish committees met next morning and designated groups for finance, transportation, relief, employment and solicitation.

The Committee on City and County Poor donated thirty iron bedstead from the county hospital, bed clothing for the women, and food for all.[42]

A warm spirit of humane benevolence marked the response of the general community. People brought food and clothing to 89 and 91 Chicago Street, Blascow's Dye Works; the Ladies Relief Sewing Society undertook to sew garments; Irish citizens met the following Sunday afternoon to assist the refugees.[43] Following the example of the Ladies' Sewing Society, the local Ladies' Aid Societies each contributed $100.[44] By July 8th, $2,000 had already been received.[45]

The old Leedom factory building on lower Broadway, to which most of the immigrants were taken, had been vacant for several years; it had broken and boarded windows and other marks of dilapidation. A visiting reporter saw:

> Its tenants swarm within it like bees in a hive, and have so far during the day-time overflowed the surrounding neighborhood in quest of fresh air and sunshine. In a room on the lower floor there were, when the reporter entered, about thirty people, men, women, and children. Much space was taken up by bedding and boxes, which were strewn about the apartment. On several mattresses spread upon the floor, men were sitting and tired-looking little children sprawled, some crying and others trying to go to sleep. Upon two of the trunks, or traveling boxes, rather, women sat, each of whom was engaged in nursing a child.[46]

However, physicians reported that the refugees were "in an extraordinary healthy condition," although one man was dangerously ill. Health Commissioner Martin found no smallpox among the refugees and many had been vaccinated at Port Huron, the port of entry from Canada.[47] The men were still wearing

> their characteristic Russian costumes, including short, peaked caps and coats with great tails reaching nearly to the ground. They wore their hair with long front locks, and their faces were balanced with heavy beards. Most of the men yielded reluctantly to the application of the razor to their chins.[48]

The leader of the entire group was Leon Blumenthal, who had conducted the party from Liverpool to Milwaukee, wearing a red ribbon badge stamped "Relief of Russian Fugitives, Liverpool Commission, Mansion House Fund." Thirty years of age, Blumenthal had been a manufacturing chemist in Odessa. Following the sack of his business by a mob in July, 1881, he fled to Galicia and made his way thence to Liverpool. From there, he obtained passage to Montreal, a voyage of about ten days. His immigrant group now totaled some 300 persons, nearly all of whom spoke "German," presumably Yiddish. Among them were six masons, four bakers, three butchers, four carpenters, and three locksmiths. Three women and eleven men had taken sick en route.[49]

Among the immigrants were David Braunstein, age, 22, and his wife, 18, who became parents a few days after their arrival in Milwaukee. A native of Chotin, Braunstein deserted the Russian army toward the end of April, 1881, and fled with his wife to Galicia. Then there was the family of Paul Krasnowitz, age 33— his wife, sister, 16, a son aged 3 (later Rabbi Nathan Krass), and a daughter aged 16. The father had been a tobacco merchant at Odessa until his business was laid waste by the Russian mob. Isaac Zimmerman, 36 years of age, eleven years the business agent of a Polish duke, had once supervised four distilleries and the sale of timber cut on the estates. Another, Joseph Chudisch, 28, had been a farmer near Odessa, until the Russian terror. Then he fled to America, leaving his wife in Europe.[50] Within a few days, eight more families, also sent from Montreal, swelled the group,[51] and about one week later, four young men and one young woman "assigned" to New York reached Milwaukee, where the committee reluctantly provided them with lodging at the Clifton House.

The Jewish communal leaders were now determined to prevent further immigrants from coming to Milwaukee. In response to the cablegrams sent on June 30, David Adler had received a cable from the Russo-Jewish Committee in London on July 4: "No further Russians coming. Am writing."[52] This was reassuring, but it was still feared that more trainloads of refugees might come from other cities. Angered by the arrival of the additional refugees from Montreal on July 7, Schram telegraphed the Montreal Committee in uncompromising terms:

Fred Boas, Montreal:
   We demand peremptorily that you send no more Russians here. All coming from Montreal hereafter will be returned without taking from depot.[53]

Replying with "great reluctance" by return mail, Boas wrote:

Montreal, July 8, 1882

Louis B. Schram, Esq., Milwaukee,

Dear Sir: Your telegram on hand. Allow me to express my surprise at the tenor of your message. The idea must be abroad that our Russian brethren are an article of trade, aceptance of which may be refused at pleasure. If any arrive in the West hereafter without your special permission, I should *advise* you—in exchange for your peremptory demand I but humbly advise—to not concern yourself [sic] about them. It would require in my opinion an anti-Russian bill to prevent the Russians from going where they please in this land of the free. At present, if they understood their position at all, they would not mind the displeasure their presence in Milwaukee even may cause some people. Here, in these British Dominions, we allow even Russians to go wherever they please, and if Milwaukee is their place of destination—with which *we* have nothing to do—we do not intend to stop them on their passage through here, except for the purpose of giving them a good meal.

Yours, very sincerely,
(Signed) Fred Boas[54]

But when two families assigned to Buffalo and Chicago arrived in Milwaukee on July 16, the local association resolved to return the newcomers and to do so thereafter in every case.[55]

Fred Boas discovered that his sharp letter did nothing to shake the resolve which prevailed in Milwaukee since the trainload's arrival on June 29th. On July 24th he received an unprecedented note:

Emigrant Aid Relief Association
of Wisconsin
Milwaukee, July 24, 1882

Mr. Fred Boas, Emigrant Aid Society,
Montreal, Ca.

Dear Sir: We send you a man tonight who is sick and is unable to do anything for his support. Please return him to Europe, and oblige.

Yours respectfully,
David Adler, President

The Montreal Committee, shocked, considered placing the unfortunate refugee in a hospital. Boas sent the correspondence to the *Jewish Messenger* in New York, observing that ". . . the action of the gentlemen in Milwaukee seems to require no comment."[56]

In other instances the Milwaukee Russian Relief Association decided to return refugees to their native land. Thus, on July 21st, a family consisting of an aged and feeble man, his wife and daughter, 14, returned to Milwaukee from Clinton, Iowa, where they failed to obtain employment. Despite the fact that his son had been murdered at Odessa, the dejected father expressed the desire to return to Russia. They were forwarded back to Russia from Milwaukee.[57] In another instance, in August, 1882, Schram informed the Hebrew Emigrant Aid Society in New York that he was returning an immigrant girl

> . . . . because she cannot earn enough to support herself, has no relatives here, and unless continually supported by us would surely go wrong. This girl came to America with her "chosen" [groom] who got tired of her and turned her adrift.[58]

From June 30 to July 20, 1882, about 350 refugees made their way to Milwaukee and approximately fifty more arrived before the end of August.[59]

During these first days, two children were born, and the new Americans, named Washington and Garfield, were circumcised by Dr. Fish and Rabbi I. S. Moses. The rabbi also married the leader of the refugee group, Leon Blumenthal, to Mathilda Bolis, one of the refugees. Four children died and were buried in the local Jewish Cemetery.[60]

Religious observance did not seriously concern either the relief association or most of the refugees. Rabbi Moses was unsympathetic:

> The Sabbath and the dietary laws form no obstacle for those among them who are decent and willing to work. And here and there emerges from among them a self-impressed "Talmudic Jew" who would have the roasted doves that he expects to fly directly into his mouth, not only Kosher-slaughtered, but also Kosher prepared.[61]

In his *Zeitgeist*, he advocated immediate steps to provide Jewish education for the youngsters, and measures to prevent their parents' ways from embarrassing the native Jews:

> It will be necessary to establish a free school for the children where, after returning from public school, they will receive their Hebrew and religious instruction under the direction of the two local rabbis . . . Also, it will be necessary to form a women's society whose duty it will be to visit the families and activate society to contribute basic needs and civilize those families, so that they do not succumb in isolation; lest left to themselves, they perpetuate their semi-Asiatic existence. We believe we are not mistaken in maintaining that through such civilizing efforts, we shall be averting from ourselves a potential danger which threatens us.[62]

More immediately, the housing question required quick solutions. Broadway residents complained at the mayor's office that immigrants' quarters on their street were "unfit for human beings," and likely to produce epidemic contagion. A report in the *Evening Wisconsin* added that there were pools of stagnant water under the building; "the whole place is reeking with filth, emitting a most horrible stench." The building, he warned, was a fire trap. A nearby store had been compelled to "throw up the lease" and vacate.[63] Although Bernhard Gross of the Russian Relief Committee denied most of the charges,[64] the building was vacated late in July. [65]

ATTEMPTS AT SETTLEMENT

The principal task was to find jobs and homes for the refugees, and Milwaukee's Russian Relief Association explored every avenue. However, it showed marked preference for jobs away from Milwaukee. By July 6th, twenty had been provided with employment in different factories in the city, while homes had been found for thirty; in addition, ten persons had been sent to farms in Rock County, and ten others to quarries near Portage. Of the 300 refugees in the city on July 4, 1882, 200 reportedly left for various points in the week following. On one day alone—July

10th—sixty-two immigrants left Milwaukee for places in Wisconsin and Iowa: Wausau, 19; Fond du Lac, 2; Appleton, 3; Eau Claire, 7; Stevens Point, 6; La Crosse, 6; McGregor, 3; Davenport, 8; and Rock Island, 8.

Homes and positions were procured for others in Minnesota and the Dakotas. Women were employed to do housework and cook at $50 per year plus board, while men employed as farm hands received board and $75 to $100 a year.[66]

Several families that had settled with their own funds in the Jewish farming colony near Bismarck, Dakota Territory, eventually gave up and sought shelter in Milwaukee in the winter of 1882 and 1883. Accommodated for a while, they were subsequently sent on to St. Paul.

Destitute and in need of food and clothing, they had to rely again in 1884 upon the Russian Relief Committee of Milwaukee for help. The Minneapolis *Evening Journal* editorially blamed Milwaukeeans who had been "instrumental in sending a lot of penniless pack peddlers, ignorant of agriculture, on the frontiers." Philip Carpeles of Milwaukee replied: "I don't see how we can be accused of sending refugees to Dakota, when the fact is we only sent them as far as St. Paul. After they reached that point, our responsibility ceased."[67]

By July 20, 1882, fourteen of the sixty families who had come to Milwaukee had been settled in the city itself besides fifteen young unmarried people. Before despatching a family, the Relief Association gave its members $15 or $20 in addition to linen and clothing, and then sent them singly or in groups of two or three to neighboring Jews who agreed to care for them and give them employment.[68] Within two months after their arrival, hardly any able-bodied refugees remained unemployed in the city or state.[69]

The Milwaukee committee, with Mayor Stowell as chairman, raised about $4,000 to aid the immigrants. Deeming its primary task completed, the Milwaukee Russian Relief Association closed its books on August 31, 1882 and formally dissolved.[70] It was decided that the community would thereafter use the Hebrew Relief Society for dealing with immigrants.[71] It reported that the number of emigrants received between June 28 and September 21, 1882 was 424, of whom 245 were male, and 231 over 21 years of age. [72]

That the Russian Jews were an unwelcome burden to the Jewish community is indicated by Rabbi Moses:

> Our Russians are singing the old song of the dissatisfied . . . we doubt very much whether the majority ever had such remunerative jobs in the old country as they have managed to find here. However, most of our new citizens . . . are very industrious and have found decent livelihoods.[73]

Many immigrants took up the occupation of peddling "only to increase the already considerable number of peddlers in our city."[74]

In 1889, when a committee of English Jews asked Jewish organizations in American cities for their views on Jewish immigration, the response from Milwaukee declared that the immigrants "have been of a class that reflects no credit upon their brethren."[75] We do not know what the immigrants thought in their turn, but dislike no doubt bred dislike. Cultural and linguistic differences, and antagonism between givers and receivers of charity, created a deep gulf between the German Jews and the East Europeans which endured well into the 20th century.

A STEADY STREAM, 1883—1900

An addition of 500 to 550 people within one year to Milwaukee Jewry, whose numbers were not many more than the 2,074 counted by Rabbi Eppstein in 1875, was an event of primary importance. Moreover, immigrants attracted their friends and relatives in Europe to join them. Native Milwaukee Jews suspected that their generosity to the first immigrants was serving as a magnet to attract others, but perhaps they overestimated their own hospitality.

The lessons of 1881—1882 were not taken to heart by the Jews in Milwaukee. They had paid little attention to the social and religious background of the Russian Jews, whom they had sent to become farmhands for Christians, or to work in towns where no other Jews lived, or where neither the Sabbath and holidays nor the dietary laws could be maintained. Men who had been peddlers and craftsmen were told to be farmers, and ultimately returned to Milwaukee. In their haste to clear their docket of the unwelcome refugees, the committee seized opportunities without investigation. Soon after the Milwaukee Russian Relief Association disbanded on August 31, 1882, its beneficiaries began returning to town.[76]

Like the rest of American Jewry, local Jews long failed to realize that Russian immigration would be permanent. They assumed that they had witnessed a flood of refugees, not the first of many waves which were to reach American soil. It lay beyond the power of Western European and American Jews to stop immigration, even if they refused relief or steamship fare. The great majority of all Jewish immigrants moved anyhow, on their own resources.[77]

Russian Jews, especially relatives and friends of those already in the city, continued to come to Milwaukee throughout the decade of the eighties. The coming of these stragglers was hardly noticed by the community, for they went directly to their relatives and friends. In 1887, it was estimated that the city's "colony of Russian Jews" contained 100 to 150 families.[78] Although some scattered about the city, a large percentage occupied an entire block of old frame houses at the junction of East Water and North Water Streets.[79] "It seems to be the very height of their ambition," commented the *Israelite*, "to marry a deutsch Maedche." Several successful young Russian Jews did marry into "some of our best German Jewish families." Most of the Russian Jewish families became self-supporting, and many of their men learned trades. Only a few needed assistance from the Hebrew Relief Society, usually where a husband left his family in order to seek work elsewhere. Nevertheless, the Society heard that "they are still very unclean in their habits."[80]

Late in 1888, we hear of a "Russian Protective Club," with I. Isaacs as president, which attracted 250 to meetings, usually on Sunday evenings in Isaacs' Hall.[81] Although this Club was probably short-lived, it was evidently the first non-synagogal immigrant association.

New anti-Jewish laws in 1891 resulted in a mass exodus of Jews from Russia. During the remainder of that year about two hundred families came to Milwaukee, and the total for 1891-1892 was reported at 1,500 immigrants.[82] Although far larger than in 1881-1882, it drew much less public attention. Many immigrants were men whose families remained abroad until they could be brought to America.[83] These new refugees had been given travel tickets from a German or other port to some particular city in America. Bearing such names as Arinovitz, Sinaiko, Safer, Primakow, Shulkin, Bezonlow, and Hurwitz, the newcomers of the early nineties did not, as did those who preceded them a decade earlier, seek assistance immediately from a local immigrant aid society. They sought to obtain employment first on their own[84] and, if need be, could also turn to their fellow Russian Jews for aid.

Among the "new" immigrants were some who had been educated in Russian universities. Such, for example, was Isadore Ladoff, who escaped from the mines of Siberia and arrived in Milwaukee with his wife and daughter on Thanksgiving Day, 1891. A graduate of the Polytechnicum at Riga, and about 35 years of age, Ladoff taught agriculture at a Russian government school until he was arrested in 1887 on suspicion of revolutionary sympathies and sentenced to imprisonment in Siberia. His wife, a graduate of St. Petersburg University, had practiced medicine in Riga and Cronstadt for eight years.[85]

In 1892, while many Russian Jews were to be found in special sections of Milwaukee, there was no density such as existed in New York or Chicago.[86] Several were wholesale merchants, and some were retail dealers and shopkeepers; there were no saloonkeepers among them. One physician had a substantial practice. The number of tailors in their midst exceeded those qualified for any other type of work. A great many were employed in tanneries, planing mills, and foundries; there were numerous carpenters, blacksmiths and locksmiths. About twenty-five families earned a good livelihood through trade in rags. Unemployment affected many during the winter of 1891-1892, particularly those who worked at the docks, in lumber yards, on street railways and other outdoor manual labor. Several then rented farms. While some failed, others profited by combining farming with logging.[87]

In 1895, between 2,500 and 3,000 Russian Jews lived in Milwaukee, concentrated in the Second and Sixth Wards. By now, there were among them five physicians, 250 tailors, and shoemakers, blacksmiths, tanners, bricklayers, cabinet-makers, tinkers, bookbinders, milkmen, butchers, bookkeepers and wholesale merchants.

By 1898, two settlements of Russian and Polish Jews existed in the downtown district. One was on the west side, near the Haymarket and bounded by Chestnut, Third, Galena and Sixth Streets. The other was on the east side, near the German market, East Water and Knapp Streets, "where they intersect, being the center of settlement." At least 2,000 lived in the two districts, observed the *Milwaukee Sentinel,* "so that they form a clearly defined 'jewry,' or 'ghetto.' . . . Besides these settlements, members of the race are scattered all over the cheaper parts of the city."

Continuing to "Glimpse Into City's Ghetto," the *Sentinel* observed:

> These people do not look like desirable acquisitions when they first arrive, but it is safe to say that the younger generation of them will turn out some valued citizens. . . . The racial desire for self-betterment is not snuffed out by the filthy environment into which their poverty forces them. . . .
>
> The language spoken by the Russian Jews . . . is what is known as Yiddish. . . . As a rule the Russian Jew is more orthodox than the American Jew. This is attested by the number of 'kosher' butcher shops to be found in the Milwaukee ghetto. These shops are, as a rule, uninviting places even to the point of offensiveness, but they proudly bear the word 'kosher' painted on their window signs . . . When it is realized that 'kosher' signifies clean or sanitary, the local uses to which it is put seem ironical. . . . Whatever of bad air and lack of soap may pertain to the average 'kosher' shop, one thing is certain, the

meat exposed for sale did not come from a diseased animal or from one not slaughtered according to the Mosaic law. . . .

The members of Milwaukee's ghetto are not all robust people, yet, they maintain fair health in spite of their decidedly unsanitary mode of living and the unsanitary forms of work some of them resort to. Many of them go into the rag business and pass day after day in the dust and exhalations of rag and refuse heaps. . . . As a rule there is little sickness among them.

Some idea of how these people live may be had from a glimpse of the 'long house' on Knapp Street, a few steps from East Water. Here twelve families are housed and no one yet has decided just the number of individual occupants. . . . Near the hay market matters are still worse. Many of these people do not know what sanitary living is.

It is well worth the trouble to walk along Sixth Street between Vliet and Cherry on a warm summer evening before the daylight has entirely vanished. Then may be seen a ghetto in full bloom for the sidewalks fairly swarm.[88]

In addition to the Russian Jewish immigration in the nineties, the community received scores of Roumanian Jews, amounting to some two hundred families in 1900. Gradually forced out of a livelihood by government policy, they too were compelled to leave their homeland. The migration of the Roumanian Jews reached America at Montreal, whence they crossed into the United States. Early in October, 1900, about 25 of 370 families who had reached Montreal a few days earlier arrived in Milwaukee. Other Wisconsin Jewish communities, such as Eau Claire and Appleton, received many. Rabbi Caro found them "an educated race, and all of them have a profession or trade."[89]

IMMIGRANTS AND NATIVES

For nine years after the crisis of 1882, the native Jewish community devoted little attention to the Russian Jews as a group. The needy could apply to the Hebrew Relief Society, but no communal effort was made for the immigrants as a group until the next crisis year, 1891, when a branch of the Jewish Alliance was established in Milwaukee. The organization aimed to teach American civics to immigrants and to encourage them to become industrial workers and especially farmers. "Jewish Americans," proclaimed an officer of the local branch, "see that the age of peddling is rapidly passing away." Officers of the Jewish Alliance contained some familiar names: Bernhard Gross, an earlier Hungarian immigrant—president; Sol Fein, a prosperous 1881 immigrant, and Rabbi Hecht—vice-presidents; L. Tobias—recording secretary; I. Goodman—financial secretary; and David Adler—treasurer. Other participants were A. W. Rich, B. M. Weil, J. M. Pereles, and L. Hammel.[90]

The Jewish Alliance decided against affiliation with the Alliance Israelite Universelle or with the Baron de Hirsch Fund in New York.[91] Instead it called a conference on April 10, 1892 of the three B'nai B'rith lodges and the Hebrew Relief Association.[92] There it was decided that the Alliance and the Hebrew Relief Association should carry on with their respective programs. The latter would continue to supply the physical needs while the Alliance would attend to their spiritual and cultural needs and would pursue its agricultural plans. They agreed to employ as agent Isadore Ladoff, the exiled Russian intellectual, who had been in the country for about eight months. An employment bureau and a temporary sheltering home for newcomers were also opened.[93]

The Milwaukee Jewish Alliance dreamed of a colony of Russian immigrants in northern Wisconsin in 1892, aided by the Baron de Hirsch Fund. They proposed to purchase a large tract in Langlade, Lincoln, Taylor and Marathon counties, at $4 an acre, and to allot part of it immediately to the colonists, together with provisions and agricultural implements. Logging was expected to provide extra income for the settlers. But the colonization possibilities in northern Wisconsin failed to persuade Julius Goldman of the Baron de Hirsch Fund, who visited this area.[94] The Fund's refusal to subsidize the colony doomed the project.

More successful was the Jewish Alliance's night school where young immigrants were enabled to secure at least a minimal English education. School was held at 561 East Water Street, the quarters of the Young Men's Hebrew Literary Society, and token tuition fee was charged to avoid the possibility of its being considered charity.[95] Instructors taught the two classes free.[96] Sixty men and ten women, aged 16 to 48, all recent arrivals, attended the school's three evening sessions on Mondays, Wednesdays and Saturdays each week from 7:30 to 9:30 p.m. Most came twice weekly. In a larger room sat fifty or sixty pupils around two long wooden tables. They paid "close attention to the lesson," after a long day's work.[97] They read aloud, and then copied dictation which had been written on the blackboard. Their instructor, Leopold Deutelbaum, a student in the German-English seminary,

> reads a lesson from the reader aloud to them and explains its meaning. Then he calls on them in turn to read the same lesson. Their writing is slow and even. The letters are formed with a care and symmetry which show that most of them have had little or no practice in writing any language whatever.

The more advanced class studied United States History two evenings a week with Rabbi Hecht, and English twice weekly with Rabbi Gerechter. The teachers proudly claimed that all students who understood little English and could not read or write it at all, could, after three months, read and write a little.

After a year the school moved to the superior facilities of the Sixth District School. Joseph Feingold, who arrived in the country a few months earlier, and was reportedly offered the chair of Latin in an Hungarian college, became principal. He was assisted by Miss Ladoff, graduate of St. Petersburg University and sister of Isadore Ladoff.[98]

The Jewish Alliance and its school disbanded, for Rabbi Victor Caro took the initiative in organizing a Hebrew Educational Society in 1899. It again established an English school and also a class for Hebrew. Daily sessions were held in a hall on Walnut Street for children, and evening classes for those who could not come during the day. Rabbi Caro served as superintendent. Instructors were Messrs. Blumberg, Wilitzkin and Rosenthal.[99] Charity and education thus remained the link between native and immigrant Jewry.

III

The Native Community:

Economic and Social Stability

As MILWAUKEE's immigrants struggled to establish themselves during the last decades of the 19th century and the opening of the 20th, the veterans of earlier immigration, and their sons and grandsons who had found assured places for themselves in the urban community, were contributing in marked measure to the city's development. Milwaukee's growth was fastest between 1870 and 1900, when its population jumped from 71,440 to 285,315. Not only foreign immigration caused this great increase, but also the "trek to the city," that feature of late 19th century American life which continued well beyond 1900. Thus, in 1920, the city's population was 457,147, a slower growth than before but still noteworthy. Milwaukeeans boasted in 1895 of their "metropolitan city," claiming that the world had seen only four other cities reach such size so quickly.[1]

Rapid growth required a broader sense of municipal responsibility. Pure water and sewage disposal by the city were spoken of in 1870 and fully developed by 1900, and the same could be said of full-time police and fire departments. Such utilities as electric lights and street cars had become common, and the telephone was on the scene, although only for a few. For young Milwaukeeans, public school facilities expanded impressively, in addition to the parallel growth of private schools. Of educational significance was the substantial public library, opened in 1898.[2]

Above all, Milwaukee's economy expanded immeasurably, while also shifting its foundations. In the early 1870's, the city ranked first in the world as a primary wheat market. But the agricultural depression of that decade lowered wheat prices, at the same time as newly tilled wheat fields in the Dakotas raised Minneapolis to a position above Milwaukee's. Both areas, however, had to compete with wheat imports from Russia and India. Farmers in the Milwaukee hinterland ultimately found renewed prosperity when they turned in the 1890's to dairy farming,[3] while the city abandoned its position in the wheat market.

Banking and insurance, railroads and real estate, facilitated Milwaukee's prominence in commerce and subsequently in manufacturing. The Merchants' Association's membership of 20 in 1861 stood at 350 in 1895,[4] and wholesale business grew equally well along with retail. Retail trade units were larger and more numerous, and chain and department stores appeared on the scene. Although the ten railroad lines and their fourteen branches which served Milwaukee in 1873 were consolidated into a few large systems, Chicago completely overshadowed the "Cream City" as a transportation point. Partly as a consequence, manufacturing replaced commerce by 1900 as Milwaukee's economic foundation. The annual value of manufactured products rose from $18,798,000 in 1870 to $43,473,000 in 1900, and touched $576,161,000 in 1919. Not only the East's desire for Western foods and raw materials, but the great Western market for manufactured goods was served by Milwaukee.[5]

Locally supported industries—milling, meat packing, tanning, brewing, and machinery—were prominent before 1900. During these years the city attained enduring fame as the nation's brewer of beer *par excellence*, although meat packing led beer in the value of the product. In the new century, steel and machinery took the lead among manufactured goods.

MANUFACTURERS AND MERCHANTS

The native Jews engaged in quite a different range of economic activity. Beer, machinery, and tanning were outside their interests.

and very few were engaged in meat packing and milling. They continued to be merchants and manufacturers of consumer goods (generally dry goods and garments) and retailers, and slowly diversified by speculation and investment in local real estate and insurance, Great Lakes mines, and public utilities for the booming city. Many sons and grandsons of immigrant businessmen became lawyers and doctors, or managers and investors of fortunes founded in the family. Two stalwart family firms, Friend and Adler, represented the older order in their men's clothing businesses, while names such as Landauer and Stern suggest the same solidity in dry goods.

When Henry Friend, eldest of five brothers and head of the Friend Brothers Clothing Company, lost his life in a sea disaster en route to Europe in 1875, his estate was estimated at $250,000.[6] By 1880, three years before incorporation, the Company was extensively mechanized, and employed 1,000 hands in a wholesale business which grossed $750,000 in 1881.[7] The last surviving brother, Emanuel Friend, retired in 1896, leaving the Friend Brothers Clothing Company in the hands of the sons—not all of them, however, for others entered the professions and other businesses.[8]

David Adler, in partnership with a brother until 1874 and a son-in-law until 1878, owned the other leading clothing factory and jobbery. This vigorous, strong-willed man was gradually joined by several sons until he too incorporated with them and Henry M. Oberndorfer in 1886, with $250,000 as capital stock.[9] Adler's quarters in 1873 made his the largest business house in Milwaukee, with 600 hands in his employ and a trade reaching the Dakotas.[10] By the nineties the Adler corporation employed 800, and its sales exceeded $1,000,000. It employed Jews for both its manufacturing and sales, generally in supervisory or skilled positions, and remained a bastion of resistance to trade unionism well into the 20th century.[11]

A smaller firm belonged to Emanuel Silverman, who took in his son-in-law to join his son in the business. When Silverman died and his son quit, L. A. Shakman, the son-in-law, renamed the firm after himself. To produce and sell an annual volume worth $400,-

ooo, Shakman employed 300 workers, besides clerks and six travellers.[12]

Many of these travellers aspired to enter business as entrepreneurs. One such person was Jacob Singer, who came from Austria in 1863 and sold Adler's goods on the road before he joined Julius Benedict, a man with a similar history, in a successful clothing firm. Its mutations show that firms like Friend and Adler were more representative than typical of Jewish business in their day. Singer left in 1883 to enter the trimmings business, and next year Charles Stein, hitherto a special partner, became a general partner. The establishment was incorporated in 1890 with a $250,-ooo stock, by Benedict, C. H. Bellack, and J. B. Schram, who had long been in the liquor business.[13] Stein was evidently out.

Although financial success rewarded an appreciable number of Jews in business, it was neither habitual nor inevitable. Even successful firms could all too easily be pushed to the wall, as the later years of the once highly profitable H. S. Mack & Co. demonstrate. Believing in Milwaukee's future as a knitting center, Herman Mack imported men and machinery from Europe to open the Northwestern Knitting Works in 1881, only to see it fail.[14] He and his brother Hugo quickly recouped, for in 1884 they employed over 300 to make their line of men's clothing. But the 1890's hit hard, when sales dropped by more than half to $80,000 in 1893. Mack suffered with most Milwaukee businessmen from the "money famine" of 1894, especially when the banks with which it dealt closed their doors.[15] This occurred at about the time when Henry Mack's able son, Edward S. Mack, was beginning a career which brought recognition as one of the city's leading lawyers.

Financial crises twice brought misfortune to Leopold Newbouer's wholesale clothing firm, conducted by his sons Charles, Edward and Nathan. When the mild depression of 1882 wrecked it for inability to collect receivables, it was subsequently re-established; but the depression of 1894 ended the Newbouer clothing firm permanently.[16] The depression of 1893-1894 did more harm to Milwaukee business and caused more human suffering than the longer and deeper depression twenty years earlier. It brought disaster to a man like Jacob Katz, an immigrant from Westphalia in 1866 who had laboriously struggled upwards. After eight years as a butcher and peddler, he opened a dry goods firm in 1874. In 1893, Katz, a son, and two sons-in-law incorporated with a $100,-000 capital. Two years later he was out of business, and had to turn to real estate and insurance brokerage. On April 16, 1897, Jacob Katz was found dead in his office of gas asphyxiation.[17]

In 1895 practically all of the thirteen clothing factories and shops in Milwaukee were Jewish-owned,[18] and remained so into the 1920's. No less Jewish was another old-time occupation, dry goods. Three firms—Goll & Frank (Goll was not a Jew), Landauer & Co., and H. Stern, Jr. & Bro. Co.—sold $7,000,000 to $8,000,000 annually in the 1890's and competed successfully with large Chicago firms, notwithstanding a thin profit margin and severe competition. Hundreds worked at home for the three companies, and Stern and Goll & Frank operated factories.[19]

The brothers Max Landauer (1837-1924) and Adolph Landauer (1847-1925), Bavarian Jews of rabbinic lineage, came to America in 1857 and 1866, respectively. After commercial study in Germany and practice in Madison, Wisconsin, they established their own business in Milwaukee in 1869,[20] and next year took in their cashier, Alfred Friedberger, as a partner.[21] Landauer & Co. made its fortune in the 1870's. In 1881, it had $250,000 capital, $875,000 in sales, and showed a $40,000 profit. While their salesmen and travellers plied the Middle West for orders, the brothers Landauer built a $100,000 headquarters in Milwaukee and took in two men named Michelbacher as partners—they may have been in-laws.[22] Within the Germanic sector of the Jewish community, Max and Adolph Landauer served as officers and patrons nearly everywhere, and typified almost to perfection the solid German-American Reform Jew.

Adolph W. Rich's (1843-1917) entrepreneurial career was more adventurous than that of his business contemporaries, as he embraced the more aggressive retailing methods of later merchants. In 1874, Rich took as his partner Lewis Silber, an immigrant of 1859 from Prussian Poland; he then employed thirty persons.[23] By 1881, 60 employees worked in retail and 53 in wholesale, nearly all women, and two years later there were 300. Rich and Silber equipped their store with elevators, a "cash railway system," and other devices "of the latest invention to expedite business," and published an 80-page mail order catalogue to be mailed throughout the Northwest.[24] They added departments of shoes and upholstery, and (symptomatic of cultural stirrings) book and art departments. When an Annex opened in 1888, a color pamphlet, "Five Minute History of Twenty-One Years' Hard Work," proudly passed the firm's story in review.[25] By the 1890's, as many as 8,000 shoppers crowded into the local merchant prince's store in one day.

A. W. Rich also manufactured some of the articles he sold, but his success was not so steady. In 1883, he and Silber joined Charles Stein in the Cream City Clothing Company, and employed 200 hands.[26] Its later annals are not known, but Stein was with Singer & Benedict one year later. Rich next began to make "Wigwam Slippers" for his customers. With a ready supply of hides from local stockyards and constant addition of electrical machinery, the A. W. Rich Shoe Company[27] within four years produced over one hundred styles of oxfords, employed over 800 people, and put out over 2,500 pairs of shoes daily.[28] Gradually, this venturesome entrepreneur concentrated on manufacturing, even after his renewed partnership with Silber in a dry goods firm collapsed in the general crash of 1893.[29] As the patron of Wisconsin's Industrial Removal Office and its Jewish agricultural movement, and in other ways, A. W. Rich was also *the* innovator and experimenter in Jewish communal life.

An array of Jewish merchant manufacturers was distributed throughout lesser trades associated with clothing and shoes. Thus, M. Heimann & Co. had a $400,000 millinery business in 1881, and one of the founder's sons made hats and bonnets for his father's firm.[30] Jacob Morawetz, once in the grocery business, joined Joseph Brandt as a hat, cap, and glove jobber.[31] Samuel Hecht, local manager of the Canada Fur and Cloak Manufacturing Company, bought out the branch and entered the ladies' cloak and millinery trade.[32] Philip Horwitz, sometime Civil War "hero" and vaudevillian, could be found in 1878 in the ladies' underwear and knit worsted goods trade.[33] In partnership with Emanuel Friend of the clothing brothers, H. L. Eisen made and sold lumbermen's and miners' raiment.[34] Lewis Silber, and later Bernard Brachman, headed companies which made suspenders.[35] Philip Gruenberg, an immigrant buttonhole maker for seven years in New York, attained modest success with his inconspicuous business in Milwaukee after 1876.[36]

As Milwaukee's manufacturing gradually surpassed its commerce between 1880 and 1900, knit goods and yarn mills owed their development to Jewish efforts. Thus, Marcus and Jonas Cohen and Sally Levy bought out Edward Friend Jr.'s two-year old National Knitting Works in 1883 and quickly made of it the largest knitting establishment in the Northwest, paying handsome dividends and accumulating proportionately huge capital reserves.[37] The Kalamazoo Knitting Company and the Northwestern Worsted Mills were both founded in 1888. Unlike clothing establishments, knitting required massive initial investments, permitting only established men of capital to enter.[38]

Department stores still grew from modest beginnings, as happened with Edward Schuster and Albert T. Friedman. Their several stores, beginning in 1884, were in then outlying sections of Milwaukee.[39] In 1897, Julius Simon arrived from Portage, Wisconsin, and founded the Boston Store downtown. Carl Herzfeld and Nathan (Nat) Stone owned the business by 1906, and developed it into a fixture of the city. Stone (1866-1931) himself was an indefatigable civic and Jewish leader during his generation.[40]

Milwaukee's branch of a celebrated firm originated in 1887, when Adam Gimbel's sons added to their stores in Philadelphia, Vincennes, Indiana, and Danville, Illinois.[41] Milwaukee's Gimbel store succeeded at once, doubling its leased space within one year and steadily expanding thereafter. Local merchants could hardly keep pace with the seven Gimbel brothers, who endowed their firm with "a surplus of capital and a surplus of Gimbels," bought in New York and Paris, and vigorously advertised their wares.[42] Their flair in displaying Paris, Berlin, and London millinery styles of 1891 thrilled local ladies:

. . . A space of 50 by 150 feet, encircled by huge mirrors and continuous glass stands, the striking effect of which is augmented by palms, plants and flowers, ribbons, etc. . . . Roses, stretched out on and attached to invisible wires which extended from the ground floor of the store to the ceiling, with a hundred white doves flying around is only one of the many pretty features. . . .[43]

The Gimbel brothers and other Jewish retailers of the city ardently created the demand which they were ready to supply.

With the demand for food constant, and for liquor and tobacco hardly less so, Jewish provisions entrepreneurs were also numerous. However, no enterprise attained the dimensions of the retail giants. The main gustatorial development apparently was a keener desire for "fancy" groceries and imported liquors. Thus, Smith & Mendel, composed of a former Governor, his son, and a leader of local German cultural activity (also David Adler's son-in-law), made its fortune by selling fancy groceries, in addition to simpler fare.[44] Such veteran firms as those headed by Schram, Patek, Morawetz, Bremer, and Scheftels, continued their prosperous wholesale grocery businesses.[45] While Louis Frank and his sons were leading meat packers,[46] the rather limited kosher meat trade (as of 1881) was catered to by S. Schwenger.[47] Passover *matzot* came from Chicago, but Milwaukee Jews could also buy theirs from Julius Kohn on Walnut Street, whose trade also extended far west of the city. For Passover, 1884, Kohn, "a robust Hebrew, with a stouter bosom companion," baked 25,000 pounds.[48]

One of the largest wholesale liquor importers was S. C. Herbst, an immigrant from Prussia of 1859, who turned from the clothing business to liquor. From 1887 to 1897 Herbst lived and operated in Europe, apparently to the profit of his firm.[49] Lesser firms like A. Blade & Son,[50] and F. W. Hartman & Co., nearly equal to Herbst,[51] also supplied Milwaukeeans.

Jews also manufactured liquor, and the most colorful was L. Rindskopf & Sons in the early 1870's.[52] Their far-flung trade even penetrated Mormon Utah when they shipped a large consignment to Brigham Young himself in 1874. "Evidently, the prophet has no fear of crusades before his eyes," commented the *Sentinel*.[53] However, the Rindskopf firm was the "Whiskey Ring," which cheated the Federal Government of liquor taxes on a gigantic scale. Retribution began in May, 1875, and required three years to complete, but proved the end of the Rindskopfs. A large fine had to be paid, and one of the brothers spent a token day in jail. The company went out of business, and the brothers Samuel (the "reform" politician), Elias, Max, and Jacob Rindskopf sank into obscurity.[54] Several other distilleries owned by Jews also operated in Milwaukee.[55]

For some time, Milwaukee was also a center of the tobacco industry. In 1891, four plants employed 325 workers. Among 200 small shops with their 1,000 workers,[56] many were owned and worked in by Jews. The leading Jew in the trade was Bernard Leidersdorf, an immigrant from Hanover in 1858, owner of the mechanized Western Steam Tobacco Works.[57] During the climactic trade union year of 1886, the relatively well-organized tobacco workers forced Leidersdorf and two large compeers to grant an eight-hour day.[58] Leidersdorf sold out to the American Tobacco Company in 1903, as did Solomon Roth, whose firm left Milwaukee for Cincinnati in 1879.[59] Lesser Jewish figures in the tobacco trade merely owned stores, like S. B. Auerbach and I. M. Lederer and J. Markwell.[60]

Behind the clothiers, merchants, grocers, and tobacconists, stood an array of trades and manufactures. Thus, Jacob E. Friend, drawing on the accumulated capital of his family's clothing business, was a founder of the Nordberg Manufacturing Company. In 1895, he became president of the firm which made engines and mining machinery.[61] Bernhard Stern was one of the city's largest flour millers,[62] and the brothers Bernhard and Jacob Gross dominated the city's soap output for many years until their firm went under in the disastrous year of 1893.[63] Julius Lando was prominent in Milwaukee's jewelry and optical trade. Like the brothers Gross, he was an immigrant from Hungary, who had come to the United States in 1861, and to Milwaukee in 1872. Later his brother Max Lando also came, equipped with optometric training at the University of Vienna.[64] Joe Heimann did not enter his father's substantial millinery business, but became a leading "artist in natural flowers, florist, and landscape gardener."[65] J. B. Schram, who appears in many trades, was Jonas Schoenmann's partner in the Milwaukee Stove Polish Manufacturing Company. This prize-winning compound polished stoves as distant as New Orleans, Pittsburgh and Denver. Together with a variety of partners, Philip Carpeles conducted a successful trunk manufacturing concern, beginning in 1870. His firm employed 200 in 1880-1881, slowly declined to a payroll of 100 in 1889, but held its valuable patents in trunk design. Besides a downtown building, Carpeles also had a factory in the industrial Menomonee Valley.[66]

Henry M. Benjamin ranked from the 1870's into the 1890's as Milwaukee's foremost coal and pig iron dealer. His bids won contracts to supply the Court House, Poor House, jail, water works, County Hospital and State Capitol.[67] It is not remarkable that Benjamin rose high in local politics, and even served briefly as Acting Mayor. At the height of his prosperity, Henry M. Benjamin utilized five outdoor yards and an extensive railroad layout to ship out 50,000 tons of coal and 75,000 tons of lumber in 1882.[68] Even he teetered on the brink of bankruptcy in 1893, but managed to survive.[69]

BROKERAGE AND INVESTMENT

Milwaukee's Jewish merchants and manufacturers were substantial but prosaic figures, lacking any mystery in their businesses. Although that potent symbol in the 19th century, the Jewish banker, did not exist in Milwaukee, Jewish businessmen could crown their success by being directors and sometimes founders of local banks.

Nathan Pereles was the first Milwaukee Jewish banker, after a career as a grocer, lawyer, and investor, and his sons became lawyers and financiers. Their Mechanics' Land Association, organized by Thomas J. Pereles[70] in 1887, and such other enterprises headed by a Pereles brother as the Milwaukee Investment Company,[71] the Lake Woods Investment Company, and Nathan Pereles & Sons and Company, typified their operations. Besides, the Citizens' Loan and Trust Company showed James and Thomas Pereles as president and vice-president.[72]

By the 1880's, other Jews could be found speculating both in urban real estate and distant tracts of virgin land. Familiar family names appeared as the accumulated capital of local Jewish enterprise poured out. Elias and Jacob Friend were incorporators of the DeHart Land and Cattle Company in 1884,[73] while Louis Shakman's, Jonas Cohen's, and Joseph Friedberg's Northwestern Land Company proposed to deal in mineral and timber lands throughout upper Wisconsin and Michigan.[74] When it was supposed that Wamduska in the Dakotas had a glowing future as a junction on the Grand Forks branch of the St. Paul, Minneapolis & Manitoba Railroad, Milwaukee Jewish businessmen joined Chicago and Grand Forks investors to sink money into the town site. The Milwaukeeans included S. Thal, Cohen Bros. & Co., Aarons Bros., and M. Rukeyser, and they planned to erect a hotel for the day in 1882 when the railroad reached Wamduska.[75] But the town site did not develop, as the investors learned painfully.

Of particular fascination to restless capital was the possibility of invisible, immeasurable wealth beneath the surface. The northern earth of Wisconsin and Michigan was known to contain mineral riches; how much, no one knew. At first, speculative capital ranged over various areas. The doughty Leopold pioneer family acquired mining interests in northern Michigan, the area they had done so much to develop, in 1874 and 1880.[76] Sam Rindskopf held financial interests in Arkansas mines,[77] while Isaac Adler, of the clothing family, had a share of a mine near Leadville, Colorado.[78] After 1883, the speculators' gaze was upon the vast wealth buried just beneath the roots of the thick timber which covered the Gogebic range.[79] Soon test pits were extracting the high-grade iron ore, and tell-tale piles of red-colored earth rose alongside.

Milwaukee capital predominated during the feverish early exploitation of the Gogebic range, and Henry M. Benjamin, the coal dealer and sometime politician who held similar investments elsewhere, led the way.[80] He was an officer and incorporator of eight mining companies in 1886 and 1887 with a combined capital of

$7,490,000, and also profited from selling lots near the sites of supposed deposits. Others rushed to join Benjamin in exploiting the mines,[81] including established businessmen like M. S. Morawetz, John Black, Simon Kander, and James M. Pereles, plus small liquor dealers, clothing contractors, and store clerks.[82] These investors only paved the way for larger and better financed combines to exploit the Lake Superior iron ore ranges. Of profits there were none, and probably few recovered the money they sank into the ventures.

A sounder investment, or one easier to see, was local real estate. Probably Milwaukee's foremost real estate figure was Benjamin M. Weil (1850-1912), a native of Baltimore who lived in Milwaukee after 1873, and by 1875 (unsuccessfully) tried to interest Eastern investors in the city's real estate. Weil described himself as a "Real Estate and Mortgage Broker" in 1876, and for a time published a real estate journal, *The Milwaukeean*. The great volume of real estate transactions which passed through his hands made him a central figure in the physical development of Milwaukee, a man whose opinions weighed heavily in such matters as street layout and urban transport. He organized and presided over the Milwaukee Real Estate Board from 1891 to 1893, and crowned his business career by a term as president of the National Real Estate Board.[83] There were other Jews in the field, such as Henry Herman, but none matched Weil.[84]

Insurance agency frequently accompanied real estate undertakings; Benjamin M. Weil was also a leader in this field. Until financial difficulties forced him out of insurance in 1879, Alexander Cohen's thriving agency represented eight national companies.[85] Theodore and Morris Weil (perhaps Benjamin Weil's relatives) represented eleven national insurers.[86]

In addition to insurance representation, Jews also made their mark upon new insurance ventures, and aided in managing some insurance companies of fraternal organizations. A local undertaking was the Mutual Hail Insurance Company, organized in 1870 with young Samuel Rindskopf, distiller and future "reform" politician, which survived until 1882.[87] David Adler and Lewis Silber served as directors of the Wisconsin Odd Fellows Mutual

Life Insurance Company,[88] while David Weil and Isaac A. Levy were incorporators of the States Mutual Benefit Society. Virtually an insurance society, it levied assessments against benefits.[89] There was only one substantial fire insurance company in Wisconsin until a group of Milwaukee merchants, including Max Landauer, Henry M. Mendel, and Moritz Seligman, organized the Merchants' Insurance Company in 1885 as a "home" institution controlled by local capital.[90] No evidence suggests that anti-Jewish policies of insurers were a stimulus, as they had been elsewhere.

Brokerage and promotion in entertainment made the fortune of Jacob Litt, the "John B. Rice" of the last two decades of the nineteenth century. Knowing what city people "expect more or less in the line of amusement," Litt provided for every level of taste. After serving as treasurer of the Grand Opera House from 1874 to 1882, he started as impresario in the summer of 1882, at the Waukesha theatre. Next year he leased the theatre in Schlitz Park and put on a series of road company "operas."[91] Successful in this too, Litt quit the Grand Opera House, disposed of his interest in the Oshkosh Opera House, and enlarged Schlitz Park for his offerings.[92] He also bought out the unsuccessful Dime Museum downtown and revamped its program. As many as 3,000 spectators daily paid 10¢ to see freaks, curiosities, and stage shows, netting the impresario $17,000 in 1884 and $10,000 in 1885.[93] When the Dime Museum troupe went successfully on the road,[94] Litt leased the Academy of Music to present such programs as Callender's Colored Minstrels and comedies like "Three Wives to One Husband."[95] Litt's entertainment network of the 1890's included the Bijou Opera House in town, a theatre in Minneapolis, and plans to build theatres in St. Paul and Milwaukee.[96]

Just as he understood and exploited the entertainment tastes of his day, "John B. Rice" accepted the prejudices of his time. On at least one occasion he offended enlightened opinion. In October, 1889, representative Milwaukee Negroes sued him for $2,500, alleging in a common law complaint that a Negro holding a ticket had been prevented from taking his seat "without cause, abruptly and with force of arm." When Litt did not deny or repudiate this, the impresario was subjected as a Jew to a severe editorial rebuke from the *Sentinel:*

> . . . it calls for exactly the same denunciation that has been directed at the prohibition of Jews at the Manhattan Beach hotels or the Catskills. It is exactly the same kind of race discrimination, taking no account of the character of individual applicants but only of race, and it is utterly indefensible on any grounds . . . We do not believe there is any prejudice among the people here that would deter them from buying seats in the same circle with respectable negroes. We do not believe that any number of intelligent people in this community would endorse any such sweeping discrimination . . . this exclusion is something new in this city. Hitherto, at the New Academy and the Opera House, colored men and women have been admitted without objection to seats in the best part of the house, and no one, as far as we have heard, has complained of it.[97]

It appears that Litt had to give satisfaction to the plaintiffs because of aggrieved public opinion.

By the 1880's and 1890's, the capital laboriously accumulated by the first generation of Jewish businessmen became increasingly available for investment and speculation. The sons of the city's Jewish pioneers did not always enter the parental businesses, but turned to brokerage, law, insurance, as well as the professions.

THE JEWISH BUSINESSMAN

The half century between the Civil War and the World War, that freest age of enterprise in American history, found Milwaukee Jewish businessmen eager participants. If there is any sign that they questioned or rejected any basic assumption of *laissez-faire* or the gospel of wealth as exemplified or preached by the captains of enterprise, the sources fail to show it.

During the 19th century, Jewish businessmen moved freely within the local business community. When the Chamber of Commerce began to publicize the commercial advantages of the city "to secure the cooperation of those most largely interested in extending . . . commercial and manufacturing facilities,"[98] Jewish entrepreneurs joined this central business body.[99] Men like Elias Friend, Benjamin M. Weil, Max Landauer, and Henry M. Mendel served on a Chamber committee to entice Eastern capital to invest in the city, and pleaded before a Congressional committee for a new Federal building.[100] When the Milwaukee Industrial Exposition was organized in 1880, Benjamin, Weil, Mendel, and A. W. Rich were among its ten incorporators,[101] and Mendel was the prime mover in the entire enterprise. The Grand Triumphal March which opened the exposition was dedicated to him for his efforts.[102] Later promotional bodies like the Association for the Advancement of Milwaukee,[103] the Merchants' Association, and the Manufacturers' Club,[104] contained Jewish officers and directors,[105] and the same could be said of such trade groups as the Knitters' Club.[106]

Just as they accepted the business ethos of their day, Milwaukee Jewish businessmen also shared the deep-seated resistance to trade unionism. Germanism in America had its socialist and trade union movement, which successful German immigrant businessmen emphatically rejected. Jewish employers made common cause with Gentiles in resisting trade union claims to speak for employees, while remaining quite paternal as long as employees were unorganized and subordinate. When Philip Carpeles feted his 150 luggage workers in 1882, the *Sentinel* doubted that so benevolent an employer would "be threatened with a strike, just at present."[107] That qualifying clause was apt, for in March, 1886, during a year of trade union ferment, sixty of Carpeles' men did strike for an increase in wages of about 25%. Claiming that none earned over $10 weekly, and some netted only 75¢ a day, the workers wanted their employer to see that they earned at least $1.25 to $1.50 daily at their piece work. Carpeles offered to pay as well as any of his competitors. These terms were probably accepted, but two months later, in May, 1886, Carpeles and two other leading Milwaukee trunk manufacturers were struck by 360 men. Underlying the men's demand for more than $5.00 weekly which some allegedly took home, and the employers' retort that none earned less than $1.50 daily, was the increasingly unskilled nature of the work. "The men say . . . that when they reach a point where they would be entitled to more pay, they are discharged and their places filled with boys, who in turn are displaced by others in the course of time."[108]

Carpeles & Hartman was only one firm affected by strikes in the spring of 1886. Nearly 12,000 striking workers gave Milwaukee its first real taste of labor strife over the eight-hour day. This demand was promulgated by the Federation of Trades in October, 1884 and May 1, 1886 was the deadline for reaching the goal. Well organized trades like beer brewers, tobacco workers, and typographers led the way.[109]

Such pacific gestures as that of Henry Benedict & Co., clothing manufacturers, which distributed $3,000 as 1885 Christmas bonuses, did not deter the employees from striking four months later.[110] The cutters at David Adler and L. A. Shakman struck, while twenty boys, 14 and 15 years old, also caught the enthusiasm and walked out of the National Knitting Works.[111] For the time, Adler conceded to his cutters, the most skilled group in his employ, nine hours' pay for eight hours' work.[112] The employees in H. M. Benjamin's coal yard returned to work only after being promised ten hours' pay for eight hours' work and double pay for overtime.[113] However, nearly all these victories were soon nullified for lack of secure labor organization.

A. W. Rich and his partner Lewis Silber were among Milwaukee's benign employers. They conducted picnics and banquets for their workers, installed a large dining room,[114] and founded a sick fund.[115] When the firm staggered during the crisis of 1893, the employees offered to accept sharply reduced wages until the company could right itself.[116]

The position of the Milwaukee Jewish businessman is eloquently described in statistics compiled by the Milwaukee *Sentinel* in 1894, in preparation for an expected Federal income tax. There were 250 firms in town rated "at above $100,000," of whom the 196 exceeding $200,000 were named. Eighteen of these 196 companies were Jewish. Four of the 62 in the $200,000 category were Jewish: Breslauer, Herbst, J. Katz, and B. M. Weil. Six of the 50 in the $300,000 bracket—Landauer, Smith-Mendel (the

Victor Caro (1856-1912)   Charles S. Levi (1868-1939)
(*Wisconsin Jewish Chronicle*)   (*Wisconsin Jewish Chronicle*)

RABBIS OF MILWAUKEE

Samuel Hirshberg (1869-1954) Solomon I. Scheinfeld, age 80
(*Mrs. Robert M. Krauskopf*)   (*Mrs. Fannie S. Grombacher*)

B'ne Jeshurun, 1886 (*Wisconsin Jewish Chronicle*)

EARLY SYNAGOGUES

Temple Emanu-El, 1872 (*Wisconsin Jewish Chronicle*)

former not a Jew), Scheftels, G. Patek, H. S. Mack, National Knitting Company—were the property of Jews. Gimbel Brothers and Henry Stern were the only Jewish concerns among the 25 with net worth over $400,000, and Pereles Brothers and J. E. Friend belonged among the 25 enterprises in the $500,000 group. Two, David Adler and Bernhard Stern, were among the twenty in the $600,000 division. Ignatius Friedman was one of ten rated at $800,000, while his clothing partner J. H. Rice was one of four Milwaukeeans whose wealth was placed at $1,500,000.[117] Of this group, only B. M. Weil, Jacob E. Friend, and the sons of Nathan Pereles and Adam Gimbel were born in the United States; many of the firms were conducted by sons of immigrant founders. These leading Jewish entrepreneurs dealt in clothing and textiles, dry goods, groceries, and retail trade. Real estate and investment, personified by B. M. Weil and Pereles, and heavy manufacturing, in the person of J. E. Friend, were not yet the source of Jewish fortunes. Later immigrant families were to have surprisingly similar entrepreneurial histories.

JEWS IN THE PROFESSIONS

Few immigrant Jews were in a profession. A notable immigrant exception was Nathan Pereles, the lawyer whose investment business was "one of the soundest private moneyed institutions in the city."[118] Regarded as "the wealthiest German in Milwaukee" with an annual income of $20,000, Pereles' estate at his death in 1879 was "above half a million . . . one of the largest that has ever come before the Probate Court."[119] His sons Thomas Jefferson and James Madison were more active in the law than in banking,[120] and had distinguished careers at the bar. The contrary was the case with Jacob E. Friend, son of Elias and Rosa Friend, an 1879 alumnus of Columbia Law School, who slowly withdrew from his large law practice to devote himself to substantial business interests.[121] Other Jewish attorneys included Friend's classmate at Columbia, Louis B. Schram, who left Milwaukee for New York City in 1886;[122] Max Lando, an attorney from 1869;[123] Nathan Glicksman, a native of Chippewa Falls, educated at Yale, who entered legal practice in the city in 1893; Edwin S. Mack, a product of Harvard Law School, who also began his notable career as a lawyer in 1893. Charles L. Aarons also opened his practice in the mid-1890's, and combined it with the public service which made him the leading Jewish lawyer of Milwaukee.[124]

Medical training, unlike legal, could be imported from abroad, as shown in the careers of such men as Dr. Louis Adler,[125] and Dr. Jacob Mendel, a native of Breslau who practiced in Milwaukee from 1873 until his death in 1895. Like his brother Henry, Jacob Mendel was an active member of Milwaukee Germandom.[126] Another was Dr. Morris Loebel, a native of Budapest and trained at Vienna, who opened practice in the city in 1878.[127] Some Jewish doctors like Samuel H. Friend followed the trend of medical education by five years of study in Berlin.[128] Milwaukee's three Jewish doctors of 1880 increased to about thirteen in 1900, and multiplied to perhaps fifty in 1925,[129] as medical practice expanded and the sons and grandsons of Jewish immigrants sought out professional fields. A similar growth occurred in the kindred professions of dentistry and oculism.[130]

The rapid expansion of the public schools developed the teaching profession, mainly for women. Two Jewish women were on the staff of the public schools in the late 1860's,[131] and twelve in the decade following.[132] During the 1880's, there were 38 Jewish public school teachers,[133] and nine more were added by the School Board between 1890 and 1900. The number of Jewish teachers thus increased at about the rate of school growth.[134] A noteworthy Jewish teacher was Bernard A. Abrams (1847-1920), an immigrant of 1871 who was a classroom instructor until he assumed the superintendency of German instruction in 1885.[135] With 63 teachers and 18,000 pupils studying German, Abrams quit classroom teaching in 1895, and was appointed Second Assistant Superintendent of Schools.[136] His practical experience was held more than equal to the value of a formal supervisory certificate.[137] Abrams was prominent within Milwaukee Germanic circles, and was for years President of the National German-American Teachers' Association.[138]

CLUBS, BALLS, AND RITUALS

The thriving Jewish entrepreneurs and their employees desired a social environment suited to their tastes to supplement always strong Jewish family ties. In this age of family firms, the father was patriarchally dominant in business, and his rule at home was confirmed by German habit and Jewish tradition. The wife gradually emerged from her exclusively domestic life to enter a less confined world, and women's organizations of broad scope appeared in the city. Milwaukee Jewry possessed social organizations for all inclinations. In addition to the synagogue and its auxiliaries, and several traditional charitable societies, the doors of Milwaukee Germandom were wide open to Jews, more than in German-American circles elsewhere.[139] Jewish social groups, Jewish branches of non-sectarian lodge organizations, and Jews in non-Jewish (usually German) bodies could all be found in profusion in the city until the later 1890's, when the organizational spirit of native Jews declined.

In general, the Jews preferred to socialize among themselves, to belong to specifically Jewish clubs and lodges, and also to vacation among each other. While Waukesha was Milwaukee's summer resort area in the 1880's, a number of Jews patronized the Rose Hill Park Summer Resort, at the outskirts of the city.[140] Many belonged to innumerable lodges of fraternal "secret societies" and orders.

Foremost among the orders was the Free and Accepted Masons,[141] distinguished for its benevolent features and possessing quasi-religious moral and spiritual momentum. Besides lodges containing Jews and Gentiles,[142] Harmony Lodge No. 142 was nearly all Jewish in membership and officers.

An anti-Semitic incident shook the brethren of Harmony in 1886, when Isaac A. Levy, a veteran member, sought to reinstate his lapsed insurance with the Scottish Rite, Good Templars and Master Masons Association of Dayton, Ohio. During a misunderstanding over the terms of reinstatement, the Secretary of the Association, one Thomas B. Hannah, returned a check to Levy accompanied by a letter which was deemed "an insult to every

Israelite in the land." Hannah ranted against the "fool Jew" who "thought, it seems, to take advantage . . . thinking . . . you could cheat us out of the former assessments you had not paid. . . ." Levy had evidently threatened to use the influence of others:

> So far as your influence is concerned we care nothing, having no use for that kind of cattle, and would only be too glad, for the good of the Association and its members to get shut [sic] of all of you. If we were accustomed to allow any one to dictate their own terms to us it would not be men of your creed and birth.[143]

Condemning this "disgraceful and abusive language," Past Master Lewis Silber unsuccessfully approached Masonic lodges in Hannah's home state of Ohio, demanding Hannah's expulsion for insulting "the entire Jewish race without any cause whatsoever."

Harmony Lodge surrendered its charter in 1893, perhaps in connection with the financial crisis of that year, and was re-established in 1895, with Moritz Mendelssohn, Alois Aarons, and Bernhard Gross as its officers.[144]

Masons conducted their ritual in private, and some also participated in Jewish worship. As befitted the symbolism of their name, it was long customary to lay the cornerstones of synagogues with Masonic ritual. Similarly, Jewish Masons were sometimes buried with both Jewish and Masonic rites, and occasionally without the former. Not all the officiants at such Masonic rites were Jews.

Many Jews were also in the Independent Order of Odd Fellows, another non-sectarian fraternal order. Like Harmony Lodge of the Masons, the members and officers of the Odd Fellows' Armenia Lodge No. 97 (German) were virtually all Jewish,[145] besides Jews scattered among other lodges in the order. David Adler, the clothing magnate, was a leading Odd Fellow, particularly in the order's financial undertakings.[146] Lewis Silber occupied such important positions as Grand Junior Warden, Grand High Priest, and Grand Patriarch of the Grand Encampment of the State of Wisconsin. He founded 50 Odd Fellow lodges ("encampments") in the State before he left Milwaukee for Cleveland in 1899.[147]

The Knights of Honor, founded in Kentucky in 1873 and appearing in Milwaukee in 1876, seem to have attracted a less affluent membership. It provided employment aid for members, besides $2,000 life insurance and mutual benefits for its 16,000 Wisconsin members.[148] Jews actively participated in the Milwaukee Knights of Honor. David Weil, insurance agent, rose to Deputy Supreme President; Moritz G. Bloch officiated as Grand Chaplain; Victor Berger was a lodge officer; Rabbi Elias Eppstein's name also appeared prominently. The officers of Abraham Linclon Council No. 40 were predominantly Jewish, suggesting that the Knights of Honor, like the Masons and Odd Fellows, had one primarily Jewish lodge plus a scattering of Jews across other lodges.[149]

Jacob Litt, the impresario, was the Esteemed Loyal Knight of the city's newly founded Elks Lodge in 1886.[150] Jews could be found in most lodges of the Ancient Order of the United Workmen,[151] but, notwithstanding the individual prominence of Sol Eckstein, not in the Royal Arcanum, nor in the Knights of Pythias, Harugari, and Order of the Iron Hall.[152]

Since fraternal organizations provided fellowship and conviviality along with material benefits, members clustered in groups of similar social standing and cultural background. The dozens of lodges and societies in the "German Athens" which conducted their affairs in German and expressed German ideals drew a high proportion of the city's German Jews. Order of the Sons of Hermann had over 2,300 of its 88,000 members living in Milwaukee during the late 1870's, and sponsored a Mutual Insurance Association headed by Jacob Brandeis, president, and Rabbi Emanuel Gerechter, vice president.[153] Brandeis also presided over the Sons of Hermann choral group and its "singing section," and other Jews were among the leaders in the local lodges.[154]

Rabbi Elias Eppstein, Grand Vice President of the Wisconsin Grand Lodge, was speaker of the day at the 1873 picnic of "800 blue-eyed sons" (of Hermann) commemorating "Cherusker's victory in the Teutoburger forest" in pagan Germany. His German-American ideology, expressed with "great earnestness and fervor," elicited "rapturous applause":

We are Germans by tongue; Germans by will of reasoning our way onwards; . . . Germans by the desire to seek knowledge and wisdom, and foster them; Germans by uniting in social life; and Germans by assisting each other in times of need . . . We are Americans, but German Americans, who are willing to amalgamate the good which we have brought from Europe with the good which we found here. . . .[155]

Even more active in attaining these lofty aims was the Milwaukee Turnverein, a transplantation of the famous German nationalist associations for physical culture, sociability, and free thought. Here Jews found so ready a welcome that in Chicago the doggerel of a song said:

Milwaukee, you are a fine little town, Your girls are so blond and your beer so brown, There the Turners build a splendid house, And no Hilton throws a Seligman out.[156]

Jacob Brandeis, the prominent Son of Hermann, was president of the Milwaukee Turnverein during the 1870's. Jews served as officers during the 1870's and 1880's, and Hugo Cohn, Joseph Benedict and B. A. Abrams taught in their German-American teachers' seminary; Jewish women were officers of the Turner Ladies' Society.[157] Most of the Jews in this milieu were quite separated from organized Jewish life. In the liberal, anti-clerical atmosphere of the Turnverein, Victor Berger became a youthful local officer, and a fluent lecturer and orator.[158] From this background, he and other Turners became founding fathers of Milwaukee socialism. After the 1890's one hears less of Jews in the Turnverein because of Jewish assimilation into Anglo-Saxon Milwaukee and the Turner movement's growing anti-Semitism.

Another revealing aspect of Milwaukee Jewish immersion in the Germanic environment was Jewish prominence in the German Association, formed in 1880 to aid "impecunious and deserving immigrants." Two years later, it had 249 members, including Elias Friend, president, Rabbi Isaac S. Moses, and the brothers Dr. Jacob and Henry M. Mendel.[159] Jews were also among the 136 Milwaukee members of the German Veterans' Association in 1882, who had once seen service in a German army.[160]

Most Milwaukee Jews, including many affiliated with Masonry and German orders, could be found in B'nai B'rith, which enjoyed its golden years as a German-Jewish group during the 1870's and 1880's. More than any fraternal body favored by German Jews, the ideal of B'nai B'rith went beyond fellowship and material aid, to affirm Judaism in terms of humanitarian idealism and broad philanthropy.[161] The city was a leading center of the order, playing host to regional conventions and supplying officers for the District Grand Lodge which covered the Middle West. Early in 1874, B'nai B'rith had about 300 Milwaukee members, over twice the enrollment of the congregations, and constituted a majority of the city's 526 Jewish males over 20.[162] During this year, three lodges —Gilead and Isaac, and the recently founded Excelsior[163]—fitted up Covenant Hall, "a large and elegant parlor," as their home. In 1879, they moved to "elegant suites" in Lipp's Hall, at the corner of Third and Prairie Streets.[164]

The lodges came together for such occasions as annual balls, picnics, and July 4th celebrations, sometimes bringing lodge brothers by special train from Chicago.[165] Such occasions as the centenary of Sir Moses Montefiore,[166] the death in 1890 of Benjamin F. Peixotto, a veteran B'nai B'rith leader and sometime United States Consul in Roumania,[167] and the case of Major Alfred Dreyfus, were marked by joint meetings of the lodges.[168] They also collaborated in humanitarian undertakings at home and abroad, contributing in 1870 to the relief of Russian Jewry and Russian Jewish immigrants.[169] Warm responses aided sufferers of the Chicago great fire of 1871,[170] yellow fever victims in Memphis in 1873,[171] and the local poor undergoing hardship from the economic collapse of that year.[172] Unsuccessful in bringing B'nai B'rith's orphan asylum to their own city, the Milwaukee lodges energetically supported the Hebrew Orphan Asylum in Cleveland with substantial individual gifts and a round of picnics, theatricals, and charity fairs.[173] David Adler, who raised $6,000 to build the Asylum's edifice and led a delegation to its opening, long served as a trustee, and in his old age served four years as President until 1900.[174]

In 1888, Excelsior and Isaac Lodges merged. One cause was

increased individual dues, now approximately $21. With severe resistance to this high charge, which provided $1,000 worth of insurance, and many threatening to quit rather than pay, Excelsior for a time paid $1.50 quarterly for each member from its $1,600 surplus,[175] but the strain was evidently too great for independent existence. This episode was one symptom of aging membership and declining interest among B'nai B'rith, and was worriedly noted in 1890. While Milwaukee Jewry doubled in the twenty years following 1874, membership in the lodges dropped from about 300 to 259. Social auxiliaries, entertainments, and even a gymnasium were proposed as attractions, but membership only reached to 300 in 1899.[176] Early in the new century, the national leadership of B'nai B'rith adopted the Industrial Removal plan as a project for the entire organization, and urged lodges throughout the country to make the nation-wide distribution of East European immigrants their business. In Milwaukee, this work was undertaken for several years by A. W. Rich and local charity, and in 1913-1914 by a local B'nai B'rith Council. [177] Nevertheless, Milwaukee Lodge (No. 141) and Isaac Lodge (No. 87) merged their reduced memberships with Gilead Lodge in 1913 and 1917, respectively, leaving only one B'nai B'rith lodge in Milwaukee until 1939.[178]

Other orders, like Kesher Shel Barzel (Iron Bond), proved unable to survive. Founded in 1860 and numbering 13,000 members in 1879,[179] the Kesher had the Daniel (German) and Mount Sinai (English) Lodges with ninety members altogether.[180] These "young and progressive Israelites" heard occasional lectures, and supported their order's home for the aged in Cleveland, in a way resembling B'nai B'rith's orphan asylum.[181] The Independent Order of Free Sons of Israel, like its fellow-orders, combined practical mutual aid with humanitarianism, aiming

. . . to unite the Sons of Israel in the interests of common humanity, and to spread intelligence and enlightenment and more firmly bind the tie which united mankind; . . . to succor the distressed—to relieve the needy—and to lend a helping hand in all that is good and noble.[182]

Two lodges, founded in 1872 and 1874 respectively, in 1881 claimed 101 members.[183] The Sons of Benjamin, a minor order, flourished in Milwaukee from the 1880's, while the Independent Order B'rith Abraham and the Independent Order of the Western Star had several lodges in the 1890's. The latter two had a large proportion of East European Jews as members, to judge from the names of the lodges' officers.[184] Most other lodges, however, were German-Jewish.

German-Jewish interest in lodges declined with the new century. Elaborate rituals were no longer in vogue, and the prosperous native Jews could by then dispense with the mutual aid features which had once been so important. Wealthier Jews gradually withdrew from the plebian lodges and built private clubs to take their pleasures. Although such bodies as Camp Barbanel of the Woodmen of the World appeared in 1898, composed of East European Jews,[185] these new immigrants had not brought with them any background of fraternal orders and rituals. Masonry and secret societies, so popular in Germany, were illegal and unknown to East European Jewry.

IN JEWISH CLUBLAND

Private social clubs enjoyed their heyday in Milwaukee from about 1880 to 1914, as the upper layer of merchants and manufacturers created an exclusive social milieu. Beginning with the Bon Ami Club in 1881, ten local clubs had 4,000 members in 1889, of whom 3,000 could betake themselves to private clubhouses.[186] Yet even the wealthiest Jews, recognized members of Milwaukee Germandom, preferred social ties with one of the city's two Jewish clubs.

The Harmonie Club,[187] originating in 1866, was reorganized in 1876 as the Concordia Club. With its fifty members paying an initiation fee of $50 and annual dues of $36, only the well-to-do belonged.[188] At the Concordia's rooms, cards and billiards and magazines were supplemented by such social events as "Phantom" and New Year's Eve parties.[189] In 1884 the Concordia Club dissolved and the Phoenix Club arose from its ashes. Composed of "the elite of Jewish society," this Club conducted a round of parties, balls, and family picnics.[190] After five years in rented quarters, the sixty-eight members of the Phoenix Club took the ambitious step of erecting a club house by means of a stock issue.[191] After spending over $50,000 for a two-story grey stone structure, which was formally opened at a sumptuous ball on New Year's Day, 1890,[192] Phoenix membership rose to 115, with $60 dues and an initiation fee of $50. A *Sentinel* reporter described the edifice just after $18,000 was spent to remodel it in 1898:

> . . . On the ground floor of the clubhouse to the right of the corridor there is now a large and attractive lounging room, decorated with Oriental furnishings. To the left of this spacious corridor is the library, which is artistically decorated with Persian blue trimmings. On the same side of the hall is a space devoted to office room, letter boxes, call bells, and telephones. Adjoining this, is the billiard and pool room, card rooms and private dining rooms. An attractive beer stuben with German decorations has been arranged in the basement, which has also been turned into bowling alleys. . . . The dining room occupies the entire space on the third floor and can accommodate 250 guests, and has been elaborately decorated and furnished. The members consider this one of the finest equipped clubhouses in the Northwest.[193]

Not longer after, in 1900, the community was surprised to learn that the Phoenix Club planned to sell its quarters for $75,000 and disband; a new club might be built in a residential section.[194] Probably this was due, in part, to the opening of the more modest Standard Club, another descendant of the original Harmonie Club.

The Standard Club's progenitor had been the Progress Club, founded by 24 men in 1877, "the successor of a former social club [i.e., the Harmonie] which had died from gout." The Progress Club was a mainly West Side association, and its home and the amusements it engaged in—debates, public readings, musicales, dancing—were modest.[195] It functioned during the 1880's and 1890's, alongside more short-lived bodies like the Union Club and the Tuxedo Club.[196] Also of West Side origin (its first meetings in December, 1892 were at B'ne Jeshurun), the Standard Club enrolled 110 business and professional men. While all its members were Jews, the Standard Club did not "restrict its membership to that race."[197] In 1899, the Standard Club began to erect its $30,000 home on Pabst Brewing Company land, on Twenty-second Street above Grand Avenue (Wisconsin Avenue today). Not equal to the resplendent Phoenix Club but "elegant in many respects,"[198] it still caused the older and stodgier clubhouse to close. The Standard Club was Milwaukee's Jewish club until the Jewish country clubs took its place.

Middle-class Jewish women, dissatisfied with the old-fashioned Jewish ladies' social and charitable societies,[199] were quickly drawn to the Milwaukee chapter of the National Council of Jewish Women. Founded in the city in 1895, it undertook an ambitious program of self-education, with rabbinic assistance, and service to immigrants.[200] The Council had East Side and West Side groups, meeting semi-monthly at synagogues, and its study circles quickly became fashionable.[201] Thus, for October, 1896, Miss Effie Silber spoke to the women on "Ghettos, their Influence and Effects on the Times," together with Miss Millie Goetz on "Attitude of Women of Leisure to their Wage Earning Sisters." In the following month, Miss Edith Rich taught "Hebrew Philosophers," accompanied by Mrs. Simon Kander's course on "Friendly Visiting Among the Poor."[202]

Aspirations to serve the poor, which were then frequent among urban ladies, found concrete realization in the Milwaukee Council of Jewish Women's volunteer social work among the city's Jewish immigrants. Classes in sewing, cooking, manual work and "treats" for immigrant children, all conducted at the Temples, were the main activities of the misnamed Milwaukee Jewish Mission.[203] When the Mission merged with the Sisterhood of Personal Service's evening classes to form the Jewish Settlement, one of the community's foremost Jewish institutions was thereby founded.[204] However, the Council of Jewish Women failed to keep up its early momentum, and lay dormant until it was revived in 1909. It resumed its study groups, and did valuable health and educational work among immigrants.

Years before these ministrations to immigrant children, local

Jewry showed mild concern for its own youth. Many elders felt uneasy over "the demoralizing influence of card-playing in our clubs"[205] and similar harmful habits. Young people's groups like the Irving Literary Society, the Montefiore Literary Club, and the Literary Circle, lacked permanence and failed to create a Jewish environment for youth.[206] Thus, a Literary and Social Life Club, with as many as 300 young members in 1895, and a program of theatrics and literary efforts, soon faded away.[207] A similar end befell an ambitious group, the Young Men's Hebrew Literary Association, founded by the Jewish Alliance in 1891. With aspirations to follow its parent into social service among the immigrants, it conducted debates, maintained a library, and heard public lectures. The night school which met in its rented quarters was the beneficiary of the Young Men's Hebrew Literary Association's balls.[208] Yet despite the manifold program, this organization also did not survive.

An effort was made during the 1880's to found a Milwaukee branch of the rapidly growing Young Men's Hebrew Association. Rabbi Moses felt "sure that congregations, as well as the rabbis, would welcome such a step"[209] for attaching to Judaism the first native generation of Milwaukee Jews.[210] However, the first steps taken in 1883 showed that religion was a secondary consideration: "social ties were to be first tightened, intellectual improvement looked to, and religious advancement considered later, if it is then thought to be the interest of the association to include it as one of the objects."[211] The preamble, signed by 119 persons, aimed broadly "to develop, foster and promote the elevation of the moral, social, religious and intellectual position of the Israelites of the city of Milwaukee."[212] Despite plans for social activities, free classes and lectures, an employment bureau, all part of a conscious design to help young Jews to find their place in the Jewish and general community, the Young Men's Hebrew Association came to nothing after a promising start,[213] notwithstanding a prominent Board of Directors (A. W. Rich, Philip Carpeles, I. J. Litt, B. M. Weil, Max Landauer, Bernhard Gross, and others), and a recognized need to draw young Jews away "from mingling with the vicious crowds that frequent the saloon and gambling room."[214] Perhaps the Y.M.H.A. did not crystallize because of low ethnic cohesion of Milwaukee Jews, blurred by Germanic associations. Ultimately, immigrant youth services outgrew their beginnings, and like their clients, climbed to middle class status. For many years, however, the lack of a Y.M.H.A. seemed to some "a fact if not to be deplored then to be wondered at." It seemed the fault of a "queer city. . . . Possibly in no other city do the votaries of Judaism or those who are Jews by virtue of their descent, display less interest in the affairs of the congregation or in the intellectual and social advancement of their race."[215]

CULTURAL EXPRESSION

Most native Jews of Milwaukee before 1900 found satisfaction in the city's rich Germanism rather than in its attenuated Judaism. Jews played an indispensable role in maintaining the German milieu and with relatively small numbers they constituted a comparatively large proportion of liberal, free-thinking Milwaukee Germans.

Sharing the enthusiasm for music, characteristic of German cultural life, Jews appeared in all the musical functions, as composers, performers, and patrons. Thus, the brothers Harry Schoenfeld (1857-1936) and Theodore Schoenfeld (1840-1881) both studied in Germany, Theodore under Joachim in Berlin and Harry at the Leipzig Conservatory. The elder settled in Milwaukee, where he had come as a boy in 1854, and became a well-known music teacher.[216] Harry Schoenfeld was already composing at Leipzig,[217] and after returning home he joined the faculty of the Hershey Music School in Chicago. There he continued a long career as a teacher and composer, apparently in European romantic style.[218] Among local talent was the violinist David Bimberg, whom the *Sentinel* deemed "a young man of surprising talent, and of remarkable attainments" when he gave a recital at the age of twenty.[219] A singer well known in German circles was Joseph Benedict, a baritone,[220] while Charles Horwitz was a writer of popular songs.[221]

Perhaps the foremost cultural institution of Milwaukee Germanism was the Milwaukee Musical Society, which during the typical year of 1873 gave its 600 members no less than ten regular orchestral and choral concerts and two "summer-night festivals." The Society was also responsible for erecting the city's Academy of Music.[222] The devoted amateurism of the Musical Society and the plays at the Stadt Theatre were not succeeded by anything comparable in the reigning English sphere. Neither a Milwaukee Symphony Orchestra nor a worthy legitimate theatre were founded in the city.

During the best years of the Musical Society, familiar German-Jewish men actively participated in its affairs: Bernhard Stern, Moritz N. Becker, A. W. Rich, C. A. Meissner, Louis Cohn, Jacob Morawetz, and especially Bernard Leidersdorf, the tobacco manufacturer, and Henry M. Mendel, clothier and wholesale grocer. Probably no Milwaukeean did more for music than Mendel, who was for many years President of the Musical Society and chairman of its Board of Directors.[223] He was president of the Arion, a German glee club,[224] and, himself an amateur musician and author of a *History of Music in Milwaukee*, was founder, patron, and lay manager of the Luening Conservatory of Music.[225] As President of the North American Saengerbund, which counted 100,000 members in German glee clubs, Mendel organized and presided over its festival, held in Milwaukee in July, 1886. With 1,200 voices singing at its opening concert, this was perhaps the largest musical event in America until its day.[226] Mendel was an early German-Jewish patron of American music, and remained within the bounds of German culture; his Jewish associations were nominal. Besides Mendel, other Jewish names regularly recur, such as M. N. Becker in the Liedertafel Society,[227] and Henry A. Adler in the Gesang-Verein.[228] Jews were particularly prominent in the Liederkranz of the Freie Gemeinde, where Jacob Brandeis served as President.[229]

The stage was another German cultural enterprise where Jewish participation was also evident. The excellent Stadt Theatre long presented classic German drama before appreciative audiences. Observed the *American Israelite* in 1895: "its Jewish patrons have taken a liberal and active interest in the theatre, contributing greatly to its success," as well, it could be added, to its rebuilding after it was swept by fire in 1895.[230] The moving spirit of the Stadt Theatre for twenty-five years until his death in 1909 was Leon Wachsner, a Jew.[231] The declining vitality of the German theatre became evident after his death.

Lesser dramatic groups also sprang up, like the Milwaukee Operatic and Dramatic Club, a Jewish amateur group of the 1890's. Its plays "in the German language and the Jewish dialect," were evidently not in Yiddish but in German with a "Jewish" accent.[232] The Milwaukee Theatre Company took over the Davidson Theatre in 1890, and was headed by A. W. Rich, with B. M. Weil, a director.[233]

The Germania Society, a liberal literary and musical association of younger Germans, steadily attracted German Jews. Names like Goldstein, Rindskopf, Hammerschlag, and Bernstein appear among its officers and trustees. A guiding spirit was B. A. Abrams, the German pedagogue,[234] and Rabbis Eppstein and Moses spoke before it.[235] Characteristically, these rabbis' successors hardly had relations with Milwaukee Germandom. After about 1890, the German sphere and the Jewish sphere hardly overlapped, and few Jews attempted to keep one foot in each.

The Jewish Press

The German-Jewish "cultural symbiosis" was not brought from Germany to Milwaukee, for Germanism and Judaism remained separate. Milwaukee's German-Jewish press made the principal attempt to synthesize the two cultures.

Isaac M. Wise's *American Israelite* and his *Die Deborah* began to print correspondence from Milwaukee in 1855, and continued to do so long after the founder's death in 1900.[236] But the news was episodic, and in later years, often trivial. A most notable German-Jewish publication appeared in Milwaukee itself, *Der Zeitgeist*, a "family paper for Israelites" published by Rabbi Isaac S. Moses with his brother, Rabbi Adolf Moses of Mobile, Alabama, later of Louisville, and Rabbi Emil G. Hirsch of Chicago.

Der Zeitgeist made its first bi-weekly appearance on January 1, 1880, and continued for three years. Its editor explained:

> Our "Zeitgeist" is not destined to be used exclusively by Jewish preachers as a background for the religious problems and contentions of our age, but, foremost, as a Jewish family periodical in the full sense of the word . . . a source of inspiration and refined entertainment. . . .

The neat, 10" x 12", sixteen-page paper was first produced by the printing house of W. W. Coleman and later by the German *Milwaukee Herold*.[237] Subscription rates for *Der Zeitgeist* and its literary section "Im Familienkreise," a total of 36 pages, were $3.00 a year.[238]

"The Spirit of the Times" appeared in German not only for opportunistic considerations, but for ideological reasons which Milwaukeeans especially could appreciate:

> We have here a strong German Jewry, filled with the spirit of German culture, which has certainly contributed a great deal to the spiritual revival of our people. By the medium of the German language, that kind of noble Jewish spirit can be preserved that was first conceived by our immortal Moses Mendelssohn, and then developed with so much faith and devotion by such teachers and leaders as Jost, Zunz, Graetz, Frankel, Geiger, Philippson, Einhorn, and other important personalities. . . .

In conscientiously defining the platform of the *Zeitgeist*, its three rabbinic editors turned to the touchy question of religion:

> . . . The *Zeitgeist* will present moderate Reform. Judaism has yet to fight great battles. And here, on one hand, we hear the call, "We want to be Jews in the traditional way; we are not allowed to transgress the limits drawn by our fathers." On the other hand: "We intend to get rid of all historical traditions, in order to form an entirely new kind of Judaism. . . ." And so we stand right in the middle of these extreme tendencies, and see how self-deception and narrow-mindedness on one side, and coarse materialism and nonsensical cynicism on the other, rank like poisonous sucklings on the stem of true Judaism.

The goal that the *Zeitgeist* tries to represent is . . . a pure reformed type of Judaism which is attuned to the age, and whose genuine eternal nucleus must remain unharmed. . . .[239]

The contributors to the *Zeitgeist* formed a notable group indeed. America's leading Reform rabbis responded to its solicitation—Kaufman Kohler, Bernard Felsenthal, Gustav Gottheil, Samuel Hirsch. Their articles dealt with basic Jewish problems, including the Sabbath, marriage and intermarriage, the ideas of the chosen people and the mission of Israel, revelation, and so forth.

Also among *Zeitgeist* contributors were some of the greatest figures of 19th century Judaism—Heinrich Graetz, the Jewish historian; Hermann Cohen, the neo-Kantian German Jewish philosopher; Adolf Jellinek, Vienna's great preacher and Talmudist. None of them had contributed to an American publication, and each turned in significant articles. Graetz wrote an original study of "The Stages in the Development of the Messianic Belief," and reprinted his "Shylock in Folklore, Drama, and History."[240] Jellinek published portions of a later book on "The Jews in Popular Proverbs."[241] Hermann Cohen's examination of the "The Historic-Cultural Significance of the Sabbath" was a profound, radical evaluation of its subject which concluded with a proposal to observe the Jewish Sabbath on Sundays. It created quite a stir when reprinted in its author's native land but apparently gained no attention in America.[242] Other scholars abroad who responded to the enterprising editors' invitations were Emanuel Schreiber and Moritz Friedlander of Vienna, and Leopold Stein of Frankfurt-am-Main. During the year which the German poet Friedrich Bodenstedt spent in Milwaukee, *Der Zeitgeist* also secured some verse from his pen.

A typical issue contained about six pages of serial novels, three or more pages of philosophical sermons, perhaps a scholarly article, prolific editorial comment, and a small ration of Jewish news. There was hardly any advertising.

After one year, Isaac Moses confessed that it had "been for the editor a year of struggles and grief." As the printing and business affairs of the periodical were in Milwaukee, most of the

burden rested upon his shoulders. "We have succeeded in win-
ning to our paper a number of the most eminent authors," wrote
the editor:

> The recognition which the *Zeitgeist* has found within Amer-
> ican Jewry cannot be proven only by wide circulation in the
> United States, but also in that it has found so great a number
> of readers in the best Jewish circles in Europe, as no other
> Jewish paper in America has found before.[243]

The editor could justifiably have boasted of this cultural link
between European and American Jewry.

As circulation grew somewhat, Julius Schwartz, editor of the
Austrian-American of New York, became correspondent from
that city. "Schwartz's reports might sound somewhat orthodox,"
but "cannot do any harm. . . . *The Zeitgeist* can only gain by the
fact that in addition to its two editors that follow radical reform,
a third now follows the somewhat conservative line."[244]

After the second year, the editors claimed that theirs was the
"only German periodical of progressive Judaism on the continent;
a paper that has succeeded in making the best writers in this
country and abroad utilize it as their mouthpiece, and a source
of instruction and entertainment for the intelligentsia among our
co-religionists." However, there was "a deficit so far," and the
editors appealed for new subscribers and prompt payments. "We
would rather have 3,000 readers at $2.50 a year rather than 1,500
who are willing to pay $5.00."[245] It is not certain that they had
the latter either; they did not reveal circulation figures.

The editor took risks. In December, 1880, one Samuel Hirsch
sued Moses, who he claimed had slandered him $5,000 worth by
the remark "Du bist ein alter ganuff" (you are an old thief).
While the suit was brought against Rabbi Moses for an oral statement, press reports left the impression that he had published it.
Moses responded that "even a Rabbi, in order to protect himself against blackmail, can risk a libel suit from time to time." But
the *American Hebrew* saw it simply:

> Our western contemporary, the *Zeitgeist*, has a real live libel
> suit on its hands for five thousand dollars. But libel suits are

excellent advertisements, and we suppose the *Zeitgeist* is correspondingly happy.

Hirsch won his case in Circuit Court the following May, the jury placing the damage at six cents. Moses bitterly asserted: "I hope that this result will satisfy the Jewish periodicals who rejoice when some one else is hurt."[246]

Moses felt "tired of carrying the entire burden of a business manager, in addition to his duties as an editor." He resentfully criticized I. M. Wise in November, 1882 for "entertaining the wishful thought" of the end of the *Zeitgeist*:

> For the enlightenment of our colleague, whose character we admire, we would like to mention that we actually consider discontinuing the publication of the "Zeitgeist" in Milwaukee . . . The "Zeitgeist" never considered it its task, as Dr. Wise claims, to find faults and weaknesses, as well as deficiencies, in the "Deborah" and the "Israelite" . . . Dr. Wise has not yet comprehended that only honest aspirations, not concerned with the acclaim of the masses, and only modest, real greatness and dignity, but not unlimited ambition, reckless will to dictate, and clownlike boasting, can earn the esteem of his contemporaries and the gratitude of these who come after us. But as to the future of the "Zeitgeist," we think that you have started too early with your jubilation, dear colleague.[247]

Nevertheless, the *Zeitgeist* ceased with the issue of December 21, 1882. The editors' hope that a reliable publisher in Chicago might continue the publication, "perhaps in a somewhat different format and partly in English," failed to materialize.[248] It died because too few German Jews would read serious writing, and as popular journalism *Der Zeitgeist* could not overcome *Die Deborah*. European readership was more of an adornment than a support.

Der Zeitgeist was a noteworthy journal which deserved a longer life, a monument to the German-Jewish synthesis which was attempted but not achieved in Milwaukee. Germanism declined and Judaism was revived by the stream of East European Jews.

IV

Civic Security and Public Service

THE ECONOMICALLY secure Jews of Milwaukee lived in unchallenged enjoyment of their civic rights, and did not hesitate to exercise fully their political rights as Americans. As vigorous upholders of church-state separation, seldom did any issue make them feel that their constitutional rights were being impaired. By a decision generally pleasing to Jewish opinion, Bible reading in the public schools was prohibited by the state's highest court. The age of sometimes doctrinaire liberalism also produced Jews who opposed the tax exemption of churches, or objected to all Sabbath legislation, although their right to keep the Jewish Sabbath instead of Sunday was written into law.

With the same freedom, the Jews of Milwaukee vigorously participated in the free-and-easy politics of the time. That a political candidate was a Jew was sometimes mentioned, but the existence of a "Jewish vote," much less its manipulation, was not suggested until a substantial Russian Jewish group resided in Milwaukee. Like liberal Germans, German Jews had been mainly Republicans, but the unallied Russian Jews' votes were eagerly solicited by the traditional parties. The rising Socialists, with Jewish and other ethnic branches, drew upon immigrant hope and idealism. Generally, East European Jews seem to have been mainly Democrats in national elections, and Socialists when they voted for municipal offices.

The 19th century Jews of Milwaukee were convinced that

they had left the old "rishus" (lit. wickedness; German Jewry's term for Jew-hatred) behind them forever, although the message of ideological anti-Semitism in Imperial Germany quickly reached Milwaukee ears. Unfaltering trust in human progress led Milwaukee Jews to regard such tremors as relapses into "medieval superstition" which would speedily be swept away by modern enlightenment. Within the city limits, they were right.

MATTERS OF LEGAL STATUS

The question whether churches and church property ought to be subject to taxation had a lengthy history. Addressing the Milwaukee *Turnverein*, in 1871, Isaac Neustadtl, a German liberal leader, advocated their taxation.[1] Toward the end of 1895, as the matter was about to be placed before the Legislature, even clergymen seemed divided on the subject, with two rabbis entertaining opposite views. Rabbi Sigmund Hecht advocated tax exemption:

> . . . Churches are unproductive as far as dollars and cents are concerned. They are built, just as hospitals, asylums or other benevolent institutions, or like parks and libraries, for the public good. . . . They are a tax upon the people who erect them, and to tax them would be equivalent to taxing a tax . . . So long as the church is not a source of revenue to those who own the property, it were wrong to burden them with a double tax. . . .[2]

But Rabbi Victor Caro opposed exemption on the principle of "the absolute separation of church and state":

> Each church must support its own with its own money and not the money of others. As a check upon ecclesiasticism, I am for the taxation of all church property. The state has no right to tax one man for the purpose of propagating another man's religion.[3]

Sunday legislation remained at issue throughout the period, especially between "Yankee" and "Teuton," for the latter's jovial Sunday habits caused social and legal controversy. In July, 1870, the case of the City of Milwaukee vs. German *Turnverein* con-

cerning the defendant's violation of the City Ordinance which prohibited public dancing on Sunday came before Judge James A.
Mallory. He held that the State Constitution

> intended to prohibit and prevent any enactment tending to
> enforce or reflect the opinions or prejudices of any sect or
> denomination of religionists, or any other persons, or class of
> persons, in any matter pertaining to or tending to interfere
> with the right of conscience. . . . If the Jews and Seventh-day
> Baptists, being a majority in any community should abstain
> from work and amusement on Saturday, nobody would hesitate
> to denounce it as a law affecting religious belief, and therefore
> unconstitutional. . . .
>   It cannot be claimed that dancing of itself is wrong; it is re-
> garded as being not only an innocent amusement, but one of
> the polite accomplishments, and its wrong would be just as
> wrong in any other part of the State, or on any other day . . .
> neither the Legislature nor the Common Council can [constitu-
> tionally] authorize or pass such an ordinance, . . .[4]

Recalling the Legislature's recent relaxation of Sunday laws, the
Court concluded that they were "a dead letter upon our statute
books, by common consent." Judge Mallory denied the Common
Council's power to pass what he deemed a religious ordinance;
moreover, since the recent repeal of statutes prohibiting dancing
on Sunday, the ordinance contravened the declared policy of the
State.[5]

Another "Sunday law" became a source of litigation in the
1890's. The Municipal Statutes prohibited all Sunday business,
"except only works of necessity and charity," as well as public
entertainment. Jewish and libertarian sensibilities were pacified
by a special clause protecting

> Any person who conscientiously believes that the seventh
> or any other day of the week ought to be observed as the
> Sabbath and who actually refrains from secular business and
> labor on that day. . . .[6]

Rabbi Hecht and members of Temple Emanu-El recorded
themselves against all Sunday closing, and, as District Attorney,

Leopold Hammel refused to prosecute Sunday violations. Business men prosecuted for Sunday business threatened to insist on closing saloons and places of amusement, and stopping street cars on the Christian Sabbath.[7]

In April, 1896, Marcus Silber, proprietor of a dry goods store at Twelfth and Walnut streets, was arrested on complaint of the Retail Clerks' Association for being open "on the [Christian] Sabbath." (He was also open on the Jewish Sabbath.) The *Turners* and the Personal Liberty League tried but failed to have the charge withdrawn, since they feared a "revival of the blue laws."[8] The prosecution successfully contended that the issue was not religious but simply a day of rest for about 4,000 Milwaukee clerks who worked from 8 A.M. to 9 P.M. five days, from 8 A.M. till 10 or 11 P.M. on Saturdays, and then also had to work from 8 A.M. till noon on Sundays. The defense only claimed that Sunday opening of stores was necessary to accommodate many laboring people, but a police court jury ruled in favor of the prosecution.[9] Silber's appeal was dismissed, on the grounds that since sentence had been suspended, there was nothing to appeal.[10]

An historic controversy over Bible reading in the public schools was decided by the State Supreme Court's decision in the Edgerton case, in March, 1890.

Teachers in the Edgerton schools had read from the King James Bible at the opening of the school day. Some Catholic parents protested the practice, and turned unsuccessfully to Rock County Circuit Court, where Judge Bennett held that the mere reading of the Bible in the schools did not violate the Constitution. The Catholic plaintiffs then appealed to the Supreme Court, which reversed the decision, saying:[11]

> . . . It logically follows that the place where the Bible is read is a "place of worship," and that as the tax payers were compelled to erect and support the school-houses and the children are under a late law compelled to attend the public or private schools during a certain period, the constitutional clauses forbid such use of the school house.
> . . . such instruction in any public school would make it a "religious seminary," . . . which is forbidden by the constitution.[12]

The Jewish community, opposed to Bible readings in the public schools, applauded the decision of the Supreme Court.[13]

The Bennett Law of 1890 split Wisconsin along religious lines and dominated the elections of that year. The law required children to attend school in the district in which they lived, and required elementary schools to teach in English. Such legislation threatened Wisconsin's Germanism, although German had been offered optionally in the public schools since the late sixties. The parochial schools heavily emphasized the language upon which the German churches, press, and theater depended. Beyond the city, many rural German communities conducted their entire school program in German.[14]

Rabbi Sigmund Hecht voiced Jewish sentiment when he found "nothing in the Bennett Law that could operate prejudicially to anyone's personal liberty. . . ." German Republicans voted Democratic on Election Day, 1890, and the G. O. P. lost the State House; the Bennett Act was repealed in 1891.[15]

From time to time, Jews had to protest to school authorities over biased teachers and lack of respect for Jewish Holy Days and the Sabbath. Thus, teachers of the First District School in 1886 punished most Jewish children who had absented themselves on Rosh Hashanah by detention after school and loss of credit for the day. This problem of Jewish holidays continued especially for immigrant children absent on the Jewish festivals. Only in 1916 was full freedom of religious observance granted to Jewish school children.

Rabbi Hecht also found it necessary to raise his voice against school commencement exercises on Friday night:

> I can see no reason why a system that claimed to be so careful not to interfere with the religious practice of the people that justly and properly regards those who keep the Sunday holy, should ignore those even though they be in the minority, who keep the Jewish Sabbath. . . . I would respectfully direct the attention of our school authorities . . . to allow everyone an opportunity to witness the achievements of our schools, without interfering with the religious duties of anyone who is inclined to perform them.[16]

Stirrings of Anti-Semitism Before 1900

Milwaukee Jews encountered generally friendly attitudes towards themselves, among the Germans to whom they were so close. Rabbi Moses rejoiced:

Not even a trace of any prejudice against Jews can be found; and if superficially unsympathetic remarks are made about Jews from time to time, those refer only to such Jews as do not wish to be Jews in the first place—who have severed any connection with their co-religionists, and only follow their own interests. In such cases, certain allegations might be justified, but they concern individuals only, and not Jewry as a whole.[17]

Yet his own words qualified Moses' opening generalization.

Events in Germany cast their shadow in Milwaukee. Bismarck's *kulturkampf* against the Catholic Church provoked a chain of unpleasant correspondence in the *Milwaukee Sentinel*, when Emil Morawetz, a son of Jacob Morawetz who had left the Jewish fold, undertook to justify the Iron Chancellor's assault on the Catholics. He pointed to the Jesuits "in whose hands the Pope is only a puppet, a corpse, . . . [who] have openly and secretly worked at the destruction of the German Confederacy." Morawetz concluded: ". . . if we Americans do not guard our liberties most jealously, in ten years from now we shall have to fight the same foes . . . Americans, rouse before it is too late!"[18]

Morawetz' effusion provoked letters to the *Sentinel* from "A Patriot," "A Roman Catholic," "A Non-Religionist," "I. Brucker," and "A Jew." The angry "Roman Catholic" asked:

. . . by what authority does Mr. Morawetz, a Jew, brand the Catholics of the United States as being dangerous to the liberties of the United States? Catholics are producers; Jews are not. Catholics sustain the military arm of the government when foes from within or without threaten it; Jews do not, with but few exceptions. Catholics recognize the binding force of the oath of citizenship; Jews do not . . . Catholics are in every position of trust and danger scattered all over this broad land and upholding its flag on every sea. Jews are found generally in cities accumulating wealth from them and others. . . .

Although slandering the Jews, the writer yet appealed to them: "There are not many Jews even who will indorse Mr. Morawetz's insult to the Catholics of Milwaukee. . . ."[19]

Reprimanding the writer for attacking the Jews in "true Catholic style," a "Non-Religionist" came to Emil Morawetz' defense:

> To my knowledge Mr. E. M. does not lay any claim to being a Jew . . . But even if he did, what prompted A. R. C. to attack all the Jews? Is not a Jew entitled to have his own individual opinion and views without dragging into it all Jews on account of the opinion of one E. M., who happens to be of Jewish descent? . . . But the most ludicrous exhalation of A.R.C. is the idea that Catholics recognize the binding force of the oath of citizenship, but Jews do not . . . The Jews recognize no higher authority than the law of the land, while the Catholics receive edicts from Rome in preference thereto . . .
>
> A.R.C. has shown his teeth. He is a Jew-hater, and not a civilized citizen.[20]

Then "A Jew" entered the controversy, disowning Morawetz who "is no Jew." He labelled the Catholic "an unscrupulous liar and defamer" yet asked him to reason calmly:

> . . . But take it for granted that Mr. Morawetz were a Jew, . . . would it be just to hold the Jews as a body, responsible for the actions or opinion of one person who might claim to be of that same denomination? . . . the world at large would be more benefited if such profound statesmen as Mr. Morawetz and A Roman Catholic would devote their entire attention to some legitimate business, instead of writing for publication sensational and inflammable articles which can create no possible good to either Jew or Catholic.[21]

This petty controversy revealed deep-seated attitudes. When the depression of the 1870's and the weakness of liberalism aided anti-Semitism to gain headway in Germany, the virus quickly crossed the Atlantic to Wisconsin. Stirred by the anti-Semitic menace in Germany, late in 1880 there was talk of protest meetings in the United States. Such a meeting was seriously considered in Milwaukee, but abandoned, since it was felt that Bismarck would defend German Jewry. Confidence in the Iron Chancellor died hard. German Jewry was discussed by the local socialists, who were then proscribed in Germany, and by Editor Biron of the *Milwaukee Journal*, who lectured to the Fortschritt Society on "Israel and the Persecution of the Jews in Germany," emphasizing the great role of Israel in civilization. The local press, English and German, was, in Rabbi Moses' words, "tactful and in every respect praiseworthy."[22] Only the *Germania*, German and Protestant, favored the cause of Court Preacher Stöcker, the anti-Semitic leader. However, upon Stöcker's arrival for an abortive American tour, *Der Herold*, another local German daily, "approached quite near the realms of anti-Semitism" in a pro-Stöcker editorial. In a subsequent issue it endeavored "to right itself with the many Jewish readers by disclaiming any intention of hurting their feelings."[23]

Toward the end of 1895, another German anti-Semite on American soil disturbed the Jewish community. On December 6 of that year, the *Germania* reported that Hermann Ahlwardt, a German anti-Semitic luminary, would undertake his Jew-baiting crusade in the United States at the invitation of Waldemir Wernich. The latter, a seed merchant on Grand Avenue, had once edited the agricultural section of the *Herold* and its subsidiary *Acker und Garten-Bau Zeitung*. Wernich denied that he had invited Ahlwardt, but confirmed "that I am an earnest anti-Semite and I am honest in my convictions on that subject." He had learned from Ahlwardt in Europe "that it would be a good thing if the eyes of the American people were opened to the fact that the Jews were rapidly ruining the commercial interests of the country, and robbing the Christians on all sides in the highwayman style. . . ."[24]

The painful news of Ahlwardt's arrival aroused Rabbi S. Hecht:

the man, . . . is a rector by profession and a libeller by trade, by supposition a man of scholarship, but in reality a man of repellent stupidity, in creed a follower of Jesus, in deed an enemy of the Jewish kinsmen of the Nazarene rabbi. His whole makeup is Jew hatred, and his ambition is to outdo

Haman of old . . . Let us combine to give him a reception that will convince him that he has struck the frigid North pole, so that he will discover that neither New York nor Milwaukee have so far retrograded as to be receptive for his sentiments.[25]

Liberal-minded Christians reassured the Jews that they had nothing to fear from Ahlwardt, and hoped that he would be ignored.[26] Ahlwardt enjoyed "no encouragement from any quarter."

> Few people go to hear his addresses. The gospel of race hatred is not congenial to the American atmosphere. We are a liberal minded, cosmopolitan people, and judge men by their acts as individuals. The Jew and the Gentile stand here upon an equal footing, and if the Jew proves the abler man he is entitled to the advantages which his ability gives him. Ahlwardt comes as the representative of provincial bigotry and the traditions of the dark ages that still linger in some quarters of the old world. His mission was foredoomed to failure.

But the *Sentinel* cautioned American Jews not to interfere with Ahlwardt's meetings:

> It is reported that they are proposing to prevent his speaking in Chicago, and intimations are given that he will be assailed with over-mature eggs and other missiles if he makes the attempt. By such conduct the Jews will simply bring disgrace on themselves, and excite sympathy for their enemies. . . . Let him talk; he can do no harm, and he will soon learn how futile are his efforts to kindle here the prejudices and hatreds that exist in some of the countries of Europe. A dignified contempt is the attitude which American Jews should assume towards him.[27]

As predicted, Ahlwardt's attempts to lay a racial groundwork for anti-Semitism proved futile. However, there were other bursts of anti-Semitism. Thus, in 1894, as on a few previous occasions, yellow posters containing an obscene and vulgar "Anti-Semitische Hymne" in German, circulated among the hucksters and farmers at the German market on Juneau avenue,[28] where Russian Jewish immigrants had gained a foothold during the preceding decade.

Liberal voices were also heard in the city, condemning anti-Semitism.

At Holy Name Church, Father James Haeffer preached about the Children of Israel, "in a manner that was rather strange in a Roman Catholic pulpit," thought the *Sentinel* reporter.

In these times it once again becomes the duty of the priest of God to warn Christians against the wrongs that are being done to the children of Israel in the intellectual and moral world . . . the Israelite stands before the world, too great and grand to be tampered with by ungodly genius. . . . It is in the . . . pure light of that divine and human truth that the Christian must form . . . a just judgment based on truth in place of preconceived notions and prejudices, a kind of appreciation grounded in charity despite every traditional hatred and antipathy . . . hatreds with which Israel has been and is too often humiliated beyond measure, are not according to the spirit of the church, but against it . . . Any uncharitable or unjust anti-Semitic movement, be it great or small, be it individual or national, shall ever receive, not her sanction, but her anathemas.[29]

During the early nineties, when murmurs of anti-Semitism were heard, a Christian Milwaukeean in whose veins ran "not a drop of Jewish blood," and who was "not connected with the Jews by the marriage of any near or distant kinsman," eloquently defended the Jews:

It is a splendid race, splendid in their patience, in their love for one another, in their endurance, in their sagacity and temperate habits, and splendid in their inflexible adherence to the Mosaic ideals . . . Do you seek aristocracy or talent? . . . the world's roll of great soldiers, authors, musicians, poets, philosophers and financiers contain more Hebrew names than I could recite in many hours . . .

It is spurious, false Christianity that hates Jews . . .

Here in Washington I have heard aspiring politicians, when beyond the reach of the reporter's pencil, sneer at Jews, and yet it was a Jew who made England's queen empress of India, [etc.]

That you never see a Jew tramp or a Jew drunkard is a proverb, that you never meet a Jew beggar is a commonplace, . . . there are relatively fewer inmates of our hospitals, jails and workhouses furnished by the Jews than any other race contributes.

Convert the Jews! Let us first convert our modern Christians to genuine Christianity.

The belief that the Jew is more dishonest than the Gentile is one-half nonsense and the other half prejudice and falsehood. The anti-Jewish feeling which now seems to be rising again is unchristian, inhuman, and un-American. No man can share it who believes in the universal fatherhood of God and the universal brotherhood of man. It is born of the devil and is detestable.[30]

In April, 1893, news of an extradition treaty with Russia disturbed American Jewish and liberal opinion, for it seemed that Russia could now seize refugee rebels against the Czarist regime. A well-attended protest meeting was held on April 10, 1893, at the Plymouth Congregational church. Speakers included the Rev. Judson Titsworth, Rabbi Hecht, Judge James A. Mallory, Robert Schilling, and Bernhard Gross. They resolved:

> Whereas, the new treaty with Russia appears to provide for the denial of the right of asylum to political offenders, and for the surrender of revolutionists whose only crime is their intense love of freedom, and their sympathy with the oppressed disinherited millions of the Russian tyrant's subjects.
>
> Resolved, that we . . . deem such provisions a gross violation of the traditions of this great republic, . . .
>
> Resolved, that we repudiate the humiliating compact with Russia and reaffirm our determination to protect the Russian revolutionists who seek the safety of our shores against the brutal arm of the czar's barbarous government.[31]

A week later, the growing left-wing in Milwaukee held its own protest meeting in the Freie Gemeinde hall. Isadore Ladoff, the Russian Jewish exile whom the treaty might endanger, related from personal experience how political offenders were dealt with in Russia. Resolutions of protest were also adopted.[32]

JEWS IN CIVIC AFFAIRS

During the early seventies, Democrats went under the label of the People's Reform Party: "Democracy thinly veiled." With the opening of the eighties, the pendulum swung in the Republican direction. Labor joined forces with the Democrats in 1882, until the Union Labor and Socialist parties appeared soon after. In the first decade of the new century, socialism slowly rose to power on the Milwaukee scene. As part of the life-stream of the city, Jews participated in local and state political affairs, and were involved in all major parties. They sought and sometimes won political office without self-consciousness, and participated in many of the political episodes of the day.

One of the most controversial politicians of the 1870's was Samuel Rindskopf, whose candidacy for Congress became a subject of wide controversy among Germans and Jews.[33] In March, 1871, Rindskopf was recording secretary of the Republican Club.[34] At the formation of the Liberal Reform Union Club a year later, Bernhard Stern was chosen recording secretary and Samuel Rindskopf an Executive Committeeman.[35] Rindskopf attended the convention that nominated Greeley for President, and was a Wisconsin elector on the Greeley ticket. He was ranked "among the most valiant of fighters, was foremost in the ranks, always giving battle which resulted in overwhelming the enemies of Reform." He was dubbed "Prince Sam."[36]

Entering politics with an "electioneering circular" in November, 1872, Rindskopf seemed "the most popular congressional candidate" in Milwaukee in 1874.[37] He and Judge Mallory and P. V. Deuster, editor and proprietor of *The Seebote*, were in contention.[38] Endorsement of "Prince Sam" came quickly from the *Milwaukee News*, the *Herold*, *Banner* and *Columbia*, with the *Banner* giving "the Prince" direct and unqualified support.[39] The *Menasha Press* (Republican) editorially embraced him, proclaiming:

He is a bold, fearless politician, and from our personal acquaintance with him we know he despises political trickery and the underhanded intrigues of scheming office seekers. He is a successful business man. He is also a man of sufficient wealth to place him head and shoulders above the corrupt evils attendant in representative lives in Washington. He is a western man, he understands thoroughly the immediate wants of the west, and no man would labor more earnestly for the advancement of our common interests than he. [40]

And Isaac M. Wise's *American Israelite* of Cincinnati enthusiastically considered

> Mr. Samuel Rindskopf . . . a gentleman of rare talents and of the highest order of integrity and honor. We hope to see him in Congress and are convinced he would be a credit to that body.[41]

On September 23, 1874, the Reform Party's Convention for the Fourth Congressional District nominated Rindskopf,[42] but his nomination somehow injected bitterness into the political atmosphere. The "Bourbon" wing of the Republican party sought a "time-honored Bourbon" to oppose Rindskopf, still hoping to defeat the upstart.[43] Bolters from the Reform party looked to the *Seebote* (Reform), which decried the "Reform farce":

> . . . we will openly and honestly oppose Mr. Samuel Rindskopf, the nominee of a "packed" convention.
> We ask every well-meaning citizen if that is reform, when by means of money, and large sums at that, the people are literally drummed together to push a certain candidate into office?[44]

The *Seebote*, whose editor-publisher had lost the nomination to "Prince Sam," found

> . . . opinion . . . gaining ground among the Germans of the other states that the nomination of Mr. Rindskopf is one that our district cannot be proud of. . . .[45]

Rindskopf's attachment to the Republican cause was recent indeed, and his qualifications as a reformer were dubious. Opponents charged that he had packed the nominating convention and had bought off delegates. Now the *Freidenker*, organ of the Freethinkers of the Northwest, denounced the "Reform Swindle," promising to

> . . . use every means in our power, and so labor before the hour of election, that your Reform candidate will be spared the opportunity to dishonor the word Reform, that we will be

Beth Israel,
Fifth Street (1901)

Anshe Lubavich,
N. 11 Street & Reservoir (1925)

Anshe Sfard, Sixth Street (1908)

Tenements in the Jewish district, *ca.* 1905
(*Bureau of Labor and Industrial Statistics*)

IMMIGRANT LIFE

Outing of the Poale Zion Folk Shule, July 16, 1916 (*Mr. Is. Tuchman*)

From left to right: Sarah Feder, I. Kopeloff, Hyman Perlmuter,
H. Deutch, Nathan Sand, Peter Ottenstein, Is. Tuchman, Joseph
Dubinsky, Meyer Dubinsky, and Golda Mabovitz (Meir).

spared the shame of seeing German Athens represented by a man who is himself in want of reform. . . .[46]

While the *Milwaukee News* (Reform) steadfastly insisted that Rindskopf was "a thorough representative of the principles of the Reform Party," the Bourbon *Sentinel* intended to "openly and honestly oppose . . . the nominee of a 'Packed Convention!' "[47]

> Rindskopf is a young, active, self-made man. He is rich. He is said to have used money to get his nomination. . . .
>
> This young man did more than all the old party-hacks of the Democratic party, . . . to elect Governor Taylor last fall; and upon every principle he is entitled to call himself the Democratic leader. It shows . . . that the Democratic party is dead.
>
> Sam has always been a Republican until he Greeleyized a year or two ago. He left the Republican party in that campaign, went over to the enemy and it seems they are his.[48]

The *Sentinel* charged that the *News* did not deny that "it had been bought up," or that "money was used to secure Rindskopf's nomination."[49]

Early in October, 1874, Rindskopf's opponents injected an explosive issue into the already bitter feud. While attempts were being made to "call" Mayor Harrison Ludington to run against Rindskopf, rumors began to circulate that "Prince Sam" was constitutionally ineligible, since he supposedly did not become a citizen until 1872,[50] as shown in District Court records.[51] *The Banner* called upon Rindskopf "to prove that his father became a citizen, and thus entailed naturalization of his son."[52] Coming to Rindskopf's defense, the *News* denounced the

> campaign roorback and falsehood. . . . The malicious fabrication is without foundation. Sam Rindskopf's father was naturalized previous to Sam's coming of age, placing all his children not then 21 years old on the same basis as native born citizens. Sam has been a citizen and voter during the past thirteen years. . . .[53]

It cited his performance of citizen's duties. Nevertheless the call to Ludington to run against Rindskopf mounted, with over 5,000 names on the call, mainly Democrats. District committee members of the People's party working for the new campaign included H. M. Benjamin, H. M. Mendel, and L. Rosenheimer of Schleisingerville. As Rindskopf gathered proofs of prior citizenship, Nathan Pereles, who had drawn up the will of his father Loebl Rindskopf, claimed to have seen the "second" papers. The candidate could not find this document among the public records.[54] The question of his eligibility was finally referred by the Reform Congressional Committee to four lawyers for their views.[55]

The *Sentinel*, endorsing Ludington, summed up the case against "Prince Sam":

1. . . . He is a young man; he has had no experience in public affairs; . . .

2. It has been openly charged, and not successfully denied, that he secured his nomination by corrupt means; that he carried the primaries by a lavish expenditure of money, and that he thus packed the convention with hirelings and hummers.[56]

On October 19, the Reform Congressional Committe reported

that Mr. Rindskopf is and has been a citizen of the United States since the year 1860, and as such is eligible to the office of member of Congress of the United States.

The fact of Mr. Rindskopf's having subsequently taken out naturalization papers for the purpose of obtaining a passport or for any other object, did not affect his allegiance or citizenship.[57]

Despite his proof of citizenship, Rindskopf withdrew from the contest on October 20. Alluding to a "Jewish issue" involved in his candidacy, he continued:

. . . It was also objected to me, in private, I am told, that I am a Jew . . . it seems to me strange that citizens of America, where every man is free to worship God according to the dictates of his own conscience, should be biased by questions that are entirely outside of the state and pertain to the realm of personal liberty. I am not ashamed of the religion of my fathers; yet, practically, I am rather the fly-leaf between the Old Testament and the New than the disciple of either. I believe in the God of the Hebrews and of the Christians, and acknowledge allegiance to the moral law.

He defended his educational qualifications:

It was further represented that I am illiterate. It was my misfortune not to receive a university education in my youth. Yet very few members of Congress have been trained up in colleges. I believe I can write correct English when I try. While the man put up to beat me is probably no more ignorant than I of English grammar and the art of English composition, I can write and speak German. He does not know a word of that noble language. I can read the divine law in the ancient and sacred tongue as it emanated from Jehovah Himself. He is ignorant of both the tongue and the law. . . .[58]

Rumors still circulated that the *News* had accepted $5,000 from Rindskopf for its endorsement, and now that Rindskopf had been "paid off" to withdraw. The *Sentinel* turned sympathetic, and could recall

no instance of such bad faith as the heartless sacrifice of Mr. Rindskopf by his political associate in this Congressional district . . . there can be no doubt that these were the controlling considerations which have driven him off the course, namely: First, Mr. Rindskopf is a Reformer and not a Democrat, and therefore only fit to serve, and not to lead; second, he is a German and a Jew . . . It worked like a charm, and the victim fell into the snare set for him, and the Reformer, Jew and German was degraded to the ranks.

Considering the political atmosphere of the "wild seventies," "Prince Sam" was not worse qualified for Congress than many who succeeded in going to Washington. But as a reform candidate he was a misfit.

Shortly after, Rindskopf Brothers, distillers, stood trial for defrauding the United States of liquor taxes, a crime subject to fine and imprisonment up to two years. Having pleaded guilty, Sam Rindskopf was sentenced to one day's imprisonment and was fined $5,000, plus costs.[59]

Only three months later, the irrepressible Rindskopf was again in politics. In April, 1875, he was nominated chairman of the Seventh Ward Democratic-Liberal Committee.[60] Shortly thereafter he disappeared from the political scene and left the city.

Of the three Jews on the Board of Aldermen,[61] Henry M. Benjamin, a Democrat, was one of the noteworthy members of the Council during this decade. He sat on the Board of Councilors for the Sixth Ward from 1872 to 1874,[62] and then on the Common Council, where he became president.[63] As a gesture of appreciation, the Council presented him with "a gold-headed cane" for Christmas.[64]

When Mayor Harrison Ludington resigned to become Governor of Wisconsin, Benjamin, as president of the Common Council, was Acting Mayor of Milwaukee from December 27, 1875 to April 18, 1876. During his brief tenure of office, one of his targets was the local gambling dens.[65] Although there was talk of Benjamin as Democratic candidate for Mayor,[66] he resigned as Alderman for personal business reasons. His Sixth Ward constituents refused to accept his resignation, and Benjamin acquiesced, retaining his Council seat. On April 18, 1876 he was almost unanimously re-elected Council president,[67] and he was similarly honored in 1877.[68]

In 1878, public sentiment sought to draft him as candidate for mayor.[69] "A Call to Mr. Benjamin," signed by a few hundred leading local businessmen, requested permission to place his name before the electorate:

> Dear Sir:—We, the undersigned voters of the City of Milwaukee, REGARDLESS OF POLITICAL PARTY, respectfully request you to allow the use of your name as a candidate for the position of Mayor of our city.
> . . . at the present time, . . . every regard of party, or of nationality, ought to be entirely done away with; . . . the voters . . . should look out for the *best men* only, of warranted ability, honesty, independence from political relations, and call them to their positions free from the intrigues of any political engagements or obligations.[70]

But Benjamin had decided to quit politics, and replied on March 26, 1878:

. . . After a continual service of seven years in public life, I feel that I ought in justice to myself give my entire attention, hereafter, to my business, and therefore decline the honor which you wish to confer upon me.[71]

Serving briefly in the Common Council at the same time as Benjamin, was Alderman F. T. Adler, an independent from the Sixth Ward.[72] Bernard Leidersdorf and Henry A. Adler were members of the Council briefly during the eighties. Representing the Eighth Ward from 1880 to 1881, Leidersdorf was chairman of the Council Committee supervising the Board of Public Works. He opposed enforcement of the law concerning employment of children in factories, citing the many boys employed in his tobacco works who earned from $3 to $4 a week. He maintained that they were better off there "than upon the streets," which would lead to jail or Reform school.[73] Adler, a Democrat, represented the Second Ward from 1888 to 1890 and was an Alderman at Large from 1906 to 1908.[74]

Other members of the Jewish community were appointed to public positions during this period. Thus, Henry Bonns was appointed Tax Commissioner of Milwaukee in January, 1881.[75] Moritz Sonnlander and Isaac Horwitz were inspectors of fruits in 1874 and 1877, respectively.[76] Thomas Jefferson Pereles was named Commissioner of Public Debt in 1896.[77] The Charter election of 1873 resulted in the designation of Bernhard Gross, of the First Ward, to fill a vacancy as Justice of the Peace.[78]

Milwaukee Jews held varied roles in political life during the 1880's and 1890's. Moritz Sonnlander was a candidate for the State Assembly, and Louis Rindskopf and A. Breslauer, unsuccessful candidates for alderman from the Second Ward in 1880.[79] Isaac and Emanuel Friend, lifelong Democrats, voted Republican after 1880 and 1888, respectively.[80] Henry M. Mendel was a delegate of the Seventh Ward to the Republican city convention.[81] The Republican convention of the First Assembly District in 1880 sent Julius Goldsmith to the State convention, while Herman Stern was chosen for the Senatorial convention of the Fifth District.[82] Bernard Schram was Second Ward delegate to the Republican County Convention of 1888.[83] During 1887 and 1888, A. W. Rich was treasurer of the Republican Club and of the First

Ward Citizens' Club. When the Republican Club merged with the Young Men's Republican Club, in 1888, Rich was also elected treasurer.[84] M. N. Lando, attorney from 1869 and a Republican, was an unsuccessful candidate for county judge in 1897.[85] Abraham E. Baer, an active Democrat, was Deputy Clerk of the Municipal Court from 1879 to 1881, and ran as an unsuccessful Democratic candidate for County Clerk in 1880 and again in 1884.[86] Also in 1884, Henry A. Adler served as vice-president of the Second Ward Cleveland Club.[87] Leopold Hammel was president of the Jefferson Club in 1899.[88] Old Bernard Schleisinger Weil participated in nominating Horace Greeley at Baltimore in 1872.[89]

Leopold Hammel was District Attorney during 1892-1893,[90] and others occupied minor positions in the courts.[91]

A goodly number of Jews showed interest in education by serving as members of the School Board. M. N. Lando sat on that body from 1879 to 1881; Jacob Poss, 1881; E. M. Oberndorfer, 1892-1895; Simon Kander, 1893-1894, 1894-1897; Charles Polacheck, 1894-1897; and Jacob Black, 1897-1898.[92] Especially noteworthy was James Madison Pereles, appointed School Commissioner in 1893 for a term of two years, who after one year was elected president of the School Board. Among his progressive recommendations as president was pensions for teachers. He also wrote an historical sketch of the Milwaukee School Board. Pereles declined reappointment, but his brother Thomas served from 1906 to 1909. Contemporary with James on the School Board was Rabbi Julius H. Meyer, a member from 1902 to 1904. Charles L. Aarons, then a young lawyer, served as school director from 1904 to 1906 and Board Chairman from 1908 to 1912; Mrs. Lizzie Black Kander, of Jewish Settlement fame, a member for thirteen years from 1906, was joined from 1912 to 1917 by Mrs. S. M. Cantrovitz. Morris Stern in 1916 became the first East European Jew to act as a part of Milwaukee's educational authority. (Mrs. Victor Berger, another long-time incumbent, was not Jewish.)[93]

J. M. Pereles' interests were not limited to school affairs. In 1897, he became a Trustee of the Milwaukee Public Library, and next year became its President.[94] He distinguished himself during a temporary appointment as Judge of the County Court in 1899-1900.[95]

The State Board of Normal School Regents included Jacob E. Singer (1889-1891) and Dr. Jacob Mendel (1891).[96] Miss Leola Hirschman (later Sure) long served, by gubernatorial appointment, as a Regent of the University of Wisconsin.

The second Jew (after B. S. Weil) to serve in the State Legislature was Moritz Nathan Becker (1872-1874). Born in Bavaria in 1827, Becker had been a cavalry lieutenant in the Bavarian army. He arrived in the United States in 1850, and moved to Milwaukee in 1852. Becker was a police justice for two years and subsequently a produce dealer.[97] As a Liberal Democrat, Becker went to the State Assembly in 1872 from a mainly Catholic district,[98] and again in 1873.[99]

Elias Friend's son, Jacob E. Friend, an attorney, served in the Assembly from 1883 until 1887.[100] Friend drafted a bill on liquor licensing and, in 1885, introduced legislation to place the Milwaukee Fire and Police departments under civil service.[101] He and other local Jews were active in the Civil Service Reform Association.[102] Rabbi S. Hecht joined other religious leaders in championing civil service reform from his pulpit:

> . . . I hold that any question, by the solution of which the moral pulse is likely to be quickened, whether such question touches the commercial, social or political sphere, may properly be handled by the pulpit . . . the civil-service reform question therefore fitly belongs to the pulpit. The cry 'to the victor belongs the spoils,' is a disgrace and a reproach to a people, and in its consequences opens the door to depravity. The people, not the party, pay for the service rendered, and therefore, the simple question arises, who can best render the service? This is the result the civil service aims at. A radical reform in this branch will do away with bossism, restore the purity of the ballot, establish justice and equity, blot out sin and reproach, and will exalt a nation to the heights of righteousness.[103]

Hecht also advocated municipal ownership of public utilities, as a means of reducing taxes.[104] Political developments of the mid-nineties were influenced by movements for municipal reform that were stirring in an urbanized nation. Their focal point was the Milwaukee Municipal League, organized in the early nineties, and dedicated to non-partisan improvement of municipal government.[105] Among its organizers in 1893 were Henry M. Mendel, Bernhard Gross, and David Adler, and its "Committee of 100" also included Leopold Heiman and James M. Pereles.[106] The Tax League, a businessmen's organization founded in 1884, aimed at relief from "over taxation, and to aid in causing manufactures to locate here," and enrolled Benjamin M. Weil.[107]

Jews also participated prominently in Milwaukee's numerous organizations for charity, education and culture. Certain family names, such as Pereles and Friend, constantly appear as directors and benefactors. A. W. Rich and Philip Carpeles were officers of the Provident Dispensary, while Mrs. Emanuel D. Friend served the Children's Hospital.[108] The Flower Mission, founded in 1876 to aid the sick and poor, had numerous Jewish ladies as officers,[109] and the same was true of the House of Mercy.[110] H. M. Mendel served on the newly founded Red Cross' local advisory board.[111] The Babies' Home, [112] the Protestant Orphan Asylum,[113] the Phonological Institute for Deaf Mutes,[114] the Humane Society,[115] and the East Water Street Free Kindergarten all owed their founding and support in large measure to Jews. The Free Kindergarten, where benevolent ladies taught impoverished children "the ways of godliness and cleanliness, without inflicting on them any particular doctrines," had immigrant Russian Jewish children in fair number alongside Irish, Italian and German pupils.[116]

Educational improvement was a favorite interest of philanthropic Milwaukee Jews. They were among the petitioners in the Seventh Ward who asked that their local school have "accomplished and efficient teachers" and one of "experience and executive ability" as Principal.[117] Jews could be found as officers of Ward and neighborhood school bodies,[118] and Jewish ladies were active in the Woman's School Alliance for sanitary improvements.[119] Mrs. J. M. Pereles was an organizer of the Milwaukee Public School Cooking Association, whose demonstrations induced the School Board to introduce the arts of the housewife into the curriculum.[120] Mrs. Pereles was also a friend of the Industrial School[121] and her husband and brother-in-law, Thomas J. Pereles, yearly supplied free text books to thousands of needy school children.[122] The Pereles brothers donated the first books for the blind to the Public Library[123] where they served as Trustees. Mrs. J. M. Pereles and H. M. Mendel were officers of the Art Museum and the local art association, respectively.[124]

Upon the city's semi-centennial in 1895, the *Sentinel* spoke laudatory words of the record of Jews in the civic and economic life of the city:

> The Jewish citizens have contributed largely to the city's prosperity; the taxes paid by them have aided . . . [public buildings and works]; the business establishments maintained by them have given employment to thousands of working men and distributed large amounts of money among the people; their charity has been always generous and general; their public spirit, broad and unquestioned. For themselves and their religion they have gained the respect of their fellow citizens.[125]

A few Jews shared in military activities. Henry Katz, a grandson of the pioneer Isaac Neustadtl, graduated the United States Naval Academy at Annapolis in 1876 and served in the Navy until 1884.[126] No Milwaukee troops saw combat during the Spanish-American War, but a scattering of Jews could be found among the soldiers from the city.[127]

RADICAL REFORM

Outside the circles of political and civic respectability, movements of radical reform were appearing in the 1880's. Their slow rise to power in the 20th century had some relation to the newer Jewish population of Milwaukee.

Jews were found in the Labor Party which flourished briefly during the late 1880's. Sam Isaacs was its candidate for supervisor in the Fifteenth Ward in 1887, and Isidore Leiser served as party treasurer.[128] The Central Club of the People's Party had F. W. Thal as its treasurer in 1884. In 1898, the party nominated William B. Rubin (1873-1959) for Congress. Then twenty-five years of age, Rubin had been practicing law in the city for about two years.[129]

The labor vote joined hands with the People's Party to support the Populists in 1892, and a few years later rallied under the banner of the Labor Party in local politics. Victor L. Berger (1860-1929), an ex-teacher in the public schools, head of the South Side *Turnverein* and representative of the People's party, the Socialist section, and the Federated Trades Council, was seriously considered in 1894 as a Mayoral nominee by the labor wing. Berger, however, believed he was "inexperienced, and that it would hardly be becoming to him to accept the nomination for so exalted an office." On the other hand, the *Sentinel* considered Berger "altogether a much more intelligent person than the people he associated with."

This was Berger's debut in Milwaukee politics, where he played a major role for 35 years, in addition to his national prominence as a Socialist Party leader. He was born in Nieder-Rehbach, Hungary, on February 28, 1860, attended gymnasium and the universities of Budapest and Vienna, and emigrated with his parents to the United States. He held odd jobs, including cattle punching, before he returned to New York and learned the trade of metal polishing. He turned to teaching German, came to Milwaukee, and became prominent in the Turner movement. In December, 1892, Berger left teaching for Socialist politics. Securing a controlling interest in *The Milwaukee Volkszeitung,* he became its editor and changed its name to *The Wisconsin Vorwaerts.* In December, 1897, he married Meta Schlichting, formerly a teacher.[130] He participated in founding the Social Democratic Party in the year of his marriage.

JEWISH VOTER OR A JEWISH VOTE: 1890-1920

As new ethnic elements poured into Milwaukee, the local political powers grasped for their votes. The new Jewish immigrants seemed attracted to the Democrats until the Socialists also came on the scene.

During the nineties, the "Jewish vote" invaded the local political arena. In the election campaign of 1892, Russian Jewish politicians involved one of the Orthodox congregations in political unpleasantness. When the Republicans nominated Mayor John C. Koch for re-election in 1894, and the Democrats offered Herman Fehr, a Hebrew Herman Fehr club was supposedly organized. Louis Rindskopf denied its existence, and David Adler investigated and discovered "only three members who are of Hebrew blood." Rindskopf, now a Republican, thereupon claimed that the majority of the city's Jews were supporting Koch![131]

The McKinley-Bryan contest of 1896 revealed Jewish politicians again placing the Jewish label on political merchandise. H. Schlomovitz, president of the Cream City Republican Club, organized the Unity McKinley and Hobart Marching Club, "consisting mostly of Russian Jews" with members from various wards. Its officers were L. Spichenetzky, president; L. Harris, vice-president; H. Leiboen, treasurer; A. Chenes, secretary; H. Caeronsky, captain; U. Nickel, first-lieut.; and Henry Apter, second-lieut. Efforts by rabbis and prominent Jews to avert religio-political organizations were of no avail against politicians desiring "to pose as bosses and acquire a political pull."[132] Rabbi Sigmund Hecht emphasized that "it was as absurd and monstrous as would be a Baptist Marching club, a Presbyterian Bryan club, or Episcopalian McKinley club or a Methodist Bicycle club," and drew sweeping generalizations:

> My dear Russian brethren, who have done much to cast a stigma on the Jewish name, are now adding this new sin to their long list of offenses which we are asked to stand responsible for. What we combat with zeal, they introduce and what we seek to dispel as unworthy they approve and establish. Such clubs I believe to be formed for revenue only. I would enlist the cooperation of all who would not have religion degraded by politics, in an effort to break up these damaging and dangerous growths. Let us emphasize it strongly that as Jews we simply stand for a particular conception of God and our relation to Him, but that in all other concerns of life we are identical with all the rest of the people.[133]

But the votes of Russian Jews were nevertheless solicited by two Jewish Republican clubs in the McKinley-Bryan contest of 1896, as in this specimen:

Dr. Gustav N. Hausman of Chicago, will address a meeting of Hebrew voters to be held at Casino hall, corner of Seventh and State streets, this afternoon at 3 o'clock, in behalf of the sound money cause. Dr. Hausman is known as the "Boy Orator of Jerusalem." He spoke to a large meeting of Hebrews at the temple Beth Hadrosh Hagadol yesterday morning.[134]

Although the Jewish voters were "politically divided," most voted Republican in 1896. In two wards Jewish votes were already so numerous that they held "the balance of power."[135]

Shortly before the election of 1898, Democratic politicians attempted to distribute political literature in the immigrant synagogues. Halted at the doors, they endeavored to "thrust a dodger" into the hands of departing worshippers. Angry members of Beth Hamidrosh Hagodol complained that the "miserable ward workers would not attempt any such thing at any of the Christian churches, and our people are indignant, that they should have less respect for us than they have for other denominations." The offending handbill had been printed in "the Hebrew language," i.e., Yiddish, in Chicago, and was headed: "Forget not the names of candidates, and elect them for your own good." Then followed the Democratic candidates' names, "printed in both English and Hebrew . . . Those are the men whom you ought to elect if you would have honest, experienced and good men to govern you."[136]

Despite repeated expressions of indignation, the immigrant congregations found it difficult to free themselves of these blandishments. Later appeals, however, became more sophisticated, and less was heard of Jewish political clubs. But the votes of Jews were energetically solicited in the language they understood. The crude efforts to win the votes of Russian Jewish immigrants made by the parties during the 1890's were replaced by growing political consciousness on the immigrants' part. Where German Jews before them had stood politically within the well-recognized

German community, East European Jews formed a group of their own in local politics, as did the Poles, Hungarians and others who had recently sailed on the immigrant ships.

The desire to vote for Jews was mixed with the wish to see one party victorious at the polls. Thus Herman Schlomovitz, for many years a Bailiff in the Federal Court and a prominent Republican, said:

> ... The Jews belonged to the Jewish nation before they became affiliates of their political parties. Therefore, it is the duty of every Jew to vote for a Jew when the duties of that position do not conflict with the principles of his party, and if the candidate is so capable and qualified an American citizen that we can be positive that his dealings in political life will not do any injury to Judaism.[137]

It was repeatedly said that Jews should vote for other Jews only when "all Jews who will vote for him will not need to be ashamed of him" in office.[138] Nevertheless, the cruder cry could be heard "that Jews should vote for Jews, whether good or bad. ..."[139] Sol Marshall advertised in his own behalf that "The Jews should have Jewish socialist representatives in the Legislature."[140]

When votes were counted, the ballots cast by Jews were carefully analyzed. Thus, in three wards "where the Jews have a good representation, the Socialist vote was heavy."[141] Peter R. Feldman, running for Alderman in 1914, ran well in the Jewish area, where Jews crossed party lines for his benefit. But he "did not receive the expected help from the non-Jewish precincts, and many Jews voted for other non-partisan candidates."[142] Charles Schiewitz and Bernhard Gettelman, victorious young Republican candidates for the State Legislature in 1916, "were elected thanks to the large Jewish vote that they received, because they are Jews."[143] Jacob H. Rubin, defeated for County Treasurer in the same election, nevertheless felt "proud and honored in that every Jew, rich or poor, Socialist or non-Socialist, wished to see me elected."[144]

Such intense combination of ethnic pride and interest in public issues sent Socialist Joseph J. Hirsch to the State Senate (1921-1923); the Jewish Sixth Ward elected Arthur Shutkin, a pharmacist, as Alderman for the eight years after 1920.

That a candidate was a Jew was only one cause for Jews to vote for him, and Jews did not always vote for Jews in preference to Gentiles. Of the early 20th century, it may be said that Jews voted for Jews in the exuberance at being able to vote or be elected to office, and for the recognition of full citizenship which their first encounters with the ballot box seemed to confer.

V

Immigrant Trades and Streets

BY 1900 Milwaukee had a full-fledged immigrant settlement, with its autonomous life, distinct trades and peculiar street scenes. Still, between 1890 and 1925 the newer Jewish community was probably less noticed than those of the Poles, Italians, Hungarians, Bohemians and Slovaks settling in the city. Like the Germans, the Jews were an old established group, well known and cordially recognized. Many new Milwaukee Jews came after living in the United States for some time, and knew something of the English language and American ways. Thus, Milwaukee Jewry was never embarrassed by being popularly regarded as "foreign." On this sensitive point the Milwaukee Jewish community differed from eastern centers of American Jewry, where third generation Jews felt the onus of "foreignness" thrust upon them. The Milwaukee community's status was hardly disturbed.

CONTINUING IMMIGRATION

The new century brought more European Jews through Eastern ports than ever before. During the 1880's, an average of 19,302 Jews had come yearly to the United States; in the 1890's it was 39,352, but during the first decade of the twentieth century an average of 97,626 Jews came annually.[1] Milwaukee of course felt this impact directly. In 1900, large scale emigration from Roumania also commenced with the dramatic "fusgayer" movement across Europe on foot, and on to America. This small but sensational movement ultimately brought into being the Industrial Removal Office,[2] which greatly influenced migration to Milwaukee.

In 1908, two-thirds of the Russian Jews in town had been in the United States less than ten years. Again, when the Arbeiter Ring polled 373 members in 1916, 270 had been in the United States less than ten years. These were the years of Milwaukee Jewry's numerical growth from about 9,000 in 1905 to an estimated 17,000 in 1917.[3]

Word about Milwaukee was long in reaching the prospective immigrant. Aside from scattered and uninformative letters from the city in the European Hebrew press, the first substantial description reached him in 1910. Among twelve cities desirable for immigrant settlement, Milwaukee stood favorably:

> Milwaukee has a considerable Jewish pupulation, about 10,000 souls. Among them, about 4,000 are of Russian origin, 3,000 from Germany, 2,000 from Roumania, and 1,000 from Galicia. . . . Anti-semitism is very little felt. . . . The Jewish population can still be very easily increased. Skilled workers can get work in Milwaukee, i.e., those who are skilled in any trade.[4]

Since personal associations were so important in selecting a destination within the United States, it is not surprising that many Jewish immigrants in Milwaukee came from the Lithuanian city of Slutsk and as many as 300 from the town of Kapulye. The predominance of Lithuanian Jews is underscored by the relatively few Galician Jews in Milwaukee; Roumanian Jews, however, were numerous. Another element was composed of Hasidic followers of the Lubavicher Rabbi, mainly from White Russia. In rough proportion, about four-sevenths of Milwaukee's East European immigrants were Russian, two-sevenths Austrian (i.e., Galician and a few Hungarians), and one-seventh from Roumania. Roumanian Jews tended strongly towards skilled and manual work, and so may have been numerous among the Jewish wage earners in Milwaukee.[5]

No immigration headquarters was maintained in Milwaukee.

Most immigrants were met on arrival by relatives or friends; otherwise a traditional Jewish method held good—go to the synagogue and await help. The local Hochnosas Orchim hospice did not concentrate on immigrants but rather helped those temporarily "down and out," and the hard core of itinerant beggars.[6]

During the vast immigration after the blood-stained failure of the Russian Revolution of 1905, a Russian Aid Society was organized in Milwaukee with about $1,400 at its disposal. It lent applicants half fare to take members of their family out of Russia. The Russian Aid Society soon succeeded "in rescuing 83 persons, mostly women and children, from the jaws of death. . . ."[6a]

Compared with the New York metropolis in 1908, the Wisconsin arrivals were more recent. Of Milwaukee's Russian Jews, 48.8% had come in the five years preceding the U. S. Immigration Commission's sample in that year, and only 9.3% had been in the United States since the 1880's. Immigrants from other countries had been in the city longer.[7] The years following 1908 kept up the flow to Milwaukee.

Immigration to Wisconsin averaged 715 each year, of whom probably 60% (429) settled in the city; about 145 more came yearly to Milwaukee through the efforts of the Industrial Removal Office. Between 1920 and the close of 1923, perhaps 300 came yearly to Milwaukee, with reduced impact in a community of some 20,000.[8]

THE INDUSTRIAL REMOVAL MOVEMENT

Early efforts to organize Jewish immigration lacked funds and experience, but the Industrial Removal Office, organized in 1900, had both. It was a branch of the Baron de Hirsch Fund, which was endowed in 1891 with the then extraordinary amount of $2,250,000, and was administered by a self-perpetuating Board of Trustees.[9]

The Fund's activities in agricultural colonization and vocational training of immigrants aimed to draw Jews away from tailoring and peddling and into other skilled fields, and to attract them out of the immigrant quarter into the countryside. But to set up one family on a farm cost several thousand dollars, and the risk was great. When the Fund became convinced that the immigrants would remain in cities, they decided on another approach. Let the Jewish immigrant be drawn out of New York, Philadelphia, Boston, and be helped to move to smaller cities where Jews already dwelt and a variety of jobs could be had. Milwaukee qualified for the Industrial Removal Program, and B'nai B'rith, the foremost national Jewish organization, was invited to take over the responsibility.[10]

The name of A. W. Rich, merchant and shoe manufacturer, dominates the Milwaukee Jewish Industrial Aid Society, which he founded and headed as the local branch of the Industrial Removal Office. Beginning by aiding the Roumanian refugees who were I.R.O.'s first clients, Rich's group undertook responsibility for about 340 persons whom it distributed in a variety of jobs.[11] By 1904, Rich had drummed up jobs for not less than "some 600 carpenters, tanners, tinsmiths, machinists, and laborers"[12] in two and a half years, including 193 heads of families who came to Milwaukee from New York in that year.[13] The effort was discontinued after 1905, "to give our community a chance to assimilate those that are already here,"[14] and not resumed until 1912.

The Industrial Removal Office sent 76,000 people throughout the United States between 1901 and 1917, and 3,700 to Wisconsin, of whom approximately 2,300 settled in Milwaukee.[15] They were sent only when there was fair certainty of a job; the settler could send for his family after becoming settled. Here is one "success story":[16]

(no date)

Gentlemen:

I shall never forget the favor you have done me in sending me to Milwaukee. In New York I suffered for fully seven years. I was always worried where to find the next day's job, where to get money to pay my rent and from whom to borrow money.

Regarding Mr. G., to whom you have sent me, I wish to state that he is a very friendly person. You cannot realize how hard he tried for us. He gave us some money and brought our baggage from the depot. The first week I earned $20.12 which actually delighted me. The coming week I shall make $18.00. I hope to be able to earn a livelihood for me and my family.

Skilled workers, however, were angry and dismayed at starting at lower wages than they had earned before: "they say that for the amount they are going to work for, they did not have to leave New York and come to a strange city. . . . Should a new removal be housed in the place where he is boarding, he makes the other man for a kicker. . . ."[17] Trade unionists insisted upon union wages, and would supposedly say: " 'If I wanted to work for that pay I did not have to come to Milwaukee,' but if B. is ready to work at a union or non-union job you can send him."[18]

However, most removal cases "say if the Industrial Removal Office would not have sent them away from New York, they would have starved or would not have been able to support their families or parents in Europe."[19]

The local Jewish immigrants gave high priority to aiding their relatives in Europe. Much of their reputed "low standard of living" originated in the poor workers' stubborn saving of pennies to bring over wives, children, and relatives. There were instances like that of Dr. Goldberg, dentist, who brought his parents to Milwaukee from New York and his brother, with a family, directly to Milwaukee from the boat.[20] Businesses specialized in this trade, for there was more money in America to buy tickets than in Europe, and many European agents earned reputations for dishonesty. The "shifskarten" dealers sent not only tickets but cash remittances, and hence dealt in currency exchange.[21] For some, this was their entry into banking. Besides the millions collected in America for European relief, millions more were sent from person to person. As a result of these efforts, "the majority" of immigrants to Milwaukee after World War I was "the wives and children of the men who had preceded them to this country by several years."[22]

Milwaukee native Jewry's attitude to immigration from Europe resembled that of American Jewry in general. Until the Kishinev pogrom of 1903 and the events afterward, it urged European

Jewish organizations not to send immigrants to America. Yet it also felt honor bound to defend free immigration, and its representative organizations and leaders did so zealously.[23]

MAKING A LIVING

Jews were not workers or entrepreneurs in Milwaukee's principal industries—beer, iron, steel, tanning, and machinery, nor in the port and railway functions of the city. A Jew at work at the vats or in the foundry was a rarity there and among his fellow-Jews, and most Jewish industrial workers sooner or later resorted to the trades usually followed by immigrants.

Early Jewish immigrants from Central Europe and, later, those from Eastern Europe used petty trade as a stepladder to retail and wholesale trade, while artisans or their sons often ended as manufacturers of that article. Yet the low number of the immigrant trades in America is striking.[24] Many trades followed in Russia and Poland could not be transferred to America, and in fact few Jews learned a trade thoroughly enough to be skilled by American standards. Moreover, a printer or clerk would have to undergo payless training, and a skilled tailor or plumber had to accustom himself to different technologies and styles, usually in trades controlled by highly restrictive craft unions. There was considerable anti-Semitism in employment which, at least once, was apprehended and suppressed in the Milwaukee office of the United States Employment Bureau.[25] Without English, the immigrant felt himself among hostile strangers, especially in the factory. An observant Jew could not work on Saturdays and Jewish holidays, as was required practically everywhere. Not only negative considerations kept the immigrant Jew from working for strangers and non-Jews. Just as he sought out relatives and former townsmen, so did he naturally turn to them for a job.

The network of retail trade, which spread over the countryside after 1900, together with mail order merchandising, completed the ruin of rural peddling. Only in obscure corners or as a convenience to customers could a peddler earn a rather scanty living.[26] Moreover, the law often required high license fees. Milwaukee

Jewish peddlers trading within the city among immigrant Germans and Poles on the north and south sides were often subjected to juvenile molestation. On one occasion, two Jewish peddlers told Mayor Rose about being assaulted by gangs and sent to the hospital. To protect their legal interests and physical safety, the peddlers organized and made their needs known in City Hall and even in Madison. When the Common Council passed an ordinance which required scales and receipts by retail traders, the peddlers —who could not carry scales about with them—registered a bitter protest at a mass meeting.[27]

The street trades fought hard to exist. Under municipal socialism, the contest between peddlers' and junk dealers' "free enterprise," versus public noise (and anti-peddling pressure by retail interests) was likelier to be resolved to the peddlers' disadvantage than when old guard Republicans controlled City Hall. There were hard fights against such regulations as those imposing high license fees and prohibiting the "barker" from proclaiming his wares.[28] The 1915 legislative session in Madison had before it a bill to restrict the "privilege" of a peddler's or scavenger's license to American citizens, which was allegedly supported by the Wholesale Junk Dealers' Association, composed of the "bosses" who bought from the street collectors. In any case, the bill was not passed, but a modified licensing bill got through in 1916.[29] These fights strengthened the union of the rag pickers as well as the trade associations of the wholesalers.[30]

Until about 1910, peddling in its varied forms—dry goods and notions, fruit stands, junk collection—prospered. "Milwaukee was a 'golden land' for peddlers, especially for rags and dry goods. . . ."[31] Even the Yiddish-speaking socialists trimmed their views to appeal to this majority of Jewish voters. They pointed out that when workers suffered from

> need and want, the small businessmen and peddlers are also in trouble. . . . You, brethren, make a living from the masses, from the poor; the rich do not buy from you, and have no business dealings with you. Your happiness, life, and contentment depend upon the happiness, life, and contentment of the masses. . . .[32]

However, peddling was sliding downhill:

> But in recent years peddling has completely lost its charm. At
> the best opportunity dozens of peddlers want to find employ-
> ment in the shops, or wish they had some trade or other with
> which to make a living.[33]

Yet during hard times, as in the 1914 recession, many unemployed Jewish metal and leather workmen "bought horse and
wagon and commenced peddling." With a mild winter, they "had
little trouble in making a living for their families."[33A] Again in
1921, "many of our Jewish skilled and unskilled factory-workers
converted themselves into fruit hucksters, practically monopol-
izing that business."[34]

Milwaukee was one of the midwestern cities where many Jews
turned to a special itinerant trade, that of waste materials. They
brought a day's pickings to the dealer who disposed of the material
to a paper mill or an iron foundry. Early in the morning the junkman's sing-song summoned housewives and storekeepers to sell
him their scrap.[35] In earlier days, the latter were supposedly relieved to be rid of old metal and rags, but later they realized that
these had value. The junkman was squeezed between the demands
of his clientele and what his wholesaler would pay. The Progressive Rag Peddlers' Union, which claimed "up to 200 members," not only offered benevolence and mutual aid, but fixed the
price on junk sold to wholesalers.

Above the itinerant traders stood the storekeeper. Ninety or
more retail Jewish grocers and delicatessen proprietors concentrated in the Jewish quarter, besides a variety of Jewish retail
stores. Clothiers, hardware dealers, pharmacists ("free advice
given"), "the only Jewish gas-fixture man in town," jewelers,
roofers, and others, knew the habits and could speak the language
of their customers. Numerous eating places served as local rendezvous: kosher or merely "Jewish" restaurants, soda fountains, drug-
and book-stores, and the like.[36] Alongside the tradesmen, a battery
of professionals resided in the immigrant quarter, to serve Jewish
immigrants. An eye, ear, nose and throat doctor was "giving up
much of his previous work for the International Harvester Com-

pany in order to be able to dedicate more of his time to his patients in the Jewish neighborhood," where he had opened an office.[37] His patients perhaps passed the nearby home of a young Jewish attorney, who informed the Jewish public that he was "at home every evening of the week" for "advice and action."[38] On Walnut Street, persons could consult one of Milwaukee's four Jewish opticians who "tests eyes free and sells eye glasses cheap on payments,"[39] and the young attorney's sister graduated as a dentist.[40] The lawyer was frequently the representative figure of the immigrant community. As a young man, Joseph A. Padway (1890-1947) moved with facility between private practice of law, local politics, real estate interests, and Jewish communal activity: each reinforced the other. Most of these Jewish physicians, lawyers, opticians, dentists, and others were the children of immigrants and sought their clienteles, especially at first, among their fellow Jews.[40A] Well-established attorneys, like the Pereles brothers or C. L. Aarons, made no particular point of serving the immigrant community.

Compared not only with New York and Chicago, and even with smaller immigrant cities like Cincinnati, Rochester, and Cleveland, the relative paucity of Milwaukee Jewish tailors seems remarkable. Moreover, the clothing manufacturers of Milwaukee were mainly Jews who employed several thousand workers.[41] Apparently, the Germans who were for a long time the predominant tailors in the United States continued coming to Milwaukee and, with Bohemians, remained the principal ethnic group among its clothing workers. They satisfied the labor requirements of the industry in Milwaukee, which did not expand greatly after the 1880's.[42]

Alongside the remarkable Jewish trade unions was the Jewish "trade association," a more typical group, uninterested in ideology, and significantly paralleling East European occupational *hebrot*. In Milwaukee the Jewish Grocers' Club, with 70 to 90 members, expanded its simple name to the "Wisconsin [or West Side] Mutual Aid Protective Association."[43] There was an Independent Fruit Dealers Association,[44] a Jewish Milwaukee Shoe Repairers Protective Association,[45] and a Jewish Butchers Association.[46]

Like traditional *hebrot*, they extended benevolent aid, and the Shoe Repairers held their meetings in a synagogue. They attempted to regulate hours: "Since Jewish grocery proprietors are also human, therefore it is no more than right that their places of business should be open less than twenty hours a day."[47] They fought for the right to be open on Sunday and closed on Saturday.[48] Junk dealing had a Wholesale Junk Dealers Association, and Milwaukee Junk Dealers' Association.[49] These groups were not essentially employers' organizations. But when Jewish bakery employees and painters struck (see below), master bakers and painters had to unite in order to bargain with their men.

The United States Industrial Commission's sample, taken in December, 1908, reveals an immigrant quarter composed of peddlers, junk dealers, and a gamut of petty storekeepers: butchers, dry-goods, crockery, grocery, shoe repairers, dairymen, restaurateurs, second-hand stores, and so forth. An appreciable proportion was composed of laborers, tinsmiths and painters working for wages.[50] An estimate of 1910 broadly covers the approximately 7,500 immigrant Jews: 500 households supported by peddling, about 300 by labor ("arbayt"); 60 householders owned work-shops, and 100 were independent businessmen, i.e., storekeepers. Perhaps 5,000 Jews derived support from these fields. About twenty-five clothing manufacturers and fifty cigar and cigarette manufacturers were included—mostly natives of Milwaukee. "In general, one does not yet see any great wealth among the immigrant Jewish population."[51] Men shifted businesses: a peddler abandoned his horse and wagon to purvey horses and hay to other peddlers.[52] A scrap metal collector entered the iron business and then plumbing and heating.[53]

The small businessmen who operated on a "shoestring," augmented by high hopes, were hit hard by any economic downswing. The brief recession in 1914 bankrupted fifteen of them,[54] and many more probably teetered on the brink. Those who survived emerged from the war period in a better position to withstand the shock of 1920-1921. The small Jewish businessman found credit hard to obtain. Besides general economic factors, Jewish credit applicants were in some instances discriminated against, and sought sources of credit within their own circles. The autonomistic tendencies of the immigrant community encouraged the founding of a bank and credit unions. The Union Bank, founded and managed by William B. and Jacob H. Rubin, attorneys, went after business aggressively, employing a man "known in radical circles as solicitor."[55] They soon had "more than 600 Jewish depositors. Many lodges and societies have deposited their money in the Union Bank."[56] Poale Zion's Jewish National Credit Association was one among many which proposed "to lend money on small payments, to deal with all kinds of ship passage, and help various cooperative undertakings."[57]

While the small businessmen were growing in numbers and wealth, the proletarian sector of the immigrant community was also advancing. Industrial work became important for a few years after 1907, when many Jewish workers again left the East to settle in Milwaukee.[58] In 1918, the number of Jews in the tailoring trade was reckoned at four hundred men and women. Their employers were mainly sub-contractors for Chicago manufacturers, besides a few of the old-time factory firms. Another immigrant trade, cap making, was definitely Jewish in Milwaukee; Local 16 of the Cap Maker's Union was reported to have but two non-Jewish members.

Bakers and house painters were indigenous Jewish unions in Milwaukee. The line between worker and employer in these trades was a thin one, and many crossed back and forth several times. The painters banded together in 1914 and struck. The dispute was settled after five days, following much caucusing by each side, by an arbitration committee whose members were J. H. Rubin of the Union Bank, J. L. Bitker, a clothing merchant, and Rabbi Charles S. Levi.[59] The men won another strike against a contractor in 1919.[60]

The Jewish Bakers' Union was founded in 1911, but did not muster a majority of the workers. In their strike of 1919, the men demanded more than $24 weekly for a first hand and $21 for a helper, and more also than the $3 increase offered by the master bakers. They pointed to inflation, and to higher productivity thanks to new machinery. The men also insisted on starting an eight-hour day from 4 a.m., rather than the wartime 1 a.m. start of an eight and a half hour day. They struck four weeks and won, supported by Jewish labor groups which urged the Jewish public to eat no "scab bread."[62]

Industrial workers were particularly vulnerable to economic downturns such as that of 1921. Jewish unemployment was light, "because our men are not all [sic] factory employees. The girls, too, seem to have steady jobs." But with "finances . . . low in all households" many undertook joint housekeeping.[63]

The immigrant Jew prospered when compared to immigrant Jews in other cities, or to non-Jewish immigrants in Milwaukee itself. In 1908, the city's average Russian Jew earned $534 annually, $81 more than the Milwaukee immigrant average, and $25 more than Russian Jews in New York.[64] On the other hand, the average Russian Jewish immigrant family subsisted on $628 a year—less by $22 than immigrants in Wisconsin, and much below the income of Russian Jewish families in other cities.[65] Higher individual income and lower family income suggests children who could not yet augment family earnings; perhaps Jewish children stayed in school longer.

IMMIGRANT HOMES

German Jews had lived among Germans, sharing a language and cultural traits. But Jews from Russia and Poland had little in common with Russian and Polish Christians, and lived separately.

Every large American city sheltered a "ghetto" of Russian and Polish immigrant Jews, situated in decaying residential areas just off the downtown district. From the Haymarket cattle market near the Milwaukee River, the Jewish immigrant quarter drifted westward on a line approximately along Vliet Street, and around 1900 crossed to the West Side. Newly built synagogues, in 1899 and 1905, also attracted settlers to the vicinity. This Jewish district, which ran from Third Street west to Thirteenth Street and from Vliet Street northward to North Avenue,[66] had once been "so predominantly German that many of the shops could be conducted by people speaking only German."[67] These Germans, including some Jews, moved north and west. By about 1905, the immigrant quarter was one of the "problem areas" of the city, and was "continually pushing out its borders."[68] It contained "a number of old and dilapidated buildings, a considerable amount of basement dwelling, insufficient and unsanitary closet provisions, unclean houses and yards due to careless habits of tenants, and the confining of chickens in basements by 'kosher' butchers. A degree of over crowding is also found in this quarter, although the evil of one-room overcrowding is not so serious as in other sections of the city."[69] New arrivals had to inhabit the worst two-story wooden houses: "The exterior is weather stained and decayed. The walls are out of plumb, the roofs are sagged. Inside the plaster is cracked and grimy, the floors are black and worn, the doors hang unevenly. And these houses rarely lack tenants. . . ."[70] Three such houses on Fifth Street sheltered fifty-six persons, including nineteen children under fourteen, in ten flats, with two toilets; three other flats stood vacant.

Jews often did business in or adjacent to their homes. One butcher kept chickens and chicken feathers in his basement, while a cobbler and his family dwelt in a basement whose corner held a smelly pile of discarded shoes.[71] Back yards were often littered: "the premises occupied by peddlars, rag-pickers and junk-dealers are too often an advertisement of the occupation of the inhabitants."[72]

The approximate Jewish area contained 2,068 little dwellings, over three-fourths of which were built in the 1890's or earlier. They were 79% frame, 11% brick veneer, 2% stucco, 8% solid brick. Although the houses were deteriorating, real estate values did not decline—possibly because the Jews paid high rents.[73] The continuing influx of immigrants steadily raised rents, and the poorest Milwaukee Jews paid an average rental of $12 per month in 1913.[74]

By the standards of the inhuman congestion in New York and Chicago, this old, drab neighborhood, among the least desirable sections of the city, was not too bad. "For this one has much to thank the healthy atmosphere and the frame houses with green grass all around, and the spacious rooms." [75] While other immigrants strained to save the money needed to buy a house, the Jews paid higher rent with less thought of becoming homeowners. Jewish families had their own toilet, and nearly all had indoor private water supply; very few lived in basement apartments. In these respects Jewish immigrants lived better than Milwaukee's other immigrant groups.[76] On the other hand, fewer Russian Jews than non-Jews owned homes.[77]

The 1920's witnessed an exodus from the immigrant district, which dropped from 17,650 in 1920 to 14,825 in 1930. The trend ran northward (above Galena Street) and westward; many moved from south to north of this central street, and those previously to its north quit the neighborhood.[78]

Impressions of better housing in Milwaukee's Jewish immigrant quarter, compared with other cities, are borne out by the United States Immigration Commission's studies in 1908.[79] A Russian Jew in Milwaukee lived in a dwelling averaging 4.62 rooms, while other immigrants in town had 4.17;[80] the Jew had 5.41 persons in his abode to 5.20 of the Christian immigrant, and paid rent of $10.98 monthly ($2.37 a room) to the Christian's $8.40 ($2.01 per room).[81] He often kept a lodger during his first years to augment his income or to aid family and friends.[82] Rents were "exorbitant" because "the newly-landed Jewish immigrant wants to live near his own people . . . and the landlord, knowing that he will not be separated from his kinfolk, charged accordingly." Adjacent non-Jewish streets rented for 25% less. The tightly packed Jewish quarter began to disperse as Greeks and Negroes infiltrated the Jewish streets and, above all, because immigrants wanted to live better.[83]

In comparison with the other ethnic immigrant communities in Milwaukee, Jewish living conditions show up quite well. Weighing the amenities and comforts against the price paid for them, the Jews lived better than immigrant Poles and Italians, and as well as the Bohemians and Germans. The Jewish immigrant in Milwaukee was economically of the "upper crust" within the American Jewish immigrant community, but was far beneath the native Jews in his own city.

VI

Naturalized Judaism and Immigrant

Piety, 1870-1900

THE INTELLECTUAL climate of 19th-century Milwaukee Jews was far different from that of their near ancestors. American optimism, humanitarianism and self-reliance pervaded their mental world, and they reshaped their Judaism to agree with this outlook. In coming to America, Milwaukee Jews had not exchanged a bitter for a sweeter exile, where they could await messianic redemption; their entire future lay in America. To them, "Jew" meant only to profess the Jewish religion, which itself required extensive change to suit the new age. All that suggested "ghetto" had to be discarded, now that the physical ghetto was a thing of the past and Jews no longer wished to live in segregation. These Jews' Judaism contained nothing mystical or contemplative; it was formulated as an optimistic, reasonable American religion, with happiness and salvation attainable by human effort. Its ground-work lay in a distinction drawn between Judaism's unchanging spiritual core, and its changeable outward observances. The essence of Judaism was only moral and ethical, while the externals of the traditional way of life were classified among outward observances and consequently abandoned. Milwaukee's approximately 3,000 native Jews in the 1890's did not profess all this explicitly, but their words and lives confirm this picture. This was also the language of their rabbis, to whom they looked as authoritative spokesmen of Judaism.

These Jews were inconsistent. For example, they still regarded as Jews persons who did not believe or practice any Jewish religious principles. They cared for poor Jews, not for fear of non-Jewish disfavor over Jews on public relief, but because these Jews were "their own." Not rejection by non-Jews stimulated the Jews to socialize with each other in Jewish clubs and at home, but a positive desire to do so. The ethnic basis of Judaism remained alive but subdued, until vigorously thrust forward by the East European settlers.

By the turn of the century, Reform had solidified as the Judaism of the "upper crust," and had lost its early enthusiasm. As the most assimilated segment of American Jewry, it was deeply affected by the liberal secular bias of American life, and by the appeal of Ethical Culture and Unitarianism. Reform Judaism weakened at the time when multitudes of East European Jews settling in the United States replenished traditional Judaism. The native Jews did not proselytize these immigrants or invite them into their temples, but endeavored instead to "Americanize" them along quite secular lines. The immigrant synagogue of East European Jews differed completely from the formality of worship in a Jewish Reform Temple. Their religious tradition encouraged small, separate places of worship, and the arrangements were highly informal. Requiring no clergy, it was possible to pray almost anywhere, including, as frequently happened, a private home. In older European communities, however, one synagogue was regarded as "central" (*shtat-shul*), and other places of worship were under its tutelage. At the central synagogue the communal rabbi would worship and might preside over the religious tribunal (Beth Din). This loose structure appeared in America wherever East European Jews settled in numbers, including Milwaukee. There were so many small immigrant synagogues, usually based upon a common town or region or origin, as to be proverbial among East European Jews. But the immigrant's synagogue was not only his place of worship. It was his club, founded and maintained by a "society" which also granted sickness and death benefits.

Reform Jews thought of the immigrants' worship as uncouth

and out of touch with the needs of modern society. To the immigrants, Reform was a caricature of Judaism for those who desired convenience above all, would make no sacrifice for their religion, and hoped to curry Christian favor. Neither harsh view is without truth. Before 1900 native and immigrant Jews felt remote from each other and kept religiously apart.

Outside the Jewish fold, religion in the growing city was developing in a changed pattern. Milwaukee's first "institutional" church, Plymouth Congregational, opened in 1889 with space for meeting rooms and social service. These were the years of the YMCA and YWCA's growth—assisting young people, many of them unattached migrants to the city. Formal religious programs were secondary to recreational and educational activity.[1]

Population change was the major source of religious change. Immigrants after the 1870's were predominantly Roman Catholics, and that Church's number of faithful rose steadily to constitute 52% of local church membership in 1890. The Lutherans, composed mainly of Germans and some Scandinavians, were 28% in the same year. The losers were the Methodists, who declined from 12% in 1870 to 4% in 1890, and other native Protestant groups: Baptists, Presbyterians, Congregationalists, and Episcopalians. With religious denominations closely connected with particular ethnic groups, late 19th century immigration profoundly affected the religious loyalties of Milwaukee. Even within the framework of the Catholic Church there was friction between older German and newer Polish elements; religious strain between the old and new Jewish immigrant groups was by no means unique.[2]

THE SYNAGOGUES: MEMBERS AND BUILDINGS

The year 1870 marks the consolidation of Reform Judaism in Milwaukee. On the West Side, B'ne Jeshurun held sway, while the newer and wealthy East Side was the seat of Temple Emanu-El, organized in the previous year. Both institutions were in the throes of building campaigns, for B'ne Jeshurun's entire building appeared in danger of collapse,[3] while Emanu-El still worshipped in Field's Hall on Wisconsin Street. Emanu-El's synagogue was ceremoniously dedicated on August 30, 1872, while B'ne Jeshurun opened three weeks later, on September 19, 1872.

B'ne Jeshurun's new brick building stood upon the same site as its predecessor, and cost about $20,000:

> A . . . stairway leads into a vestibule over which a tower rises to a height of from thirty to forty feet . . . the visitor passes into the auditorium of the temple, which is large, well-lighted and furnished with ninety-six pews.
>
> In the background in the east end of the edifice, the holy ark has a place upon a dais. On each side of the ark is a black tablet bearing the ten commandments in letters of gold—one in Hebrew and the other German. Before the ark the dais is terraced and enclosed with a neatly constructed railing, at the corners of which four candelabra are raised beside the desk and the pulpit. The latter, as well as the ark, are finished in the best of white and tastily gilded . . .
>
> In front of the ark is the perpetual lamp with a figured globe of red stained glass, and opposite this over the choir loft, a chandelier depends before the organ.[4]

The design was a compromise between a traditional reading platform (*almemar*) and a more stage-like arrangement of worship. Definitely modern was the $1700 organ, and the plans to fresco the synagogue's walls. There were three school rooms below,[5] and an adjacent lot for erecting a "parsonage."[6]

The dedication of the new B'ne Jeshurun was an elaborate affair, with a program in twenty-one sections. Thanks to Senator Alexander Mitchell, the richest man in Milwaukee, who "emptied his hot house," the "desk pulpit and Ark were in truth one flower garden." After a procession with the Torah scrolls, and an address by President L. Rindskopf, Rabbi Eppstein delivered his sermon. As the day faded, the Sabbath was ushered in, and there came a further sermon by Rabbi Eppstein in place of Rabbi Isaac M. Wise, who could not come to this dedication. Next morning ten boys and nine girls were inducted as "responsible members of Judaism." The memorable weekend closed with a banquet on Saturday night: "general glee reigned supreme until the next morning."[7]

Temple Emanu-El was also preparing for its dedication. Two

Settlement House,
Fifth Street
(*Wisconsin Jewish
Chronicle*)

Abraham Lincoln House, Ninth Street (1911) (*Wisconsin Jewish Chronicle*)

ish Community Center on Lake Michigan (1954) (*Jewish Community Center*)

Mrs. Lizzie (Simon) Kander (*Wisconsin Jewish Chronicle*)

The Ninth Edition was published in 1915. The "Liberty Supplement" suggests a special wartime printing of 1917 or 1918 (*Milwaukee Public Library*)

THE "SETTLEMENT" COOK BOOK

COMPILED BY

MRS. SIMON KANDER

ASSISTED BY

MRS. HENRY SCHOENFELD, MRS. ISAAC D. ADLER, MRS. SOL. M. CANTROVITZ

Containing Many Recipes used in The "Settlement" Cooking Classes, the Milwaukee Public School Cooking Centers, and gathered from various other Reliable Sources.

FOR THE BENEFIT OF

THE "SETTLEMENT"

———

NINTH EDITION—WITH LIBERTY SUPPLEMENT

———

PRICE $1.50, POSTPAID

SEND ALL ORDERS TO

The "Settlement" Cook Book Trustees

ABRAHAM LINCOLN HOUSE

601 NINTH STREET   MILWAUKEE, WIS.

years earlier, it had acquired a site on Main Street (now Broadway) and Martin Street for $7,500, and planned to spend up to $20,000 for a building.[8] The new congregation had employed vigorous techniques to raise the money, including a nationwide raffle[9] and a local fair.[10]

On Thursday, June 15, 1871, Milwaukeeans could see "the interesting and imposing ceremonies" of laying the cornerstone. "The crowded walks along Broadway as well as a portion of Wisconsin street gave our business center a holiday appearance, which was greatly heightened by the many fine turn-outs with their richly attired occupants and elegantly caparisoned horses." Both Jewish and non-Jewish lodges, led by Stein's Band blaring martial music, marched in procession to the appointed site, joined by judges, public officials, police, and reporters. Masonic personages, including a "Grand Tyler with Drawn Sword," "Grand Stewards with White Rods," "Principal Architect with Square, Level, Plumb and Gavel," laid the cornerstone itself with a somewhat deistic dialogue to accompany the setting of the stone. The speaker of the day was the distinguished Rabbi Max Lilienthal of Cincinnati:

> Oh, what good and glorious times are here! . . . Jew and Gentile, forgetful of their theological differences, unite as children of the one living God, to sing hymns to the day of sincere reconciliation, and to glorify the day of universal civil and religious liberty! Thanks to you, noble Masons. Thanks to your good and enlightened fraternity, that on the altar of true brotherly love we can join hands as men and brethren, indeed!

Lilienthal summarized in appealing terms the Reform Judaism of the new Temple. It would not be

> an old synagogue, with its obsolete ceremonies and antiquated customs. . . . Judaism has broken the old rusty shackles, it has cheerfully surrendered all antiquated ideas; it considers it to be its supreme duty, to reconcile religion with the progressive ideas of our age, and to bring it in full harmony with the demands made either by science or the modern state.[11]

The building itself was a striking achievement, with seats for 800:[12]

The woodwork is of black walnut and white oak throughout, giving an idea of richness and durability combined. High, narrow windows of stained glass line either side, and these, with the circular windows at each end, light the room to excellent advantage. The walls and ceilings are frescoed . . . all in all making a magnificent interior. . . . An apse to the sanctum, the latter raised and approached by circular steps, forms the east end . . . The "Holy of Holies," paintings of Evangelists and curtains of damask silk, will add much to the already handsome appearance of the edifice.[13]

The new Emanu-El was less bound to traditional synagogue architecture than B'ne Jeshurun had been.

For the dedication on August 30, 1872, Rabbi Max Lilienthal again came to Milwaukee, this time to a far less traditional service than at B'ne Jeshurun:

> Prayer by Rev. M. Spitz, rabbi of the congregation, followed; then from the choir an *Ave Marie*, in which the pure, sweet tones of Mrs. Cross's voice were distinctly heard.
>
> . . . While the holy ark . . . was opened, there was an organ prelude, when followed a quartette from Elijah while the scrolls are carried around the pulpit. "Schema Israel," by Rev. M. Spitz, and a recitative and aria from Elijah by the choir, "Thus said the Lord," in which there was a beautiful tenor solo by Colonel Jacobs, "Shehechgona," with amen by the choir, after which came a three part song, for female voices, from Elijah while the scrolls of the law are deposited in the holy ark. . . .

Lilienthal's sermon was coupled with one by the Rev. J. L. Dudley of the Plymouth Congregational Church.[14]

Jewish businesses were shut that Saturday morning, for services at the elegant new Temple, and some 200 couples attended a dinner and ball that evening.[15] The total cost of the Temple Emanu-El's edifice and land was about $60,000 of which only $14,000 was a mortgage debt payable in five years.[16]

Temple Emanu-El stood at Broadway and Martin for 51 years, adding such improvements as central heating in 1881, electric lighting in 1896,[17] and a full-scale remodeling in 1892.[18] The

Temple collected large sums for these and other needs by holding fairs.[19] But B'ne Jeshurun did not stay long on Fifth Street. In 1883, the Board, recognizing that it now stood in a business district and that its 400 seats were too few, sold the building for $12,000. On a new lot at Tenth and Cedar Streets, where the Milwaukee County Court House now stands,[20] the cornerstone was laid on September 27, 1886,[21] and the edifice was formally dedicated the following January 17.[22] Five months later, on Friday, June 17, 1887, it was consecrated.[23] The $35,000 edifice could seat 750, and its style was Moorish.[24]

During the last thirty years of the 19th century, B'ne Jeshurun was financially comfortable, while Temple Emanu-El was opulent. The elder synagogue claimed more members: it had 72 in 1875, and the number slowly rose to 145 in 1899.[25] The 35 men who formed Emanu-El in 1869 increased to about 75 in 1875, remained in the sixties for the next decade, and in the nineties during the 1890's.[26] Members' dues furnished the Temples their main source of income. They were divided into classes which corresponded to the desirability of their pews. B'ne Jeshurun's three classes paid $40, $30, and $20 yearly in the late 1870's; with the new building, dues reached $57, $42, and $27.[27] Temple Emanu-El's rates were more than twice as high, and permanent pews cost from $250 to $1,000.[28] The Temples' other income came from Sisterhoods and other auxiliaries, bequests, and from renting their facilities to outside groups, Jewish and non-Jewish. There were no offerings during services, nor were personal contributions given to the rabbi or sexton. Both congregations easily maintained themselves in a "satisfactory financial condition," as B'ne Jeshurun's officers regularly expressed themselves.[29]

Only a minority of native Milwaukee Jewry held membership in either of their Temples. Indifferent or rebuffed by high dues, they turned to the synagogue only on the High Holidays, or for weddings and funerals. The congregations reacted by high seat charges for the High Holidays; in 1900 resident non-members had to pay at least $25 for two seats. Married children of members were refused permission to occupy the parental pew.[30] B'ne Jeshurun, however, appears to have been less rigorous.

A radical step was taken by Emanu-El in 1890, followed by B'ne Jeshurun. Local Jews of means "who desire to avail themselves of the services of our minister . . . and who do not now contribute to the cost of maintaining an organization," would be "[denied] the services of our minister . . . for any occasion whatsoever. . . ." This policy was too drastic to endure, and by 1895 the congregation contented itself with a year's membership fee of $40.[31] The action reflects exasperation with the prevalent religious and communal indifference.

Synagogue membership meant not only worship, but a sphere of activity for the families in the congregation and sometimes for outsiders. B'ne Jeshurun, less wealthy than Emanu-El, was more active. Its Ladies' Society, founded in 1883, followed a tradition of synagogal women's auxiliaries by raising $1,000 toward furnishing the new building.[32] They also sponsored Purim balls, theatricals, Hanukkah festivals, Simhat Torah *Kranzchen*, picnics, and literary programs.[33] At the close of our period, it enrolled over 100 women.[34] The ladies' group at Emanu-El, organized in 1871 and reorganized in 1881, was likewise devoted to social pleasure and support of the Temple. "Sacred concerts," school picnics, and children's masquerade parties benefited the Sunday School, while calico sociables, strawberry festivals, New Year's dances, fairs, Purim and Simhat Torah balls enriched the Temple's treasury.[35]

Youth clubs also grew up within the Temples' walls. The Juvenile B'ne Jeshurun of the late 1870's and early 1880's sponsored a library, while a Dramatic and Literary Club was organized in 1887, and another, the Baron de Hirsch Literary Society, appeared in 1893. More ambitious was the organization called Knowledge Seekers, led in Bible study by Rabbi Caro during the early 1890's.[36] Emanu-El's Literary and Social Life Society, organized in 1894, quickly gathered 400 members but soon disappeared.[37]

Lay control of the American synagogue was exemplified in Milwaukee. All Temple affairs lay in the hands of the membership, which had equal electoral rights. There were usually two membership meetings yearly, and the Board of Trustees generally met monthly. Naturally, certain individuals dominated the scene. At

Emanu-El, the forceful and rich David Adler held sway from its foundation until the late 1880's. Max Landauer, dry goods manufacturer, and his brother-in-law Morris Miller, a knit goods maker, were the leaders in the 1890's, with Simon Heller and N. F. Newbouer. At B'ne Jeshurun, the Rindskopf distilling family was prominent until their commercial star declined. Simon Kahn, Edward Mahler, Leo Harris, and Leopold Baer were prominent in the 1880's; from 1882 to 1900 I. M. Hirschberg served as secretary, and Gottlieb Patek enjoyed nearly as long a tenure as Treasurer. In the closing years, Jacob Poss and Solomon Eckstein became B'ne Jeshurun's leading figures.[38] All were men of means, if not extensive wealth; by and large, they were immigrants—it was a long time before the founding generation relinquished control of the Temples which they built.

The Temples' Rabbis

The teacher and symbol of Judaism to the congregations and the general community was the rabbi. His main function was to preach and conduct religious services, and he also supervised the Sunday School, visited the ill, and performed marriages and funeral services. Seven men served the two Temples from 1870 to 1900. All were born and educated abroad, and came to the United States in their 20's. Two—Isaac S. Moses and Victor Caro—were men of distinction.

Rabbi Elias Eppstein (1831-1906) had been at B'ne Jeshurun for one year in 1870. In the fashion of German thought, his sermons on current topics, delivered alternately in German and English, treated contemporary subjects in a philosophical manner.[39] Eppstein was particularly active in non-sectarian secret orders in Milwaukee, believing that their fraternal principles constituted the future universal religion which would redeem mankind because they recognized the one essential idea of the Supreme Being.[40] He once conducted a non-sectarian burial service for a Christian child.[41] Eppstein's rather pallid diary reveals a plodding, dull person whose emotions were more engaged by the societies than by Judaism. He was a more systematic Reformer than his congregation, and chafed at their dissatisfaction over his Sabbath smoking.[42] B'ne Jeshurun cut its rabbi's salary in 1877 from $1800 to $1500 for economic reasons, but did not raise it in better times.[43]

Eppstein left for Kansas City in 1880.[44] During his decade in Milwaukee, Rabbi Eppstein's achievement for posterity was not his lectures and public activity, nor his rationalistic schoolbook of *Biblical History*,[45] but probably the unique head count of Milwaukee Jews which he conducted in 1875.[46]

Eppstein's successor, secured by advertising in the Jewish press, was Emanuel Gerechter (1842-1927), a native of German Poland who had come to the United States in 1866. Besides five years in New York City, Gerechter served in Detroit and Grand Rapids. He stayed at B'ne Jeshurun for twelve years, usually with two year appointments at a salary which rose from $1500 to $1800.[47] One young girl recalled him in Appleton about 1900:

> In stature a miniature. . . . a definitely engaging little man possessing charm and personality. . . . He walked with a slight scholarly stoop. . . , A high-bridged nose, very keen brown eyes between two pairs of glasses, one white, one blue-lensed. . . . His sermons, delivered in English on Friday nights and on Saturdays in German, were exemplars of dullness.[48]

Gerechter was eased out in May, 1892 and his next pulpit was in Appleton, Wisconsin.[49]

Temple Emanu-El's rabbis sometimes had stormier situations than the incumbents at B'ne Jeshurun. The first was Edward Benjamin Morris Browne (1843-post 1913) for whom Milwaukee was the second step in a career which included over half a dozen pulpits, a professorship of "Medical Jurisprudence and Diseases of the Mind" at Evansville Medical College in Indiana (Browne held a law degree), and much itinerant spellbinding. Upon the recommendation of Isaac M. Wise, the new Temple hired Browne unseen for three years at a lavish $2500 and soon rued the day. In August, 1870, the Board deemed the young minister "incapable" of his job "to the satisfaction of any part of said congregation . . . does not possess the necessary qualifications . . . ," and requested him to resign by November 1, 1870 or sooner.[50] He resigned and was paid $700.[51]

The chastened but wiser congregation chose as its next rabbi Moritz Spitz (1848-1920), a native of Hungary who had received rabbinic ordination from Judah Teveles of Prague. In 1870 he held his first pulpit in Chicago, which was followed by six years in Milwaukee.[52] Spitz earned the plaudits of the *Sentinel* for being "not simply a sectarian teacher but a friend of all humanity, a generous and able champion of human rights."[53] Some characteristic sermon topics were "The Monotheistic Teachers," the "Jewish Attitude toward Jesus" (the development of mutual appreciation between Judaism and Christianity was a treasured goal), "Authorship of the Five Books of Moses" (accepting Biblical Higher Criticism, but leaving non-literal reverence for the Bible unimpaired), "Hell Considered from a Jewish Standpoint" (unmentioned in the Bible and therefore un-Jewish).[54]

Rabbi Spitz' last two years were hectic. The Board of Trustees desired him to leave, but the membership wanted him to continue. When the membership again overrode the Board in the Fall of 1878 to vote Spitz a one year term, President David Adler and several prominent Trustees resigned. Rabbi Spitz thereupon resolved the problem by presenting his own resignation, having accepted the rabbinate at B'ne El in St. Louis.[55]

Isaac S. Moses (1847-1926) was Emanu-El's next rabbi for eight years beginning in 1879. Moses, native of the Duchy of Posen who was educated there and at the University and rabbinical school of Breslau, came to Milwaukee after several years in Quincy, Illinois.[56] Moses' reputation as a theological radical was confirmed in a stormy episode one year after he came to Milwaukee. In his own words:

> On the 9th of the month, Mr. Benjamin M. Goldberg was married to Miss Jennie Sibley according to the Jewish rites. The bride has previously agreed to abide by the Jewish faith. Rabbi Moses officiated.[57]

By this act Moses had violated Jewish law, whose authority he repudiated, and a regulation of his congregation which required

his president's permission before performing any marriage ceremony in Milwaukee. He had married the couple in Wauwatosa,
just over the city line, evading Emanu-El's rule—the intent of
which was to make sure that the couple paid the required marriage fee. The Board of Trustees sent a letter of censure to
Moses,[58] while the congregation was reported unhappy that its
rabbi had resorted to the "unusual *procedure*" of going to Wauwatosa, thus causing a "sensation" and "braving the censure of
his contemporaries." Indignation did not center upon the mixed
marriage itself. Moses maintained that he

> belonged to the class of radical reformers who would just as
> well have celebrated this ceremony, even without the verbal
> confession of faith which was given. . . . I do not flinch from
> carrying out what in principle has been recognized as right by
> the state. . . . This question is of great interest, from the fact
> that the reformed Judaism is still fermenting and developing to
> a more free and unprejudiced conception of its mission.[59]

The membership expressed "full confidence" in their rabbi on
May 30, 1880, holding that

> the spiritual leader of a congregation should be sustained in
> carrying out his ideas as to the best promotion of what he con-
> siders his line of duty, without any interference from the in-
> dividual members, and solely and alone under the control of the
> Board of Trustees and the Committee of Ritual, who should
> be his only superior authority to consult as regards minor mat-
> ters of form and ceremony. . . .[60]

While deciding that his actions as a Reform rabbi "have been
from conscientious motives," the members "did not assume [sic]
to approve or to disapprove the question of intermarriage . . ."[61]

Moses thus emerged practically unscathed in his own Temple,
but his act was widely noticed in the national Jewish press. Isaac
M. Wise attacked the "clandestine marriage," insisting that no
minister could

> evade the law of the land and then appeal to its authority, nor
> . . . [marry] Jew and Gentile on the strength of a momentary
> confession, so long as the synagogue has not declared this to be

right. . . . the minister is the teacher, and the congregation is the authority Halacha l'maaseh, the executive power delegated to this or that officer; and the congregation is responsible to God and Israel, while the minister has no right to any religious function interdicted by his congregation.

Wise accepted Moses' approval of the Jewish legality of the marriage because it was recognized by the State, but insisted that not "every Jewish minister claiming to be a radical can do what he pleases and as he pleases."[62] However, even Temple Emanu-El never asserted the authority over its rabbi which the Cincinnati reformer granted it. On the other hand, Wise evaded the issue of intermarriage. Rabbi Moses hotly replied to the "above dogmas . . . unfounded assertions . . . hocus-pocus of absolute dogmatism." If Wise objected to accepting as a Jew a person who made "a momentary confession," what more was required? Did the Reform leader mean to control proselytes by the same Talmud whose authority he repudiated in favor of congregational authority? The latter was also "null and void," and Wise, "one of the pioneers of an enlightened Judaism" surely could not think so.

Dr. Wise says furthermore that he had not known a rabbi who calls himself radical and yet do what he pleases. Pardon me! He can do everything as long as it conforms to his Jewish convictions.[63]

The individual conscience of the "radical reformer" was the final authority, not normative *halakhah* nor Isaac M. Wise's congregational sovereignty. Spokesmen of traditional Judaism attacked both men's consent to intermarriage:

Such procedures shatter the foundation of society and violate the sanctity of domestic life. This man Moses has only one step more to take in radical development, and that is, to approve of unions without even the formality of a [Jewish?] marriage ceremony . . . The people are heartily tired of these extreme radicals who imagine they have a divine right to do just as they choose. . . .[64]

Moses' "radical Reform" sermons were delivered on Friday evening in English and in German the following morning, and were often published in the local press. They included subjects like "Doubt," "The Attitude of Skepticism," "Sincerity, the Basis of Character," and a series on "The Origin of Religion."[65] Active in German literary circles, Moses once held a reception at his home for the visiting German poet Friedrich Bodenstedt. He delivered the main address in German at the Thomas Paine celebration, and lectured at the Germania Society and elsewhere.[66] The energetic rabbi's prayer book, which appeared in 1884, was the first Hebrew publication in Milwaukee.[67] In the fashion of rabbis of the day, Moses boarded boys who attended school and received private tuition from him.[68]

Rabbi Moses' extra-mural activities and his forthrightness so frequently expressed in *Der Zeitgeist* suggest a spirit of independence which offended leaders of his congregation. In May, 1885, when he slapped the impertinent thirteen year old son of a Trustee, every member of the Board signed a letter of rebuke. A committee also told him "that for the best interest of our congregation and himself they would deem his resignation acceptable," but Moses recouped his position by a "conciliatory" address at a membership meeting.[69] However, he was "made the target of all sorts of slurs and abuse," and in September 1887, Moses left for Nashville. Many regretted his departure, and fêted him at Schlitz Park before his farewell sermon. That sermon reportedly drew the largest attendance in the history of the congregation. Moses recalled Jacob's dream:

> When I came here I laid my head down, on a hard stone. In a dream I saw a ladder to heaven, up which I wanted to lead you. I am awake, and the stone is still hard; the circumstances are still the same, my bed has not become soft. It began to be clear, I had hoped too much and endeavored too much.

The Board of Trustees also spread a lavish tribute to its rabbi upon his departure[70] for a notable later career.[71]

Emanu-El next placed in its pulpit Sigmund Hecht (1849-1925), a native of Hungary, educated in Vienna and an immigrant in 1868. After some years in New York City, he occupied his first pulpit in Montgomery, Alabama in 1876, and stayed there until

Emanu-El elected him to a three-year term at $3000 in 1888.
While Hecht's rabbinate in Milwaukee proceeded peacefully until
his voluntary departure after eleven years,[72] Temple Emanu-El
nevertheless heard more plain talk about itself from him than
from any rabbi in its history.

Rabbi Hecht's incumbency broke with German religious influence in Temple Emanu-El; Judaism was no longer formulated
in the language of German philosophy. Hecht did not have his
predecessors' associations with Milwaukee Germandom, nor, on
the other hand, was he personally close to the immigrant community.[73] Civic activity and philanthropic and liberal causes interested him. By his associations with the liberal Protestant churches,[74]
Hecht brought Temple Emanu-El into the religious liberalism of
the times. He and his congregation must have warmly appreciated
the tribute of the *Evening Wisconsin*:

> There are few broader-minded men, few more patriotic,
> liberty-loving men. . . . He has done much to make Christians
> understand people, and to make both sects have more tolera-
> tion for each other. He is deeply interested in charitable work,
> and in many places is found working side by side with Chris-
> tian ministers. . . .[75]

Interest in the Temple surged:

> The Temple is now not only frequented by the young men
> and women, but also by those who have not been in attendance
> for a long time. Many Christians are noticed every Friday
> evening . . . his [Hecht's] sermons are full of meaning and
> common sense. . . .[76]

But matters soon drifted back. Hecht found "no truth, no
kindness, no knowledge of God in the congregation as a congregation . . . more levity, more sacrilege, more blasphemy to
the square inch here" than anywhere in the land.[77] In 1895, he
invited the congregation to choose among three possibilities:
1) If religion were not needed, they should disband; 2) If it were
the rabbi's fault, he should be replaced; 3) If the rabbi were
satisfactory, then the congregation should improve.[78]

From his pulpit, Rabbi Hecht discussed matters of science,

literature, politics, or social problems which related to Judaism. He discussed the Venezuela boundary dispute, relations with Spain, women's suffrage, civil service reform, and reconciliation between labor and capital. Before the State Board of Charity and Reform, he trod a middle way between unrestricted and drastically restricted immigration.[79] These were favorite themes of mild middle-class reform, and Hecht was not daring or original in discussing them. He also spoke before church groups, and once delivered six lectures on the Talmud at the University of Wisconsin.[80]

Hecht drew the line at performing intermarriages, "not because we are narrow-minded, but because they mean gradual and certain weakening and destroying of religion." Therefore:

> Would it not be a farce on religion were I to sanctify such nuptials? . . . There can be no unity, no happiness, and what becomes of the children of such a couple? Don't think me illiberal . . . Let us socially intermingle as friends, but not go any further. . . .[81]

He would perform the marriage where the non-Jew had converted; although "we are not anxious to receive converts, . . . we have no right to refuse them admittance if they knock at our door."[82] Hecht expected that the Jews would ultimately "plunge into the ocean of humanity," although they had not yet been invited to swim in "its invigorating waves."[83] Hecht denounced Jewish ethnic movements, and as early as 1890, considered the

> establishment of a separate and independent Jewish Kingdom [as] an event which the Jews as such neither expect nor desire. . . . The mere suggestion . . . is a reflection upon their well-known, oft tried and as often proven loyalty . . . The very idea of such a thing were little short of treason . . . The land in which we live, in which our children are born, in which our homes are, that is our fatherland, . . . every allusion to the restoration is expunged from the revised prayerbooks . . . We are striving and steering toward the temple of humanity. . . .[84]

Gradually Hecht reached the conclusion that he was having little success as architect of "the temple of humanity" at Temple

Emanu-El. In June, 1899, an invitation came to Hecht from Congregation B'nai B'rith in Los Angeles to become its rabbi, with a generous offer. Hecht hesitated:

> I can say to you that Milwaukee is not the Promised Land for a Jewish minister. . . . Am I justified in remaining, or are you justified in asking me to remain? . . . Tonight I am torn with doubts more than ever before.[85]

He finally decided to leave for Los Angeles, and asked to be released from his contract. The Board complied, realizing that it would be "exacting a great sacrifice on the part of Dr. Hecht in our efforts to retain him. . . ."[86] On Friday night, October 27, 1899, Rabbi Hecht preached for the last time at Temple Emanu-El and minced no words. He could have continued in Milwaukee only if

> I should become indifferent to the conditions existing here, as callous as the community in whose midst I am, or that you as a congregation should rise to the fullness of your power . . . I could not content myself with simply drawing the large salary you have conferred upon me, and live in peace and luxury. I felt and feel that I was not to eat the bitter bread of charity; . . .[87]

President Max Landauer admitted:

> . . . You have much to find fault in us. . . . Against apathy and indifference, you worked on with force of will and graciousness of disposition . . . We must mend our ways, and this parting will be recalled in years to come, if we profit by it and learn to help and strengthen our church affairs. . . .[88]

At the time of Sigmund Hecht's departure for Los Angeles, Victor Caro (1856-1912) had been rabbi of B'ne Jeshurun for seven years. Born in Budapest and educated in a yeshiva in Poland, Caro was ordained at the modern orthodox Rabbinical Seminary in Berlin. He came to the United States in 1881, and served in Quincy, Illinois, and Philadelphia before coming to B'ne Jeshurun in 1892.[89] In a more traditional synagogue than Emanu-El, Caro's religious and social views were about the same as Hecht's. Concerning science and religion, whose relations agitated religious thought in America, Caro held that beyond science

> there is a higher truth that speaketh of the heart, which is the mouthpiece of religion and must be cherished and esteemed to be properly understood, interpreted and obeyed as the supreme will of the all-wise and merciful God.[90]

Yet Caro declared that Spinoza "had nineteenth century ideas in the seventeenth century," to which good Jews of the new age could subscribe. From this vantage point he scornfully attacked Ingersoll's lecture on "The Bible" before 2,000 Milwaukeeans:

> We are pained less at his denials than at his coarse jokes made to win applause of the gallery. In ridiculing a faith sacred to others he robs his hearers of more than their faith—he robs them of their reverence, one of the staunchest bulwarks of character.[91]

Ostentatious living and showy funerals irritated Caro.[92]

No more than Hecht could Caro countenance Jewish separatism. Under his ban fell "separate parochial schools," a "separate Jewish ballot box," and "allegiance to any Hebrew trades union."[93] He resigned from the Hebrew Relief Association in the conviction that during normal times the Jewish poor should be aided by the general community.[94] On the other hand, he only mildly opposed Zionism:

> . . . the desired state would most likely be an unattainable Utopia. And yet, should a great number of Jews . . . [be] for that plan, the best place of establishing such a state would, undoubtedly, be old Palestine, in which those favoring that plan would then turn.[95]

Caro preferred Jewish agricultural colonies in the United States to a Jewish state in Palestine, a form of separation he otherwise opposed.[96] B'ne Jeshurun's rabbi was also dissatisfied with the condition of Judaism in the community, symbolized by "the repugnant sight of empty pews."[97] Five years after he came, Caro emphasized his intention to speak plainly from the pulpit, and not be "a mere luxury [who] should be abolished in the interests of economy":

> I know I have not pleased many of you, because I have spoken often in forcible and bold language. I have done so because I shall be held responsible before the bar of justice.[98]

Yet Caro was a beloved rabbi, a tireless worker for his congregation and in the community until his death in 1912.

WORSHIP IN THE TEMPLES

Worship in the two Temples was quite similar, and centered about the rabbi. In his absence the two weekly services, on Friday evening and Saturday morning, were cancelled. He recited much of the liturgy and led the rest, and his sermon was the main feature of the service. Emanu-El was always a Reform congregation, while its parent B'ne Jeshurun was known for some time as "the Orthodox congregation." At the end of the century its worship was "a moderate or conservative reform."[99] Although its rabbis did not consider Jewish law binding, B'ne Jeshurun changed more slowly than Emanu-El, which freely altered or abandoned traditional forms and usages. Language also divided the Temples, for B'ne Jeshurun was the more Germanic.[100]

B'ne Jeshurun used Isaac M. Wise's *Minhag America* prayer book, composed in 1855, which preserved much of the traditional liturgy but contained theological changes. In the 1880's and 1890's, the traditional prayer book composed by Benjamin Szold and Marcus Jastrow was used. Soon after Caro's arrival, he and the ritual committee eliminated some of its "untimely features" and introduced "new prayers and wordings to elevate and beautify the service."[101] In contrast, Temple Emanu-El early adopted the Reform practice of Temple Emanu-El in New York, and worshipped almost entirely in English. In 1884, it adopted Rabbi Moses' new prayer book, which it kept (with one reversion to the earlier ritual) until it introduced the official Reform Union Prayer Book.[102] The Torah was read in a triennial cycle at B'ne Jeshurun, where Rabbi Caro also read selections on Friday evening "for the benefit of those who can not attend the Saturday services."[103] In Emanu-El, the reading of the prophetic lesson (*haftarah*) was abolished in 1893, and thenceforward the Torah scroll was "taken out and put back by the minister."[104] A familiar tradition, the covered head, was banned by Emanu-El in 1870, while at B'ne Jeshurun it was slowly discarded. By 1893, the rabbi and cantor were granted permission to wear "a small covering over the head during the service."[105] Emanu-El's rabbi had doffed his *tallit* by 1873.[106] At B'ne Jeshurun, a surprised observer saw "the whole of the old [High Holiday] ritual repeated, and on *Simchath Torah* flags, banners, lights and circuits, and especially was he astonished about the huge number of *Mi Sheberach*."[107] On Purim the Scroll of Esther was read "in the traditional manner."[108] Rabbi Gerechter was known for his "wonderful melodies," but later a cantor, choir, organist, and sometimes a string ensemble was used. The congregation kept the holidays for their full length, and the hours of services long remained traditional.[109]

Emanu-El followed the path of consistent Reform Judaism.[110] Music was rendered by a voluntary choir and later a non-Jewish choir and organist. The holidays were observed for one day by abridged services.[111]

In place of the Bar Mitzvah a ceremonious group "Confirmation" on Shavuot was introduced:

> . . . the children proceeded to the platform and repeated the blessing, the boys in Hebrew and the girls in English. An address in German followed, after which the children again advanced and were examined. The Rabbi then gave them instructions for their future guidance through life . . . They were next called to the Holy Ark and confessed their faith to the Jewish religion. The blessing of the parents and its return by the children closed the services, and was so touching that many were affected to tears.[112]

Elements of civic religion were incorporated into the Reform synagogues. Both congregations held regular Thanksgiving Day services, and Washington's Birthday was also a special occasion, with G. A. R. posts often in attendance. Emanu-El's worship included "America" and the "Star Spangled Banner."[113] Special occasions, such as the assassination of President Garfield and the naval victories of the Spanish-American War, also found their way into the worship of the Temples.[114] The Milwaukee civic-religious services demonstrate the sense of full citizenship and uninhibited participation which American Jews felt, or desired to feel.

The native Jews of Milwaukee thus changed their worship within these thirty years from forms resembling immemorial synagogue practice to thoroughgoing Reform having little likeness to the old ways. While early Reform leaned heavily upon German philosophy and Jewish scholarship, by the late 1880's and early 1890's these European influences had faded. The focus on the rabbi and the passivity of the worshippers, pews for a whole family, the near disappearance of Hebrew, the emphasis on messianic deliverance of mankind by right living and good works, the solemnly stylized atmosphere of worship—all suggest a source of religious inspiration not traditionally Jewish. The imitation of Christianity in some practices was partly unconscious, but it probably also attempted to neutralize the powerful attraction of Christianity for the emancipated, assimilated native Jews of Milwaukee.

PERSONAL JUDAISM

Although the synagogues were financially well tended and care was taken with ritual changes, religious life deteriorated between 1870 and 1900. A note of defeatism crept into the preface of Rabbi Moses' *Tefillat Israel* prayer book of 1884: "The majority of those who regularly attend divine service are accustomed to the Hebrew as the language of prayer, while those for whom the English ritual was intended do not take that interest in our public worship as to justify the substitution of the English for the Hebrew." The older generation which had some Hebrew background was not replaced.

In preaching universal religion, the Reform Temples found themselves in rivalry with the fraternal lodges, whose ethical, idealistic substitute for historic religion, and offer of benefits which a temple did not provide, particularly attracted poorer people. Of approximately 500 Milwaukee Jewish families in 1881, only 125 were members of the Temples.[115]

Rabbi Caro was distressed by "the repugnant sight of empty pews" at B'ne Jeshurun.[116] At Emanu-El, Friday evening services in the 1890's "were very well attended, but mostly by Unitarians, very few of our Jews deeming it worth while to be present."[117] As for Saturday morning, it was reckoned "a veritable miracle" when "the temple was well filled, among the attendants being over two dozen men."[118] After Rabbi Hecht stated that congregational indifference impelled him to depart for Los Angeles, the committee seeking his successor castigated the membership for their absence even when candidates for the vacant pulpit were officiating.[119] Only on the High Holidays were there full congregations.

Rabbi Moses attributed the small membership to Milwaukee's "strong progressive Germanism, amongst them many Israelites. . . ." This fact "can only be considered an honor. If so many progressive Jews are unwilling to join a congregation, that is their business . . ."[120] Simon Sekles, a German journalist and the author of *The Poetry of the Talmud* (1880), visited Milwaukee in the summer of 1880 and found fewer philosophic reasons for religious indifference:

> . . . There may exist some sparks of Judaism here, but such have hardly been revealed. The greatest majority of men of Jewish descent in this city are almost unacquainted with the principles which make our religion the light of mankind . . . It is not indifferentism alone or the total absorption in business which produced the neglect of religion . . . I am credibly informed that the study of *sixty* and *sixty-six* [card games] is diligently cultivated. It is the *German spirit* and *German spirits* by which they are surrounded . . . We met in Milwaukee with Jews whose religious education was entirely neglected, and what they know about it they learned from scoffers and atheists . . . They are free-thinkers . . . They may be smart

butchers, successful grocers, but when they commence to speak about religion, they are simply ignorant fools. . . .[121]

The Sabbath, Rabbi Moses declared, was

dead in Milwaukee, and cannot by brought back to life again. Amongst the many Jewish businessmen in Milwaukee—natives of northern Germany, southern Germany, Hungary, Bohemia, Poland, Russia, etc.—there is not even one who has his business closed on the Shabbos. Even the few who attend Shabbos services demand that these services must not last more than one hour, since they cannot stay away from their stores any longer than that . . . Sabbath morning services distinguished themselves by an emptiness which is rather discouraging for both the preacher and a few mourners who desire to say their Kaddish.[122]

Saturday was the premier business day for the Jewish store-keeper, who could ill forego a day's earnings. For the well-established Jewish businessman, apparently the American doctrine of the virtue of diligent work outweighed the Jewish doctrine of Sabbath rest. Jewish working men had little choice; they had to work on Saturday for any employer. While "all Jewish stores" were closed on the Day of Atonement in 1871, by 1887 some Jews attended services but kept their businesses open as well.[123]

Rabbi Moses was also distressed by the weakness of community life:

Our beloved "German Athens" should properly be called Beeropolis, but still better, BIBOLIS, for we indeed have a sort of dual system which can hardly be surpassed. The Milwaukee River divides the city into East Side and West Side, and consequently we have an Eastern congregation and a Western congregation,

and other communal divisions drawn on social and neighborhood lines.[124]

Why was Milwaukee Jewish religious life so weak and complacent? German organizations, lodges, and later Socialism, were powerful rivals, with quasi-religious ideals. The synagogues were clubby and exclusive, and vitality and tension were drained out of Judaism. "Life is so prosaic and personal comfort so important that even the best and noblest finally lose their élan."[125]

AMONG THE IMMIGRANTS

Jewish orthodoxy almost disappeared from Milwaukee between the 1860's and 1880's. Only Anshe Emes, a little group which met in rented rooms from 1871, kept up the forms of orthodoxy. Its few members were probably orthodox "leftovers" who added some early East European immigrants; thirteen of them incorporated on May 13, 1872.[126] They were ridiculed as

> nothing more than a mere Winkelschule, wherein the attendants find divine service conducted in the old order, or rather disorder . . . . . . in practical life, even the good people who congregate there every Sabbath, disregard flagrantly the clearest laws of the Torah.[127]

By 1883, the group had 43 members and dedicated a Torah scroll, with Rabbi Gerechter as guest speaker.[128] Shortly after 1894, the congregation, which never secured a building of its own, disappeared, perhaps by joining Beth Hamidrosh Hagodol.[129] Sporadic congregations arose, mainly to observe High Holidays. In 1877, the *Sentinel* noted "two places of worship in the city supported by the Polish Israelites. . . ."[130] The sharp-tongued Rabbi Moses noted their upsurge shortly before Rosh Hashanah,

> . . . to satisfy the religious needs of everyone and anyone. For instance, a new congregation is in the making which will carry the dignified name of "Shaarey Harevach" [Gates of Profit] to whose establishment the smartest preparations are being made. The salary of the preacher is said to consist of the incoming voluntary contributions of prospective attendants, after the salary of the Shamas has been deducted. Should the contributions be in excess of a certain amount, this sum will be distributed among the members.[131]

Rootless religious figures appeared to serve some immigrants; again in Moses' words:

In the last few months, no less than five castaway (*ausrangierte*) men of God have moved to our city . . . One of these so-called reverends has distributed handbills on which he offers himself for any kind of "rabbinical" functions ever performed by a rabbi. Many may not know that any wedding certificate signed by a person not employed by an incorporated body or not authorized by a county clerk has no value whatsoever.[132]

These men probably served the growing immigrant community, which took its first steps toward congregational existence in October, 1884, when B'ne Jacob briefly appeared on the scene.[133] A firm beginning was made early in 1886, when the Moses Montefiore Gemeinde was formally incorporated, worshipping at 434 Fourth Street from 1887 until 1892. In 1890 it numbered about 60 families. Among its officers were A. Grobanski, Herman Schlomovitz, and Solomon Fein,[134] the domineering and controversial figure of the 1890's.

Soon after the Moses Montefiore Gemeinde was founded, a violent quarrel resulted in a new congregation, Anshe Jacob, which incorporated in June, 1886 and held High Holiday services in Liederkranz Hall. Jacob Glick, a butcher, served as rabbi, and Levi Cohen was teacher.[135] The ladies saw no reason to split their society, the Daughters of Eva.[136]

By 1888, the two congregations were talking of reunion, in order to build a synagogue. As contributions were scarce indeed, the financial means chosen was a tax on kosher meat, an expedient with a long and contentious history in Jewish communities. Glick and Israel Weisfeld, who objected to paying ½¢ to 2¢ a pound on their trade or, presumably, passing it on to their customers, were placed under *herem* (ban) and observant Jews were enjoined not to buy from them. Suffering severely from the boycott, the two butchers sued the trustees of the congregations. Whatever the outcome, the congregations did not build their synagogue by this means.[137]

Another immigrant congregation, the Hebrah Ohabai Sholem (Society of Lovers of Peace) incorporated in October, 1887 with about twenty members, and held High Holiday services at a hall on Third and Prairie Streets. A *Sentinel* reporter happened by its Simhat Torah celebration soon after:

> A table which was covered with a white cloth worked in silver thread—the symbol of purity—answered the purpose of what in Christian churches is called the pulpit. Around this, headed by the rabbi [sic—Abraham Cook, the volunteer cantor] walked two men bearing the sacred scrolls, followed by about forty little boys and girls, dressed in variegated clothing and bearing banners, . . . chanted the responses to the chant of the minister . . . the ladies of the congregation served refreshments consisting of cakes and wine or liquors to the half-hundred or more assembled in the hall. . . .[138]

These ladies had been organized into the Hebrah Sholem (Ladies' Society of Peace), "to practice benevolence among its members in case of sickness, misfortune, poverty, death. . . ."[139] In 1889, Ohabai Sholem changed its name to Hebrah B'ne Israel, and for almost ten years thereafter held its services in rented halls.[140]

As immigrant congregational life became more firmly founded, the 1890's closed with three congregations housed in synagogues. Moses Montefiore Gemeinde and Anshe Jacob at last reunited in January, 1892, and in June of that year had $6,000 to build their 500-seat synagogue on Fifth Street, between Cherry and Vliet.[141] The cornerstone was laid in June, 1893. A local brass band and a synagogue choir from Chicago provided music, and President Solomon Fein, Rabbis Hecht and Caro, and the Rev. Frederick Evans of First Baptist Church spoke. Max Landauer, Vice President of Emanu-El, laid the cornerstone.[142] The Beth Hamidrosh Hagodol opened its doors on September 2, 1893. It was the first building erected by the immigrant community. Members, their children, and others, moved in procession from the old synagogue to the new, bearing the Torah scrolls. The privilege of placing them in the new Ark, and of lighting the Ner Tamid, was granted "at auction."[143]

A mortgage debt of $14,000 dogged Beth Hamidrosh Hagodol for years, since the synagogue had cost not $12,500 as planned, but $20,000. Only Fein's efforts kept the mortgage from foreclosure during the depression of 1894, and again in 1900.[144]

Meanwhile, membership slowly climbed to about 100 in 1900, with 400 seats rented during the High Holidays. Income was between $2,500 and $3,000 yearly.[145]

Other immigrant congregations also aspired to leave their rented halls and attain the dignity of a synagogue building. The second congregation, Ohabai Sholem which became B'ne Israel, amplified its name to B'ne Israel Anshe Hungari ("Sons of Israel, Men of Hungary"), and reorganized itself in 1899.[146] It planned a modest home on Fourth Street, but the building itself was several years in the future.[147]

A third congregation, Anshe Sfard (Men of "Spanish" liturgy) was incorporated in October, 1889,[148] and also worshipped in rented halls for several years. Its obscure annals are illuminated by the glare of two quarrels, the first arising when Congressman Alexander Mitchell's gift of $25 in 1892 was taken by Abraham Feldman, then the rabbi. Again, two worshippers who caused a disturbance were hauled into court, but the case was settled amicably.[149] In May, 1897, a Burial Society dispute reached the courts, upon a complaint by thirty members that the President had retained funds. Other members retorted that these were disgruntled members who had been expelled, and that the *Hebra Kadisha* actually stood in debt to its President.[150] How the question was resolved remains unclear.

Despite internal conflicts, Anshe Sfard closed ranks to build its $7,000 synagogue, on Sixth Street between Vliet and Cherry, aided by some donations from native Jews. At cornerstone ceremonies on March 6, 1898, its own Rabbi Solomon Israelson, Rabbi Victor Caro, and two leading figures, Rosenberg and Schlomovitz, all spoke, the latter two "in the jargon of the people of the neighborhood, a mixture of German, English, and Hebrew words."[151] By 1900, there were 90 members and "seatholders" in the completed Anshe Sfard, and an income of approximately $2,500.[152]

The first East European rabbis were brought by Beth Hamidrosh Hagodol. In 1892 Solomon Isaac Scheinfeld (1860-1943) came, stayed one year and then lived in Louisville until 1902. The Lithuanian Rabbi Solomon Israelson (1861-1926) arrived in 1895 for an honorarium of $50 per annum plus fees and income from other sources.[153] Israelson's tenure was hectic, for he had to contend with President Solomon Fein's determination to draw the synagogue closer to the worship of the native Jews. On the last day of Passover, 1896, Rabbi Hecht occupied the pulpit. Addressing 500 immigrant Jews in German, he urged them to learn English and accept American ways, and to be more "cleanly and orderly." The pure heart and good deeds are the sources of righteousness, he explained, not merely strict and literal observance. *The American Israelite* lauded these efforts

> to inculcate American ideas into the minds of these people, though they have no desire to disturb them in their religious beliefs. He [Fein] has gradually introduced reform after reform, or rather improvement to distinguish from religious reform . . . the present condition is encouragingly superior to that existing several years ago. Naturally there has been great opposition to this work for reform. Some of the people retain their old ideas and oppose all efforts to eradicate them. They are encouraged in this by a number of so-called rabbis who have been going among them preaching and arousing them, . . . This agitation has some influence which greatly hinders the growth of the improvement, and obliges cautious and slow work. . . .[154]

Beth Hamidrosh Hagodol of 1893, where there was "no idea of order or decorum, no respect for the speakers, but continual jabber and jostle," was contrasted with its improved "order and decorum, fervency and devotion, beauty of service. . . ." But the congregants and Rabbi Israelson were more concerned with conserving their Judaism than changing it. Charges were levelled at Israelson that he "violently opposed all efforts" for "reforms, not religious, for the enlightenment of their countrymen and co-religionists."[155] It is not surprising that matters came to a climax in August, 1897 with a bitter public row between the rabbi and the president. Israelson finally stood up, resigned, and walked out.

He did not stand alone. A few days later, while members and seat-holders deliberated what to do, the 150 peddlers of the Hebrew Protective Association considered constituting themselves a congregation with Israelson as their rabbi. With so large a secession, Beth Hamidrosh Hagodol had serious qualms about meeting mortgage payments.

But matters were resolved rather quickly. Israelson, who must have been warmed by the concern for his plight, became rabbi of the newly organized Anshe Sfard until he left for Chicago in 1901. The dissident members returned to Beth Hamidrosh Hagodol, and Solomon Fein left the scene. He later joined Temple Emanu-El.[156] Rabbi Cantor came from Kansas City to Beth Hamidrosh Hagodol until 1902, when Rabbi Scheinfeld returned.[157] In addition, a cantor with a choir was considered essential for holiday services, and so a different officiant came yearly.[158]

Immigrant religion was easily seen at home or in the streets of the Jewish neighborhood. By 1900, the three synagogues—one a rented hall—stood on Fourth, Fifth, and Sixth Streets, in a line from East to West. Around them clustered kosher meat markets and milk stands, where Yiddish signs were as frequent as English. Children swarmed in the streets, playing on the synagogue steps, and women in shawls hurried back and forth.

Appearances changed on the Jewish Sabbath. Shawls were replaced by "gay headgear," and those in better circumstances wore "black satin gowns." Young men "with budding black mustaches walked in their best clothes beside their gray-bearded elders," and children also dressed in their best. Not only the kosher shops closed, for the Sabbath was fervently observed in the Haymarket district.

On the Festivals and High Holidays, deep solemnity marked the atmosphere at the three synagogues. Everyone was attired in holiday dress—men in their "blacks," relieved "by the most astonishing neckties," and women in their heavy black satins. "Every man was wrapped in his 'talith' . . . and his head was covered with a black velvet skull cap or a high silk hat."[159]

The Sukkot festival added a picturesque feature to the neighborhood:

> In many of the forlorn yards, opening on to the squalid and bad-smelling alleys, real tabernacles had been built . . . As a rule they were built box-shape of rough boards, against the wall of

the house or perhaps under or adjoining an outside staircase. The boards were uneven in length and varied in hue . . . Sheets or blankets hung at the doorway and the roofs . . . were loosely covered with . . . the green branches of trees. Within, the rough walls were decorated with fresh fruits and flowers, arranged often with much artistic effect. . . .[160]

Weddings were conducted in the spirit of Eastern Europe. "Sometimes the bride, attended by her maids, walked to the synagogue over a carpet laid . . . along the streets and under a canopy upheld by her attendants."[161] Occasionally a Jewish divorce was issued by a local or a Chicago rabbi, even at the county jail.[162] When parties in court refused to be sworn in non-Jewish form, a rabbi was summoned to administer a "Hebrew Oath."[163]

The event of death was met with utmost simplicity. Men or women

> . . . come in to make the corpse ready for the grave. The body is washed and then robed in a long white shroud of linen . . .
>
> So clothed, the body is placed in a plain, unpainted pine coffin, made when possible, by the brethren of the congregation, though the old law in this respect is usually relaxed enough to permit the coffin being purchased from the undertaker's . . . The funeral takes place from the house, unless the deceased has been a prominent member of the synagogue when it is carried thither and the services are conducted by the rabbi or cantor. But usually there are no sermons. . . .[164]

By 1890 the immigrants had a six-acre burial ground in the town of Greenfield named Second Home Cemetery, and an immigrant burial society, the *Gemilath Hesed Shel Emeth* or *Hebra Kadisha*, was founded in 1892. To be one of its approximately 100 members was regarded as a great act of piety, for the society buried without charge those who could not pay, and also cared for destitute bereaved families. The first undertaking business conducted according to "strict Orthodox rites and customs" was opened by Louis Siegel (1888-1925) in 1919. He announced that his were the "only exclusively Jewish undertaking parlors in Milwaukee."[165]

The native Jews arranged their funerals through one of several traditional burial societies, or by D. L. Schram & Co., a Jewish undertaker with a general trade. Funeral services were conducted from the house of the deceased, and burials were in Greenwood or Spring Hill Cemeteries. The Temples set aside one acre for persons unable to purchase a lot.[166]

The new century was to show how two religious wings, far distant from each other, almost imperceptibly drew closer and were transformed.

VII

Religious Tradition and Communal

Purpose, 1900-1925

TWENTIETH CENTURY Judaism in Milwaukee began to reconcile the two earlier opposites of immigrant orthodoxy and native Reform. The former adopted forms of American life and organization, while the latter slowly renewed traditionalism. Finally, the "center" Conservative movement made its appearance in the city.

REFORM CONSOLIDATION

The new century began with two Reform Temples. A third, Temple Sinai, was founded in 1900 for the small Jewish enclave on the South Side. It never rose to importance and left the scene in 1915 when its constituents rejoined the main residential areas. The generation closed with the merger of the two old Temples in 1927.

The first twenty years of the new century continued developments which had been adumbrated long before. Only in 1905 did English become the language of record at B'ne Jeshurun, and in 1909 the amended by-laws were first read in English.[1] In personal terms, the German era ended with Rabbi Caro, although Rabbi Levi agreed "to deliver a short address on Saturday morning when the services are conducted in German."[2]

Wealthy Temple Emanu-El was spiritually dormant. When Rabbi Hirshberg arrived at Emanu-El in 1904, his inaugural sermon contained sharp words. Recalling that in 1899 "the religious life here was represented as at a deplorably and desperately low ebb," he had been warned "how difficult a minister's task here must be. . . ." He learned

> that this Temple possesses within its membership a great many people who are unbelievers, skeptics and doubters, people who rejoice in and pride themselves upon their skepticism and unbelief, and take delight in boasting that they are as little Jew as it is possible to be, and that they see the interior of a Temple with such infrequency, that it is not within their power of recalling when they last were within the walls of one. . . .[3]

B'ne Jeshurun was religiously more thriving. In controverting an attack on Milwaukee's Jewish "indifference" and "Rip van Winkle slumber" by the departing Rabbi Lipkind of Congregation Sinai, Rabbi Caro admitted "some pith of truth," but insisted that there was "equally as much of indifference" elsewhere. He claimed never to have preached to less than 150 persons, and to an average of between 400 and 500 in the winter, and stated that "the Sabbath morning services are well attended."[4]

Rabbi Caro's stature increased with the years. He secured $50,000 from Abraham Slimmer, the Jewish recluse millionaire of Iowa, for Mount Sinai Hospital, and the Social Workers Tuberculosis Sanitarium owed much to his labors. In civic life, he was an active member of Milwaukee's noted Board of Park Commissioners. However, in 1909 he began to suffer from a heart ailment. In the spring of 1912, Caro left for Germany to take the baths, and unexpectedly died there in June, 1912. His body was returned home for burial amid deep sorrow in his congregation and the city. Caro's Judaism "recognized the necessity of being in harmony with the prevailing sentiment of the time and yet held fast to the traditions of the fathers."[5]

The two rabbis of Temple Emanu-El vainly combatted indifference. Young Rabbi Julius H. Meyer (1874-1944) left in 1904, after four years, to enter business. A native of the South, he had come to Milwaukee from Hebrew Union College and a pulpit in Toledo. His successor, Samuel Hirshberg (1869-1954) born in Cincinnati of old English-Jewish stock, was likewise an alumnus of Hebrew Union College. He had been educated at Harvard and served in Boston before coming to Milwaukee in 1904. Here he remained for the rest of his life, retiring in 1947. Rabbi Hirshberg was a quiet and courteous man, whose religious outlook was "classical" Reform, mixed with liberalism of a this-worldly religious rationalist. Judaism gave moral and ethical guidance to Jews in particular and the world in general, and required Jews to aid in the social and economic problems of the day. About the same outlook characterized Rabbi Charles S. Levi, Victor Caro's successor. Levi, a native of England who came to America as a child, also studied at Hebrew Union College, and as assistant in the 1890's at Cincinnati's Bene Jeshurun Temple and as a teacher at Hebrew Union College, he saw much of Isaac M. Wise. In 1898 he accepted a pulpit in Peoria, Illinois, where he remained before he moved to Milwaukee. Levi and Hirshberg were frequent speakers before Jewish and non-Jewish groups, and were directors of numerous Jewish and general organizations. In the long conflict between Zionism and its opponents, both Reform rabbis at first sided with the opposition. Like most of their colleagues in Reform Judaism, they later adopted a more favorable position, although neither became a Zionist.

The Temples' rabbis continued firmly under lay control, with the congregations possessing unobstructed right to employ as rabbi whom they pleased. Rabbinical salaries were quite good, higher than most Protestant denominations. Rabbi Caro was paid $3,600 at his death in 1912, besides a house.[6] Rabbi Julius Meyer was employed, as a man of 25, at $2,500 a year,[7] and the salary was soon raised to $3,000,[8] which his predecessor Rabbi Hecht had received after ten years' service.[9] Soon after his arrival, Rabbi Samuel Hirshberg was paid $3,500,[10] a sum which rose slowly[11] to $9,000 in 1926,[12] the year of Rabbi Joseph L. Baron's arrival at a salary of $5,500.[13] Rabbi Charles Levi started at $3,600 in 1913, and by 1922 the bachelor rabbi was paid his maximum of $7,800.[14] Rabbis were presented with purses upon anniversaries or other special occasions.[15] Their term was generally three or five years.

With this financial open-handedness went Trustees' control, not only of property but of the schedule of services and the outlines of the ritual.[16] Even the observance of Rosh Hashanah for two days was decided by their *ad hoc* vote.[17] Sermons were not passed in review, but this shows less the freedom of the pulpit than that they were inoffensive.

Reform services generally were held on Friday evening and Saturday morning, in September through June.[18] The main service was held at the former time. On the morning of the Sabbath relatively few attended, mostly children from the Sabbath school and older folk. Although the historic Sabbath was abandoned by Reform Jewry in Milwaukee, and the day was one of business, powerful sentiment opposed frequent proposals to hold the main service on Sunday instead of Friday evening. The first Sunday services were finally held in the fall of 1926.[19] Earlier that year, a series of Sunday afternoon organ recitals attracted large attendance.[20]

The Temples' scales of dues were not for poor men. In 1905, a year's pews at Emanu-El cost as follows for the several classes: $140, $95, $67.50, $45, or $30 for two seats only.[21] In 1903, Temple Emanu-El enrolled 123 members, besides seatholders,[22] while B'ne Jeshurun claimed 177 members in 1905 at lower rates.[23] Moreover, Emanu-El's rates greatly advanced by 1920.[24] The Reform Temples did not admit the unaffiliated worshippers who filled many orthodox congregations, except on the Day of Atonement, when they could be seated for $10.[25] In Caro's day, B'ne Jeshurun reached 257 members,[26] and rose further to 285 in 1914.[27] Emanu-El's membership greatly increased after the War to 257 in 1920[28] and, after the opening of the new edifice in 1923, 1048 seats were occupied in 1927[29] by members paying average dues of $110.85.[30] Outside critics could be, and were, caustic over the "rich man's club." However, the Temples had their grievances against those who desired the rabbi or the Temple for occasions: weddings, funerals, and so forth, and required them to pay one year's dues.[31]

Very gradually the influence of Zionism, Hebraism, traditionalism, the centralizing of American Jewry, international philanthropic needs, stirred Reform Judaism. Above all, the immigrant masses who poured into America between the 1880's and the 1920's replenished the movement. While these trends came to full fruition in the 1930's and 1940's, signs could be seen earlier. While the Temples opposed the American Jewish Congress of 1917, they had to participate in the elections or default their communal leadership.[32] They willingly responded to appeals from war sufferers and from the new Palestine. Within the Temple, a move was taken in 1925 towards reviving tradition by employing a *hazzan* "to revive the interests [*sic*] in Temple service, to bring back our youth into the fold."[33] Youth was believed to desire closer adherence to tradition and increased ceremony, not less. Emanu-El erected a community house alongside its new temple so that the congregation should mingle for social and cultural, as well as religious purposes. These changes of attitude are the more notable for being practically unconscious.

B'ne Jeshurun's amalgamation with Emanu-El became inevitable when the older congregation realized that

> . . . we could not build what we all wanted to have and what everybody agrees a modern temple must have, namely . . . a house of worship, and a community center.[34]

With its community house, the Temple could house a wide range of activity,[35] and outside groups could also rent the facilities.[36]

Rabbi Hirshberg alone could no longer do all that was required, and the Board engaged as Associate Rabbi Joseph L. Baron of Davenport, Iowa. Rabbi Hirshberg's uneasiness at the prospect of a young associate is understandable in a man of fifty-seven who had experienced uncertainty in his position as late as 1920, but he was set at ease with an implicit undertaking to retain him "for many years to come."[37] Rabbi Baron went to work energetically in 1926, and advanced various proposals in keeping with the trend to a broader communal, rather than congregational, outlook.[38]

Temple Emanu-El's new building in the well-to-do Jewish residential neighborhood precipitated radical congregational de-

Old Mount Sinai, 1904
(*Wisconsin Jewish
Chronicle*)

Enlarged Mount Sinai,
1922 (*Wisconsin Jew-
ish Chronicle*)

New Wing of Mount
Sinai, 1956 (*Genack
Studio*)

Charles L. Aarons
(*Wisconsin Jewish Chronicle*)

Joseph A. Padway
(*Mrs. Leo R. Weinshel*)

NOTABLES OF THE 20TH CENTURY

A. L. Saltzstein
(*Mr. Irving Saltzstein*)

Charles Friend
(*Mrs. Charles Friend*)

velopments. B'ne Jeshurun was weakening, and Rabbi Charles Levi's efforts could not overcome its unfavorable location; his complete Reform made B'ne Jeshurun appear identical with Emanu-El.[39] Its backbone of prosperous members was leaving the West Side for Emanuel-El's East Side and presently B'ne Jeshurun, which was built in 1886, found its land earmarked for the Milwaukee County Courthouse.[40]

One obstacle to amalgamation was the bitter opposition of Rabbi Levi.[41] At 58 years of age, he could expect little if the congregations should merge. On November 10, 1926, he wrote to B'ne Jeshurun's Trustees that he planned to retire after 37 years as a rabbi, "to devote myself to the general interests of American Judaism at large. . . ." Rabbi Levi continued:

> I feel that I have reached the limit of my usefulness to B'ne Jeshurun, and that at this transitional period you require the full flowering vigor of leadership which unhappily I now can no longer render to the satisfaction of our membership.

The Trustees accepted his resignation. A congregational storm arose, but since their choice was between the rabbi and amalgamation, Rabbi Levi retired as planned.[42]

The official initiative to merge came from Emanu-El in a letter to B'ne Jeshurun's annual meeting. It cited as major points Emanu-El's favorable location on the East Side, the younger Temple's space for 1,000 or more additional members, and its religious school's desire for many more children; membership rates might be reduced as more members joined; a second East Side Temple would be less desirable than one united, powerful Reform congregation in Milwaukee.[43] When amalgamation was seriously taken up early in 1927, the obstacles were overcome quickly.[44] The new institution was named simply Temple Emanu-El B'ne Jeshurun. The new partners insisted that their name appear on the Temple's cornerstone, and the old inscription was blasted away to make room for the new version.[45] Legal matters at Madison went smoothly,[46] and on August 15, 1927, the Trustees of the congregations learned that neither existed as such any more; they were now one corporate body.[47]

IMMIGRANT JUDAISM: DECLINE AND CHANGE

Around the turn of the century, immigrant religion took its first strides towards becoming American Jewish Orthodoxy. The congregations began to acquire buildings, either by construction or by purchasing and adapting Christian churches. They tried to slough off some free and easy *hebra* habits and present a more formal appearance. Outward appearances long displayed a lively traditional Jewish atmosphere. In the Jewish quarter the Sabbath was a day apart, even among those who disregarded its stricter requirements. Adults and youth dressed up, promenaded, and visited. Secular Jewish groups held their public meetings; Vizay's Hall and the North Side Auditorium could depend upon the Workmen's Circle or Poale Zion for Friday evening and Saturday. Traditional Judaism endured, even among the careless or indifferent. Long after most Jews had cast off the demanding *halakhic* discipline of Jewish life, they continued to retain Jewish habits and flavor, and their life continued to revolve about the Jewish calendar.

At the opening of the century, three congregations were established in the immigrant neighborhood. Foremost was the renamed Beth Israel, which long continued to be called Beth Hamidrosh Hagodol. Anshe Sfard had its synagogue on 6th Street with seats for 741 people. Struggling to build was the third congregation, B'nai Israel Anshe Hungari, which established its own home on Tenth Street in 1905.

The heavy immigration of 1904, 1905 and 1906 resulted in the foundation of new congregations. Thus, on November 24, 1905, eleven Jews incorporated themselves as Congregation Beth Hatfiloh (House of Prayer),[48] but left no further record. Not long after, on August 24, 1906, five men organized a synagogue "of the form of worship known as Nusach Arie . . . by the name of Congregation Anshe Leibovitz."[49] They "were originally devotees of the famous Chasidic rabbi of the city of Lubowich, Russia," but the congregation was not strongly Hasidic.[50] Agudas Achim Anshe Polen (Brotherly Association of Men of Poland) was organized in 1904, and occupied a small house on 6th and Cherry

Streets.[51] Another, Agudas Achim, of shadowy antecedents, which dissolved in 1916 and distributed its assets among charities, reappeared as Agudas Achim Anshe Polen; probably there was some fusion.[52] One other synagogue arose before World War I: Anshe Roumania, which later added "Degel Israel" (Banner of Israel) to its name, appeared on the Milwaukee scene in 1904.[53] In time the regional origin of the congregations became diluted: "Congregation B'ne Israel Anshe Ungarn is Hungarian only in name . . . there you find Jews from Russia, Poland, Lithuania, Germany, and some also who were once in Hungary."[54] As noted, Anshe Lubavich contained many who were not followers of the Hasidic Rabbi of Lubavich.

The post-1918 period saw further foundations of congregations. When Beth Israel decided not to finish its building on 11th and Lloyd streets, a Beth Medrash Hagodol Anshe Sfard, organized in 1920, took over and completed the structure.[55] A B'ne Jacob appeared on the scene in 1924,[56] and Anshe Brith Sholem incorporated on May 23, 1925.[57]

By the standards of wealth, building, learning or communal prominence, the oldest synagogue, Beth Israel, still ranked first. In 1924 it had 315 members, and such auxiliaries as a Mishnah Study Society, a Psalms Study Society, a ladies' auxiliary and the burial society. It was preparing to erect an ornate, majestic synagogue on Teutonia Avenue to seat 1,400 persons. Beth Israel was the seat of Rabbi Scheinfeld, the foremost rabbinic figure.[58] The other immigrant congregations of 1924 were:[59]

B'nai Israel Anshe Hungari, 541 10th Street.

Anshe Lubavich, 8th and Walnut Streets, planning to build at 11th and Vine Streets.

Anshe Sfard, 452 6th Street, 152 members, 741 seats.

Agudas Achim Anshe Polen, 670 11th Street, 140 members.

Degel Israel Anshe Roumania, Vine and 10th, (formerly a Presbyterian Church), 150 members, 600 seats.

Beth Medrash Hagodol Anshe Sfard, 11th and Lloyd Streets, 170 members, 700 seats.

In addition, there were services at the Talmud Torah and the Home for the Aged.

Membership charges were perhaps $10 a year, and other income came from individual fees and public offerings for synagogal honors. The immigrant congregations enjoyed balmy financial weather in the 1920's, at least compared to their early struggles and later collapse in the 1930's.[60] The over-numerous orthodox synagogues entered the depression having little spiritual or financial reserve behind the showy buildings of the 1920's.

The leader of the synagogue was the prosperous businessman, as the learned and pious, so esteemed of old, faded in importance. The character of the otherwise unknown Congregation B'ny [sic] Abraham, dated November 13, 1913, reflects dissatisfaction with lax standards. Its officers "were to be present at all times when services are performed . . . to be the first ones in the Temple every Saturday and Holiday . . . and to see that all ceremonies are performed according to the Orthodox Hebrew Laws." Punishment was provided for "conduct unbecoming a member" and for being "found guilty in any court of record" of a crime.[61]

The central figure of immigrant Judaism was Solomon Isaac Scheinfeld (1860-1943), Rabbi at Beth Hamidrosh Hagodol-Beth Israel in 1892-1893 and from 1902 until his death.[62] Scheinfeld was born in Scaudvil, Lithuania, to a rabbinic family. His somewhat westernized father was the local Crown Rabbi, appointed and recognized by the Russian Government. After teaching in the 1880's, Scheinfeld stood for a time undecided between medical and rabbinic careers, but then spent the three years from 1888 in advanced Talmudic study at the *kolel* in Kovno under its rabbi, Isaac Elhanan Spektor, who conferred rabbinic ordination in 1891. With a wife and two children, and some knowledge of English, he left for America shortly thereafter. After a year in Milwaukee and a decade in Louisville, Scheinfeld returned to Milwaukee's Beth Israel in 1902. Gradually he became the ackowledged rabbi of immigrant Jewry *par excellence*, its overseer in matters of *kashrut*, and representative in many communal institutions. Not the congregation but the community was his main field of action. As informal judge, he was regularly called upon to settle domestic, institutional, and business disputes, and to promulgate Jewish bills of divorce (*gittin*) when necessary. Few undertakings in the immigrant community, especially if they were charitable, educational, or Zionist, failed to enlist his vigorous cooperation. Rabbi Scheinfeld's interests were extensive. He was an omnivorous reader, a veteran visitor to the Milwaukee Public Library, in whose writings appear quotations from Shaw, Shakespeare, Nietzsche, Plato, and many others. Scheinfeld subscribed to the *Standard,* published by the Ethical Culture Society with whose leader, Felix Adler, he corresponded. As *Even Shayish* Scheinfeld wrote frequently in the Yiddish press. There was an intellectual cleavage within, for ultimately Rabbi Scheinfeld reached views which fundamentally differed from those of an orthodox Jew. To these he gave expression in an extraordinary article "On the Improvement of Judaism," published in 1912 in *HaShiloah,* the leading Hebrew journal of the time.[63]

In his article, Scheinfeld comes to grips straightaway with the abandonment of traditional Jewish belief and practice, not only by ignorant but also by learned Jews. In a critique of historic Judaism, he attacks expressions in the Hebrew prayers which are "vestiges of ancient times, when man conceived of his deity as a shiek who would become angry and exact vengeance, and could be soothed by pleas and gifts. . . ." No modern person could pray for the restoration of sacrificial worship. "In brief: It is impossible for an intelligent ethical moral person to come to a synagogue and imagine himself standing before some 'shiek' or tyrannical ruler and entreat him or hypocritically praise him . . . in order to act upon Him, that He might heed his plea or withdraw His wrath. . . ."

Talmudic learning fared little better from Milwaukee's orthodox rabbi. He branded most of it as obsolete subject matter from remote antiquity, and the years spent in mastering the Talmud as an interference with learning a trade or profession. He preferred that the Talmud be left to professional scholars, as classical antiquity was also turned over to them.

With traditional prayer and Talmudic study superannuated, how would Scheinfeld nourish the synagogue and houses of study, which "so long as we are in Exile . . . must after all remain the two pillars?"

I believe it would be fitting for contemporary Jewish authors and scholars to compose new prayers and poems (and not abridge and change the old ones, as the Reformers in Germany and America have done), which shall contain concepts of Deity and religious and moral doctrines suitable to the taste of educated Jews of our day. . . .

Moral and ethical matters would be the subject of synagogue sermons. Services would still differ from Ethical Culture:

Where the latter preach morals and ethics from the viewpoint of religion in general, which are common to all the adherents of various religions, we shall preach morals and ethics to ourselves in our synagogues—all from the viewpoint of Judaism and according to the Bible, the Talmud, and the Midrashim, so far as their sayings fit the spirit of the age and of the people.

(Scheinfeld carefully differentiated his program from Reform Judaism, which he considered a program to curry Christian favor and win emancipation.) A function of rabbis and scholars would be to replace the great codifications of Jewish law, which obviated the need for ordinary Jews to study the Talmud directly, with a new guide. This book would teach the Jew "the pure beliefs and habits (*ha-de'ot veha-middot*) of conduct in Judaism, and he will remain a loyal son of his people and his religion." This radical program was not only for America but for Eastern Europe, and might be implemented by youths studying in *yeshivot*.

Rabbi Scheinfeld apparently derived his ideas from an acquaintance with the Ethical Culture movement and his general reading. The hardships of maintaining Jewish observance, combined with the widespread abandonment of Jewish religious and intellectual interests, must have troubled and influenced him. Rabbi Scheinfeld was not zealous in advocating difficult ritual observances, and preferred to stress, within his own family and to others, the moral and ethical duties in Judaism. His literary output did not include the responsa and Talmudic studies characteristic of East European rabbis, but essays in excellent Hebrew on current affairs.

Solomon Isaac Scheinfeld was a man beloved by all sides, including the Jewish secularists. He does not even seem to have endured the insecurity of tenure which was the lot of the immigrant orthodox rabbi. The Anshe Lubavich congregation engaged its own rabbi in 1917 allegedly after some individuals vainly "demanded of Rabbi Scheinfeld to make the *Shulhan Arukh* (code of law) more lenient, to give a dispensation to a [unfit] *shohet* (slaughterer)."[64] These persons allegedly went to Chicago to obtain a more pliant rabbi. According to the *Wochenblat* account, the new rabbi left almost immediately, and the congregation thereupon engaged Rabbi Boaz Cohen. Again, harsh criticism was levelled at a Chicago group supposedly sponsoring him. Anshe Lubavich, however, replied that their loyalty to Scheinfeld as the communal rabbi was unimpaired.[65] Such was actually the case. Agudas Hakhilos (Associated Congregations), organized in December, 1917, included all the immigrant synagogues. It recognized Scheinfeld as "the only Milwaukee orthodox rabbi."[66] The organization apparently sank into torpor until aroused in February, 1920, when a local butcher was found selling *trefah* meat as kosher. Machzikey Hadas was then founded to promote vigilance in religious requirements, including kashrut, and shortly merged with the revived Association of Synagogues. They apparently planned to import two outside rabbis in an attempt to "create peace between all orthodox elements."[67] The Ladies' Auxiliary meanwhile busied itself with providing a mikveh bathhouse for the Jewish area.[68] However, the Agudas Hakhilos Umachzikey Hadas was too weak to overcome the individual interests of synagogues, particularly when they were enjoying prosperity and asserting their hard-won position with imposing edifices.

Within the synagogue was its pious *hebra kadisha* (burial society). That of Beth Israel buried 37 persons in 1914-1915 (5675), eight of them free of charge. The remaining 29 paid an average of $18.55, which reflects traditionally modest obsequies.[69] Anshe Lubavich's *hebra kadisha* in that year also provided both free and modest funerals.[70]

Many enlarged synagogues, uneasy in a massive building which they could not fill, sought to attract attendance and raise money by importing a famous cantor to appear. The first decades of the twentieth century were the heyday of that Jewish troubadour, the wandering *hazzan*. East European Jews, both the observant and the indifferent, were easy prey for the enchantment of a masterful *hazzan* to deliver the liturgy, and willingly paid before the sacred day to be delighted by long hours of lyric prayer. Those who objected to the concert-like performance of prayers in a house of worship were ignored or stayed away. The mass of immigrant Jews adored their mighty *hazzanim*, and chose the synagogue for the High Holidays which boasted the best *hazzan*.

Charitable appeals were also standard during holiday services, usually for the synagogue itself or some local charity. With the outbreak of war in 1914, however, the immigrant community fervently aided their own brothers and sisters and parents overseas. On Rosh Hashanah at one congregation, the officers admonished the worshippers that "the blood of brothers is being spilled everywhere as water, and the widows and orphans are writing for help"; the *shofar* would not be blown until a proper sum had been pledged. "Everyone pushed not to the door, as is customary, but rather to the pulpit where the [Gentile] writers were standing . . ." to record the amounts.[71]

The immigrant synagogues were busy places. There was constant worship and study within their walls, and on the High Holidays all were crowded to capacity. Charity, education, burials and *kashrut* lay largely within their domain. However, the immigrant congregations' religious life was steadily losing ground, and new buildings or famous *hazzanim* did not conceal this reality.

To young men and women the meticulous practices and cherished beliefs of Judaism seemed stale and outmoded in urban, industrial, scientific civilization. When the synagogue was drained of people and devotion, traditional Judaism appeared uninspired, as if withering away. Some elders, sensing the fathomless dangers that American society presented to Jewish Orthodoxy, stubbornly maintained the old ways and would not yield an inch even in such matters as the English language and proper decorum. Even in the immigrant quarter, the synagogue, with which all things Jewish were once somehow connected, became one competing institution among several.

Religious laxity and deviation showed in many ways. As among the native Jews, most immigrants attended synagogue only on Rosh Hashanah and Yom Kippur. Theatres and halls which were used for meetings and parties throughout the year were fitted up then as "mushroom" synagogues.[72] In some homes that most popular ceremony, the Passover Seder, went unobserved, for the Abraham Lincoln House and other groups conducted public Seders for young people.[73] The spiritual energies which for centuries had found their outlet in religion now flowed in channels of philanthropy, Zionism, and socialism within the community, and the gamut of liberal, progressive, and later Communist causes beyond it. A few younger people found satisfaction in the Christian Science movement, or in the older Milwaukee Rationalist Society, which carried on its free-thinking tradition from German days.[74]

Most of the Jews, however, desired to remain within the boundaries of Judaism. The growth of Conservative Judaism in Milwaukee is partly explained by this desire to adapt rather than abandon Judaism. Conservative Judaism first appeared in 1923, when B'nai Israel Anshe Hungari shifted to Conservative practice, and an explicitly Conservative congregation, Beth El, was founded. Rabbi Julius Rappaport (1863-1937) of Chicago, with extensive pulpit and social service experience, was installed as rabbi of the "Hungarians" and immediately undertook extensive changes especially to draw in younger people. Previously they did "not find [the synagogue] . . . a congenial place, nor one of interest. . . ." Men and women now sat together, and a few English prayers were introduced. The rabbi endeavored to develop a network of clubs, associations, and study groups within the refurbished immigrant congregation. But the effort did not succeed, and Rabbi Rappaport left within two years for Kenosha. The old-timers had little taste for the new order of things, and objected especially after they realized that young people were not beating a path to their old-fashioned and unattractive building in a declining Jewish neighborhood. After this experiment, B'nai Israel more or less returned to the old order of worship.

Another group had neither of these obstacles to contend with. The Oer Chodosh (New Light) Society, founded in December,

1921, was composed of Jews in the vicinity of Washington Park, northwest of the old immigrant area, which was then attracting many Jewish settlers. The pre-congregational nucleus "although far away from the Ghetto, still did not forget their obligations as Jews." Oer Chodosh appealed to

> those whose spiritual wants can not for one reason or another be taken care of by existing temples and synagogues of the city. [The group wants to build] a house of worship whose ritual will be more liberal than the orthodox synagogues and yet not reaching as far in the realm of liberalism as the Reformed temples. Synagogues of this type exist in practically every large city in the country, and are known as Conservative Temples.[75]

Rather unlike previously organized congregations, it first devoted its main attention to erecting a building and then to determining the content of its activities. It brought the widening "middle road" in religion to Milwaukee.

VIII

From Charity to Welfare

CHARITABLE EFFORT among Jews in Milwaukee changed little from its original forms until the 1890's. Aid was dispensed by mutual aid groups and ladies' charitable societies, supplemented by the Jewish lodges, and headed by the Hebrew Relief Society. They represented old-style Jewish benevolence, aiding poor Jews overcome by misfortune with food and fuel, clothing and medicine. Aside from a few dozen conscientious ladies, charitable needs so little preoccupied the Jewish community that the Hebrew Relief Society met great difficulty in merely perpetuating itself during its first 25 years of existence. However, the 1890's were a decade of radical change. Milwaukee Jewry by then had an immigrant majority, requiring extensive service over a prolonged period to augment the immigrants' own widespread self-help. At the same time, charity in America was slowly recognizing the social problems that were generated by decades of untrammeled urban growth. Rudimentary techniques of social work evolved at this time, and much was heard (and not a little done) of "personal service" to the poor. The needs of new immigrants, and the new approaches to handling them, reinvigorated Jewish charity in Milwaukee and slowly transformed its structure. At the same time, individual Jews continued to be active in supporting general charities, especially those of Milwaukee's German sector when the city's Jews were principally a German group.

WELFARE IN THE URBAN COMMUNITY

Relief and welfare activities in the general community were mainly a private responsibility. During the 1880's and 1890's a few organizations carried the burden, such as the German Relief Society, Milwaukee Mission Kindergarten and others, led by the Associated Charities of Milwaukee. Jews were prominent in the Associated Charities, especially Philip Carpeles, a founder in 1882 and vice-president for nearly twenty years, and A. W. Rich and Rabbi Hecht.[1]

The Associated Charities was a leading beneficiary of the city's annual charity ball, held each January. The ball was not without its frictions. Some Protestant quarters attacked the dancing, and in 1895 Jewish society was meagerly represented.[2] The Hebrew Relief Association received only $250 of the 1896 proceeds of $2,875.[3] In 1900, Rabbi Victor Caro condemned all sectarian charities, and proposed that relief be administered by a single non-sectarian board, but neither the sharp words nor the proposal attracted support. It was said that non-sectarianism already existed when the Hebrew Relief Association enjoyed rent-free housing in the offices of the Associated Charities.[4]

Another local charity in which Jews participated and also benefited from was the Milwaukee branch of the Needlework Guild of America, organized in 1892, which soon had 32 groups in the city. Reflecting the "personal service" emphasis of the times, each woman made two pieces of clothing, as her yearly contribution, for distribution among the poor.[5]

The city's Jews also showed charitable concern for the plight of others beyond city limits. Congregations which strained to erect their buildings, such as those at Dubuque, Appleton, Lancaster, Pa., and Gainesville, Texas, were encouraged by Milwaukee contributions.[6] A disaster evoked the greatest generosity. As soon as word reached the city of the Great Chicago Fire of 1871, the two congregations called a special joint meeting and sent a relief committee to Chicago, and made provision to house the destitute victims. All the city's Jewish organizations seem to have contributed to aid the people of Chicago.[7]

Yellow fever epidemics in 1873 at Memphis and Shreveport,

and in 1878 at New Orleans, the Johnstown flood sufferers of 1889, the Galveston hurricane-flood of 1900 were all aided by liberal contributions, generally from the congregations.[8] A. W. Rich, then a rising merchant, raised $230 among his business colleagues, mostly Jews, for victims of an Oshkosh fire in 1875.[9]

Even in the insulated decades before 1914, appeals from abroad were responded to. Sometimes they were for an individual, like Isaac Neustadtl's appeal for the philosopher Feuerbach. S. S. Weil solicited for French sufferers of the War of 1870. More often, stricken towns in Europe appealed to Jews overseas for aid, like the 100 florins gathered by Rabbi Spitz for storm victims in Miskolz, Hungary, and the brothers Morawetz' collection for Jews flooded out of their homes in Szegedin, also in Hungary.[10] Remoter places, like Persia and Salonica, as well as Russia, drew responses.[11] An occasional solicitation from Palestine did not go unanswered, as when Rabbi Abraham Hirsch Levin spoke "in costume" at B'ne Jeshurun in 1870. Simon Stampfer solicited for Jerusalem in 1880, and a school in Safed was a beneficiary in 1894.[12]

The cardinal rule of the Jewish poor was to look to fellow-Jews for aid, as the cardinal rule of the Jewish giver was to bear responsibility for him.

JEWISH CHARITY

Throughout these years, Jews continued to combine for purposes of mutual aid. A typical group, the *Chevra Bikur Cholim*, known as the Hebrew Benevolent Society, arose before 1873 to provide sick and death benefits to members. It later distributed charity from its growing surplus. The Hebrew Benevolent Society continued to 1930, but during its last twenty-five years took in few members. The membership included a few early settlers and many familiar names—Carpeles, Friend, Adler, Rindskopf, Teweles, Frisch, and others—who paid dues long after their wealth rendered them independent of assistance. Victor Berger joined in 1882 and stayed on the rolls until he died in 1929.

In 1881, the Hebrew Benevolent Society counted 75 members.[13] To attract others, it offered applicants under 30 dues of only $1 a year. But most new members were over 40 years of age, and after 1891 the Society established 44 as the maximum age for entry. Its membership stood many years at approximately 100.[14] When a member died, $75 was paid to his widow or survivor.[15] Although few if any members were religiously orthodox, some desired the rite of *tahara*, and the Society provided it.[16] True to the "sick visitation" meaning of its Hebrew name, the Hebrew Benevolent Society paid $5 weekly for illness up to thirteen weeks, sent visitors, and provided a physician to examine claimants.[17]

This traditionally patterned organization aided needy families with coal, food, and Passover supplies. Small amounts went to Jewish transients to send them on their way, and the Society participated in such campaigns as that of the Jewish orphanage at Cleveland.[18] Its assets increased steadily from $2,500 in 1881, to $4,305 in 1886, and over $6,000 in 1899. They exceeded $12,000 at the time of dissolution in 1930.[19]

Traditional long-established ladies' societies, including the True Sisters, Gemilath Chesed Society and the Hebrew Widow's and Orphans' Association, continued to aid the local needy and victims of misfortune outside the city.[20] The Gemilas Chesed Society celebrated its thirtieth anniversary on October 16, 1892, with a ball at the Germania.[21] However, the leading group during the 1880's and 1890's was the Widows' and Orphans' Society, whose purpose was indicated by its title; its parties and charity balls were "must" social functions for the leading Jewish families.[22] About 1,000 people, including "the best known members of Jewish society," graced its 28th annual ball in 1891;[23] next year came hundreds of "the fashionable Jewish society; the general wealth and fashion of Milwaukee."[24] Sizeable gifts and bequests were also left to the Widows' and Orphans' Society.[25]

With 109 members in 1880, the organization spent $264, mainly for widows, and had a capital of $1,800.[26] This rose to $1,042 in 1893-1894 to support about fifteen fatherless families, besides aid to the Cleveland Orphan Asylum where it sent children. The money came from 276 ladies who paid $2 yearly, and from a sinking fund of over $3,000.[27] However, its pensions were much too small, and the group itself dwindled in size and activity. By

1923, the Widows' and Orphans' Society was nearly dormant.[28]

Twenty women founded the Ladies' Relief Sewing Society during hard times in November, 1878:

> Only a few months ago, many families in this city, driven by cold and hunger, destitute of the very garments to clothe themselves, appealed to the benevolent for help. To answer this appeal, the Relief Sewing Society was called into existence. . . .[29]

Soon 75 women led by Mrs. A. W. Rich were sewing for the poor each Thursday afternoon, and conducted entertainments which were reputedly "the most popular amusements in the city."[30] This West Side society rivalled the East Side Sewing Society, which met at Emanu-El, and Rabbi Moses was again distressed at this additional East Side-West Side friction:

> Our beloved German Athens is on its way toward becoming a metropolis . . . in view of the rapid growth of our city, we have two ladies' sewing societies which, while at present they do not compete with each other, could do a much better job if they merged. We therefore ask the members in the name of the hungry, freezing, poor Israelites of this city . . . to consolidate these two associations, and participate in supporting our poor. It is time to get rid of the petty, separatist spirit of jealousy, and to find means toward a friendlier way of coming together.

The groups eventually consolidated.[31]

With a membership of 200 in 1885, the Ladies' Relief Sewing Society supplied thirty to forty families with clothes and bedding. Other benevolence included donations for Russian Jewish refugees, the Catholic Franciscan Hospital, and the Associated Charities. It carried on the usual balls and entertainment.[32] Its activities were long continued by a group of devoted ladies headed by Mrs. Rich.[33]

Personal association in order to uplift the poor—the philanthropic gospel of the 1890's—was undertaken by the Sisterhood of Personal Service, organized in 1893. Each member weekly visited, counseled and then reported upon the plight of one poor family.[34] The society held "school" in Temple Emanu-El, where the "daughters of the poor" learned millinery and dressmaking;

a "kitchen garden" was established on Fifth Street to teach cooking.[35] It also opened an important night school for teaching English to Jewish immigrants. The Sisterhood of Personal Service merged with the Milwaukee Jewish Mission in 1900, and brought into being the Jewish Settlement, one of the most important institutions built by Milwaukee Jewry.

Other women's charities in the 1890's were the small West Side Ladies' Aid Society[36] and the larger Society for the Relief of the Jewish Sick Poor, composed of immigrant women with a few men, including Dr. H. Brook.[37]

The 1890's were also significant for the emergence of other Russian Jewish charitable groups, such as the Hebrew Benevolent Association. Besides its officers and three trustees, there were thirty-two directors who rotated as investigators and reported to the board. The group soon had 185 members, $600 in cash, and an equal amount pledged. In addition to relief, it hoped to raise $2,000 capital to execute an ambitious program including free loans and an employment bureau aimed at making applicants self-supporting.[38] These immigrants proposed a more far-seeing program than anything the native Jews had yet planned.

THE HEBREW RELIEF SOCIETY

Aside from the steady but limited work of the ladies' societies and mutual aid groups, charity was an *ad hoc* affair—providing assistance to cases as they arose. The Hebrew Relief Society managed its affairs in this manner, living a hand-to-mouth existence out of its officers' vest pockets until the 1890's. More than once it drew near oblivion, until the new social awareness of that decade and the problems of the immigrant sub-community reawakened it. Its income was far below what was needed,[39] as is seen from the appeal to the Jewish community in 1878:

... it has been characteristic of our race, and we have received the applause of the community at large for our disinterested acts of charity, and more especially for always caring for our indigent and poor. It is desirable that we should keep on in this good labor, and show by our deeds that while we may differ in our opinions as to dogmas, be they orthodox or reform, we do stand united upon the rock of charity and benevolence.

The support you have given this society heretofore, although liberal, was barely sufficient to meet the wants and we now call on you, one and all, to come forward on Sunday afternoon next (October 6th) to participate in the deliberations of this society, and make your contributions not only what you can afford, but what necessity and circumstances may require. Unless this call is liberally responded to our Relief Association will have to disband.[40]

With but $227 on hand and over $1,000 needed for "the emergencies of the inclement season," a "canvass among the generous Israelites of the city"[41] raised $842.50, besides money from entertainment benefits.[42] Funds were still short, and President Aaron Leopold again demanded "a more united and more liberal support," insisting that "the existence of the society will have its limit" if attendance at the annual meeting were poor.[43] The meeting was well attended, but Leopold was apparently attacked for haphazard solicitation and his personal distribution of funds. A strong special committee, consisting of Bernhard Gross, A. W. Rich, R. Reichmann, Philip Carpeles, and M. Heiman, was assigned to present a reorganization plan. At least three—Rich, Gross, and Carpeles—were rising men in the Jewish and the general community. They recommended that distribution of relief be entrusted to a committee of seven from different parts of the city. This plan was adopted, and Heiman became President, Charles Stein, Vice President, and A. W. Rich, Secretary.[44]

The reorganized group next attempted to federate the Jewish charitable societies into a united relief body. They would cooperate with similar organizations elsewhere, and accumulate a surplus for a building to house the sick and destitute, or an industrial home, or to train poor children in the ways of self-dependence. Although this was the "charity organization" period of American philanthropy, Milwaukee Jewry proved unready to accept a central body. Neighborhood rivalries played their role in shelving the plan; the *Zeitgeist* again blamed "the ill-famed Milwaukee River, which splits the city into East and West sections."[45]

These brave plans were laid aside for twenty years and matters continued in the old style. With 2,100 to 2,500 Jews then residing in the city, only 106 contributed $726.50 in 1880 to the Hebrew Relief Society. It assisted eight persons, who arrived penniless, to attain "positions of trust and respectability."[46] The winter of 1880-1881 proved a cruel season for "several poor Jewish families living in deepest misery," whose children were too ill-clothed to attend school. Every Sunday morning the Society committee sat at the Progress Club to receive applications, investigate, and dispense relief.[47] Although Philip Carpeles, President in 1881, spoke of $50,000 for a hospital "exclusively for Jews," which "should be raised without delay," the immediate problem for a long period was to raise $1,000 to $2,000 each year.[48]

Although B. M. Weil attended the United States Associated Hebrew Charities at St. Louis in 1885,[49] which sought to devise a national policy to deal with transients, the sights of the Hebrew Relief Society remained fixed upon local problems. It did not significantly change its system of distributing relief in cash and in kind, depending upon the rates of unemployment and immigration. (The organization modified its name to the Hebrew Relief Association in 1889.) The highest disbursements were $3,169 in 1893-1894 (December through November), and the lowest was $990 in 1884-1885; the average was approximately $1,500.[50] During the most expensive year, 120 families in addition to 220 individuals were aided, at a time when approximately 15,000 were unemployed in Milwaukee.[51] The nature of relief is illustrated by expenses for the busy year of 1891-1892:

Bread and provisions	$ 267.45
Coal and wood	526.38
Meals, lodgings, rent	244.30
Stoves & house furnishings	358.37
Cash and other relief	869.86
Clothing, merchandise, tools	127.71
Railroad tickets, transport	148.41
Medicine and medical care	219.67
Stationery, postage, printing	27.00
	$2789.15[52]

Systematic cooperation began during hard times in 1893, when Rabbi Hecht called a meeting of Jewish charities and proposed a better system of investigation. The societies agreed to try the scheme for a few months,[53] and thereupon founded the United Hebrew Charities with delegates from the Hebrew Relief Association, the Widows' and Orphans' Society, and the Sisterhood of Personal Service. The secretary was to maintain a list of all their beneficiaries.[54] The Executive Board of the United Hebrew Charities convened almost daily during the bad months, and supported over 100 families, comprising perhaps 500 persons.[55] After the 1893-1894 winter, the United Hebrew Charities was "no longer an experiment, for the trial has already assured its success. . . ."[56] It began to systematize Jewish charity by such steps as blacklisting certain applicants, probably for dishonesty, and recommending further investigation of others.[57] The United Hebrew Charities continued to raise money for its four constituents and coordinated the disbursement of funds. In 1896-1897, it raised $3,371 and distributed $2,304.[58] Yet it only codified and refined the old methods.

Local Jews still took little interest in the Hebrew Relief Association. Bitter words spilled forth after an ill-attended annual meeting in 1894. Charity, it was complained, was of a "perfunctory nature," when "the active members comprise not more than a score"; the future looked darker still because "the young men do not come forward to share the interest and labors." If contributions were not published, "there may be some who would not give at all."[59] Two years later, in 1896, Rabbis Sigmund Hecht and Victor Caro became President and Vice President—a move suggesting an absence of willing candidates. One reason was the burden upon the officers, who were unaided by a paid staff. Isadore Ladoff was only briefly employed as agent in 1892.[60]

Nor were the Hebrew Relief Association's clients, estimated at 96% Russian Jews, very grateful. Rabbi Caro complained in 1897 that they "were insolent and imperative in their demands, freely criticizing and even cursing the almoner when their wishes were not acceded to."[61] Impoverished immigrants may have felt that a Jewish charity owed them more benevolence and less investigation.

Elections had to be postponed in 1898 in order to arouse the electorate. As usual, comments were made upon the "deplorable lack of support . . . on the part of a great number of Jewish residents. . . ."[62] It was at last decided to hire a part-time collector, investigator, and almoner, such as the Associated Charities employed.[63] Morris Miller, the new President, found much of the work still resting on his own shoulders:[64]

To systematize my relief work I set apart every Friday afternoon for meeting the poor, hearing their complaints and assisting them . . . The rooms of the Associated Charities were freely placed at my disposal, nevertheless, I could not well escape the opportunities [importunities] of the needy who sought and found me at my home and much more at my office.

Miller hoped that his administration would raise the low public standing of the Hebrew Relief Association:

The indifference, not to say bitterness and animosity that had characterized the attitude of a large portion of our coreligionists toward the association, during several years prior to my administration has made room for a more cordial sentiment and a heartier co-operation on either side of the river, and the practical result of the harmony newly created is shown in the larger collections this year as compared with the year previous.

His main practical problem was distinguishing between "imposters, who want to live without work, by cunningly begging and appealing to sympathy," and "the really deserving who are poor by no fault of theirs." A labor test, consisting of a woodyard where all able-bodied relief applicants would be required to work, was Miller's proposal for separating cheaters from the meritorious. According to the theory of the times, the former would refuse to work, while the latter would welcome the opportunity to prove good faith.

Milwaukee Jewry at last seemed ready for the plan presented in 1900 by Superintendent Rubovitz of the United Hebrew Charities of Chicago:

We find that the contributors prefer to pay a lump sum into one fund once a year . . . as the contribution is for all charitable work, [it] relieves the contributor from any further contribution. We raise $150,000 in Chicago annually, and Milwaukee ought to raise $25,000 . . . Another feature is that no paupers can under the new system receive aid from half a dozen societies at the same time.[65]

Support of the other Jewish charitable groups was finally won: the True Sisters, Ladies' Relief Sewing Societies, Sisterhood of Personal Service, Widows' and Orphans' Society, as well as local branches of the Cleveland Orphan Asylum and the Hebrew Home for Consumptives at Denver.[66] From these efforts grew the Federated Jewish Charities in 1902.

CHARITY BECOMES WELFARE

The founding of the Federated Jewish Charities opened a new period in Milwaukee Jewish philanthropy, as emphasis gradually shifted from emergency aid to systematic social service. It was symbolized by the Hebrew Relief Association's change of name in 1921 to the Jewish Social Service Association. Philanthropic activity gradually became the leading function of the Jewish community, one in which more Jews participated than any other. Only a small portion of the funds raised for charitable purposes had left Milwaukee until the outbreak of the World War. Then began in earnest American Jewry's aid to Jewry overseas, and new developments in Palestine also slowly came to the fore. Local needs gradually required a smaller proportion of funds raised.

New organizations appeared on the scene, like the Children's Outing Society, founded by a group of women in 1906. It originally intended to accommodate all children in the Kindergarten camp, but soon devoted itself to Jewish children at a site in nearby Thiensville, where they came for two to four weeks. The Children's Outing Society spent $6,500 in 1923 to care for 48 children weekly during the summer at its then outdated facilities.[67]

As noted, the Council of Jewish Women, Sisterhood of Personal Service, and Jewish Mission coalesced in 1900 to form the

Milwaukee Jewish Settlement. The Settlement rented a house on Fifth Street in 1900, moved to one larger in 1904, and in 1911 occupied its own Abraham Lincoln House. Like other settlements, the Abraham Lincoln House had a head resident, Miss Stella Loeb (Mrs. Ralph A. Bloch), who dwelled in the Settlement from 1906. Others were Miss Stella B. Rosenbaum (1916-1918), and Miss Helena Stern (1918-1922), who were followed by an Executive Director, Kurt Peiser.[68]

The House on Fifth Street teemed with activity, receiving an average of some 1,300 people weekly all year. Before it was abandoned for larger premises, as many as 17,000 adults and children yearly paid a few pennies to bathe there. There was a cooking school and a sewing school; boys' clubs, girls' clubs, and mothers' clubs drew hundreds to their meetings. No less important was the Settlement's night school, which enrolled 150 boys and men in its 1903-1904 session. The pupils, 90% adults, met from October until April to study English and American history.[69] In 1908, "48 young men and women, recent arrivals from Russia, came to the Settlement Sunday mornings and on two spare evenings" for this purpose.[70] When the Settlement took possession of its newly built Abraham Lincoln House in 1911, the Trustees of the Settlement Cook Book contributed $5,650 towards the cost of $18,000, besides a monthly allowance of $150.[71]

Like similar institutions in American Jewish communities during this age, the Milwaukee Jewish Settlement was also a meeting ground for native and immigrant young people. ". . . Fully 120 young people are giving their services to the House, as teachers, leaders of clubs, or as general helpers."[72] The clubs' names give an inkling of the ambitions of their members. There were the Arbeiter Ring, Poale Zion Singing Society, American Zionists, Yiddish Dramatic Society. Also on hand was a profusion of youthful "literary" groups: Lincoln Literary Society, The Demosthenes Club, Newsboys Literary Circle, and many more. These groups did not ignore what other clubs set in their names: All in all Progressive Athletic Club, Excelsior Athletic Club, Boxing Club, Milwaukee Hiking Club and, most candidly, Young

Men's Pleasure Club. Young girls, too, had their Little Neighbors, Campfire Girls, Daughters of Israel, and many others.

The Abraham Lincoln House opened its doors to "many . . . in our neighborhood . . . between the ages of 18 and 21 who call themselves radicals. Your resident [Miss Helena Stern] attended one of their educational meetings, and has now more than ever before, the desire to concede to their request to have open forum discussions in our House. . . ."; this was done.[73] The House compensated for the shortcomings of neighborhood Jewish education by conducting a Sabbath School, attended mainly by young girls. Approximately 100 children gathered on Saturday afternoons to join in a short service, songs, a lesson in Bible, and a "sermonette." It also conducted a Passover Seder.[74] At about the same time that the Abraham Lincoln House opened its doors, the city began to use its public schools for youthful activities. The Lapham Park Social Center, in the midst of the immigrant quarter, was a supervised social and athletic area.[75]

A unique feature emerged from the cooking classes conducted by the Settlement's "Lady Bountiful," Mrs. Simon Kander. The recipes which were taught at her classes were published experimentally in 1896 as the *Settlement Cook Book*. The simple recipes of this book won it unparalleled national success, as edition after edition was printed and sold out year after year. The accumulated royalties of the *Settlement Cook Book* reached nearly $50,000 by 1925, sufficient to finance a substantial portion of the Jewish Community Center to be built.[76] The slow departure of the Jews from their old neighborhood, and their replacement by diverse ethnic strains, indicated that the days of the Abraham Lincoln House were numbered. Now "our sidewalks are filled with Jewish boys and girls mingling with non-Jewish youth from the fast deteriorating neighborhood—a mixture of Negroes, Slavs, Italians, Greeks and other nationalities."[77] It was time to move.

Another major Jewish institution was founded early in the 20th century. The long desired Jewish hospital arose in 1903 as the Mount Sinai Hospital. The Hospital was started by immigrants who served Kosher meals, but they could not maintain it. Native Jews reorganized the hospital, gave it a new name, and abandoned the Kosher diet. It occupied a former Y.M.C.A. on Fourth and Walnut Streets, until a remarkable gift bestowed a new building upon the Hospital in 1913. Abraham Slimmer, a Jewish millionaire who lived nearly in seclusion in Dubuque, Iowa, had contributed $5,000 to the original building in 1904. Now, in 1912, he again indulged his "hobby" of endowing Jewish hospitals by donating $50,000 to Milwaukee's Mount Sinai Hospital, on condition that local Jews match his gift with an equal amount. When this was accomplished, the $160,000 edifice was opened in November, 1914. After the War, a $300,000 drive in 1921 enabled the Hospital to add operating rooms, more beds, and a nurses' residence. Since only some 25% of its patients were Jews, Mount Sinai Hospital, although near the immigrant quarter, was a non-sectarian institution in fact as well as name. Most of its attending physicians were Jews.[78]

During the same years, immigrant Jewry was actively engaged in maintaining its own charities. Of particular interest were those which aimed to preserve a Jewish atmosphere for children and aged who required institutional residence. The Home for the Aged (Moshav Zekanim) founded about 1904, fitted up a house on Galena Street in 1906, under the title of the Hebrew Institute. While suitably religious for its few inhabitants, the Home for the Aged was a shabby and depressing place, where the old people had almost nothing to do but wait to die.[79]

Concern for a Jewish environment also animated the ladies of the Society for the Care of Dependent Jewish Children, founded in 1919. Several years before, the Council of Jewish Women had contemplated founding a Jewish Home for Dependent Children, without any results. The new group rejected the traditional policy of despatching Milwaukee cases to the Cleveland Hebrew Orphan Asylum in favor of a smaller institution in the home city. By the time that it was setting up a home, voices were questioning whether institutions for children were not inferior to foster care. However, the Jewish Children's Home did open at 403 Twenty-first Street.[80]

On the same plot of ground with the Home for the Aged and the Talmud Torah stood another institution transplanted from

Eastern Europe, the Hachnosas Orchim (Hebrew Sheltering Home), giving food and temporary lodging to strangers and the homeless. Its yearly clientele were several hundred Jewish drifters, who received tickets of admission upon application to one of the officers. The Hachnosas Orchim was supported by some 300 small contributors.

Another immigrant group was the Gemilath Chesed Society (Hebrew Free Loan Association), founded in 1899. In its first 25 years the group lent $50,000 to 75 or 100 borrowers each year. The loans usually ran from $25 to $50 for business purposes. The Hebrew Free Loan Association could report with pride that the borrowers practically never defaulted.[81]

FEDERATED JEWISH CHARITIES

The Federated Jewish Charities' chartered purpose was to provide "a permanent, efficient and practical method of collecting, administering and distributing the contributions of the Jewish residents, and others of the city of Milwaukee for private, local and national charitable and educational purposes."[82] The first President was the venerable David Adler, then past 80 (1902-1903). He was succeeded by Morris Miller (1903-1910), Adolph Landauer (1910-1914), A. L. Saltzstein (1914-1917), Max Freschl (1917-1918), and Nat Stone (1918-1929). Other prominent figures during the Federated Jewish Charities' first 25 years were Max Landauer, John E. De Wolf, Nathan Glicksman, Charles Friend, M. D. Newald, J. H. Newman, Max Breslauer, Harry Krauskopf and Miss Dorothy Phillips.

Four local Jewish organizations were the original beneficiaries: the Hebrew Relief Association, the Ladies' Relief Sewing Society, the Jewish Settlement, and the Sisterhood of Personal Service, which soon merged with the Settlement. In time, three other local bodies entered: the Children's Outing Society (1916), the Council of Jewish Women (1917), which promoted education in diet and hygiene and sponsored "Americanization" classes, and the Milwaukee Talmud Torah (1924). National Jewish charities also received donations. The Hebrew Orphan Asylum of Cleveland, a traditional beneficiary of Milwaukee Jews, enjoyed particular generosity: its allotment rose from $2,100 in 1904 to $4,000 by 1922. It continued to receive Milwaukee children, of whom it sheltered 19 in 1914 at a per capita cost of $210. The Montefiore Home for the Aged, also in Cleveland, received an allotment of one-third or one-quarter of the Asylum's. In 1914 it housed five aged Milwaukee Jews. The National Jewish Hospital for Consumptives and the Jewish Consumptives Relief Society, both in Denver, the Hebrew Immigrant Aid Society and the National Farm School in Doylestown, Pa., were regular F.J.C. recipients, and were joined somewhat incongruously by the Alliance Israelite Universelle of Paris.

In its aspiration to be the sole Jewish charity appealing to the Milwaukee community, the Federated Jewish Charities combatted separate campaigns instituted by its out-of-town beneficiaries. Attempting to surpass their $50 allotment, the Hebrew Immigrant Aid Society and a few others did so, but were suppressed.[83]

The Federated Jewish Charities commenced in 1902 with 275 subscribers who contributed $9,790. The enthusiasm of its founding days slowly dissipated, to judge from the record of the pre-war years. Member-subscribers did not exceed 410 (1911) and the highest sum raised was $20,387 (1913). The founders rejoiced that they had been "among the first to adopt the idea of federation in connection with charity work," and had abolished the "old time embarrassing and wasteful method of charity entertainments, bazaars, theaters, balls, and similar undertakings. . . ."[84] But President Adolph Landauer complained in 1913 and 1914 that "we have not succeeded in arousing the conscience of a large portion of our Jewish community." He estimated that 500 prosperous Jewish families in Milwaukee were failing to contribute.[85]

The organization strode forward in the succeeding years. Before 1917, when the United States went to war, "the community at large was in a state of lethargy" concerning overseas needs; "there had never been a general community interest in this work." But the American Jewish Relief Committee, headed by Nathan Straus, called for $50,000 from Milwaukee, "and for the first time in the history of Jewish life in Milwaukee, the community interest was aroused, and 150 men and women from all walks of life took part in our campaign."[86] The heartening response raised $65,000. In speaking these words, President A. L. Saltzstein overlooked the immigrants, who had been fervently raising money nearly from the day the War began. In quick steps, F. J. C. members increased from 485 in 1915 to 1,182 in 1917, reaching an estimated 1,400 in 1922; income rose from $24,308 in 1915 to $94,196 in 1925.

Jointly with its main beneficiary, the Hebrew Relief Association, the Federated employed as its first Superintendent Jacob Billikopf (1905-1907). Morris Stern, an immigrant lawyer, succeeded him for one year, and Samuel Rabinovitch served from 1908 until 1912, as a professional leader. However, N. N. Goodman was a local man unable to handle the substantial responsibilities. Maurice B. Hexter, Isaac Rubinstein, and Isadore Kadis each served briefly until 1922, but like Jacob Billikopf before them, moved elsewhere to notable careers in Jewish social service. Simon Peiser was a middle-aged Reform rabbi who had long been a social worker when he reached Milwaukee in 1922; he made a deep impression during his tenure, which mortal illness ended after only one year. His nephew Kurt Peiser, Executive Director at the Abraham Lincoln House, succeeded him. That numerous able men served only briefly suggests that Milwaukee was not professionally satisfying; one man was required to be both a fundraiser, supported by a relative handful of people, and a social service executive for the entire community. The Federated Jewish Charities did not advance far enough beyond its first steps. Few new faces appeared among its leaders, nor did it draw many more organizations into its orbit. It seemed an exclusively "German" and "Reform" institution during a period of rising immigrant assertiveness.

The Hebrew Relief Association, which absorbed most of the F. J. C.'s income, at last converted to a modern welfare organization.[87] After a few years as Vice President, Charles Friend undertook its Presidency in 1907, and held it for more than 30 years. This leading local lawyer, delegate to the American Jewish Congress of 1917-1918, led the H.R.A. through its transformation from general relief to individualized social service. Other familiar names of the local community appear among its officers: Solomon Fein and his son Joseph S. Fein, Adolph Landauer, A. L. Saltzstein, Philip Judell. From immigrant ranks, Joseph Saffro, Zionist, Hebraist, and insurance agent, began a long tenure as Secretary in 1917.

The Hebrew Relief Association changed as the years changed the needs of its clients. The $14,545 disbursed in 1913 reached $27,810 in 1922, and the depressed postwar year of 1920 cost the maximum of $31,673. Yet the number aided did not rise greatly. Peak years were 1904, when 1302 persons were aided, and 1907, with 1391; 1912, when the H.R.A. relieved 1046 individuals; and 1920, when 1713 persons received assistance. The specimen of 1909, the first prosperous year after the 1907 depression, closely characterizes the other years: of 210 cases (710 persons) treated, unemployment counted for 45; illness, 43; "insufficient earnings," 27; tuberculosis, 23; widowhood, 23; desertion, 16.

Much effort was expended on the problem of desertion. Men often left their families to seek improvement elsewhere, and sent for wife and children later. Jewish charity would meanwhile care for the fatherless family. Well aware of this practice, the Hebrew Relief Association undertook "to make desertion as unattractive as possible, by maintaining the women and children on a plane below the minimum requirements."[88] This, it was believed, would give honorable husbands pause before they left home.

Quite different were the problems of tuberculosis. The "white plague" had "grown mightily" in 1906, and care for its victims and their families consumed about 40% of the H.R.A.'s expenditures in 1913. Jewish patients were sent to the Social Workers Sanatarium, Wales Sanatarium, and those at Blue Mound and Greenfield, all in or near the city. This scourge of urban slum life started to decline in 1914. "We are deriving the benefit of better housing conditions, and we are enjoying the advantages of the prompt and ready preventitive [sic] methods adopted by our city government."[89]

Distributing cash, food, fuel, and clothing remained the mainstay of the Hebrew Relief Association, aided by the Ladies' Relief Sewing Society. However, the Socialist administration of

Milwaukee combatted tuberculosis by vigorous health and inspection policies, and the Progressive State government initiated widows' pensions and workmen's compensation. Both pioneer measures in the movement towards a publicly assured minimum standard of living freed private charity for individualized attention to particular needs.

Nearly the entire clientele of the Hebrew Relief Association was composed of immigrants, but not the immigrants who had just arrived. The United States Immigration Commission of 1909, "which made a careful study of immigration and dependency in Milwaukee showed that out of 261 dependent cases, 149 had been living in the United States for 20 years or over, 62 from ten to twenty years, and only 13 from one to five years. This demonstrates that it is not the recent immigrant who knocks at the door of a relief organization, but he who has fallen by the wayside in the struggle for existence in our complex industry of life. . . ."[90] The needy immigrant turned first to the many charities which throve in the immigrant quarter. The Hebrew Relief Association's complaint of 1912 that not 5% of its income derived from the immigrants did not see that the latter supported a network of societies, lodges, clubs and synagogues which had charitable auxiliaries. Only when they could not help him did the immigrant approach the native Jews' more forbidding charity for such prolonged problems as widowhood, or hospitalization and medical treatment.

The Hebrew Relief Association opened a clinic at its office on Walnut and Tenth Streets in 1919, with Dr. S. H. Lippitt in charge. He soon had a nurse and an assistant, whose duties included house calls to check cases. Within three years, the H. R. A. served some 400 families (approximately 2,000 persons) "for the purpose of either curing physical ailment or preventing its occurrence."[91] The clinic spurred Mount Sinai Hospital to establish a dispensary in 1924, while the Jewish Social Service Association undertook medical social work only. Resembling its medical clinic was the H.R.A.'s dental clinic, opened in the same period and named after Solomon Fein. Employing volunteer dentists, the Solomon Fein Dental Clinic recorded 1,040 treatments in 1922.

The H.R.A. had ample reason to change its name to the Jewish Social Service Association and to add a paragraph to its Articles of Incorporation in 1922:

> To provide medical and dental care and to improve the physical well-being of the people of the neighborhood, to place children in suitable homes and to give them legal adoption; to care for the handicapped, mental and physical, to give counsel and advice to persons on their special relationships and do and perform personal service work for the Jewish community of the County of Milwaukee.[92]

The bitter taste of charity was sweetened by help coming from "a remarkable development in the neighborhood" during World War I days:

> So called "corporations" or Mutual Loan Societies; there are about 12 of these with a total paid up capital of nearly a million dollars, and a membership of about 2,500. Three of them maintain offices on Walnut St., and one intends to increase its capital to half a million dollars. An interest rate of 6% is charged to the borrower, loans being granted from amounts of $50 to $3,000. . . . Some of the corporations are paying 10%. Socially, this phenomenon is interesting to us because we have today hundreds of borderline families who tide themselves over by means of these loans. In many instances we have used the funds of these loan societies for our clients. . . .[93]

Most of the loan corporations were financially unsound, and collapsed disastrously during the 1920-1921 depression. But the immigrants and their native patrons were finding the way to transform charity into welfare, and welfare into mutual aid.

IX

The Challenge of Ideas:

Zionism and Socialism, 1890-1925

THE NEW IMMIGRANTS brought with them new ideas originating
in the profoundly Jewish environment from which they had
come. Their intellectual drive and enthusiasm for ideas set them
off decisively from older immigrants, who had been far more
conservative in their ways of thought. Being Jewish was itself
an absorbing problem to East European Jews, and the solutions
they found were propagated tirelessly. Nothing Jewish in Milwaukee was ever so fervidly or aggressively expounded as their
Zionism and Socialism, which long opposed each other.

Underneath, the Zionist movement to establish a Jewish state in
Palestine, and the Socialist movement, which sought to introduce
the Jews into the mainstream of revolutionary movements, had
the common aim of introducing the Jews as a people into the
mainstream of modern history, by linking them to the movements
which were shaping the future of Western mankind. Zionism
looked to the rights of nations, and Socialism forecast the coming
victory of the industrial workers.

As these ideologies became popular among masses of Jews,
they lost much of their opposition to each other. Movements to
reconcile or synthesize Zionism and Socialism became common,
particularly in a city like Milwaukee with strong Zionist and
Socialist movements.

SOCIALIST BEGINNINGS

Jewish socialism first appeared in 1891-1892, soon after Israel Glassman, a young leader who had already been active in Chicago and St. Louis, settled in Milwaukee. Glassman organized the Milwaukee Tailors Union of Jewish tailors who worked for Jewish contractors, which soon numbered 75 men. Like early Jewish unions everywhere, they were eager for action. As their target they selected an employer named Barnett Goldstein, who had come from Chicago, and stood in ill repute as a wage-cutter and a determined opponent of trade unions. The Milwaukee Tailors Union issued a "Call to All Workers":

> Here, too, the workers can no longer endure the bad treatment and oppression of the parasites, who wish to save up capital through the workers' toil, sweat, and blood!

At first the "parasites," frightened, reportedly became solicitous towards their workers. But Goldstein, whose hide was thickened to such assaults, reportedly led twelve Jewish contractors (or sweatshop operators) to demand that their employees quit the union. The unionists refused, and the employers responded with a lockout of fifty workers in mid-winter.

The embattled tailors, some of whom were heads of families, sought support. Max Stoler, a Jewish union organizer, was called up from Chicago, but a false telegram from the employers, who signed the workers' name, diverted him with the tale that the strike was settled. *Freie Arbeiter Stimme*, a Yiddish labor weekly, published the fifty strikers' request to "workers, basters, pressers" not to take jobs in Milwaukee during the strike. After two weeks without work, the men appealed for cash aid, to be sent to Oswald Schubert—evidently a German tailor union official. Paul Krasnowitz, an immigrant of 1881, earned the strikers' thanks by permitting those evicted from their dwellings to stay on credit in the Jewish Boarding House.[1] The terms of the workers' victory are not known, but under the chaotic labor conditions neither a defeat nor a victory lasted long.

Glassman's next step in organizing revolutionary socialism in

Temple Emanu-El B'ne Jeshurun, 1923

(From the Institutions)

CONSERVATIVE AND REFORM JUDAISM

Beth El-Ner Tamid Synagogue, 1951

Peretz Hirschbein Folk Theatre
A scene from "Hershele Ostropoler" (*Perhift Players*)

GLIMPSES OF THE CULTURAL SCENE

Beth El-Ner Tamid combined choirs in annual concert (*Beth El-Ner Tamid Synagogue*)

Milwaukee Jewry was a Workmen's Educational Club which first met on New Year's Day, 1892, in Freie Gemeinde Hall. This group had close connections with the German radical elements, who were about to organize Milwaukee's Social Democratic Party.[2]

On February 19, 1892, the *Freie Arbeiter Stimme* carried a note announcing that Israel Glassman was about to marry into a wealthy German Christian family. The local press was supposedly upset that a Jew and an anarchist should penetrate into proper society. His father-in-law reportedly gave Glassman a $1000 wedding gift, and the bridegroom spent some of it on a party for his German socialist friends. Glassman thereupon disappeared from sight, as did the organizations which he zealously built.[3]

ZIONIST BEGINNINGS

The first hint of the later Zionist movement appeared in the Milwaukee press in January, 1891, when the Blackstone petition was presented to President Harrison by several hundred Christian clergymen and public figures. Their request that he promote international recognition of Jewish rights to Palestine made little impression. A few years later, in November, 1895, Rabbi Joseph Album of Jerusalem and Chicago came to Milwaukee to organize Hovevey Zion groups, to foster Jewish colonization in Palestine. At a mass meeting at Beth Mamidrosh Hagodol he was joined by Rabbi Victor Caro. A Hovevey Zion society was organized, but soon sank into dormancy.[4]

Theodor Herzl published his *Jewish State* in 1896; the first Zionist Congress met in 1897; American Zionism, divided between the Federation of American Zionists in the East and the Order of the Knights of Zion in the West, was founded in 1898. Early in February, 1899, Zionism came to Milwaukee, as Gate No. 8 of the Order of the Knights of Zion. A group of young men met in the home of A. B. Welitzky, a Hebrew teacher, including Shnell, Safer, M. Manhoff, I. M. Shapiro, J. Saffro, J. Previant, Z. Perlman. Later in that month, President Bernard Horwich and other Knights of Zion officers came from Chicago to the first public meeting of Gate No. 8, held at Lipp's Hall.[5] With this event, Zionism commenced an uninterrupted history in Milwaukee. By 1902, Gate No. 8 had taken the name of Judah haLevi, after the medieval Hebrew poet, philosopher and lover of Zion. The group usually met twice monthly, most often in the Beth Hamidrosh Hagodol. From the time of his return to Milwaukee in 1902, Rabbi Scheinfeld became a leader. By 1902, two more Knights of Zion "Gates" existed in Milwaukee: Ahavath Zion enrolled 75 members, and Dr. Karo had 21, and the Judah haLevi group counted 170 members. With Milwaukee Jewry's 266 enrolled Zionists constituting a large proportion of the entire Order's 2,249 shekel-paying members,[6] the city was the scene of its fifth convention, beginning on January 3, 1903. Mayor David Rose, a wily Democrat and florid orator, opened the proceedings with words of greeting and sympathy:

> In our city we have a cosmopolitan people . . . we have no more progressive, thrifty, and public-spirited citizens than the Hebrews . . . Your people never transgress the laws, they are never found in our almshouses.

In addition to this unusual praise, the Mayor reassured the delegates, assembled from the breadth of the Middle West, upon a touchy point:

> I do not hesitate to say that no good American citizen does wrong to his citizenship in enrolling himself in the cause you represent. . . . Your banding yourselves together to alleviate the suffering of those who are bound to you by blood, tradition and history is noble. . . .[7]

At the convention, Rabbi Scheinfeld spoke "on the development of the Hebrew language"[8] and was elected a Second Vice Grand Master. Milwaukee Zionist membership did not rise above its peak of 1903, even during the World War years. Judah haLevi remained the main group, and other groups passed across the scene. Of interest was "Company B, Volunteers of Zion," a youthful group which dressed in uniforms and apparently had a band.[9] In 1916, Judah haLevi had 101 members, and the Hatikvah and Brandeis 42 each; the entire Knights of Zion counted 4375.[10]

The pioneer Zionists in Milwaukee had two tasks, educational and financial. The vivid contents of some early posters most clearly summarize the aims of the movement as they were presented to immigrant Jewry in Milwaukee:[11]

> Are you in sympathy with the movement to bring Jewish life into the land of our ancestors and our hope? A hope which we have not given up for 2000 years? Do you want to help in the development and spread of Hebrew thought and the Hebrew language? Do you want to be considered as a participant in the great national labor of firmly establishing the Jewish people as one body?

The purchase of a Zionist shekel could show loyalty to the great ideal. The total of the shekalim sold throughout the world

> shows the world the number of Jews who demand that the Land of Israel shall belong to the People of Israel.

The strength of the opposition, especially within the Jewish camp, was not overlooked:

> Assimilationists and common youthful idlers abound, and they work with destructive force against the survival of the Jewish people. In which camp do you belong? Are you for a Jewish people? Then
> ### BUY A SHEKEL!

Zionism was an answer to omnipresent assimilation, and to abandonment of Jewish culture by immigrants' children:

> OUR PEOPLE IS IN DANGER OF DECLINE IF WE REMAIN INDIFFERENT to the present conditions and changes in life, and *naygung* of our younger generation.

To this peril, the sole remedy was

> to build up a Jewish people and Jewish life in Palestine. There we can have our own way of life; there our children can attend our schools, study in our own tongue, till our own soil, our own cities and history. Such a kind of Jewish life in our Holy Land will have the right effect in keeping the Jewish people united in one strong body.

JUST THIS IS THE PURPOSE OF THE ZIONIST MOVEMENT.

During its early years, before the Balfour Declaration and the practical achievements in the Jewish homeland, Zionism could only be theoretical in its appeal. The movement had to attract support by the contrast between the realities of the Diaspora and the glowing hopes in Palestine. The Milwaukee Zionist who wrote these appeals looked upon Zionism as a cultural and spiritual movement to preserve and elevate Jewry, and a bulwark against assimilation.

Fund-raising also filled the days of the pre-World War Zionists of Milwaukee.

No meeting was complete without its collection for the premier fund, the Jewish National Fund. Special collections supported such early institutions as the Bezalel art school and museum, and the Hebrew gymnasium of Tel Aviv.[12] While not a fund, the Zionist shekel was also sold energetically. The Jewish Colonial Bank, Herzl's chosen instrument for large-scale development of the homeland, also sold its shares. Because the few dollars needed to purchase an equity was beyond the reach of many, "Share clubs" were founded, whose members pooled their treasuries. In 1902, 299 shares in the Colonial Bank were sold in Milwaukee.[13] Occasions when the Bank paid dividends were converted into public ceremonies, to show the viability of the Zionist cause.[14]

The growth of Zionism in the Jewish community passed without interest or sympathy from the native Milwaukee Jews. While the native Jews of the United States showed little warmth towards the movement before the Balfour Declaration, numerous individuals, uninterested in Jewish communal routine, were attracted to Zionism by its visionary boldness and its acute analysis of Jewish life. In Milwaukee, however, no native Jew of standing became connected with Zionism.

Although they were immigrants, the Knights of Zion learned the ways of politics, and did not hesitate to become embroiled with Mayor Emil Seidel upon one occasion when they thought he had given them offense. Before a convention was to be held in Milwaukee from December 31, 1910 to January 2, 1911, two members went to City Hall to invite the Mayor to greet the assemblage in person, and after a long wait, one, Joseph Previant, invited him orally. Previant later claimed that Mayor Seidel said "he would be present if possible," while the latter said that only his secretary, Carl Sandburg, had seen the Zionist spokesman, and informed him that the Mayor had conflicting engagements. In any case, Mayor Seidel did not greet the Knights of Zion either in person or by message. This was contrary to custom in the convention-hungry city, and the local Zionists were incensed. Not only they, but Poale Zion, fellow-Socialists of Seidel, passed a fiery resolution. Observing that, with fitting civic patriotism, they had drawn the convention to Milwaukee, the "Zion council" considered his negligence "as misbecoming [sic] and as a direct insult to the Jewish community of Milwaukee." Mayor Seidel retorted that if the Zionists thought themselves insulted "they are not telling the truth. A few politicians are stirring them up, because they think it is a good slap and the rest of the members are deceived."[15] The tempest died down quickly.

Sometimes Zionist leaders came to town. In 1913, Nahum Sokolow, the great Hebrew journalist, orator, and polyhistor, appeared in the city.[16] Dr. Shmarya Levin, the orator and thinker, and the Boston lawyer Louis D. Brandeis, appeared in November, 1914, during their transcontinental tour. President Wilson's confidant was also received as a guest of the native Jews. In Brandeis' words:

> The Milwaukee meeting also was successful. We had a dinner before the meeting with the Germans, who really had no sympathy with the Zionist movement, and one who came to it merely out of personal regard for me—one of them being interested in the Independent Shoe Machinery fight—another in the Fair Trade. The leader of the German community there stated to me at the dinner that he was opposed to Zionism, and no argument could move him; but when I got through my talk, he said that I had converted him, and I think that was true of some of the others. . . .[17]

Brandeis had even less difficulty, we may assume, with the largely "converted" Jews who filled Plankinton Auditorium to hear him and the famous Yiddish spellbinder. However, the German Jews were not all converted, to judge by Rabbi Charles Levi's unopposed invitation to the Board of his Temple, in 1918, to endorse as individuals the abortive anti-Zionist League of American Jews.[18]

SOCIALIST ZIONISM

The Knights of Zion were a mainly middle-class organization, and their appeal was strongly traditional in nature. To the traditional Jews and others who constituted their main membership, Zionism recalled ancient religious hopes. On the other hand, the socialist Poale Zion presented a radical appeal and a decided break with Jewish tradition. Poale Zion appeared upon the Milwaukee scene with *éclat* in 1906, when a large emigration of Russian Jewish intelligentsia arrived in America, driven from the land of the Czars by the *débâcle* of the Revolution of 1905, and the chain of pogroms which the Russian autocracy organized to crush the movement for liberty. Many of these young men fitted well into the Milwaukee atmosphere, where the Social Democratic Party was gathering strength and LaFollette's Progressivism was likewise making Wisconsin a state of national political significance.

Within one year, in 1907, Poale Zion enrolled 94 members.[19] Their public meetings were often stirring affairs, featuring debates between the speaker and articulate opponents. Poale Zion speakers had to reconcile the Socialist doctrine of class struggle with Jewish national aspirations, and maintain the necessity of Palestine while rejecting religious tradition.[20] Thus Bella Pevsner lectured first on "The Development of Zionism," emphasizing the historic hopes for restoration. Upon this occasion she had to refute a Territorialist "brought especially from Chicago." Next came a lecture on "Class Struggle and Poale Zionism," emphasizing how orthodox Socialist theory required a Zionist solution for the Jews. Miss Pevsner closed by speaking upon "The Woman's Role in Various Freedom Movements and Her Present Task."[20A] When D. Aberson appeared in the Spring of 1907, he spoke on "Zionism and Territorialism," "Socialism and Nationalism," and "The Paths Which Lead to Zion." While the Knights of Zion met little articulate opposition, Poale Zion contended with the opposition of another full-fledged Jewish ideology, that of the anti-Zionist Jewish Socialist Bund. The ideological war gave an electric tension to every meeting, where each side attempted to expose the fallacies of the other. Louis Perchonok (1888-1949) recalled Poale Zion's expectancy and elation when they secured the oratorical services of Daniel Aberson:

> As soon as Aberson was given the floor, we began to enjoy hours of pleasure, pride, and satisfaction. The audience could long not forget the profound impression.

Later the Opposition entered the crowded hall.

> After the lecture, the opponents raised a few debating points, which they shot forth, of course, from their Marx, Engels, and Kropotkin. One debater in particular presented himself as a fellow-townsman of Aberson's from Mohilev. He regretted that so learned and intelligent a young man occupied himself with mere fantasies, and recommended that Aberson read through Karl Marx' *Capital*. Then he would begin to understand what socialism is.

Aberson triumphantly refuted his fellow-immigrant from Mohilev, and all others. The audience, which had paid 10 cents admission, went home satisfied that Socialist Zionism had bested its socialist opponents. The young Poale Zionists exulted that they had made their mark in Milwaukee Jewry.

> We had the guest [Aberson] with us for three days. As our comrades expressed it, these were the most festive days in our lives.[21]

Poale Zion enjoyed generally cordial connections with non-socialist Zionists, using the Knights of Zion's hall for meetings, and securing Rabbi Scheinfeld as a speaker. (Dr. Adolph Hess, a Russian immigrant physician, worked devotedly for both groups until his early death in 1907.) But it also insisted upon demonstrating its Socialism. In 1907, a Poale Zion-Judah haLevi Gate picnic was nearly abandoned, because they insisted on marching to the picnic grounds behind the red flag. Poale Zion compromised by surrendering the flag, but played Socialist marching music.[22]

Poale Zion were also occupied in raising funds for their organ, the *Idisher Kemfer*, and the Palestine Labor Fund to aid the Jewish workingmen and labor colonies in Palestine.[23] Of the $51.00 which the Palestine Labor Fund raised in 1910, $45.95 is accounted for:[24]

Amount	Donors	Total
$1.00	2	$2.00
.50	17	8.50
.35	1	.35
.25	104	26.00
smaller	amounts	9.10
		$45.95

Poale Zionists regarded their door-to-door solicitation as an opportunity to spread their teachings.

Milwaukee contributed not only money to embryonic labor Palestine, but at least one early pioneer. On November 20, 1907, his fellow-Socialist Zionists held a modest banquet to bid farewell to Palman before his impending departure. Palman explained that "not economic conditions, but strivings for freedom compelled him to emigrate from Russia to America. Coming to America, he did not find there the freedom for which he strove. He found there the same Exile although a bit more nicely decorated—but still Exile. And therefore he is now going to Palestine, where he hopes to find true Jewish freedom."[25]

The Max Nordau Branch of the newly-founded Jewish National Workers Alliance (today Farband-Labor Zionist Order) sprang from Poale Zions in 1910.[26] The Zionist Branch sought to counter the attractions of non-Zionist fraternal organizations, particularly the Workmen's Circle, and to develop a complete Socialist Zionist milieu—social, cultural providential—for they claimed to be "true children of the Jewish people."[27] The ubiquity of the organization, its youth and verve, stood it well: "at every party or social occasion, the organization speaks up. And thus the influence of

Poale Zion grows and increasingly draws to itself the attention of Jewish workers."[28]

It prided itself on its proletarian constituency:

Milwaukee Poale Zion consists of true workers, with wives and children, who work a full day in a factory and are enthusiastic for Poale Zionism. They have not belonged to any party before.[29]

While Poale Zion was the spearhead of movements for Hebrew in the public schools, and for Hebrew and Yiddish books in the Public Library, it did not go far in civic affairs. Louis Perchonok observes that, as a recognized socialist group, Poale Zion was able to prevent the Social Democratic Party from nominating anti-Semites for public office.[30] They expected their people to vote the Social Democratic ticket.[31] Poale Zion's main role, however, lay within Milwaukee Jewry, where as a Zionist group, a cultural influence and a force for democratization of the community, its role can hardly be overestimated. Its role as a labor organization was limited; these functions were largely left to the anti-Zionist Jewish Socialists.

A Socialist Mission to the Jews

After Israel Glassman's short-lived organization of Jewish tailors in 1891-1892, Jewish trade unionism sank into near-oblivion for over a decade. There was hardly any specifically Jewish radicalism in the city of advancing Socialism until the disastrous events of 1905-1906 in Russia brought to Milwaukee philosophical anarchists, Bundists, Social Revolutionaries (descendants of Russian populism), and Social Democrats (Marxists, including Martov's Mensheviks and Lenin's Bolsheviks); a few Socialist Territorialists also came who could not accept the Zionist decision to work only towards Palestine as a Jewish homeland.

Many of these idealists had been completely detached from their Jewish origin, and immersed in Russian struggles. Now they had to return to Jewish life in some form, because it provided the only milieu in which they could work.

Probably the first Russian Jewish revolutionary exile to arrive in Milwaukee was Isadore Ladoff, in 1891, who vigorously opposed the proposed Russo-American extradition treaty of 1893.[32] Ladoff later left Milwaukee and became a Socialist writer, the author of *American Pauperism and the Abolition of Poverty* (Chicago, 1904), and *The Passing of Capitalism and the Mission of Socialism* (Terre Haute, 1901).

His secular rationalist conception of the coming social order was expressed in *Socialism the Anti-Christ* (n.p., n.d.).[33] Ladoff's successors agitated among their fellow-Jewish immigrants with indifferent success, mainly before Election Day. Sol Marshall, a moving spirit in this propaganda, summarized:

> There is very little to say about the Jewish Movement. A Jewish socialist branch exists here. There is also an Arbeiter Ring branch here; most are the same members as the socialist branch. Very little cultural and spiritual work is carried on. . . . Individualism, self-seeking, the neglect of political questions are indescribable. Pettiness and quarrelsomeness are also widespread in our movement.[34]

To a Yiddish socialist newspaper in Chicago (which he found overloaded with "metaphysics . . . abstraction . . . philosophy"), Marshall emphasized the lessons he had learned:

> We are living in America now, and American life and the American masses require enlightenment in the American style. You must give them reading material from American events. We are conducting the political and economic struggle here in America under completely different conditions than in European countries.[35]

The immigrant socialists adjusted their usual appeal to proletarians to attract the many Jewish peddlers and small storekeepers—a class which socialist theory considered inevitably doomed. The Jewish branch of the Social Democratic Party of Milwaukee claimed support because it "consists of the productive class, [and] therefore wishes to do what is right and fair for every man." It reminded peddlers and petty merchants that their prosperity depended upon the purchasing power of their working-class customers—which the Social Democratic Party would enhance. In spread-eagle terms:

> Jewish citizens of Milwaukee! We appeal to you to do your duty as a citizen, to your family, and to your suffering brethren. You have it in your power to place Milwaukee on the map as a famous city. . . .[36]

A few years sufficed to dilute the revolutionary ardor of the local Russian revolutionary refugees. H. L. Nahin's brochure *Constructive Socialism* (ca. 1911) shows reformism replacing revolutionary aspirations. The author, a Russian Jewish physician and Socialist who ran for office several times and was elected Coroner on the Social Democratic ticket, saved revolutionary appearances by insisting that reforms were merely temporary expedients:

> The rich and poor alike desire to have pure food and drink, good services and safe transportation. Then let us invite the cooperation of anyone whose object it is to improve conditions in these institutions. Let our high ideals not blind us to the immediate pressing necessities. Our long journey should not deter us from accepting the companionship of a traveller for one or two stations. On common and immediate measures we must compromise.[37]

Nahin proposed to create a socialist milieu, by such means as clubs and mutual aid societies. This the Jewish socialists attempted, especially through their rapidly growing Arbeiter Ring (Workmen's Circle).

THE WORKMEN'S CIRCLE

The path to the Jewish immigrant, whether worker or entrepreneur, lay in meeting his personal and social needs in the spirit of socialist brotherhood. Such a movement began about 1900, when a few socialist "lodges" federated in New York as the Arbeiter Ring (Workmen's Circle) and grew branches throughout the United States. In the Workmen's Circle's "secular Jewishness," the Jew who felt alienated from the synagogal environment could find a nest. Like the traditional religious society, it would support him in illness and distress, and arrange for his burial. The Workmen's Circle also possessed the moral advantage over independent lodges and benefit societies in that its member felt connected with something nobler and mightier—the struggle for justice to the workingman and for the triumph of the socialist ideal. In their way these hopes substituted for traditional religion, or for the newer Zionism. The Workmen's Circle arrived in Milwaukee in 1907, and grew steadily for twenty years. In 1916, it claimed 500 Milwaukee members, and could boast of disbursing $3,861 in benefits during the previous year.[88]

But the Workmen's Circle refused to limit itself to mere cash assistance. There was also large scale cultural activity, which made it count heavily in the cultural life of the Jewish community. During the heyday of the Yiddish lyceum, in 1915-1916, 5 cents admitted a member to hear Morris Terman, Peretz Hirschbein, Morris Winchevsky, A. Litvak and other notables lecture. That year's lecture series, conducted jointly with the Jewish Section of the Social Democratic Party "to raise the cultural level of the Yiddish-speaking public," reported 21 lectures attended by 5,300 individuals, of whom about 3,000 entered with Workmen's Circle membership cards. One wonders at the audiences which heard lectures on: "The Jewish National Question," "Religion and Socialism," "Spinoza and Bergson" (a series of three), "Hygiene and Medicine" (a series of three), "Anarchism and Socialism," "Political Economy" (both by James Larkin), "The Democratic Development of America," "Child Rearing" (a series of two), "Thoughts on Crime," "Ancient Greek Literature," "God is Justice," "Darwinism and Socialism," "Various Trends in the Labor Movement," "Military Preparedness in America," "Faith and Superstition in Life and Literature," "Tolstoy's 'War and Peace.'" The near-absence of Jewish subjects points to the organizers' desire to impart general socialist enlightenment, using Yiddish solely as the necessary linguistic means. The lectures cost $375.30, of which lecturers' fees were $268.00 ($12.76 average per lecture!). Few such lecture series in America could have mustered an average attendance of 243. The Workmen's Circle Lecture

Committee admonished its audiences that they had only begun: ". . . go to the books. Read and think about the aforementioned subjects. In the Public Library you can get Yiddish books upon all these questions. Then the Committee, together with yourself, will have done useful work."[39]

Of the aforementioned $3,861 dispensed by the Workmen's Circle in 1915, $1,400 was paid upon members' death, plus $285 for funeral benefits. Members could claim sick benefits up to 15 weeks yearly at $6.00; most "sickness" fell during strikes, for which there were no benefits. The branches paid out $1,949 in this manner. Other aid, such as "consumption benefits," and contributions to Jewish and Socialist causes, amounted to $227.[40]

The Workmen's Circle did not contain only convinced socialists. Led by the socialists in their ranks, many a lodge, composed of fellow-townsmen from Europe, joined the rising organization. Many members in the Bobruisker Branch 166 probably felt more attached to their old town of Bobruisk than to the doctrines of socialism. The earlier cosmopolitanism of the Yiddish-speaking socialists was slowly replaced by a definite Jewish program, especially during the first World War, when millions of Jews suffered as Jews, and had to be helped by Jews. As deep-seated loyalties to families and towns were stirred, the Workmen's Circle collaborated with elements whom they had long disdained: native Jews, Zionists, religious Jews. Group solidarity, not class consciousness, ruled the day. No less Jewish was the secular Yiddish school which the Workmen's Circle opened.

By the War period the Workmen's Circle wanted a "lyceum" of its own, rather than have constantly to rent Vizay's Hall or the North Side Auditorium. The Lyceum would have meeting rooms, a reading room, classrooms for its school, and facilities available to other organizations. After the War emergency had passed and the Workmen's Circle numbered in its midst men who were employers of workmen, it acquired a large house for its lyceum.

Upon the national organization's 25th anniversary in 1925, the Workmen's Circle had four branches in Milwaukee, numbered 166, 425, 484, and 549. Founded in 1907, 1910, 1913, and 1918 respectively, they enrolled 353 members in an organization of 84,791 people. By then, the main local activities were cultural, charitable, and educational.[41] Russians' affairs still profoundly interested the Medem Branch 166, some of whom were veterans of the Russian underground in the days of the Czar.

JEWISH TRADE UNIONISM

The strength of Milwaukee's socialist movement lay in its firm alliance with the city's trade unions. Jewish socialists wanted to do the same among Jewish workers, and duplicate the struggles and achievements in New York, Chicago, Philadelphia, and elsewhere. While the human material was the same in Milwaukee as in the east, Jews of Milwaukee pursued livelihoods which did not encourage the growth of trade unionism. The native Jews held their union cards in general unions, while immigrant peddlers, junk dealers and petty business men were unlikely material for unions. Immigrants who worked for wages in many cases also belonged to the general unions in their trades. Consequently, unions composed of Jewish workmen with Yiddish as their language did not develop far in Milwaukee.

During the strike of Chicago men's clothing workers in 1911, the manufacturers sought out of town shops to take on their work. When the Milwaukee Jewish tailors learned that they were unwitting "scabs," they walked out. Despite an unknown gun shot, the strikers' rights were upheld by the municipal administration, which did not permit the police or the courts to suppress the strike. It appears that the strike was won.[42]

As an old center of the cap trade, Milwaukee had a Federal local of cap-makers which became Local 16 in the new United Cloth Hat, Cap, and Millinery Workers' Union, founded in 1902. It gradually succeeded in decreasing the 59 hour week by a half hour daily, and by a half day on summer Saturdays. By 1910, the work week was 53½ hours. In 1912 and again in 1917, the Jewish cap makers suffered defeat in strikes against the Middletown Manufacturing Company, staying out in vain twelve weeks and six weeks. In 1912, the union duped the manufacturer who went

East to find scab workers. The national Union's executive then posed as strikebreakers and received free trips to Milwaukee. To their employers' bewilderment the strikers met the "scabs" at the railway station with a brass band. Nevertheless, the friendly District Attorney invoked a city ordinance to force the deceived manufacturer to give each "strikebreaker" return fare and $2.00 pocket money. Yet, the Union could not record a successful strike until 1924. What it gained otherwise came apparently from peaceful collective bargaining.

The Jewish cap-makers in Milwaukee Local 16 had

> always taken part in the local labor movement and supported the Milwaukee Socialist newspaper. The local has also constantly supported its own and outside organizations during strikes. The local now has a membership of 40.[43]

The Jewish socialists of Milwaukee, both Zionist and anti-Zionist, wanting some share in Jewish trade unionism, aided such out-of-town strikes as the New York cloakmakers in 1910 and the Chicago men's clothing workers in 1911. Poale Zion, the Workmen's Circle, and kindred organizations organized a Jewish labor council which found work in its own vineyard in Milwaukee. The Jewish cap-makers, already mentioned, and painters and bakers were aided to organize themselves by the council.[44]

Neither the workers nor their friends could break the non-union bastion of the pioneer clothing firm of David Adler & Sons, where some 600 persons were employed. It had repelled all union efforts in earlier years, and continued this policy into the changing atmosphere of the new century. A strike in 1912 came to a dead end. Then the vigorous new Amalgamated Clothing Workers, founded in 1914, enrolled Milwaukee clothing workers in its Local 151 in 1916, and on May 2, 1917, it struck David Adler & Sons. On July 11 it gave up, admitting that its failure "had a discouraging effect on the membership. . . ." However, the Amalgamated Clothing Workers, rapidly growing elsewhere, began to thrive in Milwaukee. In July, 1919, the Milwaukee Clothing Cutters' and Trimmers' Union, containing the most skilled workers, abandoned the old-line United Garment Workers and joined the Amalgamated. On August 1 of that year, most of the clothing trade in Milwaukee, headed by the Adler firm, signed three-year contracts with the triumphant union covering 1,495 workers. All the companies, or all but one, were owned by Jews. The ethnic composition of Local 151 is suggested by the names of its organizers. The manager of the cutters' and trimmers' local was Henry J. Otto, while the organizers were Nettie Richardson, Anton Johannsen, M. Conwisher, and Leo Krzycki.

The settlement of 1919 boomed the Amalgamated's membership from 75 in 1918 to 500 in 1920, and 1500 in 1922. The Cutters' and Trimmers' Union earned $6.20 more per week, while the cutters received monthly wage increases until they earned $37.00 weekly. The other tailors' wages were raised 20%. The entire scheme was based on a 44 hour week, with arbitration procedures for grievances. Once organized, the Amalgamated Clothing Workers in Milwaukee were reputed "among the most steadfast of Amalgamated members." When the contracts expired in 1922, all employers but one renewed their agreements, granting a further wage raise of approximately 10%. Nine manufacturers employed 1,830 persons, and nine contractors employed 185. The firm which would not settle, J. & S. Polacheck, conducted a lengthy struggle, complete with an injunction and a losing lawsuit. Aside from this, the garment industry of Milwaukee was fully unionized.[45]

JEWS IN THE SOCIALIST MOVEMENT

The international socialist movement was wrecked by the national divisions of the World War and splintered in each country by the Bolshevik ascent to power in Russia. These divisions appeared in Milwaukee also, although the dishonest utopianism of Communists made less headway among Jews in Milwaukee than in other large cities, because of the disciplined strength of the Social Democratic Party. Young Jews who sought radical changes in the social order possessed in Milwaukee Victor Berger's aging Socialist organization and Robert M. LaFollette's Progressivism as powerful instruments toward the realization of their ideals. The International Workers' Order, a Communist secession from the Workmen's Circle, seems not to have made headway in Wisconsin, and Jews were not prominent in the state's Communist Party. During the notorious dragnet raids conducted by Attorney General Palmer, Federal agents swooped down on Milwaukee in January, 1920, seizing two victims who appear to have been Jews, one of whom was secretary of a local Jewish pro-Communist branch.[46] Joseph A. Padway represented the entire group as attorney.[47]

However, there were bitter feelings between pro- and anti-Communist factions. Walnut Street between Seventh and Tenth Streets, long a socialist rendezvous on Sunday mornings, divided into its north and south sides, from which rival factions derided each other.[48]

The Social Democratic Party's Jewish Branch worked closely with the Workmen's Circle in sponsoring lectures. Early in 1919, it held a joint meeting to advocate national minority rights "in all countries"—actually in the new states of Eastern Europe. At this time, the branch claimed 125 members. Like Jewish branches of the Socialist Party elsewhere, it was only a propaganda arm of the Party, not an instrument for expressing Jewish desires.[49]

The services of Jews to labor and socialism in Milwaukee were notable. Foremost was Victor L. Berger (1860-1929), an immigrant from Hungary in 1882, whose early ties were with the German Freie Gemeinde. Gradually he moved from German free-thought and liberalism to a socialism which was rhetorically revolutionary but, like the German socialism which was his model, was practically much milder. By 1894 Berger was a convinced socialist who helped persuade the jailed Eugene V. Debs to join the movement. He was the principal founder of the Milwaukee Social Democratic Party in 1897, and was its undisputed leader until his accidental death in 1929. Within Milwaukee, he edited the *Leader*, the Party's news organ; in 1911 he emerged on the national stage when a principally German and Jewish district elected him as the first Socialist member of the House of Representatives. From then on, Berger's career is more of national than local significance. He sat in the House until 1915, presenting the Socialist view with persuasive cogency. In 1918, his district returned him to Congress, and again after the War from 1923 until his death. While a Jew and representing a constituency with an important segment of Jewish voters, Victor Berger did nothing to present himself as a "Jewish" candidate, nor did he associate himself with the Jewish community. On the question of free immigration, of immediate importance to every Jewish immigrant, he stood behind the Socialist Party's restrictionist policy. Other questions of moment to the Jews do not appear to have interested Berger. Presumably he felt that no Jewish question existed which the triumph of socialism would not solve.[50]

Two Jewish lawyers rendered distinguished service to labor and socialism in Milwaukee, William B. Rubin (1873-1959) and Joseph A. Padway (1890-1947). Rubin, whose family brought him from Russia to Milwaukee in 1881, won a courtroom reputation as counsel to labor unions and to workers in compensation cases. He was also a vigorous civil libertarian whose political career, while always left of center, shifted among parties and factions. Rubin was interested but not deeply committed to Jewish affairs. Upon one occasion in 1927, he engaged in a much-advertised debate on the merits of Zionism with Stephen S. Wise, but the debate disappointed the large audience which had paid 75 cents each.[51]

Joseph A. Padway was born in Leeds, and spent his early years as a lawyer mainly among immigrant Jewish clients. Then and after he was actively interested in Jewish affairs, particularly Zionism and Jewish labor. Padway served briefly as a judge and in the legislature. He accepted expulsion from the Social Democratic Party for his willingness to enter a political alliance with the LaFollette Progressives in 1926. Later he became General Counsel of the Wisconsin Federation of Labor, and then of the American Federation of Labor. Padway held these positions during a period when the constitutionality of labor legislation had to be defended up to the Supreme Court. Until he moved to Washington in the 1930's, Padway's name figured actively in Zionist and charitable appeals. His partner for many years, Robert A. Hess, was a leader of the Milwaukee Zionist District.[52]

ZIONIST TRIUMPH AND DECLINE

After the World War, Milwaukee Socialism never recaptured
the hope and vigor of its earlier days, and gradually resigned itself
to being a merely local movement with local goals. To Zionists,
the devastation of European Jewry was accompanied by the
Balfour Declaration's promise of British aid to the Jewish National Home. The granting of the Declaration was enthusiastically
greeted at a local meeting.[53] As the *Daily Wisconsin* expressed
it:

. . . The element of idealism in the Zionist movement appeals
irresistibly to the imagination, and gentiles of all lands, as well as
the descendants of Israel, are watching the outcome of the
splendid experiment with lively interest and sympathy.[54]

From Milwaukee came several who did not wish merely to be
"watching the outcome," but to be participating in it as well. We
know of 4,961 applicants for emigration to Palestine from the
United States and Canada in 1918-1919, 86 per cent of whom
were under 45 years of age, and possessed an average capital of
$3,115; among them were 72 Wisconsin Zionists.[55] Such Poale
Zionists as A. Kaplan and M. Dubinsky emigrated as did the most
celebrated, Golda Myerson Meir (née Mabovitz) who had
been intensely active in Poale Zion while still in West Division
High School. She left with her husband early in 1921. Her years
of girlhood and youth, passed among the enthusiastic young immigrant Zionists in Milwaukee, introduced her to the movement
in its most ardent years.[56]

American Zionism split in 1921 between the Brandeis and
Weizmann approaches to the development of Palestine. The
Supreme Court Justice advocated large-scale financial undertakings, while the European leader, in contrast, victoriously upheld
mass fund-raising under Zionist control. Milwaukee's Zionists,
innocent of high finance but veteran fund-raisers, staunchly supported Weizmann,[57] who came to Milwaukee in 1922 to launch
the Keren Hayesod fund.[58] Milwaukee Zionism in the 1920's was

chiefly occupied with this effort to raise funds to develop the Jewish National Home.

Acceptance by the Jewish community slowly came to the Zionists. While disavowing the political aims of Zionism, many native Jews endorsed its humanitarian accomplishments and were slowly attracted by the cultural and social goals of reborn Palestine. The Milwaukee Zionist District, a consolidation of the Knights of Zion groups, had about 250 members in the early 1920's.[59]

Poale Zion had a burst of activity in 1919 but suffered an unfavorable reaction. A project for a daily Yiddish newspaper, which sold shares to members, failed, leaving an unpleasant aftertaste. Shortly before the War Poale Zion had also organized a Jewish National Loan Fund. It operated successfully during prosperity, when borrowers could repay the loans which were generously extended, but it failed during the 1920 downturn. A credit union was established later, more modest in its scope.[60]

In the almost thirty-five years from the first appearance of Socialism and Zionism in Milwaukee, something original was added to Milwaukee Jewry. Their secular orientation, and their social and political alertness, raised storms of support and dissent. Each Jew felt personally challenged to take a stand on his ideologies, stimulating Jewish awareness and education in Milwaukee.

X

Education for Career and Community

EDUCATION, that path to distinction among Jews for centuries, was earnestly encouraged by Jewish parents. The old reverence for the study of the Torah became transferred in some measure to general educational effort. Moreover, education in America was not merely the acquisition of skills for an inherited job or the graces for a predetermined social class; it was also the stepladder to wealth and position, a means of social ascent. Thus, ideal and practical stimuli to education reinforced each other admirably among Jews.

The city of Milwaukee possessed excellent schools with marked local characteristics. A highly developed private school system was headed by the pioneer German-English Academy, which was attended by some Jewish children.[1] In addition, German Lutherans and German Catholics had parochial school systems, and somewhat later, the Polish Catholic community built a comprehensive network which combined Catholic teaching with the Polish language. Most of the German and Polish stock in the city apparently attended these schools.[2]

Public education, which originated during the German heyday, did not attempt to strip its children of their ethnic heritages. Beginning in 1867, the elementary grades studied German under special teachers, with an Assistant Superintendent of Schools, Bernard A. Abrams, a Jew, in charge of the program after 1885. Although the rule provided that pupils studied German "whose

parents wished them to study it," in practice "it [was] assumed
. . . that parents wish their children to study German, unless the
parents notify the principal of the school to the contrary." Thus,
30,000 grade school children, 93% of enrollment, studied German
in 1913. After Polish and Italian could be substituted for German
in schools where these stocks predominated, and after parents
petitioned for it, 2387 pupils studied Polish, and 770 Italian in
1913. Modern Greek was added in 1916.[3] This language policy
helped to knit the cultural fabric which had been torn in many
immigrant homes.

Several public schools contained a large proportion or a majority of Jewish children on their rolls. Around 1914, 90% of the
children at the Ninth Street School, next to the Abraham Lincoln
House, were absent on Jewish holidays, and at the Fourth Street
School about 85% of the children stayed home on these days. In
the Fourteenth Street school, on the western fringe of the Jewish
district, some 25% of the pupils were Jews, compared with 35%
at the Lloyd Street school on the southern edge.[4] The sample
taken by the United States Immigration Commission in 1908
shows that 91% of their children between the ages of six and
sixteen were attending school: the highest of any immigrant
group in Milwaukee.[5]

Most Jewish youths in the city attended the public high schools
for their secondary education, including the scions of prominent
families. Of the 514 Milwaukee Jewish school children counted
by Rabbi Eppstein in 1875, 404 attended the public schools and
110 were pupils of private and secondary schools.[6] Markham's
Academy enrolled such young members of leading Jewish families as Charles Friend, Frank B. Adler, Mark L. Patek, and Charles
Friedmann. Educational achievements of Jewish boys or girls
were proudly mentioned, such as Charles Friend's oratory prize
in 1882,[7] or young R. Robert Kahn's leading the Milwaukee high
schools' entries to the Inter-Scholastic Declamation tournament
at Madison, with Nathan Pereles, Jr. as his alternate.[8] Among the
immigrants, the completion of a high school education was sometimes a difficult achievement, in the face of many a family's need
for financial support from its growing sons. Some young children

were employed as newsboys before and after school hours, often to the detriment of their education.[9]

Laurence M. Larson, a Norwegian immigrant and later a historian, recalled his years as a high school teacher of native and immigrant Jewish students:[10]

> A strong minority of my pupils . . . were German Jews. Many of them came from cultured families and knew no citizenship, political or spiritual, except that of the country in which they lived, but some of them were not far removed from the culture of the Old World.

After this experience at West Division High School in 1902-1903, Larson met East European Jews at East Division High School, where he taught in 1905:

> They were darker, many of them, than the Jews I had known on the west side. But they all had the Jewish characteristics of energy, industry, and ability; whatever the racial mixture they were at bottom of Hebrew origin.

Teaching in the city schools early became an occupation for young men and women; as early as 1880, "the number of young Jewish ladies who devote themselves to the field of education is increasing from year to year."[11] Jews also taught in the German schools, among them Victor Berger, while B. A. Abrams was prominent at the German teachers' seminary.

College education was for the sons of the well-to-do, as a rule. Some young men attended the University of Wisconsin at Madison, while a few made the long trip east. Thus, Thomas and James Pereles graduated from the University of Wisconsin; Louis Mann, from Cornell (1877); Frederick Adler and Charles B. Schram and A. P. Frisch, from Yale (1881). The sons of the families of Mack, Friend, Benedict, Landauer, and Mendel were alumni of Harvard and took part in Milwaukee's Harvard Club.[12]

The Milwaukee school system, so accommodating to the German element in the city, and later to Poles and Italians, unbent very little for Jewish children. Venturesome Aaron Scheinfeld, then twelve years old, entered his school principal's office to complain that *The Merchant of Venice*, with its unfair portrait of a Jew, had been selected among Shakespeare's plays for study in school.[13] Immigrant children of orthodox families studying in high school found that absence from school on Jewish holidays would compel them to exceed the number of permissible absences, and they would then be denied promotion without a special examination. Immigrant protests went unheeded, and no voice was raised among the native Jews, two of whom sat on the Milwaukee School Board. The rule was relaxed when Morris Stern, an immigrant lawyer, joined the Board in 1916.[14]

One interesting attempt was made to permit Jewish children to enjoy the liberality shown to other ethnic groups by the city schools. In 1910, Milwaukee Poale Zion arrayed many immigrant organizations behind its demand to introduce Hebrew as an optional language alongside Polish and Italian, instead of German. The Zionist Socialists convened a meeting "to influence Milwaukee Jewry to demand what they are entitled to, and the present city administration will surely take the matter seriously."[15] Under the School Board's rules, a petition signed by 250 or 75% of parents in one school could introduce the language—a goal easily reached. However, the influence of the native Jews was decisively wielded against the proposal. President Charles L. Aarons of the School Board, A. W. Rich, and Rabbis Caro and Hirshberg sharply censured the movement. After a special committee of the immigrant groups took over the question, the petition for Hebrew was denied because Hebrew, unlike Polish and Italian, was not actually spoken in immigrant households.[16] Native Jews, eager for "Americanization" in the fashion of the times, saw in the public schools the major instrument towards this goal, and desired nothing even suggestive of a contrary direction. If there would be a language studied, they preferred German, virtually the second language of Milwaukee. Altogether, while Jewish children received a superior education in Milwaukee's public schools, their Jewishness was not accorded the respect which other ethnic groups enjoyed.

The education of the Jewish child did not end with the public school, for he had to be made a Jew. Native and immigrant sectors of the Jewish community both provided for the Jewish education of the young. The Reform Jews educated through Sabbath Schools in the Temples, while communal schools and private teachers were the rule among the immigrants, whether or not orthodox.

Temples Emanu-El and B'ne Jeshurun's schools met on Sunday mornings, from 9 A.M. to noon, and one hour on Saturday morning. They abolished Saturday afternoon sessions during the 1880's, and Emanu-El reduced its sessions in 1888 to two hours on Sunday, "to remedy the irregularity in the attendance."[17] Children of members attended *gratis*, while others could either pay about $6 yearly or plead poverty. The enrollment at the B'ne Jeshurun Sabbath School stood at 116 in 1875, reached 200 in 1895, and sagged to 175 in 1900; at Emanu-El, the 44 children enrolled in 1875, reached 150 in 1893, but declined to 100 in 1900.[18] Rabbi Elias Eppstein's census of 1875 had counted 514 Jewish children of school age, so that the 160 Sabbath School scholars of that year represented but 31% of Jewish children.[19] On the other hand, a considerably higher proportion of Jewish children did attend Sabbath School at some time. Besides, some children learned a few rudiments from the congregational sexton (*shammash*). Perhaps half the children among the native Jews had some exposure to Jewish study.[20]

The Reform Sabbath Schools followed a curriculum influenced by Christian catechetical methods, while retaining some Hebrew. The following was Temple Emanu-El's three year curriculum in 1877:

> Course by Rev. Spitz: curriculum:
> Second and Third Classes—First, first elements of Hebrew reading; second, translation of Hebrew words; third, prayers in Hebrew and translation in English; fourth, portions from Biblical history discoursed in the English language.
> First class—First, Hebrew reading; second, Hebrew grammar; third, translations of portions of the Bible and Prayers into English and vice versa; fourth, Biblical history and geographical explanations on the map of Palestine.
> By Benj. M. Weil, Asst. Teacher—In the first and second

classes, catechism from Rev. Szold's book, and in the first class, catechism from Rev. Dr. Wise's Judaism.[21]

When hours were shortened, the study of Hebrew was abandoned.

There were occasional "post Bar-Mitzvah" classes and special Hebrew classes and a school library. The highlight of the year was the picnic in June and prize distributions.[22] The congregations' rabbis were the principals of the Sunday schools, and also taught classes, while the staff consisted of "head teachers," who were paid from $30 to $100 annually for their services. Most of them were public school teachers, including B. A. Abrams and even Victor L. Berger, and the remainder were unpaid young "assistant teachers." The volunteers who remained to the end of a year were customarily rewarded with gifts. They were the "impetuous, frequently tactless, and nagging 'pedagogue' " whom B. A. Abrams compared unfavorably to the capable teachers of the public school.[23]

Sabbath Schools were an incidental concern to many, but a primary interest to none. From his extensive experience in Jewish and public schools, Abrams noticed the contrast and found the Jewish side sadly lacking. The children who defied the elements to "hurry to public school and pursue their studies there for five or six hours in a row" were different individuals on Sunday morning, when they "reluctantly enter the rooms of the Sabbath school . . . Attention and order on the one hand; indifference and often tumult on the other; good conduct and respect for the teacher in the public school, and here—just the opposite. . . ."

How many of the teachers who assist our preachers with the administration of the religious schools really deserve the name teacher? Besides some smattering of the Hebrew language, how many of them possess the abilities which would enable them to be in charge of a religious education. . . ? A better future can be visualized for our Sabbath Schools only if the school and the education committee will finally understand that whenever possible, only experts, men and women, who have chosen to become teachers, should be entrusted with the administration of the school.

The fault lay with the attitudes displayed by parents

who take great care to see to it that their children attend public school regularly and punctually [yet] keep the very same children at home for nonsensical reasons . . . A mere whim of the child, a party, a music lesson, are often considered important enough to justify an absence . . . a certain indifference toward religion is awakened. . . . The fact that often in the presence of the children the value of religion, in general, and of religious instruction, in particular, is judged in a negative way, and that even jokes are made on the subject . . . is still the most important obstacle which prevents a more efficient influence of the Sabbath School. . . .

Some parents "considered the Shames [sic] . . . a sufficiently competent person . . . for 'the bit of reading he can teach the children very well'."[24]

B. A. Abrams' words had validity beyond their particular time and place. Many of his observations held true in the immigrant world, where education in Judaism had been a pervasive and deeply respected tradition.

The private *melammed* and the congregational Talmud Torah served the education of East European immigrants. Immigrant synagogue charters regularly included "educational purposes," but their efforts did not reach far. The B'nai Israel of Hungarian Jews maintained a congregational *heder*, over which their cantor, Jonas Berko, presided, while Beth Hamidrosh Hagodol (Beth Israel from 1901) had a Hebrew Free School for a few years.[25] In 1900, there was a Hebrew Educational Society, whose president was H. Schlomovitz and Superintendent Rabbi Victor Caro.[26] Somewhat later, a few Beth Israel leaders rented a house and employed two teachers for a few years.[27] In 1905, Mrs. Simon Kander found that in the immigrant district around the Settlement:

We have 4 Hebrew schools; one is a *free* school. Besides this, 6 or 7 Hebrew teachers earning from $6 to $11.00 per week, go from house to house, giving religious instruction.[28]

Education by *melamdim* continued to dominate the scene. As late as 1923 "the number of children taught in private Chedarim and by Melamdim at home exceeds by far the number of children taught in established schools."[29] Most of these men taught Yiddish reading and writing, for many parents earnestly desired to see their children proficient in the "mother tongue." The ubiquitous "Bar Mitzvah teacher" provided boys with sketchy preparation for their great day in the synagogue. However, some private teachers were scholarly, capable pedagogues who would not cope with large, disorderly classes. They were among the first to stress the new educational ideals inspired by Zionism and the Hebraic revival. One of them advertised in the Yiddish press:

> Teach your children Hebrew by the same system as in the public schools, and eliminate complaints that it costs money and health, and is wasted. Do not search for a cheap teacher but rather for one who understands how to teach thoroughly. I teach beginners, six years old, just as in kindergarten—first, to speak Hebrew, and afterwards to read and write. In the course of six months, at one hour a day, I have taught the three children. . . .[30]

Ephraim E. Lisitzky arrived in Milwaukee in 1909, and likewise preferred to teach privately: "it was much more satisfactory to give lessons, where I was on my own. [But] income was unsteady. Tuition was little, and from it was deducted the teaching hours which the pupils miss, whether accidentally or intentionally. Sometimes a pupil discontinued his studies, and a replacement was not quickly found. . . ."[31] In 1923, the private teachers still kept school in "shanties in back yards, hastily put together at the cheapest possible cost. They are unsanitary, unclean fire traps." Their instruction was not considered much better, although their fees were higher than in the Talmud Torah. "The discipline was poor and in general both teachers and pupils seemed to be anxious to 'get done' with the business."[32]

From the Hebrew Free School the Milwaukee Talmud Torah developed. Ephraim Lisitzky found it "a typical American Talmud Torah" when he arrived in 1909: "a factory for Ivri [mechanical Hebrew reading] and Bar Mitzvah preparation, dismal and disorderly. . . ."[33] What its finances lacked in stability they compensated for by picturesqueness. The school's support came from "a kind of charity fund which was collected every second Sunday—two officials presented themselves for this pious deed." A good-hearted former country peddler made the collections.

> The two of them went out to make the rounds of homes, with the charity box—a red kerchief—in their hands, and call upon Jews, merciful children of merciful fathers, to contribute money to support the Talmud Torah teachers.[34]

The East European Talmud Torah had been a charity school for poor children. This background hampered the development of a satisfactory American Talmud Torah, and encouraged parents to pay little or no tuition. In the rather prosperous year of 1915, only 96 of the school's 153 pupils paid about $30 toward the weekly expenses of some $60.[35] The Talmud Torah was badly housed until 1914.[36] In 1915, it moved into a slightly better building adjoining the Home for the Aged, and then temporarily into the Abraham Lincoln House. In 1921, the Talmud Torah's supporters began to rear a new structure on Eleventh and Vine Streets. However, the area and plans were unsuitable, and the Federated Jewish Charities, which had begun to support the institution, insisted that it return to the Abraham Lincoln House to await a new Jewish Community Center.[37]

The Milwaukee Talmud Torah maintained the tradition of public semi-annual examinations, given by Rabbi Scheinfeld and other more or less learned Jews.[38] During Ephraim Lisitzky's tenure as principal of the school from 1916 to 1918 (he was out of the city from 1912 to 1916), the institution shifted to the "Hebrew by Hebrew" method of teaching, *i.e.*, the tongue became the language of instruction. Standards were elevated, and a few advanced students even studied Talmud. The school remained religiously orthodox, Zionist, and Hebraic. With Lisitzky's departure, standards declined. In 1923, two teachers, aged 39 and 55, received $160 and $140 monthly and dispiritedly taught Hebrew reading, religious customs and ceremonies, language study, and Pentateuch. The outlook was not bright.[39]

Other elements in the immigrant communities also developed

educational programs. The Socialist Zionists broke with the religious traditions which had underlain Jewish education for centuries, and educated children in their secular national philosophy. Their movement opened its first Folk Shule in 1911, and by 1915, 120 children were attending Saturday afternoon and Sunday morning classes in the Talmud Torah building and later in the Abraham Lincoln House. Their children learned Hebrew and Yiddish, Jewish history, and music, and much attention was devoted to projects and pageants for public performance. The Settlement administration was impressed by the "earnest fervor" of the "movement brewing to foster and perpetuate Yiddish language and literature."[40] Members of Poale Zion taught without salary; it may be assumed that enthusiasm filled the gaps in skill. However, the Folk Shule suspended operations, and did not resume until a later period.

These developments challenged the Yiddish Workmen's Circle, which was then embattled between its "old" and "new" ideologists. Since traditional religious or Zionistic education was unacceptable and some Jewish education was desired, they opened a Yiddish Socialist Sunday school in 1913, quartered at the North Side Auditorium. The children were taught a love for the Jewish people and its language (Yiddish), folk songs, and general sympathy for socialism and the oppressed.[41] (Nevertheless, some members of the Workmen's Circle gave their children a traditional education elsewhere.) The local synagogue presidents, scandalized, publicly warned Jewish parents "who think that their children are receiving a Jewish education, that such thinking is false." Traditional groups replied to the Yiddish secularists by establishing an orthodox Sunday school, mainly for girls, at the Beth Israel synagogue.[42]

The Workmen's Circle educational effort enrolled 80 children in 1923, mostly girls.

> No Hebrew nor religion, not even the Bible is taught. The instruction consists entirely in teaching the pupils to read Yiddish and in writing Yiddish compositions. Even for this subject no text books are used. The teacher seems to be an enthusiastic,

untrained young woman, who has become discouraged of late in her attempt to build up this type of school in Milwaukee.[43]

Approximately 25% of the 2,400 eligible Jewish children living in 1923 within the main Jewish neighborhoods had Jewish instruction. The divisions were:

Talmud Torah: 145 Children (55 girls and 90 boys)
Arbeiter Ring Schule: 80 (Yiddish-Socialist, mostly girls)
12 Chedarim: 250 to 300 (boys)
10 to 15 private Melamdim: 100 to 150 (mostly boys)[44]

The survey of 1923 formed the basis for the Federated Jewish Charities' entrance into the field of Jewish education. Its grant of $4,000 to the Talmud Torah in 1925 gave hope of broader communal interest in Jewish education, previously the concern of a small group of men.[45]

XI

World War I:

A Time of Hope and Grief

WAR CAME suddenly in 1914 while America was immersed in peacetime activities. The immediate interest of Americans in the conflict was remote, but in the State of Wisconsin Germany was favored. This was due not only to the large population of German descent, but because Germany appeared less as a militarist oligarchic state than as a land of emerging social democracy and public planning. These were ideals for which Wisconsin Progressivism had deep sympathies.

The decisive factor among American Jews was Germany's war on the hated Empire of the Czars, arch oppressor of the Jews. Germany's more exquisite forms of social and cultural anti-Semitism went generally overlooked, although men like Brandeis and Stephen S. Wise sided with the Allies from the outset and emphasized the menace of German anti-Semitism in its modern, "scientific" form. German policy in captured territories of Eastern Europe was also carefully calculated to win Jewish sympathies.

WAR RELIEF

Few people in Wisconsion more quickly sensed what war meant than Milwaukee's Jews. The majority of the city's 17,000

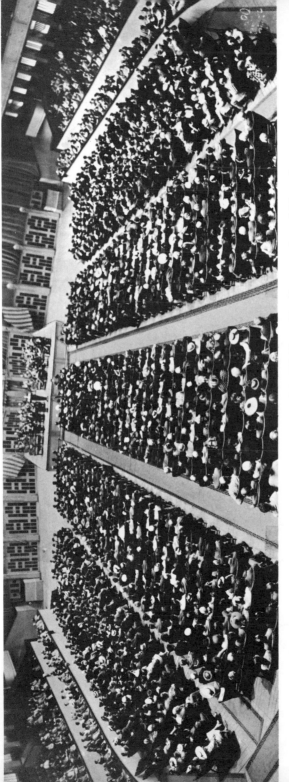

A mass meeting of the Milwaukee Jewish Welfare Fund campaign, Milwaukee Auditorium, June 3, 1940. The speaker is Rabbi Stephen S. Wise.

Ephraim E. Lisitzky, Hebrew
poet and educator
(*Mr. A. Slabot, New Orleans
Jewish Ledger*)

AGAINST THE STREAM
IN POLITICS AND CULTURE

Victor L. Berger, Socialist
(*Tamiment Institute, New
York*)

Alter Esselin, Yiddish poet
(*Sketch by J. Ribas,* 1938)

Jews had come from the areas being bombed and overrun by German, Austrian, and Russian arms. They watched impotently as brothers, sisters, fathers, mothers were stricken by hunger and disease, and were mercilessly deported into Russia before the advancing Germans and Austrians.

The first word of suffering came from Palestine, where the growing Yishuv was being atrociously treated by the Turks. A Jewish relief organization was organized about September 20, 1914, and decided upon Kol Nidrey appeals in the immigrant synagogues. Emotional scenes occurred as almost $2,000 was pledged from the Jewish pulpits of the city.[1] The relief committee named itself Ezer beTzar (Help in Distress), and quickly included representatives of immigrant organizations: every synagogue, lodge, Zionist group, Socialist society, Jewish trade union and tradesmen's association became affiliated. Nathan Sand (1880-1948), an active Labor Zionist and then an employee of a state employment bureau, was the idefatigable secretary through most of its eight year history.[2]

By the end of October, 1914, with $500 despatched, Ezer beTzar realized that its main task would lie in Europe.[3] Three fraternal orders, B'rith Abraham, B'nai B'rith, and the Arbeiter Ring, took up special collections or taxed their members, but this was an expedient which could not be regularly used.[4] A time-honored Jewish method was employed, that of ceaseless collection. Weekly house to house collections were made by volunteer committees besides regular synagogue appeals. Celebrations by organizations replenished the constantly emptying Ezer beTzar treasury, and hundreds of weddings, circumcisions, and Bar Mitzvahs produced revenue for stricken European Jewry. Passionate eagerness to raise more money was accompanied by irritation at native Jews who, many felt, showed little sympathy for the Jewish plight in the war zones.[5] Actually, native Jewry was removed from its European origins, and felt the effect of the war less keenly than recent immigrants. They contributed generously to war relief drives of the Belgians and Germans, although they undoubtedly sided with the latter. However, they took long to realize that the war had a special horror for the Jews of Europe, and their names first appeared upon the lists of Ezer beTzar in 1916. At the second wartime Jewish New Year, nearly $4500 was raised in dramatic High Holiday synagogue appeals, including the two Reform congregations and a few "mushroom" synagogues. That one of the latter failed to take up a collection shocked the communal conscience.[6]

In the fifty weeks from September 20, 1916 to August 30, 1917, the organization raised $15,550, spending merely $236 for expenses. Of this amount, $4548 came from house to house collections and $2018 from a tag day on Washington's Birthday; collections taken at weddings, circumcisions, organization functions and the like brought in $4006; a ball and a picnic netted $1651; the remainder came from synagogue appeals.[7] Among the immigrants, Ezar beTzar was a mass movement which functioned throughout the war with unusual harmony. Ideologically and economically antagonistic groups in the community worked together for the first time—a rabbi with Russified intelligentsia, small tradesmen with vehement Socialists. In the words of Milwaukee's correspondent to the New York *Forverts*:

> It is composed of all Jewish organizations, beginning with the most extreme socialists to Synagogue Jews, with Rabbi Scheinfeld at the head . . . we may rightly acknowledge that it fulfills its role brilliantly.[8]

The national labor groups were at this juncture increasingly dissatisfied with their under-representation on the central relief councils of American Jewry, and formed their own People's Relief Committee after futile requests for greater representation. However, the unity in Milwaukee was unbroken, for the Ezer beTzar allotted a sizeable grant to People's Relief.[9]

Not only money was raised. Early in 1915, the immigrant quarter enthusiastically poured out non-perishable foods for shipment to hungry Palestine Jewry aboard the U.S.N. Vulcan. Eight tons of flour, 1400 lbs. of rice, 1600 lbs. of beans, and other foodstuffs was piled up at the synogogues for shipment.[10]

Official "endorsement" of Jewish efforts came in January, 1916, from President Wilson himself, who followed the Joint

Congressional Resolution by proclaiming January 27, 1916 as Jewish Relief Day for war sufferers. Governor Philipp of Wisconsin and Mayor Bading of Milwaukee in turn proclaimed the Day for the State and city. A Milwaukee Jewish War Sufferers' Relief Committee was promptly organized and issued an impressive appeal:

> All eyes of the Jewish people abroad are turned to American Israel. Six millions of our brothers look upon their immediate surroundings as an open graveyard. We must act quickly if we would save the Jewish centers that are being destroyed, save the mothers and children who are dying of hunger and cold, the aged and infirm who are driven from town to town, shipped in freight cars like cattle.
>
> What is the answer to American Jewry in Milwaukee and Wisconsin to the horrors of helpless millions in Jewish communities desolated, of Jewish centers of culture and learning shattered, of Jewish industry paralyzed, what is our response to the haggard, terrified refugees, to the men, women, and children emaciated, who in their prayers, call upon the Jews in blessed America to save them, body and soul? Shall we withhold from them bread, water and warmth; shall we decline to drive away the plague of death that stalks by day and night? America ever generous says—No! Congress and the President answered—No! And are calling for five millions of dollars.[11]

The leading local Jews signed this declaration, which summoned Jewry to Plankinton Hall on January 27: "Obey your Jewish impulse—attend in person and with purse."[12] A prayer meeting at Beth Israel Synagogue preceded the auditorium meeting, where Rabbi Levi's appeal was joined by that of Rabbi David Lefkowitz of Duluth.[13] A goal of $30,000 was set and evidently raised.[14] Next year, inspired by America's entry into the war, Milwaukee Jewry undertook its first fund-raising campaign in modern style, with a dinner and a mass meeting, and a goal of $50,000. Dr. Judah L. Magnes and Dr. Henry Moskowitz came from New York, and Albert D. Lasker came from Chicago to the dinner. When Magnes declared that "those who have come to give should rise," all stood up. $36,000 was pledged on the spot ($3000 was the largest contribution) and the remainder soon flowed in.[15] Like the $30,000 raised the year before, this was more than Milwaukee Jewry had ever raised in one campaign.

This dinner also marked the opening of contemporary large-scale Jewish fund-raising in Milwaukee: a vivid, tragic Jewish situation, endorsement by public officials, vigorous publicity, careful behind-the-scenes solicitation of contributions, and a dinner with an important personality as main speaker to cap the appeal. Nevertheless, "three quarters of Milwaukee's wealthy Jews have not contributed to the fund."[16] In contrast, Ezer beTzar could take pride that hardly anyone in the immigrant quarter could escape its ubiquitous network. The two organizations worked independently until they gradually merged about 1920.

WARTIME MOVEMENTS

The World War gave impetus to ideas which had been circulating in the Jewish world for almost twenty years, and especially enhanced the appeal of Zionism and the movement for Jewish national minority rights in Eastern Europe. Movements for American Jewish communal democracy likewise gathered strength.[17] Immigrant intellectuals were joined by such American Jews as Louis Brandeis and, in Wisconsin, Horace Kallen, to advocate a central, democratic organization for American Jewry on the basis of direct suffrage. These groups called for an American Jewish Congress, to prepare for a projected World Jewish Congress which would articulate the post-war program of world Jewry. The Zionist hopes which were to be realized in the Balfour Declaration, and Jewish emancipation and minority rights in Eastern Europe were their main demands. The moving spirits of the Congress movement in Milwaukee centered in the Poale Zion organization, with Zionist and unsteady Socialist partnership. At a founding meeting late in June, 1915, Poale Zion met with the Judah haLevi Gate, the Arbeiter Ring branches and the Jewish section of the local Social Democratic Party.[18] They planned a local convention to nominate delegates to the regional conference in Chicago, where arrangements and rules would be made for the popular election of delegates in each community to the American Jewish Congress. The summer and fall of 1915 were spent in arousing interest, mainly in the immigrant community. Native Jews took almost no part in the entire movement. Their leaders in national Jewish organizations assailed the Congress movement, and local native Jews evidently consented by silence.

The first local conference was held at the Rumanian Synagogue on November 23, 1915, in the presence of almost 200 delegates from the synagogues, lodges, trade unions, and so on. Steered mainly by Poale Zion, the conference elected a panel of directors and delegates to the Chicago meeting.[19] Jacob H. Rubin became chairman of the local committee, which included N. Sand, L. Perchonok, Joseph Saffro, Arthur Shutkin, Isidor Cohen, M. Lazof, S. Schwab and I. M. Shapiro. Rubin and Sand were joined by Rabbi Scheinfeld, Joseph Lerner, and A. Burstein as delegates to the organizing conference in Chicago late in March, 1916.[20] Interesting to note, the Arbeiter Ring anti-Zionist socialists, whose national organization scorned the "bourgeois" and "national" Congress, were more receptive to it in Milwaukee. A majority of the organizing group was composed of Poale Zion and Arbeiter Ring elements.

The American Jewish Congress movement did not advance in 1916. Protracted negotiations lasted throughout that year but could not bring about agreement between the Congress leaders and the "official" leadership of Louis Marshall, Jacob Schiff, and their allies.

THE COMING OF THE WAR

The year of 1916 saw continued disaster in Eastern Europe and the approach of war in the United States. The belligerent armies uprooted millions of Jews from their homes, destroyed their life's possessions, and wrecked centers of culture and learning. A taste of military preparedness came when the Wisconsin National Guard was called to active service on the Mexican border in

June, 1916, and a handful of Jews was included. Like future mobilizations, there was personal hardship: wives and dependent parents had to be left behind on short notice. Frieda Mandel, a nurse, enlisted, while Rabbi Charles Levi then and later offered his services to the Army being recruited.[21] However, anti-War sentiment was powerful in Wisconsin. Morris Stern, an immigrant and School Board member who had served in the Spanish-American War, objected vigorously to the military tone: ". . . I would not want my son to read the literature that is now being sent out in order to obtain recruits."[22]

Early in 1917, Milwaukee faced the appalling likelihood that it would be called to share in a war on Germany, the native or ancestral land of most of its citizens. The city's German Jews, although out of the German cultural milieu, were lacking in enthusiasm, while the current of socialist pacifism ran very strong.

> I hardly believe that in any city in the United States has the breaking of friendly relations between the United States and Germany made such a powerful impression as in Milwaukee. Even greater is the excitement of the population at the danger that war may break out at any moment. . . . Wherever people meet one asks the other, "Well, war? Will we ourselves have to declare war? Shocking!" The peace movement has taken in all classes of the population. . . .[23]

On the brink of hostilities the Wisconsin legislature voted against war, 68 to 15. Probably no state opposed war more than Wisconsin, and these attitudes strongly influenced the Jews. The local Yiddish newspaper praised Wisconsin's Senator LaFollette for filibustering to death the President's proposal to arm merchant ships.[24]

The thought of alliance with the Czar infuriated many American Jews who had fled his pogroms and suffered his oppression. But all this changed at a critical moment, when the Czar was overthrown in March 1917, and the democratic government which replaced autocracy quickly emancipated the Jews. Milwaukee shared in the jubilation of American Jewry. During a public meeting, Ephraim Lisitzky "made mention 'in the name of all assembled, we greet free Russia,' and the hall became filled with applause. The audience clapped hands and pounded feet. They cried, "Hurrah! Bravo! Hedad!" Meetings and concerts celebrated the great event. The removal of the moral obstacle of Czarism made American Jews more receptive to entering the war.

When war was declared the great majority of the Jews abandoned any skepticism and opposition to support it. One reason was American patriotism, and another was unmistakable fear that any opposition by Jews would seriously compromise the loyalty of American Jewry at a dangerous time. When a large anti-war meeting was organized late in June, 1917—America had been at war for ten weeks—a report that Jewish socialists were also arranging a meeting caused the *Wochenblat* to tremble:

> That meeting must and should be cancelled. The war should not be made a special Jewish question. . . . it can result in much evil. It is not so much regarding what the Gentiles will say, but rather what such a meeting can bring in results. . . .

If Senator LaFollette would speak, as was expected (he did not), "he will not be arrested . . . At the Jewish meeting, it is possible that the speakers and others might be arrested, it matters not who they may be."[25] The Jewish socialists evidently held their meeting anyhow without ill effect.

Nation-wide suppression of dissent began in the fall of 1917, by which time Jewish opposition had practically ceased. On the other hand, Congressman Victor Berger, leader of Milwaukee Socialism, did not abate his hostility to the war, although more radical members of his party held their peace. Berger was re-elected in 1918 by a district which included the immigrant Jewish quarter, only to be refused his seat in the House of Representatives.[26] Opposition in Milwaukee to the United States' entry in World War I went underground and could be expressed only in the secrecy of the voter's booth.

Meanwhile, the Jews of Milwaukee contributed to the sinews of war. First of all, soldiers were needed. By the fall of 1917, masses of young Americans were flowing into hastily erected Army training camps, and Jews were among them. Most of the

Wisconsin men went to Fort Custer, Michigan, for Army basic training. While some men, like doctors, qualified for direct commissions, most, of course, entered the Army as Privates. A few joined the Navy, or the Coast Guard and Marines. Efforts were made from the beginning to maintain a record of Milwaukee Jews in the armed forces, but they remain only fragmentary. In April, 1918, Congregation B'ne Jeshurun counted 42 of its sons in the service and Temple Emanu-El, a smaller body, had 21;[27] immigrant synagogues and societies also maintained records. After the war, the Jewish community attempted to count up its men in the armed forces. By 1921, nearly 450 Milwaukeeans had been enumerated;[28] four years later, the Jewish *Blue Book* found over 1,000 from the state, of whom probably 700 to 800 came from Milwaukee.[29] Thirteen Jews from Milwaukee and eight from elsewhere in the state lost their lives in the line of duty. Two Milwaukee Jews were cited for gallantry in service, along with five others from Wisconsin.[30]

With the passage of the draft act in the summer of 1917, the war literally reached home. Weekly or monthly levies of recruits left the city constantly *en masse*. When 550 young men were bade farewell in mid-September, 1917, "Jews and non-Jews, old and young, all shed tears until the soldier train could no longer be seen. . . ."[31] It became customary for Jewish men to gather before departure for words of blessing and guidance. Rabbi Scheinfeld's remarks upon such an occasion in July, 1918 are worth quotation:

> All mothers hold their children dear, and all children have mothers who weep for them, and instead of hoping that our children should destroy the children of other mothers, let us rather follow the advice of Beruriah, Rabbi Meir's wife. And instead of cursing the wicked, let us pray to God that evil be destroyed—the leaders of war should recognize their irresponsibility, and bring an end to this world catastrophe . . .[32]

The draft affected not only single men, but began to reach heads of families. Organizations aided members claiming an exemption who were uncertain of their rights. The Arbeiter Ring engaged Peter Feldman, "the well known socialist and labor teacher, for members who wish to claim exemption. They will acquire all information and affidavits free."[33] Feldman, a young attorney and public figure, was to become one of Milwaukee's thirteen Jewish casualties.

Special recruiting took place in Milwaukee for the Jewish Legion. With permission from the Government, a drive was launched early in 1918 to enroll young American Jews in a Jewish branch of the British Army in Palestine. It seemed fitting that after England's Balfour Declaration, American Jews should aid the Jewish National Home in the Army of America's ally. In mid-April, 1918, the first four recruits were escorted down to the railroad station for the trip to Canada and thence to London. The young men were fêted and given gifts; the Mogen David group was created to keep in touch with them and send aid to the Jewish Legion.[34]

As far as can be determined, nineteen young Jews and one Irish Christian registered for service with the Jewish Legion, and at least ten actually served. One, Morris Strelzin, settled in Palestine. His was the solemn distinction of becoming American Jewry's first life sacrificed in the Jewish National Home, during the riots of 1921.[35]

Well behind the lines of battle came the enthusiastic efforts of civilians. United States participation in World War I called forth the most unpleasant display of hysteria in its history. In the State of Wisconsin some of the war effort had the appearance of a Yankee uprising against the German element, unhappy and insecure in their difficult role as Americans at war with their old homeland. The Jews were little affected by these movements, nor did they act as vigilantes. Within the Jewish community, a Jewish branch of the Liberty League proposed "to carry on the patriotic work among our Jewish brethren and to help our government in bringing about a speedy and successful end to the present world's greatest calamity. . . . We hope there are no slackers among the Jews of Milwaukee." It called upon all local Jews to march together in the Liberty Parade on Saturday, October 20, 1917.[36] Congregations and benevolent societies, as well as individuals, invested in Liberty Bonds. The Jewish restaurants on Walnut Street were pressed to join in the weekly "dairy days," a very expensive request for a kosher meat restaurant. Fulminated the *Wochenblat*: "If they will not become patriotic on Walnut Street and provide blintzes, knishes fried in butter, dairy kreplakh, and similar foods for the public—something is going to happen . . . the names of the slacker restauranteurs will be printed. . . ."[37]

There was the serious task of aiding the young men in military service.[38] Not only did Milwaukee Jews interest themselves in their own sons, but the Navy's Great Lakes Training Station, where several hundred Jewish men were to be found, was not far away. During the High Holidays, the Jewish community near Fort Custer, Michigan (evidently Battle Creek or Kalamazoo), had taken in the many Milwaukee Jewish soldiers as guests. Men in camp held services in the YMCA tent.[39] A detailed plan was prepared for any of the 1,500 Jews in Great Lakes Training Station who would come to Milwaukee, with each synagogue soliciting places among its members.[40] Early in November 1918, a portion of the United War Drive proceeds went to the newly-organized Jewish Welfare Board.[41]

JEWISH HOPES AND THE JEWISH CONGRESS

The Jewish community not only shared in America's war effort with money and men, but pressed with mounting enthusiasm the Jewish struggle, which seemed on the verge of being realized. Only a month before America went to war, a new Russia had freed her Jews. The ramshackle realm of the Hapsburgs was falling to pieces, and its nationalities were founding their new states upon its ruins. These new governments were expected to give group rights to their minorities, including the Jews. By mid-1917, reports circulated that a great victory for Zionism was possible because the British Government was sympathetically interested. The stalled American Jewish Congress movement finally scheduled a Jewish Election Day, to elect representatives to prepare the post-war Jewish program. The labor groups had withdrawn from the Congress movement because it smacked of "class collaboration," and erected their own National Labor Committee to rival the "bourgeois" Congress. However, the Congress movement was gaining remarkable momentum, and the national Jewish leadership had to accept an American Jewish Congress as graciously as it could. In Milwaukee the native Jewish leaders, realizing that their official leadership would be displaced by the potent numbers of an immigrant majority, joined it and nominated their own candidates. The adhesion of native Jews aroused some suspicion that the "assimilated elements, who have for two years fought the Congress idea, and have brought into it a demoralizing effect, are now uniting, when the great idea finally triumphed, in order to destroy it with a kiss of death" by excising the Zionist and minority rights demands supported by the Congress' leaders.[42]

After much maneuvering, the Congress nominating convention was held in Milwaukee on May 20, 1917. However, the anti-Zionist socialists finally quit the Congress movement, explaining that "with the revolution in Russia, the Jewish Congress has lost its main objective for which it was called. The Jews in Russia can do more for themselves now than we in America, for them."[43] Nevertheless, many members of the Jewish trade unions and the Arbeiter Ring voted in the Congress elections.

At the nominating convention, the Zionist-immigrant group put up Ephraim E. Lisitzky, Hebrew teacher, Zionist speaker, and later an eminent Hebrew poet and translator, and Nathan Sand, a Poale Zionist and stalwart of Ezer beTzar. The native wing nominated Rabbi Charles Levi of B'ne Jeshurun, and Charles Friend, a leading lawyer, President of the Hebrew Relief Association, and descendant of a pioneer Jewish family. Between March and June, 1917, Milwaukee Jewry witnessed a communal election campaign, something unknown in its seventy-five year history. Speeches in halls, sidewalk meetings, placards, and synagogue oratory filled the air. Their supporters declared that Lisitzky and Sand "do not represent wealth of money, but rather wealth of Jewish feelings, of Jewish knowledge, and healthy Jewish principles." Friend and Levi promised only to "strive to preserve and advance the security of our brothers in their enjoyment of the ancient home of our fathers in Palestine." They asked emancipation for all Jews, "and to win by force of public opinion the priceless blessings enjoyed by Jews in America for Jews everywhere."[44]

On Sunday, June 10, 1917, 4,123 Jews of Milwaukee paid a poll tax of 10 cents and voted for the candidates. The decision of the electorate, choosing between two sharply ideological positions, was eclectic indeed. The count was: Ephraim Lisitzky, 2265; Charles Friend, 2146; Nathan Sand, 2112; Rabbi Charles Levi, 1689. Thus, the Jewish electorate chose Ephraim Lisitzky and Charles Friend.[45] Although sharp words were exchanged concerning voting tactics, for an election without legal machinery and on short notice, this was a remarkably democratic achievement which has unfortunately never been repeated among Jews in this country.[46] Following the nation-wide elections, the White House requested that the American Jewish Congress not convene until the close of the war. The Congress did not meet until December, 1918. By that time, Ephraim Lisitzky had moved to New Orleans, and Nathan Sand, also of the Zionist bloc, took his seat.

The twelve months between November, 1917 and December, 1918 passed in an atmosphere of almost messianic tension and expectation. Apparently, incredible things were happening. Some months before, the Jews had at last won emancipation in Russia. When the Communists took over in the fall, high hopes were still held. The messianic year opened with the Balfour Declaration on November 2, that Great Britain "views with favor the establishment of a Jewish National Home in Palestine, and will use its best endeavors" to help to bring it about. The great Empire was backing the Zionist enterprise! Later events held disappointments, but this was breathtaking good fortune. The new states in Eastern Europe were to grant minority rights to their nationalities, including the Jews. As all this took place the bloody struggle was explained to hopeful Jewry as a war for world-wide freedom and democracy.

November 11, 1918 was a day not soon forgotten.

Milwaukee's East Broadway—Walnut Street—has never seen so many festive faces as illuminated it Monday. Children became pals with old people, and old people played with children, and small and large blew with shofars made of paper, storming and making tremendous noise . . . Close to 100 men and women and children marched through the various streets with Americans and Zionist flags. Near the Lubavitcher synagogue, Jews in *taleisim* blew the shofar, and in Walnut Street and Sixth Street synagogue people were reciting benedictions from early morning until late in the evening.

And late at night the people went to sleep, and with renewed courage they greeted Tuesday, in order to convince themselves that the freedom of yesterday has truly come, and with the hope that peace should never again be disturbed.

DISILLUSIONMENT: 1919

Within weeks Milwaukee's soldiers were returning home. But even before they arrived, the tidings were coming to American Jewry that there was no peace in Eastern Europe, especially not for its Jews. Reborn Poland's history was opening with violence against its Jews, while the tides of revolution and counter-revolution in Russia were bringing about a wholesale massacre of Ukranian Jewry unparalleled since the 17th century. A series of pogroms against Polish Jewry, stimulated and sometimes conducted by Polish army units, especially embittered world Jewish opinion. Other signs of anti-democratic and anti-Semitic reaction also disturbed the hopeful Jews of America. The murder of Rosa Luxemburg and Karl Liebknecht in Berlin aroused protest in Milwaukee, in which Socialist groups, including Jewish ones, participated. S. Rubin of the Jewish Socialists was chairman.[47]

The anger and despair at the violence in Poland was heard by the statesmen convened at Versailles. In no American city was there a more ringing protest than in Milwaukee's Jewish community. On May 22, 1919, fifty Jewish organizations joined a protest meeting, and still stronger measures were decided upon. The Jews of Milwaukee were summoned to march *en masse* into the municipal auditorium on Wednesday afternoon, May 28.

From Joseph A. Padway's law office the Protest Arrangements Committee worked speedily. Jewish storekeepers were called upon to shut up shop, Jewish students were invited to leave school to demonstrate, returned Jewish soldiers were told to appear in uniform, and a line of march was arranged.[48]

However, many Polish elements in Milwaukee were determined to uphold the good name of their restored fatherland. They vehemently denied that violence was taking place, except in allegedly isolated instances and against pro-Bolshevik Jews. A number of Jews, led by several who had their business in the Polish quarter of the city, also requested more moderate Jewish action. In 1917, the local Polish *Kuryer Polski* had asserted that "Poland is not a Jewish but a Polish land, and therefore the Jews should be satisfied with the rights that they have there . . ." It had recommended that "the Polish-Jewish question" be solved by "at least 80 per cent" of the Jews moving to Russia or Palestine, and the remainder becoming fully polonized.[49] It was not easy for Jews to trust later statements by Stanislaus Lempicki, its editor. Polish-Jewish relations did not begin in Milwaukee but in Poland, and the poisoned heritage made *rapprochment* in Milwaukee all but impossible at this time.

Polish propaganda in the United States argued that pogrom reports were "the best evidence that German agents in America still operate their game," in the words of Lempicki. Father Kruszka, who headed the local Polish Army Committee, agreed that they were "undoubtedly being spread by the enemies of Poland."[50] In Pulaski Hall on the North Side these charges were aired as a reply to Jewish statements.

On the day of the protest parade approximately 5000 persons of all ages were marshalled on the streets of the Jewish quarter. After zigzagging through those streets, they proceeded down Twelfth Street to Grand (now Wisconsin) Avenue, thence to Milwaukee Street, Oneida, and Wells to the Auditorium.

Following a band came two platoons of returned servicemen under Capt. H. B. Podlasky and Lt. Seidelman, and then a color guard of blue jackets with the Stars and Stripes, and then the Zionist colors, sky blue and white. . . . Thousands of women, boys and girls marched in the line, four abreast.

The assemblage "filled every seat in the south half of the Auditorium and occupied every available inch of standing room. A great crowd outside endeavored to gain admission in vain."[51] Both Mayor Hoan and Chairman Benjamin Poss emphasized the American rights of free speech which enabled the assemblage to meet, and expressed abhorrence of persecution. Bishop Samuel Fallows of Chicago, originally from Wisconsin, a Civil War veteran, spoke in the name of Christian humanitarianism. Other speakers, including several in Yiddish, emphasized the need to influence the statesmen at Versailles.

Several hours after this impressive demonstration, the largest yet conducted in Milwaukee by Jews, an overflow audience attended a Polish meeting at South Side Armory and heard reports of pogroms characterized as untrue, and Bolshevik in origin. As to the Milwaukee Jewish parade, Dr. Jacob Amsel, one of two Jewish speakers, dismissed its leaders as Socialists and its followers as ignorant.[52] The following day's *Sentinel* readers saw more serious accusations brought by a Polish Citizens' Committee in an advertisement. "Americans Reserve Your Judgment until You Have Proofs from Reliable Sources" was the heading. A series of rhetorical questions inquired why authoritative missions in Poland had failed to report pogroms. "We have many prominent Jews from Poland in this city. Why don't they participate in this anti-Polish Propaganda? Is it not significant that the leaders of Bolshevism in Russia hide their Jewish identity under assumed Russian names? Here follows a partial list:" Sixteen names followed, not all Bolsheviks and not all Jews. "It is true: Not all Jews are Bolsheviks—but almost all Bolshevik leaders are Jews." Three local Jews, Dr. Jacob Amsel, Jack Pinsel, and William B. Rubin, next exculpated Poland from anti-Semitism and "intelligent Jews of Milwaukee" from the "anti-Polish" movement.[53] This arsenal of potent anti-Semitic motifs, linking Jews with Bolshevism and German propaganda, i.e. disloyalty, was then being disseminated throughout Europe and America. Readers of the Milwaukee *Sentinel* could have turned a few pages past this advertisement to see an editorial against this "dangerous imputation." Observing that "anti-Semitism is eagerly exploiting and exaggerating the fact that some of the leaders of the Bolshevists Movement are Jews," the *Sentinel* looked askance at the advertisement it had printed: "It would be a strange anomaly should races themselves newly emancipated from oppression themselves turn oppressors of an immemorially oppressed race."[54]

Jewish-Polish relations in Milwaukee were dangerously reflecting conditions in Poland, and representative figures arranged a small conference "for the purpose of getting together on the problems confronting the two races in Europe, and preserving the harmony which has existed between the two in the United States." Those present were Rabbis Scheinfeld, Hirshberg, and Levi, Isidor Horwitz of the Yiddish *Wochenblat*, Nat Stone, J. L. Bitker, Dr. Amsel, and W. B. Rubin; Polish representatives included Father Kruszka, Professor Zowski, F. X. Swietlik, Ignatz Czerwinski, and Anton Tomkiewicz.[55] On June 3, 1919, the group met again, and urged President Wilson to appoint a fact-finding commission, and until its report "we appeal, in the name of our common Americanhood, to all citizens to withhold final judgment, and to refrain from agitations that are likely to arouse racial and religious prejudice which have no place in this country." The Jewish signatories included Rubin, Stone, Rabbis Hirshberg and Levi, Nathan Glicksman, Leopold Hammel, J. L. Bitker; Swietlik, Tomkiewicz, Zomski, Father Kruszka, and Czerwinski were joined by Father Goral on the Polish side.[56] The Polish Citizens Committee hailed the resolution, in a lengthy resolution of its own still infected with anti-Semitism. It blamed German Socialism for the "Jewish anti-Polish propaganda conducted so zealously in all American cities and throughout the world. . . ."[57]

On this bitter note the high hopes aroused during the war ended. Ezer beTzar continued, although diminished, as wartime unity gave way to individual organizations and individuals assisting their home towns and families. But thousands of dollars continued to be raised annually.

The first World War was an experience of fundamental importance for American Jewry, including the Jews of Milwaukee. It marked a final break with German associations and culture. The patriotic duties of war, as well as the defensive desire to show the Jews in the best light in a national emergency, pulled together the disparate units of the community. Socialists and bourgeois Republicans worked together. Moreover, the distress of European Jewry drew into the Jewish communal fold many who had previously shown little interest. American Jewry became nationally organized and internationally important, and these effects reached into Milwaukee, a city not in the center of Jewish affairs. The war rapidly acculturated the community's immigrants. They and their sons were called into military service not as a distinct group subject to special restrictions, but without any discrimination. Those who stayed at home were drawn into the common round of "home front" endeavor. American and Jewish affairs nearly merged in time of war.

The World War also produced negative after-effects. Fear of foreigners and immigrants oppressed a large proportion of the American people. This made for the spread of anti-Semitism in the 1920's. Certain Jews were afflicted with a passion for "Americanization," far exceeding the boundaries of necessary adjustment to American life. Over-urgent efforts were made to demonstrate Jewish "patriotism" and "Americanism," but had almost no effect in abating anti-Semitism.

PART THREE

Generation of Crises
1925-1950

Introduction

WITH THE REST of American society, the Jews of Milwaukee from 1925 to 1950 underwent a succession of shattering events. They enjoyed the glitter of prosperity of the 1920's, until its weak props buckled during the years of depression, beginning in 1929 and continuing late into the 1930's. An extraordinary burst of reform, the New Deal, exerted profound economic and social influence, and changed men's minds about the role of government in society. As a state having a long history of Progressive reform, Wisconsin was less startled by the New Deal than many other sections of the United States. But the fundamental shift in foreign policy, foreshadowing a world conflict which was to bring the United States into the center of international affairs by 1940, shook deeply the home of Progressivism. Wisconsin had been the seat of American isolationism, and abandonment of this historic attitude came hard. Four years of the greatest war ever fought by Americans decisively broke with isolationism. Young soldiers from the "American heartland" were sent to distant seas and continents, while profound changes were occurring at home. When uneasy peace came upon the world in 1945, the people of the United States entered a period of prosperity accompanied by world responsibilities and domestic restlessness.

The Jews of the United States, and those living in Milwaukee, participated intensely in these events in American life. They were also onlookers at the catastrophe of their own people, a barbarous campaign of scientific murder in which American Jews could only aid but not save. After the demoralization, destruction and dispersal of European Jewry from 1933 to 1945, the Jews of the United States witnessed and shared in a nearly miraculous renewal of the Jewish people in the new State of Israel. Between 1925 and 1950, Jewish feelings were stirred to their highest pitch since the birth of American Jewry.

Almost mute processes were transforming American Jewry during these years. The year 1924 marks the most significant single event in its history: the Johnson Act sealed the era of free immigration, and substituted drastic restrictions based on racist premises. One visible result was that by 1940, for the first time since the census was taken, the majority of American Jews were born in the United States. Other consequences were that English became the language of American Jewry, officially and unofficially; "Americanization" programs and other forms of immigrant aid lost importance except for relatively small groups of German and post-World War II refugees. The old, sharp line between native and immigrant Jews became blurred and began to be erased.

Among Milwaukee Jews, as elsewhere, greater social homogeneity was noticeable. Within these twenty-five years, the little storekeeper faded in importance, while the peddler and junk collector practically vanished, as their sons and daughters became professional and business people. The old Jewish district was liquidated, and new settlements replaced it in the northeast and northwest of the city, although the process lacked the dynamic intensity of cities like Cleveland and Detroit. Religious orthodoxy lost ground; Reform maintained its ground quantitatively; its interesting change was qualitative, for there was some infusion of long-discarded religious traditions. Conservatism, which in Milwaukee was closer to Orthodoxy than to Reform, made headway, particularly during the 1940's.

In the twenty-five years after 1925, the Jews of Milwaukee maintained and enhanced their position in the life of the city. It was no longer a matter of note for a Jew to serve as a judge or a high city or state official. When the anti-Semitic rumblings of the 1920's and 1930's were felt, local Jews were uncertain of what they might do against them; but the storms blew over within the city. Yet social separation and a certain amount of high-level social discrimination remained the rule in the city.

The Jews of Milwaukee raised their civil and economic status, beautified their homes and supported their local institutions satisfactorily; the average man had more formal education in 1950 than in 1925. However, they practiced a bare or superficial Judaism, and appeared quite satisfied with the meager Jewish cultural and educational facilities which were available. In contrast with the rather extensive Hebrew and Yiddish cultural milieu of the earlier years, there was a decline. The problem of deepening the meaning of Judaism was far from a solution, although there were hopeful signs.

I

Safety Amid Tension

POPULATION

IN 1925, about 22,000 Jews lived in Milwaukee. Twenty-five years later, the number was about 26,000. In contrast, during the twenty-five year period before 1925, the Jewish population rose from about 8,000 to 22,000. The population of Milwaukee as a whole during this period was as follows:

1920—457,147
1930—578,249
1940—587,472
1950—637,392

Thus, the city's rate of growth also slowed down during the second quarter of the century, but not as drastically as within its Jewry. Why was this decrease so extensive among the Jews? Most important, the accession of immigrants practically ceased. Other causes are less definite: decline of birth rate, emigration from the city, abandonment of Judaism. In 1923, it was estimated that 5,650 of the 20,000 Jews were between the ages of 7 and 21, and a fair projection would suggest that at least 3,000 more were children below seven. In all, almost half of the Jewish community was under 21 years of age, contrasting with the percentages for the city as a whole:

	Under 5	5-9	10-14	15-19	20-24	Tot. under 25
1920	10.0	9.5	8.3	8.1	9.8	45.7
1930	8.2	8.4	8.3	8.7	9.9	43.5
1940	6.7	6.8	7.6	8.2	8.8	38.1

During the following 25 years, the entire group under 21 would have reached, and some completed, the age of child-bearing. The high child-bearing rate of the immigrants thus contrasts sharply with the unusually low rate among their children.[1]

The other factors of physical and spiritual departure from Milwaukee Jewry left no clear record. Some descendants of early Jewish settlers disappeared from the Jewish community. Later generations of pioneer families in some instances died out, or nearly so; much spinsterhood and bachelorhood are found among some of these families. Instances of direct conversion to Christianity are very few. In any case, after 1925 the leadership of the Jewish community was no longer recruited from among people whose families came to Milwaukee seventy and eighty years earlier.

Leaving town was another, lesser reason for Jewish population stagnation from 1925 to 1950. Young Jews sought out metropolitan fields for personal fulfillment: a lawyer-financier like Alfred Strelzin, a writer-scientist like Amram Scheinfeld, anthropologist Sol Tax, and Sheldon Glueck, lawyer-criminologist. They went to New York, Chicago, and Boston; others moved where business opportunities seemed ripest. Few immigrants settled in the city, and the balance of migration was definitely outward.

IMMIGRATION

Following the end of free immigration to the United States in 1925, Jewish arrivals in Milwaukee became few until the accession to power of the Nazi regime in 1933. Then began an era of migration from disaster which extended until 1950 and beyond. Although the stream of refugees began to arrive in the United States in 1933, only several families reached Milwaukee before 1936. These few were assisted to come by other friends and relatives so that by April, 1938, between 125 and 150 German Jewish refugees resided in the city.[1a] In that year, a sharp upswing took place, caused by the annexation of Austria and vast Nazi pogroms in November, 1938; the rise was maintained until the gates closed in 1941. By then perhaps 400 victims of Nazism lived in Milwaukee of whom the majority had been in America barely two years.[2]

The great majority of Milwaukee's refugees had been business-men in Germany, engaged in sales, proprietorship or executive positions. Shoes, textiles, banks, and the cattle trade were their main industries. Professional men were sparsely represented in Milwaukee, with only three physicians, one academic, and ten to fifteen lawyers. For most of this skilled and educated group, find-ing a job was the greatest trial while the depression of the 1930's lay heavily upon the city. Men and women who had held re-sponsible and lucrative positions in Germany were compelled to become "practical nurses, unskilled factory workers, collectors, stock clerks, etc."[3] To refugee lawyers American legal prac-tice was *terra incognita*. The few doctors faced exclusionary policies. They had to return to internship and then take State medical examinations.[4]

Until mid-1938, German Jewish refugees did not seriously pre-occupy the Jewish community. They were still not many, and could be aided practically as part of the communal charitable program. In April of that year, the new Jewish Vocational Service took charge of resettlement cases sent from the East, and by the end of the year it had a much larger clientele, because of the mass departure from Germany and Austria. In the year ending June 30, 1941, the Refugee Migration Service of the Jewish Social Service Association handled 250 cases, who had overcome much greater problems in leaving German lands as the United States was being drawn into the World War. Between 1933 and 1950, Milwaukee Jewry expended over $252,000 for new Americans in its midst, aside from personal or private assistance. The Jewish community stood ready to adopt any German Jewish children who might arrive.[5] The average age of arrivals after 1938 seems to have risen, making personal adjustment and finding a job a harder task.

Not content with unaided struggle or dependence on the Jewish community, the refugees advanced through their own Society of Friends. Organized by 40 persons in 1937 under the leadership of Dr. Alfred Beutler, its membership rose to almost 200 under the subsequent chairmanship of Dr. Herman Weil, and became the New Home Club. As spokesman for Milwaukee Jewry's newest stock, it collaborated with other Jewish groups in settling German Jews in the city. At their Club, the refugees enjoyed each other's company, aided and counselled one another, and contributed as a group to the American war effort.[6]

The beginning of an economic upswing in the United States in 1940 made "a marked increase in work available to our clients. For the most part, those people who are employable have recently obtained work."[7] During 1940-41, almost half were placed in skilled and semi-skilled trades, and some were aided to enter independent business. Wages were often inadequate, and language and citizenship barriers still stood high. No account can do justice to the economic problems, vocational frustrations, or family tensions among the refugees during the eight years before German barbarity finally sealed the exits from Europe and doomed nearly all Jews who remained to an unbelievable fate.[8]

The few hundred Jewish refugees from Nazism in Milwaukee benefited from wartime prosperity and somewhat resumed their former economic and social status. Younger refugees, or children of refugees, fought the Nazi enemy as American soldiers. By 1945, these arrivals of the 1930's were a well-established group, and felt distinct from the post-war refugees who began to trickle into Milwaukee.[9]

From the war's end in 1945 until 1950 approximately 500 new Jewish refugees arrived in the city. Few were families with children; the Nazi "final solution" had seen to that. They were mainly single or recently married young men and women, generally younger than the German refugees of the 1930's. As a result of the horrors they had undergone, post-1945 refugees were more prone to be beset by personal problems. On the other hand, their relative youth and post-War prosperity eased their economic adjustment.[10]

The post-1933 immigrants did not influence the structure of the

Jewish community. Too few came to the city, and came without distinct ideas or ways of life which they wished to preserve, to alter the community. The New Home Club was the sole institution which they founded. Most of them thankfully achieved their aim of making a living and dwelling in safety, aspirations beyond the hope of European Jewry in the 20th century.

SHIFTING OF OCCUPATIONS

The majority of the city's Jews stayed in it to make their living. As before, major Milwaukee industries functioned almost entirely without Jewish ownership or labor. The beers that "made Milwaukee famous," the metallurgy which was almost as characteristic of the city as its beer, the tanneries—these the Jews had very little to do with, certainly not as workers. However, an individual like Sol Abrams became a Vice President at Schlitz, and the legal and advertising skills of Jews won them important positions. But these were notable exceptions. The Jews of Milwaukee possessed an economic profile of their own, which differed markedly from that of the city as a whole. In this, they resembled the ethnic groups which also specialized, e.g. Germans at the breweries, Poles and Hungarians at the tanneries. The city's shipping and transportation also employed few Jews, although the Leopold and Austrian firm had pioneered in Great Lakes shipping in the 1860's and 1870's.

In 1925, many poorer Jews were junk peddlers, fruit dealers, and tailors. In 1933 the figure of 300 junk peddlers is repeatedly given, and there were probably more years earlier in a trade from which Jews were drifting away. Jewish fruit peddlers were probably fewer. This trade had an active association of more than one hundred members, and probably others remained unorganized.

Several hundred Jewish storekeepers sold food, clothing, and the usual items of retail trade. Skilled Jewish artisans, such as watchmakers and shoemakers, also kept stores. A figure of 500 such retail tradesmen for 1910 certainly did not diminish before the depression of the 1930's.

How many of the city's tailors were Jews is even harder to

determine. The women's garment trade was of little importance in Milwaukee, so the main union was the Amalgamated Clothing Workers of America with 2,000 members.[11] We may conjecture that about one tenth worked for small Jewish sub-contractors and were mainly Jewish. In the large clothing firms, all (or all but one) of which were owned by Jews, there were also Jewish workers, including native Jewish artisans. Perhaps one fourth of the Amalgamated's members were Jews. One might add to this figure Jews who opened clothing, cleaning and alterations stores.

The clothing industry prospered under the terms of its contracts with the Amalgamated Clothing Workers. The original agreement of 1919 was renewed in 1922 and in 1925, with improvements for the workers each time. It was again due to expire in 1928, when, as usual, the trade was led by David Adler and Sons, employing 700 workers, four-fifths of whom were women. But an extraordinary episode put an end to stable labor relations. Two weeks before the contract's expiration on May 1, 1928, the Adler firm locked out its employees, and sought an injunction against the mass picketing which followed its action. The 700 workers sued for wages of the contractual period, and proved in court that Adler, not they, had broken the contract. But the workers never collected. Upon losing its case on appeal, the company abruptly liquidated, leaving no one who could pay the workers, and, moreover, taking away their jobs. Why the old and established firm, owned by the elderly sons of the founder, made this drastic decision is mysterious. The union had to find work for hundreds of unemployed clothing workers, who could not be absorbed into the smaller firms in Milwaukee. Its solution attracted nation-wide attention: the Amalgamated Clothing Workers itself established a factory in February, 1929, with guarantee of work from the giant Hart, Schaffner, and Marx firm in Chicago. Two hundred and ten tailors were employed in the union-owned factory for four years, until depression conditions took away the Chicago work and compelled it to close down. The remainder of Milwaukee's clothing trade remained within the fold of the Union.[12]

Retail trade increased in importance among Jews. Two of the

city's foremost department stores, Gimbel's and the Boston Store, were owned and managed by Jews. The dapper head of the Boston Store, Nat Stone (1866-1931), was a leader of mercantile interests and a principal figure in the Jewish community. Gimbel's was run by a son-in-law of the family, Oscar Brachman. Ranged behind these large emporia which were household terms to the city's shoppers, was a large collection of neighborhood stores. Besides the usual druggists, grocers, restaurateurs and merchant artisans, an apparently large number of Jews retailed new lines of consumer goods. Jews owned stores which sold radios and electrical appliances, while the home owner was appealed to by a group of Jewish roofers, fencers, coal dealers and repair men. In general, Jews were not actually the builders of the downtown area, but their financial and speculative activities raised capital and rented out some of the downtown structures which rose in the 1920's.

Two small associations of Jewish artisans, the Jewish Bakers' Union and the Jewish Painters' Club, probably had about 50 members each. The former group had won a major strike in 1918, while the latter collaborated with the Jewish Builders' Club, a trade association. In addition to their economic functions, the Jewish bakers and painters took part in the Jewish community, making charitable donations and meeting in the Labor Lyceum of the Workmen's Circle. Hard times in the 1930's, an aging membership, and the breaking down of the lines between Jewish and Gentile workers, slowly ended the existence of these interesting groups.

In addition to clothing, one other older Jewish product was prominent. This was the hosiery and knitting business, fifth in size among Milwaukee industries in 1928. Firms like Phoenix and Eagle were conspicious throughout the Middle West. Men like Morris Miller (1847-1931) typified the elder, founding generation of the trade; he was a loved figure in the city and among his fellow-Jews. The brothers Max Karger (1871-1959) and David Karger (1866-1939), owners of the Eagle firm, were not only successful entrepreneurs but maintained exemplary labor relations. A leader in the trade, Theodore Friedlander, sat on the boards of the city's largest banks.

Most of the above represents the older order of Jewish economic activity: a thin stratum of substantial merchants and clothing manufacturers, a mass of small tradesmen ranging from owners of fair-sized stores to peddlers, and a large group of working people. "Pyramid" is a misleading metaphor, for its human blocks were not fixed but mercurially mobile. Characteristically, a man's place was determined by his length of residence in the United States. Those higher up tended to be natives; the further down, the higher the proportion of immigrants.

In the 1920's, young Jews throughout the United States were gaining entry into the arts, sciences, professions. Technical and white collar work became mass employments among Jews, as the mass movement into higher education paid its economic and social dividends. Because of the problems which the would-be Jewish doctor or lawyer faced in entering and establishing himself in his profession this was not immediately visible. The depression, when even established professional practices suffered, was followed by the abnormal conditions of the war emergency. Even so, the main outlines of Jewish economic life were becoming visible long before the post-1945 years, when they became apparent to all.

In place of the Jewish proletariat several thousand Jews became clerical employees in offices, civil servants, real estate and insurance men, accountants, teachers, lawyers, engineers, physicians, dentists, scientists, and scholars. Jewish working classes endured longest in metropolitan centers, and were eliminated faster in cities where their numbers were lower. American Jewry, as a community, was a trail-blazer for nation-wide occupational tendencies, in which factory and farm employment dwindled in favor of white-collar, service, and professional work.

The strength of this shift in Milwaukee is seen in reliable estimates of the increase in Jewish doctors, dentists, lawyers, and teachers between 1930 and 1950. Although the city's 640 dentists of 1930 declined to 535 in 1950, the probable number of Jews among them rose from 55 to 70.[13] Similarly, the School Board's 2459 teachers in 1930 numbered 2418 in 1950, but the 56 Jewish teachers of 1930 ascended to 100 twenty years later.[14] The number of lawyers in Milwaukee rose and likewise the number of

Jews among them. Thus, the 860 local attorneys of 1930 counted some 155 Jews, and the 1500 in 1950 included some 250 who were Jews.[15]

Some Jews occupied notable positions at the bar. George P. Ettenheim and Charles L. Goldberg were Presidents of the Milwaukee Bar Association, while Benjamin Poss headed the Wisconsin Bar Association. Charles Aarons' judicial distinction will be noted, and Joseph Padway's eminent services beyond Milwaukee as a labor lawyer have also been mentioned.

The sharpest increase in Jewish representation occurred among the city's physicians. While the 780 practitioners of 1930 reached some 942 in 1948, the number of Jews climbed from 62 to 201 or more in the same years, as we know from a 1948 survey of Jewish medical needs in Milwaukee. The Jewish physicians were affiliated with the city's hospitals, particularly Mount Sinai, and were broadly distributed among all medical specialties—92 were exclusively specialists. These Jewish physicians were mainly (82.5%) under 50 years of age, and a substantial majority had completed their medical education after 1930. Interestingly, only 16% were natives of the city and 20% more had resided in it 25 years or more—the medical profession was rather migratory. Probably the fact that 34 had graduated from the University of Wisconsin and no less than 83 from Marquette University influenced many to settle in the state where they had been trained. In all, one Jew out of every 158 in Milwaukee was estimated to be a physician.[16]

Virtually all Jewish members of university faculties in Milwaukee were physicians and dentists at Marquette University, a Jesuit institution. In 1930, thirteen physicians were clinical teachers in its medical school and two dentists taught students of dentistry. Twenty years later, there were four Jews on the dental faculty, of whom one—Dr. Frank C. Margoles—was Head of the Division of Bacteriology. Of the 274 faculty members in the School of Medicine in 1950, 43 were Jews, of whom 36 were clinical teachers. Otherwise, the highest rank was held by an Associate Professor of Pathology.[17]

Outside medical and dental teaching, few Milwaukee Jews belonged to the local academic world in 1950. Four taught in

Der Zeitgeist, January 1, 1880. (*New York Public Library*)

MILWAUKEE
JEWISH
PUBLICATIONS

Wisconsin Jewish Chronicle, 1921 (*Wisconsin Jewish Chronicle*)

Beth Israel, dedicated 1925 (*Mr. A. Weiss*)

COMMUNAL BUILDINGS OF THE 1920'S

Jewish Home for the Aged, 1930

other branches of Marquette University, and a handful taught at Milwaukee State Teachers College (later the University of Wisconsin-Milwaukee). The University of Wisconsin at Madison did number many Jews on its faculty.

CIVIC AND SOCIAL STATUS

It was no longer notable in the 1920's for a Jew to hold public office in Milwaukee.[18] In 1925, Victor L. Berger was the city's veteran Socialist Congressman and continued to be so until he died in 1929. During most of the 1920's and 1930's the colorful immigrant banker of Madison, Solomon Levitan, was State Treasurer as a La Follette man. The State Legislature counted among its members Senator Bernhard Gettelman, a Republican (Progressive) from a considerably Jewish constituency, who served between 1923 and 1955, and Ben Rubin, Socialist in 1931-1933 and Progressive from 1937 to 1943. The Sixth Ward, center of Milwaukee Jewry until post-World War II years, constantly sent Jews to the Common Council: Arthur Shutkin until 1928, followed by Samuel M. Soref until 1940, who was succeeded by Fred P. Meyers. The only Jew elected to city-wide office was Max Raskin, Socialist City Attorney from 1932 to 1936. In Milwaukee's complex politics, the legislators' national party labels meant little, for they were all on the political left.

More common than Jews in elective position was service by Jews on city commissions. Thus, Harry V. Meissner was a School Director for 22 years after 1925. Other Jews sat on the Board of Assessments and the Board of Appeals, the Safety Commission, the Motion Picture Board, the Sewerage Commission, the Art Commission, and the Board of Trustees of the Milwaukee Public Library. Well before 1950, Norman N. Gill, Municipal Reference Librarian from 1940 to 1945, had made himself the non-partisan authority on municipal affairs, and was a storehouse of specialized information. Benjamin Glassberg was County superintendent of public assistance for the critical eleven years from 1933 until he entered the service of UNRRA.[19]

Charles L. Aarons, lawyer and past President of the School

Board, sat as a Circuit Court Judge from 1926 until his retirement in 1950. In this capacity he was perhaps the most representative Jew in public life, and enjoyed general esteem for his judicial service.[20]

If Jews were well represented in civic office, this was less the case in some quasi-public bodies such as the Milwaukee Association of Commerce. Only four professing Jews sat on its Board between 1925 and 1950—two less than in the years between 1875 and 1900—of whom three had minimal two-year terms. No Jew was an officer throughout its history.[21]

Beginning in the 1920's, the secure status of the Jews in Milwaukee society was no longer taken for granted. This was coincident with a sharp rise of anti-Semitism in America. Earlier outbreaks, such as those in the 1860's and the 1890's, passed Milwaukee with barely a trace. That of the 1920's, whose roots lay in the resentment of small town against big city, and the exaggerated fear of Bolshevism, made some mark. Anti-Semitism in the 1930's, bred by depression and propagated as part of the Nazi onslaught, held great dangers in a city badly hit by hard times with the Germans its major ethnic group.

Early in the 1920's, Jews in the city were disturbed by the sale of Henry Ford's anti-Semitic *Dearborn Independent*. At this time the Reform Temples pointedly invited Gentiles as well as Jews to attend their services, in the belief that exposure to the reality of Judaism would purge anti-Semitic sentiments. The rabbis spoke as often as possible before non-Jewish audiences for "good will" purposes. However, the basic attitude of the Jewish community as a community was to ignore or treat silently the whole problem. Accordingly, anti-Semitism in Milwaukee was very seldom mentioned, while publicly expressed anti-Semitism was nearly unknown. There seems to have been little in the field of education, for the two universities attended by local Jews, the state University of Wisconsin and the Catholic Marquette University, displayed none in the admission or treatment of their students. But it was common knowledge among Jews that certain banks would hire no Jews, and that in some firms the fact of one's Jewishness was an insuperable barrier to advancement. And certain businessmen's clubs in the city, such as the Wisconsin, would not vote in a Jew as a member, thus excluding Jews from the intimate business discussions which took place within their walls. One resort hotel which found itself labeled anti-Semitic took pains to deny using any such tactics, and to observe that its new management intended to maintain a democratic policy as had the old. Residential anti-Semitism does not appear to have existed in the city. Jews who left the old Jewish quarter moved further northwest without difficulty, while those who settled on the East Side joined a long established but less centralized Jewish group. As before, the South Side attracted very few Jews. Exclusionary policies do not appear to have played any consequential role in these movements.

The prosperity of the 1920's was very apparent in Milwaukee. The city's employment rose from 88,000 to 117,000 during the decade, thousands of homes were built, and a major industrial expansion visited the city. As usual during good times, the sharp edge of anti-Semitism and other hatreds was blunted. The depression years held dangers, especially when the efforts of Nazism were distinctly felt in the United States. The Hitler regime made special efforts to infiltrate American Germandom, and subsequently chose to build and subsidize generously its own American Nazi network. A Nazi Bund operated in Milwaukee, and there as elsewhere agitation against the Jews was one of its major activities. It is estimated that perhaps 15% of the population of Milwaukee were overt anti-Semites. They demonstrated their conviction by abuse or personal insult: anti-Semitic tradesmen to Jewish customers and the reverse, occasionally on the street, while at work, and the like. Physical attacks, however, did not occur. The same estimate holds that about 10% of the city's people were good friends of the Jews, and the city government cooperated fully in combatting anti-Semitism.

There were differences of opinion in the community on how to deal with the problem, tied into larger ideological considerations. The traditional leadership of the community, interlocked in the Reform Temples, Federated Jewish Charities, Mount Sinai Hospital, and prominent in the life of the city, preferred that the matter be kept quiet. Others, particularly among Zionists and socialists, demanded a more aggressive approach. On March 29, 1933, they sponsored an anti-Nazi meeting which 4,000 persons attended at Plankinton Hall. With Judge Charles L. Aarons in the chair, Protestant and Catholic speakers joined the Jews in denouncing the Nazi government in Germany, then only eight weeks in power. The meeting aroused dissent, apparently among those who believed that American Jewish activism might further endanger German Jewry; an "undercurrent of sharp criticism" complained of the "unrepresentative" character of the meeting.[22] Another anti-Nazi meeting, held late in 1939, included clerical spokesmen of the Polish and German communities. Ernest Goerner, a leading local Nazi, threatened the clergymen, apparently without effect.[23]

The domestic anti-Semitic danger, incited by German Nazism, brought about the organization of the Milwaukee Jewish Council in 1938. For several years the Anti-Defamation League of B'nai B'rith had informally conducted its work in Milwaukee through its chairman, Bert C. Broude. Another good-will group was the Round Table of Christians and Jews, which sought to promote good will through the churches. Rabbi Baron was the main Jewish figure, and liberal Protestant clergy collaborated with him. The Catholic Church showed very little interest, however. In July, 1939, Archbishop Stritch of Milwaukee (later Cardinal Archbishop of Chicago) addressed a letter to Rabbi Baron in which he denounced in rather cool, deliberate terms the attacks upon Jews being made by "certain individuals." Echoing Pope Pius XI's attack on racist anti-Semitism, the Archbishop emphasized: "At the bottom it is atheism."[24] Although the Catholic Archdiocese thus reprehended anti-Semitism, it still did not lend support to the efforts to combat it. Neither did the more conservative Protestant churches in Milwaukee join in. The active Christian associates of the Jews in the fight were Protestant churches of more "old American" sources—Episcopal, Unitarian, Presbyterian, and some Baptist and Methodist: together they comprised a minority of Milwaukee Protestantism.

The Milwaukee Jewish Council[25] did not debate with anti-

Semites, but attempted to channel the democratic traditions of the community against anti-Semitism and against group hatreds generally. Commencing its activities on a rising tide of revulsion against anti-Semitism which began at the close of the 1930's, the Council distributed masses of printed matter among various groups in the community. A helpful speech by a Catholic bishop; material on intercultural education at a teachers' convention; "Cohn Answers" the questions of labor union members; scholarships in intercultural education at a University of Wisconsin summer session, illustrate the educational effort against anti-Semitism. In the eighteen wartime months ending June 30, 1945, the Milwaukee Jewish Council distributed 91,000 pamphlets and about 5,000 other pieces of literature in defense of democracy and Jewish rights.

This positive program aimed to counter local incursions of anti-Semitism. The most menacing forms were wartime tales of Jewish profiteering or shirking danger, and the promotion of hatred through ethnic groups within the city. The local German *Herold* had been pro-Nazi in the 1930's, and ceased publication during the war period. However, it came to life again around 1950, and resumed its slurs on Jews in more careful disguise. Unlike most German newspapers in the United States, it reprinted Hitler's last harangue in full, including his tirade against the Jews. The city's Polish and Hungarian newspapers also showed proneness to fall in step with the anti-Semitic regimes in their homelands. These newspapers were read by followings which were always growing smaller, but their capacity for causing harm concerned the Milwaukee Jewish Council. Also of concern was the strongly anti-Israel line taken by the *Herald-Citizen*, organ of the Catholic Archdiocese, when the new state was founded.

Rumors and incidents kept the Council occupied, with an average of 75 complaints referred yearly to a Complaints Committee. These were mainly personal encounters, such as a foul-mouthed anti-Semitic buyer in a Jewish store, and the like. Anti-Semitism in the field of education, such as the refusal of a suburban School Board to hire Jews as teachers, and the discriminatory treatment of Jewish students in a dental school, were settled satisfactorily.

Since the scrap metal industry in Milwaukee was almost entirely owned by Jews and scrap was essential to armaments, rumors of monopolistic price-fixing were of deep concern. The Polish press, beset by fear that post-war Poland would come under Russian domination, harped on supposed Jewish pro-Communism. Near the end of the war, the line expected of the anti-Semites was ultra-nationalism. One local anti-Semite visited the Milwaukee Jewish Council to deny his anti-Semitism and to "invite" Jewish cooperation in this new program. On the other hand, those who kept the pulse of the city's inter-group relations looked with foreboding to a revival of anti-Semitism during the tensions and possible economic depression of the post-war period. To the relief of pro-democratic forces this did not occur.

Its key position in dealing with this menace to every Jew enabled the Milwaukee Jewish Council to enforce a modicum of communal self-discipline. A dishonest Jewish merchant was forced to mend his ways. The Jewish People's Committee, a Communist front, found itself hard put to find speakers or to rent halls, owing to its pretense at representing true Jewish interests. A perennial problem, the keeping of kosher meat quarrels out of the public courts, and the maintenance of the beleaguered Vaad HaKashruth, occupied the Council from time to time. It may have overreached itself in attempting to require local rabbis to consult with it before speaking at public meetings or sending letters to the press; however, three leading local rabbis helped to frame this proposal.

In World War II

The decade of the 1940's marked certain positive advances against the disease of anti-Semitism. The ultimate horrors of Hitler's program of extermination, combined with the fact that he was the enemy of America, made active anti-Semitism politically impossible and sharply reduced its appeal. To wartime patriotism should be added wartime and post-war prosperity as buffers against hatred. In 1944, the Milwaukee Common Council passed an ordinance banning the public distribution of literature bearing a message of group hatred. The Milwaukee *Journal*, the nationally known afternoon newspaper, adopted the policy of refusing to publish discriminatory advertising.

The approximately 28,000 Milwaukee Jews in 1941 plunged whole-heartedly into the four years of America's war effort. Most directly involved were the young men, and some women, who served during World War II in every branch of service and theatre of operations. In October, 1941, an estimated 250 Jews were in the armed forces.[26] Just two years later, Jewish communal sources were able to name almost 2,000 who were serving,[27] and a total of about 2,400 Milwaukee Jews wore military uniforms. Of the 2,208 who are definitely ascertainable, 1,816 were in the Army (about 240 as officers), and 392 in other branches of the service including 57 women (about 72 as officers).[28] Thirty-six sons of German Jewish refugees went to war on their demonic persecutor, and two lost their lives.[29] Interesting to note, by June 1943 almost half the local Jewish lawyers were in the armed forces, and more than half (104) of the Jewish physicians were serving in July, 1943.[30]

Of the 2,400 Jews from Milwaukee in their country's service, 197 received some decoration for wounds or gallantry in action. The ultimate sacrifice was made by 64 men.[31]

The statistics conceal an endless variety of wartime experiences. Alongside the boredom of garrison service were exploits which reached extremes of bravery and resourcefulness. Few, if any, were more remarkable than those of Army Air Force Captain Arthur L. Post, the son of a Russian immigrant. From his base in New Guinea, he voluntarily undertook a photographic reconnaissance mission over New Britain in June, 1943, where Japanese forces were concentrated. He parachuted into the jungle from his unarmed and unescorted plane after it was attacked and set fire by a group of Japanese aircraft. Missing and presumed dead, Post spent the following 101 days in the New Guinea jungle, where native tribesmen sheltered him. Despite his injuries, he used his time to advantage in spying on nearby Japanese bases and learning what he could from his primitive hosts. At last he was rescued, brought to Pearl Harbor, promoted to Major, awarded the Distinguished Flying Cross and given home leave. One year later, Major Post was killed in the Pacific during a test flight, aged 27.[32]

The Milwaukee Zionist Emergency Council and the overseas aid campaigns of the Jewish Welfare Fund symbolized the special stake of the Jews in the War, while the Milwaukee Jewish Council defended democratic attitudes and maintained Jewish rights at a critical hour. The Jewish community, with most of its young men in uniform, required no stimulation to share in the toils of the war effort with the rest of the community. Jewish communal participation, aside from what was done by each individual Jew, was directed by the Milwaukee Army and Navy Committee, affiliated with the Jewish Welfare Board, and organized in the Fall of 1941. It included representatives from each congregation and every major organization. From its headquarters in the Milwaukee Center, the Army and Navy Committee divided its activities among several sections. Its Personal Service Committee maintained connections with local men through cards, gifts, food packages, and the like. The Social and Hospitality served soldiers of all faiths who came to Milwaukee. A Record Keeping Committee maintained a full account of Milwaukee Jews in the armed forces, and lesser committees dealt with budgetary matters, religious affairs, and publicity.[33]

Around 1950, Milwaukee Jewry was as free of public, avowed anti-Semitism as ever in its history. Its representative body practiced the rule that safety from anti-Semitic assault depended upon the health of American society. It collaborated with religious, ethnic, and Negro groups to this end.

II

The Jewish Community Consolidates

COMMUNAL STRUCTURE AND LEADERSHIP

IN TWENTY FIVE YEARS, from 1925 to 1950, two sub-communities of Jews in Milwaukee became one community. The Milwaukee River had divided the two groups of different backgrounds, divergent ways of life, even opposing conceptions of what it meant to be Jewish. A synonym for "native" was "Reform," while "Orthodox" equalled "immigrant" in 1925.

The manner in which the sub-communities organized themselves for Jewish purposes clarifies many of these differences. The established native Jews of the city recognized the Temple as their focus of Jewish identification. The other Jewish institutions which they supported did not detract from this special status of the Temple, even during the Temple's lean years. The most characteristic Jewish activity in these circles was charitable aid to other Jews, at their own doorstep in Milwaukee and abroad. A small group of men were the informal governing group, many of whom were related by ties of kinship and business. Names like Stone, Saltzstein, Ruscha, Daneman, and Freschl were the pacesetters. The Jewish merchants and manufacturers who dominated the community in the old days were followed as leaders by the lawyers and brokers. Both in feeling and principle they were hostile to formal community organization.

West of the Milwaukee River dwelt the larger and poorer immigrant group in 1925, also called the "orthodox" community.

However, they were less synagogue-centered than the native Jews. While their numerous places of worship were prominent, both observant and non-observant immigrants seemed to regard them as one major element in communal life, not as its fount or focus. Zionist organizations, socialist groups, trade associations, and benevolent societies rivalled the synagogues in communal status. Several Jewish ideologies would have organized the Jewish community upon a secular, representative basis. Thus, the Labor Zionists desired representative Jewish communal organization in almost every sphere, including education, charity, and protection of the civil status of the Jews. Although ultimately unsuccessful, they strongly influenced communal development.

The immigrant body had its leaders also. Substantial learning, religious piety and adequate means ideally qualified a communal leader in the old communities of Eastern Europe. To be sure, they were often distant ideals even in Eastern Europe, and in America these qualifications for communal leadership were discarded quickly. The new standards were wealth, a respected profession such as doctor, lawyer, dentist, and prestige derived from non-Jewish sources. The man who could offer no more than devotion probably attained only minor rank—usually that of secretary. All in all, this crudely reflected what the immigrants sought in America: they desired to prosper, to enter or see their children enter professions which were closed to them in Europe, and to enjoy equal civil status with Gentiles. Thus, a minor official of a Federal court in Milwaukee long held sway among his fellow-immigrants. Doctors who showed an interest in Jewish affairs—which was seldom—were rewarded with high status. More commonly, a lawyer rose to leadership, especially in organizations which aimed to persuade the public. Above all, money talked, not only for the power it conferred, but because it spelled "success" and the realization of a vulgarized "American dream."

Among Milwaukee's Jewish organizations, Poale Zion's leaders were the best qualified intellectually. These men often combined old-time learning with knowledge of modern Jewish literature and thought, and awareness of world affairs and the Jewish position. Ideology was the essence of Poale Zion, and its leaders had to expound it, while organizations with simpler purposes were led by simpler figures.

Until the unprecedented pressures from foreign and domestic problems of the 1930's, the established leadership of the native community remained limited in view. On the other hand, the immigrant leaders, who stood on shaky ground between the richness of the old cultural life and ideals, and the newer demands of American Jewish communal affairs, were personally inadequate. The Zionists provided the explicit leadership of West Side Jewry in Milwaukee, as the record of attempts at communal union show.

In 1930, the wartime American Jewish Congress was revived not as a suffrage body but as a policy-making federation of national organizations. Under Zionist leadership in Milwaukee, a barrage of newspaper articles in the Yiddish *Shtimme*, letters to officers, and speakers before membership gatherings attempted to interest the synagogues, lodges, and benevolent societies in a Congress to represent American Jewry during the crisis over the Passfield White Paper on Palestine and the deteriorating conditions in the lands of Eastern Europe. West Side Jewry followed the lead, but the city's native Jews declined to participate. After several local conferences, two delegates, Robert A. Hess (a General Zionist) and Nathan Sand (a Labor Zionist) went to the national meeting in New York. However, all efforts—and there were arduous ones—to infuse life into the Milwaukee American Jewish Congress came to naught.[1]

Eight years later, a more enduring attempt at limited communal union was made. Rabbi Joseph L. Baron and Nathan M. Stein, representing the American Jewish Committee, convened representatives of the Jewish Labor Committee, the American Jewish Congress, and B'nai B'rith to hold the first meeting of the Milwaukee Jewish Council on December 2, 1938. It proposed "to consider and act upon proposals for safe-guarding the rights of Jews," and it struggled hard for a few years to pay the small part-time salary of its first Executive Director, George Gratz. However, it sharply rejected the Welfare Fund's offer of support in 1942, on condition of being taken over by that body. In the following year, the

Milwaukee Jewish Council did agree to become the Regional Office of the Anti-Defamation League. Without abandoning its representative character, the Council served thenceforward as the autonomous local arm of the Jewish defense organization, from which it derived a substantial part of its budget. Its Presidents were Bert C. Broude, Abe Rice, Max Raskin, Eugene Mahler, Norman N. Gill, and Harry A. Kovenock. Messrs. Stein and Broude were among the most active members before 1950, together with George Gratz, Executive Director until 1943, Ben Goldman, his successor, and Sidney H. Sayles, who assumed the Directorship in 1946.

The Council reached its definitive shape in 1945. Besides the original constituents, the Jewish War Veterans were also represented. Each had three delegates elected by the Council at large from a slate presented by fifteen members at large. The Milwaukee Jewish Council, while representative, thus also tended to be a closed corporation of groups functioning in the field of intergroup relations.[2]

American Jewry's post-war objectives were partly stated in 1943, when the American Jewish Assembly was convened by B'nai B'rith, with intense Zionist support. The name "Conference" soon replaced "Assembly." Unlike the American Jewish Congress in 1917, it made no move towards general elections. Instead, 74 Milwaukee Jewish organizations sent 242 representatives who elected three delegates. Hyman M. Seidelman (a General Zionist), Morris Weingrod (a Labor Zionist), and Rabbi Louis J. Swichkow (Chairman of the Milwaukee Zionist Emergency Council) went to the Conference in New York as Milwaukee's delegates.[3] The American Jewish Conference began to sink when the American Jewish Committee withdrew, together with the Jewish Labor Committee, on account of the Conference's pro-Zionist declaration in the name of American Jewry. In mid-1945, the American Jewish Committee, smarting under the severest criticism in its 40-year history on account of its withdrawal, attempted to become a more representative organization with local chapters. With Judge Charles L. Aarons as Chairman, the non-Zionist nuclei in the Milwaukee community were recruited. However, the Milwaukee Chapter of the American Jewish Committee made little progress.

Central representative councils thus failed to establish themselves. The successful central bodies were those with specific functions, notably the Jewish Welfare Fund, organized in 1938, and the Zionist Emergency Council, originating in 1940.

The Jewish Welfare Fund's roots reached back to the beginnings of Jewish charity in the city, when the Hebrew Relief Society was founded in 1867. From the Hebrew Relief Society and several lesser charities grew the Federated Jewish Charities in 1902. The Federated Jewish Charities remained the bell-wether of local Jewish charity, but it failed to move with the times, remaining distinctly the organ of the native Jews even after the immigrants were no longer objects of charity. In 1930, the Yiddish *Shtimme* expressed what must have been widespread doubts about its representative character.[4] The Federated Jewish Charities ultimately dissolved in 1937, four years after turning over its beneficiaries to the Milwaukee Community Chest for support. A year later, a broader and more representative body was formed, the Jewish Welfare Fund. Like its predecessor, it proposed merely to raise money to be distributed locally, nationally, and overseas. But the responsibility for the allocation of monies raised could not be sidestepped, and its implications made the Jewish Welfare Fund the powerhouse of the Jewish community.

If money made the Jewish Welfare Fund powerful, the Zionist Emergency Council's sway depended on the Jewish feeling of responsibility for their brethren. Representing the large Zionist constituency in Milwaukee and in intimate touch with headquarters in New York, it presented the Zionist view to the Jewish community and the non-Jewish world with marked success. Its authority increased as its membership bodies' enrollment skyrocketed during the 1940's. Within American Jewry as a whole, and in Milwaukee, all effective opposition to the Zionist program faded, and the Milwaukee Zionist Emergency Council's role was practically unimpeded by dissenting views in the community.

Thus, three central bodies arose in Milwaukee Jewry to serve specific objectives. Its philanthropic structure was overhauled by the Jewish Welfare Fund in 1938. In the same year, the community erected a Milwaukee Jewish Council to protect its status and to combat its detractors. Two years later, the increasingly urgent Zionist program was centralized in the Zionist Emergency Council.

Professional employees gradually emerged in the foreground of the Jewish community structure. After the synagogues, the charities and welfare bodies had been the first to employ salaried aides, at first in merely clerical positions, and after the turn of the century in executive and policy-recommending capacities. The Federated Jewish Charities was assisted by professional personnel. Elkan Voorsanger, who was employed by the Jewish Welfare Fund as Executive Director, built the fund-raising machinery of the Jewish community. George Gratz was part-time director of the Milwaukee Jewish Council and Anti-Defamation League, and Ben Goldman and Sidney Sayles continued in the same joint arrangement. The Zionist Emergency Council had no professional employee, and its affairs ran directly under its chairman's direction. The widely noticed influence of professional employees in the direction of the American Jewish community's affairs did not register in Milwaukee before 1945.

Religious Life

Twenty-five years almost sufficed to eradicate the old orthodoxy. By 1950, there were very few orthodox Jews left in the city, even among the membership of the orthodox congregations.[5] During the same span the Reform situation did not change much on the surface. However, the Conservative body which was new in 1925 moved into a leading position, particularly in the years immediately following World War II, and inherited most of the strength of the orthodox congregations.

Jewish religious life depended less upon the number or prosperity of congregations, than upon the mass individual observance of Judaism. This greatly declined in Milwaukee. Well before 1930, the Walnut Street area supported some restaurants which did not serve Kosher food. The number of daily worshippers at the synagogues shrank precipitously; those who came in the evening for Talmudic study were the elderly and retired. Whatever the superiority of their general education, the Jewish educational level of the youth stood much below their elders'. Moreover, the general concerns of the times between 1929 and 1945 were not religious but secular. The local synagogues somehow did not express or interpret the deepest interests of local Jewry—or so the latter felt, to judge by their general disinterest. The condition of Beth Israel exemplified a congregation which no longer desired to be a characteristically immigrant synagogue but could find no other basis to stand on. In 1925, Solomon Isaac Scheinfeld was still its rabbi, and continued to be until his death in 1943, aged 83. Universally respected, he was less the rabbi of Beth Israel specifically than the communal rabbi of the orthodox.

During the 1920's, Beth Israel came under the presidency of I. J. Rosenberg, then a flamboyant banker. It built a tremendous structure on the northern edge of the immigrant settlement, with seats for 1400—far more than it could fill with worshippers. Since Beth Israel, like other immigrant synagogues, derived its main income from the sale of seats for the High Holidays, it advertised a different cantor and choir yearly. Moreover, to attract younger people it engaged younger rabbis alongside the aging Rabbi Scheinfeld. The first was Rabbi Max Mintz, who served for three years from 1926; he was followed by Rabbi Charles Rubenstein. Like the "Hungarian" synagogue a few years earlier, Beth Israel continued as an orthodox congregation but introduced late Friday evening services containing prayers in English as well as a sermon. The innovation seems to have enjoyed no particular success, but it was continued for several years.

In 1933, when many had involuntary leisure and were prematurely retired, we have a first-hand glimpse of a day at Beth Israel. Some arrived at the Synagogue as early as 5:00 A.M. to recite Psalms: they stayed through the morning services. This was followed by a study session in the popular compendium of Jewish law *Hayyey Adam*. Again, at 4:00 P.M., there was a class in *Midrash* for retired persons, followed by late afternoon service and a lesson in *Mishnah* by Rabbi Rabinowitz. Following the evening service, Rabbi Rubenstein conducted a session in *Talmud*. On Saturday afternoon Rabbi Scheinfeld conducted a class in Jewish ethics.[6]

Beth Israel's auxiliary groups included a men's club, a youth group, a Psalms society, a free Sunday School mainly for girls, and its burial society. But the heavy schedule of daily classes and study groups was described exclusively as existing for the elderly and retired; young people did not appear. In fact, the Jewish educational facilities in Milwaukee could not have prepared anyone to participate with comprehension in the Talmudic studies at the synagogue.

As the 1930's flowed into the 1940's, the orthodox congregations lost ground as their memberships became older and younger people did not join. The orthodoxy which they represented dwindled away. To this account of congregational senescence one exception may well be made. In 1929, Rabbi Jacob Twerski, scion of a long line of Hasidic rabbis, established himself in the city and gradually drew about him a considerable and devoted following. The congregation which developed differed from all others in that it revolved entirely about its Hasidic leader. Jews who recalled Hasidic life from their boyhoods returned to that enthusiastic style of worship once it appeared in Milwaukee. Rabbi Twerski's personal qualities and his reputation for sage personal counsel aided the cause.[7]

Rabbi Scheinfeld had no recognized successor as he aged and slowly retired from active life in the 1930's. His seventieth and eightieth birthdays were celebrated widely, not only by his immediate orthodox circles but by the Zionists and Hebraists of whom he was one, and by the common folk of the Jewish district. When Scheinfeld died of cancer in April, 1943, his funeral was typical of his life. Having more than once refused to eulogize others whom he would not praise during their lives, his own funeral was of utmost modesty. It took place in a room in his house, and was attended only by his immediate family and the burial society. Despite his unusual acquisition of Western culture, Rabbi Scheinfeld belonged to the immigrant generation. The rabbis who served orthodox congregations after him were usually men who had received their *yeshiva* training in Europe and had come here directly afterwards. On the other hand, Rabbi Harold Baumrind was American but went abroad to be ordained. He came to Beth Israel from Long Island, N. Y., in 1939.

As Solomon Israelson had done in the 1890's, it was not extraordinary for the orthodox rabbis to shift pulpits within the city. Rabbi Ben Zion Manesewitz served Anshe Sfard for eleven years, until he moved to Degel Israel in 1936 for one year; he then returned to Anshe Sfard until his death in 1939, at the early age of 49.[8] Rabbi Charles Rubenstein, who was at Beth Israel with Rabbi Scheinfeld from 1932 until 1939, served Anshe Sfard from 1941 to 1947. The latter synagogue brought Rabbi David S. Shapiro from Indianapolis in 1948, to assume its rabbinate.[9]

Following the decline of orthodoxy during the 1920's and 1930's and the prosperous immobility of World War II, two congregations achieved the consolidation which they had spoken of for 20 years. Degel Israel, the old "Roumanian" congregation, and B'nai Israel, the old "Hungarian" congregation, merged to form a "United Synagogue," and in haste and enthusiasm began to erect a new synagogue at Burleigh and North 55th Street. But to their disappointment, neither members nor funds could be attracted to complete the building. No choice remained but to sell the place to the local Labor Zionists (Poale Zion, Farband, Pioneer Women) who converted it to a Beth Am Center. The unfortunate congregation, their old homes sold and the new home a fiasco, had to take over a small old church at Garfield and North 47th Street.[10] Ultimately the "United Synagogue" merged with the Beth Hamidrash Hagadol, and acquired the name of Beth Hamidrash Hagadol B'nai Sholem.

Five years after the close of the War, Jewish orthodoxy in Milwaukee was a very tenuous affair. Beth Israel, the oldest and once the largest, harbored an aging body of men. Many members lived far away, but maintained membership for old times' sake. The learning and vigor of Rabbi Shapiro could not change a similar situation at Anshe Sfard. The others—Anshe Lubavich, Degel Israel, B'nai Israel, Beth Medrash Hagodol, Agudas Achim, B'ne Jacob—remained fast in the old neighborhood, where Jews were fewer each year and orthodox worshippers at an exiguous minimum. Rabbi Twerski's Hasidic followers held faithful to their leader. Funerals, once the province of the congregations' *Hebrot Kadishot*, gradually moved to the commercial firms of Harry B. Goodman and his sons (successors to L. Siegel) and Sender Bensman and his grandson (partners and successors to D. Schram).[10a] The orthodox manner of burial slowly yielded to other styles.

The communal impact of orthodox requirements was also weak. General communal institutions did not observe the Sabbath; Jewish patients at Mount Sinai, the Jewish hospital, did not receive kosher food; public communal dinners were also not kosher.

Out of this orthodoxy grew Temple Beth El. The first rabbi of this Conservative congregation, Eugene Kohn, resigned in 1926, and was succeeded by Rabbi Philip Kleinman, like his predecessor an alumnus of the Jewish Theological Seminary. Rabbi Kleinman stayed for ten years and had to struggle against adverse circumstances. The impetus which founded the congregation and built its synagogue had dissipated, due to religious indifference compounded by economic depression. The congregation's school, built in 1929, stood at a low level, with most children entering for Sunday instruction or Bar Mitzvah training only. The congregation's membership was approximately 100 families. Rabbi Kleinman was succeeded by Rabbi Louis J. Swichkow, then 25 years old, a native of Chicago and holding orthodox rabbinic ordination from its Beth Midrash laTorah (Hebrew Theological College). During the 13 years of his tenure within our period, Temple Beth El underwent its second period of major growth. With membership exceeding 300 families in 1945, it decided to construct a large synagogue and attract some orthodox congregations to merge with it for the purpose. A temporary organization called the Milwaukee Greater Temple was founded to achieve this end, of which Rabbi Swichkow was Executive Director, in addition to his incumbency at Temple Beth El. The Milwaukee Greater Temple drew in members of orthodox congregations and unaffiliated Jews, but failed to effect a union with any other congregation. The ambitious and risky endeavor was dropped, but Ner Tamid (Eternal Light) was added to the name Beth El to signalize the new elements which had entered its fold.

The visible result of these unusual maneuvers was the erection of the new building, at Fond du Lac Avenue and Sherman Boulevard. The sale of seats in the rising structure was so heavy that plans were altered to add 300 seats for a total of 1300. The new Beth El Ner Tamid Synagogue opened in September, 1951, in a round of celebrations. By that time, it was an active congregation, with such arms as a Men's Club, Sisterhood, United Synagogue Youth, and so forth. Its affiliation with the Jewish Theological Seminary became an important feature of the congregation, and financial support was requited by religious orientation and educational guidance.[11]

On the ladder of social status, Beth El Ner Tamid by the year 1950 had acquired practically the same level as old Temple Emanu-El B'ne Jeshurun. Where the Conservative congregation stood in the "right wing" (closer to orthodox) of its movement, the Reform congregation would be termed on its movement's "left-wing"—further removed from Jewish tradition. However, they shared certain important features in common, such as their rabbis' central role in the worship. They both increasingly centered Jewish expression within the walls of the synagogue.

The Reform Temple Emanu-El B'ne Jeshurun, formed by the union of the two old Temples in 1927, did not fulfill the high hopes for its expansion. The approximately 900 families which were affiliated with the Temple on East Kenwood Boulevard did not increase during the years when it was the "status" congregation of the city and the sole Reform congregation. Its two rabbis were Samuel Hirshberg (1869-1954), serving since 1904, and Joseph L. Baron (1894-1960), who arrived in 1926. Aside from the contrast in personalities between the elder rabbi, a "gentleman of the old school," and his junior, there was some difference in their religious outlooks. Rabbi Baron was sympathetic to Zionism and interested in Jewish cultural expression such as art and music, while Rabbi Hirshberg held true to "classical Reform" which denied the ethnic values in Judaism. He was also non-Zionist.

With 750 families in 1930—a number which fluctuated from

600 to 700 during the 1930's—President A. L. Saltzstein complained of "woeful attendance" at services. He regretted the abolition of "practically all forms of ceremonialism. We have removed much of the colour and left but little to appeal to our hearts." Responding to his appeal, the congregation by a 2-1 majority decided to hire a cantor—an office which had never existed in Emanu-El and had disappeared by the turn of the century at B'ne Jeshurun.[12] The history of the Reform congregation during the twenty years following Saltzstein's remarks consists to a large extent of a search for the old "ceremonialism," "color," "appeal to our hearts." The catastrophes and achievements in world Jewry during these years did their part in enhancing such feelings and creating a desire to express them liturgically.

Temple Emanu-El B'ne Jeshurun continued to move in a direction which was sympathetic to Zionism. Bert C. Broude, its President from 1934 to 1937, also served as President of the Milwaukee Zionist Organization. However, a substantial element of Reform Jews did not approve of the new direction, and they constituted the 60 members of the Milwaukee American Council for Judaism, an anti-Zionist organization, at a meeting in 1945. Rabbi Hirshberg participated as chairman, and A. L. Saltzstein was the host.[13] His son, Jerome Saltzstein, was a principal local spokesman for the movement. While this group ultimately rejected the anti-Zionist extremism of the American Council for Judaism, it comprised the spiritual nucleus of a "classical Reform" congregation which was organized after 1950. However, from 1925 to 1950, Temple Emanu-El B'ne Jeshurun had the Reform field to itself in Milwaukee.[14] During the 1940's it more than recovered the ground which it had lost in the 1930's and emerged with a membership of 1,076 families in 1950—the largest Jewish congregation in the city and the state. Rabbi Baron was its active leader throughout the period. Rabbi Harry B. Pastor came from Peoria in 1947 as Associate Rabbi at Emanu-El B'ne Jeshurun until 1951, when he became rabbi of the old institution's new offshoot, Congregation Shalom.

In sum, 1925 through 1950 were lean years for Jewish religious life in Milwaukee. However, after 1945, the congregations became the acknowledged foci of Judaism and Jewish life in the city. The Reform and Conservative wings entered upon a period of material growth and Jewish interest without precedent in the annals of the Jews in Milwaukee.

JUDAISM AND THE COMING GENERATION

Bringing up the Jewish child in Milwaukee as a synthesis of Jew and American remained an (or better *the*) unsolved problem of Milwaukee Jewry. The struggles of the immigrant generation to establish itself in Milwaukee took the form in their children of a desire to become fully acclimatized in American culture and society. Dilemmas of Jewish status in a Gentile world preoccupied Jews during these years. Thus, one season at the Jewish Center included a course in "Jewish Problems" (a highly characteristic term) which sought to inculcate "a positive, non-cringing attitude toward Judaism. . . ."[15] A pessimistic view, expressed during the depression years, concluded that

> . . . Jewish youth is going far away from the Jewish people and the Jewish people is sentenced to decline, because our growing generation will be far removed from the ideals of our people and will no longer wish to continue our national exist-ence.[16]

The majority of Jewish parents in the city, contrasting the importance of public education with Jewish education, apparently concluded that their children did not require systematic Jewish education. As one thoughtful educator expressed it:

> The larger part of the American Jewish parents satisfy themselves with sending their children to the American public school. They do not understand at all that while their children acquire a general education which makes a career for them, they receive no humanizing (*menshlikh*), moral, ethical education and certainly not a Jewish education.[17]

The strictures on the public school were certainly exaggerated, but it was an accurate intuition that the dominance of the public school without the balance of adequate Jewish education helped to make the Jewish background seem trivial yet burdensome.

. . . the less the parents know about their children's studies in the public school, the more respect they have for it. They then look down on the Jewish school.[18]

Jewish education itself underwent a transformation in Milwaukee between 1925 and 1950. Where in previous years schools had been maintained by communal societies, they tended slowly to return to the practice of 19th century Milwaukee Jewry by becoming the responsibility of the congregations. In place of the faltering support which the orthodox congregations gave the communal Talmud Torah, Beth Israel and Beth El established their own schools. A city-wide superstructure was also erected, aiming at the coordination of Jewish educational effort.

The picture in 1925 was not particularly different from that reported in a survey two years earlier. The Talmud Torah then had 145 children (55 girls and 90 boys), and the Yiddish school conducted by the Arbeiter Ring taught 80 children, mainly girls. Twelve private *hadarim* taught 250 to 300 boys, and 10 to 15 private teachers had 100 to 150 students, mainly boys, among whose houses they made their daily rounds. Other elements were the Sunday school and weekday school conducted by Temple Beth El, with perhaps 50 children, and the Sunday schools of the soon-to-merge Reform Temples, which together taught nearly 500 children. Of approximately 2400 Jewish youth of elementary school age on the West Side, only 25% received Jewish education at any given time.[19] The proportion of those who had Jewish education at some time may have exceeded 50%. In the Reform and Conservative Temples, members customarily sent their children to the Sunday School. Not enrollment but enriching the thin curriculum was the problem for the latter group.

Until the last years of our period, Milwaukee Jewish education had four sectors. The first was the Sunday schools of the Reform and Conservative congregations. (Beth El retained an optional weekday school also.) They followed an English curriculum, emphasizing Jewish history, Bible stories, and ethics. The West

Side area supported the three other educational sectors. These were the Talmud Torah, private schools and teachers, and the Yiddish schools. The private schools and teachers, with their 350-450 pupils, were for the most part preoccupied with *Bar Mitzvah* preparation—trivial in content and fleeting in interest. Most of the teachers were men who pursued other vocations, besides synagogue functionaries and the like. On the other hand, several scholarly teachers selected private pupils for intensive training; this was the choice of some conscientious parents who were dissatisfied with the school facilities.

The principal Jewish school was the Milwaukee Talmud Torah, housed in Beth Israel synagogue until 1944. It desired to give a comprehensive course of Jewish study in ten hours weekly, but was bedevilled by short-term students sent by parents for Bar Mitzvah training. According to its curriculum, the Talmud Torah was taught by the "Hebrew by Hebrew" method, using the original tongue as the language of instruction. The school was orthodox in its outlook, with a large admixture of Jewish national elements. There was strong emphasis on mastering the Hebrew language. The staff of the Talmud Torah, while learned Jews, had a training and background far removed from that of their children, making rapport difficult between teachers and students. Haim Margalith, a Palestinian, was appointed principal in 1925, and succeeded in elevating the institution's standards. He also became director of the Board of Jewish Education when it was founded in 1928 with Federated Jewish Charities aid. Although Beth Israel's school merged with the Talmud Torah, the Board did not obtain real cooperation from the jealously independent private and communal schools. Margalith subsequently resigned and returned to Palestine in 1932.[19a]

The finances of the Talmud Torah were shaky. Tuition ranged from 50¢ to $1.00 weekly, but many fell deep in arrears, and others could not pay at all. The school appears to have attained financial security when the Federated Jewish Charities granted it an annual subsidy. Thus, the 1926 expenses of $11,915 came from $2,615 in tuition, and $4,850 in membership payments, appeals, and so forth. Besides a loan of $750, the Talmud Torah also received $3,700 from the Federated Jewish Charities.[20] However, depression severely damaged the school: the subsidy was sharply cut and tuition could not be collected. The communal Hebrew school was waning throughout the country, and in Milwaukee it suffered also.

The same decline overtook the Yiddish school system. Schools with Yiddish as the central feature of their curriculum were associated with Jewish socialism, both Zionist and non-Zionist. The Workmen's Circle established a school in 1919.[21] Its Yiddish and secular emphasis found few sympathizers, and its exclusion of religious training, including Bar Mitzvah preparation, insured that few students except girls would enroll.

Poale Zion and the Farband re-established their Folk Shule in 1924 at the Folk Institute, and had 60 children after one year. Three years later there were 100, besides 22 others in a branch in the northwest.[22] When the depression set in, enrollment dropped to a level fluctuating between 80 and 100, and touched a high of 114 in 1939. The Folk Shule taught not only Yiddish but Hebrew, and was traditionalist enough for a merger with the Talmud Torah to be considered as early as 1930. Under S. Shapiro, principal and Poale Zion's secretary from 1935, traditional emphases were especially introduced. After insistent Poale Zion pressure failed to secure Federated Jewish Charities subsidy, the Folk Shule collaborated with the Talmud Torah and the Beth El school in an appeal for funds.[23]

In 1941, 1,435 children were attending the Jewish schools of Milwaukee, which amounted to approximately 30% of all Jewish children aged 6-14. Of this total, 865 attended Sunday School (40 at high school level), 294 the three Hebrew schools, and 172 the two Yiddish schools. Three schools, enrolling about 163 children, were conducted privately, and perhaps 85 children received lessons from private teachers. The Hebrew schools' registration was mostly of boys, pointing to *Bar Mitzvah* preparation as a dominant factor. As a result the average weekday Jewish education lasted from 1.2 to 2.2 years in schools which kept such records. Outside the Sunday Schools, the teachers were ill-paid men of

European background. The situation was most unpromising, and improved little during the 1940's.[24]

The schools survived the depression and held firm during the war, but they could not withstand the changing neighborhoods. The Talmud Torah moved to the Northwest in 1944, where the Folk Shule already had its main branch. As the period drew to its close, the ideological lines which separated the Talmud Torah (orthodox, Hebraic, national) from the Labor Zionist Folk Shule (secular, Yiddish, national) became more blurred in the Milwaukee setting. By 1947, the two shrinking schools merged to become the United Hebrew School. (Ten years later, the Workmen's Circle school joined the union.)

The communal Jewish schools were slowly losing ground to the congregational school of Temple Beth El. During these years it struggled to raise its standards. The maximum age for beginning Hebrew studies was lowered from eleven to ten, and then to nine, as internal opposition to each step was surmounted, and enrollment steadily ascended. If a far-reaching reason for this increase was greater Jewish consciousness among American Jews, an immediate cause was the movement of Jews into Beth El's Northwest neighborhood.

As the communal schools slowly declined, a movement towards communal responsibility for Jewish education rose. In 1927, the Women's League for Jewish Education was organized to aid the Talmud Torah by such committees as Scholarship, Textbook, Prizes, Home Visiting, Entertainment and School Furnishings.

From these beginnings and Haim Margalith's efforts grew the Milwaukee Board of Jewish Education, to serve and guide the city's Jewish schools.[25] Its efforts, including an Extension Department, were crippled by the depression. Not until 1944 did the renewed Bureau of Jewish Education, supported by the Jewish Welfare Fund, engage a full-time Director, Meyer Gallin.[25a] In 1948, it opened an East Side Hebrew School for the Jews of that area.

A short-lived all-day Jewish School appeared in the city in 1948, beginning with a Mizrachi kindergarten. Its existence provoked a lively debate when an adversary condemned the new school as "a return to ghettoism." Rabbis Schulson and Shapiro and several parents urged in reply that the public schools had a fundamentally Christian bias, and that children could attain emotional security as Jews and receive adequate Jewish study only in a full-time Jewish school.[26] However, the institution failed to perpetuate itself.

There is little information concerning Jewish children in the public schools. As elsewhere, a high school education became the norm for Jewish youth, and college education was achieved by many. Within Milwaukee, where most Jewish youth perforce remained while attending college, there was a branch of the University of Wisconsin, and Catholic Marquette University. The latter, with schools of law, business, dentistry and medicine, provided a gateway into these careers for hundreds of young Jews. A small sample taken during the 1930's shows a substantial majority of the city's Jewish high school graduates attending college, full time or part time, in a higher proportion than any ethnic group in the city, including the old Yankee-Yorker stock.[27] This proportion of Jews undoubtedly rose still higher as economic conditions improved.

Among Milwaukee's Jewish academic youth there was some Jewish ferment. A local branch of Avukah, the student Zionist organization, was organized in 1927, and provided a forum for students and young graduates to share the Zionist stimulus. The Milwaukee Avukah lasted into the 1930's and was briefly re-established upon a purely collegiate basis in 1945.[28]

THE JEWISH ENVIRONMENT

The Jewish community was not only a complex of institutions, nor merely a psychologically unity; it was also a social environment. This was especially true in the older Jewish neighborhood, which retained a distinct color of its own. Its main streets remained characteristically Jewish until the 1940's, with Jewish stores and food specialties, Yiddish widely spoken, and several points of "hangout" for casual groups.

The ideological battles of the immigrant years on Walnut Street, one participant fondly recalled, were past:

> . . . Walnut Street now is stuffed with wurst, corned beef, tongue, sour pickles, and "hot dogs". . . . In the old days things were brought to Walnut Street—thoughts, ideas, opinions, principles. And today they are taken from Walnut Street—chopped livers, fish, corned beef, Sabbath loaves, cake . . .
>
> I see how the old-timers have become fatter, paunchier, broader, and my Walnut Street has alas become paler, narrower, and plainer.[29]

The exodus from Walnut Street and its environs went on rapidly during the 1920's, more slowly during the 1930's, and was completed in the 1940's. By 1945, the center of Jewish population had shifted from North Central (Wright Street to Brown Street, N. 7th to N. 20th) to North West (West Keefe to West Lloyd, N. 41st to N. 64th). Areas of settlement had grown up in the far North East along Lake Michigan, Whitefish Bay and Shorewood. The newer Jewish districts, like those of the established native Jews, showed no Walnut Street traits, but were only areas of private homes and gardens, no different from their Gentile neighbors.

Among native Jewry, social entertainment centered about the home, while the club served the recent immigrant group. The downtown businessmen's club was primarily economic in motivation, while native Jews could also relax at their two country clubs. The Woodmount Club reached back to 1907 while newer and younger elements founded the Brynwood Club in 1926.[30] These were social centers and places of fashionable relaxation for the merchant and professional group, and a place to advance into the "right circles."

The Sholom Aleichem Circle, a luncheon club organized by younger Jewish business and professional men, was a peculiarly significant group. Intentionally avoiding formal organization, its about 120 members could sit daily around a large round table and hear speakers on matters of the day. Almost every Jewish notable who appeared in the city was brought before this influential group to "state his case" and be part of the informal discussion, so that men like Stephen Wise and Chaim Weizmann sat with the Sholom Aleichem Circle. The Circle also gave charity informally, and was an informal communal meeting place until wartime pressure caused its dissolution in 1942.

The newer sections of Milwaukee Jewry socialized extensively among themselves. The family visiting of earlier days was succeeded by the social organization, usually a benevolent society. The synagogues partly served this function for their members, as did the Labor Zionists and the Workmen's Circle for their clienteles. The city's leading Jewish social and benevolent society was the Austrian Sick Benefit Society (OKUV—Ostraykher Kranken Untershtitsn Farayn), founded in 1905 by Galician Jews but including Jews of all East European origins as well. During its prosperous years in the late 1920's, the OKUV had about 400 members, a women's auxiliary and a youth society. When the Society celebrated its 25th anniversary, it possessed a capital of $35,000, and a home building on North Avenue valued at $55,000. A savings and loan association, confined to members, claimed a $125,000 capital on the brink of the depression. Benefits to members, the primary reason for the OKUV's existence, were disbursed to a limit of ten weeks yearly of sick benefit, a $50 consumption benefit (unclear in its terms), and a $500 death benefit. It also aided needy members.[31] Because of the substantial reserves available for charitable purposes, the OKUV's good will was assiduously cultivated by local institutions.

Other Jewish lodges provided similar satisfactions for their members. The Progressive Order of the West had three groups in the city, one of which, Degel Israel, was also associated with a synagogue.[32] The only lodges equalling the OKUV were those of the Workmen's Circle. There were three, numbered 166, 425, and 802, a women's branch. They all granted benefits, supported a Yiddish school, and conducted educational forums for their members.[33] Both the Workmen's Circle, an ideological organization, and the OKUV, without such a basis, began to concern themselves with their posterity. The OKUV established the Junior OKUV, while the Workmen's Circle's Young Circle attempted likewise to enroll their sons and daughters. The Jewish National Workers Alliance (Farband), connected with Poale Zion, enjoyed more success with its Labor Zionist youth movements.

The fraternal organizations suffered badly during the 1930's. Their benefits could not begin to cope with distressed members' needs, and they could not collect dues. Aside from economic problems, the mainly Yiddish lodge organizations were aging without finding youthful successors.

The strength of the immigrant lodges and benefit societies passed into an organization much older than they, B'nai B'rith, which had existed in Milwaukee since 1861. Hitherto a pronouncedly native organization, which maintained its German tradition into the 20th century, it had been uninviting to the new majority of the city's Jews. However, by the later 1930's both B'nai B'rith and the East European Jewish stock of Milwaukee were receptive to each other. Intensive membership drives between 1940 and 1944 pushed up the membership rolls to 4,400—2,800 men in five lodges and 1,600 women in six auxiliaries.[34] This astonishing total also resulted from a surge of Jewish feeling during those years, which drew previously unattached Jews into communal association. In any case, B'nai B'rith was the largest Jewish organization which had ever existed in Milwaukee. Its program included the defense of Jewish rights, the collegiate Hillel Foundations, and was shortly to turn towards Jewish cultural activity. Nonsectarian service was its most conspicuous project. Unlike the sons of the lodges, B'nai B'rith's youth met outstanding organizational success.

Changing communal needs and social habits also transformed the old settlement house into a community center. The Abraham Lincoln House stood on a large lot in the midst of the declining Jewish quarter, in a small building inadequate for its purposes. It had only nine rooms for activities and no athletic facilities. On a typical weekday, seven English classes met at the Abraham Lincoln House, besides classes in music, cooking, and nutrition. While these were being conducted under the aegis of the Milwaukee Council of Jewish Women, other activities were under way in the game room. Each evening the meeting rooms were filled with youthful social clubs, literary and debating societies, athletic groups, glee clubs, and so forth. The Abraham Lincoln House encouraged some older cultural groups and Zionist societies to meet within its walls, conducted youth services several times yearly, and celebrated Jewish holidays.[35]

The Abraham Lincoln House's services were supplemented through the city's Lapham Park Social Center, a municipal community house within the Jewish district. The Jewish institution, receiving some 1,500 regular visitors an average of 75,000 times annually, acquired its new home thanks to a unique and lucrative asset, the Settlement Cook Book. Its royalties had been held in trust by the Grand Old Lady of the institution, Mrs. Lizzie Kander. With $75,000 at hand from the famous book of recipes, besides several bequests, and the proceeds of the sale of the old House to the Urban League, the Abraham Lincoln House took over the discarded University High School downtown for a mere $60,000 and converted it to its needs. This fortunate *coup* supplied Milwaukee Jewry with a substantial Jewish Community Center (its new name) for twenty years.

The new building, dedicated in March, 1931, was perhaps five times larger than the old. It could offer a substantially richer program, including open forums on problems of the day, courses of cultural and vocational content, and discussion programs on Jewish problems. The musical program included a School of Music and Allied Arts, junior and senior orchestras and a choral society; dramatics were as extensively cultivated. In cooperation with the city's social services, there was a child guidance clinic. Of course, the program of sports and social activity was the Jewish Community Center's staff of life. On the other hand, the old "Americanization" program was practically abandoned, except for the German Jewish refugees of the 1930's, and the needs of the times produced vocational guidance, an employment bureau, and a room registry. The Jewish Community Center made itself a community-wide institution, rather than a service from wealthier Jews to their poorer brethren. During the War, the building on Milwaukee Street was the center of Jewish war activity: hospitality within its walls was offered to Jewish and Gentile soldiers, wrappings and packages were sent out, and statistics of Jewish war service kept.[36] With the end of the War, plans were drawn up for the most elaborate Jewish structure to be erected in the city. This was the new Jewish Community Center on the lakefront, dedicated in 1955—the fifth building in the odyssey of Mrs. Lizzie Kander's "Jewish Mission" of 1896.

THE CULTURAL SCENE

By 1925, the general cultural milieu of the city's Jews was English. Milwaukee's Germanism had practically disappeared by that time, and in any case most of the city's Jews were no longer of German origin. However, German theatres continued to advertise in the *Wisconsin Jewish Chronicle* a few years longer. What frail threads of Germanic associations survived were broken forever by the advent of Nazism in Germany. The German Jewish refugees had no connection with local Germanism.

While Milwaukee's native Jews maintained considerable social separateness they were culturally assimilated. Jews appeared prominently on the boards and as patrons of such cultural enterprises as the Public Library, the Layton Art Museum, and musical organizations, and enjoyed the same films and radio and other entertainments as their Gentile neighbors. Nor did Yiddish terms, Yiddishisms, and Jewish food specialties noticeably infiltrate local folkways before 1950.

The cultural diversity in the immigrant world thinned out considerably after its richer years from about 1910 to 1930. There was the old rabbinic learning, usually modified by a degree of western culture; Hebrew humanism, invariably combined with Zionism; and most strongly, Yiddishist secularism, connected with socialism and sometimes combined with Zionism. By 1930, signs of dissolution in each of these spheres were apparent and the decline ran a steady course throughout the 1930's and 1940's. The activities of these circles did not embrace original creation, but rather support for their cause, and lectures and discussions. Rabbinic Judaism received moral reinforcement from such occasional visitors as the Lubavicher Rabbi in 1932, and R. Meir Shapiro, head of the Lublin Yeshiva. Such men as Samuel Charney-Niger graced the Yiddishist circles, and Menaham Ribalow spoke to the local Hebraists. However, these were only passing stimuli.

The leading figure in the rabbinic and Hebraic fields was Rabbi Scheinfeld, in life a European Rabbi, but in thought a contemporary Hebraist. He wrote several volumes of moral and ethical reflections such as *Ziyyunim beDerekh haHayyim (Way-Marks in the Path of Life)*, published in two volumes, 1922 and 1928; *Adam HaMa'alah (The Superior Man)* (1931) a picaresque fantasy on the ethical life; *Olam HaSheker (The Lying World)* (1936); and *Divrei Hakhamim (Words of the Wise)* (1941), a collection of proverbial wisdom, mainly from Western thinkers. A common theme seems to pervade his works: the duality between profession and performance, thought and deed, with no affirmative, clear-cut solution offered. More typical of *maskilic* activity was that of Louis Heifetz, an immigrant of 1911, businessman and Hebrew teacher, who composed a Biblical chronology, a Hebrew grammar, and a volume of essays and reminiscences,[37] all of slight value.

The most significant figure in Hebrew and Yiddish letters in Milwaukee, after the departure of Ephraim Lisitzky in 1917, was Alter Esselin, who settled in the city in 1925. Esselin was born in Russia in 1889, came to America in 1908, and lived in several cities before his arrival in Wisconsin. But he did not earn his bread from poetry:

> To the other workmen of the Stark Construction Co who are putting up the St. Mary's Hospital, Alter Esselin is just a good carpenter who reads during the half hour lunch period instead of discussing women or ball scores or moonshine. . . . At 1709 Meinecke Avenue, Alter is husband and father . . . "A poet and carpenter?" says Alter, "Yes. And I don't know of which I am the more proud." His first book was published last year . . . A second book will be published in the next few months.
>
> "No, I do not publish them myself," Esselin says, "that would take money. There are bills and children and a wife and lots

of things to do with money. All Jewish poets must have trades, too. One must live."

"When I am working I can think of things. At noontime and in the evening I can read. I think life is beautiful. Almost any subject has a poem in it that one may sing about."

But there's nothing of the absent-minded dreamer to Esselin. He doesn't tell his fellow workmen that he is a poet because they would misunderstand him, he says. "They would make fun of me," he says. "But you know Jesus Christ was a carpenter and he wrote some excellent poetry, too." Esselin is obviously very proud of his trade.[38]

Fame in his own city eluded the modest poet-carpenter, where he remained little known. In addition to incidental essays he was the author of *Knayten* (1927), *Unter der Last* (1948), and *Lider fun a Midbornik* (1954). It is lyric poetry written in a quiet, reflective spirit, sometimes breaking into fierce complaint. The Peretz Society, a local group of lovers of Yiddish literature, subsidized the publication of Alter Esselin's books.[39]

Jewish literary creativity in English was very slender. Rabbi Joseph L. Baron earned fame by his collections, *Candles in the Night*, and *Stars and Sand*. These two anthologies, widely circulated by the Jewish Publication Society, consisted of quotations about Jews and stories of Jewish life, all by Gentiles. Rabbi Baron's *Treasury of Jewish Quotations* was a large collection of quotations by and about Jews and Judaism. Studies in the sciences and works of scholarship by Milwaukee Jews would go too far afield, but a book which attracted international attention by its fluent combination of scientific accuracy with literary skill was *You and Heredity* by Amram Scheinfeld, who grew to manhood in the city in the home of his father, Rabbi Scheinfeld.

Like every considerable American Jewish community, Milwaukee was visited by troupes of Yiddish actors during the golden years of Yiddish cultural life before 1930. They appeared at the Columbia Theatre, until depression and the advent of talking films replaced these troupers with Yiddish movies. But Milwaukee also boasted a cultural asset which was matched nowhere else—an expert amateur Yiddish dramatic company, which originated as the Young Literary and Dramatic Society (1920), and became the Yiddish Drama League (1931). After inaction during World War II, it revived as the Perhift Players, a name assumed in 1949 in memory of the playwright Peretz Hirschbein.[40]

Starting merely as a reading group, the group presently staged one-act Yiddish plays, and ultimately full length dramas, both comic and serious. Howard Weinshel was the amateur actors' long-time Secretary and President, and their director after 1945 was Maurice Mason of Chicago. Plays by Hirschbein, Sholom Aleichem, David Pinsky, H. Leivick, I. J. Singer, and others filled the programs, and usually two or three works were performed annually. The Perhift Players, by becoming a communal fixture in which local Jewry took pride, perpetuated itself long after the disappearance of Yiddish as a major cultural force.

During the 19th century there had been but one Jewish newspaper in Milwaukee, the short-lived but notable *Zeitgeist*, in German. The *Wochenblat* began publication in 1914 as a Yiddish newspaper, and continued to appear weekly throughout this period. However, by 1925 it lost what distinction it had had, and remained an inconsequential mouthpiece for its editor, printer, and publisher, Isidor Horwitz. One cause of its decline was the publication from 1921 of the substantial *Wisconsin Jewish Chronicle*, jointly by Nathan J. Gould and Irving G. Rhodes. The partners brought out their weekly without interruption until Gould's death in 1941, when Rhodes became sole publisher.

The *Wisconsin Jewish Chronicle* began to appear when the English-reading audience existed in sizable numbers, and interest in local and general Jewish affairs had been stimulated by the World War. It maintained editorial dignity to match the unusual dignity of its physical appearance, which hardly any Jewish newspaper in the United States equalled. It reported local Jewish news comprehensively, especially the activities of the native English-speaking Jews, and reported on Jewish affairs elsewhere mainly through the dispatches of the Jewish Telegraphic Agency.

Editorially, the newspaper followed a moderate course of least resistance. It endorsed the rebuilding of Palestine without being wholly Zionist, and appeared to favor a middle-of-the-road policy in religious life. The *Wisconsin Jewish Chronicle* remained aloof in politics, although in the 1936 Presidential election no reader could have had difficulty in divining its pro-Roosevelt enthusiasm.

Well-edited and handsomely produced, the *Wisconsin Jewish Chronicle* was never a combative journal. In fact, it generally swept communal issues and disputes under the rug; from reading its pages one would not suppose the Milwaukee Jewish community harbored serious differences. Such unpleasantnesses as local anti-Semitism were rarely mentioned. It seldom reviewed books or showed interest in the Jewish cultural scene, in Milwaukee or elsewhere. On the other hand, its dignity and moderation made the *Chronicle* respected, and it suffered no serious opposition in the Jewish community. Throughout the years between 1925 and 1950, it was unquestioned as the local Jewish organ.

One more attempt was made to publish a serious Yiddish newspaper. This was the Milwaukee *Idishe Shtimme*, which made its first appearance on September 22, 1930, and its last apparently on September 25, 1931.[41] Making its debut when the Great Depression was fastening its hold upon the country, the *Shtimme's* chances of survival were slim. During its year of life, however, the newspaper distinguished itself. Its contents were mostly editorial comment, humor, *feuilletons*, and other features, with actual news given in small amounts. Most of the news was bulletins of local organizations' activities.

The publisher of the *Shtimme* was Arthur Spiegel and on its staff were A. Posey and Joseph L. Malamut. Its policies may be summarized briefly as Labor Zionism. The Zionist message was constantly repeated, and it urged readers to join the protests against the Passfield White Paper. Within Milwaukee, it tirelessly advocated a representative community organization, Jewish education, and the perpetuation of the Yiddish language. The economic events which were shaking the country did not make much impression, except for semi-humorous complaints about hard times and a general air of bewilderment. Many *Shtimme* contributors were Poale Zion activists, some of whom showed native literary talent when they set pen to paper. The *Shtimme's* death ended the last effort to produce a Yiddish newspaper in Milwaukee. From then on, New York and Chicago Yiddish newspapers had to satisfy Yiddish readers.

Gradually, some elements of Yiddish culture were transferred into English garb. Thus, the Jewish Community Center conducted a Jewish Folklore Revue in 1936 and 1941,[42] and produced a Yiddish play in English translation in 1938.[43] The impact of the new Palestine, hardly visible outside small circles in 1925, slowly increased, but aside from some songs and dances it remained a focus of feeling rather than a cultural force before 1950. But this was not enough to prevent the 1925-1950 years from representing a net cultural loss, in terms of a European cultural heritage lost in America and not replaced by a rich, serious native Jewish culture.

PHILANTHROPY

Not by common religious beliefs and practices, nor by cultural environment, did most Milwaukee Jews identify themselves as Jews. They did so through the medium of financial aid to other Jews within the city and beyond its boundaries, in which more Jews participated than in any other Jewish activity. The original terms "relief" and "charity" were replaced by "philanthropy" and then "welfare"—symbolic of the great broadening of Jewish eleemosynary activity during these years. Not only did the amount of money donated show an extraordinary increase, but the entire technique was revised, and as the period ended philanthropy became more studied than ever before.

In 1925, the Jewish community supported three philanthropic institutions: Mount Sinai Hospital, the Jewish Children's Home, and the Hebrew Sheltering Home. The first was a full-scale hospital, providing complete medical and surgical service. It had been built and was conducted by a close group of native Jews, who supported it generously. The Jewish Children's Home was a charity of immigrant origin, which was gradually taken over and supported by native Jews. The Hebrew Sheltering Home (Hochnosas Orchim) was a common transient shelter corresponding to the European *hekdesh*, with American improvements. It was supported entirely from within the immigrant group.

Mount Sinai Hospital, at 12th and Cedar Streets, bordered downtown Milwaukee and the vanishing immigrant neighborhood. It contained 130 ward beds, but the only distinct department was the obstetrical; other cases were scattered about the institution. There was an attending staff of 26 physicians, and 134 outside physicians could use its facilities. The Hospital had also conducted a nurses' training school since 1914, and in 1925 was just embarking upon an out-patient clinic and social work connected with its medical service. The annual budget rose steadily from $153,000 in 1925, although bed rates in wards and semi-private rooms were below average at $2.25 to $3.50 a day. In 1927, Mount Sinai added a free dispensary and clinic at a cost of $35,000. With these facilities, the institution reached its mature development, at which point it remained until a new pavilion was added in 1938. During the late 1940's it began to conduct medical research.

About 25% of Mount Sinai Hospital's patients in 1925 were Jewish, a ratio which did not change much throughout the years following. This was the lowest ratio of any sizeable Jewish hospital in the country, and stirred considerable discussion. One hint came from a Yiddish source, that Jewish patients felt no different in a Jewish hospital which celebrated Christmas than in any other hospital. The unavailability of kosher food was another probable cause. It was estimated that only half the city's Jewish hospital cases entered Mount Sinai, which was the principal local beneficiary of Federated Jewish Charities and Jewish Welfare Fund campaigns, and the sole Jewish association for some of its members.[44] Milwaukee's Jewish hospital was as much a service by the Jewish community to the wider community as a service to its own sick.

The Jewish Children's Home acquired a building of its own in 1923, and expanded it in 1928, notwithstanding misgivings of the wisdom of settling dependent children in institutions. Despite sharp opposition from the Federated Jewish Charities, the Jewish Children's Home maintained itself until 1948. In that year, its merger with the Jewish Social Service Association formed the Jewish Family and Children's Service.

Early in 1930, the Home for Aged Jews entered its new premises on 50th Street between Wright and Meinecke, with 26 rooms accommodating two aged persons each—a far cry from the unsafe and dilapidated old quarters on 8th Street. Instead of the old house's depressing atmosphere of lingering until death, the new Home undertook seriously to occupy its elderly residents.[45] The Home for Aged Jews became prominent among the Jewish philanthropies of the city, quite a remove from its bedraggled beginnings among poor immigrants.

A survey of communal structures completed during the 1920's, before depression and war imposed a 15 year hiatus on such projects, is of interest:[46]

1922:	Mount Sinai Hospital, expansion from 100 to 160 beds and quarters for 70 nurses	$350,000
1923:	Milwaukee Jewish Orphan Home (enlarged in 1928)	50,000
1923:	Temple Beth El Synagogue and school building (1928)	75,000
1923:	Home for Aged Jews (enlarged in 1928)	125,000
1924:	Temple Emanu-El	450,000
1924:	Beth Medrash Hagodol	40,000
1925:	Anshe Sfard	75,000
1926:	Anshe Lubavich	75,000
1927:	Mount Sinai Hospital Free Dispensary and Clinic	35,000
1926:	Beth Israel	200,000
1929:	Camp Sidney Cohen	40,000
1929:	Building for Milwaukee Jewish Center	60,000
		$1,475,000

Practically every Jewish institution was rehoused during the 1920's. Of major institutions, only Mount Sinai did not change entirely, but it was substantially increased. The Workmen's Circle, OKUV, and Poale Zion bought and remodeled older buildings, and are on that account omitted. The conservative habits of Milwaukee's Jews served them faithfully during the economic collapse. The Hebrew schools, Home for Aged Jews, and the Jewish Center (acquired in "bargain basement" style) were practically free of debt. In the words of Benjamin Glassberg, Director of the Federated Jewish Charities:

> Milwaukee Jewry faced this period of depression in fairly good shape, not because of any special foresight on our part, but because we were slow moving. It has no institutions with enormous mortgages and fixed interest charges eating up funds which should be used for relief or service.[47]

If the city's Jewish institutions were strong enough to withstand economic collapse, the fund-raising apparatus proved itself unequipped for demands which constantly grew greater. Cases served by the Jewish Social Service Association reached 226 cases, totaling 758 persons, by the autumn of 1931, and went up higher as the depression cut deeper.[48] The old sentiment stating that the Jews had to "take care of their own" had to be abandoned when perhaps every tenth Jew required help; Jews applied to local and then to New Deal agencies for relief along with the rest of the impoverished citizenry. Only in the case of the German Jewish refugees, a group over which feelings were very sensitive, did local Jewry carefully "take care of its own." Actually, it was difficult to do social case work when the numbers were so large and the needs so apparent; instead, there was a reversion to old-time relief.

In the later 1920's, the Federated Jewish Charities supported established local institutions and a few national Jewish charities. It raised $100,000 in 1925, and reached a peak during its 1927 and 1929 campaigns, which yielded $145,000 each. In 1930 it dropped to $126,500, and in the following year, greatly increased local relief needs were supported by only $115,000. The depression was the deepest but not the sole cause of the drop in income. The Federated Jewish Charities had become a relic of an older order of things, when rich Jews, generally natives, charitably aided poor Jews, generally immigrants.[49]

Alongside the Federated Jewish Charities, campaigns for overseas aid were conducted whose impetus came from various national headquarters in the East. After several Joint Distribution Committee campaigns came the realization that aid to overseas Jewry would be a permanent necessity. The United Jewish Appeal of Wisconsin, a name pregnant for the future, was established to combine the overseas campaigns of 1926, 1927, 1928, and 1929. During these four years, $185,462 was raised in Milwaukee. Aid to Palestine was not included, except in the United Palestine Appeal in 1926 and 1928.[50] The Keren Hayesod independently raised $50,000 in 1927 and $30,000 in 1929.[51] It would be appropriate to include as overseas aid the cash remittances which hundreds of Milwaukee Jews sent to close relatives abroad. There is no way to tell how much was sent, but it is not improbable that it equalled the amount officially raised. Aid to Palestine must include the Poale Zion's Palestine Labor (Geverkshaften) campaigns, which began with $1,700 in 1926 and reached $8,600 in 1930. After 1932 it joined in the local United Palestine Appeal.[52] The overseas commitments of American Jewry had a hand-to-mouth organization in Milwaukee, in contrast to the solid but hidebound Federated Jewish Charities. It is unfortunate but not remarkable that the weak structure of Jewish charity in Milwaukee collapsed in the 1930's. As the depression continued, the Federated Jewish Charities leaned more and more heavily upon the Community Chest. Within the Chest, a Jewish unit was constituted which raised funds for the city's non-sectarian agency.[53] Finally, the Federated Jewish Charities found itself impotent by 1933, and turned its beneficiaries over to the Community Chest. No such débâcle had ever occurred in the annals of the city's Jews, and it happened when the pall of depression was gradually lifting and overseas needs were becoming more urgent.

Early in 1933, an emergency appeal for German Jewry, conducted under the shock of the adoption of Nazi rule in Germany, had raised an unimpressive $8,362.[54] Two overseas campaigns were conducted in 1936. The eloquence of Rabbi Stephen S. Wise at a United Palestine Appeal dinner in 1936 inaugurated that year's campaign, which went $3,000 beyond its $25,000 goal.[55] When this drive ended in March, the Joint Distribution Committee's campaign for overseas Jewry exclusive of Palestine commenced, and it too attained its $25,000 goal.[56] In 1938-39, the enduring local and national structure of Jewish fund-raising was erected. The United Palestine Appeal and the Joint Distribution Committee were joined by several minor bodies to found the United Jewish Appeal—the greatest fund-raising organization ever seen in America. Correspondingly (but not by design), Milwaukee Jewry at last developed an instrumentality adequate to needs which were never diminishing. This was the Jewish Welfare Fund, which incorporated the leading local Jewish charitable institutions and the major foreign drives.[57] The local beneficiaries of the defunct Federated Jewish Charities, and the national constituents of the United Jewish Appeal, were to derive most of the benefit. In addition, comparatively small donations were made to a few national Jewish institutions (such as the Los Angeles Hospital, the National Jewish Hospital at Denver, the American Jewish Congress, and small amounts to cultural groups) and a few overseas causes, particularly the Palestine Labor Fund (Geverkshaften). As a constituent of the Council of Jewish Federations and Welfare Funds, the Welfare Fund was influenced by that body's studies and implied suggestions.

The first Board of Directors incorporated some of the old names of the Federated Jewish Charities, supplemented with some drawn from the newer elements in the community. There was Zionist representation upon the Board, and congregations besides Emanu-El B'ne Jeshurun "arrived" in terms of seating some of their members upon it. Nathan M. Stein was first President and Campaign Chairman. He was a lawyer, of Russian immigrant stock, with affiliations in the Reform wing. The same could be said of his two successors, Aaron Scheinfeld (son of Rabbi Scheinfeld) and Bert C. Broude. B. E. Nickoll and Dr. Norbert Enzer completed the roster of Jewish Welfare Fund Presidents before 1950. The local rabbis sat upon the Board from time to time. Elkan C. Voorsanger, a descendant of 19th century American rabbis and a man of extensive organizational experience, became professional head of the Jewish Welfare Fund in 1939 and continued throughout our period.

The Jewish Welfare Fund not only raised money but had to allocate it. Where the first was a matter of technique and organization, the latter raised questions of fundamental Jewish outlook. Should the monies of Milwaukee Jewry emphasize the relief and reconstruction of world Jewry in their scatterings, or be centralized in Palestine? Should "territorial" solutions of refugee homelessness be financially stimulated or, again, was Palestine the only refuge meriting full support? What were the relative merits of claims by hospitals and educational institutions? How could domestic and overseas requirements be equitably balanced? Scientific studies could illuminate these questions to a point beyond which personal philosophies of Jewish life had to decide. With so broad a spectrum of Jewish opinion seated upon the Board of the Milwaukee Jewish Welfare Fund, there was no doubt that debates were sharp even though their details do not remain. Yet less than one generation later, it is clear how uncontrollable forces answered most of the questions.

The first Jewish Welfare Fund campaign was conducted in the fall of 1938, and went $10,000 beyond its modest $75,000 quota.[58] In June, 1939, Rabbi Stephen S. Wise again visited Milwaukee to address the "largest Jewish rally in the city's history" which opened a campaign for $265,500. With the White Paper of 1939 just issued and Word War II on the near horizon, the old orator inspired the exertions of 1,000 volunteers. They raised some $235,000—a sum which grew larger with each later campaign— and collected it from 8,220 persons.[59] In terms of family units, this was a substantial majority of the Jews of the city. It was far more persons than had ever before been reached by fundraising efforts, and more than twice as many as the Federated Jewish Charities reached during its best years in the 1920's. Thenceforward, the main efforts of the Jewish Welfare Fund lay in increasing individual contributions in a city reputed for conservatism in donations. In the climactic 1946-1950 period, the number of contributors ranged between 8,960 and 10,055— testimony to the effectiveness of the Fund's original job in canvassing the city's Jews. The Jewish Welfare Fund drive in 1942 raised approximately $262,000.[60] The Fund merged its appeals during the war years of 1943, 1944, and 1945 with those of the Community Chest. During the latter two years, it had $395,890 and $476,665 to allocate, of which 66 per cent and 71 per cent was devoted to overseas Jewry, principally through remittances to the United Jewish Appeal.

The campaign of 1946 was undertaken immediately after the end of the war, following the full disclosure of the fate of European Jewry. That year and those following illustrate the extraordinary upsurge in Jewish feelings which the European carnage and the birth of Israel aroused.

Year	Total Allocations	UJA Allocation	Percentage Overseas	Percentage Nat'l	Percentage Local
1946	$ 954,188	$ 775,000	84	4	7
1947	1,292,856	1,015,000	79	4	11
1948	1,653,973	1,218,000	75	3	10[a]
1949	1,219,917	802,079	67	3	18[b]
1950	931,765	600,000	66	5	22

[a] $100,000 additional given to the new Jewish Community Center Building.

[b] $85,000 additional given to the new Jewish Community Center Building.

As the number of contributors changed relatively little, the extraordinary increase was due to doubling and trebling by individual contributors. In the peak year, a quota of $2,500,000 was actually announced, and $1,750,766 actually came in by the official close of the drive. In the feverish spring of 1948, the Jewish Welfare Fund negotiated a $500,000 loan for immediate dispatch abroad, using campaign proceeds as collateral.[61] This was a far cry from the conservative habits of the old days, but times had changed beyond recognition in less than twenty years.

Local needs also asserted themselves. As shown above, an increasing proportion of the budget was set aside for local purposes after 1948, much of which was devoted to aid for recently arrived refugees. Mount Sinai's allocation doubled from its $25,000. The various Jewish schools received subsidies through the Bureau of Jewish Education, which distributed about $40,000 annually, and the Milwaukee Jewish Council's allowance rose from $7500 to $12,000. The Jewish Welfare Fund's decisions and allocations mirrored the thinking of the Jews of Milwaukee, or at least that of the men whose views weighed heavily in policy deliberations.

Other philanthropies served Milwaukee Jewry during these years. An array of old-time charities merged into larger units. Thus, the Children's Outing Society and the Ladies' Relief Sewing Society merged into the Jewish Social Service Association. The latter's name and function changed when it absorbed the Jewish Children's Home and was redesignated the Jewish Family and Children's Service in 1948: a long stride from the Hebrew Relief Society organized in 1867, and one which suggests the transition from material relief to social work and psychological services. The Jewish Vocational Service was organized in 1937, to give professional vocational educational guidance to youth and adults. It also bore responsibility for the economic adjustment of the German and post-war refugees through its Department for Refugee and Migration Service established in 1938. A considerable proportion of its clientele was not Jewish, and the Jewish Vocational Service considered itself as rendering a service to the youth of the city in the Jewish community.[62]

III

Milwaukee Jewry's Expanded Horizon

NATIONAL AND international events influenced the thinking of Milwaukee's Jews between 1925 and 1950 as never before. An essentially insular Jewish community, with restricted Jewish connections beyond the city limits, became absorbed in the far-flung affairs of their people. Unquestionably stimulated in doing so by the United States' abandonment of isolationism, the broader Jewish interests nevertheless transcended America's reluctant assumption of world responsibility.

As an immigrant community, news of the "old country" was of consuming interest to the city's Jews; before they turned catastrophic, the reports had long been bad. The *Wisconsin Jewish Chronicle*, not to mention the short-lived *Idishe Shtimme*, devoted more attention to foreign news than any newspaper in the city, including the eminent *Milwaukee Journal*. A flow of representatives from abroad also served to inculcate a world Jewish outlook. National Jewish newspapers and magazines played unceasingly upon the problems of world Jewry and the oneness of American Jewry. Although these periodicals, like the visitors, avowedly had partisan ends in view, nonetheless they raised the level of Jewish interest above bare provincialism.

Above all, local Jews in 1925 were still mainly immigrants, whose near relations still lived in dozens of cities and towns throughout Eastern Europe. Although trans-Atlantic family ties of long settled German Jews had grown faint, this was not so for the throngs of recently arrived Russian, Polish, and Roumanian Jews. Hundreds corresponded with relatives in Europe and sent money.

In 1925, the national connections of local Jewish organizations were important only in the case of the Zionists and the Workmen's Circle. Reform Jewry was affiliated with the Union of American Hebrew Congregations and its rabbis were members of the Central Conference of American Rabbis. Temple Beth El was connected with the United Synagogue; an orthodox network hardly existed. B'nai B'rith and other fraternal and benevolent groups had such organizations beyond the city. However, the congregations' and societies' preoccupations were necessarily local, and their affiliations were to a large extent signs of loyalty and fellowship rather than vital necessities.

The Zionists and to some extent the socialists in the Workmen's Circle were ideological, and held that their programs were of validity for all American Jewry; local differences were unimportant. But the Workmen's Circle was enmeshed in its benefit system, and hamstrung by the general decay of socialism; local interests nearly surmounted its wider outlook. Not so the Zionists. The tragedies of Jewish history between 1925 and 1950 gave irresistible impetus to their program, and swept practically all local Jewry into fervent support of Jewish Palestine which became the State of Israel. In the city of Milwaukee, the growth of Zionism, in the loose sense of sympathy and support for the Jewish National Home, registered the development of a broad Jewish consciousness.

Zionism centered in the Milwaukee District of the Zionist Organization of America, and Poale Zion and its fraternal organization, the Farband. Mizrachi's orthodox religious Zionism never struck deep roots, and the political radicalism of the Revisionists seems not to have existed in Milwaukee at all. One characteristic of Milwaukee Zionism was the gradual growth of women's and young Zionist groups. In early years, men and women had belonged equally in the Zionist Organization and Poale Zion. During the years following 1925, practically all women Zionists enrolled in Hadassah (founded 1920) and the David Pinsky

Women's Club (established 1922); the Pioneer Women's Organization came on the scene in 1926. Mizrachi Women showed the vitality which the men did not.

In organizational terms, the city's Zionists kept up a somewhat wavering strength during the 1920's. The Zionist District, which claimed 250 members "a few years" before 1927, had 750 in that year. However, the 1930's brought reverses, with only 250 enrolled in 1933 and 500 early in 1939.

From then through the establishment of the State of Israel, the Zionist Organization of Milwaukee increased by large strides yearly. Several Zionist old-timers like Saffro, Hess and Seidelman, were still on the scene; but new men, generally the sons of East European immigrants, were appearing to direct Zionist affairs. Significantly, Jews who were prominent in public life also assumed membership among Milwaukee's Zionists. In 1944, the Milwaukee District of the Zionist Organization had about 600 members, and a year later the total was 988. By 1947, all Milwaukee Zionist groups had 2300 members.[1] This demonstrates less the extensiveness of Zionist education than the aroused affirmation of Jewish loyalty during crisis years. A Zionist member was not asked to do much; the appeal to join stressed the importance of large numbers and a united Jewry during a period of catastrophe. The Zionist Organization enjoyed its greatest vogue during crisis periods, and declined swiftly thereafter.

Poale Zion was an important organization but declined in relative strength after 1925.[2] Clubs of younger members were organized in 1927 and 1946; yet, unlike the Zionist Organization, it did not succeed in developing a succession to its hard-working veterans like Perchonok, Sand, Tuchman, and Weingrod. The Labor Zionists grew mainly in their fraternal arm, the Jewish National Workers' Alliance, or Farband. As its third branch in Milwaukee, the Farband won over the strong Ostraykher Kranken Untershtitsn Farayn (OKUV). While Poale Zion's two branches in 1944 contained 110 members, the three Farband branches, including the old OKUV, had 425 persons. The language question was a rather ambiguous matter. Poale Zion's devotion to Yiddish no doubt decreased its potential influence in a city where its mild socialism and Zionism with a pioneering emphasis otherwise held much attraction. Its English speaking League for Labor Palestine had a short and unsuccessful existence, from 1933 to 1937. Poale Zion, which interlocked with the Far-band, provided a social and cultural milieu for its people in its home on Eleventh Street.

On the other hand, the orthodox Zionists of Mizrachi did not make much impact in the city. Rabbi Charles Rubenstein was their main rabbinic mover, and Chaim Siegel, a learned layman, served as president when Mizrachi, following one unsuccessful attempt, organized 118 men. In 1944, it claimed 160.[3] Mizrachi conducted its activities mainly within the orthodox synagogal environment, and the weakness of Jewish orthodoxy in Milwaukee is reflected in Mizrachi's failure to impress itself upon the city's Jewry.

Unlike Mizrachi and Poale Zion, membership in the Zionist Organization tended to symbolize the acceptance by the Jewish communities of the Zionist idea. One congregation, Temple Beth El, affiliated as a body with the Z.O.A. Reform Temple Emanu-El Bne Jeshurun as a body demanded the abrogation of the British White Paper of 1939, but did not officially favor the Jewish Commonwealth. By the end of World War II, no articulate anti-Zionism, outside a small American Council for Judaism chapter, remained in the Jewish community. The great preponderence of Jewish Welfare Fund receipts sent overseas went mainly to Palestine.

Although political decisions were left to the men, the women's Zionist organizations offered more activity to their members. The Pioneer Women, part of the Poale Zion group, grew to 225 women by 1944, and claimed 1,000 in 1948. The 300 Mizrachi Women in 1936 reached 450 by 1944. Largest of all was Milwaukee Hadassah, which by 1945 divided its 1450 women into four districts in the city.[4] The women Zionists undertook charitable projects, and conducted a round of parties, fashion shows, theatre benefits, and so forth. Gradually a more intensive Jewish program was undertaken, including Jewish arts at meetings and Jewish subjects as the basis of programs.[5] Hadassah had its Youth

Aliyah and medical services, while the Pioneer Women aided the women workers in labor Palestine; the Mizrachi Women supported religious and educational institutions in the Jewish National Home. The Jewish National Fund's land purchase and reforestation programs struck deep Jewish feelings, and were popular among all Zionists and many non-Zionists. Through a round of house-to-house collections, Golden Book certificates, dinners, and other means, the city's J. N. F. Council collected $362,000 during the 1940's. Wisconsin was the first state to acquire its *nahalah* (landholding) in the Land of Israel, in 1947.

Zionism in its most intensive form was found among relatively small circles in the city's Jewish youth. Poale Zion youth groups, many of whom had graduated from the Folk Shule, assumed the name of Habonim in 1934; in 1944 they claimed about 50 members, and 135 in 1948. Hashomer Hatzair, organized in 1935, claimed no parent organization, but had a direct connection with the Palestinian kibbutz movement. Hashomer Hatzair synthesized Zionism and Marxism, while Habonim was more broad-based in its socialism and Zionism. These youth organizations sought to inculcate in their members settlement in Palestine, preferably on a kibbutz. In June, 1939, Aryai Ben-Hillel and Sara Tucker left Milwaukee to settle on a Hashomer Hatzair Kibbutz in Palestine, and some others went also.[6] However, the youth organizations did not set the tone of Zionism in Milwaukee, although their fire and zeal were welcomed.

Through the American Jewish Conference, the Zionists made their program the official position of Milwaukee Jewry. The four conveners of the local Conference to elect delegates in May, 1943 were Rabbis Baron and Swichkow, Hyman Seidelman, and Nathan Stein: the city's Zionist President, Vice President, a member of the Zionist Executive, and a pro-Zionist (Rabbi Baron). After the Board of Elections met, and nominations and elections by organizations' delegates took place, the two Zionist officers were joined by a Poale Zion stalwart, Morris Weingrod, for the trip to the Conference in New York. They went with the Jewish Commonwealth platform of American Zionism, which had been adopted in 1942, as the avowed program of the Milwaukee delegates. Thus, 45 years after the first Zionist circle met in the home of a Milwaukee Hebrew teacher, the city's Jews as a body officially endorsed the full Zionist program. To be sure, not every Jewish group in the city was so minded, and Zionism in its cultural implications remained generally unfulfilled. But during the years of American political effort and mass publicity preceding the Jewish State, Milwaukee's Zionists could speak for the city's Jews to Governors, Mayors, Congressmen, and the press.

Zionism appealed to the public through the Zionist Emergency Council, composed of thirty-eight representatives from all the city's Zionist organizations. They elected as their Chairman Rabbi Louis J. Swichkow, who set about the direction of affairs with indefatigable energy. A Public Relations Committee sought local groups, Jewish and Gentile, to pass a model resolution favoring free immigration to Palestine. A second duty of the Public Relations Committee was to convince the Wisconsin members of Congress of the Zionist program. By a significant accident, several sat upon the Committee on Foreign Affairs, including Milwaukee's Representatives McMurray and Zablocki, while Senator Wiley was a ranking member of his chamber's Committee on Foreign Relations. The Emergency Council's Educational Committee assumed the task of persuading not only the Jewish organizations of Milwaukee but those of the entire city of the justice of Zionism. Labor unions, Christian ministers, veterans' organizations, nationality groups, women's organizations, all received close attention from special Zionist subcommittees which stood ready to supply speakers and literature. Jews having entree to these bodies solicited their sympathy and support as part of American Zionism's intensive campaign to win over public opinion. The peak of this effort came in 1944. Within its first months, the Emergency Council solicited every one of Milwaukee Jewry's 79 organizations and secured pro-Zionist resolutions from the great majority; nearly all the rest condemned the British White Paper. After careful preparation, it passed through the Milwaukee Common Council a resolution which expressed sympathy for the Jewish victims of Nazism, denounced the White Paper, and showed "favor [to] the continued development of the Jewish National

Home in Palestine for the absorption of as many Jews as may be required by the urgent needs of the Jewish people." The County Board of Supervisors soon followed suit, and later in that year of 1944 Acting Governor Goodland proclaimed Balfour Day as the state's Palestine Day, brushing aside political objections in order to do so. In February, the Wisconsin State Federation of Labor passed a pro-Palestine resolution, as did the Milwaukee Ministerial Association and the local Council of Church Women. Especially appreciated was a similar resolution passed by the Catholic Archdiocesan Holy Name Union, since very few Catholic lay or clerical groups in the United States were on record for Zionism. The energy of the Milwaukee Zionist Emergency Council, particularly its Chairman and Steering Committee, produced these results. However, a positive feeling of sympathy for the worst victims of the Nazi enemy and the inherent justice and reason of the Zionist program made the way an easy one. Never before had a general Jewish issue been brought before the general community in a sustained manner by the Jewish community as a whole.

The *Milwaukee Sentinel,* a Hearst newspaper, followed the policies of that chain in endorsing Zionist goals. The *Milwaukee Journal,* the city's outstanding newspaper, published a sympathetic feature article but long withheld comment on the entire subject. Finally, it editorially advocated the abrogation of the White Paper under the significant title "Appeasement and Palestine," on March 23, 1944. A report to New York expressed pleasure:

> For us this is very significant, because it indicates that public opinion—non-Jewish as well as Jewish—is overwhelmingly behind the demand that the White Paper be abrogated. Thus, instead of the *Milwaukee Journal* molding public opinion, *public opinion compelled the Milwaukee Journal to state the case in the light that it does.*

The greatest effort was directed at the Congressional delegation to secure passage of the 1943 Palestine resolution pending before the House Foreign Affairs Committee. A campaign of letters and telegrams was directed at Milwaukee's Congressmen McMurray and Waiselewski, of whom the former sat on the decisive Foreign Affairs Committee. At the behest of the War Department, the resolution was postponed, to arise again after the 1944 elections. Once again, the resolution, which now commanded the support of the rather aloof Senator LaFollette, was set aside by the Senate Foreign Relations Committee at the State Department's urging. In the internal uproar following the shelving of the resolution, Rabbi Abba Hillel Silver resigned as National Chairman, after having been the leader of the activist school of Zionist politics which the Milwaukee Zionist Emergency Council exemplified. As one of the most active local Councils, Milwaukee's vigorous espousal of Rabbi Silver's position materially aided his restoration to unchallenged direction of American Zionist affairs.

The year 1943 had featured the Jewish community's official endorsement of Zionism, while 1944 was notable for the general community's widespread acceptance of the Zionist appeal. From 1945 until 1950, Jewish pro-Zionism and the warm favor of the general community were called upon repeatedly during the epochal struggle of Palestinian Jewry. In Spring of 1945, branches of the American Palestine Committee, consisting of pro-Zionist Christians, and the American Christian Palestine Committee, whose members were friendly Protestant ministers, were founded in Milwaukee. The American delegation to the San Francisco Conference which founded the United Nations in April, 1945, was petitioned by the city's Jewish organizations to recognize the Jewish Agency's right to speak for the Jews in connection with Palestine. The *Journal* and *Sentinel* echoed these views, which Dr. Norbert Enzer broadcast on a local radio station. Step by step, in day-to-day collaboration with New York headquarters, the Jewish community and its allies petitioned, urged, persuaded. Of particular importance was the friendship of the state's senior Senator, Alexander Wiley, who attended the fateful General Assembly of the United Nations which voted to accept the partition plan. The temporary reversal of United States support of the partition plan in March, 1948, brought a telegraphic and journalistic storm of bitter criticism, while President Truman's prompt recognition of the new State of Israel was hailed with enthusiasm little less than that greeting the founding of the State itself.

The Milwaukee Zionist Emergency Council was incidentally concerned with keeping the record straight upon the occasion of each terrorist act in Palestine committed by the dissident Irgun Zvai Leumi. Rabbi Swichkow repeatedly explained in the *Milwaukee Journal* that his body was unrelated and opposed to the terrorists and their methods. The friends of the Irgun Zvai Leumi did not publicly organize in Milwaukee, despite their vogue in many American Jewish communities.

Milwaukee could well feel that its share in the birth of the Jewish state had been second to no other American Jewish community in proportion to its size. A tiny trickle of Palestine settlers, mainly drawn from members of Zionist youth organizations, had followed in the footsteps of the post-World War I emigration to Palestine. In place of the vanished European ties of Milwaukee's Jewish immigrants, the second century of Jewish life in the Wisconsin city began to build ties with the developing center of world Jewry in the historic Home.

NOTES

LIST OF ABBREVIATIONS

AJYB	*American Jewish Year Book*
Am. Heb.	*American Hebrew*
Am. Isr.	*American Israelite*
Andreas	A. T. Andreas, publisher, *History of Milwaukee from Prehistoric Times to the Present Date*. Chicago, 1881.
Blue Book	*The Jewish Community Blue Book of Milwaukee and Wisconsin*. Milwaukee, 1924.
Buck	James S. Buck, *Pioneer History of Milwaukee*. 2 vols., Milwaukee, 1876 (rev. ed., 1890), 1881. *Milwaukee Under the Charter*. 2 vols., Milwaukee, 1884, 1886. These are referred to as volumes III and IV.
Conard	Howard L. Conard, ed., *History of Milwaukee from Its First Settlement to the Year 1895*. 3 vols., Chicago, n.d.
Ev. Wis.	*Evening Wisconsin*
Gregory	John G. Gregory, *History of Milwaukee, Wisconsin*. 4 vols., Chicago, 1931.
J. Mess.	*The Jewish Messenger.*
Kemfer	*Idisher Kemfer*
PAJHS	*Publications of the American Jewish Historical Society.*
Sent.	*Milwaukee Sentinel*
Sent.-Gaz	*Milwaukee Sentinel and Gazette*
Shtimme	*Milwauker Idishe Shtimme*
Still	Bayrd Still, *Milwaukee: The History of a City*. Madison, 1948.
WMH	*Wisconsin Magazine of History.*
Watrous	Jerome A. Watrous, ed., *Memoirs of Milwaukee County*. 2 vols., Madison, 1909.
Wchblt.	*Milwauker Wochenblat.*
Wisc. JC	*Wisconsin Jewish Chronicle.*

PART ONE: PIONEERING YEARS, 1844-1870

I. FROM FUR TRADING POST TO COMMERCIAL CENTER

1. *New York Jewish Chronicle*, Oct., 1849, p. 128; cf. *Occident*, Sept. 1849, pp. 330-31; *Jewish Chronicle* (London), Nov. 2, 1849, p. 30; *Sent.-Gaz.*, Dec. 12, 1849, p. 2.
2. Jacob R. Marcus, ed., *Memoirs of American Jews, 1775-1865*, II (Phil., 1955), pp. 272-73.
3. *Ibid.*, II, p. 157.
4. Andreas, p. 35.
5. Still, pp. 52-53.
6. By 1842, twenty-five stores were doing business of $70,000 to $150,000 annually. Buck, II, p. 117.
7. The panic of 1837 drove nearly all but the grocers out of business. Gregory, I, p. 424.
8. Still, pp. 52-53.
9. Gregory, I, pp. 202, 270-271.
10. Still, p. 45 ff.
11. By 1845, Milwaukee's tonnage was one steam and 26 sailing vessels, totaling 2,475 tons. Edward D. Holton, "Avenues to the Town," quoted in Gregory, I, pp. 279-280; Buck, II, p. 214.
12. Still, p. 51.
13. See copy of a handbill announcing an auction sale of lots, dated Oct. 8, 1835. Buck, I, p. 80.
14. I. A. to D Lapham, July 7, 1836; I. A. Lapham to Dr. C. W. Short, August 17, 1836, Lapham Papers, cited by Still, p. 26.
15 Gregory, I, p. 72.
16. Juneau to Martin, May 30, 1837, Martin Papers, cited by Still, p. 27.
17. A. W. Kellogg, "Recollections of Life in Early Wisconsin," *WMH*, VII, 1924, p. 484.
18. In 1836, Milwaukee's population was listed as 1206; in 1838, due to the depression the number had declined to 700. In 1840, the number rose to 1751; and in 1842, to 2700. The population of Wisconsin for 1840 and 1842 was 30,945 and 44,478 respectively. These figures are based on the census returns of 1840 and 1842, *Wisconsin Territorial Census; Directory, 1848-49*, p. 61.
19. Solomon Juneau was elected first mayor of the city. The Democrats elected all but one of their candidates. Andreas, p. 262; *Sent.*, Oct. 16, 1895.
20. Still, p. 105.
21. Gabriel Shoyer was Treasurer of a Sack Company in 1852; Nathan Pereles was a Fire Warden in 1854, and Herman S. Mack was also active. *Sent.*, Jan. 10, 1852, p. 2; *Directory, 1854-55*, p. 334; *The U. S. Biographical Dictionary*, Wis. vol., pp. 137-38; James S. Buck, *Milwaukee Under the Charter*, III (Milwaukee, 1884, 1886), pp. 234-35; IV, p. 28.

22. Gabriel Shoyer was a member of the Washington Guards, which had about 70 members in 1851. Formed in Jan. 1845, with about 50 Privates and Officers, and a band, the Washington Guards met at Military Hall, which became the center of German activities in the city. *Sent.*, May 14, 1851, p. 2; *Directory, 1851-52*, p. xxviii

23. Milwaukee Chamber of Commerce, *Report, 1863*, p. 4; Frederick Merk, *Economic History of Wisconsin During the Civil War Decade* (Madison, 1916), I, pp. 221-222.

24. A Chamber of Commerce grew from these beginnings in 1858. Watrous, I, p 579.

25. During the period 1835-41, the value of imports was close to $6,000,-000, while that of exports was less than $500,000. Even in 1849, imports amounted to $4,000,000; exports, $2,000,000. Ray H. Whitbeck, *The Geography and Economic Development of Southeastern Wisconsin*, Wisconsin Geological and Natural History Survey, Bulletin no. 58, (Madison, 1921), p. 59, cited by Still, p. 61; Conard I, p. 282.

26. *Directory, 1847-48*, p. 71. Dealers in Milwaukee negotiated with the farmers in the vicinity of the village. Gregory, I, pp. 287, 454.

27. *Sent.*, Oct. 16, 1895; Still, p. 64.

28. Still, p. 184.

29. Henry Stern, "The Life Story of a Milwaukee Merchant," WMH, IX, 1 (Sept., 1925), p. 69.

30. Still, p. 185; Conard, I, p 285.

31. Among them were 7 architects, 17 insurance agents, 64 physicians and surgeons, 202 saloons, 224 groceries. Still, p. 200.

32. Gregory, I, p. 512.

33. Gregory, p. 517. Matches were still a novelty in many parts of the country.

34. Gregory, p. 538. This brewery, built by Reutelshofer, was situated on the South Side.

35. William George Bruce, ed., *History of Milwaukee City and County*, I (Chicago, 1922), p. 200; *Directory, 1848-49*, p. 61.

36. Still, p. 73. The first German in Milwaukee was Edward Wiesner. He left Germany in 1828 and arrived in Milwaukee in December of 1835. The first child of German parentage born in Milwaukee was Louis Bleyer (Dec. 25, 1837). *Sent.*, June 26, 1887, p. 3.

37. Bernard Heller, a Jewish settler of 1848, spent six weeks in crossing the Atlantic on board a sailing vessel, and six weeks more in traveling by boat down the Erie Canal and the Great Lakes before he reached his destination; obituary, Bernard Heller, *Sent.*, March 15, 1891, p. 1; Marcus, *op. cit.*, II, p. 272.

38. Stern, *op. cit.*, p. 63.

39. Kate A. Everest, "How Wisconsin Came By Its Large German Element," *Wisconsin Historical Society, Collections* (1892), p. 300. Of a population of 4,872 in the Second Ward in 1851, 2,715 were born in Germany, Austria, and Switzerland, 424 in England, 272 in other European states, 208 in Holland; of 1,471 Americans, 775 were born in Wisconsin. Buck, III, p. 334.

40. Still, pp. 112, 574; Table 4.

41. On April 17, 1848, Milwaukeeans of many nationalities had participated in a public demonstration greeting the revolution in Germany. *Sent.*, Dec. 2, 1851; obit., Isaac Neustadtl, *Sent.*, Dec. 3, 1877, p. 8; Still, pp. 112-114.

42. *Sent.*, Oct. 16, 1895.

43. Still, pp. 81, 131. Bohemians came to Milwaukee in large numbers as a result of the Austrian revolution of 1848. The first Polish settler, Anthony Kochanek, arrived in 1848. In 1860, there were about 50 Polish families in Milwaukee. Watrous, I, pp. 612-13.

44. *Sent.*, Oct. 16, 1895. Jacob Franks was a member of the Franks family of Montreal. An early Michigan trader, and prominently identified with Northwest beginnings, Jacob Franks was an English Jew who arrived in Green Bay in 1794, to open a trading post for his Montreal employers. A certain Capt. Anderson refers to him and his sister's son as "an English gentleman, Jacob Franks and his nephew, John Lawe, Jews extensively embarked in the fur trade here." When Franks retired to Mackinac during the War of 1812, he was a prominent person. The first saw mill and the first grist mill operated in Wisconsin were due to his endeavors. *Wisconsin Historical Collections*, III, pp. 252-53, 255; IX, p. 145; XV, p. 3; *PAJHS* (1905), pp. 52-53.

45. Wisconsin *Territorial Census*, 1836-42 *passim*; cf. Gregory, II, p. 630, who credits the Shoyer family and Henry Newhouse with having been "Jewish settlers of 1836."

46. The following names and descriptions are listed: Henry Newhouse, 2 males and 3 females, total, 5; Myer Shoyer, 11 males and 6 females, total 17; and Moses Weil, 8 males and 4 females, total 12.

47. The "Great Fire in Milwaukee," on April 6, 1845, resulted in "Two square miles in ruins," and "over $90,000 in property destroyed . . . Shoyer, Merchant Tailor, loses $150." *Sent.-Gaz.*, April 7, 1845, p. 2; Gabriel Shoyer married Louisa Shoyer, and Justice James B. Cross solemnized the ceremony; *ibid.*, Sept. 7, 1847, p. 2; Obit., Isaac Neustadtl, *Sent.*, Dec. 3, 1877, p. 8; April 28, 1871, p. 4; Buck, IV, p. 115.

48. *Am. Isr.*, Aug. 22, 1856, p. 53. City directories and census returns do not adequately reflect an all-inclusive picture of the actual population; many names may have been omitted. Moses Frank was the second Jewish child born in Milwaukee, according to his brother, Mr. Louis Frank; interview of March 3, 1956. *Am. Isr.*, Dec. 15, 1910, p. 2.

49. See Appendix for dates of arrival and countries of origin; cf. William George Bruce, *op. cit.*, who asserts that "The first Jews to arrive here were of English and Holland birth, and later came the Bohemian and German." Lands of origin are described in the Old Jewish Cemetery Record Book, pp. 4-10, 15, 17-18, 21, 23-24, 27-29, 31.

50. In 1855, the Second Ward was bordered by Walnut Street and West North Avenue, the Milwaukee River, Twenty Seventh Street on the west, West Kilbourn on the south, and the Milwaukee River on the east. *Wisconsin State Census, 1855, Milwaukee County*, II.

51. Fredrika Bremer, *The Homes of the New World; Impressions of America*, I (N.Y., 1854), pp. 615-17; Still, p. 112.

52. A. C. Wheeler, *The Chronicles of Milwaukee* (Milwaukee, 1861), p. 279.

53. Still, pp. 75-78.

54. Joseph Schafer, "The Yankee and the Teuton in Wisconsin," *WMH* VII (Dec., 1923), p. 158.

55. The first baseball club was organized on April 5, 1860; Still, p. 227.

56. *Sent.-Gaz.*, April 7, 1845, p. 2; March 14, 1846, p. 1; June 14, 1850, pp. 1, 2; *Sent.*, Sept. 9, 1853, p. 4; Aug. 25, p. 2; Sept. 9, p. 3; Oct. 9, 1854, p. 2; April 28, 1855, p. 2; Oct. 28, 1861, p. 1; *Directories, 1847-48*, pp. 118, 122; *1851-52*, p. 141; *1854-55*, p. 245; Buck, IV, p. 115.

57. Others were L. Newbauer, A. Breslauer, Abraham Fischel, and Isaac J. Litt. *Sent.-Gaz.*, March 1, 1850, p. 3; *Sent.*, Jan. 7, 1864, p. 1; *Am.* Isr., Jan. 7, 1897, p. 2; *Directories, 1847-48*, pp. 65, 110; *1851-52*, p. 171; *1854-55*, p. 37.

58. *Sent.*, Aug. 1, 1861; *Directory, 1856-57*, p. 32.

59. Buck, III, pp. 27, 146-47; *Directories, 1847-48*, pp. 90, 120; *1854-55*, p. 18; *Sent.*, Aug. 1, p. 4; Sept. 1, 1860, p. 2; Sept. 16, 1862, p. 1; April 28, 1871, p. 4; Jan. 1, 1873, p. 1; Feb. 17, 1875, p. 8; Andreas, pp. 1241-1242; *Am. Isr.*, Oct. 15, 1896, p. 7; Conard, II, pp. 430-32. Jacob Adler died in New York City in Feb., 1875.

60. *Sent.*, Feb. 27, 1858, p. 1; Andreas, pp. 1240, 1574.

61. *Sent.*, Sept. 9, 1853, p. 4; May 3, p. 3; July 9, p. 4; Dec. 13, 1856, p. 1; Aug. 8, 1860, p. 1; May 9, 1895, p. 3; *Directory, 1851-52*, p. 52; Buck, III, pp. 309-310; Andreas, p. 1241; *The U. S. Biographical Dictionary*, Wisconsin vol., pp. 372-76.

62. *Sent.*, Oct. 3, 1862, p. 1.

63. *Sent.-Gaz.*, June 8, 1848, p. 2; *Directory, 1848-49*, p. 200.

64. *Sent.*, Sept. 10, 1853, p. 3; Nov. 21, 1854, p. 2; July 9, 1856, p. 4; Oct. 13, 1857, p. 4; *Directory, 1854-55*, pp. 170-71; *1856-57*, p. 200; Buck, III, pp. 234-35; *The U. S. Biographical Dictionary*, Wisconsin vol., pp. 137-38.

65. Stern, pp. 64-68.

66. Goll & Frank grew from year to year. By 1881 they headed the dry goods jobbing trade in Milwaukee. Andreas, pp. 1235-36. The "Jr." after "Henry Stern" in the firm name, was added to distinguish him from another merchant bearing the same name. *Directory, 1851-52*, pp. 57, 148; *1854-55*, p. 255; Elmer E. Barton, *Industrial History of Milwaukee—The Commercial, Manufacturing and Railway Metropolis of the Northwest* (Milwaukee, 1886), p. 154.

67. Stern, p. 74.

68. *Directory, 1866*, p. 310; Conard, II, p. 370-71; *The U. S. Biographical Dictionary*, Wis. vol., pp. 86-87; *Sent.*, Aug. 26, 1899, p. 3. On the Heimann millinery firm, see *Sent.*, April 19, 1872, p. 4; July 26, 1888, p. 3; Andreas, p. 1271; See also *Sent.*, Aug. 1, 1860, p. 2; Feb. 14, 1887, p. 3.

69. *Sent.*, Nov. 3, 1856 p. 1; *The U. S. Biographical Dictionary*, Wis. vol., pp. 84-85.

70. *Sent.*, Sept. 12, 1866, p. 1; Oct. 4, 1886, p. 1; July 18, 1867, p. 1.

71. *Ibid.*, Oct. 21, 1867, p. 1; May 27, 1869, p. 1.

72. *The U. S. Biographical Dictionary*, Wis. vol., pp. 84-85; *Sent.*, Apr. 4, 1887, p. 2; Barton, p. 123; Andreas, p. 1245.

73. A fire in 1866, which destroyed his entire stock, left Schram with a loss of $50,000. *Sent.*, Nov. 17, 1866, p. 1; May 14, 1872, p. 4; May 15, 1872, p. 4; Andreas, p. 1594.

74. *Sent.*, March 15, 1891, p. 1; *Am. Isr.*, Oct. 15, 1896, p. 7; Marcus, II, p. 270; Andreas, pp. 1224, 1225.

75. *Sent.*, Feb. 5, 1856, p. 3; May 14, 1896, p. 3; *Directory, 1856-57*, Adv.

76. *Sent.*, May 31, 1862, p. 1; *Am. Isr.*, May 14, 1858, p. 359.

77. The Leopolds came from Riechen, Grand Duchy of Baden, Germany, where their family name was Freudenthaler; the Austrians, whose original name was Oesterreicher, came from Wittelshofen, Bavaria. D. E. Heineman, "The Leopold and Austrian Families," *PAJHS*, 1905, p. 59.

78. Lewis F. Leopold married Babette Austrian. Shortly after his arrival at Mackinac, Samuel F. Leopold purchased a one-mast sloop, the "Agate," with which he gathered up the product of the different fishing points, becoming the first in that section to enter the fishery trade. The Leopold brothers sent a thousand barrels of salted fish to Cleveland each year. This venture, together with the sale of supplies to fishermen, Indian trading, and the purchase of furs, laid the foundation for an extensive business. *Ibid.*, p. 58.

79. Optimism regarding prospects of the Lake Superior Navigation Company grew following Aaron F. Leopold's two-months' visit to the Lake Superior mining districts, in 1869. Passage of the "copper-tariff" bill inspired general industrial and business improvement. Small mines, which had been lying idle for years, re-opened; at the beginning of the navigation season, it was anticipated that there would be work for at least 2,000 additional men. *Sent.*, March 11, 1868, p. 4; March 12, 1869; p. 1; *Directory, 1869-70*, p. 403. Henry F. Leopold remained active in transportation until 1869, when he came to Chicago and entered the wholesale packing business. However, the Chicago fire destroyed his entire plant. Thereafter he retired, spending the rest of his days in Milwaukee where he died Sept. 3, 1896. *Am. Isr.*, Sept. 17, 1896, p. 2.

80. *Sent.*, Sept. 9, 1853, p. 1; *Directories, 1851-52*, p. 97; *1854-55*, pp. 172, 246; Andreas, p. 1483.

81. "Ethical Letter—Benjamin M. Roth to his son Solomon, 1854," *American Jewish Archives*, VI, 1 (Jan., 1954), pp. 6-7; *Sent.*, June 4, 1869, p. 1; Oct. 23, 1886, p. 3.

82. Andreas, p. 1481; For other tobacconists, see *Sent.*, Feb. 1, 1868, p. 1; Sept. 30, 1869, p. 1; *Directory, 1865*, p. 295.

83. *Sent.*, May 11, 1854, p.2.

84. According to Mr. Nathan Pereles, Jr., his grandfather prepared himself for the study of law by buying and studying an English Bible. His law certificate, now in the possession of Nathan Pereles, Jr., is dated Sept. 22, 1859, and was signed by the judge of the Second Judicial Circuit of Wisconsin, Arthur McArthur. Interview with Nathan Pereles, Jr., Oct. 11, 1954.

85. *Directories, 1848-49*, p. 113; *1851-52*, p. 121; *1862*, p. 298; *1868-69*, p. 335; Buck, IV, pp. 217-219; *Am. Isr.*, April 23, 1896, p. 7; Watrous, pp. 553-554; Andreas, p. 665.

86. Simon Levy, J. S. Abrams, M. N. Lando, and Philip Stein. Stein moved to Chicago, where he subsequently became a judge. He spent his early boyhood on a farm near Milwaukee, moving there in 1859. He married Emma Stein in April, 1875. Valedictorian of the University of Wisconsin, class of 1865, Stein delivered the dedicatory address at the opening of the Standard Club, Chicago, in 1870. *Sent.*, Jan. 30, 1865, p. 1; Jan. 11, 1870,

p. 1; Feb. 28, p. 1; April 6, 1875, p. 5; July 13, 1894, p. 3; *Am. Heb.*, June 29, 1895, p. 397; *Directories, 1858*, p. 275; *1859-60*, p. 276; *1860-61*, p. 276.

87. *Sent.*, Aug. 2, 1881, p. 5; *Directories, 1851-52*, p. 141; *1867*, p. 49; *1870-71*, p. 337; Andreas, pp. 1026-1027.

88. *Am. Isr.*, Aug. 22, 1856, p. 53.

89. Watrous, I, p. 123.

90. Still, pp. 133-34.

91. *Sent.*, May 13, 1851, p. 2; Buck, IV, p. 219; Watrous, I, p. 54; Conard, II, 370-71.

92. *Sent.*, Feb. 27, p. 2; March 3, 1852, p. 2; Jan. 1, 1853, p. 1. The Second Ward contained the largest segment of Milwaukee's Jewish population.

93. Gabriel Shoyer, Independent candidate for alderman in 1855, and Jacob Steinhardt, a Reformer candidate in 1858, were both unsuccessful. *Sent.*, Oct. 23, p. 2; Nov. 15, 1854, p. 2; Mar. 5, 6, and 7, 1885, p. 2; Apr. 6, 1858, p. 1; Apr. 4, p. 1; Apr. 8, 1868, p. 1.

94. *Sent.*, April 9, 1857, p. 2.

95. Rindskopf served on the Finance, Police and Plats committees of the Council. *Sent.*, April 7, p. 1; April 10, 1869, p. 1; April 6, 1870, p. 1; *Directory, 1869-70* (1869), App., p. 398.

96. *Sent.*, April 8, p. 1; April 18, 1861, p. 1; March 24, p. 1; April 3, p. 1; April 11, p. 1; Oct. 17, 1862, p. 1; *Directory, 1862*, p. 14. Mack resigned as alderman in Oct., 1862. He had served on the standing committees of Judiciary, Licenses, and Railroads.

97. The county board was composed of a representative from each assembly district who held office for two years. Mack sat on the standing committees for Circuit and Municipal Courts, and Roads and Bridges. *Sent.*, May 8, p. 1; Oct. 19, p. 2; Oct. 28, 1861, p. 1; *Directory, 1862*, pp. 21, 22.

98. *Sent.*, April 10, 1860, p. 1; *Directory, 1860-61*, p. 290.

99. *Sent.*, March 24, 1860, p. 1; Oct. 29, 1861, p. 1.

100. *Sent.*, April 1, 1867, p. 1.

101. *Sent.*, Feb. 19, 1867, p. 1.

102. Born as Schleisinger, Weil added the name of his second wife to his own, as "a compliment often paid by Frenchmen to their wives." *Sent.*, July 8, 1858, p. 2.

103. *Sent.*, July 11, 1854, p. 2; July 8, 1858, p. 2; Jan. 11, 1871, p. 3. According to one source, Weil bought 20,000 acres of land lying between Cedar Lake and the site of the present town of Slinger, at 25 cents an acre, which brought the investment to $5,000. *Milwaukee Journal*, July 1, 1954, p. 8.

104. Originally known as Rubicon, the name of the village was changed to Polk in 1848; it was named after Baruch Schleisinger Weil in the spring of 1850. During World War I, a wave of anti-German feeling throughout the country moved the leaders of the community to de-Germanize the name of the village. On April 1, 1920, the name was officially changed to Slinger. *Milwaukee Journal*, July 1, 1954, p. 8.

105. *Sent.*, Sept. 2, p. 2; Oct. 27, p. 2, Nov. 8, 1851, p. 2.

106. *Sent.*, Sept. 30, p. 2; Nov. 6, p. 2, Nov. 13, 1852, p. 2.

107. *Sent.*, April 8, p. 2, April 12, 1853, p. 2.

108. Weil received 657 votes against 515 for Mitchell Delaney (Indep. Dem.) and 465 for Dr. G. F. Hunt (Rep.). *Sent.*, July 8, 1858, p. 2; Jan. 11, 1871, p. 3.

109. Weil was delegate to the Democratic State Convention in Madison in 1853; and a Senatorial delegate to the Waupan Democratic Congressional Convention from Washington County, in Sept., 1854. *Sent.*, Sept. 6, 1853, p. 3; Sept. 26, p. 2; Oct. 11, p. 2; Nov. 1, 1854, p. 2; Nov. 13, 1855, p. 2; Jan. 8, p. 2; Nov. 8, 1856, p. 2.

110. *Sent.*, June 2, p. 3; Sept. 4, p. 1; Sept. 10, 1857, p. 2.

111. *Sent.*, July 3, 1858; June 21, p. 1; June 22, p. 1; June 23, p. 2; July 8, 1858, p. 1.

112. *Sent.*, Nov. 3, p. 2; Nov. 17, 1870, p. 2; Jan. 11, 1871; *Blue Book*, pp. 16–17; *The Wisconsin Blue Book* (Madison, 1915), pp. 262, 313.

113. *Sent.-Gaz.*, Oct. 3, 1849, p. 2; *Sent.*, Nov. 4, 1852, p. 2; Oct. 20, 1859, p. 2. The Wisconsin *Territorial Census* of 1848 (as of Dec. 1, 1847) lists "L. Silverman" as a resident of Milwaukee County; *Directory 1848-49*, p. 123.

114. Port Washington *Blade*, cited by *Sent.*, April 22, 1853, p. 2.

115. According to the Governor's statement of June 4, 1853, Paul A. Weil had been authorized to remove them from Port Washington to West Bend, in Washington County. This directive was in accordance with the law enacted in that year, which divided Washington County and set up Ozaukee County. Port Washington was in Ozaukee County. Lion Silverman prevented Weil, a brother-in-law of B. S. Weil, from taking possession of the records, and had Weil assaulted and arrested. The Milwaukee *News* attacked the Governor for this dismissal; the *Sent.* and the Sheboygan *Lake Journal Democrat* endorsed it. The latter contended that it was the "duty of a public officer to execute, not resist, the laws of the State." Silverman's unimpaired prestige in his own community is reflected by the fact that the County Supervisors allowed him $1500 for damages sustained in resisting the law. *Sent.*, June 6, p. 2, June 7, p. 2, June 9, p. 2, June 10, p. 2, Sept. 24, 1853, p. 2.

116. *Ibid.*, Sept. 2, 1853, p. 2. Silverman's political influence is indicated by the Governor's action. He revoked an earlier appointment by merely explaining that as Governor he had power to remove an officer of his own creation without showing cause. *Ibid.*, Feb. 18, 1854, p. 2; Feb. 2, p. 2; Feb. 3, 1855, p. 2; Sept. 27, 1855, p. 2; April 10, 1857, p. 2; Nov. 6, 1858, p. 1.

117. *Ibid.*, Aug. 6, p. 2; Sept. 15, 1859, p. 2; *Am. Isr.*, Sept. 2, 1859, p. 71; Sept. 9, 1859, p. 78; *J. Mess.*, Sept. 16, 1859, p. 85.

118. The Madison *Journal* attacked Silverman for the "orthography and capitalization" in his letter. This same paper published a letter from Mansfield, Ohio, accusing Silverman of having swindled in that community 18 years earlier. All three German Democratic papers, the *Seebote*, *Banner & Volksfreund*, and *Phoenix*, labored for Silverman's defeat. *Sent.*, Oct. 3, p. 1; Oct. 4, p. 2; Oct. 10, p. 2; Oct. 20, p. 2; Nov. 15, 1859, p. 1.

119. *Sent.*, Nov. 15, p. 1; cf. Nov. 23, p. 2; Nov. 30, p. 2; Dec. 2, p. 1; Dec. 6, p. 2; Dec. 14, 1859, p. 2.

120. Quoted in *Sent.*, Nov. 23, 1859, p. 2.

121. *Sent.*, Nov. 30, 1859, p. 2. During his declining years, "Col." Silver-

man took up resident in Pine Bluff, Ark. In his seventy-fifth year, he ended his life by suicide. *Ibid.*, April 28, 1894, p. 2.

122. Otterbourg married Mathilde Bruno shortly after his arrival in Milwaukee. Their son, Eugene, was born in 1854. Following the death of his wife, he married Augusta Stroheimer in 1858. Their child George was born in 1859. Ruth L. Benjamin, "Marcus Otterbourg, United States Minister to Mexico in 1867," *PAJHS*, XXXII (1931), pp. 65-66; *Am. Isr.*, Dec. 14, 1893, p. 5; *AJYB*, 5698 (1937-38), p. 737.

123. *Sent.*, Dec. 3, 1858, p. 1; Jan. 17, 1859, p. 1.

124. *Sent.*, June 23, p. 1; Nov. 30, 1859, p. 1; Aug. 16, 1867, p. 1; Feb. 6, 1860, p. 1; Aug. 13, 1860, p. 1; Platterville *Witness*, cited by *Sent.*, Oct. 2, 1860, p. 1.

125. *Ibid.*, Aug. 16, 1861, p. 1.

126. Benjamin, *op. cit.*, pp. 65, 96; *Am. Isr.*, Dec. 14, 1893, p. 5; *Sent.*, June 29, p. 2; Aug. 16, 1867, p. 1; Aug. 7, 1875, p. 2.

127. *Sent.*, May 21, 1858, p. 1.

128. Judge McArthur was the grandfather of General Douglas MacArthur of World War II fame. *Sent.*, March 1, p. 1; March 2, 1859, p. 2; March 19, 1958, p. 14; *Am. Isr.*, April 1, 1859, p. 306.

129. *Sent.*, March 2, 1859, p. 1.

130. *Am. Isr.*, Sept. 4, 1857, p. 68. Only the Washington, D.C. *Star* and the Dubuque *Express* and *Herald* editorially supported the discriminatory treaty. See Morris U. Schappes, ed., *A Documentary History of the Jews in the United States, 1654-1875* (N.Y., 1950), p. 321.

131. *Sent.*, Oct. 22, p. 1, and Oct. 23, 1857, p. 2. The Milwaukee Jewish mass meetings were held under the joint sponsorship of congregations B'ne Jeshurun and Anshe Emeth. The meetings on October 20 resulted in the election of Dr. David Einhorn of Baltimore as Milwaukee's delegate. This produced an unpleasant exchange between him and Rabbi Isidor Kalisch. *Sinai*, II, 11 (Dec., 1857), pp. 756, 758, 761; *Asmonean*, Nov. 20, 1857, p. 45.

132. Bertram W. Korn, *The American Reaction to the Mortara Case: 1858-1859* (Cincinnati, 1957), p. 95.

133. *Ibid.*

134. Milwaukee *News*, cited by *Sent.*, Dec. 4, 1858, p. 2; Dec. 28, 1858, p. 2.

135. *Am. Isr.*, Dec. 17, 1858, p. 191.

136. Stern, *op. cit.*, p. 75. The second war meeting founded the Milwaukee Volunteer Relief Association, designed to relieve soldiers' families. In a single day, members of the Chamber of Commerce subscribed over $11,000 to the fund, and over $12,000 was subscribed the same day by merchants in the city. That organization functioned until the close of the war, and often called for contributions. Watrous, I, p. 594.

137. "I was one of the helpers," wrote Sophia Heller Goldsmith. Marcus, *op. cit.* II, p. 276; Still, p. 158.

138. Watrous, I, p. 594; Still, p. 157.

139. Still, pp. 158-59; Watrous, I, 595. During the Fall of 1862, the 24th was sent to Kentucky, leaving Milwaukee on Sept. 5. The 26th Wisconsin Regiment left Milwaukee to join Sigel on the Potomac, Oct. 6, 1862. It was a German regiment, of which almost two-thirds came from Milwaukee. Andreas, p. 720; Watrous, I, p. 595.

140. Still, p. 159.
141. Stern, *op. cit.*, p. 75.
142. *Sent.*, Oct. 12, 1874, p. 1.
143. *Sent.*, July 14, 1937, p. 8c; Certificate of Service, Adjutant General's Office, State of Wisconsin, dated Jan. 31, 1956; *Roster of Wisconsin Volunteers—War of Rebellion, 1861-1865*, II (Madison, 1886), p. 275; William de Loss Love, *Wisconsin in the War of Rebellion: a History of all Regiments and Batteries* (Chicago, 1866), p. 1097; *Sent.*, Dec. 22, 1863, p. 1.
144. Certificate of Service, Adjutant General's Office, State of Wisconsin, dated March 22, 1956; *Roster of Wisconsin Volunteers*, II, pp. 313, 317.
145. Old Jewish Cemetery Record Book, page 7: "Jonas Goldschmied, of Prague, Bohemia, born 1837 Shemine Atzeres, killed in battle near Murfreesboro on February 1, 1863—buried on February 9, 1863—soldier—no fee." *Sent.*, Feb. 9, 1863, p. 1. A search in the Wisconsin Adjutant General's Office for the name "Goldschmied," "Goldsmith," or "Goldschmidt" failed to disclose any record of Goldsmith.
146. *Roster of Wisconsin Volunteers*, I, p. 446; II, p. 264.
147. *Directory* for 1860-61 contains the earliest listing of Phillip Horwitz, as proprietor of an "intelligence office" at 234 East Water. After the Civil War, he was a cigar manufacturer and a policeman. In 1881, he was clerk to the Mayor. Divorced from his first wife, Sophie, on Jan. 14, 1874, he married Rosa Strued, 33 years his junior, on May 27, 1874, and fathered two children, Olga, born March 27, 1875, and Alex, born Dec. 15, 1877. Horwitz died on Nov. 8, 1886, at the age of 64, of a disease "incurred while in the service of the United States." He was buried in the Greenwood Cemetery. Certificate of Service, Adjutant General's Office, State of Wisconsin, dated Jan. 12, 1956; *Sent.*, Sept. 25, 1861, p. 2; Aug. 12, p. 1; Aug. 20, p. 1; Oct. 3, 1862, p. 1; Dec. 28, 1880, p. 8; Jan. 1, 1881, p. 2; Nov. 9, pp. 3, 5; Nov. 11, 1886, p. 5; *Roster of Wisconsin Volunteers*, I, p. 306, II, p. 312; photostat of Declaration for an Original Invalid Pension, dated Oct. 1882; photostat of Certificate of Service, Adjutant General's Office, War Dept., dated June 5, 1883; photostat, Widows' Declaration for Pension, dated August 3, 1887; *Directory, 1860-61*, p. 116; *1867-68*, p. 208; Andreas, pp. 700, 720.
148. Other Milwaukee Jewish soldiers were unrecorded by Simon Wolf. Charles Neubauer enlisted June 18, 1861, and was transferred to Co. A, Ind. Batt., on July 13, 1864. Herman Perlewitz enlisted for three months; he served in Co. A, 26th Regiment Infantry, on Aug. 15, 1862, with the rank of Sergeant, and was discharged March 19, 1863 for disability. Roth, attached to Co. A, 26th Regiment, and whose residence was given as Cedarburg, served from Aug. 21, 1862. He attained the rank of Sergeant. He was mustered out June 13, 1865. It appears that he was the younger brother of Solomon and Moses Roth, who came to Milwaukee in 1854. *American Jewish Archives*, VI, 1 (Jan., 1954), p. 6. Louis Seligman, of Co. C, 24th Regiment Infantry, entered the service on April 15, 1864; he was transferred to Co. K, 13th Wisconsin Infantry, on June 7, 1865. *Roster of Wisconsin Volunteers*, I, pp. 307, 446; II, pp. 264, 315.
149. *Sent.*, June 19, 1865, p. 1; July 14, 1866, p. 1.
150. *Sent.*, Nov. 28, 1861, p. 1. He was an Army purveyor.
151. *Sent.*, Sept. 20, 1861, p. 2.

152. *Sent.*, June 9, 1865, p. 1; Bertram Wallace Korn, *American Jewry and the Civil War* (Phil., 1951), p. 208.

153. Note the following schedule of incomes:

	1865	1866	1867	1868
Henry Stern		$12,277.	$8,026.	$9,352.
Herman Stern		12,277.	8,026.	9,352.
M. Friend		7,328.	6,777.	5,802.
E. Friend		7,465.	6,748.	5,760.
H. Friend		7,227.	8,666.	5,782.
David Adler	$10,088.	6,962.		
Solomon Adler	10,022.	6,962.	6,199.	5,098.
J. Morawetz		5,139.	5,083.	6,264.
M. L. Morawetz			5,235.	5,235.
J. Friedman		5,925.		
G. Bremer		5,080.		6,255.

In 1867, the number of persons whose incomes exceeded $5,000 fell to 113, of whom 8 were Jewish. Records for the year 1868 revealed that 109 individuals earned more than $5,000; 9 were Jews.

The income tax law was in operation from 1863 until 1872. The highest tax paid in 1866 was by Alexander Mitchell, $13,200, on a total income of $132,000. *Sent.*, Aug. 1, 1866, p. 1 and Dec. 24, 1893, p. 9.

154. Letter of Maria Heller Shakman, Jan. 29, 1866, in authors' possession.

155. *Am. Isr.*, Sept. 29, 1865, p. 101. *Occident*, XXIV, no. 8 (Nov., 1866), p. 383; "We learn that between two and three hundred Jewish families reside in Milwaukee who are, we suppose, all emigrants from Europe . . ."

II. FOUNDING A JEWISH COMMUNITY

1. Letter of August 28, 1845, in Sidney Glazer, "Wisconsin as Depicted in the Michigan Press," *WMH*, XXVII, p. 89.

2. Milwaukee *Courier*, May 8, 1844, cited by Gregory, II, pp. 894, 842; Still, pp. 89-90.

3. *Sent.*, August 9, 1885, p. 7; Gregory, II, pp. 840-842.

4. Gregory, II, p. 841.

5. Gregory, II, p. 850; Still, p. 91; *Sent.*, June 26, 1887, p. 8.

6. Gregory, II, pp. 841, 867-868.

7. Still, pp. 79, 92.

8. Still, p. 92.

9. *Sent.*, October 9, 1856, p. 2. See *Am. Isr.*, October 10, 1856, p. 110: "All the stores were shut during the last holidays . . ." A similar account is in *Sent.*, Sept. 6, 1869, p. 1.

10. *Sent.*, April 7, 1858, p. 1; May 17, 1861, p. 1; April 10, 1868, p. 1; July 29, 1868, p. 1; March 17, 1870, p. 1.

11. *Allgemeine Zeitung Des Judenthums*, XXXIV, 14 (April 5, 1870), p. 272.

12. Most of the stone inscriptions are in German. A few early monument inscriptions read: "Isaac, died March 21, 1850, aged 4 years.—Sarah, died August 7, 1848, aged 5 mos. 15 days, children of J. & F. Steinhart"; "Gertrude, daughter of H. & M. Newhouse, born June 15, 1849, died June 21,

1851"; "S. Neustadtl, Oct. 3, 1849"; "William, son of S. & L. Adler, died July 26, 1850, 4 yrs." Supplementary Typed Burial List, 1936.

13. Those attending the meeting were Solomon Adler, Samuel Engel, Isaac Stransky, A. Weil, S. Raudnitz, E. Schram, A. Greenfeld, J. Schoenmann, E. Heller, Moses Kahn, C. Beckard, M. Michelstadter, A. Bellock, A. Mayer, E. Taehaw, Charles Zikenex, T. Fuchs, S. Schram, Isaac Neustadtl, Jacob Morawetz, Jacob Steinhart, and I. Fuchs. Record, Religious Societies, Milwaukee County, I, p. 6.

14. The one acre cost $1200. Originally bought by Congregation Ahabath Emuno, all congregations arranged to use it. Legal description of cemetery ground: "Lot 24 in Block 2, in Assessment Subdivision No. 33, in the city of Milwaukee." Abstract of Title, Old Jewish Cemetery. Deed recorded in Office of Register of Deeds, 42:62; *Directory, 1854-55*, p. 347.

15. Burial records from August 27, 1861 to Sept. 7, 1876, contained 356 burial entries in German. They give names, places of origin, dates of birth and death, and other data. "Record Concerning Bodies Which Have Been Buried On the Burial Ground of the Congregation B'ne Jeshurun from September 1861 and Thereafter." This Record Book, well preserved, is presently in the possession of Temple Emanu-El B'ne Jeshurun of Milwaukee. The last burial in the Old Jewish Cemetery took place in 1888. *Wisc. JC.*, Sept. 28, 1951, p. 13. According to the most recent report, drawn up in 1936, 87 bodies still remain interred in that cemetery.

16. *Sent.*, January 1, 1883, p. 9; June 17, 1887, p. 5; October 16, 1895; *Directory, 1848-49*, p. 111; Andreas, p. 948; Rabbi S. Hecht, "The Jews and Judaism in Milwaukee," *History of Milwaukee* . . . , in Conard, ed. II, pp. 233-234.

17. "Synagogues and Churches are not built for ourselves alone but for our children and our children's children to worship therein . . . ; their numbers warrant then in incurring an outlay exceeding their present capital; if they go into a new building with a moderate debt, there is every prospect of liquidating it in a few years . . . Doctoring old buildings is never advisable, more particularly where there exists deficiencies which cannot be remedied or removed . . ." *Asmonean*, II, 18 (August 23, 1850), p. 140.

18. *Asmonean*, XI, 25 (April 6, 1855), p. 196.

19. The City Directory listed Congregation Imanu-Al as "Jews' Synagogue." *Directories, 1854-55*, p. 324; *1856-57*, p. 449; *Am. Isr.*, Aug. 22, 1856, p. 53.

20. Record of Religious Societies, Milwaukee County, Certificate of Incorporation of Imanu-Al Congregation, p. 3; *Asmonean*, XI, 25 (Apr. 6, 1855), p. 196..

21. *Am. Isr.*, Nov. 23, 1855, p. 166; August 22, 1856, p. 53; *Directories, 1854-55*, p. 324; *1856-57*, p. 449; *Sent.*, Jan. 1, 1883, p. 9; J. J. Benjamin II, *Reise in den ostlichen Staaten der Union* (Hamburg, 1862), p. 37, cited by Leo Goldhammer, "Jewish Emigration from Austria-Hungary in 1848-1849," *YIVO Annual of Jewish Social Science*, IX (1954), p. 360; (I. J. Benjamin, *Three Years in America, 1859-1862* II, [Phila., 1956], p. 175); Andreas, p. 948; Warranty Deed, "Richardson Houghton and Eliza P. Houghton to Congregation Ahaveat Emuno," dated Jan. 10, 1854, Abstract of Title, Old Jewish Cemetery.

22. "An act to incorporate the 'Ahabath Emuno Congregation' of the

city of Milwaukee," *General Acts Passed by the Legislature of Wisconsin in the year 1856* (Madison, 1856), ch. 47, p. 48.

23. *Am. Isr.*, August 22, 1856, p. 53; Sept. 5, 1856, p. 66.

24. *Ibid.*, August 22, 1856, p. 53; Superficially, it would seem that a discrepancy exists in the official records of Congregation Anshe Emeth, since the introduction to the Constitution states: "We, the undersigned members of the religious congregation of the Israelites in the city of Milwaukee, founded on the 14 of October, 1856, 5617, a congregation consisting of 15 members, and accept the following constitution and its by-laws . . ." Both the *Israelite* and the *Occident* carried news of the congregation from early 1855. Furthermore, the congregation was officially incorporated on March 31, 1856. In all probability, the society existed informally until October 14, 1856, when the members decided to organize on a permanent basis.

25. Letter of M. H. Schwartzenberg dated August 10, 1855, in *Am. Isr.*, August 24, 1855, p. 54; *Occident*, May, 1856, pp. 94-95.

26. "An Act to incorporate the Anshe Emeth Congregation of the city of Milwaukee," *General Acts Passed by the Legislature of Wisconsin in the year 1856* (Madison, 1856), ch. 382, p. 806.

27. *Am. Isr.*, May 9, 1856, p. 357; *Occident*, Dec., 1856, p. 454.

28. Anshe Emeth Record Book, pp. 28-29. For the Rules of Order, Constitution and By-Laws of Congregation Anshe Emeth, see Appendix 4.

29. *Ibid.*, Article XI, Sec. 1, 2, 7.

30. *Ibid.*, Articles XIII and XIV.

31. *Ibid.*, Article IV, Sec. 2.

32. *Ibid.*, Articles II, III, Record Book, Congregation Anshe Emeth.

33. *Ibid.*, Article IV, Sec. 4, 10; Article VI, Sec. 3.

34. *Ibid.*, Article X.

35. *Ibid.*, Article IX.

36. *Ibid.*, Article XII.

37. *Ibid.*, Articles VII, XV. However, Masonic services frequently took place.

38. *Ibid.*, Article IV, Sec. 3.

39. "Mrs. Friend was five years long a pupil of mine when I kept school in Albany, N. Y." Elias Friend married Rose Stern in Albany on Sept. 24, 1855, the Rev. S. Falk officiating. *Am. Isr.*, August 22, 1856, p. 53; *Sent.*, October 5, 1855, p. 2.

40. *Am. Isr.*, Aug. 22, 1856, p. 53.

41. *Am. Isr.*, Aug. 29, 1856, p. 62. Following Isaac Leeseer's plan for the establishment of a school for the training of American-born rabbis and teachers, Isaac M. Wise, in 1854, proposed the establishment of the Zion Collegiate Institute for that same purpose. Moshe Davis, "Jewish Religious Life and Institutions in America (A Historical Study)," Louis Finkelstein ed., *The Jews, Their History, Culture, and Religion*, I, (Phila., 1949), p. 374.

42. On September 18, 1856, M. H. Schwarzenberg, vice-president of Anshe Emeth, wrote to the *Israelite*: "At the last meeting of the three congregations of this place it was resolved to unite into one congregation under the name of *Bene Jeshrun* . . . Among the resolutions past [sic] . . . was one which says: 'The Reformed *Minhag* of the new congregation shall be as the Minhag in K. K. *Bene Jeshurun*, Cincinnati, Ohio.'" *Am. Isr.*, Sept. 26, 1856, p. 94.

43. *Sent.*, January 14, 1857, p. 3: *Am Isr.*, Nov. 17, 1856, p. 142; Andreas, p. 948.

44. *Am. Isr.*, Nov. 7, 1856, p. 142.

45. *Ibid.*, Jan. 23, 1857, pp. 230-231.

46. *Ibid.*, May 1, 1857, p. 342; *Occident*, June, 1857, pp. 154-55; Andreas, p. 948.

47. *Am. Isr.*, Dec. 25, 1857, p. 198.

48. The congregation existed "celebrating divine worship according to the rites of the Jewish church and for burying their dead according to the said rites." The certificate of incorporation, dated September 21, 1858, and recorded October 5 of the same year, was signed by Solomon Adler and Rev. Dr. Isidor Kalisch. Certificate of Organization of Congregation *Bene Jeshurun*, Record of Religious Societies, Milwaukee County, pp. 14-15.

49. *Sent.*, May 11, 1859, p. 1; Andreas, p. 948.

50. *Occident*, Feb., 1857, p. 551; June, 1857, pp. 154-55; *Asmonean*, XV, 15 (Jan. 22, 1857), p. 117; *Directory, 1858*, Appendix, p. 16.

51. *Am. Isr.*, July 30, 1858, p. 31.

52. *Sent.*, Jan. 1, 1883, p. 9: Oct. 16, 1895; Sworn statement by Lewis Rindskopf, Abraham Fischel, and Abraham Breslauer, dated March 17, 1896, Abstract of Title, Old Jewish Cemetery. *Am. Isr.*, May 20, 1859, p. 366; June 10, 1859, p. 391.

53. *Sent.*, Sept. 17, 1859, p. 1.

54. *Am. Isr.*, Sept. 30, 1859, p. 102.

55. *Ibid.*, Aug. 26, 1859, p. 63; June 10, 1859, p. 391; Marcus, *op. cit.* II, p. 273.

56. One of the girls was Sophia Heller, only 11 years old at the time. In her memoirs, written in 1908 and continued in 1918, she wrote: "Two girls and myself were the happy children robed in white with baskets of flowers. We walked in front of Dr. Wise as he carried the *Safratorah* around in the temple. We strewed flowers in front of him . . . About seven years later I was married in the same temple . . ." (to Phillip Goldsmith). Marcus, *op. cit.*, II, pp. 268-269, 273.

57. *Sent.*, Sept. 17, 1859, p. 1; *Am. Isr.*, Sept. 16, 1859, p. 84.

58. Officers of the congregation at this time were: Solomon Adler, president; Jacob Adler, secretary; other members of the Administration were: M. H. Schwarzenberg, J. Hyman, S. Lewald, M. Friend, I. Stransky, M. Otterbourg, and Henry Bonns. *Am. Isr.*, Sept. 30, 1859, p. 102; Oct. 7, 1859, p. 110; *Sent.*, Sept. 20, 1859, p. 1; *J. Mess.*, Oct. 12, 1859, p. 117; Oct. 28, 1859, p. 125.

59. *Am. Isr.*, Sept. 30, 1859, p. 102.

60. For reference to Wise's call for complete consolidation of all congregations, see: *Am. Isr.*, May 1, 1857, p. 342; May 20, 1859, p. 366.

61. David de Sola Pool, "Judaism and the Synagogue," *The American Jew, A Composite Portrait*, Oscar I. Janowsky, ed. (New York, 1942), p. 33.

62. Isaac Mayer Wise, *Reminiscences* (Cincinnati, 1901), p. 45. In 1855 there were only nine ordained rabbis in the United States. *Ibid.*, p. 308.

63. Joseph Schafer, "The Yankee and the Teuton in Wisconsin," *WMH*, VI (1922-23), pp. 368-402; Still, pp. 80, 93.

64. His father, Burnham (?) Kalisch, died September 1, 1856, at Krotschin; Sarah Kalisch passed away on March 14, 1883, in New York, at

the age of 87. Mrs. Marcus Cohn, a sister of Rabbi Kalisch, lived in Milwaukee for many years, and died there in September, 1882. A son of Rabbi Kalisch, Samuel, became Justice of the Supreme Court of New Jersey. *Der Zeitgeist*, Oct. 12, 1882, p. 320; *Am. Isr.*, April 6, 1883, p. 334.

65. Samuel Kalisch, "Rabbi Isidor Kalisch, a Memoir," *Studies in Ancient and Modern Judaism* . . . *Selected Writings of Rabbi Isidor Kalisch,* Samuel Kalisch, ed. (New York, 1928), pp. 1-7.

66. *Ibid.*, pp. 242-247.

67. The original German title was *Wegweiser fuer rationelle Forschungen in den Biblischen Schriften.* The English edition was published by Bloch & Co., publishers of the *Israelite* and *Deborah*.

68. Kalisch's wife died on March 25, 1856, at the age of 37. Samuel Kalisch, *op. cit.*, pp. 19-22, 26.

69. Isidor Kalisch was an active participant in the conference of moderate Reform elements in Cleveland on October 17, 1855. Rabbis Lilienthal, Merzbacher, Rothenheim, and Wise had been appointed by the Conference with Wise as chairman, to report on a revised prayer book at a subsequent gathering. Due to the death of Merzbacher, and the inability of Lilienthal, Kalisch cooperated in the editorial work of the *Minhag America*, and was thus an author of that Prayer Book. Prayers for the return to Eretz Yisrael, the rebuilding of the Temple in Jerusalem, and the restoration of the Davidic dynasty were eliminated. *Am. Isr.*, May 15, 1857, p. 355; Jan. 15, 1858, p. 221; April 30, 1858, p. 342; *Occident*, April 26, 1860, p. 32; Davis, *op. cit.*, pp. 369, 371.

70. In 1882, when the Society of True Sisters celebrated its twenty-fifth anniversary, a "telegram of thanks," together with $50, as "a gift of honor" were sent to "the courageous old fighter." *Der Zeitgeist,* Nov. 23, 1882, p. 368.

Upon leaving Milwaukee, Rabbi Kalisch moved to New York City. After serving in some communities, he occupied pulpits in Indianapolis (1862-1864), Detroit (1864-1866), and Leavenworth, Kansas (1866-1868). In 1863, Kalisch's application for an Army chaplaincy was rejected. In 1869, he conducted a Day and Boarding School on West 36th Street in New York City. After a year, he entered the lecturing field. From 1870-1872, he served as rabbi of Congregation B'nai Abraham, of Newark, New Jersey; from 1872 to 1875, rabbi of Congregation Ohabei Sholom, Nashville, Tennessee. He returned to Newark in September, 1875, where he devoted himself to literary work. Kalisch wrote Hebrew poems, tales, fables, and translated into Hebrew German and English poets, which never appeared in print. He translated into English prose Lessing's *Nathan der Weise,* and an elaborate English translation of *Sepher Yesirah, A Book on Creation or The Jewish Metaphysics of Remote Antiquity.* In 1880, a selection of Kalisch's German poems was published in Newark, New Jersey.

Kalisch died May 11, 1886, survived by his widow (whom he married in New York in 1864), five sons and a daughter. For a list of biographical sketches of Isidor Kalisch, see Samuel Kalisch, *op. cit.*, pp. 59-60; *J. Mess.*, June 8, 1860, pp. 172-173; March 11, 1870, p. 3; Aug. 9, 1872, p. 2; *Am. Isr.*, Sept. 7, 1860, p. 78; Aug. 15, 1862, p. 51; May 22, 1863, p. 362; Sept. 2, 1864, p. 75; Dec. 14, 1886, p. 4; Jan. 25, 1878, pp. 4-5; April 30, 1880, p. 6; May 14,

1886, p. 9; May 21, 1886, p. 2; *Am. Heb.*, May 14, 1886, p. 8; *Jewish Times*, June 11, 1869, p. 7; Dec. 17, 1869, p. 15; June 12, 1874, p. 247; *Jewish Chronicle*, Feb. 21, 1873, p. 675; *Allgemeine Zeitung des Judenthums*, Jan. 1, 1878, p. 11; Bertram Wallace Korn, *American Jewry and the Civil War* (Phil., 1951), pp. 81-82.

71. The entire correspondence between Kalisch and Buchanan appeared in the *Jewish Chronicle*, (London), Oct. 29, 1858, pp. 6-7.

72. Copies of Buchanan's reply were published in the *Sent.*, Sept. 22, 1858, p. 1; *Archives Israélites*, XX (Jan., 1859), pp. 54-55; *Am. Isr.*, Sept. 24, 1858, p. 94. Commenting on the above incident some 68 years later, Samuel Kalisch attributed it to his father's "intense love for religious liberty, and his zealous care of the honor and future of the Jewish people, even to the most exacting minutiae." Samuel Kalisch, *op. cit.*, p. 28.

73. The German title of the work, published in 1865, is *Tone des Morgenlandes*. *Am. Isr.*, May 4, 1860, p. 547; *Occident*, May 24, 1860, p. 54. An admirer of Kalisch wrote to the *Sentinel*: ". . . . Milwaukee, and the Jewish community foremost, loses a man of distinction and great reputation in literature . . . The learned gentleman was one of the only three on this globe who were able to decipher the Phoenician scriptures found in Zidon, Palestine, and was acknowledged as such by the Cyron Historical Society in London . . . May another city, in better pecuniary circumstances, acknowledge our loss by giving him a support, and afford him a greater sphere of action, so that he may never be in trouble as to his earning a living." *Sent.*, May 10, 1860, p. 1.

74. Stuart E. Rosenberg, *The Jewish Community in Rochester, 1843-1925* (New York, 1954), pp. 30-34.

75. *Directory, 1860-1861* (publ. 1860), p. 293. *Am. Isr.*, Sept. 7, 1860 p. 78; July 12, 1861, p. 14. Entries of "offerings" recorded in the congregation's journal show three donations by "Dr Sarner" during September and October, 1860. Anshe Emeth Record Book (B'ne Jeshurun), pp. 35, 36, 37,

76. After the War he engaged in lecturing in New York City and was joint editor and publisher of a German-Jewish monthly, *Die Rebekah*. Sarner returned to the pulpit as rabbi of the Orthodox Congregation Beth El, of Memphis, Tennessee, where he remained until his death in August, 1878, during an epidemic of yellow fever. Bertram W. Korn, *op. cit.*, pp. 84-85; Rosenberg, *op. cit.*, pp. 30-34.

77. Heiman was listed as "Rev. M. Heiman, Rabbi." *Directory, 1862*, p. 18.

78. *Ibid., 1863*, p. 73; *1865*, p. 192; *1866*, p. 136; *Am. Isr.*, May 27, 1863, p. 299; March 19, 1866, p. 285; Nov. 16, 1866, p. 5; For donations of Dr. Falk to the congregation from May, 1863 to June, 1865, see Anshe Emeth Record Book (B'ne Jeshurun), pp. 62, 63, 67, 68, 69, 72, 75, 78, 82, 85, 87. Samson Falk was born on Feb. 7, 1827 in Höchburg, Württemberg. He studied at the University of Württemberg and was probably ordained in Germany. He came to the U. S. in 1853, serving as rabbi in Albany before coming to Milwaukee. From there he moved to Buffalo, N. Y., where he remained 20 years, leaving "an indelible mark on the city." See Selig Adler and Thomas E. Connolly, *From Ararat to Suburbia* (Phila., 1960), p. 137.

79. *Am. Isr.*, Sept. 29, 1865, p. 101; Nov. 16, 1866, p. 5.

80. Commenting on this development, Isaac M. Wise wrote: "It might have been adopted sooner, had we used any personal influence with our friends there . . ." *Am. Isr.,* Nov. 30, 1866, p. 6.

81. Letter of Rabbi Falk, *Sent.,* Oct. 31, 1863, p. 2.

82. *Sent.,* Sept. 11, 1863, p. 1.

83. *Directory, 1868-69,* pp. 46, 96; Bertram W. Korn, *op. cit.,* p. 87.

84. *Am. Isr.,* Jan. 1, 1869, p. 2.

85. *Ibid.,* Oct. 8, 1869, p. 6; *Sent.,* March 13, 1869, p. 1.

86. *Am. Isr.,* Dec. 21, 1866, p. 6; April 8, 1870, p. 7; *AJYB,* 5664 (1903-04), p. 53.

87. *Am. Isr.,* Aug. 24, 1855, p. 54; July 30, 1858, p. 31; *Sent.,* Jan. 1, 1883, p. 9; *The Jewish Encyclopedia,* s. v., "Milwaukee"; Andreas, p. 948. During the summer of 1858, Congregation B'ne Jeshurun advertised for "a gentleman competent to act as *Hazzan,* Teacher in the Hebrew Branches, and who is capable of instructing a Choir, 'three times a week'." A salary of $500 to $600 a year was offered, "besides perquisites amounting to about $100." *Am. Isr.,* June 4, 1858, p. 379; July 30, 1858, p. 27.

88. *Am. Isr.,* March 13, 1863, p. 287; Jan. 25, 1867, p. 3.

89. *Am. Isr.,* July 30, 1858, p. 31.

90. Salo Wittmayer Baron, *A Social and Religious History of the Jews* II, (New York, 1937), p. 104.

91. A review of the lay leadership of Milwaukee's earliest congregations reveals the following: Congregation Imanu-Al was officered by Solomon Adler, president, and Jonas Schoenmann, secretary; Ahabat Emuno: Simon Levi and M. Markwell, president and vice-president, respectively, in 1856; Anshe Emeth: 1855, Simon Levi, president, M. H. Schwarzenberg, vice-president; 1856, J. M. Hart, president, M. H. Schwarzenberg, vice-president, B. Oettinger, sec'y; 1857, Gabriel Shoyer, president, M. H. Schwarzenberg, vice-president, J. Hyman, treas., B. J. Oettinger, sec'y; 1858, Gabriel Shoyer, president, M. H. Schwarzenberg, vice-president, B. Willner, secretary. The wives of most of the officers simultaneously headed the congregation's Hebrew Benevolent Society. Officers of B'ne Jeshurun were: 1856, Nathan Pereles, president, Isaac Levy, vice-president, M. Markwell, secretary; 1857, Simon Levy, president, M. Markwell, secretary; 1858, Solomon Adler, president, M. Markwell, vice-president, M. Friend, treasurer, Sig'd Bachmann, secretary; 1859, Solomon Adler, president, M. H. Schwarzenberg, vice-president, J. Hyman, treasurer, Jacob Adler, secretary; 1860, Solomon Adler, president, J. H. Adler, secretary; 1861, Henry Bonns, president, M. H. Schwarzenberg, vice-president; 1863, Henry Bonns, president; 1866, Isaac Stransky, president; Loebl Rindskopf; 1867, I. Stransky, president, J. Nathanson, rec. secretary; 1869, David Adler, president, J. Nathanson, rec. secretary. Certificates of incorporation, Congregation Imanu-Al, 1853, Ahabat Emuno, 1856, B'ne Jeshurun, 1858; *Sent.,* April 30, 1857, p. 3; *Occident,* Dec., 1856, p. 454; Sept. 1857, pp. 307-308; *Asmoneon,* XV, no. 15 (Jan. 22, 1857), p. 117; *J. Mess.,* Sept. 28, 1860, p. 100; *Am. Isr.,* Aug. 24, 1855, p. 54; Nov. 7, 1856, p. 142; Dec. 25, 1857, p. 198; July 30, 1858, p. 31; July 30, 1858, pp. 27, 31; Sept. 30, 1859, p. 102; Feb. 24, 1860, p. 267; July 12, 1861, p. 14; March 13, 1863, p. 287; March 2, 1866, p. 277; Jan. 18, 1867, p. 3; Jan. 1, 1869, p. 2.

92. *Der Zeitgeist,* April 29, 1880, p. 148.

93. Still, pp. 122-123, 126.

94. *Am. Isr.*, Aug. 22, 1856, p. 53.

95. *Asmonean*, XI, 25 (April 6, 1855), p. 196. Apparently they were non-believers in organized religion, but desired a Jewish community which had to be built by religious affiliation.

96. *Am. Isr.*, Aug. 22, 1856, p. 53.

97. Quoted in Marcus, *op. cit.*, II, p. 154; *Der Zeitgeist*, April 29, 1880, p. 148.

98. *Am. Isr.*, Aug. 22, 1856, p. 53.

99. *Ibid.*, Aug. 24, 1855; July 30, 1858, p. 31; March 2, 1866, p. 277; *Occident*, Dec., 1856, p. 454; June 18, 1857, pp. 154-155; *Sent.*, May 1, 1859, p. 1; May 11, 1859, p. 1; Jan. 1, 1883, p. 9; June 17, 1887, p. 5; Anshe Emeth Record Book, pp. 28-29; Andreas, p. 948.

100. *Am. Isr.*, Aug. 12, 1870, p. 8.

101. *Occident*, Sept., 1857, pp. 307-308.

102. *Am. Isr.*, Nov. 30, 1866, p. 6.

103. During the ministry of Rabbi Kalisch, *Mincha* services were also held on Saturday afternoons at three o'clock. *Sent.*, Sept. 18, 1858, p. 1; June 29, 1861, p. 1; April 10, 1869, p. 1; Dec. 24, 1869, p. 1; *Directories, 1862*, p. 18; *1865*, p. 131, *1866*, p. 87; *1868-69*, p. 46.

104. *Am. Isr.*, June 17, 1859, p. 399.

105. Marriage of Sophia Heller and Phillip Goldsmith, Aug. 27, 1865; Marcus, *op. cit.*, II, p. 280.

106. *Sent.*, July 3, 1858, p. 1; June 9, 1865, p. 1.

107. *Am. Isr.*, Sept. 30, 1859, p. 102; July 12, 1861, p. 14; March 2, 1866, p. 277. In 1861, M. Heiman was *Hazzan;* the choir was directed by the organist, Mr. Louis Hillmantel.

108. *Occident*, Nov., 1866, p. 383.

109. *Am. Isr.*, April 8, 1870, p. 7.

110. *Occident*, Nov., 1866, p. 383.

111. *Sent.*, March 18, 1869, p. 1; Jan. 1, 1883, p. 9; Andreas, pp. 948-951.

112. *Blue Book*, pp. 33, 35.

113. *Sent.*, Nov. 16, 1869, p. 1; Feb. 1, 1870, p. 1; Andreas, pp. 946-948; *Blue Book*, p. 35.

114. *Blue Book*, p. 36.

115. Korn, *op. cit.*, p. 5.

116. New England had instituted free schools, maintained by public taxes. During the thirties, New Yorkers and Pennsylvanians were endeavoring to establish a free school system. Joseph Schafer, "Origin of Wisconsin's Free School System," *WMH*, IX, (Sept., 1925), 28-31, cited by Still, p. 81ff. *Evening Wisconsin*, Oct. 15, 1895; *Sent.*, June 7, 1845.

117. *Constitution of the State of Wisconsin . . . 1846*, Article IX, sections 3 and 4; *Constitution of the State of Wisconsin, 1848*, Article X, section 3. Still, p. 216; Buck, IV, p. 79; Laurence M. Larsen, *A Financial and Administrative History of Milwaukee* (Madison, 1908), cited by Still, p. 219. J. B. Schram, one of Milwaukee's Jewish pioneers, served as president of the Second Ward Free School Society during 1859-60. *Directory, 1859-60*, p. 302; Buck, IV, p. 385.

118. Still, p. 220; Watrous, I, p. 393.

119. Obituary notices of Henry Katz, Elizabeth Katz, and Isaac Neustadtl, *Sent.*, Dec. 3, 1877, p. 8; Aug. 3, 1891, p. 3; Dec. 30, 1891, p. 3; Gregory, II, p. 1176.

120. Patrick Donnelly, "The Milwaukee Public Schools," John W. Stearns, ed., *Columbian History of Education in Wisconsin*, pp. 458-459, cited by Still, p. 122; William George Bruce, ed., *History of Milwaukee City and County* I (Chicago, 1922), p. 638.

121. *Sent.*, July 14, 1937, cited by Still, pp. 221-224; Gregory, II, pp. 1179-1180; Watrous, I, p. 420.

122. *Sent.*, April 30, 1857, p. 3.

123. *Am. Isr.*, May 22, 1857, p. 366.

124. *Occident*, Sept., 1857, pp. 307-308.

125. For a brief interval, in 1866, it appears that classes were conducted three times a week. *Directory, 1869-70*, p. 405; *Am. Isr.*, July 12, 1861, p. 14; March 2, 1866, p. 277.

126. *Sent.*, Dec. 3, 1869, p. 1; March 24, 1870, p. 1; Oct. 1, 1870, p. 1; Nov. 12, 1870, p. 4; *Occident*, Nov., 1866, p. 383.

127. Still, pp. 235-236.

128. Still, p. 237; Andreas, pp. 982, 989.

129. The Deborah Ladies' Hebrew Benevolent Society, in 1859, was headed by Mesdms. S. Feist and Rebecca Schwarzenberg; in the same year, the Society of True Sisters was officered by Mesdms. Theresa (J. B.) Schram and Eva Stransky. The Independent Order of True Sisters was organized in 1846, but there is no evidence that Milwaukee's True Sisters were connected with the Independent Order of that name. Samuel Kalisch, *op. cit.*, ed., pp. 26-27; *AJYB*, 5670 (1909-1910), p. 155; *Directory, 1858*, App., p. 17; *1859-60*, p. 300; *Am. Isr.*, July 30, 1858, p. 31; Feb. 4, 1859, p. 245; Sept. 30, 1859, p. 102; May 4, 1860, p. 347; *Der Zeitgeist*, Nov. 23, 1882, p. 368; Hyman B. Grinstein, *The Rise of the Jewish Community of New York, 1654-1860* (Phil., 1945), p. 154.

130. Officers of the organization for the year 1869-70 were: Mesdms. J. P. Frisch, president; A. Breslauer, vice-president; Eichmann, treasurer; and A. Steiner, secretary. *Sent.*, Jan. 18, 1858, p. 1; Jan. 22, p. 4; Jan. 23, p. 1; Feb. 10, 1868, p. 4; Sept. 9, 1870, p. 1; *Directory, 1869-70*, p. 409.

131. Officers for 1869 were: L. Rindskopf, president; I. Stransky, vice-pres.; D. S. Lederer, sec'y.; and M. Teweles, treasurer. *Sent.*, Feb. 7, 1868, p. 1; March 3, 1868, p. 4; *Directory, 1869-70*, p. 409; *AJYB*, 5668 (1907-1908), p. 428; Andreas, p. 983.

132. *Am. Isr.*, March 2, 1866, p. 277; Oct. 27, 1892, p. 5; I. J. Benjamin, *Three Years in America, 1859-1862* II (Phila., 1956), p. 275; *Sent.*, June 1, 1870, p. 1; Dec. 27, 1891, p. 3; *Directory, 1869-70*, p. 409. Its first officers were: David Adler, president; Meyer Friend, vice-president; M. Littauer, secretary; I. Stransky, treas.; L. Rindskopf, S. Feist, A. Abraham, directors.

133. Officers elected in September, 1869, were: David Adler, president; L. Rindskopf, vice-president; M. Katzenstein, secy.; H. S. Mack, treasurer; trustees: A. F. Leopold, S. Feist, and E. Friend. In August, 1870, the society received a bequest of $100 from the estate of their late vice-president, Loebl Rindskopf. *Sent.*, Aug. 27, 1870, p. 1; *Directory, 1869-70*, p. 409; *1870-71*, p. 371; *AJYB*, 5668 (1907-1908), p. 428; *Blue Book*, pp. 75-76; Andreas, p. 982.

134. *J. Mess.*, March 2, 1860, p. 70; *Am. Isr.*, Feb. 24, 1860, p. 267.

135. *Am. Isr.*, April 13, 1860, p. 326.

136. *Sent.*, Jan. 6, 1874; Jan. 10, 1875, p. 8.

137. *Daily Wisconsin*, Dec. 15, 1849, cited by Gregory, II, p. 624. Milwaukee Lodge, No. 1, was organized April 20, 1848. Germania Lodge was formed May 21, 1856. Andreas, p. 978.

138. *Sent.*, Dec. 17, p. 1; Dec. 22, 1858, p. 1; Dec. 27, 1866, p. 1; Dec. 25, p. 1; Dec. 27, 1867, p. 1; Feb. 5, p. 1; Dec. 14, 1869, p. 1; *Directory, 1854-55*, p. 326; *1856-57*, p. 452; *1859-60*, p. 301; *1860-61*, p. 293; *1869-70*, pp. 406, 407.

138a. *Sent.*, Oct. 27, 1865, p. 1; *Directory, 1859-60*, p. 301; *1860-61*, p. 294; *1869-70*, p. 407; *Blue Book*, p. 151; *The U.S. Biographical Dictionary*, Wis. vol., pp. 137-138.

139. Grinstein, *op. cit.*, pp. 109-110.

140. Korn, *op. cit.*, p. 4.

141. *Ibid.;* Grinstein, *op. cit.*, p. 113.

142. *Am. Isr.*, Apr. 19, 1861, p. 334; July 12, 1861, p. 14.

143. *Ibid.*, July 12, 1861, p. 14. Wise estimated the Jewish population of the city at this time at about 1,000. *Sent.*, June 22, 1874, p. 3.

144. *Am. Isr.*, July 12, 1861, p. 14; Sept. 29, 1865, p. 101.

145. *Sent.*, June 22, 1874, p. 3; Andreas, p. 976. Officers of both lodges for 1869-70 were: Gilead Lodge, No. 41: Dr. L. Adler, pres.; Albert Steiner, vice-pres.; B. Gross, rec. sec.; G. Hirschberg, fin. sec.; Isaac Lodge, No. 87: E. Silverman, pres.; E. Rindskopf, vice-pres.; William Katzenstein, rec. sec.; S. Heller, fin. sec. The former group met every Thursday evening at 302 W. Water; the latter, every Tuesday evening at the same place. *Directory, 1869-70*, p. 407.

146. *Sent.*, Mar. 24, 1870, p. 1; June 22, 1874, p. 3; *Am. Isr.*, April 8, 1870, p. 7; Andreas, p. 976.

147. *Sent.*, Jan. 22, p. 1; Feb. 28, 1868, p. 1.

148. *Sent.*, July 2, p. 1; July 22, p. 1; July 23, p. 1; July 25, 1868, p. 1.

149. *Sent.*, Sept. 14, 1868, p. 1; *Jewish Chronicle* (London), Oct. 16, 1868, p. 6.

150. *Am. Isr.*, May 27, 1870, p. 10.

151. *Ibid.*, July 26, 1867, p. 6; *Sent.*, July 15, 1867, p. 1; Jan. 22, 1868, p. 1; June 22, 1874, p. 3. At the convention of 1869, R. Reichmann of Milwaukee was elected trustee of the Cleveland Orphan Asylum. *Sent.*, July 29, 1869, p. 1; Jan. 4, 1870, p. 1; Jan. 10, 1870, p. 1; Jan. 11, 1870, p. 1. Within 26 years the Order grew to 135 lodges, divided into six districts.

152. *Sent.*, July 16, 1867, p. 1; *Occident*, Aug., 1867, pp. 264-265. For a detailed history of B'nai B'rith in Milwaukee, see: Louis J. Swichkow, "A Century of B'nai B'rith in Milwaukee," in *B'nai B'rith Centennial Publication, A Century of Service*, (Milwaukee, 1962).

153. J. J. Schlicher, "Hans Balatka and the Milwaukee Musical Society," *WMH*, XXVII, (Sept., 1943), p, 45; cited by Still, p. 117. For a summary of the principal orchestral and choral works performed from 1850 to 1870, see Andreas, pp. 584-585.

154. *Sent.*, April 11, 1851, p. 2; March 18, p. 2; May 4, 1852, p. 2; May 3, 1853, p. 2; May 3, 1855, p. 2; May 6, 1858, p. 1; May 5, 1859, p. 1; May 29, 1866, p. 1; May 8, 1867, p. 1; May 4, 1869, p. 1; *Directory, 1856-57*, p. 454; *1858*, p. 16; *1869-70*, p. 409; Gregory, II, p. 1091; Still, p. 117.

155. Still, pp. 119-120.
156. Still, p. 121; Andreas, p. 611.
157. Still, p. 123 ff.
158. Andreas, p. 984.
159. *Sent.*, Dec. 2, 1857; Lillian Krueger, "Social Life in Wisconsin," *WMH*, XXII, June, 1939, pp. 421-425, cited by Still, pp. 214-215.
160. The library was transferred to the city in 1878. Gregory, II, p. 1078; Watrous, I, p. 417.
161. Still, pp. 211-213.
162. *Am. Isr.*, March 9, 1866, p. 285; *Directory, 1869-70*, p. 408.

PART TWO: YEARS OF GROWTH, 1870-1925

I. INTRODUCTION: GROWTH IN POPULATION AND IDEAS

1. Board of Delegates of American Israelites and Union of American Hebrew Congregations, *Statistics of Jews of the United States* (Philadelphia, 1880) p. 3, cited by: Benjamin Rabinowitz, "The Young Men's Hebrew Associations" (1854-1913), *PAJHS*, XXXVII (1947) pp. 286-287; David Sulzberger, "Growth of Jewish Population in the United States," *PAJHS*, VI (1897) pp. 141-149; H. S. Linfield, "Statistics of the Jews and Jewish Organizations in the U. S.: An Historical Review of Ten Censuses, 1850-1937," in the *AJYB*, XL (1938-1939) [5999] pp. 61-84; *ibid.* (1899-1900) [5660] (Philadelphia, 1899) pp. 283-284; (1901-1902) [5662] (Philadelphia, 1901) p. 157; (1914-1915) [5675] (Philadelphia, 1914) p. 353; *Der Zeitgeist*, vol. II, no. 1 (January 6, 1881) p. 20. In his preface, Hackenburg stated that his questionnaires had frequently remained unanswered by a number of individual communities, and concluded that the actual total probably amounted to 250,000. Others estimated the figure at 400,000 to 500,000. Rabbi Moses maintained that the statistics released "cannot be considered a reliable source because of many deficiencies." "Instead of giving us such an incomplete and deficient estimate," he commented in the *Zeitgeist*, "it would have been better to have saved the money for something worthwhile." *Ibid.*, p. 11.

2. *Sent.*, February 17, 1873, p. 4. The conclusion of the authors is based on an average family of five; this would approximate the size of the average Jewish family of 1875.

3. *Ibid.*, August 9, 1875, p. 8; *Ev. Wis.*, August 8, 1875, p. 4.

4. *Ibid.*

5. Rabbi S. Hecht, "The Jews and Judaism in Milwaukee," *History of Milwaukee County from its First Settlement to the Year 1895*, Howard Louis Conard, ed. (Chicago, n.d.), vol. II, p. 234. An estimate of 10,000 for the Jewish population in 1892, announced at an Alliance meeting, must be discounted. In 1895, the *Israelite* ventured to suggest a Jewish population of 7,000. *Sent.*, April 11, 1892, p. 4; June 16, p. 13; July 31, p. 1; August 7, p. 1;

October 16 and October 19, 1895, p. 5; *Am. Isr.*, October 10, 1895, p. 2.
6. *Sent.*, December 27, 1890, p. 1.

II. IMMIGRATION FROM EASTERN EUROPE

1. Samuel Joseph, *Jewish Immigration to the United States*, 1881-1910 (New York, 1914), p. 173. The figure given is minimal, and there were perhaps 100,000—200,000 more.
2. Few if any Jews arrived in Milwaukee from Turkey or the Levant during this period.
3. Ismar Elbogen, *A Century of Jewish Life* (Philadelphia, 1946), pp. 63-64.
4. *Ibid.*; Moshe Davis, "Ha-Zofeh ba-Arcz ha-Hadashah: A source for the History of East European Jews in the United States," (Hebrew) *Sefer ha-Yovel li-Khevod Alexander Marx* (New York, 1950), p. 116
5. Elbogen, *op. cit.*, p. 62; Davis, *op. cit.*, p. 117.
6. Solomon Grayzel, *A History of the Jews* (Philadephia, 1953) p. 657; Cyrus Adler and Aaron M. Margalith, "American Intercession on Behalf of Jews in the Diplomatic Correspondence of the United States, 1840-1938," *PAJHS*, XXXVI (1943) p. 215; Samuel Joseph, *op. cit.*, pp. 93.
7. *Sent.*, Aug. 3, p. 4; Oct. 18, p. 1; and Dec. 11, 1890, p. 1; May 26, 1891, p. 1; March 20, 1892, p. 4.
8. Old Cemetery Record Book (B'ne Jeshurun), pp. 31, 35, 40, 41, 42, 44, 46; *Sent.*, August 9, 1875, p. 8; *Daily Wisconsin*, August 8, 1875, p. 4.
9. *Sent.*, Jan. 4, p. 7; Jan. 23, p. 4; July 3, 1882, p. 2; *Der Zeitgeist*, vol. III, no. 8 (April 13, 1882), p. 128: interview with Moses Abraham Hiller, May 22, 1955.
9a. *Der Zeitgeist*, vol. I, no. 8 (April 15, 1880), p. 128; no. 10 (May 13, 1880), p. 149; vol. II, no. 21 (Oct. 13, 1881), p. 344.
10. Alliance Israelite Universelle in Paris, Copies of Letters, vol. 95, pp. 12, 118, cited by Zosa Szajkowski, "The Attitude of American Jews to East European Jewish Immigration (1881-1893)" *PAJHS*, XL, 3 (March, 1951), pp. 251-252.
11. *Der Zeitgeist*, vol. II, no. 21 (Oct. 13, 1881), p. 344
12. *Ev. Wis.*, October 13, 1881, p. 4.
13. *Ibid.*; *Der Zeitgeist*, vol. II, no. 22 (October 27, 1881), p. 360; *Am. Isr.*, October 21, 1881, p. 135. Moses Abraham Hiller, a member of the group, related that he left Riga after Shavuot, 1881. "We sailed on the ship 'Polaria'; there were 2,300 Jews aboard. We traveled via Hamburg. Among the ten emigrants who arrived with me in Milwaukee were 'the two Cohens,' Ben Hiller, Jackie and Louis Geisenfeld, S. Fein, S. Margolus, and Abe Birnbaum." Interview with Moses Abraham Hiller, May 22, 1955.
14. *Sent.*, November 16, 1881, p. 7.
15. Russian refugees, it was pointed out, were then entering the United States at the rate of 200 to 300 per week. Ellinger advised the meeting that he wished Milwaukee Jewry to provide for eight or ten families, at $500 per family, one-half of which was to be loaned by the Relief Committee, and the other half by the local Jewish group. The entire amount was to be due from the refugee borrower after a reasonable lapse of time. Nothing came of this plan. *Sent.*, November 30, p. 3; December 1, 1881, p. 7; *Der Zeitgeist*,

vol. II, no. 25 (December 8, 1881), p. 408; no. 26 (December 22, 1881), p. 424.

16. *Sent.*, January 4, p. 7; January 7, p. 10; January 23, 1882, p. 4; *Der Zeitgeist*, vol. III, no. 2 (January 19, 1882), p. 32.

17. *Sent.*, January 23, 1882, p. 4.

18. The Milwaukee Relief Association had received a call from the vicinity of Escanaba, Michigan, for eight men to cut telephone poles during the winter and engage in general farm work during the summer. *Ibid.*, *Der Zeitgeist*, vol. III, no. 3 (February 2, 1882), p. 48.

19. *Sent.*, February 6, 1882, p. 5.

20. *Der Zeitgeist*, vol. III, no. 8 (April 13, 1882) p. 128; no. 9 (April 27, 1882), p. 144.

21. *Sent.*, May 5, 1882, p. 4.

22. *Der Zeitgeist*, vol. III, no. 2 (January 19, 1882), p. 32.

23. *Sent.*, January 23, p. 4; January 27, 1882, p. 3. The Association unofficially substituted "Emigrant" for "Immigrant" in its name. Later changes were similarly made.

24. *Der Zeitgeist*, vol. III, no. 3, (February 2, 1882), p. 48.

25. *Ibid.*, no. 11 (May 25, 1882), p. 176; *Sent.*, May 27, p. 2; May 29, 1882, p. 2.

26. *Sent.*, May 29, 1882, p. 2.

27. *Ibid.*, June 3, 1882, p. 2.

28. *Ibid.*, June 7, 1882, p. 2; *Der Zeitgeist*, vol. III, no. 12, (June 8, 1882) p. 192; no. 13 (June 22, 1882) p. 208; *Am. Heb.*, vol. II, no. 6 (June 23, 1882) p. 68.

29. The total shipped by HEAS was 1542 men, 356 women, 719 children. *Sent.*, Jan. 31, 1892; p. 13; Zosa Szajkowski, "The Attitude of American Jews to East European Jewish Immigration (1881-1893), *PAJHS* XL, 3 (March, 1951), Appendix C, pp. 272-273.

30. *Sent.*, June 30, 1882, p. 8; *Ev. Wis.*, June 29, 1882, p. 8. European Jewish societies had just instituted their plan of sending refugees to the interior of the United States, by way of Canada. This they found necessary to do, since about the middle of June the New York committee had informed the Commissioner of Immigration at Castle Garden that it could not undertake to provide for refugees who might arrive. For a similar story, see W. Gunther Plaut, *The Jews of Minnesota* (New York, 1959), pp. 92-94.

31. *Der Zeitgeist*, vol. III, no. 14 (July 6, 1882), p. 224.

32. *Ev. Wis.*, June 29, 1882, p. 8.

33. *Sent.*, June 30, 1882, p. 8; reprinted in the *Am. Isr.*, July 14, 1882, p. 12.

34. *Sent.*, June 30, p. 8; July 1, p. 2; July 3, 1882, p. 2; *Ev. Wis.*, June 29, 1882, p. 8.

35. *Sent.*, June 30, 1882, p. 8.

36. *Ibid.*

37. *Sent.*, July 1, 1882, p. 2.

38. Zosa Szajkowski, "The Attitude of American Jews to East European Jewish Immigration (1881-1893)," *PAJHS*, XL, 3 (March, 1951) p. 238.

39. *Sent.*, June 30, 1882, p. 8.

40. *Ibid.*, July 1, 1882, p. 2; *Ev. Wis.*, July 1, 1882, p. 8.
41. *Ev. Wis.*, July 1, 1882, p. 8.
42. *Ibid.*
43. *Ev. Wis.*, July 8, 1882, p. 2; *Sent.*, June 30, p. 8; July 2, p. 12; July 3, p. 2; July 8, 1882, p. 10.
44. *Der Zeitgeist*, vol. III, no. 15, (July 20, 1882), p. 237.
45. *Ev. Wis.*, July 3, p. 8; July 6, p. 2; July 8, 1882, p. 8. On July 17, the chairman of the finance committee stated that thus far, $1,430 had been expended. *Ibid.*, July 17, 1882, pp. 8, 10.
46. *Sent.*, July 3, 1882, p. 2.
47. *Sent.*, July 1, 1882, p. 2; *Ev. Wis.*, July 1, 1882, p. 8.
48. *Sent.*, July 3, 1882, p. 2.
49. *Ibid.*
50. *Ibid.* The Russian atrocities left their inescapable mark. An example was the unfortunate Samuel Cohen who arrived in 1882, at the age of 15. Four years later, then the son of a well-to-do Russian refugee and 19 years of age, young Cohen was taken to the Asylum at Wauwatosa after he attempted to shoot his mother and himself. It was revealed by medical authorities that the recollection of a squadron of Cossacks tormenting and frightening his parents and younger sister resulted in a devastating shock. *Ibid.*, Sept. 26, 1887, 3.
51. *Ibid.*, July 7, p. 3; July 11, 1882, p. 3; *Ev. Wis.*, July 8, 1882, p. 8.
52. *Sent.*, July 6, 1882, p. 2; *Eve. Wis.* July 6, 1882, p. 2; *J. Mess.*, July 14, 1882, p. 2.
53. *J. Mess.*, August 4, 1882, p. 5.
54. *Ibid.*
55. *Sent.*, July 15, p. 10; July 17, 1882, p. 10.
56. *J. Mess.*, Aug. 4, 1882, p. 5.
57. *Sent.*, July 21, 1882, p. 5.
58. Quoted by Zosa Szajkowski, "The Attitude of American Jews to East European Jewish Immigration (1881-1893)," *PAJHS*, no. XL, part 3 (March, 1951) p. 243.
59. *Sent.*, July 15, p. 10; July 17, p. 10; July 18, p. 2; July 21, 1882, p. 5; *Ev. Wis.*, July 17, 1882, p. 8. Significant are the following statistics of the distribution of the 6,694 emigrants sent to the United States by the London Mansion House Fund up to June 17, 1882:

No. of Refugees	Sent to
2,926	New York City
672	Philadelphia
415	Boston
359	Winnipeg
263	Buffalo
193	Chicago
340	Milwaukee
113	Detroit
105	Montreal

Seventeen other cities received groups numbering 11 to 99. Groups of less than ten went to twenty cities. Fifty were sent to Australia. Alliance

Israelite Universelle, Paris, Correspondence file No. 358, letter of June 23, 1882, cited by Zosa Szajkowski, "The Attitude of American Jews to East European Jewish Immigration (1881-1893)," *PAJHS*, XL, 3 (March, 1951), p. 236.
The destinations of 605 emigrants shipped by the Hebrew Emigrant Aid Society of New York from June 1 to August 1, 1882, included "Milwaukee— 32½." *Ibid.*, Appendix D, p. 274. According to the *Am. Heb.*, the number of Russian refugees sent to Milwaukee in June and July, 1882 by the Hebrew Emigrant Aid Society of New York was 321. *Am. Heb.*, XI, 13 (August 11, 1882) p. 152.

60. *Der Zeitgeist*, vol. III, no. 15 (July 20, 1882), pp. 236-237; *Sent.*, July 7, 1882, p. 3; *Ev. Wis.*, July 11, 1882, p. 8.

61. *Der. Zeitgeist*, vol. III, no. 15 (July 20, 1882), 236-237.

62. *Ibid.*

63. *Sent.*, July 10, 1882, p. 9; *Evening Wisconsin*, July 11, 1882, p. 8.

64. *Sent.*, July 12, 1882, p. 6.

65. *Sent.*, July 15, 1882, p. 10.

66. *Sent.*, July 3, p. 2; July 6, p. 2; July 7, p. 9; July 11, p. 3; July 15, p. 10; July 18, p. 2; July 20, p. 7; July 21, 1882, p. 5; *Evening Wisconsin*, July 6, p. 2; July 8, p. 8; July 11, 1882, p. 8; *J. Mess.*, July 14, 1882, p. 2; February 2, 1883, p. 5.

67. *Sent.*, February 27, p. 3; March 1, 1884, p. 3; *Der Zeitgeist*, vol. III, no. 17 (August 17, 1882) p. 272; *J. Mess.*, February 2, 1883, p. 5.

68. *Der Zeitgeist*, vol. III, no. 15 (July 20, 1882) pp. 236-237.

69. *Sent.*, October 16, 1895, p. 43; *Am. Heb.*, vol XII, no. 4 (September 8, 1882), p. 44.

70. Contributions of the Hebrew Emigrant Aid Society of New York for the month of August amounted to $186.55. *Sent.*, August 29, p. 2; August 30, 1882, p. 2; January 31, 1892, p. 13; *J. Mess.*, September 8, 1882, p. 2.

71. *Der Zeitgeist*, vol. III, nos. 20, 21 (October 12, 1882), p. 320.

72. Of these, 49 single men and families were settled on farms, and 91 went to various towns and cities in Wisconsin, Minnesota, and Iowa.

Although the Wisconsin Emigrant Relief Association was offically dissolved in September, 1882, it continued to exist as a committee for the needy former colonists at Grand Forks, D. T.

The officers of the Association from the time of organization in October, 1881 up to September 21, 1882, when it ceased to exist as a body, were: David Adler, president; Philip Carpeles, vice-president; Louis B. Schram, secretary; Bernhard Gross, treasurer. In reviewing the causes of the wholesale exodus of refugees, David Adler stated that the first few who came were treated so well that they wrote glowing accounts of the promised land found, and that "the rush to share the unheard of benefits narrated by letters was of a mad crowd from poverty and oppression to comfort and ease." The total receipts of the Association were $3,978.84; disbursements, $3,964.42. Among the largest contributors were the Hebrew Aid Society of the United States, $200; Gemilas Chesed Ladies' Society, $100; Treue Schwestern Ladies' Society, $100; Widows' and Orphans' Ladies' Society, $100; Ladies' Sewing Society, $100; H. Friend & Bro., $100; David Adler,

$50; Landauer & Co., 50; Marshall & Ilsley, $50; E. P. Allis & Co., $50; Alexander Mitchell, $50; *Sent.*, December 22, 1882, p. 2.
73. *Der Zeitgeist*, vol. III, no. 18 (August 31, 1882) p. 288.
74. *Ibid.*, no. 25 (December 7, 1882) p. 384.
75. Reports to the Board of Trade on Alien Immigration. C. 7113, 1893, pp. 263, 282-283.
76. *Sent.*, July 3, p. 2; July 6, p. 2; July 7, p. 9; July 11, p. 3; July 15, p. 10; July 18, p. 2; July 20, p. 7; July 21, 1882, p. 5; *Ev. Wis.*, July 6, p. 2; July 8, p. 8; July 11, 1882, p. 8; *J. Mess.*, July 14, 1882, p. 2; February 2, 1883, p. 5.
77. Mark Wischnitzer, *To Dwell in Safety* (Philadelphia, 1949) pp. 66, 99.
78. *Sent.*, September 26, p. 3, and September 28, 1887, p. 3; January 31, 1892, p. 13. The statement by the *Israelite* that the "Russian settlement in the city numbers at least 200 families or—considering their great domestic fertility *unbescrieen*—nearly 1,200 persons," is a gross exaggeration. See *Am. Isr.*, August 6, 1886, p. 10.
79. *Sent.*, September 26, 1887, p. 3.
80. *Ibid.*, p. 3, and September 28, 1887, p. 3; *Am. Isr.*, August 6, 1886, p. 10.
81. *Sent.*, October 23, 1888, p. 5.
82. *Sent.*, October 16, 1895, 43.
83. *Sent.*, January 31, 1892, p. 13.
84. *Sent.*, December 29, 1891, p 2.
85. *Sent.*, November 30, 1891, p. 1.
86. *Sent.*, Oct., 16, 1895, 43.
87. *Sent.*, January 31, 1892, p. 13.
88. *Sent.*, July 10, 1898, p. 5. *The Sentinel's* estimate that "the population of Russian and Polish Jews reaches something like 5,000 persons," is exaggerated.
89. *Sent.*, September 25, 1900, p. 3.
90. As early as July, 1884, Rabbi Henry Illowizi of Minnesota came to re-establish a Milwaukee Alliance Israelite Universelle; however, nothing came of his endeavors. *Sent.*, July 29, 1884, p. 3. The Jewish Alliance, whose head-quarters were in Philadelphia, drew upon the Baron de Hirsch Fund to provide immigrants with a start in their new places of settlement. The Milwaukee branch of the Jewish Alliance did not receive any subsidy from the Hirsch Fund during 1891. Bernhard Gross, president of the Milwaukee branch, subsequently became a member of the National Committee on Russian Relief. *Ibid.*, July 7, p. 3, October 5, p. 8, November 7, p. 3, and December 29, 1891, p. 2; *Ev. Wis.*, November 9, 1891, p. 3.
91. *Ev. Wis.*, January 28, 1892; *Sent.*, April 18, p. 3, and April 25, 1892, p. 3.
92. *Sent.*, November 9, 1891, p. 3; April 9, p. 3, and April 11, 1892, p.4; *Am. Isr.*, April 21, 1892, p. 7.
93. *Sent.*, April 25, 1892, p. 3.
94. *Ibid.*, January 29, 1892, p. 3; *Ev. Wis.*, January 28, 1892.
95. This was based on the practice of the Alliance school in Baltimore, whose pupils paid thirty cents a month, or one penny a day. *Sent.*, October 5, 1891, p. 8.
96. *Sent.*, October 15, p. 3, and October 20, 1891, p. 3.

97. *Sent.*, October 27, 1891, p. 3, and January 31, 1892, p. 13.
98. *Sent.*, November 16, 1892, p. 3.
99. *Sent.*, October 4, 1899, p. 11; *The Reform Advocate*, vol. XVIII, no. 9 (October 14, 1899), p. 256.

III. THE NATIVE COMMUNITY: ECONOMIC AND SOCIAL STABILITY

1. *Sent.*, June 22, p. 8; July 2, p. 8; Aug. 20, 1880, p. 2; July 20, 1890, p. 1; *Ev. Wis.*, Oct. 15, 1895, cited by Still, p. 258. For percentages of increase in population over each decade, see Still, Table 1, pp. 570-571.

2. Watrous, I, pp. 397, 404; Still, pp. 359-360.

3. Still, pp. 322-325.

4. Still, p. 345.

5. Still, pp. 321, 327, 345.

6. Of the 395 passengers aboard the Schiller, 311 lost their lives, including Joseph Schlitz of Milwaukee. The remains of the Friends were brought to Milwaukee on June 2. The Masonic Fraternity, the Chamber of Commerce and Merchants' Association, together with Congregation Emanu-El, took part in "the cortege, the largest ever witnessed in this city." A "requiem" by the choir of Temple Emanu-El and a eulogy by Rabbi M. Spitz comprised the religious service, followed by the ritual of the Masons. Henry Friend and his wife were survived by eleven children, ranging from three to twenty-four years of age. *Sent.*, May 10, p. 4; May 11, p. 1; May 12, p. 5; May 31, p. 8; June 2, p. 8; June 3, 1875, p. 8; Aug. 29, 1879, p. 8; May 12, 1880, p. 2.

7. *Sent.*, Feb. 10, p. 8; Mar. 8, 1876, p. 5; Feb. 26, p. 8; May 12, 1880, p. 2; Jan. 8, 1881, p. 2; Jan. 10, p. 7; July 10, 1882, p. 7; Jan. 24, 1883, p. 5 Andreas, p. 1241; *Directory*, 1883, p. 32.

8. Isaac Friend met his death in 1889 by falling down an elevator shaft in the company's factory. Elias Friend passed away in November, 1890, leaving an estate of $1,000,000. Meyer Friend died at Frankfort-on-Main, Germany, in May, 1895, where he had been living several years. *Sent.*, Nov. 7, 1890, p. 5; May 9, 1895, p. 3; Dec. 15, 1898, p. 1; *Am. Isr.*, Nov. 20, 1890, pp. 4, 6, 8; W. J. Anderson and Julius Bleyer, eds., *Milwaukee's Great Industries*, Association for the Advancement of Milwaukee (Milwaukee, 1892), p. 222.

9. *Sent.*, Dec. 21, 1886, p. 3.

10. *Sent.*, Jan. 1, p. 1; Feb. 7, p. 4; Mar. 20, 1873, p. 5; *Directory*, 1875-1876, p. 56.

11. J. H. Rice and Friedman, originating in 1855, was a manufacturer and jobber nearly as large as Friend and Adler. *Sent.*, Feb. 8, 1881, p. 2; Jan. 3, 1884, p. 7; Oct. 18, 1886, p. 3; Jan. 25, p. 3; Feb 14, 1887, p. 3; Feb. 28, 1890, p. 3; Oct. 20, 1894, p. 3; Conard, II, pp. 431-432; *Directory*, 1895, p. 775; *Milwaukee Industrial Exhibition Association, Report* (Milwaukee, 1881), p. 17.

12. Emanuel Silverman left an estate of about $200,000. *Sent.*, Sept. 16, 1874, p. 8; May 9, 1879, p. 8; Nov. 5, 1880, p. 8; Andreas, p. 1240.

13. *Sent.,* Dec. 17, 1884, p. 2; Nov. 20, 1890, p. 1; Elmer E. Barton, *Industrial History of Milwaukee-The Commerical, Manufacturing and Railway Metropolis of the Northwest* (Milwaukee, 1886), p. 148; Andreas, pp. 1241-1242.

14. *The U. S. Biographical Dictionary,* Wisconsin Volume (Chicago, 1877), pp. 137-138; *Sent.,* Oct. 24, 1872, p. 4.

15. Mortgages totaling $163,000 were filed against the concern in December, 1894. *Sent.,* Dec. 20, 1894, p. 4: James S. Buck, *Milwaukee Under the Charter (1847-1853),* III (Milwaukee, 1884), pp. 234-235.

16. *Sent.,* Nov. 28, 1882, p. 2; Mar. 28, 1891, p. 3; Mar. 6, 1899, p. 3.

17. *Sent.,* June 5, 1880, p. 5; Mar. 16, 1893; April 17, 1897, p. 1; Andreas, p. 1264. His life insurance policies, it was said, amounted to $50,000. *Sent.,* July 28, 1895, p. 1; April 17, 1897, p. 1.

18. *Directory,* 1895, p. 1087.

19. *Sent.,* Feb. 24, 1899, p. 3.

20. *Sent.,* Feb. 24, 1899, p. 3; Gregory, IV, p. 430; Andreas, pp. 1235-1236.

21. *Sent.,* Jan. 10, 1870, p. 1.

22. *Sent.,* Oct. 30, 1881, p. 3; Jan. 1, 1896, p. 12; Feb. 24, 1899, p. 3; Andreas, p. 1236.

23. Silber was born in Kalish in 1843, and came to America in September, 1859. He worked and attended night school in New York for six months. From 1860 to 1863, he conducted a small business in Orange County, New York. Having accumulated $400, in 1863 he embarked in the dry goods business with his brother in Paterson, New Jersey. In 1865 they moved to Milwaukee, but gradually transferred their business to Waupun, Wisconsin in 1868. After seven years, Silber returned to Milwaukee where he entered into partnership with A. W. Rich. *Sent.,* April 4, 1887, p. 2; *The U. S. Biographical Dictionary,* Wisconsin volume (Chicago, 1877), pp. 54-55; Andreas, p. 1245.

24. *Sent.,* Oct. 20, p. 4; Oct. 21, p. 4; Nov. 12, 1883, p. 5; April 5, p. 6; Oct. 21, 1885, p. 3. Lewis Silber retired in 1884 and became associated with the Milwaukee Cloak & Suit Co. *Sent.,* Dec. 30, 1884, p. 3; Jan. 19, 1893, p. 5.

25. *Sent.,* Feb. 14, 1886, p. 3; Nov. 18, 1888, p. 3; Oct. 20, 1890, p. 3.

26. *Sent.,* Feb. 25, p. 5; Sept. 29, 1883, p. 8.

27. *Sent.,* Jan. 18, 1888, p. 3; Aug. 2, 1890, p. 2; Jan. 6, p. 3; Jan. 12, 1891, p. 5.

28. *Sent.,* Jan. 12, p. 5; Oct. 6, 1891, p. 5.

29. *Sent.,* Oct. 6, 1891, p. 5; Jan. 19, p. 5; Jan. 29, p. 3; April 9, p. 6; Dec. 26, 1893, p. 1; Jan. 19, p. 3; Feb. 6, p. 1; July 14, 1894, p. 3; *Directory,* 1895, p. 776; 1900, p. 1185.

30. Marcus Heiman passed away in July, 1888. *Sent.,* July 12, 1876, p. 8; April 2, 1885, p. 8; July 26, 1888, p. 3; Andreas, p. 1271.

31. L. Morawetz had been a member of G. Bremer & Co., wholesale grocers, for nearly thirty years. *Sent.,* Nov. 9, p. 7; Nov. 15, 1881, p. 3; Jan. 3, 1882, p. 6.

32. *Sent.,* Aug. 30, p. 3; Dec. 29, 1885, p. 3; April 8, 1886, p. 3. The Canada

Fur and Cloak Manufacturing Company tanned, dressed, and dyed its furs in Chicago, and they were then manufactured in Milwaukee.

33. Andreas, p. 1275.

34. The firm was dissolved in 1883. *Sent.*, March 24, 1879, p. 1; Jan. 8, 1881, p. 2; Nov. 2, 1883, p. 5.

35. *Sent.*, Jan. 4, 1882, p. 7; March 22, p. 3; April 3, 1887, p. 3; Barton, p. 184.

36. Andreas, p. 1659.

37. *Sent.*, May 21, 1881, p. 2; Dec. 28, 1883, p. 7; Jan. 17, p. 4; June 8, p. 8; Aug. 18, p. 5; Dec. 26, 1884, p. 3; Jan. 8, 1885, p. 3; Oct. 4, 1886, p. 3. The firm encountered a brief but stormy labor strike in March, 1886. *Sent.*, March 11, p. 4; March 18, 1886, p. 3.

Born in Germany on March 28, 1835, Marcus Cohen, son of a prosperous merchant, migrated to New York at the age of twenty. He undertook general merchandising in Wautoma, Wisconsin for seven years, and thereafter conducted a boot and shoe business in Milwaukee. After two years, he transferred to Berlin, Wisconsin. Three years later, he returned to Milwaukee with substantial capital. In 1870, he became a member of the firm of Strass, Cohen and Co., wholesale furnishers. After two years he purchased the interest of Strass and the firm became Cohen Bros. Co., his partner being Jonas Cohen. Marcus Cohen married Gertrude Water of Baltimore in 1871. Conard, II, pp. 444-445.

38. *Sent.*, Jan. 10, p. 8; July 6, 1888, p. 3; Feb. 6, 1889, p. 3.

39. The size of the merchandise carried may be surmised from the loss of $100,000 as a result of the fire. The business was incorporated on May 25, 1901; a warehouse was built adjacent to the new store. *Sent.*, May 1, 1893, p. 1; William George Bruce, *Builders of Milwaukee* (Milwaukee, 1946), pp. 73-74.

40. *Sent.*, April 29, 1900, p. 8; Bruce, p. 73; Still, p. 400.

41. *Sent.*, May 15, p. 3; Sept. 30, 1887, p. 4.

42. *Am. Isr.*, Nov. 6, 1890, p. 5; *Yenowine's News*, VIII, 187 (Oct. 21, 1888), pp. 1-3 *Ev. Wis.*, Oct. 15, 1895, p. 22. Adam Gimbel visited Milwaukee frequently. *Sent.*, Nov. 9, 1888, p. 3; March 24, 1889, p. 3; Dec. 8, 1892, p. 3; April 6, 1893, p. 2; June 30, 1896, p. 3.

43. When, in February, 1894, the firm bought out Haines & Co. in Philadelphia for $1,000,000, two of the brothers moved there. Simultaneous with the expansion of the Milwaukee branch came even greater expansion in Philadelphia, where in June, 1900, Gimbel Bros. purchased almost an entire block to erect its store. *Sent.*, Sept. 24, 1891, p. 3; Feb. 21, 1894, p. 3; Oct. 10, 1897, p. 4; July 17, 1898, p. 3; June 1, 1900, p. 3; *Am. Isr.*, March 1, 1894, p. 2.

44. Mendel entered the firm of his father-in-law, David Adler, where he stayed until 1879. After a turn at the Leidersdorf business, he founded Smith & Mendel, a grocery firm. Mendel's brother practiced medicine in Milwaukee for many years. *Sent.*, Jan. 27, p. 3; Mar. 14, 1882, p. 6; April 2, 1885, p. 5; Aug. 20, 1886, p. 3; May 30, 1888, p. 3; June 1, 1895, p. 7; Jan. 1, p. 12; Apr. 21, 1896, p. 3; Mar. 26, 1897, p. 1; Barton, p. 88; Conard, II, pp. 370-371.

45. *Sent.*, May 14, p. 4; May 15, 1872, p. 4; Jan. 11, p. 5; Jan. 13, p. 8; Feb.

22, p. 4; Dec. 18, 1875, p. 2; Aug. 9, 1897, p. 6; *Directory*, 1875-1876, p. 56; Andreas, p. 1632.

46. *Am. Isr.*, Nov. 20, 1890, p. 8; Oct. 15, 1896, p. 7; Andreas, p. 1224. Another dealer was E. M. Nathan, a native of Prussia who came to Milwaukee in 1869. After engaging in the livestock trade with his son, from 1871 they developed a lively wholesale and retail business. Max Loebel came to America from Austria in July, 1870. He arrived in Milwaukee where he established this business seven years later. *Sent.*, July 19, 1881, p. 7; Andreas, p. 1233.

47. *Der Zeitgeist*, vol. II, no. 6 (Mar. 17, 1881), p. 104.

48. *Der Zeitgeist*, vol. I, no. 3 (Feb. 5, 1880), p. 47; vol. II, no. 7 (Mar. 31, 1881), p. 120; *Sent.*, Apr. 6, 1884, p. 7.

49. *Sent.*, July 3, 1883, p. 5; *Ev. Wis.*, Oct. 15, 1895, pp. 10, 22; *Directory*, 1900, p. 1191; Andreas, p. 1540.

50. *Sent.*, Oct. 8, 1897, p. 3.

51. F. W. Hartmann was born in Prussia in 1835, and came direct to Milwaukee in 1855. Henry Schoenfeld, a native of Syracuse, N. Y., settled in Milwaukee in 1866. See Barton, *op. cit.*, pp. 118-120.

52. In 1868, the firm acquired property "at the foot of East Water Street," for its liquor warehouse. *Sent.*, June 14, 1867, p. 1; Mar. 9, 1868, p. 1.

53. *Sent.*, Feb. 7, p. 8; Apr. 24, 1874, p. 8.

54. Indicted with many others as members of the "Whiskey Ring," were Samuel, Jacob, Elias, and Max Rindskopf. *Sent.*, May 29, p. 8; June 1, p. 8; July 1, p. 8; July 21, 1875, p. 5; Jan. 26, p. 4; May 29, p. 8; July 4, 1876, p. 8. For disposition of the Government's case against the Rindskopfs, see: *Sent.*, July 11, 1876, p. 2; for liquidation of the liquor interests of Sam, Elias and Siegfried Rindskopf, see: *Sent.*, Nov. 13, 1876, p. 8; Aug. 26, p. 8; Sept. 3, p. 8; Sept. 18, p. 8; Sept. 20, p. 8; Sept. 23, 1878, p. 8; Mar. 20, p. 8; May 1, p. 8; July 3, 1879, p. 8. Other "Ring" defendants tried at the time were Leopold Wirth, Aaron Schoenfeld, Edward Wirth, Henry Schoenfeld, and Isaac A. Levy. *Sent.*, Jul. 10, 1875, p. 2; May 30, p. 4; Sept. 26, p. 8; Sept 28, 1876, p. 8.

From 1877 to 1878, Sam Rindskopf operated the Blatz Bottling establishment, specializing in bottled export Lager beer, at Broadway and Knapp streets. *Sent.*, Feb. 12, p. 8; Apr. 9, 1877, p. 8; June 26, p. 8; June 28, 1878, p. 8; J. Louis Rindskopf's distillery also suffered a similar fate. *Sent.*, July 9, p. 4; Oct. 1, 1872, p. 4. For details concerning the case against Louis Rindskopf and the financial problems arising from his grain brokerage activities, see: *Sent.*, June 15, 1874, p. 8; May 11, p. 1; May 24, p. 8; Oct. 9, p. 8; Oct. 13, p. 8; Oct. 16, 1875, p. 4; Mar. 31, p. 2; Apr. 10, p. 4; June 2, 1876, p. 8; Apr. 20, p. 3; Apr. 21, p. 3; June 18, p. 8; Oct. 2, p. 3; Oct. 5, 1877, p. 3; Sept. 11, p. 2; Oct. 19, 1878, p. 2; June 21, 1879, p. 8; Jan. 23, p. 8; Jan. 29, 1880, p. 2.

55. *Sent.*, May 5, 1880, p. 8; June 1, 1884, p. 6.

56. *Milwaukee's Great Industries*, p. 206.

57. *Sent.*, Jan. 9, p. 4; Dec. 9, 1872, p. 4; Jan. 3, p. 4; Feb. 10, p. 4; July 14, 1873, p. 8; Jan. 1, p. 8; Apr. 13, p. 8; Nov. 24, 1874, p. 1; Aug. 12, 1876, p. 3; Apr. 22, p. 5; July 23, 1878, p. 8; Jan. 16, p. 8; Jan. 29, 1879, p. 8; Dec. 19, 1881; Sept. 26, 1882, p. 2; Mar. 18, 1884, p. 3.

58. *Sent.*, Feb. 7, 1886, p. 3; Sept. 27, 1888, p. 1.

59. *Sent.*, July 20, 1872, p. 4; Feb. 29, pp. 5, 8; Mar. 1, 1880, p. 8; "An Ethical Letter, Benjamin M. Roth to his son Solomon, 1854," *American Jewish Archives*, vol. VI, no. 1 (Jan., 1954), p. 7.

60. *Sent.*, May 28, 1873, p. 8; Jan. 23, 1880, p. 8; Jan. 9, p. 3; Apr. 24, 1887, p. 3; Andreas, p. 1485.

61. Gregory, IV, p. 684.

62. *Milwaukee's Great Industries*, pp. 149, 151, 224, 300; *Directory*, 1881, p. 35; 1882, p. 35; Gregory, I, p. 534.

63. Bernhard Gross, "Soap Manufacturing Business," *Milwaukee's Great Industries*, p. 183; *Sent.*, Sept. 14, 1872, p. 4; Apr. 20, 1878, p. 2; May 21, 1881, p. 5; May 16, 1883, p. 5; July 23, 1893, p. 3; *Der Zeitgeist*, vol. I, no. 23 (Nov. 11, 1880), p. 372; Barton, *op. cit.*, p. 219; *Milwaukee's Great Industries*, pp. 238, 344.

64. *Sent.*, May 4, p. 5; Nov. 11, 1882, p. 2; June 1, 1888, p. 3; May 6, 1897, p. 3; Andreas, p. 1268; *Der Zeitgeist*, vol. II, no. 13 (June 23, 1881), p. 216.

65. Andreas, p. 1540.

66. Philip Carpeles was president of the Northwestern Trunk Manufacturers in 1876. *Sent.*, Dec. 20, 1875, p. 4; Mar. 30, p. 8; Apr. 17, 1880, p. 8; Aug. 8, p. 2; Aug. 11, 1881, p. 4; Jan. 3, 1882, p. 3; Jan. 2, p. 7; Jan. 25, p. 3; Dec. 7, 1889, p. 3; Barton, *op. cit.*, p. 210.

67. *Sent.*, July 31, 1872, p. 4; Nov. 19, 1873 p. 8; July 14, p. 8; July 26, 1876, p. 8; May 15, p. 3; July 3, p. 10; July 4, 1881, p. 8; Aug. 9, p. 2; Aug. 16, 1882, p. 2; Oct. 15, 1884, p. 3; June 10, 1887, p. 3; May 30, 1889, p. 1.

68. *Sent.*, Apr. 13, 1875, p. 8; May 5, p. 8; June 14, 1876, p. 8; July 4, p. 8; Aug. 14, 1880, p. 3; *Milwaukee's Industrial Exposition & Grand Union Dairy Fair of 1882*, Appendix, p. 179; Andreas, p. 1316; Barton, *op. cit.*, p. 212.

69. *Sent.*, July 26, 1893, p. 1; *Directory*, 1895, p. 1088; 1900, p. 1194.

70. *Sent.*, June 26, 1887, p. 11; May 12, 1888, p. 3.

71. *Sent.*, Apr. 12, 1888, p. 4.

72. *Sent.*, Aug. 31, 1888, p. 3; Nov. 5, 1892, p. 3; Apr. 11, 1894, p. 3; Jan. 13, 1898, p. 3.

73. *Sent.*, Aug. 22, 1884, p. 3.

74. *Sent.*, Aug. 28, 1886, p. 3.

75. *St. Paul Daily Dispatch*, quoted in *Sent.*, June 14, 1882.

76. *Sent.*, Aug. 14, 1874, p. 8; Jan. 1, 1881, p. 2.

77. *The Hot Springs Arkansas Sentinel*, quoted in *Sent.*, Oct. 18, 1879, p. 8; Apr. 8, 1880, p. 8.

78. *Sent.*, July 9, 1879, p. 8.

79. The Gogebic range, running from east to west, is divided near its center by the Montreal River, which in turn divides upper Michigan and Wisconsin.

80. *Sent.*, Jan. 22, 1882, p. 2; Mar. 22, 1885, p. 3; Barton, *op. cit.*, p. 214.

81. *Sent.*, Jan. 10, pp. 3,5; Mar. 19, pp. 1,4; Apr. 1, p. 3; Apr. 8, p. 3; Apr. 9, p. 3; Apr. 15, p. 8; Apr. 18, p. 10; May 18, p. 3; June 4, p. 3; Nov. 2, p. 3; Nov. 18, 1886, p. 3; Jan. 21, p. 3; Feb. 5, p. 3; Mar. 18, p. 3; May 20, 1887, p. 4; Sept. 21, 1889, p. 3.

82. *Sent.*, Jan. 11, p. 3; July 20, p. 4; Nov. 30, p. 3; Dec. 1, 1886, p. 3; Jan. 15, p. 5; Jan. 20, p. 3; Jan. 23, p. 3; Apr. 22, p. 3; May 4, 1887, p. 8.

83. *Sent.*, Aug. 12, 1875, p. 8; Sept. 1, 1876, p. 8; Mar. 16, 1877, p. 8; Mar. 17, 1881, p. 7; Sept. 11, 1891, p. 6; May 2, 1893, p. 9; *Ev. Wis.*, Oct. 15, 1895, p. 22.

84. *Milwaukee's Great Industries*, pp. 239, 347.

85. *Sent.*, Apr. 9, 1877, p. 8; Apr. 24, p. 5; Apr. 30, p. 8; May 1, p. 8; May 9, 1879, p. 8.

86. *Sent.*, Nov. 22, p. 8; Nov. 23, 1878, p. 8; Apr. 5, 1880, p. 8; Mar. 16, 1881, p. 2.

87. *Directory*, 1875-1876, p. 43; 1876-1877, p. 35; 1877-1878, p. 36; 1878, p. 28; 1879, p. 33; *Sent.*, Mar. 6, 1877, p. 3; Dec. 8, 1882, p. 2.

88. *Sent.*, Nov. 5, 1880, p. 8; Jan. 21, 1893, p. 3.

89. *Sent.*, Mar. 18, 1885, p. 3.

90. *Sent.*, Sept. 14, 1885, p. 3.

91. *Sent.*, July 2, p. 2; July 4, p. 6; July 30, 1882, p. 4; Feb. 4, p. 4; Mar. 28, p. 5; June 21, 1883, p. 4; *Der Zeitgeist*, vol. II, no. 25 (Dec. 8, 1881), p. 408; Still, p. 402. Schlitz's Park, covering eight acres and accommodating 20,000 persons, was at the north end of 8th Street, near Walnut. It also provided hotel accommodations. It was a popular resort in the German style for many years. Barton, *op. cit.*, p. 118.

92. *Sent.*, Mar. 30, p. 3; May 14, p. 4; June 4, 1884, p. 3; Oct. 15, 1895, p. 10.

93. *Sent.*, July 26, 1884, p. 3; Mar. 16, 1885, p. 4; Nov. 7, 1889, p. 4; Barton, *op. cit.*, p. 194.

94. *Sent.*, Feb. 2, 1885, p. 3.

95 *Sent.*, Mar. 4, p. 4; Mar. 16, 1885, p. 4; Barton, *op. cit.*, p. 194.

96. *Sent.*, Nov. 7, 1889, p. 4; May 12, 1893, p. 3; Apr. 11, 1894, p. 3; Feb. 11, 1895, p. 3; Still, p. 403.

97. *Sent.*, Sept. 13, p. 4; Sept. 14, p. 2; Oct. 22, 1889, p. 3.

98. Still, pp. 345-346; *Milwaukee's Great Industries*, p. 85.

99. *Sent.*, May 11, p. 8; May 18, p. 8; Aug. 17, 1873, p. 8; May 27, 1875, p. 5; Oct. 16, 1878, p. 8.

100. *Sent.*, Nov. 27, 1871, p. 4; Apr. 13, 1887, p. 3; Jan. 11, p. 3; Jan. 15, p. 3; Mar. 28, 1888, p. 1; Still, p. 346; Gregory, I, p. 492; *Directory*, 1879, p. 46; 1880, p. 47; 1881, p. 51; 1882, p. 51; 1885, p. 52. Bernard Leidersdorf was a member of the Merchants' Association committee to relieve the victims of the Rochester, Minn. cyclone. *Sent.*, Aug. 31, 1883, p. 5.

101. Many bought $10 shares in the capital stock of $300,000. A financial success, it was repeated for 21 years. The final exposition was held in 1902, when the State Fair began to wrest away its function. Articles of Association, By-Laws and Rules and Regulations of the Milwaukee Industrial Exposition Association, *Milwaukee Exposition Reports*, 1882, p. 8.

102. *Sent.*, Mar. 16, p. 8; Mar. 25, p. 5; Apr. 26, 1880, p. 8; May 6, p. 2; June 12, p. 4; July 9, p. 5; Aug. 26, p. 2; Sept. 2, 1881, p. 3; Apr. 21, p. 5; Apr. 29, 1883, p. 3; May 3, 1884, p. 3; Mar. 14, p. 3; May 27, 1885, p. 3; Feb. 2, p. 3; Nov. 12, 1886, p. 3; Mar. 12, 1887, p. 3; Jan. 11, 1890, p. 3; *Directory*, 1886, p. 52; *Milwaukee Exposition Reports*, 1881-1887.

103. *Sent.*, Apr. 8, 1888, p. 3; *Milwaukee's Great Industries*, p. xiii; Still, pp. 348-349; Gregory, I, p. 507.

104. The Manufacturers' Club had been organized in the early nineties

to supply information, lend money to worthy projects, and promote the manufacturers' interests in the state Legislature. Still, p. 350; Gregory, I, pp. 494-495.

105. *Sent.*, Feb. 5, 1895, p. 3; Oct. 9, 1896, p. 3.

106. *Sent.*, June 29, 1889, p. 3.

107. *Sent.*, Jan. 3, 1882, p. 3.

108. *Sent.*, Mar. 9, p. 4; Mar. 10, p. 4; May 8, 1886, p. 1.

109. Still, pp. 287-288, 292.

110. *Sent.*, Dec. 25, 1885, p. 3; Mar. 16, p. 3; Apr. 24, 1886, p. 3.

111: *Sent.*, Apr.. 24, p. 3; Mar. 10, 1886, p. 4.

112. *Sent.*, May 1, 1886, p. 1.

113. *Sent.*, May 4, 1886, p. 3.

114. *Sent.*, May 17, 1881, p. 3; May 9, p. 6; Dec. 1, 1882, p. 7; *Am. Isr.*, July 17, 1890, p. 5.

115. *Sent.*, Dec. 6, 1882, p. 6; *Directory*, 1884, p. 53; 1886, p. 49. Because of his unique role as employer, A. W. Rich was selected a member of a special arbitration committee, which included Mayor Wallber, to settle labor disputes. *Sent.*, Mar. 10, 1886, p. 4.

116. Employees voluntarily suggested a reduction of ten per cent on salaries of from $4.50 to $11, fifteen per cent on salaries of from $11 to $20, and twenty per cent on salaries over $20. *Sent.*, Jan. 19, 1894, p. 3.

117. *Sent.*, Sept. 30, 1894, p. 9. Omitted by the *Sentinel* were scores of other businessmen whose net worths were below the $200,000 mark. See Appendices 1 and 2.

118. *Sent.*, July 29, 1876, p. 5; *Directories*, 1870-71, p. 337; 1871-72, p. 346; 1880, p. 616; 1881, p. 658.

119. Pereles' will, dated April 20, 1878, was "obviously written with a view to concealing from the curiosity of the public the value of the estate." Although a Jew by birth, in the words of Isaac Mayer Wise, Nathan Pereles "had long ago ceased to identify himself with any Jewish place of worship and was, in fact, an outspoken, so called free thinker; but in his dying moments, it appears, he clung to the faith of his ancestors." His wife, Fanny, died in April, 1892, at the age of 68; Rabbi Sigmund Hecht officiated at her burial. Survivors were her three sons, Benjamin Franklin, James Madison, and Thomas Jefferson, and a daughter, Julia. *Sent.*, April 24, p. 4, and April 29, 1878, p. 8; Jan. 29, p. 5, Jan. 30, p. 8, Jan. 31, p. 8, Feb. 1, p. 8, and March 5, 1879, p. 3; *Am. Isr.*, Feb. 7, 1879, p. 2; April 14, 1892, p. 7; April 23, 1896, p. 7.

120. *Sent.*, March 16, 1875, p. 8; June 24, 1876, p. 8; Jan. 11, 1881, p. 3; May 12, 1899, p. 2; June 21, 1900, p. 5; *Directories*, 1890, p. 986; 1895, p. 1136.

121. Jacob E. Friend married Alice Levy of Cincinnati on April 29, 1885. *Sent.*, Nov. 9, 1882, p. 2; Jan. 11, p. 4, April 29, p. 3, and April 30, 1885, p. 3. Ellis Baker Usher, *Wisconsin Its Story and Biography, 1848-1913* (Chicago, 1914), cited by Gregory, IV, pp. 680-684; *Directory*, 1900, p. 1243.

122. *Sent.*, July 20, 1876, p. 5; June 18, 1878, p. 2; June 18, 1879, p. 3; March 7, 1884, p. 7; Feb. 11, p. 3, and Feb. 14, 1886, p. 7; *Directory*, 1881, p. 658.

123. *Sent.*, Jan. 11, 1870, p. 1, and March 14, 1897, p. 3; *Directories,* 1881, p. 658; 1890, p. 986; 1895, p. 1136; 1900, p. 1243.

124. Louis Sax was a graduate of the Law Department of the University of Michigan, class of 1881. S. R. Simon was admitted to the bar in October, 1887. *Sent.*, April 25, 1878, p. 8; March 4, 1882, p. 6; March 23, p. 4, and Oct. 8, 1887, p. 6; June 18, p. 9, and June 29, 1893, p. 3; June 12, 1896, p. 3; Jan. 23, p. 3, and Sept. 21, 1897, p. 3; Sept. 1, 1898, p. 3; *Der Zeitgeist,* vol. II, no. 16 (Aug. 4, 1881), p. 264; *Directories,* 1880, p. 616; 1881, p. 658; 1890, p. 986; 1895, pp. 1135-1136; 1900, pp. 1242-1244; Gregory, *op. cit.,* vol. IV, pp. 731-732; "In Memoriam—Edwin S. Mack," Memorial of the Milwaukee County Bar Association (Milw., 1943), p. 1; photostat of Mack's Milwaukee High School Report Card, 1885-1886, in the writers' possession.

125. *Sent.*, Nov. 24, 1893, p. 3; *Am, Isr.,* Nov. 30, 1893, p. 2; *Directory,* 1870-71, p. 337; 1880, p. 627; 1890, p. 1006.

126. *Sent.*, Sept. 17, 1881, p. 8; Oct. 4, 1882, p. 3; Oct. 31, 1888, p. 3; March 8, 1893, p. 3; Nov. 18, 1895, p. 3; *Der Zeitgeist,* vol. II, no. 15 (July 21, 1881), p. 248; *Am. Isr.,* Nov. 21, 1895, p. 2; Gregory, *op. cit.,* vol. II, p. 976; *Directory,* 1880, p. 627; 1890, p. 1006; 1895, p. 1162.

127. *Directory,* 1881, p. 670; Andreas, p. 1028.

128. *Sent.*, May, 10, 1888, p. 3, and Oct. 1, 1893, p. 3; *Directory,* 1895, p. 1161; 1900, p. 1269.

129. *Sent.*, March 10, 1894, p. 3; *Directory,* 1890, pp. 1006-1007; 1895, pp. 1161-1162; 1900, pp. 1268-1270. Dr. Ferdinand Rosenthal, a native of Nordhausen in the Hartz, was born in 1814; he studied chemistry in his early years and later became a student of medicine at Halle, Jena, and Berlin. After a year in Milwaukee, he moved to Good Hope, in the suburbs. It was said that a precaution he never neglected was the use of sterilized water. After the Civil War, Dr. Rosenthal made his home at Thiensville, where he died in 1884. Gregory, vol. II, pp. 962-963.

130. *Directory,* 1880, p. 600; 1890, p. 959; 1895, p. 1099; 1900, p. 1203; *Am. Isr.,* April 21, 1904, p. 2; *Der Zeitgeist,* vol. II, no. 1 (Jan. 6, 1881), p. 19.

131. *Annual Reports of the Board of School Commissioners of the City of Milwaukee,* 1867-68, pp. 17, 21, 22, 59, 61; 1868-69, pp. 55, 57; 1869-70, pp. 22, 23.

132. Bernard Abrams, Esther Hermann, Rosa Kirschner, Leah Herrmann, Frederick Hirsch, Julia Kaufer, Bertha Kahn, Nellie H. Scheftels, Jennie C. Bennisch, Minnie Schoenmann, Julia A. Jacobs, and Sarah Kahn. *Ibid.,* 1870-1880, Secretary's Reports; *Am. Isr.,* Feb. 5, 1875, p. 2. Julia Kaufer graduated from the High School in 1875 and completed the Normal School course of studies in 1876; Julia Adeline Jacobs, a graduate of the High School, 1878, was graduated from the Normal Department in 1879. Among other graduates of the Normal School were: Bertha Kahn, 1877, Nellie Helena Scheftels, 1878, Sarah A. Kahn and Minnie Schoenmann, class of 1879. *Annual Reports of the School Board of the City of Milwaukee,* 1879-80, pp. 65, 66, 71, 72.

One teacher was Victor L. Berger, who came to Milwaukee in 1881 and began his teaching career in September, 1883, as instructor of German in the Eighth District School at $800 per annum. In February, 1889, he underwent investigation for remarks allegedly made in class, which, it was charged by some parents and ministers, cast an unfavorable reflection on the Bible. He was, however, exonerated. Berger resigned his position on December 31, 1892, when his remuneration was $1,100 a year. *Sent.*, Aug. 31, 1883, p. 5; July 17, 1887, p. 6; Feb. 5, p. 1, Feb. 6, p. 3, and Feb. 7, 1889, p. 1; *Annual Reports of the School Board of the City of Milwaukee,* 1882-1889, Secretary's Report; *Idem*, p. 160.

133. Bernard A. Abrams, Esther Hermann, Rosa Kirschner, Leah Herrmann, Frederick Hirsch, Julia Kaufer, Bertha Kahn, Nellie Scheftels, Jennie C. Bennisch, Minnie Schoenmann, Julia A. Jacobs, Sarah Kahn, Clara Horwitz, Sigmund Cohn, Sallie Berkenwald, Sallie Herz, Anna Salzman, Frances Heimann, Elizabeth De Wolf, Clara Metzl, Lottie Markwell, Victor Berger, Elizabeth Harris, Alma Patek, Adeline Kahn, Fannie Herbst, Anna Harris, Rachel Becker, Belle Reichenbaum, Ray Bernstein, Tillie Epstein, Rebecca Apple, Julia Stern, Sophia Hauser, Minnie B. Goodman, Adele Hauser, Henrietta Kussel, and Lena Rich. *Sent.*, Sept. 5, 1880, p. 8; Jan. 2, p. 8, Jan. 4, p. 2, Feb. 6, p. 8, Oct. 6, p. 9, and Dec. 2, 1881, p. 5; Aug. 4, 1886, p. 3; June 21, 1890, p. 3; *Annual Reports of the School Board of the City of Milwaukee,* 1880-1890, Secretary's Report. Graduates of the Normal Department included: Clara Horwitz, class of 1878; Sallie Birkenwald and Annie M. Salzman, 1880; Clara Metzl, 1881; Tillie Epstein, 1886; and Sophia Hauser, 1889. *Ibid.*, 1879-1880, pp. 71, 72; 1880-1881, p. 87.

134. *Annual Reports of the School Board of the City of Milwaukee,* 1890-1900, Secretary's Reports. An indication of the growth of the Milwaukee Public Schools is reflected in the following figures: in 1879, there were 258 teachers employed; in 1880, 272; by 1887, the number was 340; there were 676 instructors in the system in 1894. *Idem*, 1880-1881, p. 39; 1893-1894, p. 27.

135. B. A. Abrams married Esther Harris, who was born in New York. Interview with Mr. Sol Abrams, son of B. A. Abrams, February 9, 1955; *Annual Reports of the Board of School Commissioners,* 1873, Secretary's Reports, p. 180; 1876, p. 309; 1879, p. 192; *Der Zeitgeist*, vol. I, no. 14 (July 8, 1880), p. 228; *Sent.*, Aug. 16, 1883, p. 5; *25th Annual Report of the School Board,* 1886, Secretary's Report. In discussing his appointment in 1891, the School Commissioners voted 25 to 4 in his favor. *Sent.*, Jan. 6, p. 3, Jan. 26, p. 3, Feb. 3, 1886, p. 3; June 30, 1889, p. 3; Aug. 5, 1891, p. 3; July 1, 1893, p. 3.

136. The total cost to the city in 1895 for this area of education was $45,875. *Sent.*, March 22, p. 3, and June 21, 1894, p. 3; June 20, 1895, p. 3; June 10, 1896, p. 3; *Thirty-Eighth Annual Report of the School Board of the City of Milwaukee,* 1897, p. 5.

137. Appearing before the Board in his own defense, Abrams contended that twenty years earlier he would have been able to pass an examination and secure a certificate; but the lapse of time had dimmed his memory "of many of the things he had mastered when a school boy." He insisted that he had devoted "all his life to the study of one particular branch and he thought himself competent in that." *Sent.*, Jan. 25, p. 3, and Nov. 13, 1898, p. 6.

138. *Sent.*, Oct. 16, 1874, p. 8; Feb. 2, 1878, p. 8; Sept. 5, 1880, p. 8; Jan.

2, p. 8, Jan. 14, p. 2; April 30, p. 3, June 11, p. 3, Sept. 26, p. 3, Oct. 4, p. 3, and Oct. 26, 1881, p. 3; July 18, 1882, p. 2; April 16, p. 3, Aug. 8, 1886, p. 3; Sept. 5, 1887, p. 3; Jan. 27, p. 3, and July 10, 1889, p. 3; July 4, 1896, p. 3; April 6, 1897, p. 3; *Der Zeitgeist*, vol. II, no. 9 (April 28, 1881), p. 152. Speaking before the National Association of German-American Teachers meeting in convention in Milwaukee on July 7, 1892, Abrams asserted that children should begin with the study of German during their first school year, and condemned the efforts then being made to exclude German from lower classes in the public schools. "The German language," he said, "is, as it were, the second mother tongue of our German school children." *Sent.*, July 8, 1892, p. 3. B. A. Abrams served as editor of the *Jugend Post* and *Kinder Post* for the *Milwaukee Herold*, and subsequently taught German and French at Marquette University. In addition, he taught Sunday School at Temple Emanu-El. Interview with Mr. Sol Abrams, his son, February 9, 1955; *Sent.*, March 9, 1880, p. 8.

139. Rudolf Glanz, *Jews in Relation to the Cultural Milieu of the Germans in America up to the Eighteen Eighties*, (N. Y., 1947), pp. 26-48.

140. *Der Zeitgeist*, vol. III, no. 11 (May 25, 1882), p. 176.

141. *Sent.*, Jan. 10, 1875, p. 8; Jan. 6, 1877, p. 8.

142. *Sent.*, Dec. 22, 1875, p. 8; Dec. 18, 1876, p. 8; Dec. 21, 1881, p. 7; Dec. 17, 1884, p. 3; *Directory*, 1870-1871, p. 369; 1871-1872, p. 378; 1872-1873, p. 351; 1873-1874, p. 395; 1875-1876, pp. 35-37; 1876-1877, pp. 42-43; 1877-1878, pp. 43-44; 1879, p. 40; 1880, p. 40; 1881, p. 42; 1882, pp. 42-43; 1883, p. 41; 1884, p. 41; Milwaukee Chapter No. 32 was chartered in 1867; however, it surrendered its charter to the Grand Encampment on March 5, 1878. Andreas, p. 961.

143. *Am. Isr.*, Aug. 20, 1886, pp. 4, 9.

144. *Sent.*, June 26, 1895, p. 3; *Am. Isr.*, July 4, 1895, p. 3.

145. *Directory*, 1875-1876, p. 38; 1881, p. 44; 1882, p. 44; 1883, p. 43; 1884, p. 42; 1885, p. 41; 1886, p. 38; *Sent.*, Jan. 7, 1876, p. 8; June 7, p. 8; July 13, 1877, p. 8; July 6, 1878, p. 8; June 4, 1880, p. 7; June 3, p. 2; Dec. 19, 1881, p. 7; Oct. 7, 1884, p. 3.

146. *Idem.*, 1870-1871, p. 369; 1872-1873, p. 351; 1877-1878, p. 46; 1878, p. 38; 1879, p. 42; 1881, p. 44; 1882, p. 45; 1883, p. 43; 1884, p. 42; 1885, p. 41; 1886, p. 38; 1887, p. 36; 1888, p. 51; 1889, p. 48, 1890, p. 47; *Sent.*, Dec. 4, p. 4; Oct. 10, 1878, p. 8; June 3, 1880, p. 4; June 8, 1883, p. 5; June 4, 1885, pp. 4, 8; June 3, 1886, p. 8; Conard, II, pp. 430-432.

147. *Sent.*, June 10, 1881, p. 8; Feb. 19, 1886, p. 3; May 2, 1899, p. 3; *The U. S. Biographical Dictionary*, Wis. vol. (Chicago, 1877), pp. 54-55. Silber also served as treasurer of I.O.O.F. Uniform Degree Camp—Camp Elliot No. 1 in 1884. *Directory*, 1884, p. 43.

148. *Sent.*, June 13, 1876, p. 8; Feb. 16, p. 6; July 10, 1882, p. 3.

149. *Sent.*, May 28, p. 8; Oct. 24, 1880, p. 8; Jan. 18, p. 3; Mar. 17, p. 2; Dec. 24, 1881, p. 3; Jan. 6, p. 7; Jan. 11, p. 7; Mar. 24, p. 6; Dec. 22, 1882, p. 2; July 22, 1884, p. 3; *Directory*, 1881, p. 47; 1882, pp. 46-47; 1884, p. 45; 1885, p. 44; 1886, pp. 41-42; 1890, p. 48.

150. *Sent.*, Apr. 29, 1886, p. 3; *Directory*, 1886, p. 43.

151. *Sent.*, Jan. 23, 1887, p. 3; *Directory*, 1880, p. 44; 1884, p. 44; 1885, p. 43; 1887, p. 38; 1888, p. 53; Andreas, pp. 977-978.

152. *Sent.*, May 3, 1895, p. 3; Ignatz Langer was a secretary of the Harugari Widows' and Orphans' Fund in 1884-85. David and Alex Weil were officers of Milwaukee Branch No. 176, Order of Iron Ball. *Directory*, 1884, pp. 43, 46; 1885, p. 45.

153. For the year 1876-1877, receipts of the Order were $4,489,870, and disbursements amounted to $1,689,485. *Sent.*, Aug. 2, 1871, p. 4; Sept. 20, 1877, p. 8; July 29, 1879, p. 8; *Directory*, 1878, p. 40.

154. *Sent.*, Oct. 9, p. 8; Oct. 19, 1874, p. 8; Jan. 22, p. 8; Apr. 12, 1875, p. 8; Apr. 10, 1876, p. 8; Mar. 29, 1877, p. 8; Oct. 14, 1878, p. 8; *Directory*, 1881, p. 47; 1882, p. 50; 1883, p. 49; 1885, p. 49; 1886, p. 42; Andreas, pp. 978-979.

155. *Sent.*, Sept. 8, 1873, p. 8; Sept. 5, p. 8; Sept. 7, 1874, p. 8; Jan. 25, 1875, p. 4; Sept. 15, 1877, p. 8; *Directory*, 1873-1874, p. 396; 1875-1876, p. 40.

156. Cited in Glanz, *op. cit.*, p. 37; "Milwaukee, du bist ein gar herrliches Städchen,/ So braun ist dein Bier und so blond deine Mädchen,/ Dort beut dem Turner manch gastlich Haus,/ Und es schmeisst dort kein Hilton nen Seligman 'naus'." This referred to the famous episode of Joseph Seligman's exclusion by "Judge" Hilton from the Grand Union Hotel at Saratoga in the summer of 1877, explicitly because of Seligman's Jewishness.

It is also worth noticing that Jews were prominent in Milwaukee's Old Settlers Club, while in other cities they (and sometimes all Germans) were excluded by devising the latest date of a "pioneer's" arrival just before the first Jew arrived. Among the 60 Old Settlers in Milwaukee were James and Thomas Pereles (pioneer's sons), Max Landauer, H. S. Mack, and David Adler. T. J. Pereles and Adler served as officers. *Sent.*, Jan. 5, 1888, p. 3; Apr. 9, 1891, p. 6; Feb. 23, 1892, p. 3; *Directory*, 1889, p. 62; Conard, II, p. 431; Glanz, *op. cit.*, pp. 23-25.

157. *Sent.*, Jan. 14, p. 3; Mar. 5, 1887, p. 1; *Directory*, 1883, p. 49; 1884, p. 50; 1885, pp. 46, 48.

158. *Directory*, 1870-1871, p. 371; 1871-1872, p. 381; 1872-73, p. 353; 1875-1876, p. 40; 1876-1877, p. 47; 1887, p. 43; *Sent.*, Jan. 5, 1871, p. 4; Jan. 5, 1872, p. 4; Jan. 4, 6, 1873, p. 4; Apr. 9, 1880, p. 8; Apr. 1, 1882, p. 11; Apr. 8, p. 2; May 21, 1888, p. 2; Aug. 9, 1889, p. 2; Apr. 6, 1890, p. 1; Oct. 23, p. 3; Dec. 11, 1891, p. 3.

159. *Sent.*, June 1, 1880, p. 8; Feb. 4, p. 6; Oct. 6, 1882, p. 2.

160. *Sent.*, Aug. 22, 1882, p. 3; *Directory*, 1883, p. 50; 1885, p. 47.

161. Midwestern officers included: Louis Rindskopf, first vice president (1873) and president (1876); R. Reichmann, first vice president (1878) and president (1879); Adolph Loeb, secretary (1879-1880); Solomon Weil, sergeant-at-arms (1885); Henry Hermann, second vice president (1888) and president (1891); Max Ascher, second vice president (1891). Louis Rindskopf was chosen treasurer of the Endowment Fund, of which David Adler long served as trustee. *Sent.*, Jan. 10, 1876, p. 8; Feb. 17, p. 5; Feb. 18, p. 3; Feb. 21, 1879, p. 8; Jan. 27, 1880, p. 8; Jan. 12, p. 3; Jan. 13, 1885, p. 3; Dec. 6, 1890, p. 3; Feb. 2, p. 5; Feb. 3, 1891, p. 3; *Am. Isr.*, Feb. 1, 1878, p. 5; Jan. 23, 1885, p. 2; June 22, 1888, p. 8; *Jewish Times*, vol. IV, no. 50 (Feb. 7, 1873), p. 987; vol. VI, no. 4 (Mar. 20, 1874), p. 57. R. Reichmann had joined B'nai B'rith's first lodge in New York City—Hebron

Lodge, in 1845. He died in March, 1881. *Der Zeitgeist,* vol. II, no. 5 (Mar. 3, 1881), p. 88; *Am. Isr.,* Mar. 14, 1879, p. 5.

162. *Sent.,* June 12, p. 8; June 20, p. 8; June 22, 1874, pp. 3, 8.

163. *Sent.,* June 22, 1874, p. 3.

164. Excelsior Lodge met at Boynton's Hall, corner of Milwaukee and Mason Streets. *Sent.,* Feb. 17, 1879, p. 8; *Directory,* 1881, p. 48; 1882, p. 48.

165. *Sent.,* July 27, p. 4; Aug. 3, 1871, p. 4; Oct. 24, 1874, p. 8; June 27, 1876, p. 8; Aug. 24, 1880, p. 8; *Der Zeitgeist,* vol. I, no. 18 (Sept. 2, 1880), p. 292.

166. *Sent.,* Oct. 25, 1884, p. 3.

167. *Sent.,* Feb. 2, 1891, p. 2.

168. *Sent.,* Feb. 22, p. 5; Mar. 2, 1898, p. 3.

169. *J. Mess.,* June 17, 1870, p. 3; *Jewish Times,* vol. II, no. 11 (May 13, 1870), p. 166; vol. III, no. 38 (Nov. 17, 1871), p. 605.

170. *Sent.,* June 22, 1874, p. 3.

171. *Sent.,* Oct. 8, 1873, p. 8.

172. *Sent.,* Dec. 12, 1873, p. 8.

173. *Directory,* 1870-1871, p. 371; 1871-1872, p. 381; 1872-1873, p. 354; *Jewish Times,* vol. V. no. 49 (Jan. 30, 1874), p. 775; *Am. Isr.,* Jan. 14, 1881, p. 221; Feb. 1, p. 7; July 25, 1884, p. 5; Nov. 19, 1886, p. 3; May 13, 1887, p. 6; Aug. 31, p. 8; Oct. 5, p. 9; Oct. 26, 1888, p. 2; *Der Zeitgeist,* vol. II, no. 2 (Jan. 20, 1881), p. 36; no. 5 (Mar. 3, 1881), p. 88; no. 18 (Sept. 1, 1881), p. 296; Collections from Milwaukee firms and individuals were published annually in the *Israelite.* In January, 1881, David Adler contributed $500 in memory of his wife, Fannie. *Sent.,* May 14, 1875, p. 8; Apr. 12, p. 8; Apr. 19, p. 8; Apr. 20, p. 8; Dec. 25, 1878, p. 8; Sept. 23, 1880, p. 3; July 9, p. 8; July 10, 1881, p. 3; May 25, 1887, p. 3; July 29, 1889, p. 3.

174. *Am. Isr.,* Feb. 1, 1878, p. 5; June 22, 1888, p. 8; *Sent.,* Feb. 17, 1879, p. 5; Jan. 15, 1882, p. 3; July 29, 1889, p. 3; July 10, 1895, p. 7; July 30, 1896, p. 3; July 10, p. 3; Nov. 16, 1900, p. 4.

175 *Am. Isr.,* July 16, 1886, p. 6; *Am. Hebr.,* July 29, 1894, p. 397.

176. *Sent.,* July 16, 1894, p. 3; Aug. 24, 1899, p. 5; *Am. Isr.,* July 19, 1894, p. 2; June 25, 1896, p. 2; *Am. Hebr.,* July 29, 1894, p. 397. For a list of officers of the local B'nai Brith lodges, see Appendix B.

177. *Proceedings of Annual Convention, District Grand Lodge No. 6,* 1913, p. 33.

178. For full details on B'nai B'rith, see Swichkow, Louis J., "A Century of B'nai B'rith in Milwaukee," in *A Century of Service: Gilead Lodge No. 41....* (Milwaukee, 1962), pp. 6-27.

179. It maintained an endowment fund, and applicants were required to undergo medical examinations as prerequisite for joining. *Sent.,* Feb. 3, p. 8; Feb. 4, 1879, p. 8; *AJYB,* 5670 (1909-1910), p. 164; *Directory,* 1879, p. 44; 1883, p. 47; 1884, p. 46; 1885, p. 46; 1886, p. 44; 1887, p. 42; 1888, p. 55; 1889, p. 51; 1890, p. 51; Andreas, p. 983.

180. *Directory,* 1881, p. 48; 1882, p. 48; 1883, p. 47; 1885, p. 46; 1886, p. 44; 1887, p. 42; 1888, p. 55; 1889, p. 51; *Am. Isr.,* Jan. 15, 1875, p. 6; Andreas, p. 983.

181. *Am. Isr.*, Feb. 16, p. 275; July 20, 1883, p. 6; July 25, 1889, p. 4; June 2, 1892, p. 5; July 15, 1897, p. 3; Aug. 4, 1898, p. 3; July 13, 1899, p. 6.

182. *Sent.*, Jan. 29, 1877, p. 3.

183. *Sent.*, Jan. 29, 1877, p. 3; Feb. 14, 1887, p. 3. At the 1882 convention, with 24 lodges represented, the question of consolidating the four Orders of "benevolent Hebrew societies in one organization" was seriously considered. The organizations under discussion were the Free Sons of Israel, the Improved Free Sons of Israel, B'nai B'rith, and Kesher Shel Barzel. The motion made no progress. *Sent.*, Jan. 30, 1882, p. 3. In 1894, there were 106 lodges in the Order, with an aggregate membership of 13,000. *Sent.*, Jan. 27, 1894, p. 2.

184. In May, 1898, Baron Hirsch Lodge forgave the dues of all members enlisting for the Spanish-American War. In 1899, there were 188 lodges, with 14,046 members in this Order. *Sent.*, July 14, 1896, p. 3; May 4, 1898, p. 3; *Directory*, 1885, p. 46; 1886, p. 44; 1887, p. 42; 1888, p. 55; 1889, p. 51; 1890, p. 50; 1896, p. 34; *Am. Isr.*, Jan. 21, 1897, p. 2; *AJYB*, 5660 (1899-1900), pp. 76, 91; 5661 (1900-1901), p. 132.

185. *Sent.*, Dec. 21, 1897, p. 3; Jan. 3, 1898, p. 3.

186. *Sent.* Nov. 5, 1899, Sect. II, p. 1.

187. *Sent.*, Jan. 25, 1876, p. 8; Feb. 5, 1877, p. 8; *Directory*, 1870-1871, p. 370; 1871-1872, p. 381; 1872-1873, p. 353; 1873-1874, p. 398; 1878, p. 43; *Am. Isr.*, Feb. 17, 1871, p. 7.

188. *Sent.*, Feb. 5, p. 8; Feb. 19, 1877, p. 8; *Directory*, 1877-1878, p. 50.

189. *Directory*, 1878, p. 42; 1879, p. 46; 1880, p. 46; *Am. Isr.*, Mar. 14, 1879, p. 5; *Der Zeitgeist*, vol. I, no. 2 (Jan. 15, 1880), p. 32; no. 3 (Feb. 5, 1880), p. 48; *Am. Hebr.*, Jan. 23, 1880, p. 115; *Sent.*, Apr. 11, 1877, p. 3; Andreas, p. 567.

190. Officers in 1886 were: Joseph Friedberg, president; B. M. Weil, vice president; D. H. Friend, secretary; H. S. Mack, treasurer; for 1887: Joseph Friedberg, president; B. M. Weil, vice president; J. H. Newman, secretary; H. S. Mack, treasurer. *Sent.*, May 5, 1895, p. 9; *Am. Isr.*, Feb. 19, p. 6; Feb. 26, 1886, p. 2; Nov. 18, 1887, p. 3; Aug. 31, 1888, p. 8; *Directory*, 1886, p. 52; 1887, p. 51.

191. *Am. Isr.*, Apr. 20, 1888, p. 8; Aug. 31, 1888, p. 8; *Directory*, 1889, p. 62.

192. The attempt to hold a New Year's ball on a Friday night, December 31, 1897, evoked protests from a few board members. *Sent.*, May 5, p. 9; Oct. 27, 1895, p. 3; May 3, 1896, p. 3; Jan. 22, 1899, p. 4; *Am. Isr.*, July 18, 1895, p. 3; Nov. 7, 1895, p. 2; Nov. 18, 1897, p. 7.

193. *Sent.*, Nov. 12, 1899, p. 5.

194. *Sent.*, Dec. 22, 1900, p. 3; *AJYB*, 1900-1901, p. 489.

195. *Sent.*, Jan. 7, p. 4; Feb. 22, p. 4; Mar. 21, p. 8; Apr. 26, p. 8; May 23, p. 8; Dec. 29, 1880, p. 7; Jan. 3, 1881, p. 2; Jan. 9, 1882, p. 7; Mar. 21, 1899, p. 3; *Der Zeitgeist*, vol. I, no. 2 (Jan. 15, 1880), p. 32; no. 3 (Feb. 5, 1880), p. 48; no. 21 (Oct. 14, 1880), p. 340; no. 23 (Nov. 11, 1880), p. 372; vol. II, no. 2 (Jan. 20, 1881), p. 36; *Directory*, 1878, p. 43; 1879, p. 47; 1880, p. 47; 1881, p. 51; *Am. Isr.*, Feb. 14, p. 2; Mar. 14, 1879, p. 5; Andreas, pp. 566-567.

Officers for the period 1879-1882 were:

year	president	vice president	secretary	treasurer
1879	Wm. Katzenstein	Theo. Weil	A. L. Baer	Jos. Schiller
1880-81	A. W. Rich	L. H. Harris	I. S. Klein	J. Schiller
1882	A. W. Rich	J. Pollack	I. S. Klein	J. Schiller

196. *Sent.*, Oct. 14, 1884, p. 3; May 11, 1890, p. 3; *Am. Isr.*, Aug. 21, 1890, p. 7; Conard, II, p. 235.

197. Officers of the Standard Club during the nineties were:

year	president	vice president	secretary
1894	M. D. Newald	Wm. Kohn	L. Heilbronner
1895	M. D. Newald	H. Friedlander	L. Heilbronner
1896	M. D. Newald	M. Lamfrom	L. Heilbronner
1897	M. D. Newald	H. Friedlander	Max. J. Loeb
1899	H. Friedlander	Ed. Mahler	Max. J. Loeb
1900	H. Friedlander	Ed. Mahler	Max. J. Loeb

treas.	fin. sec'y.
H. Eckstein	I. M. Hirschberg
H. Eckstein	I. M. Hirschberg
H. Eckstein	I. M. Hirschberg
H. Eckstein	I. M. Hirschberg
H. Eckstein	I. M. Hirschberg
A. Tiefenbronner	I. M. Hirschberg

Sent., Jan. 15, p. 16; Apr. 2, p. 13; Dec. 31, 1893, p. 3; May 10, p. 3; May 17, 1895, p. 3; Jan. 2, 1896, p. 3; *Am. Isr.*, Jan. 11, 1894, p. 3; Mar. 21, 1895, p. 2; May 23, 1895, p. 3; Jan. 16, 1896, p. 7; *AJYB*, 1900-1901, p. 489; Conard, II, p. 235.

198. *Sent.*, Nov. 9, 1899, p. 5.

199. Some such were the German Ladies' Association, the Minnehaha Pleasure Club, the E. T. C. Club, the Young Ladies' Thursday Afternoon Club, the Jewish Women's Club. *Sent.*, Mar. 29, 1883, p. 5; Oct. 28, 1888, p. 5; *Directory*, 1869-1870, p. 409; 1870-1871, p. 371; 1871-1872, p. 382; 1872-1873, p. 354; *Am. Isr.*, Jan. 29, 1886, p. 10; Mar. 26, 1886, p. 7; June 4, 1886, p. 7; Feb. 26, 1886, p. 2; Oct. 2, 1888, p. 5; Sept. 14, 1888, p. 8; Apr. 11, 1889, p. 3; Sept. 5, 1889, p. 5.

200. Initial officers elected were: Mrs. S. R. Levy, president; Mrs. B. M. Weil, vice president; Miss Sophie Katz, secretary; Mrs. V. Caro, treasurer. *Sent.*, Oct. 27, p. 3; Oct. 28, 1895, p. 3; *Am. Isr.*, Oct. 31, 1895, p. 2; Monroe Campbell, Jr. and William Wirtz, *The First Fifty Years—a History of the National Council of Jewish Women*, 1893-1943 (1943), p. 91. Mrs. Emanuel Friend, Mrs. J. C. Hyman, and Miss Sophie Katz were the Milwaukee delegates to the Women's Congress at the Parliament of Religions during the World's Fair in Chicago in 1893. *Am. Isr.*, Sept. 7, 1893, p. 3. The National Council of Jewish Women came into being as a result of that conference. In 1895, there were sections in 21 cities and a membership of 2,500.

201. *Sent.*, Nov. 11, 1895, p. 3; *Am. Isr.*, Nov. 28, 1895, p. 2.

202. *Am. Isr.*, Oct. 1, 1896, p. 3; *The Reform Advocate*, XII, 11 (Oct. 31, 1896), p. 171.

203. *Sent.*, Apr. 2, p. 3; Apr. 5, p. 3; June 13, 1897, p. 9; *Am. Isr.*, Jan. 16, p. 7; Mar. 12, p. 3; Apr. 2, 1896, p. 3; Feb. 11, p. 2; Apr. 8, p. 3; June 17, 1897; *Directory*, 1898, p. 57; *Blue Book*, p. 84.

204. *Am. Hebr.*, Mar. 30, 1900, p. 647; *Blue Book*, p. 85.

205. *Der Zeitgeist*, vol. I, no. 3 (Feb. 5, 1880), p. 48; no. 23 (Nov. 11, 1880), p. 372.

206. *Sent.*, Feb. 5, p. 8; Feb. 7, 1876, p. 8; Oct. 27, 1888, p. 3; Jan. 26, p. 2; Mar. 3, 1889, p. 11; Nov. 13, 1891, p. 3; *Am. Isr.*, Jan. 29, 1886, p. 10; Feb. 5, 1886, p. 2; Oct. 26, 1888, p. 2; May 15, 1890, p. 8; Jan. 15, 1891, p. 4; Sept. 28, 1893, p. 2; Nov. 14, 1895, p. 2.

207. *Am. Isr.*, Apr. 28, 1892, p. 7; Conard, II, p. 235.

208. *Sent.*, July 4, 1891, p. 3; Jan. 3, 1892, p. 3; Dec. 9, 1893, p. 3; *Am. Isr.*, May 7, 1891, p. 2; Nov. 30, 1893, p. 2.

209. *Der Zeitgeist*, vol. I, no. 3 (Feb. 5, 1880), p. 48; no. 23 (Nov. 11, 1880), p. 372.

210. Benjamin Rabinowitz, "The Young Men's Hebrew Associations (1854-1913)," *PAJHS*, XXXVII (1947), pp. 222-226, 245, 247, 249.

211. *Sent.*, Nov. 8, p. 12; Nov. 19, 1883, p. 4.

212. *Sent.*, Nov. 19, 1883, p. 4.

213. The arrangements committee for the latter event included Victor Berger. *Sent.*, Dec. 2, p. 12; Dec. 3, p. 5; Dec. 7, 1883, p. 5; Jan. 8, p. 5; Jan. 28, p. 3; Feb. 2, p. 7; Mar. 27, p. 3; Mar. 28, 1884, p. 3; *Am. Isr.*, Feb. 1, p. 5; Feb. 29, 1884, p. 6; *Directory*, 1884, p. 54.

214. *Sent.*, Dec. 10, p. 5; Dec. 17, p. 5; Dec. 23, 1883, p. 12.

215. *Am. Isr.*, Feb. 1, 1894, p. 2.

216. *Sent.*, Aug. 2, 1881, p. 5.

217. *Sent.*, June 26, p. 5; Sept. 11, 1875, p. 2; May 20, p. 5; July 29, 1876, p. 3; Mar. 22, p. 8; Sept. 30, 1878, p. 8; Sept. 27, p. 3; Oct. 17, 1879, p. 3.

218. *Sent.*, Nov. 6, 1879, p. 8; Jan, 13, p. 4; Feb. 15, 1880, p. 4; Jan. 9. p. 4; Feb. 12, 1881, p. 3.

219. *Sent.*, Feb. 2, p. 8; Feb. 3, 1882, p. 5; Nov. 22, 1885, p. 3; Jan. 29, 1889, p. 2; *Der Zeitgeist*, vol. III, no. 6 (Mar. 16, 1882), p. 96.

220. *Sent.*, Feb. 1, p. 2; Aug. 28, 1887, p. 6; Jan. 18, 1890, p. 3; *Der Zeitgeist*, vol. II, no. 5 (Mar. 3, 1881), p. 88.

221. *Sent.*, Apr. 14, 1885, p. 3.

222. *Sent.*, May 6, 1873, p. 8; May 13, 1880, p. 8; *Am. Isr.*, Aug. 8. 1895, p. 3; Andreas, p. 584.

223. *Sent.*, May 7, p. 8; May 13, 1880, p. 8; May 9, 1882, p. 5; May 3, 1883, p. 5; May 20, 1886, p. 3; May 10, p. 3; June 7, 1887, p. 3; Oct. 9, 1889, p. 3; *Directory*, 1872-1873, p. 353; 1882, p. 50; 1883, p. 49; 1886, p. 47.

224. *Sent.*, June 7, 1893, p. 3; Mar. 26, 1897, p. 1; Organized in November, 1877, membership of the Arion Musical Club was composed of about fifty per cent of the principal male singers of the city. In 1881, the maximum number of active members was about 60. Andreas, p. 586.

225. *Sent.*, May 1, p. 8; Sept. 24, 1888, p. 3; May 26, 1889, p. 1; June 1, 1890, p. 3; Conard, II, pp. 370-371.

226. *Sent.*, Nov. 24, 1884, p. 3; Nov. 25, 1885, p. 3; Sept. 15, 1886, p. 3;

Mar. 26, 1897, p. 1; *Directory*, 1884, p. 50; 1885, p. 49; *Am. Isr.*, July 16, 1886, p. 6; Conard, II, pp. 370-371; Still, p. 407.

227. The Milwaukee Liedertafel, organized in July, 1858, was a social singing society. In 1881, its membership was 74. *Directory*, 1871-1872, p. 381; Andreas, p. 586.

228. *Directory*, 1883, p. 49.

229. *Sent.*, Jan. 10, p. 8; June 3, 1880, p. 8; Mar. 11, p. 8; May 12, 1881, p. 8. The Freie Gemeinde, a free religious association and musical society, was founded in 1867. Its membership was 170 in 1881. Andreas, p. 588.

230. *Am. Isr.*, Jan. 24, 1895, p. 3.

231. *Am. Isr.*, Apr. 22, 1909, p. 3

232. *Sent.*, Jan. 19, 1894.

233. *Sent.*, Aug. 12, 1890, p. 4.

234. *Directory*, 1882, p. 51; 1883, p. 50; 1884, p. 51; 1885, p. 3.

235. In 1880, Germania's membership was 125. *Sent.*, Jan. 7, p. 4; Feb. 2, p. 4; July 7, 1871, p. 4; Jan. 5, 1872, p. 4; Jan. 6, 1873, p. 4; Jan. 10, 1880, p. 8; Feb. 19, p. 2; Mar. 26, 1881, p. 2; *Der Zeitgeist*, vol. II, no. 5 (Mar. 3, 1881), p. 88; *Directory*, 1870-1871, p. 370; 1871-1872, p. 380; 1872-1873, p. 353.

236. M. Shulhof was local agent of the *Israelite* in 1876. *Am. Isr.*, July 7, 1876, p. 4.

237. *Der Zeitgeist*, vol. I, no. 1 (Jan. 1, 1880), pp. 1, 8; vol. II, no. 12 (June 9, 1881), p. 200; *Sent.*, Dec. 30, 1879, p. 8.

238. The *Zeitgeist* alone, $2.50 per year; the *Familienkreise* alone, $1.50 a year. Foreign, $3.00 for the *Zeitgeist*, and $4.00 for both papers. *Der Zeitgeist*, vol. I, no. 20 (Sept. 30, 1880), p. 324.

239. *Idem*, vol. I, no. 1 (Jan. 1, 1880), p. 1.

240. The latter (Shylock in der Sage und in Geschichte) appeared simultaneously in the learned *Monatsschrift für Geschichte und Wissenschaft des Judentums*, XXIX (1880), pp. 337-354, 387-403. *Die Entwicklungsstadien des Messiasglaubens* has remained unnoticed and does not appear in the bibliography of Graetz's writings.

241. Adolf Jellinek, *Der jüdische Stamm in nicht-jüdischen Spruchworte*, 3 parts (Vienna, 1882.)

242. "Der Sabbat in seiner kulturgeschichtlichen Bedeutung," in Hermann Cohen, *Judische Schriften*, II (Berlin, 1924), pp. 45-73, 469-470. Like nearly all his works, it has, unfortunately, not been translated.

243. *Der Zeitgeist*, vol. I, no. 26 (Dec. 23, 1880), p. 412.

244. *Ibid.*, vol. II, no. 18 (Sept. 1, 1881), p. 296. On October 27, 1881, Chicago was added to the Milwaukee by-line.

245. *Ibid.*, vol. II, no. 26 (Dec. 22, 1881), p. 409.

246. *Sent.*, Dec. 30, 1880, p. 2; May 20, 1881, p. 3; *Der Zeitgeist*, vol. II, no. 2 (Jan. 20, 1881), p. 36; no. 11 (May 26, 1881), p. 184; *Am. Hebr.*, Dec. 31, 1880, p. 73.

247. *Der Zeitgeist*, vol. III, no. 24 (Nov. 23, 1882), p. 360.

248. *Ibid.*, vol. III, no. 26 (Dec. 21, 1882), p. 392.

IV. CIVIC SECURITY AND PUBLIC SERVICE

1. *Sent.*, March 24, 1871, p. 4.

2. *Sent.*, December 24, 1894, p. 5.

3. *Ibid.; Am. Isr.,* June 21, 1894, p. 3; Dec. 27, 1894, p. 2. Jewish congregations' property was then valued at about $150,000.

4. Quoted, *Jewish Times,* vol. II, no. 20 (July 15, 1870), p. 312. See in general Herman J. Deutsch, "Yankee-Teuton Political Rivalry in Wisconsin Politics in the Seventies," *Wisconsin Magazine of History,* XIV, 3 (March, 1931), pp. 262-281; 4 (June, 1931), pp. 403-418.

5. *Am. Isr.,* July 15, 1870, p. 11. Although not relating to dancing, a dance-band prelude was prohibited in the Theater Comique on Sunday by Acting-Mayor H. M. Benjamin. *Sent.,* Feb. 5, 1876, p. 8.

6. Quoted, *Am. Isr.,* Aug. 2, 1894, p. 2; *Sent.,* Feb. 26, 1890, p. 3.

7. *Am. Isr.,* Dec. 5, 1889, p. 1; Aug. 2, 1894, p. 2; *Sent.,* Feb. 26, 1890, p. 3.

8. *Sent.,* April 15, 1896, p. 3.

9. *Sent.,* April 17, 1896, p. 1.

10. *Sent.,* Sept. 23, 1896, p. 3.

11. The case was "The State ex. rel., vs. Frederick Weiss, John Cornett, W. H. Morressey, Thomas Mooney, James McBride and J. C. Burnes, plaintiffs and appellants, against the District Board of School District No. 8, of the city of Edgerton, Rock county, Wisconsin."

12. *Sent.,* Jan. 26, p. 4, March 19, p. 1, March 20, 1890, p. 4; *Am. Isr.,* April 24, 1890, p. 5; Aug. 7, 1890, p. 6.

13. *Sent.,* March 22, p. 3, and June 20, 1890, p. 4

14. The Bennett Law was opposed by a coalition of Catholic and Lutheran Germans. German liberal and secular groups, including Jews, generally joined Yankee elements to support it. In supporting the enactment, the *Sentinel* pointed out that 50,000 children did not attend school. In attacking the law, the three German Catholic bishops denied the right of the State to provide for the compulsory education of children as "an infringement of superior parental rights." The German Lutheran church, too, denied the right of the state "to prescribe a certain measure of secular education." Watrous, *op. cit.,* vol. I, p. 400; Still, *op. cit.,* pp. 260-261, 296; *Sent.,* March 15, p. 4, and March 27, 1890, p. 4.

15. *Sent.,* March 22, p. 3, and June 20, 1890, p. 4; Louise Phelps Kellogg, "The Bennett Law in Wisconsin," *Wisconsin Magazine of History,* II, 1 (Sept., 1918), pp. 3-25.

16. *Sent.,* June 20, 1890, p. 4.

17. *Der Zeitgeist,* II, 3 (Feb. 3, 1881), p. 52.

18. *Sent.,* Dec. 16, 1874, p. 3.

19. *Sent.,* Dec. 25, 1874, p. 3.

20. *Sent.,* Dec. 28, 1874, p. 2.

21. *Ibid.*

22. *Sent.,* Dec. 2, p. 8; Dec. 8, p. 8; Dec. 12, 1880, p. 8; Jan. 13, 1881, p. 2; *Der Zeitgeist,* II, 3 (Feb. 3, 1881), p. 52.

23. *Der Zeitgeist,* II, 7 (March 31, 1881), p. 120. In a sermon, Rabbi Victor Caro denounced the attitude of the newspaper. *Am. Isr.,* Sept. 28, 1893, p. 2; Oct. 12, 1893, p. 3.

24. *Germania,* quoted in *Sent.,* Dec. 7, 1895, p. 5; Dec. 16, 1895, p. 3

25. *Sent.,* Dec. 7, 1895, p. 5.

26. *Sent.,* Dec. 8, 1895, p. 4.

27. *Sent.,* Dec. 17, 1895, p. 4.

28. *Am. Isr.,* Sept. 27, 1894, p. 2.
29. *Sent.,* Nov. 23, 1885, p. 3.
30. *Sent.,* Jan. 31, 1892, p. 13.
31. *Sent.,* April 8, p. 3, and April 11, 1893, p. 1.
32. *Sent.,* April 15, p. 3, and April 16, 1893, p. 3.
33. *Sent.,* Oct. 21, 1874, p. 1.
34. *Sent.,* March 14, 1871, p. 4.
35. In response to a call issued by the Liberal Missouri Convention, held at Jefferson City, Mo., on January 24, 1872, for a convention to be held at Cincinnati the following May, a meeting of "liberal citizens, without distinction of party or nationality," took place at the West Side Turner Hall on March 19, 1872. C. J. Palme, editor of the *Daily Herold,* who presided, urged complete reform in public service. It was resolved that the meeting "organize itself into the Liberal Reform Union Club, for the purpose of working in the interests of the reform movement, and having our city and state represented in the Cincinnati Convention." Resolutions adopted were based on a printed circular drawn up by Carl Schurz. The group resolved "That Republicanism makes it our imperative duty to expose corruption wherever it is found, . . . and work for the reforms necessary to public welfare. . . ." *Sent.,* March 25, 1872, p. 4.
36. *Am. Isr.,* Sept. 18, 1874, p. 2.
37. *Sent.,* Nov. 11, 1872, p. 4, and Aug. 31, 1874, p. 8.
38. *Sent.,* Sept. 11, p. 4, Sept. 15, p. 5, and Sept. 18, 1874, p. 8.
39. *Sent.,* Sept. 21, p. 8, and Sept. 24, 1874, p. 4.
40. *The Menasha Press,* July 16, 1874, quoted by *Am. Isr.,* Sept. 18, 1874, p. 2.
41. *Sent.*
42. *Sent.,* Sept. 22, p. 8, and Sept. 24, 1874, p. 1.
43. *Sent.,* Sept. 25, p. 1, Sept. 26, pp. 1, 4, and Sept. 28, 1874, p. 4.
44. Quoted by *Sent.,* Sept. 29, p. 1, and Oct. 7, 1874, p. 4.
45. *The Seebote,* Oct. 8, 1874, quoted by *Sent.,* Oct. 9, 1874, p. 1.
46. Quoted by the *Sent.,* Oct. 9, 1874, p. 1.
47. *Sent.,* Sept. 25, p. 1, and Oct. 7, 1874, p. 4.
48. *Sent.,* Sept. 24, 1874, p. 4.
49. *Sent.,* Sept. 30, p. 4, and Oct. 5, 1874, p. 4.
50. *Sent.,* Oct. 2, p. 8, Oct. 9, p. 1, Oct. 10, pp. 1, 8, and Oct. 13, 1874, p. 1.
51. Quoted by *Sent.,* Oct. 12, 1874, p. 1.
52. Quoted by *Sent.,* Oct. 12, 1874, p. 1.
53. Quoted by *Sent.,* Oct. 12, 1874, pp. 1 and 3.
54. *Sent.,* Oct. 14, p. 1, Oct. 15, p. 1, and Oct. 19, 1874, p. 1.
55. Rindskopf's eligibility especially interested the foreign elements of the city. *Sent.,* Oct. 19, 1874, pp. 4 and 8.
56. *Sent.,* Oct. 19, 1874, p. 4.
57. *Sent.,* Oct. 20, 1874, p. 3. The investigating committee, which included Judge L. S. Dixon, H. L. Palmer, Geo. B. Goodwyn, and John I. Thompson, found that Loebl (Leopold) Rindskopf, the father, a native of Austria, migrated to this country and settled in the county of Shenandoah, Va., in 1852, bringing with him a wife and several minor children, including Samuel Rindskopf, then a boy of about 11. Leopold Rindskopf remained in

Virginia with his family until 1854. On February 7, 1853, he declared his intention of becoming a citizen.

In 1854, the family removed to Milwaukee, where Leopold resided until his death in 1870. After two years in Milwaukee, he voted. While naturalization papers had not been produced, proof of their existence and subsequent loss existed. It was established that Leopold Rindskopf appeared in Municipal Court, Milwaukee, on business connected with his full naturalization on or about November 5, 1860. Nathan Pereles and Judge Erastus Foote testified to the existence of such papers. Sam Rindskopf, then under 21, became a citizen upon the naturalization of his father in 1860.

58. *Sent.*, Oct. 21, pp. 1 and 4, Oct. 22, pp. 4 and 8, and Oct. 24, 1874, p. 4.

59. Rindskopf was placed in the custody of the Deputy-Marshal, occupying a room at the Park Hotel. *Sent.*, Dec. 11, p. 4, Dec. 19, p. 1, and Dec. 30, 1874, p. 1.

60. *Sent.*, Apr. 5, 1875, p. 8.

61. Louis Rindskopf, brother of Samuel Rindskopf, represented the Fourth Ward; he served on important Council committees. *Sent.*, May 12, 1871, p. 4; Mar. 29, p. 4, and Apr. 3, 1872, p. 4; Mar. 26, 1898, p. 3; *Directories*, 1870-71, p. 341, and 1872-73, p. 341.

62. From 1858 to 1873, the Common Council was composed of two bodies, the Board of Councilors and the Board of Aldermen. In the latter year, the two groups were again merged. In the election of April, 1872, H. M. Benjamin was unopposed. He served on the Harbor, Flats, and Sewer committees. *Sent.*, Apr. 3, 1872, p. 4, and June 21, 1873, p. 8; *Directories*, 1872-73, p. 341; 1873-74, p. 386.

63. *Sent.*, Mar. 4, p. 8, and Mar. 23, 1874, p. 8; Apr. 22, 1874, p. 4. Commenting on the selection of Benjamin, the editor of the *Israelite* sarcastically wrote: "H. M. Benjamin, Esq., may be the next president of the United States, for he has been elected (29 out of 30 votes) president of the City Council of Milwaukee, as grave a body as there is one in this country. That Mr. Benjamin is an Israelite, you know, but there is something about him besides all that: he is an honest man. Therefore we have some grave doubts of his nomination for the presidency of the United States, especially since the defeat of Horace Greeley." *Am. Isr.*, May, 1, 1874, p. 6. Isaac M. Wise was a life-long Democrat.

64. During the absence of Mayor Ludington, Benjamin was Acting Mayor. *Sent.*, May 18, p. 8, and Dec. 28, 1874, p. 8; Oct. 11, 1875, p. 8.

65. *Sent.*, Dec. 30, p. 4, and Dec. 29, 1875, p. 4; Jan. 3, p. 4, and Jan. 21, 1876, p. 8; *Directory*, 1875-76, p. 25; *Am. Isr.*, Nov. 25, 1897.

66. *Sent.*, March 15, 1876, p. 8.

67. Benjamin delivered his "valedictory" before the Common Council, giving up his position as Acting Mayor on April 18, 1876. *Sent.*, March 28, p. 2, April 17, p. 4, and April 19, 1876, pp. 2, 8; *J. Mess.*, April 28, 1876, p. 2; *Directory*, 1876-77, p. 27.

68. *Sent.*, April 5, p. 8, April 18, p. 2, and July 3, 1877, p. 3; *Directory*, 1877-78, p. 27.

69. At a fair given for the benefit of the Little Sisters of the Poor, Benjamin was voted "the most popular candidate for the office of mayor." *Sent.*, Feb. 27, 1878, p. 8.

70. *Sent.,* March 25, 1878, p. 8.

71. A resolution of tribute to Benjamin was adopted by the Common Council, and was lithographed and hung in the Council chambers. *Sent.,* March 26, p. 2, and June 17, 1878, p. 3.

72. *Sent.,* Oct. 31, p. 8, Nov. 2, 1874, p. 4; March 31, p. 8, April 7, 1875, p. 1; March 9, p. 8, March 28, 1876, p. 2; *Directories,* 1875-76, p. 25; 1876-77, p. 27.

73. *Sent.,* March 29, p. 8, March 7, p. 5, April 16, 1880, p. 5; Jan. 25, p. 3, March 17, 1881, p. 7; *Directory,* 1880, pp. 23, 24. It was estimated then that at least 3,000 children were employed in the factories of the city "that ought to be at school." *Sent.,* Nov. 9, 1880, p. 2. A complimentary resolution by the Council, upon the resignation of Leidersdorf, was opposed by two aldermen, one of whom accused Leidersdorf of having referred to his colleagues as "black sheep." *Sent.,* March 25, 1881, p. 3.

74. *Sent.,* March 26, p. 3, and April 3, 1889, p. 1; *Directory,* 1888, p. 25; 1889, p. 19; 1890, p. 15. In 1894, he was again nominated for alderman from the same ward. *Sent.,* March 20, 1894, p. 1.

75. Despite confirmation by the Council, Bonns resigned shortly after his appointment. *Sent.,* Jan. 3, p. 8, Jan. 4, p. 2, Jan. 6, p. 2, Jan. 13, 1881, p. 2; *Der Zeitgeist,* vol. II, no. 1 (Jan. 6, 1881), p. 20.

76. *Sent.,* Sept. 29, p. 8, Sept. 30, p. 8, Oct. 6, 1874, p. 8; May 8, p. 8, May 28, p. 8, June 4, p. 8, June 27, p. 8, and Aug. 8, 1877, p. 8.

77. *Sent.,* Mar. 18, 1897, p. 3.

78. *Sent.,* Apr. 2, 1873, p. 8; *Directory,* 1873-74, p. 386; Andreas, p. 1226.

79. *Sent.,* Oct. 28, p. 5, and Nov. 4, 1880, p. 4; Jan. 26, 1895, p. 3.

80. *Sent.,* Oct. 21, 1880, p. 8, and Sept. 21, 1888, p. 1.

81. *Sent.,* Mar. 24, 1882, p. 8, and July 21, 1884, p. 1.

82. *Sent.,* May 2, 1880, p. 4.

83. *Sent.,* May 2, 1888, p. 3.

84. On October 12, 1888, it was reported that "since the beginning of this campaign, A. W. Rich has sold 23,000 Republican buttons and 3,700 Cleveland buttons." *Sent.,* Dec. 11, 1887, p. 3; Jan. 4, p. 3, Feb. 12, p. 3, Oct. 12, p. 1, and Dec. 16, 1888, p. 3.

85. *Sent.,* March 14, 1897, p. 3.

86. *Sent.,* Oct. 7, p. 5, and Nov. 2, 1880, p. 8; Sept. 24, p. 2, Oct. 27, p. 1, and Nov. 15, 1884, p. 8.

87. *Sent.,* Aug. 3, 1884, p. 3.

88. *Sent.,* April 15, p. 1, and Dec. 12, 1899, p. 3.

89. *Sent.,* July 8, 1872, p. 4.

90. Watrous, I, p. 535; *Am. Isr.,* Nov. 2, 1893, p. 2; Aug. 2, 1894, p. 2.

91. Gottlieb Engel, Office Clerk, County Court in Probate, 1875-76; Moritz Becker, Deputy Sheriff of Municipal Court, 1875-77; *Sent.,* May 25, 1876, p. 8; Mar. 12, 1877, p. 8; Feb. 20, 1879, p. 8; Jan. 4, p. 2, Dec. 25, 1881, p. 5; *Directories,* 1875-76, pp. 26, 30; 1876-77, p. 28; 1879, p. 24; 1880, p. 24; 1881, p. 26. A. L. Baer was born in France in 1846, and came to Wisconsin in 1852. He eventually engaged in journalism, serving for seven years as editor of the *West Bend Democrat.* Elected Circuit Clerk of Washington County, he held that office for two years. Also engaged in banking business,

he was a member of the firm Hirsch and Baer for six years. He resigned his position on January 1, 1882. Andreas, p. 660.

92. *Sent.*, May 7, p. 4, and May 8, 1895, p. 1; Apr. 21, 1897, p. 3; *Directories*, 1879, p. 27; 1881, p. 28; *Annual Reports of the School Board of the City of Milwaukee*, 1879, p. 7; 1880, p. 7; 1888; 1892; 1893; 1894, pp. 7, 8; 1895; 1896, pp. 7, 8; 1897, pp. 7, 8. Jacob Black, whose term was to expire in 1899, resigned on February 8, 1898. *Ibid.*, 1898, p. 7.

93. *Annual Reports of the School Board of the City of Milwaukee*, 1893; 1894, pp. 7, 8; 1895. Commenting on retirement provisions for teachers, Pereles said that "grounds exist for the pensioning of teachers . . . to enable teachers who have been in the service 25 years to retire on half pay. . . ." *Idem*, 1895, President's Annual Address, p. 36 J. M. Pereles' retirement from the School Board also necessitated his retirement from the Public Museum Board as ex-officio member. *Idem*, 1894, p. 33; *Sent.*, May 2, 1894, p. 3; Apr. 3, p. 3, Apr. 12, p. 3, Apr. 17, p. 3, May 7, p. 4, May 8, p. 1, May 9, p. 5, and Nov. 3, 1895, p. 3; May 12, 1899, p. 2.

94. *Sent.*, May 11, 1898, p. 4; May 11, 1898, p. 4; May 10, p. 3, May 12, 1899, p. 2; May 15, 1900, p. 5.

95. "Twenty-eight rules with reference to the practice in the County Court were formulated; a calendar of causes was made up for each month, and a daily calendar for each succeeding day was drawn up for the convenience and information of the attorneys. Telephone service was introduced, and the arrangement of the rooms altered to give the public access to the records." *Sent.*, May 7, p. 3, May 12, 1899, p. 2; June 3, 1900, p. 4.

96. *Sent.*, Dec. 24, 1889, p. 4, and July 28, 1891, p. 3.

97. Moritz Becker married Miss Minnie Gutman, a native of Württemburg, in Milwaukee, in 1863. *The Legislative Manual of the State of Wisconsin*, A. J. Turner, complr. (Madison, 1873), p. 449; Andreas, p. 1474. B. S. Weil returned to politics as an Assemblyman in 1871 and 1872, but was defeated for State Senator in 1874. Aged 77 and "very infirm," he again was Assemblyman in 1880.

98. *Am. Isr.*, Nov. 17, 1871, p. 7. The election returns gave 1,006 votes to Becker, while 518 were won by his Republican opponent. *The Legislative Manual of the State of Wisconsin, 1873*, p. 449; *Sent.*, Oct. 27, 1871, p. 4. For legislation introduced by Becker during his first term in office, see: *Sent.*, Jan. 25, p. 4, Feb. 15, p. 4, and Feb. 20, 1872, p. 4.

99. *Sent.*, Oct. 24, p. 4, and Nov. 12, 1872, p. 4.

100. Friend was chosen corresponding secretary of the Republican "Committee of 100" in August, 1884. *Ibid.*, Oct. 26, pp. 2, 4, Nov. 8, p. 4, and Nov. 9, 1882, p. 2; Aug. 3, p. 3, Oct. 24, p. 4, Oct. 27, p. 1, Nov. 3, p. 4, Nov. 6, p. 5, and Nov. 15, 1884, p. 8; *Der Zeitgeist*, vol. III, no. 23 (Nov. 9, 1882), p. 352.

101. *Sent.*, March 11, 1885, pp. 1, 4; Gregory, *op. cit.*, vol. IV, p. 684.

102. *Sent.*, Nov. 4, 1884, p. 4.

103. *Am. Isr.*, Dec. 5, 1889, p. 1.

104. *Sent.*, Nov. 29, 1897, p. 8.

105. Still, *op. cit.*, p. 299.

106. *Sent.*, Jan. 22, p. 9, Feb. 8, p. 1, and March 10, 1893, p. 1.

107. *Sent.*, May 11, 1884, p. 3.

108. *Sent.*, Oct. 16, 1895.

109. *Sent.*, Oct. 8, 1885, p. 3, and Oct. 17, 1889, p. 3. Mrs. J. M. Pereles served as secretary for almost two decades. *Sent.*, May 5, 1896, p. 2.

110. *Am. Isr.*, March 8, 1894, p. 2.

111. *Sent.*, April 16, 1883, p. 5.

112. *Sent.*, Aug. 5, 1886, p. 3.

113. *Sent.*, July 31, 1885, p. 3; Dec. 4, 1889, p. 3.

114. *Sent.*, June 29, 1878, p. 8; Jan. 14, 1879, p. 2; Feb. 15, p. 5, and Nov. 4, 1881, p. 8; *Directory*, 1887, p. 51; Watrous, I, pp. 418-419.

115. In 1893, Hecht was instrumental in organizing a branch of the association at Ft. Atkinson, Wisconsin. *Sent.*, Jan. 1, p. 2, and Nov. 26, 1884, p. 4; Dec. 1, 1886, p. 3; Feb. 29, p. 3, and Nov. 28, 1888, p. 3; Nov. 27, 1889, p. 3; Oct. 11, 1893, p. 3; Nov. 30, p. 3, and Dec. 1, 1897, p. 3; *Am. Isr.*, Nov. 16, 1893, p. 2.

116. The association graduated five youngsters in June, 1896, at Ethics Hall. Rabbi S. Hecht delivered the address and presented the diplomas. *Am. Isr.*, Mar. 8, 1894, p. 3; Sept. 13, 1894, p. 2; June 27, 1895, p. 2; July 4, 1895, p. 3; *Am. Hebr.*, July 10, 1896, p. 258.

117. *Sent.*, Aug. 2, 1871, p. 4. Signers included Isaac, Elias, and Henry Friend, David Adler, H. Mahler, Aaron F. Leopold, and J. P. Frisch.

118. *Sent.*, Oct. 16, 1874, p. 8; Sept. 27, 1886, p. 3; May 27, 1900, p. 3; *Directories*, 1884, p. 53; 1885, p. 53; 1886, p. 53.

119. *Sent.*, May 13, 1893, p. 2.

120. *Sent.*, Oct. 28, 1887, p. 4; May 5, 1896, p. 4; Watrous, I, p. 401.

121. *Sent.*, Sept. 27, p. 8, Sept. 28, 1875, p. 8; June 15, 1876, p. 5; July 22, 1878, p. 8; May 5, 1896, p. 4; Watrous, I, p. 423.

122. *Sent.*, Nov. 22, 1896, p. 9; *Am. Isr.*, Sept. 30, 1897, p. 3. J. M. Pereles took a special interest in the pupils of the Seventh District school. In memory of his sister Mrs. Nathan Markwell, who was a graduate of that school, he arranged at his expense in October, 1893, to have all pupils of the fifth to eight grades of the school who had not yet visited the Chicago Exposition (about 35 youngsters) travel there to see it. *Sent.*, Oct. 28, 1893, p. 3.

123. *Sent.*, June 3, 1900, p. 8.

124. *Sent.*, July 14, 1882, p. 7; Feb. 12, p. 6, and April 22, 1888, p. 3; May 6, 1890, p. 3; *Directory*, 1883, p. 49.

125. *Sent.*, Oct. 16, 1895.

126. Edward Katz was born at Nauvee, Illinois, and when two years old moved with his family to Eagle, Wisconsin, taking up residence in Milwaukee in 1867. *Sent.*, May 13, p. 4, and June 15, 1872, p. 4; June 23, 1875, p. 8; July 29, p. 8, Aug. 24, 1876, p. 4; April 25, 1879, p. 8; Letter from National Archives and Records Service, General Services Administration, dated April 4, 1958.

127. *Sent.*, June 21, 1898, p. 5; Sept. 11, 1898, p. 8; *Wchblt.*, June 23, 1916, p. 4; Watrous, I, pp. 604-605; Brigadier General Ralph M. Immell, publ., *Roster of Wisconsin Troops in the Spanish American War* (Madison, 1899), pp. xi, xii, xiii, xxviii, xxx, xxxii, and xxxiii.

The Jewish population of the country in 1899 was estimated at 1,043,800. There were 32 Jewish officers in the Regular Army and Volunteers; 26 Jewish officers in the Navy and Marine Corps; and 172 non-commissioned

Jewish officers and privates, regular army and volunteers. Letter from National Jewish Welfare Board, dated Dec. 23, 1957. Cf. news dispatch dated September 13, 1898 concerning issuance of orders by Adjt. Gen. Corbin, in response to request of Union of Orthodox Jewish Congregations, "that 4,000 Jewish volunteers who had either joined volunteer regiments, or had seen fighting at the front during the late Spanish-American war should receive furloughs to enable them to participate in the celebration of the approaching Jewish holidays. . . ." *Sent.,* Sept. 14, 1898, p. 2.

128. *Sent.,* Apr. 1, p. 3, and Apr. 4, 1887, p. 3; Jan. 10, 1888, p. 3.

129. *Sent.,* Dec. 2, 1884, p. 3, and Sept. 1, 1898, p. 3.

130. *Sent.,* Dec. 22, 1892, p. 3; Mar. 27, 1894, p. 3; Mar. 2, 1895, p. 3, and Dec. 8, 1897, p. 2; Frederic Heath, *A Brief History of Socialism in America* (Terra Haute, Ind., 1900), p. 107, cited by Still, p, 303 ff; Frederick I. Olson, *The Milwaukee Socialist Party, 1897-1941* (Harvard University thesis 1952), ch. II.

131. *Sent.,* Mar. 31, 1894, p. 3.

132. *Am. Isr.,* Oct. 15, 1896, p. 7.

133. *Am. Isr.,* Oct. 8, 1896, p. 2; *Sent.,* Oct. 4, 1896, p. 3.

134. *Sent.,* Nov. 1, 1896, p. 3.

135. *Am. Isr.,* Nov. 12, 1896, p. 3.

136. *Sent.,* Oct. 27, 1898, p. 6.

137. *Wchblt.,* Oct. 20, 1916, p. 1.

138. *Wchblt.,* Oct. 20, 1916, p. 1.

139. *Wchblt.,* April 5, 1918, p. 1.

140. *Wchblt.,* Oct. 30, 1914, p. 4.

141. *Wchblt.,* April 10, 1914, p. 1.

142. *Wchblt.,* March 27, 1914, p. 1.

143. *Wchblt.,* Nov. 10, 1916, p. 1. Schiewitz served from 1917 to 1919, and Gettelman was State Senator from 1923.

144. *Wchblt.,* Nov. 10, 1916, p. 1. Full listings of Jews in public office may be derived from the following official annuals: *Manual of the Common Council and of the Municipal Government of the City of Milwaukee,* 1900-1920; *Municipal Government and Activities of the City of Milwaukee, Report of the Common Council,* 1921-1925; *Manuals of the County Government of the Board of Supervisors,* Milwaukee County, 1911-1925.

V. IMMIGRANT TRADES AND STREETS

1. S. Joseph, *History of the Baron de Hirsch Fund* (N. Y., 1935), Tables VIII, XXVII, XXIX, pp. 162, 172, 173.

2. Mark Wischnitzer, *To Dwell in Safety,* (Philadelphia, 1949), pp. 83-85; Joseph, *op. cit.,* Table XVIII, p. 167.

3. *Jewish Encyclopedia,* s.v. "United States of America" (by Joseph Jacobs); *AJYB,* 1918-1919, pp. 50, 73.

4. Jewish Colonization Association, *Amerikanishe Shtedt,* (Petrograd, 1911). "A collection of articles on several cities in the United States where Jewish immigrants may well establish themselves" *(aynordnen).* The list of cities is: Baltimore, Pittsburgh, Cincinnati, Cleveland, Detroit, Grand Rapids, Milwaukee, St. Paul, Davenport, St. Joseph, Omaha, Kansas City.

5. *Ibid.*, p. 27; S. Joseph, *op. cit.*, Tables VI and VII, pp. 93-94. Cf., however, the "nationalities of applicants" to the Hebrew Relief Association, which were collected in 1908, 1910, 1914, and 1915: of 1054 applicants in four years, 67% were "Russian," 8% "Galician" and "Austrian," 6% "Hungarian," 6% "Roumanian," 6% "German," and the remainder scattered. Federated Jewish Charities, *Sixth, Eighth, Twelfth, Thirteenth, Annual Report* (1908, 1910, 1914, 1915).

6. This may be seen from its records, now in the authors' possession.

6a. President's Report, November 4, 1906, in Federated Jewish Charities, *Fourth Annual Report* (1906).

7. U. S. Immigration Commission, *Reports.* vol., 26, (Immigrants in Cities, I) (Washington, 1911) Table 23, p. 701.

8. Commissioner General of Immigration, *Annual Reports.* The estimate of 60% is based on the fact that the population estimates of 1905, 1912, 1917, and 1922 show that this proportion of Wisconsin Jewry resided in Milwaukee.

9. S. Joseph, *op. cit.*

10. On the Industrial Removal Office, see S. Joseph, *op. cit.*, pp. 184-205.

11. *Am. Isr.*, October 8, 1903.

12. *Ibid.*, November 24, 1904. In 1904, the Office sent from New York forty-one families, 228 cases, 347 individuals. The relations between the three categories are hazy. For an account of a Jewish agricultural colony founded in Arpin, Wis., at this time by A. W. Rich and the I.R.O., see a forthcoming article in the *American Jewish Historical Quarterly* (PAJHS), LIII, by the present authors.

13. Report for 1904 of the Hebrew Relief Association in *The Jewish Conservator*, II, 19, Nov. 4, 1904.

14. Report of President of Hebrew Relief Association, October 29, 1905, in Federated Jewish Charities, *Third Annual Report* (1905). However, the I. R. O. continued to aid persons sent by the New York office at the request of Milwaukeeans. *Idem.*, 1907, n.p.

15. I.R.O., *Annual Reports.* Figures for Milwaukee are not available yearly. The sum of 2,300 is reached by assuming a constant ratio between I.R.O. clients sent to Wisconsin and those sent to Milwaukee. In other words, 62½% of those despatched to Wisconsin went to Milwaukee in the nine years for which we have figures. It is assumed that the same 62½% holds for the other eight years.

16. *Distribution*, III, 9 (April, 1917), p. 6.

17. G. Glickman, Milwaukee to D. M. Bressler, N. Y., April 24, 1912; I.R.O. Papers, Baron de Hirsch Fund archive, Invoice 100.

18. G. Glickman, Milwaukee to D. M. Bressler, N. Y., April 23, 1912, *loc. cit.*

19. G. Glickman, Milwaukee to Philip L. Seman, N. Y., June 22, 1912, *loc. cit.*

20. *Yiddisher Record* (Chicago), June 14, 1913.

21. Advt. in *Wchblt.*, Feb. 19, 1915, p. 4; Dec. 3, 1915, p. 1.

22. Report of Head Resident of the Abraham Lincoln House, in Federated Jewish Charities, *Twentieth Annual Report* (1921); cf. *Idem.*, 1920.

23. In general, see Z. Szajkowski, "The Attitude of American Jews to East European Jewish Immigration (1881-1893)," *PAJHS*, XL, 3 (March, 1951), pp. 221-280; John Higham, *Strangers in the Land: Patterns of American Nativism 1860-1925* (New Brunswick, N. J.), 1955, pp. 123-30; *Louis Marshall, Champion of Liberty: Selected Papers and Addresses*, ed. Charles Reznikoff, 2 vols. (Philadelphia, 1957) I, pp. 109-243.

24. S. Joseph, *op. cit.*, Tables 52, 53, 54, pp. 187-88. The proportion of "merchants and dealers" is unduly low. Doubtless many of these preferred to claim a trade.

25. *Wchblt.* (*Jewish Daily Press*), April 6, 1919, p. 1.

26. E. Tcherikower, ed., *History of the Jewish Labor Movement in the United States* (Yiddish), 2 vols. (N. Y., 1943) I, pp. 235-253, 338-355.

27. Chicago *Yiddisher Record*, June 14, 28, 1913; *Am. Isr.*, August 27, 1908; Federated Jewish Charities, *Fourteenth Annual Report* (1916), n.p.

28. *Wchblt.*, June 12, 1914. On the attempted withdrawal of a junk dealer's license, see *idem*. December 18, 1914 and January 29, 1915.

29. *Wchblt.*, March 26, 1915, April 9, 30, 1915; Federated Jewish Charities, *loc. cit.*

30. We know of the Milwaukee Jewish Dealers Association (*Wchblt.*, July 10, 1914), the Wholesale Junk Dealers Association of Milwaukee (with about forty members and a capital of $2,000). *Idem*, July 2, 1915. The pickers had the Progressive Rag Peddler Union.

31. *Forverts*, undated clipping, September, 1918.

32. *Yiddisher Arbeter Velt* (Chicago) October 30, 1908.

33. *Forverts*, undated clipping, September, 1918.

33a. Report of Superintendent of Hebrew Relief Association, in Federated Jewish Charities, *Thirteenth Annual Report* (1915), n.p.

34. Federated Jewish Charities of Milwaukee, *Annual Report*, 1920-1921, p. 30.

35. *Forverts*, May 11, 17, 1919; *Chicago Yiddisher Record*, August 2, 1913.

36. *Am. Isr.*, November 18, 1915; *Chicago Yiddisher Record*, June 7, 1913; also retail stores' advertising in Jewish press, *passim*.

37. *Wchblt.*, March 20, 1914, p. 1.

38. *Wchblt.*, March 12, 1915, p. 3; cf. *idem*, Mar. 20, 1914, p. 1.

39. *Wchblt.*, December 11, 1914, p. 4; August 13, 1915, p. 1.

40. *Wchblt.*, August 7, 1914, p. 1.

40a. "Some twenty Jewish lawyers, doctors, and professional people have organized themselves in a Jewish collegiate club." All were from the immigrant sphere. *Wchblt.*, Oct. 29, 1915, p. 1.

41. *Directory, 1895*, p. 1087 lists twelve clothing manufacturers by name, of whom all were Jews.

42. 20.3% in a sample taken of Bohemian immigrants were tailors. In the same sample only 7.2% of immigrant Jews were thus occupied in Milwaukee, to 37.9% of the New York City sample. U. S. Immigration Commission, *Reports*, vol. 27 (Immigrants in Cities, II), Washington, 1911, Table 300, pp. 309-314. On the other hand, peddlers were much fewer in New York, reaching only 7.9% of the sample just quoted.

43. *Wchblt.*, July 10, 1914; *Am. Isr.*, November 18, 1915.

44. *Wchblt.*, March 3, 1916.

45. *Wchblt.*, February 19, 1916. This group, with a membership of sixty, held its meetings in a synagogue.

46. *Wchblt.*, June 5, 1914.

47. *Wchblt.*, July 10, 1914.

48. *Am. Isr.*, November 18, 1915; *Wchblt.*, September 18, 1914; October 2, 1914; October 15, 1915. Sunday closing was an issue not made easier by some Jewish stores' habit of being open seven days.

49. *Wchblt.*, March 26, April 9 and 30, 1915.

50. U. S. Immigration Commission, *Reports*, vol. 27, Washington, 1911 (Immigrants in Cities, II), Table 245, pp. 244-246. *Forverts*, undated clipping, September, 1918.

51. Jewish Colonization Association, *Amerikanishe Shtedt*, p. 27.

52. *Wchblt.*, May 28, 1915, p. 1; February 25, 1916, p. 1.

53. *Ibid.*, April 26, 1915, p. 1.

54. *Ibid.*, January 22, 1915, p. 1.

55. *Ibid.*, March 20, 1914, p. 1.

56. *Ibid.*, December 4, 1914.

57. *Ibid.*, June 8, 1915; August 20, 1915, p. 1. There was also a Jewish share corporation, the Modern Mutual Association, with one hundred forty members and $13,500 capital.

58. *Forverts*, March 14, 1918.

59. *Am. Isr.*, May 21, 1914; *Wchblt.*, March 27, May 22, May 29, 1914.

60. *Forverts*, May 17, 1919.

61. *Wchblt.*, June 5, 1914; March 26, 1915.

62. *Forverts*, April 5, 1919; *ca.* May 4, 1919; May 10, 17, 1919.

63. Report of Head Resident, Abraham Lincoln House, in Federated Jewish Charities, *Twentieth Annual Report* (1921).

64. U. S. Immigration Commission, *Reports*, vol. 26, Table 64, p. 738; cf. *ibid.*, Table 62, p. 224.

65. *Ibid.*, Table 66, p. 740..

66. *Forverts*, March 31, 1919.

67. Report of the Mayor's Housing Commission, 1933, p. 13.

68. *Ibid.*, p. 316.

69. Bureau of Labor and Industrial Statistics, *Twelfth Annual Report*, 1905-1906, Part IV, *The Housing Question in Wisconsin*, pp. 289, 294.

70. *Idem.*, p. 294.

71. *Idem.*, p. 295.

72. *Idem.*, p. 327.

73. Report of the Mayor's Housing Commission, 1933, pp. 12, 14. These figures hold good for earlier years.

74. Report of the President of the Hebrew Relief Association, October 28, 1906, in Federated Jewish Charities, *Fourth Annual Report* (1906); Report of Hebrew Relief Association in *Am. Isr.*, November 13, 1913, p. 6.

75. *Idisher Kemfer*, II 13, June 28, 1907, p. 11.

76. U. S. Immigration Commission, *Reports*, vol. 42, Table 50, p. 725; Table 45, p. 720; Table 47, p. 722.

77. *Ibid.*, Table 51, p. 726.

78. Board of Public Land Commissioners, "Population Changes by Census Tracts . . . 1920-1940," p. 20.

79. U.S. Immigration Commission, *Reports.* Volumes 26 and 27 are entitled "Immigrants in Cities." Volume 26, pp. 680-765, is devoted to Milwaukee. Two categories are devoted to Jews, "Hebrews, Russian" and "Hebrews, Other." Of the former, 102 households were investigated to 23 of the latter. The "Other" means ten Roumanians and ten Austrians, evidently Galicians, and two Germans. The statistics used here omit these "Hebrews, Other" because twenty-three seems an unduly small sample, and because they are longer in America (26 of 68 persons reporting were here over ten years) and therefore less an "immigrant" group than Russian Jews.

80. *Ibid.,* Table 25, p. 703.

81. *Ibid.,* Table 55, p. 729.

82. Twenty-nine of 552 were lodgers (5.3%), compared to fifteen of thirty-four who had arrived within the previous five years (44.1%). Proportions among non-Jews are very similar. *Ibid.,* Tables 40-41, p. 717.

83. *Milwaukee Journal,* December 28, 1907, p. 3; U. S. Immigration Commission, *Reports,* vol. 26, pp. 562, 558; cf. Table 50, p. 210; Table 45, p. 206.

VI. NATURALIZED JUDAISM & IMMIGRANT PIETY
(1870-1900)

1. *Still,* pp. 424-425.

2. *Ibid.,* pp. 419-420. See Colman J. Barry, *The Catholic Church and German Americans* (Milwaukee, 1953), p. 47, and Benjamin J. Blied, *Three Archbishops of Milwaukee* (Milwaukee, 1955), p. 59.

3. *Sent.,* Sept. 10, 1870, p. 1

4. *Sent.,* Sept. 16, 1872, p. 4.

5. *Sent.*

6. *Sent.,* Oct. 8, 1872, p. 4.

7. Quotations are from *Am. Isr.,* Oct. 14, 1872, p. 6. It was also described in the Sept. 21, 1872 editions of the *Sentinel,* (p. 4) and the *Ev. Wis.* (p. 4).

8. Emanu-El, *Minutes,* Nov. 7, 1869; Jan. 30, April 3, July 17, Aug. 28, Oct. 23, 1870; *Sent.,* Aug. 25, 1869, p. 1; Nov. 15, 1869, p. 1; Oct. 13, 1870. The lot was paid by $2,000 cash and the remainder in installments within five years. The interest was low at 4%.

9. Emanu-El, *Minutes,* June 11, 1871; *Sent.,* July 20, 1871, p. 4; *Am. Isr.,* Feb. 17, 1871, p. 7; *J. Mess.,* Feb. 17, 1871, pp. 5 and 12, Mar. 24, 1871, p. 5. The fair was planned for August, 1871. On October 14 of that year, the committee explained the delay arose from the Chicago fire and other disasters in the region. These misfortunes "will necessarily tax the benevolence of the people of our city and state to its utmost extent, and it seems to the committee that all other undertakings of the nature of this fair should be postponed until the terrible effect of these calamities are [sic] at least partly erased...." *Sent.,* Oct. 16, 1871, p. 4.

10. Emanu-El, *Minutes,* Jan. 14, 1872; *Sent.,* Nov. 25, p. 4; Dec. 6, p. 4; Dec. 7, p. 4; Dec. 8, p. 4; Dec. 9, p. 4; Dec. 11, p. 4; Dec. 15, p. 4; Jan. 5, 1872, p. 4; *J. Mess.,* Dec. 6, 1871, p. 6.

11. The quotations and the description of the cornerstone ceremony are

taken from *Sent.*, June 13, 1871, p. 4; June 14, p. 4; June 16, p. 4. See also *Jewish Times*, June 23, 1871, p. 259; Emanu-El, *Minutes*, June 15, 1871.

12. *Ev. Wis.*, Aug. 31, 1872, p. 4.

13. *Sent.*, July 13, 20, 29, 31, Aug. 8, 16, 1872 (all p. 4); *Am. Isr.*, Sept. 13, 1872, p. 10.

14. *Sent.*, Aug. 31, 1872, pp. 1-4; also described in *Ev. Wis.*, Aug.. 31, 1872, p. 4 (reprinted in part in *Blue Book*, p. 34). The choir was apparently the renowned Milwaukee Musical Society, conducted by Hans Balatka. *Sent.*, Aug. 23, 1872, p. 4.

15. *Sent.*, Aug. 31, 1872, p. 4; *Am. Isr.*, Sept. 13, 1872, p. 10.

16. Emanu-El, *Minutes*, Aug. 4, 1872, Dec. 21, 1872, Jan. 9, 1873, July 29, 1873. This may not include $4,500 still due in 1872 on the land purchase. See above, note 8.

17. Emanu-El, *Minutes*, Jan. 14, and Mar. 10, 1896; *Der Zeitgeist*, I, 1 (Jan 1, 1880), p. 16; *Sent.*, Nov. 11, 1881.

18. Emanu-El, *Minutes*, Dec. 12, 1892, June 3, 1893; *Sent.*, May 13, Oct. 18, 19, 21, Nov. 5, 1892 (all p. 3); Mar. 16, May 3, 6, Aug. 23, 1893 (all p. 3).

19. *Sent.*, Nov. 12, Dec. 14, 15, 16, 17, 1880 (all p. 8); Dec. 19 (p. 4), 20 (pp. 3, 8), 1880; May 13, Oct. 18 19, 21, Nov. 5, 1892 (all p. 3); Mar. 16, May 3, 6, Aug. 23, 1893 (all p. 3); *Der Zeitgeist*, I, 20 (Sept. 30, 1880), p. 325; 25 (Dec. 9, 1880), p. 404; 26 (Dec. 23, 1880), p. 420; II, 1 (Jan. 6, 1881), p. 20; *Am. Isr.*, Jan. 1, 1882, p. 215; Mar. 30, 1888, p. 7; June 2, 1892, p. 3; Emanu-El *Minutes*, Jan. 2, 1881.

20. B'ne Jeshurun, *Minutes*, June 10, Sept. 16, 1883; March 8, June 8, 21, July 5, 1885. The old synagogue was used as a factory. *Sent.*, Dec. 10, 1899, p. 3.

21. *Sent.*, Sept. 28, 1886, p. 3; *Am. Isr.*, Oct. 8, 1886, p. 6.

22. *Sent.*, Jan. 18, 1887, p. 3.

23. *Sent.*, June 15, 1887, p. 3; *J. Mess.*, July 8, 1887, p. 2; *Am. Isr.*, July 1, 1887, p. 8.

24. *Sent.*, May 13, 1888, p. 11.

25. *Am. Isr.*, Sept. 3, 1875, p. 5; B'ne Jeshurun, *Minutes*, Sept. 3, 1882, Sept. 1, 1889, Sept. 4, 1892, Sept. 8, 1895; *Sent.*, Aug. 18, 1895, p. 9; *Am. Isr.*, Sept. 17, 1896, p. 2; Sept. 16, 1897, p. 2; *AJYB*, 1899-1900, p. 270; 1900-1901, p. 488.

26. *Sent.*, Feb. 17, 1873, p. 4; Sept. 29, 1875, p. 8; Sept. 4, 1876, p. 5; Sept. 3, 1877, p. 2; Feb. 6, 1888, p. 3; May 6, 1888, p. 3; Aug. 18, 1895, p. 9; Nov. 5, 1899, p. 9; Emanu-El *Minutes*, Aug. 17, 1874, Feb. 26, 1879, April 12, 1888, March 11, 1890, Sept. 20, 1900; *Am. Isr.*, Sept. 24, 1875, p. 6; May 9, 1895, p. 2; May 6, 1897, p. 2; *AJYB*, 1899-1900, p. 270.

27. B'ne Jeshurun, *Minutes*, Aug. 10, 1879, Sept. 5, 1880, June 5 and Sept. 11, 1887.

28. Emanu-El, *Minutes*. Oct. 19, 1869, Aug. 4 and Dec. 21, 1872; Jan 9 and July 29, 1873; Jan. 11, 1874, June 24, 1877, May 23, 1880, July 2, 1882, July 11, 1884, Dec. 18, 1887; *Am. Isr.*, May 9, 1895, p. 2; May 6, 1897, p. 2.

29. Emanu-El's budget rose from about $4,000 when founded to $6,500-$7,000 in 1899; in that year, B'ne Jeshurun spent about $6,000. Emanu-El, *Minutes*, 1869-1900, *passim*; B'ne Jeshurun, *Minutes*, 1869-1900, *passim*; *Am. Isr.*, May 6, 1897, p. 2; *AJYB*, 1899-1900, p. 27; *Sent.*, May 6, 1895, p. 3.

30. Emanu-El, *Minutes*, Sept. 8, 1879, Aug. 9, 1880, Aug. 12, 1890, March 13, 1900; *Sent.*, Sept. 13, 1879, p. 3, Sept. 12, 1884, p. 3. In any case, the rabbi required a permit from the president to officiate at a wedding or funeral, and this was strictly enforced. B'ne Jeshurun, *Minutes*, Dec. 22, 1895.

31. Emanu-El, *Minutes*, July 6, 1890. See also *Sent.*, July 18 (p. 1), 19 (p. 3), 20, 1890 (p. 7); *Am. Isr.*, May 9, 1895, p. 2.

32. *Am. Isr.*, Oct. 22, 1886, p. 7.

33. *Sent.*, Aug. 17, 1872, p. 4; Oct. 13, 1884, p. 3; March 6, 1887, p. 3; Dec. 8, 1890, p. 3; Oct. 1, 1897, p. 2; Dec. 21, 1897, p. 3; *Am. Isr.*, Oct. 22, 1886, p. 7; May 6, 1887, p. 8; Sept. 30, 1887, p. 9.

34. *Sent.*, Nov. 16, 1898, p. 2.

35. Emanu-El, *Minutes*, Jan. 14, 1872; *Sent.*, Mar. 2, 1872, p. 4; Apr. 5 (p. 8), 25 (p. 8), June 10 (p. 8), July 21, 1873; Feb. 28 (p. 8) and Mar. 3, 1874, p. 8; July 24, 1877, p. 8; Mar. 5, 1895, p. 3; Feb. 6, 1875, p. 8; June 21, 1876, p. 8; Jan. 3 (p. 8) and 18, 1877, p. 8; Oct. 7, 1879, p. 8; Oct. 24 (p. 3) and 28, 1883, p. 3; April 6, 1884, p. 3; *Am. Isr.*, Mar. 5, 1886, p. 7; Mar. 19, 1886, p. 10; Mar. 26, 1886, p. 7; *Der Zeitgeist*, I, 2 (Jan. 15, 1880), p. 32; 5 (Mar. 4, 1880), p. 80; 20 (Sept. 30, 1880), p. 324; II, 22 (Oct. 27, 1881), 360; II, 26 (Dec. 22, 1881), p. 424.

36. Andreas, *op. cit.*, pp. 948-951; *Am. Isr.*, Nov. 18, 1887, p. 3; Oct. 5, 1893, p. 2; Oct. 26, 1893; Nov. 9, 1893, p. 2; Nov. 16, 1893, p. 2; Mar. 29, 1894, p. 3; *J. Mess.*, Nov. 25, 1892, p. 2; *Am. Heb.*, Aug. 30, 1895, p. 408.

37. *Sent.*, Nov. 21, 1891, p. 3; Sept. 15, 1894, p. 5; Jan. 8, 1894, p. 3; *Am. Isr.*, Feb. 11, 1897, p. 2.

38. These names come from impressions of the Temples' *Minutes*, *passim*.

39. Typical pulpit "lectures" are: "The Tendency of Our Time," "The Achievements of the Present Century and Their Bearing on Mankind." The *Sentinel* often published his sermons; Aug. 26, 1870, p. 1; Dec. 1, 1870, p. 4; Feb. 20, Mar. 6, Oct. 30, 1874 (all p. 8); Sept. 21, 1874, p. 5; Oct. 1, 1875, p. 1; April 19, 1878, p. 2; Sept. 30, 1878, p. 3; Sept. 19, 1879, p. 2.

40. *Am. Isr.*, Feb. 13, 1874, p. 2.

41. *Sent.*, Sept. 26, 1874, p. 8.

42. This diary, covering 1871 through 1874, has been kindly made available by the American Jewish Archives.

43. He was re-elected from year to year. B'ne Jeshurun, *Minutes*, Sept. 17, 1876, Aug. 13, and Sept. 2, 1877; Jan. 17 and Dec. 6, 1878; Sept. 7, 1879; *Sent.*, Sept. 4, 1877.

44. B'ne Jeshurun passed the customary resolutions of regret and good wishes. B'ne Jeshurun, *Minutes*, Jan. 18, 1880, *Sent.*, Feb. 28 (p. 8), Mar. 9, (p. 2) and 10, 1880 (p. 4); *Der Zeitgeist*, I, 2 (Jan. 15, 1880), p. 2; 3 (Feb. 5, 1880), p. 48.

45. This little book stirred some controversy. I. M. Wise, who upheld Biblical literalism, was lukewarm to the author whose "attempt . . . deserves encouragement." *Am. Isr.*, Mar. 21, 1873, p. 4. The *Jewish Times* of Philadelphia, a more conservative paper, assailed the book for leaving Biblical history "denuded of all poetic charm of that legendary halo and glory, by a rude uncouth grasp, which can have no other effect than to destroy the last vestige of respect and veneration yet remaining." It noted that Rabbi

Felsenthal had repudiated his prefatory approbation. *Jewish Times*, March 28, 1873, p. 73.

46. *Sent.*, August 9, 1875, p. 8; *Ev. Wis.*, August 8, 1875, p. 4.

47. *Sent.*, June 17, 1887, p. 5; Andreas, *op. cit.*, p. 951; *Am. Isr.*, May 14, 1880; B'ne Jeshurun, *Minutes*, Dec. 26, 1880; Sept. 11, 1881, Sept. 3, 1882, Sept. 6, 1884, Sept. 4, 1887.

48. Edna Ferber, *A Peculiar Treasure* (N. Y. 1939), p. 72. He remained there as rabbi and teacher of Hebrew and German at Lawrence College until his retirement in 1912.

49. B'ne Jeshurun, *Minutes*, Sept. 20, 1891, May 8 and 15, 1892; July 31, 1892; *Sent.*, Sept. 22, 1891, p. 3, July 26, 1892, *J. Mess.*, Sept. 9, 1892, p. 3; *AJYB*, 1903-1904, p. 57; *Am. Isr.*, Nov. 21, 1912, p. 3.

50. Emanu-El, *Minutes*, Aug. 21 and 28, 1870.

51. Emanu-El, *Minutes*, Sept. 4, 11, 25, 1870. Browne remained to conduct High Holiday services. He received an LL.B. from the University of Wisconsin in 1871; a letter from the University Recorder's office dated Aug. 18, 1955 confirms the conferral of the degree. Browne ostentatiously demanded an explanation of his discharge in *Am. Isr.*, May 5, 1871, p. 5, but he was ignored. His later vicissitudes are summarized in Morris U. Schappes, *A Documentary History of the Jews in the United States, 1654-1875*, (New York, 1950), p. 733, note 9.

52. Alma Spitz, "Biographical Sketch of Moritz Spitz," *American Jewish Archives*, VI, 1, (Jan., 1954) p. 66; *AJYB*, 1903-1904, p. 101.

53. *Sent.*, Sept. 6, 1877, p. 4. Spitz's contracts were renewed in 1872, 1874, 1875, 1877, all at $1500. Emanu-El *Minutes*, Oct. 13, 1872, Oct. 18, 1874, Oct. 17, 1875, Jan. 27, 1878.

54. Spitz also opposed the Ethical Culture Movement founded in 1877 mainly by Jews. *Sent.*, Dec. 18, 1875, p. 2; Nov. 11, 1876, p. 7; June 30 (p. 2), Oct. 20 (p. 2), Nov. 10, 1877 (p. 8); Feb. 9 (p. 2), March 30 (p. 2), April 24, 1878 (p. 8).

55. He remained in St. Louis until his death in 1920. Emanu-El, *Minutes*, Jan. 27, Oct. 20 and 27, 1878; Jan 13, 1879; *Sent.*, Jan 31 (p. 2), Oct. 15 (p. 8) and 21 (p. 8) and 29 (p. 8), 1878; Nov. 8, 1878 (p. 8); *Am. Isr.*, Jan. 17, 1879, p. 5. In later years, Spitz visited Milwaukee and lectured there. Alma Spitz, *op. cit.*; *Sent.*, May 2, 1879, p. 8; June 28 (p. 7) and July 10, 1881, p. 3.

56. *AJYB*, 1903-1904, p. 83. His acquaintanceship included his teachers Hermann Cohen, the neo-Kantian philosopher, and Heinrich Graetz, the historian, who both contributed to Moses' *Zeitgeist*. Rabbinic ordination from Felsenthal perhaps signified acceptance as a Reform rabbi in the United States.

57. *Der Zeitgeist*, I, 6 (March 18, 1880), p. 96.

58. Emanu-El *Minutes*, March 25 and April 5, 1880.

59. *Sent.*, Mar. 12, 1880, p. 8; *J. Mess.*, Mar. 26, 1880, p. 2. The idea of a Jewish "mission" to the world was developed by reform Jewry in Germany, with which Moses had deep personal and intellectual connections. The mission neant that the Jews were to diffuse prophetic ethical monotheism among the nations. Few Reformers agreed with Moses in countenancing marriages between Jews and Christians to achieve this end. Nor did Reform Judaism in America accept the Jewish legality of all marriages sanctioned

by the state, and Moses' statement reflects a rather German subjection to the state and its "moral." Moses cited Rabbi Felsenthal of Chicago in support of his position, to which, he admitted, most Reform rabbis stood opposed.

60. Emanu-El, *Minutes*, May 30, 1880. The resolution requested that it be kept private, but it was published anyhow. *Am. Isr.*, June 18, 1880, p. 2.

61. *Am. Isr.*, June 18, 1880, p. 2; *Sent.*, June 1, 1880, p. 7. The Board of Trustees resigned as a body for reasons which are not given, but likely in annoyance at the members' emphasis upon the rabbi's freedom in all religious matters except "minor matters of form and ceremony." After a two-month hiatus, practically the same men took office again. At the general election, an opposition slate to the trustees was presented by R. Reichmann, one of whose partners was the father of the Christian bride in the cause célèbre. Emanu-El, *Minutes*, July 8, Aug. 1, Aug. 9, Sept. 5, 1880.

62. *Am. Isr.*, Mar. 19, 1880, p. 4. Wise's argument, which vests in a Jewish congregation the comprehensive legal authority which he had removed from *halakhah*, is legally and historically untenable. It could be said that congregational sovereignty was pragmatically useful under isolated frontier conditions, where rough-and-ready decisions had to be made.

63. *Der Zeitgeist*, I, 7 (April 1, 1880), p. 104.

64. Jewish *Record* (Philadelphia), quoted in *Sent.*, Mar. 30, 1880, p. 8.

65. Specimen texts and summaries of Moses' sermons are in the *Sentinel*: April 9 (p. 3), and 11 (p. 8), May 9 (p. 8) and Sept. 8, 1879 (p. 8); Sept. 6 (p. 8) and 15, 1880 (p. 8); April 29 (p. 5), Oct. 21 (p. 5) and 28, 1881 p. 7); June 24, 1882, p. 2; May 14 (p. 8) and Oct. 20, 1883 (p. 4); March 2 (p. 3), July 10, (p. 3), Oct. 23, 1885 (p. 3); April 26, 1886 (p. 3).

66. *Sent.*, March 16, 1880, p. 8; Jan. 29, 1881, p. 8; Mar. 2, 1885, p. 3; *Der Zeitgeist*, II, 2 (Jan. 20, 1881), p. 36; 7 (Mar. 31, 1881), p. 120; 25 (Dec. 8, 1881), p. 402; 26 (Dec. 22, 1881) p. 424. Moses spoke at the State Unitarian Conference in 1886. *Am. Isr.*, June 4, 1886, p. 7.

67. Moses' writings in Milwaukee include: *The Pentateuch* (1881)—an edition for children which omitted embarrassing passages; *The Historical Books of the Bible* (1884); *Man and Humanity* (1886), a sermon; *Religion and Mysticism*, (1880), a lecture delivered to the Unitarian Church at Quincy, Illinois; *The Inner Light* (1883), Rosh Hashanah sermons; *Tefillat Yisrael, Orders of Prayers and Responsive Readings for Jewish Worship* (1884, 2nd ed., 1887); *A New Ritual* (1887). The last contained prayers and psalms both in English and Hebrew.

68. *Am. Isr.*, July 16, 1886, p. 3.

69. Emanu-El, *Minutes*, May 22, and June 7, 1885. The *Sentinel* recalled "the troubles which existed between them (Moses and the Board) for some time culminated (in the Mack incident) . . . this meeting was called, it was said, to settle the matter of whether Moses or his congregation should leave." *Sent.*, June 8, 1885, p. 3; cf. *Sent.*, May 31, 1885, p. 3; July 6, 1885, p. 3. Moses was then serving under a three year contract which began on April 1, 1885. Emanu-El, *Minutes*, Aug. 10, 1884.

70. *Am. Isr.*, May 27, 1887, p. 8; Emanu-El *Minutes*, May 1, July 3, 1887; *Sent.*, July 8 (p. 3) and Aug. 27 (p. 4), Aug. 28, (p. 3), and 30, 1887 (p. 4), Sept. 3, 1887, p. 2; *Am. Isr.*, Sept. 9, 1887, p. 6; Sept. 16, 1887, p. 2.

71. He served in Nashville, Chicago, and from 1900, at the Central Syna-

gogue in New York, one of the city's leading Reform congregations. *Am. Isr.*, Dec. 13, 1900, p. 3; Dec. 13, 1917, p. 3; *1869-1919; Golden Anniversary, Congregation Emanu-El*, pp. 20-21.

72. Emanu-El *Minutes*, Jan. 31, Feb. 5, Mar. 2, 1888; *Sent.*, Feb. 24, 1888, p. 3, Aug. 18, 1895, p. 9; *Ev. Wis.*, quoted in *Am. Isr.*, April 21, 1892, p. 4; *Idem*, Feb. 17, 1888, p. 8, Mar. 9, 1888, p. 3; *AJYB*, 1903-1904, p. 62.

73. His *Epitome of Post-Biblical History* (1881) for which the University of Alabama awarded him a D.D. in 1886, was expanded and republished in 1895 in two parts as *Post Biblical History of the Jews*. A third section, from 1657 to the author's day, was added in 1897. The *Am. Isr.* commended it (Aug. 29, 1895, p. 7), but the *Am. Heb.*, criticized its "heavy, dull, and cumbersome style" which was "partly excusable" because of Hecht's German birth. Hecht retorted to this criticism. *Idem*, Mar. 19, 1897, p. 537; Mar. 26, 1897, p. 564. The Jewish Sunday School Union adopted it as a text for advanced classes. Hecht's *Epitome* is derived from standard works of Jewish history, and possesses no independent value. Its highly optimistic, liberal view of the future is an interesting specimen of that outlook.

74. Hecht was a member of the local Central Committee of the Associated Charities and the Wisconsin Humane Society. He spoke at the Western Unitarian Conference, and delivered an invocation at the opening of a session of the Wisconsin Legislature.

75. Quoted in *Am. Isr.*, April 21, 1892, p. 4.

76. *Am. Isr.*, May 4, 1888, p. 2.

77. *Sent.*, Sept. 7, 1889, p. 3; cf. *J. Mess.*, Sept. 20, 1889, p. 4.

78. *Sent.*, Mar. 15, 1895, p. 3; *Am. Isr.*, Mar. 21, 1895, p. 2.

79. *Sent.*, Nov. 29, 1889, p. 5; Nov. 16, 1895, p. 3; Dec. 21, 1895, p. 3; April 8 (p. 4) and 16, 1898 (p. 3); *Am. Isr.*, Nov. 29, 1894, p. 3; Jan. 25, 1894, p. 2; *J. Mess.*, June 22, 1888, p. 3.

80. *Sent.*, Feb. 7, 1896, p. 3; *Reform Advocate*, Sept. 1, 1894, p. 26; June 25, 1898, p. 311; *Sent.*, July 8, 1895; *Am. Isr.*, July 25, 1895, p. 3. A Hebrew Lectureship and Scholarship Society supported these lectures. *Sent.*, May 10, 1899; *Reform Advocate*, April 8, 1899, p. 230; *Am. Isr.*, June 1, 1899, p. 2; *Am. Heb.*, April 7, 1899, p. 764. Hecht held various offices in Reform Jewish organizations, including that of Treasurer of the Central Conference of American Rabbis from 1892 to 1900.

81. *Sent.*, Mar. 1, 1890, p. 1.

82. *Ibid.*; for specimens, see *J. Mess.*, 1, 1889, p. 2; *Am. Heb.*, June 7, 1895, p. 122.

83. *J. Mess.*, July 20, 1894, pp. 4-5.

84. *Sent.*, Nov. 30, 1890, p. 11. He attacked Herzl's Zionist movement on the same grounds. *Am. Isr.*, Sept. 23, 1897, p. 2.

85. *Sent.*, July 8, 1899, p. 1.

86. Emanu-El, *Minutes*, Aug. 14, 1899; cf. *Sent.*, Aug. 17, 1899, p. 5.

87. *Sent.*, Oct. 28, 1899, p. 3.

88. *Sent.*, Nov. 1, 1899, p. 3; *Am. Isr.*, Nov. 9, 1899, p. 2.

89. *Sent.*, Sept. 8, 1892, p. 3; Aug. 18, 1895, p. 9; *AJYB*, 1903-1904, p. 48.

90. *Am. Isr.*, Feb.. 15, 1894, p. 3.

91. *Ibid.*, Jan. 17, 1895, p. 2; Nov. 23, 1893, p. 2.

92. *Sent.*, Oct. 27, 1894, p. 3; *Am. Isr.*, Nov. 1, 1894, p. 2.

93. *Sent.*, Nov. 26, 1899, p. 5.
94. *Sent.*, Jan. 26, 1900, p. 6.
95. *Sent.*, Oct. 11, 1897, p. 3.
96. *Ibid.*
97. *J. Mess.*, July 14, 1893, p. 2.
98. *Sent.*, Sept. 4, 1897, p. 3; Sept. 2, 1898, p. 5.
99. *Ibid.*, Sept. 8, 1877, p. 3; Conard, *op. cit.*, p. 234. The author of this article is Rabbi Hecht.
100. By 1870, the yearly cycle of Torah readings was changed to a three year cycle, shortening the length of the weekly readings. *Sent.*, Oct. 20, 1870, p. 4; April 4, 1873, p. 8; Oct. 30, 1874, p. 8; Feb. 19, 1875, p. 8; June 24, 1887, p. 3; Sept. 14, 1894, p. 3; Feb. 7, 1896, p. 3; April 19, 1898, p. 5; Sept. 2, 1898, p. 5; *Am. Heb.*, Aug. 30, 1895, p. 409.
101. B'ne Jeshurun, *Minutes*, June 2, 1889, p. 287; *Am. Heb.*, Oct. 8, 1886, p. 139; Nov. 2, 1893, p. 2.
102. *Minhag America* had been used briefly during Browne's tenure. Emanu-El, *Minutes*, May 25 and 29, Aug. 28, 1870; Sept. 26, 1884; Sept. 12, 1886, Nov. 3, 1887, Feb. 5, 1888, April 11 and May 7, 1893; Sept. 17, 1894; *Sent.*, Sept. 8, 1877, p. 3; Aug. 18, 1895, p. 9; Sept. 29, 1894, p. 3; *Am. Isr.*, July 1, 1870, p. 11; Aug. 26, 1887, p. 7; Sept. 30, 1887, p. 7; May 17, 1894, p. 3; Oct. 11, 1894, p. 7; *Reform Advocate*, Sept. 29, 1894, p. 93.
103. *Am. Heb.*, Nov. 2, 1893, p. 2; *Reform Advocate*, Sept. 29, 1894, p. 93.
104. Emanu-El, *Minutes*, May 15, 1893.
105. *Sent.*, May 9, 1872, p. 4, May 22, 1893, p. 8; B'ne Jeshurun, *Minutes*, Sept. 2, 1888, Sept. 3, 1893.
106. Emanu-El, *Minutes*, Sept. 4, 1873.
107. *Am. Isr.*, Oct. 20, 1876, p. 3.
108. The old-style Purim reading was later abolished. B'ne Jeshurun, *Minutes*, Nov. 6, 1881; *Sent.*, Sept. 19, 1879, p. 2; Oct. 9, 1894, p. 3; Mar. 8, 1895, p. 3; *Der Zeitgeist*, II, 7 (Mar. 31, 1881), p. 120.
109. Andreas, *op. cit.*, pp. 948-951; *Der Zeitgeist*, III, 20-21 (Oct. 12, 1882), p. 320; B'ne Jeshurun, *Minutes*, July 3, 1881, Nov. 6, 1881, Oct. 30, 1887; Aug. 5, 1894; Jan. 2 and Feb. 6, 1898; *Sent.*, April 26, 1880, p. 8; Oct. 8, 1878, p. 8; Sept. 14, 1882, p. 2; April 10, 1884, p. 3; Sept. 14, 1874, p. 5; Sept. 8, 1877, p. 3; Sept. 13, 1882, p. 3; Sept. 9, 1885, p. 3; Sept. 25, 1889, p. 3; Sept. 18, 1895, p. 3; Sept. 7, 1896, p. 5; Sept. 23, 1900, Sect. I, p. 12. *Kol Nidre* was chanted at sunset and Yom Kippur services, which began at 7:30 A.M. until 1882, commenced at 9 A.M. from 1894.
110. Emanu-El, *Minutes*, May 25 and 29, 1870.
111. *Idem.*, *passim.*
112. *Sent.*, June 2, 1873, p. 8. There were five children upon this occasion, and the number reached as high as twelve. During the 1890's, the children were publicly examined on the Friday evening before Shavuot. *Am. Isr.*, June 10, 1897, p. 3; *Reform Advocate*, May 13, 1899, p. 362.
113. *Sent.*, Nov. 16, 1869, p. 1; Nov. 26, 1879, p. 8; Nov. 30, 1888, p. 3; Nov. 25, 1890, p. 3; Feb. 21, 1890, p. 3; Feb. 28, 1891, p. 3; Feb. 22 (p. 2) and 23, 1895 (p. 3); Feb. 22, 1896 (p. 3). Christian ministers addressed B'ne Jeshurun on some of these occasions. Emanu-El, *Minutes*, April 8, 1889.
114. *Der Zeitgeist*, II, 21, (Oct. 13, 1881), p. 344; *Sent.*, May 28, 1898, p. 9; Oct. 7, 1898. p. 3.

115. *Der Zeitgeist*, II, 12 (June 9, 1881), p. 200; 19 (Sept. 15 1881), p. 312; III, 18 (Aug. 31, 1882), p. 288.

116. *Sent.*, Oct. 11, 1897, p. 3.

117. *Am. Isr.*, July 16, 1886, p. 1. The Milwaukee correspondence of the *American Israelite* during the 1880's and 1890's had a tone antagonistic to Temple Emanu-El.

118. *Am. Isr.*, Aug. 6, 1886, p. 10.

119. *Mobile Jewish Chronicle*, quoted in *Reform Advocate*, Dec. 16, 1899, p. 516.

120. *J. Mess.*, Oct. 9, 1885, p. 5.

121. *Jewish Advance*, quoted in *J. Mess.*, Aug. 27, 1880.

122. *Der Zeitgeist*, II, 16 (Aug. 4, 1881), p. 264.

123. *Sent.*, Sept. 25, 1871, p. 4; *Am. Isr.*, Sept. 30, 1887, p. 9.

124. *Der Zeitgeist*, I, 9 (April 29, 1880), p. 148.

125. *Ibid.*, I, 8 (Apr. 15, 1880), p. 128.

126. Milwaukee County, Record of Religious Societies, vol. I, p. 79. *Sent.*, Feb. 17, 1873, p. 4; Sept. 4, 1873, p. 8; April 7, 1874, p. 8. C. Turk and Florian Schauer are mentioned as ministers at various times. The latter was legally authorized to perform marriages. *Sent.*, Feb. 3, 1882, p. 2.

127. *J. Times*, Jan. 27, 1873. Rabbi Eppstein, whose diary speaks in derogatory terms of the group, may be the author of this piece.

128. *Sent.*, March 26, 1883, p. 5. Lewis Silber, of the Rich-Silber firm, conducted High Holiday services in 1881. *Ibid.*, Sept. 27, 1881, p. 11.

129. In 1894, Jacob Rosenberg, a Trustee of Beth Hamidrosh Hagodol, requested a "Paroches" (Ark curtain) of Emanu-El "in behalf of Congregation Anshe Emes." Emanu-El replied that it had "nothing to give for such purposes." Emanu-El, *Minutes*, April 10, 1894.

130. *Sent.*, Sept. 8, 1877, p. 3. One was Anshe Emes.

131. *Der Zeitgeist*, I, 17 (Aug. 19, 1880), p. 276.

132. *Idem.*, (Nov. 9, 1882), p. 352. Moses himself had neglected to file his credentials with the county clerk. *Sent.*, Feb. 3, 1882, p. 2.

133. *Sent.*, Oct. 15, 1884, p. 3.

134. Milwaukee County, Record of Religious Societies, p. 114; *Sent.*, Jan. 28, 1886, p. 3; Nov. 29, 1890, p. 3; *Directory*, 1887, p. 32; 1888; p. 47; 1889, p. 45; 1890, p. 43; 1891, p. 57; 1892, p. 56. Max M. Kaufman is listed as "rabbi" in the 1886 *Directory*, p. 34.

135. *Am. Isr.*, Aug. 6, 1886, p. 10; *Sent.*, June 18 (p. 3), Sept. 26 (p. 3) and 30, 1886, p. 3; *Directory*, 1887, p. 32; 1888, p. 47; 1890, p. 43.

136. *Sent.*, Sept. 28, 1886, p. 3.

137. *Ibid.*, May 18, 1888, p. 3; *Am. Isr.*, May 25, 1888, p. 9; *J. Mess.*, April 17, 1888, p. 3.

138. *Sent.*, Aug. 23, 1887 (p. 3), Sept. 18 (p. 3), 27 (p. 3), 29 (p. 3), Oct. 11, 1887, p. 3, Oct. 23, 1887, p. 3.

139. *Sent.*, Nov. 1 (p. 3), 18 (p. 1), 21 (p. 8), 1888.

140. *Sent.*, Aug. 14, 1889, p. 3.

141. *Am. Heb.*, July 8, 1892, p. 324; June 23, 1893, p. 256; *Am. Isr.*, June 9, 1892; *Sent.*, Oct. 22, 1892, p. 3.

142. *Sent.*, June 23 (p. 3) and 26 (p. 3), 1893, p. 3.

143. *Sent.*, Sept. 1 (p. 3) and 2, 1893, p. 3; *J. Mess.*, Sept. 15, 1893, p. 2; *Am. Isr.*, Sept. 7, 1893, p. 3.

144. *Am. Isr.*, Feb. 8, 1894, p. 3; June 21, 1894, p. 3; *Sent.*, Mar. 28, 1900, p. 5.

145. *AJYB*, 1900-1901, pp. 487-488; *Am. Isr.*, Sept. 2, 1897, p. 2.

146. *Milwaukee Corporation Record*, vol. N, pp. 141-42. "Anshe Hungari" was dropped in 1924. *Ibid.*, vol. 54, p. 377.

147. *Sent.*, Nov. 28 (p. 3) and Dec. 11, 1898, p. 3. Its ladies group Daughters of Israel had been founded in 1898, and counted about 65 ladies. *Sent.*, Oct. 6, 1898, p. 3; Feb. 14, 1900, p. 3.

148. *Sent.*, Oct. 26, 1889, p. 3.

149. *Sent.*, Dec. 20, 1892, p. 3.

150. *Sent.*, May 31, 1897, p. 3.

151. The largest was Landauer & Co., $25; Among lesser amounts was Gimbel Brothers, $5. *Sent.*, Feb. 26, 1898, p. 5; Mar. 7, 1898, p. 3.

152. *Sent.*, Dec. 20, 1892, p. 3; Mar. 7, 1898; p. 3; *Directory*, 1894, p. 55.

153. Solomon Israelson composed two works of rabbinic novellae, *Neveh Shalom* (Chicago, 1900) and *Divrey Shalom* (Chicago, 1920). *Sent.*, Nov. 20, 1895, p. 3. It was not clear at the time what Israelson's functions were. Some opponents held that he was only to deliver sermons, while Israelson considered himself rabbi in the East European sense. *Ibid.*, Aug. 18 and 23, 1897, p. 3; *Am. Isr.*, Aug. 26, 1897, p. 3.

154. *Am. Isr.*, April 9, 1896, p. 3.

155. *Ibid.*, April 9, 1896, p. 3; Oct. 18, 1894, p. 2.

156. *Sent.*, Aug. 23 (p. 3), 25 (p. 3), 28, 1897, p. 3; *Am. Isr.*, Sept. 2, 1897, p. 2.

157. *AJYB*, 1900-1901, p. 270; *Sent.*, May 26, 1899, p. 3.

158. Occasional preachers also spoke in the city. *Sent.*, July 24, 1897, p. 3; May 28, 1899, p. 6. Among the cantors were J. Michalowsky of Paris, E. Samuels, and Israel Kapper.

159. *Ibid.*, Oct. 8, 1894, p. 3; April 2 (p. 7) and Sept. 6, 1899, p. 6; April 15, 1900, Sec. III, p. 8.

160. *Ibid.*, Sept. 20, 1899, p. 3.

161. *Ibid.*, April 15, 1900, Sec. III, p. 8.

162. *Ibid.*, Sept. 26, 1895, p. 3; Aug. 18, 1897, p. 3.

163. *Ibid.*, Nov. 19 (p. 3), 20, 1895, p. 3.

164. *Ibid.*, May 13, 1900, Sec. III, p. 8.

165. *Ibid.*, Nov. 29 (p. 3) and Dec. 25, 1890, p. 2; Feb. 12 (p. 3) and April 27, 1891, p. 3; April 29, 1900, p. 3. A commonly accepted tale derives the name "Second Home" from the immigrants' corrupt pronunciation of the non-Jewish Forest Home Cemetery as "First" Home Cemetery. Second Home actually originates in the traditional Jewish view of the cemetery as the "eternal home." *Wisc. JC*, Mar. 31, Apr. 28, May 26, 1922; Jan. 16, April 17, May 1, 1925.

166. Spring Hill was the B'nai B'rith cemetery. Greenwood was independent, but closely connected with the Reform Temples. The old Hopkins Road cemetery was used as late as 1888. Emanu-El, *Minutes*, Oct. 19, 1869, Aug. 13, 1870, May 21, 1871, Mar. 24, 1872, April 7, 1872, Jan. 9, 1873, May 4, 1873, Sept. 6, 1874; Nov. 2, 1874; B'ne Jeshurun, *Minutes*, June 7, April 12, Oct. 4, 1896; Abstract of Title, Old Jewish Cemetery; *Register of Deeds*,

vol. 182, p. 62; Milwaukee County, *Record, Religious Societies*, I, p. 85; *Sent.*, June 28 (p. 8) and 30, 1873, p. 8; *Am. Isr.*, Sept. 17, 1896, p. 2.

VII. RELIGIOUS TRADITION AND COMMUNAL PURPOSE 1900-1925

1. B'ne Jeshurun, *Minutes*, Sept. 17, 1905; July 4, 1909.
2. C. S. Levi to S. Eckstein, Jan. 7, 1913, in B'ne Jeshurun, *Minutes*, Jan. 5, 1913.
3. *The Jewish Conservator*, II, 11, Sept. 9, 1904, pp. 4-8.
4. *Am. Isr.*, Aug. 31, 1911.
5. *Ibid.*, June 27, 1912.
6. B'ne Jeshurun, *Minutes*, Sept. 3, 1911. When Caro left the old house, he was granted $300.00 annually for rent. *Ibid.*, Sept. 1, 1901. He also received $10.00 for each wedding or funeral at which he officiated. *Ibid.*, Nov. 4, 1906.
7. Emanu-El, *Minutes*, Dec. 17, 1899.
8. *Ibid.*, April 8, 1902.
9. *Ibid.*, Sept. 19, 1898.
10. *Ibid.*, May 7, 1905.
11. *Ibid.*, May 11, 1919.
12. *Ibid.*, May 20, 1926.
13. *Ibid.*, Aug. 17, 1926.
14. B'ne Jeshurun, *Minutes*, Dec. 22, 1912; Aug. 5, 1918; Sept. 1, 1918; Sept. 29, 1920; Oct. 11, 1922. He declined a raise to $8,400. Oct. 7, 1925.
15. Emanu-El *Minutes*, Nov. 26, 1900; Oct. 4, 1921.
16. *Ibid.*, Feb. 2, 1908. It was a concession to permit ritual changes for these three months by the rabbi with only the concurrence of the Ritual Committee and not the Board. On one occasion, the Rabbi had a lengthy conference with two officers, who reported that he "would in all respects comply with the wishes of the Board. . ." *Ibid.*, Jan. 2, 1918. The Board did not feel that its control of worship necessarily obligated it to attend services. *Ibid.*, Sept. 18, 1918.
17. B'ne Jeshurun, *Minutes*, Sept. 25, 1910.
18. A "Kaddish Service" was held on Friday evening during many summers for members in mourning or observing the anniversary of a relative's death. For example, Emanu-El, *Minutes*, June 3, 1913.
19. *Ibid.*, Aug. 17, 1926.
20. *Ibid.*, Feb. 2, 1926.
21. *Ibid.*, April 16, 1905. The seatholders were also categorized according to the location of the seats they occupied. They paid $85, $60, $40 and $25 respectively. *Ibid.*, April 13, 1900. A half pew cost was $95, $68, $45, $30 for the four classes of members. *Ibid.*, March 5, 1907.
22. *Ibid.*, April 7, 1903.
23. They were $66, $48, $36, $33, and $27. B'ne Jeshurun, *Minutes*, Sept. 17, 1905. The dues fell $6.00 annually by 1912 (*Ibid.*, Sept. 1, 1912), but rose about 25% in the higher memberships and declined by $3 to $24 at the lowest rate. (*Ibid.*, March 7, 1915).
24. Emanu-El, *Minutes*, May 20, 1923.
25. *Ibid.*, Sept. 6, 1910.

26. B'ne Jeshurun, *Minutes*, Feb. 2, 1913.

27. *Am. Isr.*, June 25, 1915. Membership fluctuated much and rose as high as 300 in 1923, and stood at 284 in B'ne Jeshurun's last independent year, 1926. Of course, this did not keep pace with Emanu-El or population growth. B'ne Jeshurun, *Minutes*, Sept. 30, 1926.

28. Emanu-El, *Minutes*, Nov. 2, 1920.

29. *Ibid.*, Jan. 4, 1927.

30. There were 48 seatholders, whose average contribution was $37.20. *Ibid.*, Oct. 12, 1926.

31. *Ibid.*, May 16, 1909.

32. *Ibid.*, Jan. 4, 1916; May 6, 1917.

33. *Ibid.*, May 6, 1925.

34. H. V. Meissner, in B'ne Jeshurun, *Minutes*, March 24, 1927.

35. Emanu-El *Minutes*, Jan. 2, 1924.

36. *Ibid.*, May 1, 1923; March 6, 1923.

37. *Ibid.*, July 15, 1925; April 6, 1926; May 3, 1926. The mollifying words were: "Dr. Hirshberg has served us long and faithfully; we express our full confidence in him, and trust that he may continue to be with us for many years to come." *Ibid.*

38. *Ibid.*, Jan. 4, 1927; Mar. 1, 1927.

39. The Union Prayer Book was adopted in 1915 (B'ne Jeshurun, *Minutes*, Sept. 6, 1914; March 7, 1915). Services were longer than Emanu-El's, lasting from 7:30 P.M. to 9:15 P.M. on Fridays and 10:00 A.M. to 11:30 A.M. on Saturdays. *Ibid.*, June 2, 1918.

40. The suggestion of public acquisition appeared years before. B'ne Jeshurun, *Minutes*, March 6, 1910. Serious negotiations began in 1922 and the Temple was sold for $100,000 in 1924. B'ne Jeshurun, *Minutes*, May 21, 1922 and Dec. 7, 1924, and *passim*.

41. Emanu-El, *Minutes*, Oct. 6, 1925; March 8, 1927; Dec. 30, 1919.

42. Rabbi Levi's letter is in B'ne Jeshurun, *Minutes*, Nov. 14, 1926. See also *idem.*, Dec. 5, 9, and 26, 1926; Jan. 9 and 30, 1927.

43. *Ibid.*, Oct. 6, 1925.

44. They included such matters as a common treasury, memorials, Mrs. Caro's pension, and the old cemetery. *Ibid.*, March 11, March 30, 1927 and April 7, 1927.

45. *Ibid.*, n. d. (ca. July 28-Aug. 14, 1927).

46. *Ibid.*, May 3, 1927.

47. *Ibid.*, Aug. 15, 1927.

48. Milwaukee County, *Corporation Record*, Vol. W, pp. 50-52.

49. Milwaukee County, *Corporation Record*, Vol. X, p. 307.

50. *Blue Book*, p. 61.

51. *Blue Book*, p. 63; *Wchblt.*, Oct. 4, 1918.

52. *Wchblt.*, March 31, 1916, p. 2.

53. *Blue Book*, p. 64. "We feel that the time has come when we should give ourselves a more Jewish name . . . the name of our congregation should now be Degel Israel, and the congregation should be known as Degel Israel Anshe Roumainia." *Wchblt.*, Feb. 12, 1920, p. 1.

54. *Wchblt.*, March 10, 1919, p. 3.

55. *Blue Book*, p. 65.
56. *Ibid.*, Supplement (Feb., 1926), p. 39.
57. Milwaukee County, *Corporation Record*, Vol. 58, p. 7.
58. *Blue Book*, pp. 47-50.
59. *Ibid.*, pp. 51-55, 61-65.
60. The habit of selling old synagogues and building larger structures a few streets to the west was already apparent in 1914. (*Wchblt.*, Aug. 7, 1914, p. 1). Anshe Polen considered purchasing a Baptist Church on 6th and Walnut in 1916. (*Ibid.*, June 16, 1916, p. 1). Anshe Sfard considered selling to a Negro group in 1920, or tearing down the synagogue and selling the lot, but it did neither. (*Ibid.*, April 7, 1920, p. 1). "The Negroes have up to now purchased all churches of the until recently Jewish neighborhood, and they are planning also to acquire the synagogues that are situated south of Walnut Street." *Ibid.*, June 18, 1920. However, the synagogues held fast and moved slowly. Similarly, Beth Israel made many gestures before it actually moved, and sold its building on 5th Street to a Negro church. *Ibid.*, Jan. 18, 1918, p. 1; June 18, 1920, p. 1; June 25, 1920, p. 1; April 3, 1921, p. 1; April 22, 1921, p. 1; Aug. 3, 1921 (announcing the laying of the cornerstone for a new synagogue which others completed); Feb. 23, 1923, p. 1 (announcing a different site, which was finally used). These shifts in plans probably caused the formation of the Beth Medrash Hagodol Anshe Sfard in 1920, who were satisfied with the plans for the building at 11th and Lloyd. The dominant group, led by I. J. Rosenberg, was more ambitious.
61. Milwaukee County, *Corporation Record*, vol. 35, p. 159.
62. *Blue Book*, p. 49; "I Remember," reminiscences by Amram Scheinfeld in *Wisc. JC*, Sept, 28, 1951; oral statements by Mr. Scheinfeld.
63. "LeTakanat HaYahadut," *HaShiloah*, XXVI (1912), pp. 193-197. The quotations following are from this article.
64. *Wchblt.*, Dec. 28, 1917, p. 4.
65. The episode is discussed *Ibid.*, and in the issues of Nov. 23, 1917, p. 4; Nov. 30, 1917, p. 1; Dec. 7, 1917, p. 2; Dec. 28, 1917, p. 1. The real motives and background of this episode are obscure.
66. *Ibid.*, Dec. 21, 1917, p. 4; Jan. 11, 1918, p. 3.
67. It began with 125 members. *Wchblt.*, Jan. 7 (p. 1), Feb. 20 (p. 1), Feb. 22 (p. 1), Feb. 26 (p. 1), March 1, (p. 1), March 12 (p. 1), April 22, 1920, p. 1.
68. *Ibid.*, April 3, 1921, p. 1.
69. *Ibid.*, Dec. 3, 1915, p. 1.
70. *Ibid.*, Dec. 17, 1915, p. 4.
71. *Wchblt.*, Oct. 2, 1914, p. 1.
72. A typical advertisement:
"I hope that you will patronize me and reserve tickets and come and pray with all of us on Rosh Hashanah and Yom Kippur in the large and airy Vizay's Hall, where we will pray for a good year for us and all Israel. Your devoted friend, Rev. E. Vogel." *Ibid.*, Sept. 23, 1919, p. 2. The North Side Auditorium was also put to use.
73. *Wisc. JC*, April 6, 1923, p. 1.
74. *Wchblt.*, May 15, 1914, p. 1—slightly alarmist, emphasizing the

synagogal affiliations of many Jews who allegedly are "the most enthusiastic" Christian Science believers. See *Ibid.,* Feb. 25, 1919 for obituary of Joel Rubin (1887-1919), of Russian Jewish parentage, President of the Milwaukee Rationalist Society.

75. *Wisc. JC,* Feb. 17, 1922, p. 1.

VIII. FROM CHARITY TO WELFARE

1. The Associated Charities was incorporated in August, 1886. *Sent.,* Jan. 15 (p. 11), and Mar. 3, 1882, p. 3; Nov. 25, 1884, p. 3; Jan. 27, 1885, p. 3; Jan. 5 (p. 3), Aug 25 (p. 3), and Nov. 17, 1886, p. 3; Jan 11, 1888, p. 3; Jan. 23, 1891, p. 3; *Am. Isr.,* Jan. 31, 1895, p. 2; *Directory,* 1883, p. 49; 1884, p. 50; 1885, p. 50.

2. Dr. E. L. Eaton, a Methodist minister, had attacked charity balls because of the evils of dancing. In a sermon at Temple Emanu-El entitled "Holy and Unholy Zeal," Rabbi Hecht opposed him, while Rabbi Caro supported him in minor respects in a sermon "True Liberty." Eaton replied to the rabbis in a sermon styled "After the Bawl." In any case, the Hebrew Relief Association was dissatisfied with its small proceeds. *Am. Isr.,* Jan. 25, 1894, p. 2; Jan. 31, (p. 2), Feb. 7, (p. 2), and May 2, 1895, p. 2.

3. *Am. Isr.,* Feb. 6, 1896, p. 2.

4. *Sent.,* Jan. 26, 1900, p. 6.

5. For the year 1894, a total of 4,141 pieces of apparel was distributed, of which 191 came from the Hebrew Relief Association, and 197 from the Ladies' Relief Sewing Society. *Am. Isr.,* Nov. 9 (p. 2) and 23, 1893; Dec. 20, 1894, p. 3.

6. *Sent.,* April 3, 1880, p. 2; Dec. 30, 1883, p. 12; *Emanu-El, Minutes,* Feb. 18, 1889 and Dec. 12, 1892.

7. *Sent.,* Oct. 16, 1871, p. 4; *J. Times,* Nov. 3, 1871, p. 567.

8. Emanu-El, *Minutes,* Oct. 6, 1873, Sept. 1, 1878; Jan. 17, 1899; Oct. 16, 1900; *Sent.,* Oct. 9 (p. 8), 13 (p. 8) and Dec. 6, 1873, p. 8; Aug. 21 (p. 8), 22 (p. 1) and Oct. 9, 1878, p. 8; Oct. 18, 1888, p. 3. *Am. Isr.,* Oct. 24, 1873, Oct. 17, 1889.

9. *Sent.,* May 27, 1875, p. 3. Rich was also Secretary of a Committee of Twelve which raised $5,000 for victims of Ohio River floods in 1884. *Sent.,* Feb. 29, 1884, p. 6.

10. *Ibid.,* March 1, 1871, p. 2; Jan. 8, 1872, p. 4; Nov. 8, 1878, p. 8; March 24, 1879, p. 8.

11. *J. Mess.,* June 7, 1872; *Sent.,* Nov. 7, 1891, p. 3; Emanu-El, *Minutes,* Sept. 21, 1890, Nov. 6, 1891.

12. *Sent.,* Aug. 9 (p. 1) and 11, 1870, p. 1; Dec. 2, 1880, p. 8; *Am. Isr.,* March 22, 1894, p. 2; March 29, 1894, p. 3. For the latter, a short-lived joint committee was organized.

13. Andreas, p. 983.

14. Chevra Bikur Cholim, *Minute Book,* April 15, 1883, July 11, 1886, April 26, 1891, July 23, 1891, Jan. 4, 1900, and *passim.*

15. *Ibid.,* Oct. 21, 1883, April 17, 1887. In 1889, the society voted to tax each member 25¢ in case of a man's death, and 15¢ in the event of a woman's. *Ibid.,* Oct. 13, 1889.

16. *Taharah* is the ablution of a body before enshrouding it. Attempts to draft members to perform *taharah* did not succeed. In 1891, the rite became voluntary, and was performed by an *ad hoc* group upon a family's request. *Idem.,* May 9, 1886 and July 23, 1891.

17. Regulations of 1894 granted the full benefit of $65 to a member suffering chronic disease, and only $1 weekly for 13 weeks thereafter. *Idem.,* April 29, 1894. Victor Berger, incidentally, collected $10 in sick benefits for two weeks. *Ibid.,* Jan. 24, 1897. See also *Ibid.,* Jan. 1, 1884, Sept. 5, 1899; Aug. 19, 1900.

18. *Ibid.,* April 15, July 22, and Oct. 21, 1883; Oct. 17, 1886; Nov. 8, 1891, Jan. 19, 1896, Jan. 1, 1899.

19. Most of the assets were mortgages yielding 5% to 7%. *Ibid.,* March 23, 1884, April 15, 1888, Jan. 1, 1889; Andreas, p. 983.

20. *Sent.,* Oct. 16, 1873, p. 8; May 24, 1879, p. 5; *Directory,* 1870-71, p. 371; 1871-72, p. 382; 1872-73, p. 354; 1873-74, p. 398; 1875-76, p. 41; 1876-77, p. 48.

21. *Am. Isr.,* Oct. 27, 1892, p. 5; cf. *Sent.,* June 27, 1876, p. 8; Jan. 27, 1877, p. 8; Jan. 14, 1878, p. 8; Oct. 17, 1879, p. 8.

22. *Sent.,* Oct. 23, 1876, p. 8; Nov. 29 (p. 8) and Dec. 28, 1878, p. 8; Nov. 18, 1881, p. 7; Dec. 14, 1890, p. 1; *Am. Isr.,* Jan. 17, 1879, p. 5; Oct. 15 (p. 6), Nov. 19, (p. 3) and Dec. 10, 1886, p. 3; June 7, 1894, p. 2.

23. *Sent.,* Dec. 27, 1891, p. 3. For its 25th anniversary, see *Sent.,* Jan. 18 (p. 2) and Feb. 3, 1889, p. 2; *Am. Isr.,* Dec. 26, 1889, p. 5.

24. *Sent.,* Dec. 10, 1892, p. 3.

25. Such as Mrs. Solomon Adler's gift and Marcus Cohn's bequest. *Sent.,* Feb. 3, 1889, p. 2; Feb. 25, 1891, p. 3.

26. *Der Zeitgeist,* Aug. 19, 1880, p. 276.

27. *Sent.,* June 1, 1894, p. 3; May 24, 1895, p. 3; *Am. Isr.,* June 7, 1894, p. 2.

28. *Community Survey,* 1923, p. 34.

29. *Am. Isr.,* Feb. 15, 1884, p. 6; *Sent.,* Dec. 19, 1878, p. 8; *AJYB, 5668 (1907-1908),* p. 428.

30. *Der Zeitgeist,* Aug. 5, 1880, p. 260; *Am. Isr.,* Jan. 17 (p. 5), Feb. 14 (p. 6), and Mar. 14, 1879, p. 5.

31. *Der Zeitgeist,* Aug. 19, 1880, p. 276; Jan. 20, 1881, p. 36; Nov. 10, 1881, 376; *Am. Isr.,* Dec. 24, 1880, p. 206.

32. *Sent.,* Oct. 11, 1885, p. 3; Jan. 2, 1890, p. 2; Jan. 6 (p. 3), Nov. 24, 1893, p. 3; Dec. 6, 1894, p. 3; Jan. 6, 1895, p. 7; Oct. 26, 1899, p. 5; *Am. Isr.,* Feb. 16, 1883, p. 275; Feb. 15, 1884, p. 6; Mar. 5 (p. 7), Apr. 2 (p.7), Oct. 8 (p. 6), Oct. 22, 1886, p. 7; Feb. 18, 1887, p. 6. Monthly coffees were held at Germania Hall, in addition to its charity balls. *Am. Isr.,* Jan. 15, 1891, p. 4; *Sent.,* Dec, 7, 1890, p. 3; Nov. 20, 1892, p. 3. The society received a $250 bequest upon the death of Elias Friend. *Sent.,* Nov. 28, 1890, p. 3; *Am. Isr.,* Dec. 4, 1890, p. 6. During 1893, about 4,000 pieces of clothing were distributed, including values of $400 in dry goods, $750 in shoes, $100 in clothing, *Sent.,* Jan. 5, 1894, p. 3. In 1897, membership decreased to 196, and 102 families were supplied with clothing. *Reform Advocate* (Chicago), Jan. 30, 1897, p. 383. In 1898, only 188 members assisted 60 families, with expenses of $800 against income of $1,100. *Sent.,* Jan. 6, 1899, p. 3.

33. *Community Survey,* 1923, pp. 42-44.

34. The Sisterhood also included a Quilting Bee. *Am. Isr.*, Aug. 24 p. 2, Sept. 28 p. 2, and Nov. 30, 1893, p. 2; *Sent.*, May 23, 1894, p. 3; *Am. Hebrew.*, June 8, 1894, p. 197.

35. *Am. Isr.*, Nov. 8 (p. 2), and 15, 1894, p. 2; Nov. 21, 1895, p. 2; *Reform Advocate*, Nov. 24, 1894, p. 226.

36. *Am. Isr.*, Nov. 15, 1894, p. 2.

37. *Sent.*, May 6, 1897, p. 3.

38. *Sent.*, Nov. 24, 1899, p. 5; Jan. 2, 1900 p. 5; *Directory*, 1900, p. 58.

39. The Hebrew Relief Society incorporated in February, 1872. *Sent.*, Feb. 16, 1872, p. 4; Dec. 5, 1876, p. 8; Dec. 6, 1877, p. 8.

40. *Sent.*, Oct. 1, 1878, p. 8.

41. *Sent.*, Oct. 7, (p. 8), Oct. 8, 1878, p. 8.

42. *Sent.*, Nov. 11, 1878, p. 4; Jan. 20 (p. 8), Jan. 21, 1879, p. 8.

43. *Sent.*, Oct. 10, 1879, p. 8.

44. *Sent.*, Oct. 14 (p. 8), Oct. 23 (p. 8), Oct. 27, 1879, p. 8. Only annual subscribers could be voting members. The Board met every Sunday morning at the Progress Club to receive relief applications, hear investigative reports, and personally distribute relief. Andreas, p. 982; *Blue Book*, p. 76.

45. *Sent.*, Apr. 24 (p. 8), April 26 (p. 8), Nov. 15, 1880, p. 8; *Der Zeitgeist*, May 13, 1880, p. 149; Nov. 11, 1880, p. 372. For the names of the constituents of the proposed organization, see *Blue Book*, p. 76.

46. *Sent.*, Nov. 15, 1880, p. 8; *Der Zeitgeist*, Nov. 25, 1880, p. 388.

47. *Der Zeitgeist*, Dec. 9, 1880, p. 404; Andreas, p. 982.

48. Carpeles made his pioneering proposal at the society's 14th Annual Meeting, in November, 1881. *Sent.*, Nov. 14, 1881, p. 7; cf. *Der Zeitgeist*, Nov. 24, 1881, p. 392; Nov. 23 (p. 368), Dec. 7, 1882, p. 384; *Am. Isr.*, Nov. 25, 1881, p. 170.

49. *Sent.*, Sept. 14, 1885, p. 3; *Blue Book*, p. 77.

50. *Sent.*, Sept. 28 (p. 3), Nov. 13 (p. 3), Dec. 6, 1885, p. 3; Oct. 5, 1886, p. 3; Sept. 26, 1887, p. 3; Oct. 5, 1888, p. 3; Sept.. 30, 1892, p. 3; Mar. 8 (p. 3), Oct. 8, 1895, p. 2; Sept. 28, 1896, p. 3; Jan. 17, 1897, p. 22; Sept. 29, 1897, p. 3; *Am. Isr.*, Oct. 1 (p. 2), Oct. 15, 1886, p. 6; Oct. 7, 1887, p. 9; Oct. 26, 1888, p. 5; Aug. 10 (p. 2), Sept. 28, 1893, p. 2; Oct. 18, 1894, p. 2; Oct. 10, 1895, p. 2; Oct. 1, 1896, p. 3; Jan. 28 (p. 2), Oct. 7, 1897, p. 2; *J. Mess.*, Oct. 9, 1885, p. 2; *Am. Heb.*, Oct. 9, 1896, p. 583; Oct. 22, 1897, p. 749; *Blue Book*, p. 77. Beginning in 1893, small sums were added annually to a sinking fund.

51. *Am. Isr.*, Oct. 26, 1888, p. 5; Sept. 28, 1893, p. 2. The individuals were probably transients. *Sent.*, Oct. 5, 1888, p. 3.

52. *Sent.*, Sept. 30, 1892, p. 3.

53. *Ibid.*, Oct. 18, 1893; p. 1; *Am. Isr.*, Sept. 28 (p. 2), Oct. 19, 1893, p. 2.

54. *Sent.*, Oct. 29 (p. 3), Oct. 31 (p. 3), Nov. 8 (p. 3), Dec. 26, 1893, p. 3; *Am. Isr.*, Nov. 9, 1893, (p. 2).

55. *Sent.*, Dec. 26, 1893, p. 3.

56. *Am. Isr.*, Dec. 28, 1893, p. 2; Mar. 22, 1894, p. 2.

57. *Am. Isr.*, Nov. 15, 1894, p. 2; *Sent.*, Jan. 17, 1897, p. 22.

58. *Am. Heb.*, Feb. 1, 1895, p. 387; *Sent.*, Jan. 17, 1897, p. 22. The United Hebrew Charities' officers in 1897 were: Rabbi S. Hecht, president; Mrs. A. W. Rich, vice-president; Mrs. S. M. Rukeyser, secretary-treasurer. *Directory*, 1897, p. 58; *Reform Advocate* (Chicago), Oct. 16, 1897, p. 571.

59. *Am. Isr.,* Oct. 11, 1894, p. 7.
60. *Sent.,* Sept. 28, 1896, p. 3; Jan. 17, 1897, p. 22; *Am. Isr.,* Oct. 1, 1896, p. 3; *Am. Heb.,* Oct. 9, 1896, p. 583.
61. *Am. Isr.,* Feb. 11, 1897, p. 2; *Reform Advocate,* Feb. 27, 1897, p. 29. It was upon this occasion that he resigned, demanding that Jewish cases be handled by the Associated Charities.
62. *Sent.,* Oct. 11, 1898, p. 3; *Blue Book,* p. 79.
63. *Sent.,* Oct. 25 (p. 3), Nov. 3 (p. 5), Nov. 11, 1898, p. 5; *Blue Book,* p. 79
64. The following quotations are from the President's Report in the *32nd Annual Report of the Hebrew Relief Association,* Sept. 24, 1899.
65. *Sent.,* Oct. 15, 1900, 5.
66. *Sent.,* Oct. 15, (p. 5), Oct. 20, 1900, 5.
67. *Blue Book,* pp. 89-92; *Community Survey,* 1923, pp. 38-41; *Report of the Superintendent,* in *14th Annual Report of the Federated Jewish Charities* (1916)—hereafter F.J.C., *Ann. Rep.*
68. *Blue Book,* pp. 81-88; *Community Survey,* 1923, pp. 86-192. Each F.J.C. *Ann. Rep.* discusses Settlement affairs.
69. F.J.C., *2nd Ann. Rep.* (1904).
70. F.J.C., *6th Ann. Rep.* (1908).
71. F.J.C., *9th Ann. Rep.* (1911). $5,000 was subscribed in a 1907 campaign, but the project was "dropped temporarily (due to financial conditions)." F.J.C., *5th Ann. Rep.* (1907).
72. F.J.C., *15th Ann. Rep.* (1917).
73. Report of the Head Resident, F.J.C., *18th Ann. Rep.* (*1920*).
74. Independent schools, such as the Talmud Torah and the Folk Shule of the Labor Zionists, at different times were quartered in the Abraham Lincoln House. F.J.C., *6th, 14th, 23rd Ann. Reps.* (*1908, 1916, 1924*).
75. F.J.C., *6th Ann. Rep.* (*1908*).
76. The 3rd edition appeared in 1907, and the 8th in 1916, the latter in 15,000 copies "with bright prospects for ready sale." In 1918 and 1919 about 1,000 were sold each year. See the F.J.C. *Ann. Reps.* for the years mentioned. The Settlement Cook Book was not "Kosher."
77. Report of the Acting Director of Abraham Lincoln House, F.J.C., *24th Ann. Rep.* (*1925*). The Lapham Park Social Center was becoming unusable for Jews for a similar reason, as the neighborhood was on the frontier of ethnic change. It was estimated that 4,000 Negroes had moved into its immediate area, and "20 different retarded nationalities. . . . Even the most enthusiastic assimilationist would not wish that our Jewish children should form their character in such association. Any impartial sociologist knows that in such areas demoralization and delinquency grow up. . . ." F.J.C., *23rd Ann. Rep.* (*1926*).
78. *Blue Book,* pp. 105-110; *Community Survey, 1923,* pp. 66-85. Of 26 attending physicians in 1922, 14 were Jews, while 20 of the 134 who used its facilities were Jews. Among 2747 admissions in 1922, 63% were surgical cases. In distinction to its low proportion of Jewish patients, Mount Sinai's maternity ward was "almost entirely Jewish." *Ibid.,* p. 74. On Abraham Slimmer, see *Am. Isr.,* Feb. 19, 1914, p. 1.
79. *Blue Book,* p. 124; *Community Survey, 1923,* pp. 26-29. The tale of its

origin is found in a Yiddish MS., n.d. (recent), among the Home's records which were kindly made available.

80. The institution kindly made some of its records available to us. See also Reports of the Executive Director in F.J.C., *24th and 26th Ann. Reps. (1924-1926)*; *Blue Book*, p. 134; *Community Survey, 1923*, pp. 35-36; on the Council of Jewish Women's plans, see President's Report to Hebrew Relief Association, F.J.C., *10th Ann. Rep.* (1912).

81. *Community Survey, 1923*, pp. 31-32; *Blue Book*, p. 136. The *Blue Book* (p. 126 ff.) mentions numerous other charitable groups, mostly of immigrant origin: Ladies Benevolent Society, Ladies of Peace, True Sisters, Milwaukee Ladies' Aid, Ukrainian Ladies' Society, and others.

82. This is Article I, Section 2 of the *Articles of Organization, By-Laws, and Rules of Order* of the F.J.C., adopted Nov. 13, 1902. The incorporators, in order of signature, were David Adler, Paul Sidenberg, L. H. Heller, A. W. Rich, Max Landauer, Julius H. Meyer, Geo. W. Patek, M. D. Newald, Victor Caro, Morris Miller, Charles Friend. Each constituent of the F.J.C. was entitled to one representative on the F.J.C. Board of eleven, chosen by the F.J.C. membership from among nominees submitted by that institution. By-Laws, Article V, Section 1. Membership in the F.J.C. cost $5.00 or more annually, according to the Fifth Article of Organization.

83. This is derived from the *Annual Reports* of the F.J.C., *passim;* specific points mentioned will be found in the *Ann. Rep.* of the respective year.

84. F.J.C., *3rd Ann. Rep.* (1905).

85. F.J.C., *12th Ann Rep.* (1914).

86. F.J.C., *15th Ann. Rep.* (1917).

87. The yearly reports of the H.R.A. are incorporated in the F.J.C. Annual Reports, and the specific facts given below are to be found in the report of the given year.

88. Report of the Superintendent of the H.R.A., in F.J.C., *14th Ann Rep. (1916)*. Succeeding years recorded the diminution of the problem, probably owing to general prosperity and to the location work of the National Desertion Bureau. By 1919, desertion was "a very negligible problem." *Idem.*, in F.J.C., *17th Ann. Rep.* (1919).

89. President's Report to H.R.A., in F.J.C., *12th Ann. Rep.* (1914).

90. Report of the Superintendent of the H.R.A., in F.J.C., *15th Ann. Rep.* (1917).

91. President's Report to H.R.A., in F.J.C., *21st Ann. Rep* (1922).

92. Quoted in *Ibid.*

93. Report of the Superintendent of the H.R.A., in F.J.C., *18th Ann. Rep.* (1920).

IX. THE CHALLENGE OF IDEAS: ZIONISM AND SOCIALISM (1890-1925)

1. *Freie Arbeiter Stimme*, Dec. 11, 1891, p. 3; Dec. 25, 1891, p. 5; Jan. 1, 1892. The local English press seems to have taken no notice of the strike.

2. *Ibid.*, Jan. 22, 1892, p. 3.

3. *Ibid.*, Feb. 19, 1892, p. 3.

4. *Sent.*, Jan. 30, 1891, p. 1; Nov. 8, p. 3, and 11, 1895, p. 3.

5. *Ibid.,* Feb. 28, p. 3, and Mar. 1, 1899, p. 5; *Directory*, 1899, p. 34; *Blue Book*, pp. 124-125.

6. *The Maccabaean*, II, 6 (June, 1902). It is not clear who "Dr. Karo" was. Could it have been Rabbi Victor Caro? However, the spellings are different; Victor Caro did not have the title of doctor; moreover, he was anti-Zionist.

7. *Ibid.,* IV, I (Jan., 1903), p. 52.

8. *Ibid.,* IV, I (Jan., 1903), p. 55.

9. *Ibid.,* VI, 2 (Feb., 1954). In 1913, only Judah haLevi existed. *Ibid.,* XXIII, 7 (July, 1913), p. 201.

10. Federation of American Zionists, *Report of Executive Committee,* June 1, 1917.

11. The following quotations are from the collection of Joseph Saffro (1878-1959). Most carry no date, but their provenance is 1904 to 1917. They were probably written by Saffro.

12. J.N.F. collections for a 12 month period in 1904-1905 realized $435. *The Maccabaean*, IX, I (July, 1905), p. 54; *Idisher Kemfer*, I, 39 (Dec. 31, 1906).

13. *The Maccabaean*, II, 2 (Feb., 1902), p. 96.

14. *Idisher Kemfer*, II, 18 (Aug. 2, 1907); II, 35 (Dec. 13, 907); *Wchblt.,* March 27, 1914, p. 1.

15. *Sent.* and Milwaukee *Journal*, Jan. 3, 1911. The "Zion Council" is probably an *ad hoc* group, composed for the occasion.

16. *Yiddisher Record* (Chicago), April 18, 1913.

17. From a letter to his brother Alfred Brandeis, Nov. 27, 1914, quoted in Alpheus T. Mason, *Brandeis: A Free Man's Life* (N.Y., 1946) p. 447.

18. B'ne Jeshurun, *Minutes*, Nov. 3, 1918.

19. *Idisher Kemfer*, I, 51 (Mar. 16, 1907).

20. *Ibid.,* II, 16 (July 19, 1907).

20a. *Ibid.,* 1, 39 (Dec. 31, 1906).

21. These quotations are taken from pp. 6-9 of the MS. Yiddish memoirs of Louis Perchonok (1888-1949), a founder and long-time Secretary of the Poale Zion in Milwaukee. The memoirs were written *ca.* 1947-49 and are in 158 pp. They supply a detailed picture of Milwaukee immigrant life and early Socialist Zionist movement, and appear accurate at all points where they could be checked against contemporary sources.

22. *Idisher Kemfer*, I, 15, July 6, 1906; *Perchonok Memoirs*, pp. 1-10, 58.

23. *Idisher Kemfer*, May 11, 1906, June 1, 1906, June 20, 1906, July 6, 1906, July 27, 1906, Aug. 20, 1906, Sept. 7, 1906, Dec. 31, 1906, June 10, 1910.

24. *Ibid.,* June 17, 1910.

25. *Ibid.,* Dec. 13, 1907, The Yiddish spelling is uncertain. Nothing further could be found of this early Palestine settler.

26. *Perchonok Memoirs*, passim.

27. *Idisher Kemfer*, I, 51, Mar. 15, 1907.

28. *Ibid.,* III, 18, July 22, 1910.

29. *Ibid.,* II, 13, June 28, 1907.

30. *Perchonok Memoirs*, p. 50.

31. *Wchblt.,* Mar. 27, 1914, p. 1.

32. *Sent.,* April 16, 1893, p. 3.

33. Donald D. Egbert and Stow Persons, eds., *Socialism and American*

Life, 2 vols. (Princeton, 1952), II, pp. 149, 263, 409. Ladoff's article "Sexual Slavery" was excised from the February, 1905 issue of the *International Socialist Review*. It evidently dealt with the prostitution traffic and the editors feared legal action.

34. *Yiddisher Arbeter Velt* (Chicago), Sept. 17, 1909.

35. *Ibid.*, June 11, 1909.

36. *Ibid.*, Oct. 30, 1908.

37. H. L. Nahin, M.D., *Constructive Socialism*, n.d. The general contents suggest a date of publication between 1910 and 1915.

38. Circular letter to membership, March 1, 1916, in microfilm of Milwaukee material in the YIVO Archive, New York City.

39. This information derives from two placards, n.d., *ca.* Mar., 1916, in microfilm of Milwaukee material in the YIVO Archive, New York City.

40. Circular letter, *supra* note 38.

41. A. S. Sachs, *Di Geshikhte fun Arbeiter Ring*, 2 vols. (N.Y., 1925), II, end papers, pp. xiv, xxix, xxxii, xxxvi.

42. Herz Burgin, *Di Geshikhte fun der Idisher Arbayter Bavegung in Amerika, Rusland un England* (N.Y., 1915), p. 711.

43. J. M. Budish, *Geshikhte fun di Cloth Hat Cap un Millinery Arbayter*, 2nd ed. (N.Y., 1926), pp. 323-324; *Wchblt.*, April 20, 1917, p. 4.

44. *Perchonok Memoirs*, pp. 59-60; *Forverts*, Mar. 25, 1917, (for Tom Mooney and Montreal tailors).

45. Amalgamated Clothing Workers of America, *Proceedings of the Third Biennial Convention* (1918), pp. 128, 207; . . . *Fourth Biennial Convention* (1920); pp. 139, 141; . . . *Fifth Biennial Convention* (1922), pp xiii, 181, 182; . . . *Sixth Biennial Convention* (1924), pp. 119-20, lxxii; *Wchblt.*, May 4, 1917, p. 4; April 25, 1919, p. 1.

46. *Wchblt.*, Jan. 12, 1920, p. 1.

47. *Ibid.*, Jan. 16, 1920, p. 1.

48. Edward Friebert, *Memoirs* (MS.), p. 281-282. On their author (1875–1960), see *Milwaukee Journal*, Feb. 9, 1960.

49. *Forverts*, Mar. 31, 1919. The Milwaukee Socialists had numerous ethnic branches—German, Polish, Finnish, Italian, Hungarian. However, most of them lay dormant until shortly before Election Day.

50. F. I. Olson, *The Milwaukee Socialist Party*, 1897–1941 (doctoral thesis, Harvard University, 1952). Berger was a life-long member of the Chevra Bikur Cholim from its foundation in 1883, as is to be seen from its Minutes (MS.) *passim*. He taught in the Sunday School of congregation B'ne Jeshurun from 1882 until probably the end of 1884. B'ne Jeshurun, *Minutes*, Sept. 3, 1882, Nov. 5, 1882, Dec. 3, 1882, Dec. 7, 1884.

51. *Milwaukee Journal*, Feb. 3, 1959; *Wisc. JC*, Mar. 18, 1927, p. 1.

52. *Wchblt.*, Jan. 7, 1916, p. 1; Oct. 26, 1917, p. 1; information from Mr. Robert Hess. Rubin and Padway became partners for a time. The earlier sources give 1888 as his year of birth.

53. *Wchblt.*, Nov. 23, 1917. *Perchonok Memoirs*, pp. 115-116.

54. *Daily Wisconsin*, Feb. 25, 1918.

55. Zionist Organization of America, *Report of the National Executive Committee*, 1918-1919, pp. 14-19; cf. Zionist Organization of America, *Record of Zionist Achievement in America, 1918-1919*, p. 50.

56. *Perchonok Memoirs,* pp. 71, 99, 110-11.
57. Statement of Mr. Bert C. Broude.
58. *Wchblt.,* Nov. 25, 1921, p. 1; *Wisc. JC,* Dec. 16, 1921, p. 1; Apr. 27, 1923, p. 1.
59. *Wisc. JC,* Mar. 18, 1927, p. 1.
60. *Perchonok Memoirs,* pp. 75-78.

X. EDUCATION FOR CAREER AND COMMUNITY

1. Cf. *supra,* p. 52.
2. Still, pp. 121-22, 260-61, 268-72.
3. Board of School Directors, *54th Annual Report* (1913), pp. 82, 119-21; George LaPiana, *The Italians in Milwaukee* (Milwaukee, 1916), pp. 39-40; *Wchblt.,* Oct. 6, 1916. German was thus taught in the elementary schools until the anti-German hysteria during World War I. B. A. Abrams' successor in charge of German instruction, Leo Stern (a Jew?), was a leading pro-German partisan until 1917. Still, p. 462.
4. *Wchblt.,* May 1, 1914, p. 1; June 26, 1914, p. 1; Sept. 18, 1914, p. 1; June 18, 1915, p. 1; April 21, 1916, p. 1. The reports of the Jewish Settlement for 1908, 1910, and 1921, incorporated in the F. J. C. *Ann. Reps.* for those years, show similar proportions of Jewish pupils.
5. U. S. Immigration Commission, *Reports,* vol. 26, Tables 62 and 63, pp. 736-737.
6. *Sent.,* Aug. 9, 1875, p. 8.
7. *Der Zeitgeist,* July 8, 1880, p. 228; *Sent.,* June 22, 1880, p. 8; May 17 (p. 6) and June 23, 1882, p. 2.
8. *Sent.,* May 26, 1899, p. 3; Cf. also *Der Zeitgeist,* July 8, 1880, p. 228; *Sent.,* June 26, 1887, p. 11, June 27, 1890, p. 3; May 16, 1896, p. 3.
9. In an address to Poale Zion, Rabbi Scheinfeld censured this practice. Louis Perchonok, *Memoirs* (Yiddish MS.), pp. 19-20.
10. Laurence M. Larson, *The Log Book of a Young Immigrant* (Northfield, Minn., 1939), pp. 283-84.
11. *Der Zeitgeist,* July 8, 1880, p. 228; *Am. Isr.,* June 26, 1890, p. 5.
12. *Der Zeitgeist,* Aug. 4, 1881, p. 264; Cf. also *Sent.,* July 20, 1876, p. 5; July 12, 1877, p. 3; July 17, 1881, p. 11; Aug. 27, 1884, p. 3; Dec. 23, 1894, p. 17; Cf. *supra,* pp. 109-110.
13. *Am. Isr.,* Feb. 20, 1913, p. 6.
14. *Wchblt.,* Sept. 24, 1915, p. 1.
15. *Idisher Kemfer,* July 22 and 29, 1910. This appears to have been the first effort made in the modern Hebrew movement in the secondary schools. Poale Zion was otherwise strongly devoted to Yiddish.
16. *Am. Isr.,* July 24 (p. 7), Aug. 11 (p. 7), Aug. 18, 1910, p. 5; Perchonok, *op. cit.,* pp. 51-57.
17. B'ne Jeshurun, *Minutes,* April 17, 1876, Nov. 5, 1876, Nov. 2, 1879, Dec. 26, 1880, Sept. 18, 1881; Emanu-El, *Minutes,* Aug. 10, 1873, Nov. 24, 1876, Aug. 5, 1888, May 6, 1889; *Der Zeitgeist,* Sept. 15, 1881, p. 312; Aug. 31, 1882, p. 288; *Sent.,* Nov. 13, 1891, p. 3; the *Directory* yearly mentions the schools briefly.
18. Emanu-El's enrollment was only about 40 when Rabbi Moses left in

1888, but almost doubled when Rabbi Hecht succeeded him. Neither school grew after the 1890's. The congregations' *Minutes* refer to the Sunday Schools *passim.*

19. *Sent.,* Aug. 9, 1875, p. 8.

20. However, B'ne Jeshurun's President L. H. Heller remarked that "less than half our our children have attended our school. . . . We regret to observe an indifference on their [parents'] part. . . ." *Am. Isr.,* Sept. 17, 1896, p. 2.

21. *Sent.,* Sept. 3, 1877, p. 2. The textbooks are Isaac M. Wise, *Judaism: Its Doctrines and Duties* (Cincinnati, 1872), and Benjamin Szold, *Reshith Da'ath: Catechism designed for the Religious instruction of Israelitish children* (Baltimore, 1874). On Jewish education during this period, see Moshe Davis, *Yahadut Amerika Be-Hitpathutah: The Shaping of American Judaism* (New York, 1951), pp. 101-19, 250-256 (in Hebrew; an English version is in preparation).

22. In 1914, B'ne Jeshurun's President warmly endorsed the recent resumption of Hebrew teaching, as a means of appreciating the beauty of Hebrew prayers. B'ne Jeshurun, *Minutes,* Sept. 6, 1914. In 1923, Emanu-El was considering the introduction of week-day Hebrew instruction. *Community Survey, 1923,* p. 48.

23. B'ne Jeshurun, *Minutes,* Nov. 5, 1882; Dec. 3, 1882; Sept. 6, 1884; Dec. 7, 1884; *Am. Isr.,* May 10, 1894, p. 2; *Sent.,* Sept. 4, 1876, p. 5. B'ne Jeshurun's teachers were paid as high as $15 monthly in 1923; *Minutes,* Oct. 7, 1923. At Emanu-El, a proposal to raise salaries from $10 to $20 monthly in 1925 was settled by granting a 50% raise; *Minutes,* Feb. 3 and April 13, 1925.

24. These quotations from B. A. Abrams come from his article "The Discipline in Our Sabbath Schools," *Der Zeitgeist,* Jan. 15, 1880, p. 23. Forty-three years later, a professional observer still noted: "Lack of time, indifferent or antagonistic home influence, inadequately equipped teachers, and the general tendency to provide the barest minimum of instruction are to be noted here as everywhere in the Sunday schools of Reform temples." *Community Survey, 1923,* p. 48. The Settlement also conducted a Sunday school. Cf. *supra,* p. 227.

25. Milwaukee County, *Record of Religious Societies,* I, p. 114; *Directory,* 1888, p. 47; *Blue Book,* pp. 53, 102-103; *Sent.,* Jan. 20 (p. 3), Sept. 2, 1893, p. 3; *Am. Isr.,* June 21, 1894, p. 3. The Hebrew Free School had rooms in the Beth Hamidrosh Hagodol's basement, and was a bone of content on between Rabbi Israelson and President Solomon Fein. *Am. Heb.,* June 23, 1893, p. 256; *Am. Isr.,* Aug. 26, 1897, p. 2; *Sent.,* Aug. 23, 1897, p. 3.

26. *AJYB, 1900-1901,* p. 489.

27. *Blue Book,* pp. 102-103.

28. F.J.C., *3rd Ann. Rep.* (1905).

29. *Community Survey, 1923,* p. 49.

30. *Wchblt.,* Jan. 8, 1915, p. 1; "Shostok's Sabbath and Sunday School," *Ibid.,* Jan. 27, 1916.

31. Ephraim E. Lisitzky, "The Beginning of a Period" (Hebrew), *Moznayim,* n.s. IV, 4 (March, 1957), pp. 241-42.

32. *Community Survey, 1923,* p. 49.

33. Ephraim E. Lisitzky, *loc. cit.* He took the Talmud Torah position in order to have a relatively steady income while studying pharmacy.
34. *Idem.*
35. *Wchblt.*, Nov. 29, 1916, p. 1. The weekly payments were: 12¢—2; 15¢—2; 17¢—3; 18¢—2; 25¢—49; 37¢—2; 40¢—3; 50¢—20; 62½¢—2; 75¢—6. *Wchblt.*, Nov. 5, 1915, p. 1; Nov. 27, 1914, p. 1. From November, 1921 to November, 1922, some 37% of the $8964 income came from tuition, and the remainder from subscriptions, collections, and benefits. Expenses were $9750, of which $6195 was paid to teachers. *Community Survey, 1923*, p. 54.
36. *Wchblt.*, June 26, 1914, Jan. 1, 1915, p. 1; August 20, 1915, p. 2.
37. *Wchblt.*, Nov. 29, 1916, p. 1; *Community Survey, 1923*, pp. 50-54; Reports of the Settlement in F. J. C., *Ann. Reps., 1920, 1924.*
38. *Wchblt.*, Oct. 9, 1914, p. 1.
39. *Community Survey, 1923*, pp. 56-65 by Alexander M. Dushkin, presents a detailed description and offers numerous suggestions; Louis Heifetz, *Negohot: Reflections* (My Life) (Milwaukee, 1942), is the Hebrew Memoir of one of the teachers; oral statement by Mr. Lisitzky to authors, November, 1959.
40. *Wchblt.*, Jan. 22, 1915, p. 1; May 22, 1914, p. 1; Report of the Settlement, in F. J. C., *13th Ann. Rep.* (1915). In the following year, these were "three periods weekly"; *idem, 14th Ann. Rep.* (1916). The *Community Survey, 1923*, makes no reference to this Folk Shule. See also Louis Perchonok, *Memoirs* (M.S. in Yiddish), pp. 81-83, 100-102, 135.
41. *Wchblt.*, Dec. 24, 1915, p. 1; in general, see J. Levin in *Die Tsukunft*, May, 1921, pp. 277-280; S. Niger Charney, *In Kamf far a Nayer Dertsiung* (N. Y., 1940).
42. *Wchblt.*, Feb. 25, 1916, p. 4; Jan. 19, 1917; p. 1.
43. *Community Survey, 1923*, p. 50.
44. *Ibid.*, p. 49.
45. F.J.C., *23rd and 24th Ann. Reps.* (*1924, 1925*).

XI. WORLD WAR I: A TIME OF HOPE AND GRIEF

1. *Wchblt.*, Oct. 2, 1914, p. 1.
2. *Ibid., passim.*
3. *Ibid.*, Oct. 30, 1914, p. 1.
4. *Ibid.*, Dec. 18, 1914, p. 1; Jan. 1, 1915.
5. *Ibid.*, Dec. 4, 1914, p. 1.
6. *Ibid.*, Sept. 24, 1915, p. 1; Nov. 5, 1915, p. 4.
7. *Ibid.*, Sept. 21, 1917, p. 4.
8. *Forverts*, undated clipping, early February, 1917.
9. Attempts were made by representatives of the People's Relief to establish a separate committee in Milwaukee in 1917, but they drew little support in the city. People's Relief was satisfied to receive a larger allocation of Ezer be Tzar funds. *Forverts*, undated clippings: early Sept., 1917; late Sept., 1917.
10. *Wchblt.*, Feb. 12, 1915, p. 1; Feb. 19, 1915, p. 1; Feb. 26, 1915, p. 1.
11. *Ibid.*, Jan. 21, 1916, p. 2.

12. *Idem.*
13. *Ibid.*, Jan. 27, 1916 (Special Edition) p. 1.
14. *Ibid.*, Feb. 4, 1916, p. 1.
15. *Ibid.*, Apr. 20, 1917, p. 1; May 11, 1917, p. 1.
16. *Ibid.*, May 11, 1917, p. 1.
17. See in general Oscar I. Janowsky, *The Jews and Minority Rights 1898-1919*, (N. Y., 1933), on the ideological and central aspects of these movements. See also Charles Reznikoff, ed., *Louis Marshall, Champion of Liberty; Selected Paper and Addresses*, 2 vols. (Phila., 1956), II, 305-675.
18. *Wchblt.*, July 2, 1915, p. 1.
19. *Ibid.*, Nov. 5, 19, 1915.
20. *Ibid.*, Nov. 26, 1915, Jan. 7, 1916.
21. *Ibid.*, June 23, 1916; July 14, 1916.
22. *Ibid.*, June 23, 1916.
23. *Forverts*, n.d., early March, 1917.
24. *Wchblt.*, Mar. 8, 1917.
25. *Ibid.*, June 29, 1917.
26. *Wchblt.*, Mar. 23, Apr. 6, 1917. *Yiddisher Record*, Apr. 12, 1917; Frederick I. Olson, *The Milwaukee Socialist Party, 1897-1941* (Harvard University thesis, 1952).
27. *Wchblt.*, Apr. 19, 1918, p. 1.
28. *Wchblt.*, Apr. 1, 1921, p. 1. An early committee began the job: *Ibid.*, Aug. 23, 1918
29. *Blue Book*, p. 173.
30. *Idem.* Their names were: Dan Cohen, Peter R. Feldman, Raymond Fredman, Joseph Galatz, Edward Hamilton, Max Heimer, Alfred H. Israel, Albert C. Labutsky, Harry Assovsky, Emil Reitman, Joseph Silverberg, Hyman Tishler, Sidney Weller. A memorial tablet is affixed in the lobby of the Jewish Community Center.
31. *Wchblt.*, Sept. 21, 1917.
32. *Ibid.*, July 19, 1918. In the talmundic tractate Berakhot 10a, the story is told that Rabbi Meir's wife Beruriah heard him pray for the death of wicked neighbors who were embittering his life. Quoting Psalms 104:35, she enjoined him to pray instead that wickedness vanish, and that evildoers would thus disappear. Rabbi Meir did so, with a salutary effect upon his neighbors.
33. *Forverts*, undated clipping, early September, 1917. Poale Zion, torn between its pacifism and Zionism, debated the Jewish Legion call at length before deciding "to remain neutral." Perchonok, *Memoirs*, p. 116.
34. *Wchblt.*, Mar. 22, 1918; April 12, 1918; April 19, 1918; April 26, 1918; June 28, 1918.
35. *Ibid.*, Aug. 9, 1918; Aug. 16, 1918; Aug. 23, 1918; Aug. 30, 1918; Sept. 27, 1918; Apr. 25, 1919; Sept. 21, 1919; Nov. 2, 1919; Sept. 5, 1920; June 8, 1921. Strelsin taught English at Herzliah High School in Tel Aviv, and was a member of Haganah. "When the riots broke out in 1921 and when he heard that Arabs were killing Jews, he immediately decided to go to Jaffa to help. He approached one of our Palestinian Legionaires, the late Nahum Hertzberg, to join him. Hertzberg asked him whether he had any fire arms. The answer was 'No', but he pulled out a knife and said: 'With

this I will go to defend Jewish lives.' He went by himself and was killed (actually stoned to death) in one of Jaffa's side streets." From a statement by Mr. Sam Dror, forwarded by Mr. L. Cheifetz, Secretary, Bet Hagdudim Ltd., Avichail, Israel, dated February 3, 1960. We are much indebted for this valuable reminiscence.

36. *Ibid.*, Oct. 9, 1917.
37. *Ibid.*, Oct. 5, 1917.
38. *Ibid.*, Aug. 2, 1918.
39. *Ibid.*, Oct. 12, 1917.
40. *Ibid.*, Aug. 23 and 30, 1918.
41. *Ibid.*, Nov. 1 and 8, 1918.
42. Ephraim E. Lisitzky in *Wchblt.*, Mar. 8, 1917. As a Hebrew educator and Zionist he was leading spokesman of the Congress movement. He became an eminent Hebrew poet and translator.
43. *Wchblt.*, May 18, 1917. Although the correspondence from Milwaukee in the *Forverts* belittled the movement, as did the *Forverts* itself (n.d., early June, 1917), the local Arbeiter Ring and Jewish unions made their own decision whether or not to participate. *Wchblt.*, June 1, 1917. It is not clear what they decided.
44. *Wchblt.*, June 8, 1917; Louis Perchonok, *Memoirs*, p. 113.
45. *Wchblt.*, June 15, 1917. Each affiliated organization paid $5.00 per fifty members, up to $25.00.
46. *Ibid.*, Nov. 15, 1918.
47. Advt. in *Forverts*, Apr. 12, 1919; Apr. 19, 1919.
48. *Sent.*, May 22, 1919, p. 4; May 23, 1919, p. 6; *Wchblt.*, May 25, 1919.
49. Quoted in *Wchblt.*, June 29, 1917. This was published soon after the American Jewish Congress elections, and is probably connected with the demands made for Jewish national minority rights in post-war treaties which were widely publicized.
50. *Sent.*, May 25, 1919, part II, p. 1.
51. *Ibid.*, May 29, 1919, p. 20; *Wchblt.*, May 26, 27, 28, and 29, 1919.
52. *Ibid.*, May 29, 1919.
53. *Ibid.*, May 29, 1919, p. 6.
54. *Ibid.*, May 29, 1919, p. 14.
55. *Ibid.*, June 1, 1919, part II, p. 1.
56. *Ibid.*, June 3, 1919. cf. E. Lifschutz, "The Pogroms in Poland of 1918-1919, the Morgenthau Committee and the American State Department" (Hebrew with English summaries), *Zion*, XXIII-XXIV, 1-2, 3-4, (1958-59), pp. 66-97, 194-211.
57. *Sent.*, June 5, 1919, p. 8.

PART III: GENERATION OF CRISES 1925-1950

I. SAFETY AMID TENSION

1. These figures come from the *Community Survey* of 1923, and it is of interest to compare them with a *Summary Report, Study of Group Needs, Services and the Jewish Community Center*, of December, 1961.

The latter survey, which passes the chronological bounds of this book, found 7,598 Jewish households in Milwaukee, and on that basis estimated 30,000 Jews in the city. The age proportions were:

	Est. Percentage	Est. Number
Under 5	8.2	2,460
5-13	16.4	4,920
14-17	4.8	1,440
18-25	8.2	2,460
26-59	46.4	13,920
60+	16.0	4,800
	100.0	30,000

The figure of 30,000 appears too high by about 2,000, since due allowance is not made for the childless and the unmarried and smaller families. An average of 1.96 children per Jewish household appears excessive.

1a. *HDS Report to Vocational Board*, April 20, 1938, p. 1 (mimeographed); interview with Miss Rebecca B. Tenenbaum, June 27, 1961.

2. *Report to Refugee Committee by Michael M. Galazan, Director, Jewish Vocational Service*, September 18, 1941, p. 1.

3. Interviews with Miss Tenenbaum (*supra*, note 1a) and Mr. Harri Hoffmann, June 20, 1961; *Wisc. JC*, March 17, 1939, p. 3.

4. Interview with Miss Tenenbaum (*supra*, note 1a); Milwaukee Jewish bodies also aided a refugee doctor to settle successfully in a small town in Illinois. *Report read before Refugee Committee*, September 18, 1941, pp. 2-3 (Typescript).

5. *HDS Report* (*supra*, note 1a), pp. 1-2; *Report to Jewish Vocational Service Board of Trustees*, Nov. 15, 1938 (typescript); *Report . . . Refugee Committee* (*supra*, note 4), p. 1; Helen D. Sadow, *German-Jewish Refugee Children*, Mar. 14, 1939 (typescript).

6. Personal statement by Dr. Herman Weil; *Wisc. JC*, Sept. 28, 1951, Sept. 7, 1956.

7. *Report . . . Refugee Committee* (*supra*, note 4), p. 1.

8. *Ibid.*, pp. 2-3.

9. Interview with Miss Tenenbaum (*supra*, note 1a).

10. Melvin S. Zaret, *Report on Services for Jewish Immigrants in Milwaukee*, Milwaukee Committee for Jewish Refugees, November, 1950.

11. This is based on passing references in the *Shtimme*, and the *Annual Reports* of the Amalgamated Clothing Workers; cf. Louis Levine, *The Women's Garment Workers* (N. Y., 1924), pp. 519, 551.

12. *Life and Labor Bulletin*, No. 68, Jan., 1929, pp. 1-2; *The Nation*, Nov. 7, 1928; *Men's Wear*, Sept. 5, 1928.

13. The figures derived from the City Directory's listing of dentists and identifying the names of Jews among them.

14. Information kindly supplied by Mr. Aaron Shansky.

15. The 1930 figure is drawn from the City Directory's list of lawyers and by identifying Jewish names among them. For 1950, see article by Harry A. Kovenock in *Wisc. JC*, Sept. 28, 1951, pp. 12-15.

16. The 1930 figure is drawn from the City Directory's list of physicians and by identifying Jewish names among them. However, only 635 physicians

were members of the Milwaukee County Medical Society. In 1950, 1075 belonged to the Society, and estimated 95% of the city's physicians. The number of Jewish physicians in 1948 may be as high as 224. In other words, the proportion of Jews mong the city's physicians rose from about 8% in 1930 to approximately 20% twenty years later. The 1948 figures are derived from Jacob J. Golub, M. D., *A Survey of the Health and Hospital Situation of the Jewish Community in Milwaukee, Wisconsin* (Milwaukee, 1948), pp. 73–80 (mimeographed). Dr. Mischa J. Lustok's figures in *Wisc. JC,* Sept. 28, 1951, p. 14, are derived from Golub.

17. See *General Bulletin of Marquette University, 1929-1932,* and *Bulletin* of Marquette's colleges for 1949-1951.

18. The data which follow are drawn from the annual *Municipal Government and Activities of the City of Milwaukee* and the *Milwaukee County Directory of Public Officials.*

19. Milwaukee Army and Navy Committee Bulletin (Jewish Welfare Board), II, 6 (July, 1944), p. 4.

20. The political behavior of Milwaukee Jews requires separate investigation. There is little question that they were among the Social Democratic Party's faithful groups in the city, and in state affairs they generally followed the La Follette tradition until its eclipse. The New Deal of Franklin D. Roosevelt drew their overwhelming support.

21. Based on *Annual Committee Organizational Reports of the Milwaukee Association of Commerce,* kindly made available for the years 1926 to 1950 by Mr. Robert F. Buntrock of the Association.

22. *Wisc. JC,* March 31, 1933, p. 1 ff.

23. *Ibid.,* Dec. 29, 1939, p. 1 ff.

24. *Ibid.,* July 28, 1939, p. 1.

25. Material on the Milwaukee Jewish Council and the problems it coped with was drawn from its full Minutes. We are greatly indebted to Mr. Sidney Sayles, then Director of the Council, for permission to use them. We are also grateful to Mr. Sayles and to Mr. Bert C. Broude for oral statements on Feb. 4, 1960.

26. Report of the Army and Navy Committee, Jewish Center of Milwaukee, Oct. 6, 1941.

27. "A Report to the Community," by the Milwaukee Army and Navy Committee, September, 1943.

28. Milwaukee Jewish Military Service Records, MS. Section, Wisconsin State Historical Society, Boxes 1, 2, and 6 SJ; interview with Mrs. Ned Alpert, Secretary, Milwaukee Army and Navy Committee, 1942-1946, July 4, 1961.

29. "Jewish Refugee List—from Milwaukee," June, 1946, Box SJ (as cited *supra,* note 28).

30. *Milwaukee Army-Navy News,* I, 3 (June, 1943), p. 4; I, 4 July, 1943), p. 4.

31. Box 6 SJ (as cited in note 28); 25th Silver Anniversary Ball (Booklet), Department of Wisconsin, Jewish War Veterans of the United States, Nov. 12, 1960.

32. Major Post's military record is cited from his personal effects. *Mil-*

waukee Army-Navy News, I, 5 (Nov., 1943), pp. 1-3; *The Overseas Sentinel*, National Jewish Welfare Board, July-August, 1945, pp. 40-41.
33. "A Report to the Community" by the Milwaukee Army and Navy Committee, Oct., 1943.

II. THE JEWISH COMMUNITY CONSOLIDATES

1. *Shtimme*, Sept. 22, 1930. p. 1; Oct. 10, 1930, p. 3; Oct. 31, 1930, p. 3; Nov. 7, 1930, p. 2.
2. Milwaukee Jewish Council, *Minutes*, Dec. 2, 1938, Dec. 9, 1938, Feb. 3, 1940, June 12, 1940, July 16, 1940, June 15, 1942, Sept. 22, 1942, May 5, 1943, Aug. 5, 1943, July 9, 1945.
3. *Wisc. JC.*, June 18, 1943.
4. *Shtimme*, Oct. 31, 1930, p. 6; Nov. 14, 1930, p. 6; Nov. 23, 1930, p. 5
5. In spite of many errors and inaccuracies, an article by Howard Polsky "A Study of Orthodoxy in Milwaukee: Social Characteristics, Beliefs, and Observances," in Marshall Sklare, ed., *The Jews: Social Patterns of an American Group* (Glencoe, 1958), pp. 325-335, gives a good impression of the situation.
6. *Wisc. JC.*, Sept. 15, 1933, p. 1 f.
7. Shortly after arrival, Rabbi Twerski became rabbi of Anshe Sfard, a connection which lasted until 1940. *Congregation Anshe Sfard Dedication Book*, January 31, 1960. Rabbi Twerski's personal synagogue was Beth Yehudah. Its articles of incorporation have no local precedent for establishing the position of a rabbi. He "shall supervise and direct the affairs of the congregation and give instructions to the directors as to the mode of conducting services and the affairs of the congregation. . . . " Corporation *Record, Milwaukee County*, 70, p. 212, Jan. 31, 1929.
8. *Wisc. JC*, Sept. 4, 1936, p. 4; Apr. 7, 1939, p. 7.
9. *Ibid.*, Dec. 3, 1948, p. 1; *Congregation Anshe Sfard Dedication Book*, January 31, 1960.
10. *Wisc. JC*, Oct. 26, 1945, p. 7.
10a. *Milwaukee Journal*, March 8, 1960; interviews with Fred W. and Dr. Burton Goodman, Seymour Bensman and Max Silberg, March 8, 1960.
11. *Minutes*, Temple Beth El., Oct. 21, 1945; Articles of Incorporation, Milwaukee Greater Temple, Dec. 23, 1945; Beth El Ner Tamid Synagogue Dedication (booklet), Sept. 7-9, 1951.
12. *Wisc. JC*, May 23, 1930, p. 1. f.
13. *Ibid.*, Apr. 27, 1945, p. 2.
14. One might mention Rabbi Morris J. Urich's Youth Free Synagogue, which met during 1933 at the North Side Auditorium. It attempted "to enlist the young and middle-aged professional and businessman," with "a free pulpit," forums, social activities, and so forth. *Wisc. JC*, Aug. 25, 1933, p. 3.
15. *Ibid.*, Sept. 25, 1931, p. 5.
16. *Shtimme*, Oct. 31, 1930, p. 7.
17. *Ibid.*, Sept 18, 1931, p. 5.
18. *Ibid.*
19. *Jewish Community Survey of Milwaukee*, 1923, pp. 1-3, 45-65

(mimeographed). A perhaps unique copy is at the Council of Jewish Federations and Welfare Funds, New York, and was kindly made available. The section on education was prepared by Alexander M. Dushkin.

19a. Federated Jewish Charities, 28th Annual Statement.

20. *Wisc. JC*, Dec. 31, 1926, p. 4; the Annual Statements of the Federated Jewish Charities included financial reports of the Talmud Torah.

21. Survey, 1923, p. 50.

22. *Wisc. JC*, Jan. 7, 1927, p. 6.

23. These data are derived from Poale Zion, *Minutes*, 1929-1940, *passim*.

24. Israel B. Rappaport, *Report on a Preliminary Survey of Jewish Education in Milwaukee, Wisconsin, submitted to the Milwaukee Jewish Welfare Fund*, August 7, 1941 (hectographed). A copy is at the Council of Jewish Federations and Welfare Funds, New York, and was kindly made available. In 1950, Aharon Kessler of the American Association for Jewish Education published his *Evaluation of the Bureau of Jewish Education of Milwaukee, Wisconsin* (mimeographed), which found 1579 children at Jewish schools in the city. It contained detailed statistics, as well as administrative recommendations for the future.

25. *Wisc. JC.*, April 1, 1927, p. 9; March 21, 1930, p. 5; March 6, 1931 p. 1.

25A. *Ibid.*, Sept. 7, 1956.

26. *Ibid.*, Oct. 22, 1948.

27. Helen Bertha Goetsch, *Parental Income and College Opportunities*, Teachers College, Columbia University, Contributions to Education, No. 795, (New York, 1940) pp. 111-115, 141.

28. Records of Avukah, *passim*; *Wisc. JC*, July 6, 1945, p. 5.

29. M. Weingrod, in *Shtimme*, Sept. 22, 1930, p. 4.

30. *Wisc. JC*, Aug. 6, 1926, p. 5.

31. *Shtimme*, Sept. 22, 1930, p. 2.

32. *Idem.*, p. 7.

33. *Shtimme*, Sept. 11, 1931, p. 2.

34. *Wisc. JC.*, April 13, 1945, p. 2.

35. Survey, 1923, pp. 86-102, gives elaborate information.

36. *Wisc. JC.*, Mar. 20, 1931, pp. 1, 8; Mar. 27, 1931, p. 1; Sept. 25, 1931, p. 5; Mar. 23, 1945, p. 11; Apr. 27, 1945, p. 10.

37. His published works are: *Luah haDorot* (Chronology), Milwaukee, 1923; *Negohot:* (Reflections), Milwaukee, 1942. The grammar exists in MS.

38. *Milwaukee Journal*, Sept. 30, 1928.

39. *Shtimme*, Sept. 22, 1930, p. 2; interview with Mr. Esselin, Milwaukee, May 25, 1960. His poems won a national award of the Jewish Book Council for 1955. *Milwaukee Journal*, June 5, 1955.

40. Records of the group were kindly made available by Mr. Howard Weinshel. *Wisc. JC.*, Nov. 19, 1948, p. 9.

41. A perhaps unique incomplete file of the *Shtimme* is in the Jewish Division of the New York Public Library. Mr. Arthur Spiegel claimed that the *Shtimme* "was issued for at least two years." Interview, December 29, 1960.

42. Programs of these events, dated March 21-29, 1936, March 29-31, 1941.

There also existed a "Jewish Band" and the "Halevy Chorus." Several vocal ensembles existed in the city at various times.

43. Program of this event, March, 19-21, 1938.

44. Survey, 1923, pp. 66-85; "The Duties of the Community", *Shtimme*, Oct. 10, 1930, p. 6; J. J. Golub, *Survey*, 1948; *Wisc. JC.*, Dec. 2, 1955. The Annual Reports of the Federated Jewish Charities suppy detailed information about the hospital.

45. Records of the Jewish Home for the Aged were kindly made available. Survey, 1923, pp. 8, 26-29, 35-36. On the Jewish Children's Home, see the Federated Jewish Charities *Annual Report*, 1927; interviews with Mr. Frank Grossman, past president of the Home, and Miss Rebecca B. Tennenbaum, December 20, 1960; Ben L. Grossman, *Home for Aged Jews, Milwaukee, Wisconsin. Survey Report* (Milwaukee February, 1951). A copy of this mimeographed report was kindly made available by the Council of Jewish Federations and Welfare Funds, New York.

46. *Wisc. JC.*, April 18, 1930, Sec. 4, p. 1.

47. *Ibid.*, Nov. 21, 1930.

48. *Wisc. JC.*, Nov. 20, 1931, p. 5; the J.S.S.A. Annual Reports, and a historical booklet which it published for its 72nd Annual Meeting, Sept. 25, 1940.

49. *Wisc. JC.*, Apr. 18, 1930, p. 1 ff.; Nov. 20, 1931, p. 1 ff.; the *Shtimme* regularly attacked the structure of the Federated Jewish Charities, while pleading with its readers to contribute during campaigns.

50. *Wisc. JC.*, Jan. 10, 1930, p. 1.

51. *Ibid.*, Apr. 18, 1930, Sec. 4, p. 1 ff.

52. Louis Perchonok, *op. cit.*, pp. 126-127.

53. In 1933, the Jewish unit raised $66,323 of the $864,851 raised by the Chest. *Wisc. JC.*, Oct. 27, 1933, p. 1 ff. Not all money donated by Jews was given through the Jewish unit.

54. *Wisc. JC.*, Aug. 4, 1933, p. 1.

55. *Ibid.*, Feb. 28, 1936, p. 5; March 20, 1936, p. 1.

56. *Ibid.*, May 29, 1936, p. 1.

57. We are greatly indebted to Mr. Melvin S. Zaret, Executive Director of the Fund, for furnishing us with valuable factual material concerning its activities.

58. *Wisc. JC.*, Jan. 6, 1939, p. 1.

59. *Ibid.*, June 9, 1939, p. 1 ff; July 7, 1939, p. 1.

60. The goal was $344,538. *Ibid.*, May 8, 1942, p. 1 ff; June 12, 1942, p. 3.

61. *Ibid.*, Feb. 6, 1948, p. 1; Mar. 12, 1948, p. 1; June 11, 1948, p. 1; June 18, 1948, p. 1.

62. See Walter A. Lurie, *A Study of the Milwaukee Jewish Vocational Service.* June 30, 1952. A copy of this mimeographed report was kindly made available by the Council of Jewish Federations and Welfare Funds, New York.

III. MILWAUKEE JEWRY'S EXPANDED HORIZONS

1. *Wisc. JC.*, March 18, 1927, p. 1; Jan. 27, 1939, p. 3; *Membership List of the Zionist Organization Milwaukee District*, 1942-1943, leaflet. Most of

the material upon which this chapter is based comes from the files of the Milwaukee Zionist Emergency Council, in the possession of Rabbi Louis J. Swichkow, its Chairman from 1943 to 1960.

2. Louis Perchonok, *op. cit.*, pp. 103-159.

3. *Wisc. JC.*, April 17, 1936, p. 3; the Milwaukee Zionist Emergency Council files contain a list of every local Jewish body in 1944, and their membership.

4. *Wisc. JC.*, Sept. 30, 1945.

5. This is based on the scrapbook of Milwaukee Hadassah, which was kindly made available.

6. *Wisc. JC.*, June 23, 1939, p. 5.

BIBLIOGRAPHY
APPENDICES
INDEX

Bibliography

I. MANUSCRIPT MATERIAL

A. *Jewish Institutions*

Avukah. Minute Book, 1927-1929. In the possession of Dr. Eugene C. Heifetz, former president of Avukah.

B'nai B'rith, Gilead Lodge No. 41. Minute Book, 1906-1914.* Abstract of Title, Spring Hill Cemetery.

Chevra Bikur Cholim. Minute Book, 1883-1930. In German until 1910. Congregation Emanu-El B'ne Jeshurun.

Congregation Anshe Emeth. Constitution, By-Laws, and Rules of Order, 1856; Record Book, 1860-1865. Congregation Emanu-El B'ne Jeshurun.

Congregation Beth El. Minute Book, 1943-1949; list of charter members; initial officers, directors, and members of the Sisterhood (typed).

Congregation Beth El-Ner Tamid. Minute Book, 1949-1951.

Congregation B'ne Israel Anshi Hungari. Chevra Kadisha. Minute Book, 1909-1950. German and English.

Congregation B'ne Jeshurun. Minute Book, 1875-1927. In German until 1906. Congregation Emanu-El B'ne Jeshurun.

Congregation Emanu-El. Minute Book, 1869-1927. Congregation Emanu-El B'ne Jeshurun.

Congregation Emanu-El B'ne Jeshurun. "Record concerning bodies which have been buried on the Burial Ground of the Congregation B'ne Jeshurun from

September, 1861 and thereafter" [Old Jewish Cemetery Record Book, 1861-1876]. Abstract of Title, Old Jewish Cemetery. Supplementary Burial List, Old Jewish Cemetery, 1936 (typed).

Ezra BeTzar. Minute Book, January 23, 1917-February 12, 1918.*

Hachnosas Orchim (Hebrew Sheltering Home). Minutes and Accounts, 1901-1937.*

Hebrew Relief Association. Minute Book, 1867-1898. In German until 1879. Milwaukee Jewish Family and Children's Service.

Home for Aged Jews, Milwaukee.
Origin of the Home [n.d.] (Yiddish MS).
B'nos Israel Society, officers, 1906-1930 (Yiddish MS).
Minute Book, 1931-1949.
Officers of the Home, 1909-1930 (Yiddish MS).

Industrial Removal Office Papers, Baron de Hirsch Fund Archive. American Jewish Historical Society, New York.

Jewish National Fund Council, Milwaukee. Minute Book, 1939-1950.

Milwaukee Army and Navy Committee (Jewish Welfare Board). Individual records of Milwaukee Jews who served in World War II (Boxes 1 and 2 SJ).
List of Casualties and Awards; June, 1946 (Box 6 SJ).
List of Commissioned Officers from Milwaukee, June, 1946 (Box 6 SJ).
Military Record of Jewish Refugees of Milwaukee, June, 1946 (Box 6 SJ).
Box 6 SJ contains various data, such as names of wounded and lost in action, and correspondence. Wisconsin State Historical Society, Madison, MS Section.

Milwaukee Jewish Council. Minute Book, 1938-1950.

Milwaukee Zionist Emergency Council. Correspondence, resolutions, press releases, clippings, and a list of all Jewish organizations in the city, 1942-1950.*

Poale Zion (Labor Zionist Organization of America), Milwaukee. Minute Book, 1926-1945.*

*Custody of authors

B. Public Records—Local, State, Federal

Milwaukee County (Offices of the Clerk and Register of Deeds). Corporation Records. Record of Religious Societies. Records of Deeds.

Anshe B'rith Sholem (May 23, 1925), vol. 58, p. 7.

Association of the Home for Aged Jews (November 5, 1928), vol. 69, p. 185; amended (Milwaukee Home for Aged Jews, March 5, 1948), vol. 199, p. 380.

Beth El-Ner Tamid Synagogue (September 10, 1949), vol. 176, p. 587.

Congregation Agudas Achim (March 24, 1920), vol. 43, p. 293.

Congregation Anshe Emes (May 13, 1872), vol. I, p. 79.

Congregation Anshe Leibovitz (August 24, 1906), vol. X, p. 307.

Congregation Anshe Roumania (February 20, 1904), vol. T, p. 216; amended (Congregation Degel Israel Anshe Roumania, December 21, 1919), vol. 44, p. 602.

Congregation Anshe Sfard (July 30, 1908), vol. 27, p. 198; amended (July 11, 1926), vol. 61, p. 101.

Congregation Beth El (November 6, 1922), vol. 49, p. 610.

Congregation Beth Hatfiloh (November 24, 1905), vol. W, pp. 50-52.

Congregation Beth Israel (May 25, 1901), vol. l, p. 114.

Congregation Beth Yehudah (January 31, 1929), vol. 70, p. 212.

Congregation B'nai Jacob (February 17, 1924), vol. 58, p. 152; amended (January 26, 1926), vol. 59, p. 338.

Congregation B'ne Israel Anshi Hungari (August 7, 1899), vol. N, pp. 141-142; amended (May 25, 1924), vol. 54, p. 377.

Congregation B'ne Jeshurun (October 5, 1858), vol. I, pp. 14-15.

Congregation B'ny Abraham (November 13, 1913), vol. 35, p. 159.

Congregation Imanu-al (September 30, 1854), vol. I, p. 3.

Congregation Sinai (November 14, 1900), vol. O, p. 282.

Daughters of Israel Society (March 10, 1906), vol. W, p. 475.

Gilead Lodge No. 41, B'nai B'rith (February 14, 1867), vol. 115, pp. 179-180; Spring Hill Cemetery, Records of Deeds (July 6, 1876), Instrument No. 1439, vol. 149, p. 20; (July 28, 1936), Instrument No. 2095407, vol. 1466, p. 139.

Greenwood Cemetery Association (February 1, 1873), vol. I, p. 85.

Imanu-al Cemetery Association (May 4, 1850), vol. I, p. 6.

Jewish Hospital Association (May 26, 1902), vol. Q, pp. 250-253; amended (Mt. Sinai Hospital Association, December 12, 1913), vol. 35, pp. 195-197; articles amended (Mt. Sinai Hospital, November 7, 1950), vol. 189, pp. 406-413.

Milwaukee Greater Temple (December 18, 1945), vol. 133, p. 603.

Moses Montefiore Gemeinde (January 27, 1886), vol. I, p. 114.

Old Jewish Cemetery [B'ne Jeshurun], Records of Deeds (January 18, 1854), vol. 42, p. 62.

State of Wisconsin

At the State Historical Society, Madison.

First Wisconsin Territorial Census, Milwaukee County, 1836.

Wisconsin Territorial Census, Milwaukee County, 1836-1842.

Wisconsin Territorial Census, Milwaukee County, June, 1846.

Wisconsin Territorial Census, Milwaukee County (as of December 1, 1847), February, 1848.

Wisconsin State Census, City of Milwaukee, June, 1885, vol. II.

"An Act to incorporate the Ahabath Emuno Congregation . . . ," *General Acts Passed by the Legislature of Wisconsin in the Year 1856*, Chapter 47, page 48 (Madison, 1856).

"An Act to incorporate the Anshe Emeth Congregation . . . ," *General Acts Passed by the Legislature of*

Wisconsin in the Year 1856, Chapter 382, page 806 (Madison, 1856).

"An Act to incorporate the Congregation Emanuel . . . ," *General Laws Passed by the Legislature of Wisconsin in the Year* 1870. Chapter 63, pages 127-129 (Madison, 1870).

Adjutant General's Office:

Phillip Horwitz. Certificate of Civil War Service, dated January 12, 1956.

Jonas Goldschmied. Letter, dated February 21, 1956.

Jacob Mahler. Letter, dated January 31, 1956.

Alexander Metzel. Certificate of Service, dated March 22, 1956.

Nathan E. Neustadtl. Certificate of Service, dated January 31, 1956.

United States Government

General Services Administration, National Archives and Records Service, Washington, D.C.

Phillip Horwitz. Records of Service in the Mexican and Civil Wars.

Edward Katz. Letter, dated April 4, 1958.

(Major) Arthur L. Post. Military records, 1941-1944, now in the possession of Mr. and Mrs. John Post.

C. *Memoirs and Family Records*

Eppstein, Elias. Diary, 1871-1874. Comments on his tenure in Milwaukee. American Jewish Archives, Cincinnati, Ohio.

Friebert, Edward, Sr. Memoirs. Pertinent portions were made available through the courtesy of his son, Joseph Friebert. Jewish radicals during early twentieth century.

Mack Family:

Family history (typescript, 1 page).

Mack, Edwin S. Photostat of high school report card, 1885-1886.

Mack, Solomon. Passport, May, 1856, Germany. Obtained through courtesy of Mrs. Walter Mack Goldsmith.*

Perchonok, Louis. Memoirs (Yiddish). Courtesy of Mrs.

Louis Perchonok. Covers *ca.* 1905-1948. Important for Labor Zionism and American Jewish Congress activity.

Post, Arthur (Major). Diary, 1943. Recorded on New Britain Island during 101 days after his plane was shot down on June 20, 1943. In the possession of Mr. and Mrs. John Post.

Shakman, Maria Heller, Letter to Elenora and Jacque Riese, Milwaukee, January 29, 1866. Translated from German; made available by Mr. and Mrs. Walter Goldsmith.

Spitz, Alma, "Biographical Sketch of Moritz Spitz." MS at the American Jewish Archives, Cincinnati, Ohio.

D. *Interviews and Personal Statements*

Sol Abrams, February 9, 1955; information regarding the career of his father, B. A. Abrams.

Mrs. Eva Adelman, of Chicago, August 7, 1955; granddaughter of Joseph Glick who arrived in Milwaukee in the early 1880's and served as *mohel* and *shohet*; his activities in the Jewish immigrant community.

Mrs. Ned Alpert, July 4, 1961; information on the activities of the Milwaukee Army and Navy Committee from 1942 to 1946 of which she was Secretary.

Glenn E. Burg, of the Milwaukee Medical Society, Milwaukee County, June 26, 1961; statistics on physicians affiliated with the Milwaukee County Medical Society.

Bert C. Broude, February 4, 1960; information on the Jewish Welfare Fund during the 1940's, and the Anti-Defamation League in Wisconsin.

Isidor Cohen, past president of the Milwaukee Talmud Torah and the Milwaukee Home for Aged Jews, November 12, 1957; recollections of Jewish life between 1898 and 1920.

Sam Dror, written statement re: Moshe Strelzin; forwarded by Mr. L. Cheifetz, Secretary, Bet Hagdudim, Ltd., Avichail, Israel, dated February 3, 1960.

Louis Frank, brother of Moses Frank (second Jewish child born in Milwaukee), March 3, 1956.

Walter Goldsmith, great grandson of Maria Heller Shakman, October 5, 1954; family history.

Mrs. Walter Mack Goldsmith, October 5, 1954; information concerning her father Edwin S. Mack, and her grandfather, Herman S. Mack.

Fred W. and Dr. Burton Goodman, and Seymour Bensman, November 30, 1960; the origin of the Goodman and Bensman Funeral Homes, founded by Harry Goodman and Sander Bensman.

Morris Gordon and Morton Wax, December 30, 1960; membership of the Milwaukee Zionist District, Z.O.A., in the 1940's.

Frank Grossman, December 20, 1960; early history of the Milwaukee Jewish Orphan Home, of which he was co-founder and president.

Robert A. Hess, February 4, 1960; recollections of immigrant Jewish life; impressions of social, political, and Zionist activities.

Moses Abraham Hiller, May 22, 1955; one of the first group of nine Russian-Jewish immigrants who arrived in Milwaukee in October, 1881. Reminiscences of the voyage; religious and economic life in the city at the close of the nineteenth century.

Harri Hoffmann, June 25, 1961; German Jewish refugees, *ca.* 1933-1950.

Samuel Kaufman, January 30, 1956; brought to Milwaukee in 1887, at the age of one month; Jewish life at the turn of the century; Jews in the cap-making trade; labor conditions; the treatment of Jewish peddlers.

Mrs. George Keller, Executive Secretary of the Milwaukee Jewish National Fund Office, December 30, 1960; data on finances of the Jewish National Fund, 1939-1950.

Dr. Ephraim Lisitzky, oral statement, November, 1959. Reminiscences on Jewish education and cultural and communal activities in Milwaukee, 1908-1912; 1914-1917.

Nathan Pereles, Jr., October 11, 1954; recollections concerning his grandfather, Nathan Pereles.

B. F. Saltzstein, December 11, 1962; information regarding collapse of the Federated Jewish Charities.

Sidney Sayles, Executive Director of the Milwaukee Jewish Council, February 4, 1960; activities of the Council.

Amram Scheinfeld, New York, oral statement, November, 1959; Jewish life in Milwaukee and recollections of his father, Rabbi Solomon I. Scheinfeld.

Miss Rosalie Scheinfeld, November 6, 1958; reminiscences of her father, Rabbi Solomon I. Scheinfeld; social and economic conditions in the city.

Hyman Seidelman, December 30, 1960; recollections of Zionism and the Milwaukee Jewish National Fund.

Max Silberg, June 18, 1961; description of funerary practices in Milwaukee, *ca.* 1900, before the establishment of the first Jewish Funeral Home.

Arthur Spiegel, December 29, 1960; information on the Milwaukee *Idishe Stimme* which he published.

Miss Rebecca B. Tenenbaum, June 27, 1961; German refugees during the 1930's and 1940's and the Milwaukee Jewish Family and Children's Service.

Isidor Tuchman and Morris Weingrod, December 25, 1960; early history of the Poale Zion, Farband, and Pioneer Women's Organization.

Dr. Herman Weil, June 25, 1961; information on the New Home Club and Jewish refugees in Milwaukee after 1933.

Melvin S. Zaret, Executive Director of the Milwaukee Jewish Welfare Fund, February 4, 1960; information and statistics on J. W. F. campaigns.

Mrs. Sol (Flora Rubin) Zien, October 27, 1955; recollections of Jewish social and political activities; information on William B. Rubin and Jacob H. Rubin; comments on descendants of early Jewish families, including those who intermarried.

II. GOVERNMENT PUBLICATIONS

Milwaukee (City and County)

Annual Reports of the School Board of the City of Milwaukee, 1867-1900; 54th Annual Report of the Board of School Directors (1913).

Board of Public Land Commissioners, "Population Changes by Census Tracts . . . , 1920-1940," Milwaukee.

Manuals of the Common Council and of the Municipal Government of the City of Milwaukee, 1900-1920.

Manuals of the County Government of the Board of Supervisors, Milwaukee County, 1911-1925.

Milwaukee County [annual] Directories of Public Officials, 1925-1950, County Clerk, Milwaukee.

Municipal Government and Activities of the City of Milwaukee, Report of the Common Council (Compiled and edited by the Municipal Reference Library), Milwaukee *Annual Reports*, 1921-1950.

Report of the Mayor's Housing Commission, Milwaukee, 1933.

State of Wisconsin

Bureau of Labor and Industrial Statistics, State of Wisconsin, *Twelfth Biennial Report, 1905-1906*, Part IV, "The Housing Question in Wisconsin."

The Legislative Manual of the State of Wisconsin, A. J. Turner, complr., (Madison, 1873).

United States and Foreign

United States Commissioner General of Immigration, *Annual Reports*, 1905, 1912, 1917, 1922.

United States Immigration Commission, *Reports*, 42 vols. (Washington, D.C., Government Printing Office), 1908-1913. Volumes 26 and 27 are entitled "Immigrants in Cities" (Senate Document 338, 61 Cong., 2 sess., Washington, 1911). Volume 26 (pp. 680-765) includes Milwaukee.

Great Britain. Parliament. Reports to the Board of Trade on Alien Immigration. C. 7113, 1893, pp. 263, 282-283.

III. NEWSPAPERS AND PERIODICALS

A. *Local Newspapers*

The Milwaukee *Journal*, 1907-1949; 1954-1961; scattered.

Milwaukee *Sentinel*, 1837-1901; scattered, 1908-1959.

Daily Wisconsin (Milwaukee), August 8, 1875; February 25, 1918.
Evening Wisconsin (Milwaukee), 1872-1875, scattered; 1881-1882; November 9, 30, 1891; January 28, 1892; October 15, 1895.
Yenowine's News (Milwaukee), October 21, 1888.

B. *Jewish Newspapers: Local and Out of Town*
Allgemeine Zeitung Des Judentums, Leipzig, 1837-1880.
American Hebrew, New York, 1879-1900.
Archives Israélites, Paris, 1840-1880.
The Asmonean, New York, 1849-1858.
Forverts, New York, 1916-1919. (Microfilm collection of Yiddish press clippings on Milwaukee in the YIVO Archive.)
Freie Arbeiter Stimme, New York, 1891-1892.
Der Iddisher Arbeiter, New York, November 7, 1930.
Idisher Kemfer, New York, 1906-1907; 1910.
Jewish Chronicle, London, 1844-1880.
Jewish Chronicle, New York, 1844-1855.
The Israelite [or *The American Israelite*], Cincinnati, 1855-1922.
The Jewish Conservator, Chicago and Milwaukee, 1904-1905.
The Jewish Messenger, New York, 1857-1900.
Jewish Times, New York, 1869-1879.
Milwauker Idishe Shtimme (Milwaukee Jewish Voice), Milwaukee, 1930-1931.
Milwauker Wochenblat (The Jewish Daily Press), Milwaukee, 1914-1932.
The Maccabaean, New York, 1901-1920.
The Occident, Philadelphia, 1843-1869.
The Reform Advocate, Chicago, 1893-1900.
Sinai, Baltimore, 1856-1862.
Die Tsukunft, New York, May, 1921.
The Wisconsin Jewish Chronicle, Milwaukee, 1921-1961.
Yiddisher Arbeter Velt, Chicago, 1908-1909.
Yiddisher Record, Chicago, 1913.
Der Zeitgeist, Milwaukee, 1880-1882 (German).

C. *Other Periodicals*

Men's Wear, September 5, 1928.
The Nation, November 7, 1928.

IV. SCRAPBOOKS AND COLLECTIONS

Avukah. Scrapbook. In the possession of Dr. Eugene C. Heifetz, former president of Avukah.

Hadassah. Scrapbooks. Six volumes, 1920 to 1959; include newspaper clippings, programs, and organizational bulletins.

Horwitz, Isador S. Scrapbook. Undated newspaper clippings, mostly written by Horwitz prior to 1914 for the Milwaukee *Leader*. In the possession of his son, Mr. Hy Howard, West Los Angeles, California.

Perhift Players. Scrapbook. Covers the history of the Young Literary and Dramatic Society, Jewish Dramatic League, and the Perhift, from 1920 to 1961; photographs, programs, and newspaper clippings. In the possession of Mr. Howard Weinshel.

Joseph Saffro Collection. A rich variety of handbills, advertisements of meetings, newspaper clippings, and other printed material dealing with Milwaukee Zionism and Jewish education. Most items date from 1905 to 1919, and were probably written by Saffro.*

V. BOOKS AND ARTICLES

A. *Books*

Adler, Selig, and Connolly, Thomas E., *From Ararat to Suburbia* (Philadelphia, 1960.)

Amalgamated Clothing Workers of America, *Proceedings, Third, Fourth, Fifth, Sixth Biennial Conventions* (1918, 1920, 1922, 1924).

The American Jewish Year Book (Philadelphia), 1899–1900—1903-1904; 1905-1906—1907-1908; 1909-1910; 1914-1915; 1918-1919; 1937-1938.

Anderson, W. J., and Bleyer, Julius (eds.), *Milwaukee's Great Industries*, Association for the Advancement of Milwaukee (Milwaukee, 1892).

Andreas, A. T., publ. [Frank A. Flower], *History of Milwaukee from Prehistoric Times to the Present Date* (Chicago, 1881).

Baron, Salo Wittmayer, *A Social and Religious History of the Jews*, 3 vols. (New York, 1937).

Barry, Colman J., *The Catholic Church and German Americans* (Milwaukee, 1953).

Barton, Elmer E. (publr.), *Industrial History of Milwaukee—The Commercial, Manufacturing and Railway Metropolis of the Northwest* (Milwaukee, 1886).

Benjamin, I. J., *Three Years in America*, 1859-1862, 2 vols., translated by Charles Reznikoff (Philadelphia, 1956).

Blied, Benjamin J., *Three Archbishops of Milwaukee* (Milwaukee, 1955).

B'nai B'rith Manual, edited by Samuel S. Cohon (Cincinnati, 1926).

B'nai B'rith, *Proceedings of Annual Conventions*, District Grand Lodge No. 2, 1862-1869 District Grand Lodge No. 6, 1869-1950.

———, *Proceedings of the Constitution Grand Lodge Convention*, 1915, 1935.

Bremer, Fredrika, *The Homes of the New World: Impressions of America*, 2 vols. (New York, 1954).

Bruce, William George (ed.), *History of Milwaukee City and County*, 3 vols. (Chicago, 1922).

———, *Builders of Milwaukee* (Milwaukee, 1946).

Buck, James S., *Pioneer History of Milwaukee*, 2 vols. (Milwaukee, 1876 [rev. ed., 1890], 1881.)

———, *Milwaukee Under the Charter*, 2 vols. (Milwaukee, 1884, 1886).

Budish, J. M., *Geshikhte fun di Cloth Hat Cap un Millinery Arbayter*, 2nd ed. (New York, 1926).

Buntrock, Robert F. (ed.), *A Century of Organized Progress, Milwaukee Association of Commerce 1861-1961* (Milwaukee, 1961).

Burgin, Herz, *Di Geshikhte fun der Idisher Arbayter Bavegung in Amerika, Rusland un England* (New York, 1915).

Campbell, Monroe, Jr., and Wirtz, William, *The First

Fifty Years—A History of the National Council of Jewish Women, 1893-1943 (New York, 1943).

Charney, S. Niger, *In Kamf far a Nayer Dertsiung* (New York, 1940).

Conard, Howard Louis (ed.), *History of Milwaukee from its First Settlement to the Year 1895,* 3 vols. (Chicago, n.d.).

Davis, Moshe, *Yahadut Amerika Behitpathutah* (The Shaping of American Judaism) (New York, 1951).

Directories of the City of Milwaukee, 1847-1950.

Egbert, Donald D., and Persons, Stow (eds.), *Socialism and American Life,* 2 vols. (Princeton, 1952).

Elbogen, Ismar, *A Century of Jewish Life* (Philadelphia, 1946).

Ferber, Edna, *A Peculiar Treasure* (New York, 1939).

Glanz, Rudolf, *Jews in Relation to the Cultural Milieu of the Germans in America up to the Eighteen Eighties* (New York, 1947).

Goetsch, Helen Bertha, *Parental Income and College Opportunities,* Teachers College, Columbia University, Contributions to Education, No. 795 (New York, 1940).

Grayzel, Solomon, *A History of the Jews* (Philadelphia, 1955).

Gregory, John G., *History of Milwaukee, Wisconsin,* 4 vols. (Chicago, 1931).

Grinstein, Hyman B., *The Rise of the Jewish Community of New York, 1654-1860* (Philadelphia, 1945).

Hecht, Sigmund, *Epitome of Post-Biblical History* (Cincinnati, 1882).

Heifetz, Louis, *Luah HaDorot* (Chronological Tables) (Milwaukee, 1923).

———, *Negohot (Reflections)* (Milwaukee, 1942).

Higham, John, *Strangers in the Land; Patterns of American Nativism, 1860-1925* (New Brunswick, N.J., 1955).

Israelson, Solomon, *Neveh Shalom* (Sermons and Novellae) (Chicago, 1900).

———, *Divrey Shalom* (Sermons and Novellae) (Chicago, 1920).

Janowsky, Oscar I., *The Jews and Minority Rights, 1898-1919* (New York, 1933).

The Jewish Community Blue Book of Milwaukee and Wisconsin, The Wisconsin Jewish Chronicle, complr. and publr. (Milwaukee, 1924).
————, *Supplement,* The Wisconsin Jewish Chronicle, complr. and publr. (Milwaukee, 1926).
Jewish Encyclopedia, 12 vols. (New York, 1902-1906). s.v. "Milwaukee" (by Julius H. Meyer), vol. VIII. s.v. "United States of America" (by Joseph Jacobs), vol. XII.
Joseph, Samuel, *History of the Baron de Hirsch Fund* (n.p., 1935).
————, *Jewish Immigration to the United States from 1881 to 1910* (New York, 1914).
Kalisch, Isidor, *A Guide for Rational Inquiries into the Biblical Writings* (Cincinnati, 1857).
————, *Studies in Ancient and Modern Judaism . . . Selected Writings,* edited by Samuel Kalisch (New York, 1928).
Korn, Bertram W., *American Jewry and the Civil War* (Philadelphia, 1951).
————, *The American Reaction to the Mortara Case: 1858-1859* (Cincinnati, 1957).
La Piana, George, *The Italians in Milwaukee* (Milwaukee, 1916).
Larson, Laurence M., *The Log Book of a Young Immigrant* (Northfield, Minn., 1939).
Love, William D. Loss, *Wisconsin in the War of Rebellion; a History of all Regiments and Batteries* (Chicago, 1866).
Marcus, Jacob R. (ed.), *Memoirs of American Jews,* 1775-1865, 3 vols. (Philadelphia, 1955-1956).
Mason, Alpheus T., *Brandeis: A Free Man's Life* (New York, 1946).
Merk, Frederick, *Economic History of Wisconsin During the Civil War Decade,* Publication of the State Historical Society, *Studies* (Madison, 1916).
Nahin, H. L., M.D., *Constructive Socialism* (Milwaukee, 1910-1915).
Plaut, W. Gunther, *The Jews of Minnesota* (New York, 1959).

The First Convention of the National Council of Jewish Women held in New York, November 15-19, 1896, *Proceedings* (Philadelphia, 1897).

Reznikoff, Charles (ed.), *Louis Marshall, Champion of Liberty: Selected Papers and Addresses*, 2 vols. (Philadelphia, 1956).

Rosenberg, Stuart E., *The Jewish Community in Rochester, 1843-1925* (New York, 1954).

Roster of Wisconsin Troops in the Spanish American War, Ralph M. Immell, publr. (Madison, 1899).

Roster of Wisconsin Volunteers—War of Rebellion, 1861-1865, 2 vols. (Madison, 1886).

Sachs, A. S., *Di Geshikhte fun Arbeiter Ring*, 2 vols. (New York, 1925).

Schappes, Morris U. (ed.), *A Documentary History of the Jews in the United States, 1654-1875* (New York, 1950).

Scheinfeld, Solomon I., *Ziyyunim beDerekh HaHayim*, 2 vols. (Milwaukee, 1922, 1928).

———, *Adam HaMa'alah* (Milwaukee, 1931).

———, *Olam HaSheker* (Milwaukee, 1936).

———, *Divrei Hakhamim* (Milwaukee, 1941).

Still, Bayrd, *Milwaukee—The History of a City* (Madison, 1948).

Tcherikower, E. (ed.), *History of the Jewish Labor Movement in the United States* (Yiddish), 2 vols. (New York, 1943).

The U. S. Biographical Dictionary, Wisconsin volume (Chicago, 1877).

United States Census, 1870, *Population*, vol. I.

Watrous, Jerome A. (ed.), *Memoirs of Milwaukee County*, 2 vols. (Madison, 1909).

Wischnitzer, Mark, *To Dwell in Safety* (Philadelphia, 1948).

Wheeler, A. C., *The Chronicles of Milwaukee* (Milwaukee, 1861).

The Wisconsin Blue Book, 1915, 1927, 1935, 1944, 1958 (Madison).

Wise, Isaac, Mayer, *Reminiscences*, edited by David S. Philipson (Cincinnati, 1901).

Wolf, Simon, *The American Jew as Patriot, Soldier and Citizen*, edited by Louis E. Levy (Philadelphia, 1895). Jewish Colonization Association, *Amerikanishe Shtedt* (Petrograd, 1911). ("A collection of articles on several cities in the United States where Jewish immigrants may well establish themselves.") Zionist Organization of America, *Record of Zionist Achievement in America, 1918-1919.*

B. *Articles*

Adler, Cyrus, and Margalith, Aaron M., "American Intercession on Behalf of Jews in the Diplomatic Correspondence of the United States, 1840-1938," *Publications of the American Jewish Historical Society*, XXXVI (1943).

Benjamin, Ruth L., "Marcus Otterbourg, United States Minister to Mexico in 1867," *Publications of the American Jewish Historical Society*, XXXII, 65-98 (1931).

Davis, Moshe,"*Ha-Zofeh ba-Arez ha-Hadashah*: A source for the History of East European Jews in the United States" (Hebrew) *Sefer ha-Yovd li-Khevod Alexander Marx* (New York, 1950), 115-141.

Davis, Moshe, "Jewish Religious Life and Institutions in America (A Historical Study)," in *The Jews, Their History, Culture and Religion*, I, 354-453, edited by Louis Finkelstein (Philadelphia, 1949).

Deutsch, Herman J., "Yankee-Teuton Political Rivalry in Wisconsin Politics in the Seventies," *Wisconsin Magazine of History*, XIV, 3, 262-281 (1931); XIV, 4, 403-418 (1931).

Engelman, Uriah Zvi, "Jewish Statistics in the U.S. Census of Religious Bodies (1850-1936)," *Jewish Social Studies*, IX, 2, 128-140 (April, 1947).

Everest, Kate A., "How Wisconsin Came By Its Large German Element," Wisconsin Historical Society, *Collections*, XII, 295-330 (1892).

Goldhammer, Leo, "Jewish Emigration from Austria-Hungary in 1848-1849," *YIVO Annual of Jewish Social Science*, IX, 332-362 (1954).

Heineman, David E., "Jewish Beginnings in Michigan

before 1850," *Publications of the American Jewish Historical Society*, XIII, 47-70 (1905).

Kellogg, Amherst W., "Recollections of Life in Early Wisconsin," *Wisconsin Magazine of History*, VII, 478-490 (June, 1924).

Kellogg, Louise Phelps, "The Bennett Law in Wisconsin," *Wisconsin Magazine of History*, II, 3-25 (September, 1918).

Kisch, Guido, "The Revolution of 1848 and the Jewish 'On to America' Movement," *Publications of the American Jewish Historical Society*, XXXVIII, 3, 185-234 (March, 1949).

Korn, Bertram W., "Jewish 48'ers in America," *American Jewish Archives*, II, 1, 3-20 (June, 1949).

Lifschutz, E., "The Pogroms in Poland of 1918-1919, the Morgenthau Committee and the American State Department" (Hebrew with English Summaries), *Zion*, XXIII-XXIV, 1-2, 3-4, pp. 66-97, 194-211 (1958-1959).

Linfield, H. S., "Statistics of the Jews and Jewish Organizations in the United States: An Historical Review of Ten Censuses, 1850-1937," in *The American Jewish Year Book*, 1938-1939 (Philadelphia, 1938), 61-84.

Lisitzky, Ephraim E., "The Beginning of a Period" (Hebrew), *Moznayim*, n.s. IV, 4, 241-242 (March, 1957).

Pelling, Henry M., "The Rise and Decline of Socialism in Milwaukee," *Bulletin of the International Institute of Social History*, X (1955), 91-103.

Polsky, Howard, "A Study of Orthodoxy in Milwaukee: Social Characteristics, Beliefs, and Observances," in *The Jews: Social Patterns of an American Group*, edited by Marshall Sklare (Glencoe, 1958), 325-335.

Pool, David de Sola, "Judaism and the Synagogue," in *The American Jew, A Composite Portrait*, edited by Oscar I. Janowky (New York, 1942), 28-55.

Rabinowitz, Benjamin, "The Young Men's Hebrew Associations, 1854-1913," *Publications of the American Jewish Historical Society*, XXXVII, 221-326 (1947).

Roth, Benjamin M., "An Ethical Letter: Benjamin M. Roth to his Son Solomon, 1854" (translated by Albert H. Friedlander), *American Jewish Archives*, VI, 1, 6-9 (January, 1954).

Schafer, Joseph, "The Yankee and the Teuton in Wisconsin," *Wisconsin Magazine of History*, VII, 147-160 (December, 1923).

Scheinfeld, Amram, "I Remember," *The Wisconsin Jewish Chronicle*. September 28, 1951.

Scheinfeld, Solomon I., "LeTakanat HaYahadut," *Ha-Shiloah*, XXVI, (1912) 193-197.

Shpizman, L., "Etapn in der Geshikhte fun der Tsionist-isher Arbeter-Bavegung in di Faraynigte Shtatn," in *Geshikhte fun der Tsionistisher Arbeter-Bavegung in Tsofn-Amerike*, 2 vols. (New York, 1955).

Stern, Henry, "The Life Story of a Milwaukee Merchant," *Wisconsin Magazine of History*, IX, 1, 63-79 (September, 1925).

Sulzberger, David, "Growth of Jewish Population in the United States," *Publications of the American Jewish Historical Society*, VI, (1897) 141-149.

Swichkow, Louis J., "A Century of B'nai B'rith in Milwaukee," in *A Century of Service*, Gilead Lodge, B'nai B'rith Centennial Publication (Milwaukee, 1962).

Szajkowski, Zosa, "The Alliance Israelite Universelle in the United States, 1860-1949," *Publications of the American Jewish Historical Society*, XXXIX, 4, 389-443 (June 1950).

Szajkowski, Zosa, "The Attitude of American Jews to East European Jewish Immigration, 1881-1883," *Publications of the American Jewish Historical Society*, XL, 221-280 (March, 1951).

VI. PAMPHLETS AND UNPUBLISHED MATERIAL

"A Report to the Community," by the Milwaukee Army and Navy Committee of the Jewish Welfare Board, Sept., 1943.

Annual Committee Organizational Reports of the Milwaukee Association of Commerce, 1875-1950 (typescript). Made available through the courtesy of Mr. Robert F. Buntrock, Manager of the Association's Public Relations Division.

Annual Report of Milwaukee Bureau of Jewish Education, submitted by Meyer Gallin, Executive Director, to the Third Annual Meeting, July, 1951 (mimeographed).

Chernov, Ben L., "Twenty Years of Progress, a Report to the Community," by the President of the Milwaukee Jewish Council, December 8, 1959.

Congregation Anshai Lebowitz [sic.,] "Golden Anniversary Book," 1954.

Congregation Anshe Sfard, "Dedication Book," January 31, 1960.

Congregation Beth El, Bulletins, 1937-1949.

———, "Mortgage Redemption Jubilee," March 12, 1944.

Congregation Beth El Ner Tamid, Bulletins, 1949-1951.

———, Dedication Booklet, September 7-9, 1951.

Congregation Beth Israel, "60th Anniversary Publication, 1884-1944," 1944.

Congregation Emanu-El,
Charter and By-Laws, revised May 27, 1908.
Dedication Booklet, November 2-4, 1923.
Golden Anniversary (1869-1919) (booklet), Nov. 8, 1919.
Silver Jubilee Banquet Program, Oct. 18, 1894.

Congregation Emanu-El B'ne Jeshurum, Centennial Banquet Program, 1956.

"Dedication of Honor Roll," June 12, 1943, sponsored by the Milwaukee Army and Navy Committee of the Jewish Welfare Board.

Ezra B'tzar Reporter, September 27, 1916 (4 pp.).

Federated Jewish Charities of Milwaukee, Annual Reports, 1904-1930. Include annual reports of:
The Settlement; Abraham Lincoln House
Hebrew Relief Association; Jewish Social Service Association
Sisterhood of Personal Service
Mt. Sinai Hospital Association
Milwaukee Section, National Council of Jewish Women
Ladies' Relief Sewing Society
Children's Outing Society
Milwaukee Talmud Torah Association

————, Articles of Organization, By-Laws, and Rules of Order, November 13, 1902.

Federation of American Zionists, Report of Executive Committee, June 1, 1917.

Golub, Jacob J., M.D., "A Survey of the Health and Hospital Situation of the Jewish Community in Milwaukee, Wisconsin." (Milwaukee, 1948) (mimeographed). Council of Jewish Federations and Welfare Funds, New York, Library.

Grossman, Ben L., "Home for Aged Jews, Milwaukee, Wisconsin. Survey Report." (Milwaukee, February, 1951) (mimeographed). Council of Jewish Federations and Welfare Funds, New York, Library.

Hebrew Relief Association, Annual Reports, 1894-1899. Milwaukee Jewish Family and Children's Service.

"In Memoriam—Edwin S. Mack," Memorial of the Milwaukee County Bar Association. 1943.

"Jewish Community Survey of Milwaukee." 1923 (typescript). The section on Jewish education was written by Dr. Alexander Dushkin. Council of Jewish Federations and Welfare Funds, New York.

Jewish Social Service Association, 72nd Annual Meeting, September 25, 1940.

Kessler, Aharon, "Evaluation of the Bureau of Jewish Education of Milwaukee, Wisconsin." 1950 (mimeographed).

Life and Labor, Bulletin No. 68, January, 1929.

Lurie, Walter A., "A Study of the Milwaukee Jewish Vocational Service," Milwaukee, June 30, 1952 (mimeographed). Council of Jewish Federations and Welfare Funds, New York, Library.

Marquette University, General Bulletin, 1929-1932 (Milwaukee, 1929).

————, Bulletins of Marquette's Colleges, 1949-1951.

"Milwaukee Army-Navy News." Bulletins of the Milwaukee Army and Navy Committee of the Jewish Welfare Board, June, 1943 to December, 1945. Bulletins in the possession of Mrs. Ned Alpert.

Milwaukee Chamber of Commerce Report, 1863.

Milwaukee Exposition Reports, 1881-1905, Milwaukee

Industrial Exposition Association (Milwaukee, 1881-1906).

Milwaukee Home for Aged Jews, Annual Financial Statements, 1940-1942.

Milwaukee Zionist District, Zionist Organization of America. Membership list for 1942-1943 (typed).

Olson, Frederick I., "The Milwaukee Socialist Party, 1897-1941." (Ph.D. Thesis, Harvard University, 1952).

"The Overseas Sentinel," National Jewish Welfare Board, July-August, 1945.

"Perhift Players of the Jewish Community Center Celebrating 40 Years of Yiddish Theatre in Milwaukee, 1921-1961."

Rappaport, Israel B., "Report on a Preliminary Survey of Jewish Education in Milwaukee, Wisconsin." Submitted to the Milwaukee Jewish Welfare Fund, August 7, 1941 (hectographed).

Report at Joint Meeting, Ladies Auxiliary and Women's Aid: "Which Improvements Can We Expect with the Addition of the New Building?" by the Superintendent, November 14, 1949. Milwaukee Home for Aged.

"Report of the Army and Navy Committee," Jewish Center of Milwaukee, Bert C. Broude, Chairman. October 6, 1941.

Report to Jewish Vocational Service Board of Trustees, November 15, 1938 (typescript). Milwaukee Jewish Family and Children's Service.

Report to Refugee Committee, by Michael M. Galazan, Director of Jewish Vocational Service, September 18, 1941 (typescript). Milwaukee Jewish Family and Children's Service.

Report of the National Executive Committee of the Zionist Organization of America, 1918-1919.

Sadow, Helen D., "German-Jewish Refugee Children," March 14, 1939 (typescript). Milwaukee Jewish Family and Children's Service.

————, Report to Vocational Board, April 20, 1938 (mimeographed). Milwaukee Jewish Family and Children's Service.

"Summary Report, Study of Group Needs, Services and

the Jewish Community Center." Co-Sponsoring organizations: United Community Services, Jewish Welfare Fund, Jewish Community Center (mimeographed) (Jewish Community Center, Milwaukee, December, 1961).

25th Silver Anniversary Military Ball, Department of Wisconsin, Jewish War Veterans of the United States, November 12, 1960 (booklet).

Zaret, Melvin S., "Report on Services for Jewish Immigrants in Milwaukee," Milwaukee Committee for Jewish Refugees (mimeographed) (Milwaukee Jewish Family and Children's Service, November, 1950).

List of Appendices

		Page
1.	Jewish Immigration to Milwaukee, 1844-1855	466
2.	Inventories of Jewish Firms (1893)	468
3.	Values of Property Owned by Some of the City's "Heaviest Tax Payers" (1894)	469
4.	Congregation Anshe Emeth (1856)	469
	Constitution	
	By-Laws	
	Rules of Order	
5.	Rabbis of Milwaukee Congregations, 1857-1962	482
6.	Presidents of Milwaukee Congregations	485
	Congregation Imenu Al (1850)	
	Congregation Ahabath Emuno (1854)	
	Congregation Anshe Emeth (1855)	
	Congregation B'ne Jeshurun (1856)	
	Congregation Emanu-El (1869); Congregation Emanu-El B'ne Jeshurun (1927)	
	Congregation Anshe Emes (1871)	
	Congregation Anshe Jacob (1886)	
	Moses Montefiore Gemeinde (1886)	
	Congregation Beth Hamidrosh Hagodol (1892); Congregation Beth Israel (1901)	
	Congregation B'ne Israel (1887) [Anshe Hungari]	
	Congregation Anshe Sfard (1889)	
	Congregation Sinai (1900)	
	Congregation Agudas Achim [Anshe Polen] (1904)	
	Congregation Degel Israel [Anshe Roumania] (1904)	

Page

Congregation Anshe Lubavich (1906)
Congregation Beth Medrash Hagodol Anshe Sfard (1920)
Congregation Beth El (1921); Beth El Ner Tamid Synagogue (1949)
Congregation B'ne Jacob (1924)
Congregation Beth Yehudah (1929)
United Synagogue B'ne Sholom (1945)
Congregation Shalom (1951)
Congregation Sinai (1955)
Congregation Beth Hamedrosh Hagodel B'nai Sholom (1957)
Congregation Anshe Emeth (1958)

7. Memberships of Jewish Congregations in Milwaukee, 1950   493
8. Presidents of District Grand Lodge, B'nai B'rith (from Milwaukee)   493
9. Presidents of all B'nai B'rith lodges of Milwaukee   494
10. Independent Order, Free Sons of Israel—Presidents, 1879-1890   499
11. Past Masters of Harmony Lodge No. 142, F. & A. M., 1867-1895   499
12. Presidents of Chevra Bikur Cholim, 1868-1930   500
13. Presidents of Ladies' Relief Sewing Society, 1878-1931   500
14. Presidents of Hebrew Relief Society, Hebrew Relief Association, Jewish Social Service Association, and Jewish Family and Children's Service, 1867-1962   501
15. Circular of Hebrew Relief Society (calling for formation of United Relief Society), 1880   501
16. Income by year of Hebrew Relief Society and Hebrew Relief Association, 1877-1900   503
17. Presidents and Superintendents of Federated Jewish Charities, 1902-1937   503
18. Income and Number of Contributors by Year of Federated Jewish Charities, 1903-1931   504
19. Presidents and Campaign Chairmen of Milwaukee Jewish Welfare Fund; Executive Directors; 1938-1962   505
20. Milwaukee Jewish Welfare Fund—Funds Raised and Allocated, 1938-1961   506
21. Milwaukee Jewish Welfare Fund—Number of Givers by Categories, 1946-1961   507
22. Presidents, Judah ha Levi Gate No. 8, Order of the Knights of Zion and Milwaukee Zionist District, 1899-1962   508
23. Milwaukee Poale Zion—Presidents
Branch 1, Dr. Nachman Syrkin Branch, Dr. Nachman Syrkin

Page

Branch, Poale Zion, and Brandeis Branch; 1906-1962   509
24. Presidents of Mizrachi of Milwaukee, 1935-1962   510
25. Presidents, Milwaukee Chapter of Hadassah, 1920-1962   511
26. Milwaukee Council of Pioneer Women, 1949-1962   511
27. Presidents, Jewish National Fund Council of Milwaukee, 1925-1962   512
28. Presidents, Milwaukee Jewish Mission; The Settlement; Abraham Lincoln House, and Head Residents and Directors, 1896-1931   512
29. The Jewish Community Center of Milwaukee, Presidents and Directors, 1931-1962   513
30. Presidents, Milwaukee Jewish Council, 1938-1962   513
31. Presidents, Milwaukee Bureau of Jewish Education, 1944-1962   514
32. Milwaukee Jews who held public office, 1852-1962   514
33. Milwaukee Jews who died in World War II   519

APPENDIX 1

Jewish Immigration to Milwaukee, 1844–1855

Name	Land of Origin			Year of Arrival	
	Germany	Austria, Hungary, Bohemia	Other lands	1844–48	1849–55
Moses Weil			France	1844	
Isaac Neustadtl		Bohemia		1844	
Solomon Adler	Germany			1844	
J. B. Schram		Bohemia		1844	
Adolph Weil		Prague, Bohemia, Austria		1846	
Mrs. Isaac Neustadtl	Buck, Bavaria			1847	
Henry Friend	Antenhausen, Bavaria			1847	
Elias Friend	Antenhausen, Bavaria			1847	
Nathan Pereles		Sobotist, Neutra, Hungary		1847	
Mrs. Nathan Pereles		Prague, Bohemia		1847	
Henry Katz		Neustadtl, Bohemia		1847	
Emanuel Friend	Antenhausen, Bavaria			1847	
Bernard Heller		Citow, Bohemia		1848	
Marcus Otterbourg	Landau, Rhenish Palatinate, Bavaria			1848	
Albert Seligmann	Oppenheim, Germany			1848	
I. M. Hirschberg		Austria			1849
Jacob Morawetz		Bohemia			1849
Herman L. Mack	Altenkondstadt, Bavaria				1850
Jonas Schoenmann		Bohemia			before 1850
Moritz N. Becker	Bavaria				1852
Henry Stern	Markt-Breit, Bavaria				1850

Name	Place of origin	Country	Year
Isaac Stransky	Boehmisch, Leippe, Bohemia		1850
Marcus Teweles	Prague, Bohemia		1851
Louis Frank	Bavaria		1851
David Adler	Neustadt, Bohemia		1852
Mrs. David Adler	Lungendoerfels, Bohemia		1852
Leopold Newbouer	Prague, Bohemia		1852
A. L. Baer		France	1852
Gottlieb Patek	Radmitz, Bohemia		1852
Henry Mahler	Karlsruhe, Gy.		1852
Emanuel Silverman	Bavaria		1853
Moritz L. Morawetz	Radmitz, Bohemia		1853
Herman Stern	Karkt-Breit, Bav.		1853
A. W. Rich	Hungary		1853
Henry M. Mendel	Breslau, Gy.		1854
J. P. Frisch	Berlin, Gy.		1854
Theo. Schoenfeld	Bohemia		1854
Hugo Mack	Altenkundstadt, Bavaria		1854
Leo Sax	Bavaria		1854
Alex. Billstein	Hesse, Darmstadt, Germany		1854
Solomon Roth	Hechingen, Wuerttemberg, Germany	London, Eng.	1854
Louise Hyman	Germany		1854
Nathan Cahn			1854
Loebl Rindskopf	Bohemia		1854
Leopold Harris	Germany		early 1850's
Samuel Michael Cohn	Prussia		early 1850's
M. Markwell	Germany		early 1850's

SUMMARY

Immigrants from German lands	24
Immigrants from Hapsburg lands:	
Austria, Bohemia, and Hungary	20
Immigrants from France	2
Immigrants from England	1
Total	47

APPENDIX 2

Inventories of Jewish Firms (1893)*

David Adler and Sons	$140,000
Friend Bros. Clothing Co.	135,000
Landauer & Co.	80,000
Gimbel Bros.	60,000
Rich & Silber Dry Goods Co.	50,000
Leidersdorf & Co.	40,000
J. Katz & Co.	35,000
H. S. Mack & Co.	35,000
Benedict & Co.	30,000
H. Sheftels & Co.	25,000

*Sent., August 21, 1893, p. 3

APPENDIX 3

Values of Property Owned by Some of the City's "Heaviest Tax Payers" (1894)*

	Real Estate	Personal Property	Total
David Adler	$166,000	$149,000	$315,000
J. E. Friend & Bros.	165,000	125,000	290,000
H. S. Mack & Co.	235,000	26,000	261,000
B. & H. Stern	112,000	85,000	217,000
Pereles Brothers	124,000		124,000
B. M. Weil	82,000		82,000
L. A. Shakman	25,000	50,000	75,000
J. Friedmann	86,000	15,000	101,000

* *Sent.*, September 30, 1894, p. 9.

APPENDIX 4

(Translated from the German)

CONSTITUTION OF THE CONGREGATION ANSHE EMETH

Introduction

We, the undersigned members of the religious congregation of the Israelites in the city of Milwaukee, founded on the 14th of October, 1856-5617, a congregation consisting of 15 members, accept herewith the following constitution and its by-laws as a basis for this congregation, and guarantee that we shall observe same.

Article I

Name of the congregation

The name of the congregation shall be Kehillas Anshe Emeth.

Article II

Officers of the congregation

The business of the congregation shall be managed by a president, a vice president, treasurer, five trustees, and one secretary.

Article III

Election of Officers

Sec. I. The officers of the congregation shall be elected by secret ballot at an annual meeting which shall take place on the first Sunday after Rosh Hashanah, by a majority vote of those present at the meeting.

Sec. II. No member of the congregation living outside the city limits and no member who has not paid up his dues shall be eligible to become an officer.

Article IV

Powers and duties of the president and his officers

Sec. I. The president, vice president, treasurer, and trustees shall be the administrators of the congregation. They shall be responsible for the management of the affairs of the congregation; they, as well as their successors, shall administer all the property of the congregation in the interest of the congregation.

Sec. II. They shall not be permitted to bequeath or sell the real estate of the congregation without the consent of the congregation, given at a previous general meeting.

Sec. III. They shall not be permitted to legislate or carry out any transaction which, according to the by-laws, can be transacted only by all the members of the congregation.

Sec. IV. The president shall be permitted to dispose of up to $25.00 of the funds of the congregation, but shall be required to obtain the consent of the committee of trustees for an amount in excess of (the latter figure).

Sec. V. It shall be the duty of the president to see to it that the constitution and by-laws shall be observed by the congregation.

Sec. VI. The president shall chair each meeting. He shall vote only if there is a tie, so that his vote will be the deciding factor.

Sec. VII. The president may call meetings of the congregation or of the Executive Committee whenever he finds it necessary; it shall also be his duty, whenever either three members of the Executive Committee or any 15 members of the congregation ask for it in writing, to call a meeting.

Sec. VIII. The president must countersign any voucher of the treasurer.

Sec. IX. The president or any member of the Executive Committee shall be entitled to examine the books of the secretary or the treasurer.

Sec. X. The president and vice-president shall have their seats at the services on both sides of the Holy Ark, and shall be responsible for decorum and order during the services.

Sec. XI. Neither the president nor the vice-president, the treasurer, or any member of the Executive Committee shall receive any payment for their services.

Article V

Duties of the Vice-president

Sec. I. In case of absence of the president at the meetings, or in the synagogue, in the case of his resignation, in case of illness or death, the vice-president shall replace him and countersign the vouchers of the treasurer.

Sec. II. In such cases, the vice-president shall chair the meetings of the Board of Trustees.

Article VI

Duties of the Treasurer

Sec. I. The treasurer shall take charge of all monies of the congregation. He shall honor all orders signed by the president and countersigned by the secretary.

Sec. II. Before he assumes his office, he shall give a bond to his fellow officers. The amount of this bond is to be stipulated by the president and his fellow members.

Sec. III. The treasurer shall pay the congregation 7% interest per annum for any amount above $50.00 of any funds which belong to the congregation.

Sec. IV. He shall keep a correct account of all the income and expense of the congregation.

Sec. V. At every quarterly meeting, he shall render a report concerning the past three months, and at the annual meeting, a report concerning the financial status of the congregation.

Sec. VI. Upon relinquishing his office, he shall hand over all money, papers and everything else that belongs to the congregation in public meeting without any alterations, to his successor.

Article VII

Duties of the Executive Committee

Sec. I. The Executive shall be present at each meeting of the Executive Committee, and shall deal with any problem brought to the assembly by the president.

Sec. II. The chairman of the Executive Committee shall be the supervisor of the cemetery and assume the title of Gabe Bays Chaim.

Sec. III. It shall be the duty of the Executive Committee to examine each payment made, with the exception of such payment as rent, salary of officials, and etc.

Article VIII

Duties of the Secretary

Sec. I. The secretary shall be present at each meeting of the congregation and the Board of Trustees, and he shall record all the proceedings in German, in a special journal, with his signature.

Sec. II. He shall also have a book containing the constitution and its by-laws signed by all the members of the congregation and

Sec. III. He shall keep a record and main book [*haupt buch*] in which shall be recorded all sums paid to any member of the congregation, as well as contributions made to organizations or individuals from out of town.

Sec. IV. He shall receive all dues which he then will hand over to the treasurer against the receipt. He shall countersign each voucher issued by the president. He shall carry out all correspondence of the congregation.

Sec. VI. He shall render a quarterly report of all the expenses and income of the congregation, and shall furthermore give a bond which will be stipulated by the president and the Board of Trustees.

Sec. VII. He shall keep all documents and papers for the congregation, and upon relinquishing his office, he shall hand over all books, papers, etc., to his successor at a public meeting.

Article IX

Salaried Officials and Their Duties

Sec. I. Salaried officials, such as the *Shamash*, the *Shochet*, and the *Chazan*, shall be elected annually by majority vote at the general meeting, and contracts shall be drawn up in writing, wherein their salaries and duties shall be stipulated.

Sec. II. No *Shochet* may be accepted by the congregation unless he possesses a valid Kabbalah.

Sec. III. Any accusations against a salaried official concerning neglecting his duties or immoral conduct shall be brought in writing before a public meeting; the accused shall be given a copy and he shall have the right to defend himself at a public meeting. Should he be found guilty, the president may give him a warning for his first transgression, or suspend him, or dismiss him entirely from his office.

Article X

Meetings

Sec. 1. The four quarterly meetings shall be followed by an annual meeting, to be held on the first Sunday after Rosh Hashanah for the purpose of electing officials; and a quarterly meeting shall be held on the first Sunday of February, May, and August of each year.

Sec. 2. The president shall have the right to call a special meeting of the members of the Executive Committee whenever he finds it necessary.

Sec. 3. The Executive Committee shall meet on the first Sunday of every month.

Sec. 4. A quorum for the general meeting and any special meeting shall consist of one-third of all members within the city limits.

Sec. 5. The quorum at the meeting of the Executive Committee shall be reached when the president, vice-president, and three officers are present.

Sec. 6. Additional laws concerning meetings shall be stipulated in the by-laws.

Article XI

Qualifications for Membership and Eligibility for Office

Sec. 1. Only Israelites that observe the Covenant of Abraham may become members.

Sec. 2. Any individual whose wife happens not to be a member of the Jewish faith, cannot become a member of the congregation.

Sec. 3. No one with a deficient moral background may be accepted as a member.

Sec. 4. The initiation fee shall not be less than $5.00.

Sec. 5. An application for membership must be signed by the candidate and the initiation fee must be enclosed. Said application shall remain dormant for four weeks, and a committee shall be appointed to investigate and report on the candidate.

Sec. 6. A secret ballot shall then be cast, and if a majority can be found for his acceptance, he shall be declared accepted and shall be so informed by the secretary.

Sec. 7. He shall be acknowledged as a member only after having signed the constitution and by-laws. His refusal to sign shall exclude him from membership, in which case he shall also lose his initiation fees.

Sec. 8. In case he is not accepted by the majority of voters, his initial fee shall be refunded to him, and the secretary shall inform him concerning the decision.

Sec. 9. He can then re-apply after a period of six months.

Article XII

Schools

Sec. 1. This congregation shall, as soon as it finds it necessary, establish a school to instruct Jewish children, and a general meeting shall engage the necessary teachers and stipulate their salaries and duties in the form of written contracts.

Sec. 2. Each member shall have the right to send his children to the aforementioned school.

Sec. 3. A committee consisting of members familiar with Jewish educational problems shall be appointed, whose duty it shall be to supervise the school, and the teachers shall follow their directives.

Sec. 4. Children of non-members may be accepted. Applications shall be made to the school committee. Fees shall be stipulated later.

Sec. 5. Complaints against the teachers shall be addressed to a school committee. No member shall be allowed to contact the teachers directly. If he does so, he shall be fined $5.00.

Article XIII

Assessments

Sec. 1. The annual membership fees shall not be less than $9.00 a year or 75 cents a month.

Sec. 2. All bequests and gifts to the congregation shall be entered in addition to the name of the donor, into a special ledger, by the secretary of the congregation.

Article XIV

Rights and Privileges of Members

Sec. 1. Rights and privileges shall be the same for all members. However, if a member should join another congregation in the city, he shall no longer be eligible for any office, and shall lose his right to vote.

Sec. 2. A member who has not paid his dues for six months shall lose his right to vote. If he is delinquent for 12 months, he may be excluded.

Sec. 3. Members who have been excluded for this reason may be reinstated, provided they have paid all delinquent dues up to the date of such reinstatement.

Article XV

Concerning the Burial Place

Sec. 1. The cost of burial for members, their wives, children, mothers and fathers who are supported by their children, unmarried sisters or brothers under the age of 21, or people unable to bear the cost, shall be buried at the expense of the congregation.

Sec. 2. The burial expense for relatives of members shall not be less than $5.

Sec. 3. Non-members may, upon application to the president, be admitted to the burial place, provided they make a down payment of not less than $5 and not more than $50.

Sec. 4. If the president of the congregation and the officers are satisfied that the bequest of the deceased is insufficient to cover the expense of his burial, the difference shall be paid by the congregation.

Sec. 5. Persons not belonging to the Covenant of Abraham, or who refuse to be buried according to the Jewish ritual, cannot be buried at the burial grounds of the congregation.

Article XVI

Supplements

Sec. 1. This constitution shall, at all times, constitute the laws of the congregation, and all by-laws and regulations shall agree with it. No article and no section shall be excluded or withdrawn. The entire constitution, however, may be changed if, at any general meeting, an application, signed by 15 members, is turned over to one of the officers. It shall then be brought on the agenda of the next general meeting, and if two-thirds majority support it, it shall be accepted.

Sec. 2. As long as the congregation counts ten members, it shall not cease to exist, and its laws and regulations cannot be discontinued.

Sec. 3. This constitution shall immediately be signed by all its members and shall come into effect at once, this 22 day of December, 1856.

[50 names appear; signed personally by individual members]

F. M. Hardt	Gabriel Shoyer
M. Schwarzenberg	Emanuel M. Shoyer
Lazarus Schwarzenberg	M. Abraham
Henry Abraham	A. Blade
Joseph Weinberg	L. Blade
Louis Frank	J. Hochstadt
Jakob Bach	Jacob Mayer
B. I. Oettinger	Marcus Oberhouser
Aron Abraham	Jacob Herz
Si. Feist	Simon Herz
M. N. Becker	Simon Friebert
Michael Cohen	Hirsh
Jacob Kahn	Marcus Dryfoos
A. Mock	M. Engelman
Benjamin Mock	S. Stern
Henry Theobalt	B. Mock
Joseph Hyman	H. Kubitshek
Emanuel Friend	B. Millner
I. Blum	H. Cohen
Jacob Frank	H. Mak
M. Sohn	Solomon Roth
Isaak Frank	A. Boskawitz
Benoit Shwab	Nathan Schwarzenberg
Jacob Wirth	Moses Bach
Isaac Friedberg	Moses Kahn

(Translated from German)

BY-LAWS

Article I Decorum in the Synagogue

1. Ritual and order of prayers shall follow the Minhag Frankfurt.
2. Upon entering the Synagogue, each shall go to his seat.
3. No one shall leave his seat unless he is called to the Sefer Torah.
4. Talking in the Synagogue or disturbance of services is prohibited and is subject to payment of fine.
5. No one except the Cantor (*Chazan*) shall pray aloud and only in responsive readings is praying aloud permissible.
6. While the Torah is being read, no one may leave the Synagogue. But if it should be unavoidable, it shall be done without disturbing the congregation.
7. When the Torah is taken out or returned, or when the *Borchu* or *Kaddish* is being said, the congregation shall rise.
8. Calling up to the Torah shall be carried out by an officer and shall follow the order of affiliation with the congregation, in which all members shall participate.
9. Any member who is a chiuf shall inform the congregation.
10. Not more than three names, besides those of the family, shall be included in any *Mishe Berach*.
11. No one except the *Chazan* shall have the right to conduct the services publicly without special permission of the officers.
12. The distribution of the prayers on the Holidays shall be made by the Executive Committee which shall also set the hour for the commencing of each service.

Article II Cemetery and Burial

1. In the case of death among the members of the congregation or their families, as described in Article XV, Section 5 of the Constitution, the following By-Laws shall be added:
It shall be the duty of the Superintendent of the cemetery to appoint two members, in alphabetical order, to remain for six hours with the deceased, and this service shall be continued to the hour of his burial.
2. The *Gabbai* of the Beth Chaim (Superintendent) shall ask each member to accompany the deceased, and the *Gabbai* of the Beth Chayim shall also obtain a hearse and carriage at the expense of the congregation. However, if a member of the congregation desires to bury the deceased at another burial place, or if he does not desire to follow the Hebrew ritual, then the congregation, as well as the *Gabbai* of the Beth Chaim, are relieved of their duties.

3. The *Gabbai* of the Beth Chaim shall perform the Tharah and provide Tachrichim, and he shall be present at the Orahron. He is also to designate the grave and to arrange for the time of the burial.
4. The *Gabbai* of the Beth Chaim shall sign each bill connected with the burial ceremony before the Executive Committee shall make any payments.
5. Each member who lives within the city limits and who insists on a Minyon during the seven days of mourning shall obtain such a Minyon. The *Gabbai* of the Beth Chaim shall appoint ten members for the first three days and another ten members for the last three days. Any violation of these regulations shall be subject to fine by the Executive Committee.

Article III   Regarding Committees

1. All committees shall be appointed by the president.
2. A standing committee of three (including the president) shall be appointed for one year, whose duties it shall be to supervise the kindergarten.
3. A committee may be appointed whenever necessary for any specific purpose. It shall have full power, and report its decisions to the congregation.
4. The first appointee of its committee shall be called chairman of the committee. In case of his absence, the second appointee shall become chairman.
5. A written report shall be turned in by each committee, and it shall be signed by the chairman and the majority of the committee.
6. No member of any committee may ask to be refunded for expenses or compensation of loss of time, unless he had previously informed the congregation.
7. Any neglect in duty by any member of a committee shall be subject to a fine, to be set by the president.

Article IV   Expenses, Taxes, and Cash

1. The annual membership fee of a member shall amount to not less than $9.00 payable in monthly installments.
2. Widows or widowers shall have the same rights as all the other members, but shall pay only half of the membership dues. If such person declares himself unable to pay any dues or fees, the Executive Board shall decide whether an exemption shall be granted.
3. Any person who wishes to be married by the minister of the congregation shall receive a permit from the president which shall be sent to the minister, and must pay $3.00 to the congregation, $2.00 to the copulant, and $1.00 to the servant of the congregation.

Article V   Concerning Meetings

1. Written notices shall be sent out by the secretary to all members of the congregation for all regular meetings, as well as for special meetings called by the president.
2. Each member shall receive a written invitation for the annual meeting—on this invitation the fine for his non-appearance shall appear. If a member lives outside the city this invitation shall be mailed to him.

Article VI   Regarding Fines

1. Each member who has been suggested and has accepted appointment must be willing to carry out his office. In case of refusal he shall pay a fine of $5.00.
2. Members who accept to work on a committee but do not attend the meetings of said committee, shall pay $1.00.
3. Each member who has been asked to come to a funeral and who fails to appear shall be fined $1.00. This shall also apply to the watch over the dead. He shall, however, be allowed to send another honorable man to be his substitute. In case of sickness or absence from the city, he shall be exempted from paying the fine.
4. Members who congregate in front of the residence of a deceased member and who do not conduct themselves properly or decently, or are not properly dressed, shall pay $1.00 fine.
5. Anyone who does attend the Minyon in a house of mourning shall have to pay 25¢ each time he does not appear.
6. If someone has been called to order by the president and disregards it, he shall pay a fine from 25¢ to $2.00. Any disobedience or uncouth behavior at meetings or during services may lead to an expulsion of said member from the congregation.
7. For not being present at the meetings, members shall be fined 25¢; officers, 50¢; and the president, $1.00.
8. Fines may be modified if a member makes application and the majority of the meeting decide in favor of such action.

Article VII   Amendments

1. None of these By-Laws or their additions may be changed, amended, or nullified, except through a written application which must find a two-thirds majority of those present at the meeting. It shall then rest in abeyance for a month, and after its expiration, shall become law.

(Translated from German)

RULES OF ORDER

Article I   Order of Business

1. Thirty minutes after the official beginning of each meeting, provided there is a quorum, the President shall take his chair and call the meeting to order. This shall be done in the following order:
   a. The calling of the names of the official members, recording the names of those absent.
   b. Reading of the minutes of the last meeting and acceptance of same.
   c. Listening to the excuses of those who were absent at the last meeting.
   d. Acceptance of candidates.
   e. Acceptance of applications for membership.
   f. Reports of the committees.
   g. Reports of officers.
   h. Election of officers.
   i. Pending business.
   j. New business.
2. These rules concerning the order of business may be changed by a vote of two-thirds of the members present.

Article II   Conduct

1. During the meetings all should observe complete silence. Nobody shall leave the room without special permission of the president.
2. No one shall use the real name of the previous speaker, but shall designate him as the previous, and so on.
3. No one shall use insulting language.
4. No one shall disturb a speaker. If one speaks out of order, he shall be called to order by the president.
5. No one shall be allowed to say anything without permission; and then he shall rise and remain standing while speaking; and he shall limit himself to the subject under consideration.
6. No one shall speak more than three times on any particular subject.
7. No one shall speak before the question has been raised.
8. No one shall be permitted to speak for more than fifteen minutes except with the agreement of the meeting.

Article III   The Chair

1. The president shall see to it that at the meetings personal attacks shall be avoided, shall see that the speaker sticks to his subject, and shall decide to whom he shall give the floor.

2. If a motion has been made and seconded, such motion shall be read once more before debate is over. When the house is ready for the vote, the president shall rise and ask the house to decide on this question, whereupon the debate shall be closed.
3. The president shall give up his chair whenever he desires to express his opinion.
4. A motion may be rescinded before the debate has been opened.
5. All questions shall be decided justly, and it shall be the duty of the president to inform the meeting about the decision taken. Each member shall be entitled, in case of doubt, to ask for a rising vote.
6. If there is an appeal from the decision of the president, the following questions shall be put to those present: Does the house wish to support the president in his decision? Whereupon the ayes and the nayes shall be counted. The president himself shall have no vote in this case.
7. Whenever there is a tie vote, the president shall cast the decisive vote (Article III, Section 6 shall be exempted from this rule).

Article IV   Discussion

1. Whenever someone is called to order by the president, he shall be seated immediately and shall wait for permission to continue his remarks.
2. When a regular question is being presented, it can be dealt with in the following way:
    a. It can be postponed.
    b. It can be tabled.
    c. By the preceding question.
    d. By investigation.
    e. By amendments.
    f. To give more time for consideration.
The above mentioned order must be observed and is not debatable.

Article V   Motions and Procedure

1. Any member who presents a motion has a right to give the reasons for such motion.
2. No question can be debated unless supported and announced by the president.
3. If a motion is presented, the affirmative shall be considered first.
4. No one shall be allowed to vote if he was outside the room when the question was being discussed; but everyone who was present shall vote, unless he has a direct or indirect interest in the question under discussion, or if he had been excused from voting by the president.
5. All questions . . . shall be decided by a majority vote.

6. All questions that are not dealt with in these rules shall be decided by parliamentary law.

Supplement

These rules and regulations may be changed, amended, or rescinded in the same way as the By-Laws, and in no other way. The house, however, shall have the right to rescind them for just one meeting or for a short period, provided it receives a two-thirds majority of those present.

Milwaukee, November 4, 1856

1. Gabriel Shoyer, President
2. M. H. Schwarzenberg, Vice President
3. Joseph Hyman, Treasurer
4. Benoit Schwab, Secretary
5. Joseph Weinberg, Superintendent of the Cemetery
6. Henry Theobald ⎱ Members
7. Aron Abraham ⎸ of the
8. Simon Feist ⎹ Executive
9. Leo Sax ⎰ Committee
10. J. M. Hardt
11. L. Schwarzenberg
12. Louis Frank
13. Jacob Bach
14. M. N. Becker
15. A. Mock
16. D. Blum
17. Jacob Frank
18. Isaac Frank
19. Jacob Wirth
20. Isaac Friedberg
21. Moses Abraham
22. A. Blade
23. I. Hochstadter
24. Jacob Mayer
25. Marcus Otterburg
26. Jacob Herz
27. Simon Herz
28. Simon Hirsh
29. L. Blade
30. Henry Abraham
31. Benjamin Mock
32. E. M. Schoyer
33. S. Kuppershack
34. M. Engelman
35. Marcus Dryfoos
36. W. L. Schoyer
37. L. Mock
38. S. Weil of Merton
39. S. Stern of Green Bay
40. N. Levy of Green Bay
41. A. Marx of West Bend
42. W. Hirsh of Janesville
43. M. Hirsh of Janesville
44. Aron Newhof of Janesville

APPENDIX 5

RABBIS OF MILWAUKEE CONGREGATIONS, 1857-1962

(In order of founding)

Congregation B'ne Jeshurun

Rabbi Isidor Kalisch	1857-1860
Rabbi Ferdinand Leopold Sarner	(Sept.-Oct.) 1860
Rabbi Samson Falk	1863-1866
Rabbi G. M. Cohen	1868
Rabbi Elias Eppstein	1869-1880
Rabbi Emanuel Gerechter	1880-1892
Rabbi Victor Caro	1892-1912
Rabbi Charles S. Levi	1913-1927

Congregation Emanu-El

(after 1927:) *Congregation Emanu-El B'ne Jeshurun*

Rabbi Edward Benjamin Morris Browne	(Apr.-Sept.) 1870
Rabbi Moritz Spitz	1872-1878
Rabbi Isaac S. Moses	1879-1887
Rabbi Sigmund Hecht	1888-1899
Rabbi Julius Meyer	1900-1904
Rabbi Samuel Hirshberg	1904-1947
Rabbi Joseph L. Baron	1926-1951
Rabbi Harry B. Pastor	1947-1951
Rabbi Herbert H. Friedman	1951-1955
Rabbi Dudley Weinberg	1955-

Congregation Anshe Emes

Rabbi Florian Schauer	1873-1882

Congregation B'ne Israel

(Originally known as *Hebrah Ohabai Sholem,
Hebrah B'ne Israel, B'ne Israel Anshe Hungari*)

Rev. Jonas Berko	1894-1919
Rabbi Julius Rappaport	1923-1925
Rabbi David S. Savitz	1925-1927
Rabbi Joseph H. Snapir	1936-1938

Congregation Anshe Sfard

Rabbi Abraham Feldman	1892
Rabbi Louis Lazarus	1894
Rabbi Solomon Israelson	1897-1901
Rabbi Ben Zion Manesewitz	1925-1936; 1937-1939
Rabbi Jacob Twerski	1928-1940
Rabbi Charles Rubenstein	1941-1947
Rabbi David S. Shapiro	1948-

Congregation Beth Israel

(Originally known as *Congregation Beth Hamidrosh Hagodol*)

Rabbi Solomon I. Scheinfeld	1892-1893
Rabbi Solomon Israelson	1895-1897
Rabbi Samuel Cantor	1897-1901
Rabbi Solomon I. Scheinfeld*	1902-1943
Rabbi Max J. Mintz	1926-1929
Rabbi Samuel S. Spivak	1931
Rabbi Charles Rubenstein	1932-1939
Rabbi Harold H. Baumrind	1939-1958
Rabbi Milton Arm	1959-1960
Rabbi Joseph A. Gorfinkel	1961-

Congregation Sinai

Rev. E. Kahn	1900-1902
Rabbi H. Newman	1903
Rabbi Henry Friedman	1904-1905
Rabbi H. Elias	1906
Rabbi Max Rosenstein	1906-1907
Rabbi G. Lipkind	1910-1911
Rabbi U. Shayeson	1911
Rabbi Bennett Grad	1912-1914

Congregation Degel Israel

(Originally known as *Congregation Degel Israel Anshe Roumania*)

Rabbi Samuel Hurwitz	1928-1929
Rabbi Ben Zion Manesewitz	1937
Rabbi David Korb	1939-1940

* Rabbi Solomon I. Scheinfeld was the recognized rabbinical head of all the Orthodox congregations during his tenure.

Congregation Agudas Achim

(Formerly known as *Congregation Agudas Achim Anshe Polen*)

Rabbi Boaz Cohen	1923
Rabbi Israel Feldman	1949-

Congregation Anshe Lubavich

Rabbi Boaz Cohen	1917-1918
Rabbi Charles S. Taylor	1922-1932
Rabbi Simon Winograd	1939-1944
Rabbi Solomon Schulson	1944-

Congregation Beth Medrash Hogodol

Rabbi Boaz Cohen	1921-1923
Rabbi Julius Hyatt	1934-1936
Rabbi Yedidiah Gurnansky	1940-1942
Rabbi Charles Rubenstein	1956

Congregation Beth El
Beth El Ner Tamid Synagogue

Rabbi Eugene Kohn	1923-1926
Rabbi Philip Kleinman	1926-1937
Rabbi Louis J. Swichkow	1937-

Congregation B'ne Jacob

Rabbi Jacob Becker	1938-

Congregation Beth Yehudah

Rabbi Jacob Twerski	1929-

United Synagogue—B'ne Sholom

Rabbi Paul S. Greenman	1953-1957

Congregation Shalom

Rabbi Harry B. Pastor	1951-

Congregation Sinai

Rabbi Jay R. Brickman	1955-

Congregation Beth Hamedrash Hagodel—B'nai Sholom

Rabbi Paul S. Greenman	1957-1959
Rabbi Emanuel Lifschutz	1959-1962

Congregation Anshe Emeth

Rabbi Harold H. Baumrind	1958-1960

APPENDIX 6

PRESIDENTS OF MILWAUKEE CONGREGATIONS
CONGREGATION IMENU-AL

(Founded in 1850; consolidated with Congregation Ahabath
Emuno in 1856, to form Congregation B'ne Jeshurun)

Presidents

David Adler	1851-1852
Solomon Adler	1853-1856

CONGREGATION AHABATH EMUNO

(Founded in 1854; consolidated with Congregation
Imenu Al in 1856, to form Congregation B'ne Jeshurun)

President

Simon Levy	1854-1856

CONGREGATION ANSHE EMETH

(Founded in 1855; consolidated with
Congregation B'ne Jeshurun in 1859)

Presidents

Simon Levy	1855
J. M. Hart	1856
Gabriel Shoyer	1856-1859

CONGREGATION B'NE JESHURUN

(Established in 1856, as a result of the consolidation of congregations
Imenu Al and Ahabath Emuno in 1856, and Anshe Emeth in 1859)

Presidents

Nathan Pereles	1856	Simon Kahn	1883-1888
Simon Levy	1857	E. B. Friend	1888-1890
Solomon Adler	1858-1860	S. B. Auerbach	1890-1891
Henry Bonns	1861-1863	L. H. Harris	1891-1892
Isaac Stransky	1866-1867	Ed. Mahler	1892-1894
David Adler	1868-1869	L. H. Heller	1894-1897
Loebl Rindskopf	1869-1873	Jacob Poss	1897-1900
H. A. Kusel	1873-1875	Elias Rindskopf	1900-1902
M. Teweles	1875-1876	Jacob Poss	1902-1911
Jacob Eichman	1876-1877	S. A. Eckstein	1911-1917
Leo Harris	1877-1879	L. Ullman	1917-1920
M. Berliner	1879-1880	Max Breslauer	1920-1926
Leo Harris	1880-1883	Arthur Polacheck	1926-1927

CONGREGATION EMANU-EL
(Founded in 1869)
Presidents

David Adler	1869-1871	Morris Miller	1891-1894
Henry Friend	1871-1873	David Adler	1894-1895
David Adler	1873-1878	Morris Miller	1895-1896
Elias Friend	1878-1879	Max Landauer	1896-1900
David Adler	1879-1885	A. W. Rich	1900-1906
H. S. Mack	1885-1886	Paul Sidenberg	1906-1907
Lewis Silber	1886-1887	Max Landauer	1907-1917
J. P. Frisch	1887-1888	A. L. Saltzstein	1917-1921
David Adler	1888-1889	Joseph G. Daneman	1921-1925
J. P. Frisch	1889-1891	A. L. Saltzstein	1925-1927

CONGREGATION EMANU-EL B'NE JESHURUN
(Amalgamation of congregations Emanu-El and B'ne Jeshurun, in 1927)
Presidents

A. L. Saltzstein	1927-1934
Bert C. Broude	1934-1937
George P. Ettenheim	1937-1947
Benjamin F. Saltzstein	1947-1953
Edward R. Prince	1953-1957
Herman A. Mosher	1957-1961
Charles L. Goldberg	1961-

CONGREGATION ANSHE EMES
(Organized in 1871; probably merged with Congregation Beth Hamidrosh Hagodol shortly after 1894.)
Presidents

Joseph Platke	1874
E. M. Nathan	1883
Jacob Rosenberg	1894

CONGREGATION ANSHE JACOB
(Founded in 1886; consolidated with Moses Montefiore Gemeinde in 1892 to form Congregation Beth Hamidrosh Hagodol which was reorganized as Congregation Beth Israel in 1901.)
Presidents

Markus Katz	1888	J. Luleschnik	1890
Herman Schlomovitz	1889	S. Fink	1891

MOSES MONTEFIORE GEMEINDE

(Established in 1886; consolidated with Congregation Anshe Jacob in 1892 to form Congregation Beth Hamidrosh Hagodol which, in 1901, was reorganized as Congregation Beth Israel.)

Presidents

M. Rosenstein	1886	Max Kaufman	1890-1891
A. Grobanski	1887	Sol. Fein	1892

CONGREGATION BETH HAMIDROSH HAGODOL

(Organized in 1892, as a result of a merger of Congregation Anshe Jacob and the Moses Montefiore Gemeinde in the same year.)

Presidents

B. Goldstein	1892	Sol. Fein	1896
Herman Schlomovitz	1892	Herman Schlomovitz	1896
Sol. Fein	1893-1894	Samuel Margoles	1897-1898
Herman Schlomovitz	1895	J. Rosenberg	1899-1901

CONGREGATION BETH ISRAEL

(Reorganization of Congregation Beth Hamidrosh Hagodol in 1901 resulted in establishment of Congregation Beth Israel.)

Presidents

Sol. Fein	1901-1904	I. J. Rosenberg	1920-1926
Alexander Mosher	1904-1909	Ely Miller	1926-1928
I. J. Rosenberg	1911-1915	Isaac Cohen	1928-1941
P. Fein	1915	Oscar Willis	1941-1948
I. J. Rosenberg	1916	Sam Jacobson	1948-1953
Herman H. Schlomovitz	1917	George Glicksman	1953-1955
		Abe Shlensky	1955-1960
Alexander Mosher	1918-1919	Aaron Weiss	1960-

HEBRAH OHABAI SHOLEM
HEBRAH B'NE ISRAEL
CONGREGATION B'NE ISRAEL ANSHE HUNGARI
CONGREGATION B'NE ISRAEL

(Founded in 1887 as Hebrah Ohabai Sholem; name amended to Hebrah B'ne Israel, in 1889, to Congregation B'ne Israel Anshe Hungari, in 1899, and to Congregation B'ne Israel, in 1924.)

Presidents

Edward May	1887-1888	Max Traxler	1919-1921
L. Segall	1888-1889	S. Hoffman	1921-1922
Jacob Marks	1889-1892	Philip Suran	1922-1923
B. Brachman	1892-1893	M. Sogolowich	1923-1924
M. Brachman	1893-1894	Leopold Greenblatt	1924-1926
H. Brachman	1894-1895	Max Traxler	1926-1932
Bern. Brachman	1895-1898	Aaron Cohen	1932-1940
Herman Kraus	1898-1902	I. D. Hecht	1940-1942
Victor Montwid		Frank Stark	1942-1943
M. Breslauer		Joseph Neubauer	1943-1944
Max Stern		Louis Weiss	1944-1945
Adolph Suran	1909-1918	Bela Reisman	1945-1946
H. Trintz	1918-1919		

CONGREGATION ANSHE SFARD

(Incorporated 1889)

Presidents

Sam Kulla	1889-1893	Wolf Forman	1931-1933
Jacob Forman	1894-1897	Harold Shapiro	1933-1937
N. Rabenovitz	1898-1900	Louis Belin	1937-1939
S. Kops	1901-1904	Harry Malawsky	1939-1941
Jacob Forman	1905-1908	Meyer Tarnow	1941-1943
Jacob Maller	1909-1912	Harry Malmon	1943-1944
Harry Rubinovitz	1913-1916	Sidney Saichek	1944-1946
M. Zuker	1917	Ben Katz	1946-1948
J. Radoff	1918-1919	Morris Lewis	1948-1951
Michael Katz	1919	David Lippow	1951-1955
J. Lerner	1919-1920	Morris Malavsky	1955-1957
Harry Rubinovitz	1920-1921	Erv. Wolkenstein	1957-1959
J. Radoff	1921-1923	Samuel Oxman	1959-1961
Harry Rubinovitz	1924-1928	Henry Mayer	1961-
Morris Duckler	1929-1931		

CONGREGATION SINAI
(Organized, 1900; disbanded, 1915)
President
Arthur S. Kahn   1900-1915

CONGREGATION AGUDAS ACHIM ANSHE POLEN
CONGREGATION AGUDAS ACHIM
(Founded, 1904, and dissolved in 1916; reorganized in 1917)

Presidents

Meyer Boruszak	1904-1906	Max Karp	1934-1936
Max Holzman	1907-1916;	Jacob Karp	1937-1945
	1917-1919	Louis Goldberg	1945-1950
M. Wetter	1919-1920	David Cash	1950-1951
Max Holzman	1920-1932	Ben Yopack	1951-1952
N. Grossman	1932-1934	Hyman Epstein	1952-

Louis S. Berkoff   Honorary President

CONGREGATION ANSHE ROUMANIA
CONGREGATION DEGEL ISRAEL ANSHE ROUMANIA
(Organized and incorporated as Congregation Anshe Roumania in 1904; name changed to Congregation Degel Israel Ansche Roumania, in 1919.)

Presidents

Joseph Simon	1904-1910	B. Herman	1920-1921
Nathan Singer	1911-1912	L. D. Fisher	1921-1922
M. B. Rottman	1913-1915	B. Herman	1922-1923
Joseph Brill	1915-1918	L. D. Fisher	1924-1935
L. D. Fisher	1918-1919	Sam Rosenfeld	1935-1938
B. Herman	1919-1920	Max Stein	1938-1945
M. Vigdor	1920		

CONGREGATION ANSHE LUBAVICH
(Organized 1906)

Presidents

Robert Wasserman	1906-1908	A. Davidoff	1925-1926
J. Schefrin	1908-1910	J. Schefrin	1926-1940
Max Eisenberg	1910-1912	Samuel Schefrin	1940-1942
Herman Ruppa	1912-1914	Joseph Saffro	1942-1944
Max Schefrin	1914-1915	Jack Segel	1944-1945
H. Padway	1916-1917	John Ruppa	1945-1948
Herman Ruppa	1917	Robert Perlson	1948-1951
H. Padway	1917-1918	Morris Segel	1951-1959
Max Sverdlin	1918-1920	Robert Perlson	1959-1961
Morris Padway	1924-1925	Charles Refkin	1961-

CONGREGATION BETH MEDRASH HAGODOL
ANSHE SFARD
(Organized 1920)

Presidents

Max Sverdlin	1920-1925	Henry Silberman	1940-1946
M. Grossman	1926-1930	Abe Saichek	1946-1948
B. Schnoll	1925-1926	Max Orenstein	1948-1954
S. Lookatch	1930-1934	William Apter	1954-1955
Edward Weinshel	1934-1936	David S. Wollach	1955-1957
Jacob Nashban	1936-1940		

CONGREGATION BETH EL
(Founded 1921; original name, "Oer Chodosh")

Presidents

Henry D. Eder	1922-1925	Joseph Arenson	1935-1938
Michael Stein	1925-1927	Ben Gill	1938-1939
Joseph Sable	1927-1929	Sam Rosen	1939-1940
Herman D. Schwartz	1929-1931	Dewey Erbstein	1940-1943
Ben Gill	1931-1932	Morris Gordon	1943-1945
Joseph Arenson	1932-1933	Nathan Stein	1945-1947
Isidor Cohen	1933-1935	George Rosenberg	1947-1949

BETH EL NER TAMID SYNAGOGUE
(Founded 1949)

Michael Shapiro	1949-1950	A. L. Skolnik	1955-1958
Nathan Stein	1950-1952	Morris Gordon	1958-1960
Oscar Plotkin	1952-1953	Dewey Erbstein	1960-1962
George Rosenberg	1953-1955	Eliot M. Bernstein	1962-

CONGREGATION B'NE JACOB

(Organized in 1924 by a group of dissident members of
Congregation B'ne Israel who left that congregation that
year to establish the Orthodox Congregation B'ne Jacob.)

Presidents

L. Feldman	1924-1926	M. Goldman	1943-1948
Max Shumow	1926-1928	B. Switzky	1948-1951
R. Spiegel	1928-1929	M. Schwartz	1951-1953
S. Shumow	1929-1930	J. Hirschbein	1953-1957
Morris Feldman	1930-1935	M. Kramer	1957-1959
A. Orenstein	1935-1937	H. Rittberg	1959-1960
I. Glatter	1937-1939	Louis Sherman	1960-1961
I. Eckstein	1939-1941	H. Rittberg	1961-
R. Kupferberg	1941-1943		

CONGREGATION BETH YEHUDAH

(Incorporated in 1929. Sponsoring organization, Ahavat
Reyim Society, 1929-1941. Officers of Congregation
elected from 1941.)

Presidents

Eli Forman	1941-1943	Phil Levin	1951-1953
Isaac Weinstein	1943-1945	Sam Bass	1953-1961
Nathan Stein	1945-1946	Frank Grossman	1961-
Harry Bass	1946-1951		

UNITED SYNAGOGUE B'NE SHOLOM

(The merger of Congregation Degel Israel and Congregation B'ne Israel in 1945 resulted in the founding of
United Synagogue B'ne Sholom.)

Presidents

Sam Holtzman	1946-1947	L. D. Fisher	1951-1952
Joseph Schiller	1947-1948	Millard Durchslag	1952-1954
L. D. Fisher	1948-1949	Louis Baer	1954-1955
Philip Pinkus	1949-1950	Irving Baer	1955-1956
Max Stein	1950-1951		

CONGREGATION SHALOM

(Established, 1951)

Presidents

David R. Pasch	1951-1952	Jacob Beck	1956-1958
Edward H. Meldman	1952-1953	Daniel W. Howard	1958-1960
Isador Abrams	1953-1954	Herman Williams	1960-1962
Robert M. Gill	1954-1955	Paul J. Spector	1962-
David R. Pasch	1955-1956		

CONGREGATION SINAI

(Established 1955)

Presidents

Richard Teweles	1955-1959	Charles D. Ashley	1959-
Herbert Leeds	1959		

CONGREGATION ANSHE EMETH

(Established 1958)

Presidents

George Glicksman	1958-1960	Abraham Silverstein	1961-1962
Myron Marks	1960-1961	Irving Benedon	1962-

CONGREGATION BETH HAMEDROSH HAGODEL B'NAI SHOLOM

(Established in 1957 when Congregation Beth Medrash Hagodol Anshe Sfard and United Synagogue—B'ne Sholom consolidated to form this congregation.)

Presidents

David S. Wollach	1957-1961
Sam Kraus	1961-1962
David S. Wollach	1962-

APPENDIX 7

MEMBERSHIPS OF JEWISH CONGREGATIONS IN MILWAUKEE, 1950

Beth El Ner Tamid Synagogue (C)	650
Congregation Agudas Achim (O)	125
Congregation Anshe Lubavich (O)	150
Congregation Anshe Sfard (O)	160
Congregation Beth Medrash Hagodol Anshe Sfard (O)	130
Congregation Beth Israel (O)	658
Congregation Beth Yehudah (O)	175
Congregation B'ne Jacob (O)	100
Congregation Emanu-El B'ne Jeshurun (R)	1076
United Synagogue—B'ne Sholom (O)	65
	3289

(C) = Conservative   (O) = Orthodox   (R) = Reform

Summary

Orthodox affiliates in all congregations	47%
Conservative and Reform affiliates	53%

APPENDIX 8

PRESIDENTS OF DISTRICT GRAND LODGE NO. 6 B'NAI B'RITH

1875-1876	Lewis Rindskopf
1879-1880	R. Reichmann
1890-1891	Henry Herman
1899-1900	Max Ascher
1914-1915	Charles L. Aarons
1929-1930	Leo Reitman
1935-1936	I. B. Padway
1951-1952	Morris F. Jacobs
1922	Benjamin Braun, Honorary President

APPENDIX 9

PRESIDENTS OF B'NAI B'RITH LODGES
GILEAD LODGE NO. 41
(Instituted June 23, 1861)

Past Presidents

1861	M. Heiman	1908	Alfred Teller
1868	Moritz N. Becker	1909	Moritz Zarne
1869	Dr. Louis Adler	1910	Ralph F. Oberndorfer
1870	L. Frank	1911	Rabbi Goodman Lipkind
1871	S. Cahn	1912	Benjamin Braun
1872	M. Docter	1913	Isidor B. Goetz
1880	M. Seligman	1914	Mark L. Helfar
1881	Jacob Katz	1915	Mark L. Helfar
1882	Alex. Spiegel	1916	Abe Carlsruh
1883	S. Weil	1917	Dr. A. N. Baer
1884	M. Seligman	1918	Roland Meissner
1885	Fred. Becker	1919	Leo Reitman
1886	Simon Bach	1920	Michael Sadek
1887	I. Eisen	1921	Maurice Goldberg
1888	Samuel E. Mossler	1922	Hyman E. Padway
1889	Samuel E. Mossler	1923	David Sondel
1890	Samuel E. Mossler	1924	Nathan Eder
1891	Samuel E. Mossler	1925	Max Diamond
1892	Sol. Herz	1926	Louis Roos
1893	Sol. Herz	1927	Mervyn Braun
1894	Jacob Marks	1928	I. B. Padway
1895	Jacob Marks	1929	Nathan Boruszak
1896	Jacob Marks	1930	Ben Z. Glass
1897	Jacob Marks	1931	I. B. Padway
1898	Simon Epstein	1932	Louis Roos
1899	H. L. Eisen	1933	I. B. Padway
1900	Abe Braun	1934	Benjamin Zelonky
1901	A. Kreielsheimer	1935-1936	Mathew Horwitz
1902	H. Herz	1936-1937	Bert C. Broude
1903	Sam Schram	1937-1938	Paul L. Moskowitz
1904	Nathan L. Stein	1938-1939	Robert A. Hess
1905	Louis Lachman	1939-1940	Jesse J. Habush
1906	Max Teweles	1940-1941	Morris F. Jacobs
1907	Alex P. Greenthal	1941-1942	Dr. Joseph Weiss

1942-1943	Avin Sable	1952-1953	Norman Sussman
1943-1944	Dr. Joseph Weiss	1953-1954	Henry Goodman
1944-1945	Alfred G. Goldberg	1954-1955	Riley Cohen
1945-1946	Noah N. Shapiro	1955-1956	Sol T. Goodsitt
1946-1947	Harry G. Marcus	1956-1957	Sol T. Goodsitt
1947-1948	Albert A. Mayer	1957-1958	Barnett Franks
1948-1949	Bernard Fine	1958-1959	Henry Goodman
1949-1950	Benjamin I. Dolnick	1959-1960	David Lippow
1950-1951	Samuel J. Ansfield	1960-1961	Riley Cohen
1951-1952	Norman Sussman	1961-1962	Sam Eisenstadt

ISAAC LODGE NO. 87

(Instituted, 1866; consolidated with Gilead Lodge No. 41, in 1917)

Past Presidents, 1866-1917

1868	Lewis Rindskopf	1894	E. Aarons
1869	Emanuel Silverman	1895	Rabbi Sig. Hecht
1870	H. M. Benjamin	1896	Rabbi Sig. Hecht
1871	H. A. Kusel	1897	L. H. Heller
1872	M. N. Lando	1898	L. H. Heller
1873	M. N. Lando	1899	L. H. Heller
1874	M. N. Lando	1900	L. H. Heller
1875	Gottlieb Engel	1901	Harry Marks
1876	Gottlieb Engel	1902	Charles L. Aarons
1879	Ed. B. Friend	1903	Rabbi Julius H. Meyer
1880	Ed. B. Friend	1904	Rabbi Julius H. Meyer
1881	David H. Blascow	1905	Benjamin Poss
1882	H. Herman	1906	Benjamin Poss
1883	Wm. De Wolf	1907	Albert Oberndorfer
1884	Charles Polachek	1908	S. F. Wetzler
1885	Max Ascher	1909	S. F. Wetzler
1886	Abe L. Baer	1910	Joseph Hirschberg
1887	Abe L. Baer	1911	Joseph Hirschberg
1888	Max Ascher	1912	Harry Glicksman
1889	E. B. Friend	1913	Harry Glicksman
1890	H. M. Oberndorfer	1914	Harry Marks
1891	L. E. Katzenstein	1915	Harry Marks
1892	L. Rindskopf	1916	Alfred Newlander
1893	Charles Kahn	1917	Charles L. Aarons

MILWAUKEE LODGE NO. 141
(Instituted, 1870; merged with Gilead Lodge No. 41, in 1913)

Past Presidents, 1870-1913

1870	Leopold Heller	1894	Julius Manasse
1871	Isaac Stransky	1895	A. Kahn
1872	M. Teweles	1896·	M. Cahn
1873	E. Eppstein (Rabbi)	1897	M. Cahn
1874	B. Gross	1898	M. Cahn
1875	B. Gross	1899	M. Cahn
1878	Sol. Eckstein	1900	M. Cahn
1880	K. D. Davidson	1901	B. Eckstein
1881	A. Meissner	1902	Henry Eckstein
1882	S. H. Baum	1903	Gustav Hartstein
1883	Julius Manasse	1904	Gustav Hartstein
1884	Ignatz Polachek	1905	A. Rosenberg
1885	Ignatz Polachek	1906	Rabbi Victor Caro
1886	Sigmund Scheftels	1907	Rabbi Victor Caro
1887	Kaufman Baer	1908	H. Susag
1888	David Seelig	1909	Abe Braun
1889	S. Thal	1910	R. Marx
1890	S. Thal	1911	Leo Silberman
1891	J. Hirsch	1912	S. De Nosaquo
1892	Sigmund Scheftels	1913	S. De Nosaquo
1893	Sigmund Scheftels		

EXCELSIOR LODGE NO. 170
(Instituted, 1872; consolidated with Isaac Lodge No. 87 in 1888)

Past Presidents, 1872-1888

1872	Dr. Kahn	1882	M. Oberndorfer
1874	Joseph Pollack	1883	E. D. Adler
1876	S. H. Goodman	1884	D. H. Friend
1877	J. Nathanson	1885	H. M. Oberndorfer
1879	E. M. Oberndorfer	1886	W. Katzenstein
1880	A. W. Rich	1887	Charles Kahn
1881	S. B. Auerbach	1888	Charles Kahn

SHOREWOOD (BAY SHORE) LODGE NO. 1373
(Instituted June 15, 1939)
Past Presidents

1939-1940	Abe Rice	1951-1952	Hyman B. Parks
1940-1941	Herman J. Scholl	1952-1953	Sidney Melvoin
1941-1942	Dr. Carl O. Diamond	1953-1954	Sidney Sayles
1942-1943	Joe E. Smith	1954-1955	Jack Berland
1943-1944	Sol Raskin	1955-1956	Bernard J. Hankin
1944-1945	Lawrence S. Katz	1956-1957	Dr. Benj. L. Feldman
1945-1946	Samuel Goldenberg	1957-1958	Philip E. Lerman
1946-1947	Dr. Sam Granof	1958-1959	Louis Heller
1947-1948	I. E. Lample	1959-1960	Louis Heller
1948-1949	Edwarde E. Perlson	1960-1961	Armin Solomon
1949-1950	Ervin R. Abramson	1961-1962	Bernard Goldstein
1950-1951	Marvin Klitsner		

SHOFAR LODGE NO. 1388
(Instituted November 19, 1939)
Past Presidents

1939-1941	Avrum Chudnow	1952-1953	Arthur Hirschbein
1941-1942	Bernard Solochek	1953-1954	Dr. Charles Goldstein
1942-1943	Nathan J. Rakita	1954-1955	Saul Rapkin
1943-1944	Sidney A. Levner	1955-1956	Oscar Eisendrath
1944-1945	Milton Holzman	1956-1957	Dr. Bernard Sharp
1945-1946	Lionel Rosenberg	1957-1958	Alex Zaidins
1946-1947	Harry Weintrob	1958-1959	Louis Silberman
1947-1948	Hy Cofar	1959-1960	Matthew J. Berlowitz
1948-1950	Ben Sax	1960-1961	Leonard Edelstein
1950-1951	Philip Zarem	1961-1962	Louis Riches
1951-1952	Ervin Abrams		

WASHINGTON PARK LODGE NO. 1460
(Instituted May 4, 1941)
Past Presidents

1941-1942	Herman Schwartz	1953-1954	Davis Cohen
1942-1943	Sol Forman	1954-1955	Joe Radoff
1943-1945	Max Raskin	1955-1957	Dr. Jack C. Biller
1945-1947	Manuel Holtzman	1957-1958	David Gutkin
1947-1948	Maurice Marks	1958-1959	Harry Sicula
1948-1949	Clarence Goldberg	1959-1961	Ervin Wolkenstein
1949-1951	Abe Parelskin	1961-1962	Irving Fields
1951-1953	William Kay		

SHOLOM ALEICHEM LODGE NO. 1559

(Instituted March 25, 1945)

Past Presidents

1945-1946	Joseph Bursten	1950-1951	Leon Goldberg
1946-1947	Ben Trosch	1951-1952	Simon Hoffman
1947-1948	Sam Korelstein	1952-1953	Jacob Joseph
1948-1949	Sam Schneiderman	1953-1962	Abraham Gecht
1949-1950	Simon Hoffman		

MILWAUKEE MEMORIAL LODGE NO. 1692

(Instituted July 22, 1947)

Past Presidents

1947-1948	Leo Lichter	1955-1957	Hyman W. Rubin
1948-1949	C. Irvin Peckarsky	1957-1959	Leslie Bern
1949-1951	Lawrence Cohen	1959-1960	Leonard S. Marcus
1951-1952	Norman Saichek	1960-1961	Edwin Goldman
1952-1953	Philip Croen	1961-1962	Samuel Gilbert
1953-1955	Arthur L. Kahn		

LAKE SHORE LODGE NO. 1985

(Instituted June 27, 1954)

1954-1955	Thomas Kaufman	1958-1959	Jack Shlimovitz
	Gerald Kahn	1959-1960	Robert M. Rice
1955-1956	A. L. Meyer	1960-1961	Gerald Minkoff
1956-1957	Adolph Stern	1961-1962	Robert Lessin
1957-1958	Arthur Posner		

FLAGSTONE LODGE NO. 2266

(Instituted April 2, 1960)

1960-1961	Norvall O. Winnik	1961-1962	Shale Yanow

CENTURY LODGE NO. 2304

(Instituted February 12, 1961)

1961-1962   Robert Temkin

APPENDIX 10

INDEPENDENT ORDER, FREE SONS OF ISRAEL
Presidents, 1879-1890

HARMONIE LODGE NO. 52		CREAM CITY LODGE NO. 63	
Max Ascher	1880	A. Boguslawski	1879
Adolph Goldstein	1881	Lewis Silber	1880
Fred. Becker	1882	Bernhard Gross	1881
M. N. Lando	1883-1884	Lehman Aarons	1882
M. Sonlander	1885	Lewis Silber	1883
Martin Berliner	1886	M. Modler	1884
L. Teweles	1887	B. Brachman	1885-1886
Isaac Gottschalk	1888-1889	I. J. Litt	1887
M. N. Lando	1890	Lewis Silber	1888
		M. Boguslawski	1889
		Josh. Gross	1890

APPENDIX 11

PAST MASTERS, HARMONY LODGE NO. 142,
FREE AND ACCEPTED MASONS, 1867-1895
(Instituted June 10, 1863)

Henry Bonns	1867	David Adler	1877-1878
Julius Nathanson	1868	Sol H. Goodman	1879
Henry Bonns	1869	Julius Nathanson	1880-1881
David Adler	1870	Lewis Silber	1882-1885
Julius Nathanson	1871	Louis Lachman	1886
Henry Bonns	1872	William Kohn	1887-1888
William Kohn	1873	Samuel J. Decker	1889-1890
Leopold Heller	1874-1875	Moritz Mendelssohn	1895
Moritz Mendelssohn	1876		

APPENDIX 12

CHEVRA BIKUR CHOLIM (HEBREW BENEVOLENT SOCIETY)

(Founded, 1861; dissolved, 1930)

Presidents

Loebl Rindskopf	1868-1870	Louis Rindskopf	1888-1898
S. Eckstein	1871-1872	Louis Lachman	1899-1909
S. Feist	1873-1876	Elias Rindskopf	1909-1923
L. Eigmann	1877-1881	David Zarne	1924-1930
Leopold Baer	1882-1887	Emil Pentler	1930

APPENDIX 13

LADIES' RELIEF SEWING SOCIETY

(Organized 1878)

Presidents, 1879-1931

Mrs. A. W. Rich	1878-1883
Mrs. Lewis Silber	1884-1887
Mrs. J. Gross	1888-1890
Mrs. Lewis Silber	1891-1892
Mrs. E. Friend	1893
Mrs. Simon Kander	1894-1895
Mrs. W. Kohn	1896
Mrs. Jacob Gross	1897-1900
Mrs. Sig. Wollheim	1904-1911
Mrs. Emanuel M. Phillips	1911-1921
Mrs. Albert Kreielsheimer	1921-1925
Mrs. Sig. R. Levy	1925-1926
Mrs. F. C. Mock	1926-1928
Mrs. Fanny Burgheim	1928-1930
Mrs. Armin Rosenberg	1930-1931

APPENDIX 14

THE HEBREW RELIEF SOCIETY (1867);
THE HEBREW RELIEF ASSOCIATION (1889);
JEWISH SOCIAL SERVICE ASSOCIATION (1921);
JEWISH FAMILY AND CHILDREN'S SERVICE (1948)

Presidents

David Adler	1867-1872	Morris Miller	1898-1902
Simon Feist	1872-1877	A. L. Saltzstein	1902-1905
Aaron F. Leopold	1877-1879	Solomon Fein	1905-1907
Marcus Heimann	1879-1880	Charles Friend	1907-1941
Philip Carpeles	1880-1883	Leo Mann	1941-1943
J. P. Frisch	1884-1886	Ralph L. Heilbronner	1943-1947
S. Hermann	1887-1891	Raymond Scribner	1947-1949
J. P. Frisch	1892-1894	Mrs. Harold L. Miller	1949-1954
Simon Heller	1894-1896	Marvin Klitsner	1954-1958
Rabbi S. Hecht	1896-1897	Donald Michelstetter	1958-
Simon Heller	1897-1898		

Miss Rebecca Tenenbaum, Executive Director, 1932-

APPENDIX 15

CIRCULAR OF HEBREW RELIEF SOCIETY
CALLING FOR FORMATION OF
UNITED RELIEF SOCIETY, March 21, 1880*

Hebrew Relief Society, Secretary's Office, Milwaukee, March 21, 1880—To the Officers and Members: At a recent meeting of the Board of Trustees of this Society, the following resolution was unanimously adopted: Resolved, to issue a circular which shall be addressed to all the different Hebrew organizations in this city, requesting their co-operation in forming a UNITED HEBREW RELIEF SOCIETY in our midst. The objects to be attained by a United Relief Society are various; among the most prominent points which suggest themselves are the following: A positive assurance of a well organized praise-

* *Milwaukee Daily Sentinel*, November 15, 1880, p. 8.

worthy Hebrew charity, in the welfare of which all the Jewish people of the city shall feel interested; That all deserving, poor, unfortunate and sick will be systematically relieved from immediate destitution, and aided, if possible, to improve their condition in life by rendering them assistance in obtaining proper employment, etc., etc.; That all application for relief shall be made to one source where charity will be dispensed with uniformity according to the condition and character of the applicant, and not bestow the most upon the one that understands begging the best, as is now frequently the case; to discriminate against the so-called professional beggars, who are too indolent and too lazy to care for their own support, and who prefer to trust to Providence, and to their benevolent co-religionists than to use their own energies for the purpose of elevating themselves to a higher sphere of life than perpetual pauperism, and who make it a point to always get all they can wherever they can; to cooperate with similar organizations which are now in existence in many cities in the United States, thereby protecting the generously inclined from imposition, which is now almost daily practiced, and rather devote the surplus of the charity fund—if at some future time a sufficient amount accrues—toward the maintenance of an institution for destitute sick, or for a temporary Industrial Home for poor women, and the education of poor children, thereby diminishing the source of destitution and misery, elevating indigent children through a proper mental as well as physical training until they are fitted to care for themselves, thereby fulfilling the true and noble principles of charity to its fullest extent; to effect this laudable enterprise, we propose the following mode: That for every yearly contribution of $25.00 from any Temple, Lodge, Sewing Society, or other Jewish organization in this city, such organization shall be entitled to one delegate to represent it in the U.H.R.S. Delegates from the different societies with the Board of the present Relief Society shall constitute the United Hebrew Relief Society Board. We are aware that, at best, we can present this matter only in an imperfect shape in the space of this circular, but hope that the principle of our intention will be understood and taken into consideration by your honored society. Should this circular, or any part thereof, meet with your approval, we should be pleased to have you act upon it at once, or should you have any suggestion to make, whereby our aim may be better effected, we shall be happy to receive such suggestions, and the same shall have our thorough consideration.

APPENDIX 16

HEBREW RELIEF SOCIETY
HEBREW RELIEF ASSOCIATION (1889)
INCOME BY YEAR, 1877-1900

1877	$ 660.	1891-1892	$2157.
1878	842.	1892-1893	2789.
1880	726.	1893-1894	3000.
1881	780.	1894-1895	2866.
1883	1500.	1895-1896	2200.
1884-1885	1025.	1896-1897	2400.
1885-1886	2622.	1897-1898	1626.
1886-1887	1686.	1898-1899	2035.
1887-1888	1465.	1899-1900	2868.

APPENDIX 17

THE FEDERATED JEWISH CHARITIES OF MILWAUKEE

(Founded in 1902; initially representing the local constituent societies: Hebrew Relief Association, The Settlement, Ladies' Relief Sewing Society, Sisterhood of Personal Service; and the Jewish Orphan Asylum of Cleveland, Ohio, the Moses Montefiore Home for the Aged, Cleveland, Ohio, and the National Jewish Hospital for Consumptives at Denver, Col.)

Presidents

David Adler	1902-1903	M. A. Freschl	1917-1918
Morris Miller	1903-1910	Nat Stone	1918-1929
Adolph Landauer	1910-1914	Benj. F. Saltzstein	1929-1935
A. L. Saltzstein	1914-1917	A. L. Saltzstein	1935-1937

Superintendents

Jacob Billikopf	1905-1907	I. Rubinstein	1916-1918
Morris Stern	1907	Isadore Kadis	1919-1922
Samuel Rabinovitch	1908-1912	Dr. Simon Peiser	1922-1923
N. N. Goodman	1912-1914	Kurt Peiser	1923-1926
Maurice B. Hexter	1914-1916	Benjamin Glassberg	1927-1933

APPENDIX 18

FEDERATED JEWISH CHARITIES

(Founded 1902)

INCOME AND NUMBER OF CONTRIBUTORS
BY YEAR, 1903-1931*

Year	Income	Number of Contributors
1903	$ 9,790.	275
1904	10,940.	375
1905	10,813.	380
1906	10,780.	369
1907	14,716.	400
1908	14,230.	343
1909	16,772.	370
1910	17,572.	370
1911	20,433.	410
1912	20,037.	
1913	20,387.	
1914	18,459.	388
1915	24,308.	485
1916	26,867.	610
1917	31,322.	1,182
1918	45,180.	
1919	45,429.	
1920	50,490.	
1921	52,036.	
1922	53,331.	1,400
1924	73,375.	1,500
1925	94,196.	
1926	84,049.	
1927	133,588.	2,500
1928	131,000.	2,400
1929	138,493.	2,560
1930	131,000.	
1931	115,000.	

* Figures taken from Annual Reports of the Federated Jewish Charities of Milwaukee.

APPENDIX 19

MILWAUKEE JEWISH WELFARE FUND
(Organized 1938)

Presidents		Campaign Chairmen	
Nathan M. Stein	1938-1941	Nathan M. Stein	1938-1940
Aaron Scheinfeld	1941-1944	B. E. Nickoll	1941-1942
Bert C. Broude	1944-1946	(War Chest, 1943-1945)	
B. E. Nickoll	1946-1948	Irving G. Rhodes	1946-1948
Dr. Norbert Enzer	1948-1950	Sol J. Kahn	1949
B. F. Saltzstein	1950-1953	H. H. Ribner	1950
Harry L. Epstein	1953-1955	Sol J. Rosenberg	1951
Harry Bloch, Jr.	1955-1958	Solly Bazelon	1952
B. J. Sampson	1958-1961	Harry Bloch, Jr.	1953
Harry J. Plous	1961-	B. J. Sampson	1954-1955
		Lawrence S. Katz	1956-1957
Executive Directors		Marvin Glasspiegel	1958-1959
H. A. Goldsmith	1938-1939	Albert Adelman	1960-1961
Elkan C. Voorsanger	1939-1955	Ben D. Marcus	1962-
Melvin S. Zaret	1955-		

APPENDIX 20

MILWAUKEE JEWISH WELFARE FUND
FUNDS RAISED AND ALLOCATED, 1938-1961

Year	Fund Raised	Fund Allocated	Percentage of Allocations UJA Overseas	National	Local
1938	$ 85,107	$ 74,157	45. % 16.3%	17.3%	8.5%
1939	235,000	190,017	42.5 6.7	4.4	27.3
1940	250,000	202,771	41.0 5.9	5.8	28.6
1941	250,000	219,599	42.2 6.1	4.6	34.8
1942	261,739	236,223	44.1 7.2	4.7	34.3
1943	348,969	326,159	50.1 10.5	7.7	25.1
1944	395,890	370,425	56.8 9.5	9.1	18.1
1945	476,665	454,565	62.9 8.3	8.6	15.5
1946	995,400	954,188	77.9 6.2	4.4	7.4
1947	1,381,598	1,292,856	73.5 5.1	4.1	10.9
1948	1,750,766	1,653,973	69.6 5.3	3.3	16.3
1949	1,295,757	1,219,917	61.9 5.1	3.4	23.7
1950	995,634	931,765	60.3 5.9	5.1	22.2
1951	998,175	916,996	60.1 6.2	5.3	20.3
1952	882,232	806,705	56.8 6.2	6.1	22.4
1953	856,745	766,819	54.3 5.8	6.7	22.7
1954	807,161	722,110	53.7 5.8	6.5	23.5
1955	771,819	701,902	53.6 5.9	6.5	25.0
1956	986,925	919,711	60.5 5.1	5.4	22.2
1957	1,166,424	1,102,850	63.9 4.8	5.2	20.6
1958	1,022,000	914,382	51.3 5.3	5.7	22.9
1959	1,176,572	1,054,105	56.5 5.1	5.9	22.1
1960	1,300,739	1,129,072	53.9 4.9	5.8	22.2
1961	1,335,208	1,177,989	52.9 4.9	5.8	24.9

APPENDIX 21

NUMBER OF GIVERS BY CATEGORIES—1946 thru 1961

Size of Contribution	1946	1947	1948	1949	1950	1951	1952	1953	1954	1955	1956	1957	1958	1959	1960	1961
Under $5.	1219	1209	1409	1826	1832	1807	1775	1913	2070	2016	1318	1387	1522	1420	1419	1381
$5 to 9.99	2149	2011	2188	2206	2309	2266	2264	2329	2280	2130	2029	2117	1993	1942	1953	2000
$10 to 24.99	2158	2037	2151	1980	2123	2059	1868	1878	1748	1669	1861	1964	1840	1740	1690	1692
$25 to 49.99	1184	1133	1316	1288	1274	1314	1180	1228	1153	1121	1183	1182	1132	1098	1148	1125
$50 to 99.99	748	755	817	722	727	729	712	708	741	685	710	779	757	739	751	783
$100 to 249.99	866	961	1113	1085	1039	991	939	919	846	788	890	916	910	924	947	940
$250 to 499.99	288	349	393	363	341	335	322	312	285	280	320	366	372	397	386	385
$500 to 749.99	172	186	235	209	165	159	149	138	124	112	149	177	182	196	222	213
$750 to 999.99	18	48	60	50	30	34	28	38	37	37	46	63	45	55	49	45
$1000 to 2,499.99	132	173	207	171	154	150	132	121	112	117	139	165	164	174	171	180
$2500 to 4,999.99	31	48	60	35	30	30	29	26	31	32	44	50	46	51	55	47
$5000 to 9,999.99	25	29	33	32	21	21	19	16	13	15	19	24	13	17	25	25
$10,000 to 24,999.99	14	17	28	15	10	11	7	8	7	3	3	9	7	12	17	20
$25,000 and over	—	4	4	1	—	—	—	—	—	—	2	1	1	1	1	2
GRAND TOTAL	9004	8960	10,015	9983	10,055	9906	9421	9634	9447	9005	8713	9200	8984	8766	8834	8838
Junior Division, Organizations and Specials															50	613
															8884	9451

APPENDIX 22

JUDAH HALEVI GATE NO. 8, ORDER OF THE KNIGHTS OF ZION
(Organized 1899)

Presidents

L. Rotter	1899	Paul Sondel	1914-1915
S. Krasnow	1900	I. Schefrin	1915
A. Lifschitz	1901-1903	L. Shapiro	1915-1916
Joseph Previant	1904-1907	Harry Seidelman	1916-1917
M. Gottlieb	1908-1911	L. Weiss	1917-1918
Joseph Saffro	1911-1912	I. J. Rosenberg	1918
I. Schefrin	1912-1914	I. M. Shapiro	1919

MILWAUKEE ZIONIST DISTRICT
ZIONIST ORGANIZATION OF AMERICA

Presidents

Joseph Grossman 1920
Frank Grossman 1921

(Zionist District No. 1)

Robert A. Hess	1921-1922
I. V. Brossel	1923-1924

Milwaukee Zionist District

Robert A. Hess	1924-1925
Arthur Shutkin	1925-1929
Joseph Saffro	1929-1930
Herman D. Schwartz	1930-1931
Arthur Shutkin	1931-1932
Dr. Eugene H. Heifetz	1932-1934
Bert C. Broude	1934-1935
Alex Himmelman	1935-1938
Hyman M. Seidelman	1938-1939
Morton Wax	1939-1941
Hyman M. Seidelman	1941-1943
Herman D. Schwartz	1943-1945
Morris Gorden	1945-1947
Dr. L. W. Blumenthal	1947-1949
Leo J. Salzstein	1949-1950
Alex Himmelman	1950-1952
Morton Wax	1952-1954
Hyman M. Seidelman	1954-1955
Rabbi Louis J. Swichkow	1955-1956
George Rosenberg	1956-1959
Herbert Arnstein, Jr.	1959-1962
John Post	1962-

Zionist District No. 2

(Organized 1921; merged with District No. 1 in 1924)

President

A. P. Rosenberg 1921-1924

Henry Monsky Group

(Organized, 1947; consolidated with Milwaukee Zionist District in 1949)

Presidents

Avin Sable	1947-1949
Robert Agulnick	1949

Ner Tamid Group

(Organized, 1947; consolidated with Milwaukee Zionist District, 1949)

Carl Millman	1947-1949
Herbert Lelchuk	1949

APPENDIX 23

MILWAUKEE POALE ZION

Branch 1	*Dr. Nachman Syrkin Branch*
(Organized 1906)	(Organized, 1928; consolidated with Branch 1 in 1945 to form Dr. Nachman Syrkin Branch, Poale Zion.)

Presidents		*Presidents*	
Louis Perchonok	1906-1907	Jack Rosenthal	1928
Leo Feinman	1907-1909	Hyman Fishman	1929
Abraham Kaplan	1909-1910	William Richman	1930
Peter Ottenstein	1910-1913	Dr. Joseph Bursten	1931
Meyer Dubinsky	1913-1915	William Richman	1932
Morris Meyerson	1915-1917	Morris B. Ellman	1933
I. Tuchman	1917-1920	Oscar Hianny	1934
Nathan Sand	1920-1923	Max Orenstein	1935
Louis Perchonok	1923-1925	William Richman	1936-1937
Eli Zavel	1925-1926	Morris B. Ellman	1938
Louis Perchonok	1926-1928	Oscar Hianny	1939
Nathan Sand	1928-1930	Sam Kahn	1940
G. A. Zavel	1930-1932	Dr. Joseph Bursten	1941
Peter Ottenstein	1932-1933	William Richman	1942
Morris Weingrod	1933-1935	Sam Kahn	1943
I. Tuchman	1935-1937	Ivan Weinstein	1944
Nathan Sand	1937-1940	Sam Kahn	1945
Mayer Hiken	1940-1942		
I. Tuchman	1942-1944		
Louis Perchonok	1944-1945		

Dr. Nachman Syrkin Branch, Poale Zion

(Formed in 1945 through the consolidation of Branch 1 and Dr. Nachman Syrkin Branch.)

Presidents

Morris Weingrod	1945-1948	Peter Ottenstein	1957-1958
William Becker	1948-1950	Morris B. Ellman	1958-1959
Arthur Spiegel	1950-1951	Morris Weingrod	
Sam Kahn	1951-1954	Sam Kahn	1959-
Morris Weingrod	1954-1957	Sam Ziegelman	

Brandeis Branch
(Organized in 1946 as English-speaking group)
Presidents

Louis Sand	1946-1948
Herman Weingrod	1948-1950
Joseph Hirshberg	1950-1951
Paul Melrood	1951-1952
Dr. Zacharie Schlomovitz	1952-1953
Dr. Avrom Kniaz	1953-1954
Mrs. Julia Rabinovitz	1954-1955
Dr. Reuben Beezy	1955-1956
Dr. Irving I. Lutsky	1956-1958
Lawrence Orenstein	1958-1960
Paul Melrood	1960-

APPENDIX 24

MIZRACHI OF MILWAUKEE

Religious Zionists of America
(Organized, 1935)
Presidents

Chaim Siegel	1935-1937
J. Schefrin	1937-1938
Isaac Cohen	1938-1940
Robert Wasserman	1940-1944
Paul Lichter	1944-1948
Rabbi Solomon Schulson	1948-1954
Rabbi Harold Baumrind	1954-1958
Jacob Paler, Moses Wolfe, Rabbi Solomon Schulson	1958-1959
Jacob Paler and Moses Wolfe	1959-

APPENDIX 25

MILWAUKEE CHAPTER, HADASSAH
(Organized, 1920)
Presidents

Miss Sarah Margoles 1920-1921
Mrs. Isidore Greenberg 1921-1924
Mrs. Charles T. Cohen 1924-1925
Mrs. Helen Machlis 1925-1926
Mrs. Isidore Greenberg 1926-1929
Mrs. Louis Cohen 1929-1930
Mrs. I. G. Strauss 1930-1932
Mrs. Louis Bernhard 1932-1933
Mrs. Herman Levitz 1933-1935
Mrs. Simpson Markson 1935-1938

Mrs. Harry Brody 1938-1941
Mrs. Charles T. Cohen 1941-1944
Mrs. Robert Agulnick 1944-1948
Mrs. Hyman Peckarsky 1948-1951
Mrs. Ben Rosenfeld 1951-1953
Mrs. Edward M.
  Lazarus 1953-1957
Mrs. Gustav Wand 1957-1961
Mrs. George J. Laikin 1961-

APPENDIX 26

MILWAUKEE COUNCIL OF PIONEER WOMEN
(Pioneer Women, organized in 1926; Council of Pioneer Women formed in 1949)
Presidents

Mrs. Mendel Safer 1949-1952
Miss Goldie Sosoff 1952-1955
Mrs. Jack Futterman 1955-1957
Mrs. Harry Luck 1957-1959
Mrs. Peter Pikofsky 1959-

APPENDIX 27

JEWISH NATIONAL FUND COUNCIL OF MILWAUKEE

(Organized 1925)

Presidents

John A. Post	1925-1927	Peter Ottenstein	1935-1939
Isidor Cohen	1927-1930	Mayer Hiken	1939-1941
S. Tussman	1930-1934	Arthur Shutkin	1942-1945
S. N. Goodman	1934-1935	Hyman M. Seidelman	1945-

APPENDIX 28

MILWAUKEE JEWISH MISSION

(Organized 1896)

President

Mrs. Simon (Lizzie B.) Kander   1896-1900

THE SETTLEMENT

(The Milwaukee Jewish Mission and the Sisterhood of Personal Service merged to organize The Settlement in 1900.)

ABRAHAM LINCOLN HOUSE

(The Settlement was renamed Abraham Lincoln House in 1911.)

Presidents

Mrs. Simon (Lizzie B.) Kander	1900-1918
Mrs. Sol (Belle) Cantrovitz	1918-1921
Mrs. Edwin S. Mack	1921-1927
Mrs. Joseph (Minette F.) Daneman	1927-1930

Head Residents and Directors

Miss Stella A. Loeb	1906-1916
Miss Stella B. Rosenbaum	1916-1918
Miss Helena Stern	1918-1922
Kurt Peiser	1922-1923
Jack Landesco	1924
Benedict Gorowitz	1926
Mrs. Ralph A. (Stella Loeb) Bloch	1929-1931

APPENDIX 29

THE JEWISH COMMUNITY CENTER OF MILWAUKEE
(Founded, 1931)

Presidents

Joseph L. Daneman	1931-1941
Eugene H. Mahler	1941-1947
Edward H. Meldman	1947-1949
Sol J. Kahn	1949-1955
Edward A. Miller	1955-1958
Bernard Solochek	1958-1961
Julius R. Atkins	1961-

Executive Directors

George M. Peizer	1931-1944
Jacob Mirviss	1944-1954
Harold E. Katz	1954-1955
Meyer Bass	1956-

APPENDIX 30

MILWAUKEE JEWISH COUNCIL

(Organized, 1938; comprising the following agencies: American Jewish Committee, American Jewish Congress, B'nai B'rith, Jewish Labor Committee, and the Jewish War Veterans of the United States; also, an equal number of members from the community-at-large.)

Presidents

Bert C. Broude	1938-1940	Robert A. Polacheck	1951-1953
Abe M. Rice	1940-1943	Lawrence S. Katz	1953-1955
Max Raskin	1943-1945	Myron L. Gordon	1955-1957
Eugene H. Mahler	1945-1947	Ralph L. Heilbronner	1957-1959
Norman N. Gill	1947-1949	Ben L. Chernov	1959-1961
Harry A. Kovenock	1949-1951	Richard L. Weil	1961-

Executive Directors

George Gratz	1939-1943
Ben Goldman	1944-1946
Sidney H. Sayles	1946-1962

APPENDIX 31

MILWAUKEE BUREAU OF JEWISH EDUCATION
(Organized 1944)

Presidents

Norman N. Gill	1944-1947	Bernard Solochek	1958-1959
Sam Rosen	1947-1951	Eliot M. Bernstein	1959-1961
Frank Grossman	1951-1954	Carl Millman	1961-
Morris Gordon	1954-1958		

Executive Directors

Meyer Gallin	1947-1952
Dr. Isaac Levitats	1952-1956
Dr. William B. Furie	1956-1962
Dr. Benjamin L. Yapko	1962-

APPENDIX 32

MILWAUKEE JEWS WHO HELD PUBLIC OFFICE

House of Representatives
Victor L. Berger   Fifth District   1911-1913; 1919-1929

U.S. Diplomatic Service
Marcus Otterbourg   U.S. Consul at Mexico City   1861-1867
U.S. Minister to Mexico   1867

Wisconsin State Legislature

Senators

Baruch [Bernard] S. Weil (Dem.) West Bend 1853, 1856, 1857
Washington County
Joseph J. Hirsch (Soc.)   Sixth District   1921-1923
Bernhard Gettelman (Rep.)   Fifth District   1923-1955
Joseph A. Padway (Soc.)   Sixth District   1925

Assemblymen

Baruch [Bernard] S. Weil (Dem.) West Bend, Wash. County 1852,
1880
Schleisingerville, Wash. County   1871, 1872, 1873

Moritz N. Becker (Lib. Dem.) Ninth District 1872, 1873
Jacob E. Friend (Rep.) Seventh District 1883-1885; 1885-1887
Charles Polacheck (Rep.) Wards 2 and 4 1897-1899
Simon Kander (Rep.) Wards 8 and 23 1907-1909
Arthur Kahn (Soc. Dem.) Tenth District 1911-1913
Bernhard Gettelman (Rep.) Seventh District 1917-1918
Charles S. Schiewitz (Rep.) Sixth District 1917-1919
Ben Z. Glass (Rep.) Sixth District 1925-1927
Harry G. Slater (Rep.) Twelfth District 1929-1931
Ben Rubin (Soc.) (Prog.) Sixth District 1931-1933; 1937-1943
Ben G. Slater (Rep.) Fifteenth District 1939-1941

Aldermen

	Ward	
Isaac Neustadtl (Rep.)	2	1852-1853
M. Heiman	9	1857; 1858 (Board of Councilors)
Lewis S. Mack (Dem.)	1	1861-1862
Louis Rindskopf (Dem.)	4	1869-1870; 1870-1871; 1872-1873
Henry M. Benjamin (Dem.)	6	1872-1874 (Board of Councilors) 1874-1877; 1877-1878
Fred T. Adler (Indep.)	6	1875-1876
Bernard Leidersdorf (Rep.)	8	1880-1881
Henry A. Adler (Dem.)	2	1888-1890
	Ald. at Large	1906-1908
Arthur Shutkin	6	1920-1928
Samuel M. Soref	6	1928-1940
Fred P. Meyers	6	1940-

County Board of Supervisors

Lewis S. Mack (Dem.) 1 and 7 Wards 1861-1862
Henry M. Benjamin (Dem.) 6th Ward 1874-1877; 1878

Judiciary

James M. Pereles	County Court	May, 1899-June, 1900
Samuel D. Stern	Police Court, West Allis	1922-1927
Joseph A. Padway	Civil Court, Branch 4	1924; 1926
Charles L. Aarons	Circuit Court, Branch 8	1926-1950
Myron L. Gordon	Civil Court, Branch 1	1950-1956
	County Court	1956-1961
	Wisconsin State Supreme Court	1962-

District Attorney

Leopold Hammel 1892-1893

Assistant District Attorney

Leo Reitman	1906-1912
Joseph Hirshberg	1911
Sol Simon } Louis Koenig }	1914-1922
Samuel E. Gross	1922-1928
Louis S. Wiener	1928-1932
Herman A. Mosher	1933-1937
Nathan W. Heller	1937-1943
Ben J. Wiener	1943-

City Attorney

Max Raskin (Soc.)	1932-1936

Assistant City Attorney

Benjamin Poss	1909
Louis L. Cohen	1916

Assistant U.S. Attorney for Eastern Dist. of Wis.

David A. Sondel	1918-1923

Minor Court Officials

Gottlieb Engel	Office Clerk, County Court in Probate	1875-1876
Moritz N. Becker	Deputy Sheriff, Municipal Court	1875-1877
Abraham L. Baer	Deputy Clerk, Municipal Court	1879-1881
Herman Schlomovitz	Baileff, Federal Court	1899-1919
	Deputy Marshall	1919
Bernhard Gettelman	Deputy Sheriff	1912
	Chief Deputy	1918-1919
Abraham Rosman	Deputy Sheriff	1915-1916

County Coroner

Dr. H. L. Nahin	1911-1912
Dr. S. N. Franklin	1918-1920

Board of School Directors

Max N. Lando	1879-1881
Jacob Poss	1881
E. M. Oberndorfer	1892-1895
James M. Pereles	1893-1895
Simon Kander	1893-1897
Charles Polacheck	1894-1897
Jacob Black	1897-1898
Rabbi Julius H. Meyer	1902-1904
Charles L. Aarons	1904-1906; 1908-1912

Thomas J. Pereles   1906-1909
Mrs. Simon Kander   1906-1919
Mrs. S. M. Cantrovitz   1912-1917
Morris Stern   1916-1921
Harry V. Meissner   1925-1947

Milwaukee School Board

Bernard A. Abrams   Assistant Supt. of Schools   1885-1908

Board of Trustees, Milwaukee Public Library

James M. Pereles   1897-1899; 1902-1910
Henry A. Adler   1906-1911
Victor L. Berger   1910-1912
Arthur Shutkin   1922-1928
Samuel M. Soref   1936-1938

Tax Commissioner   Henry Bonns   1881

Commissioners of Public Debt

Thomas J. Pereles   1896-1898
Isaac D. Adler   1904-1906
Bernard Leidersdorf   1906-1907
Emanuel D. Adler   1916-1928

Board of Fire and Police Commissioners

Jacob E. Friend   1901-1904
Joseph Stein   1920-1935

Board of Park Commissioners

Dr. Victor Caro   1906-1912
Benjamin Poss   1912-1918

Public Welfare Commission   Sol A. Eckstein   1918-1920

City Sewerage Commission   Bruno V. Bitker   1931-1950

Board of Estimates

Max Raskin   1932-1936
Fred P. Meyers   1947-

Board of Appeals

Morris Stern   1927-1933
Robert A. Hess   1936-1940
Michael Levin   1941-1944
Mrs. Michael Levin   1945-1947
Maurice M. Spracker   1948-1962

Safety Commission

	Dr. M. W. Sherwood	1932-1944
	Bert C. Broude	1934-

Board of Assessments

	Morris Stern	1933-1939
	Milton R. Polland	1940-1946

Municipal Reference Librarian   Norman N. Gill   1940-1945

Board of Harbor Commissioners   Milton R. Polland   1946-1949

Civic Progress Commission

	Ben Barkin	1947-1953
	Mrs. Michael Levin	1947-1953

APPENDIX 33

MILWAUKEE JEWS WHO DIED IN WORLD WAR II

Marvin A. Abrams
David Robert Altman
Phillip Askotsky
Norman R. Bensman
Sanford Morton Brooks
Norman Cabot
Sam Chudacoff
Irwin Cohen
Leonard E. Domb
Solomon S. Doren
Ervin Eisenstadt
Benjamin Frankel
Robert W. Gash
Robert Glaessner
Harvey Glick
Daniel Golland
Lawrence L. Gollin
Irving Grant
Arthur J. Grossman
Morris J. Guten
Armand L. Hankin
Edward J. Harris
Peter R. Hirshberg
Jacob J. Horwitz
Louis Kadwit
David Kramer
Arnold Libman
Isidore Lichter
Jack Lorber
Jack Mantell
Stanley Marsack
Milton Mendelblatt
Kurt David Meyer

William (Billy) Miller
Ben Moronovitz
Lawrence L. Moser
Robert J. Nathan
Arthur Nedbeck
Lester Roy Ordens
Robert J. Pentler
Alexander Perlin
Milton A. Perlin
Louis S. Peterman
Arthur L. Post
Harry A. Rattner
William Rosen
Matthew Rosenblum
Kenneth Ruskin
Louis Sadoff
Curtis E. Sanders
Bernard Schuster
Samuel Schwartz
Gerald E. Shapson
Joseph R. Sherr
Norman Siegel
Harry Silverstein
Jack Silverstein
Herbert Urich
David Velie
Leonard D. Vogel
Daniel F. Wallock
Edward G. Weisfeldt
Charles M. Willis
Sol C. Zaichick
Edward A. Zaidens

INDEX

(Covering text and notes only)

Aarons, Alois, 112
Aarons, Charles L., 110, 146, 163, 260, 300, 301-302, 304, 312
Aberson, Daniel, 242, 243
Abraham Lincoln House, 213, 226-227, 329
Abrams, Bernard A., 110, 114, 123, 257, 259, 262, 263, 389 n. 132, 390 n. 133, n. 135, n. 137, 391 n. 138, 428 n. 24
Adler, David, 14, 56, 71, 75, 78, 79, 81, 82, 91, 95, 104, 108, 109, 112, 115, 148, 151, 177, 229
Adler, David, & Sons, 251, 297
Adler, Frank B., 258
Adler, Frederick, 259
Adler, F. T., 145
Adler, Henry A., 122, 145, 146
Adler, Isaac D., 14, 103
Adler, Jacob, 14, 56, 360 n. 59, 372 n. 91
Adler, Dr. Louis, 18, 110
Adler, Solomon, 11, 14, 34, 40, 372 n. 91
Adler, Mrs. Solomon (Sarah), 40
Agudas Achim Synagogue, 207, 317
Agudas Achim Anshe Polen Synagogue, 206, 207, 419 n. 60
Agudas Hakhilos (Associated Congregations), 211
Ahabath Emuno Synagogue, 34-35, 38, 39, 367 n. 14, 372 n. 91
Album, Rabbi Joseph, 237
Alexander, 46
Aliyah (to Palestine), 255
Alliance Israélite Universelle, 71, 91, 230; Milwaukee branch, 72

Amalgamated Clothing Workers, 251, 297
"Americanization," 170, 229, 260, 285, 290, 330
American Christian Palestine Committee, 352
American Council for Judaism, 320, 348
American Israelite, 123, 397 n. 236, 415 n. 117
American Jewish Committee, 311, 312
American Jewish Conference, 312, 349
American Jewish Congress, 204, 272, 273, 278, 279, 280, 311
American Jewish Relief Committee, 230
Amsel, Dr. Jacob, 283, 284
Anshe Brith Sholem Synagogue, 207
Anshe Emes Synagogue (1871), 192, 415 n. 129
Anshe Emeth Synagogue, 35, 36-37, 39, 49, 368 n. 24, 372 n. 91
Anshe Jacob Synagogue, 193
Anshe Lubavich (Leibovitz) Synagogue, 206, 207, 211, 317, 338
Anshe Sfard Synagogue, 195, 197, 206, 207, 317, 338, 419 n. 60
Anti-Defamation League, 304, 312
Anti-Nazi meetings, 304
Anti-Semitism, 21, 23, 24, 64, 111-112, 133, 135-136, 142, 156, 160, 161, 245, 284, 285, 290; (1920's), 302, 303, 304; (1930's), 305, 308
Apter, Henry, 151

Art, 60
Assimilation, 63, 64, 293
Associated Charities, 216
Attorneys, see Occupations and Professions—Law
Auerbach, S. B., 101
Austrian, Julius, 17, 361 n. 77
Avukah, 326

Baer, Abraham, E., 146, 401 n. 91
Baer, Leopold, 177
Balfour Declaration, 255, 280-281
Bar Mitzvah, 264, 323, 324
Baron, Rabbi Joseph L., 202, 204, 304, 311, 319, 320, 333, 349
Baron de Hirsch Fund, 91, 158, 381 n. 90
Baumrind, Rabbi Harold, 317
Becker, Moritz, N., 122, 147, 402 n. 97
Bellack, C. H., 96
Ben-Hillel, Aryai, 349
Benedict, Henry, & Co., 108
Benedict, Joseph, 114, 121
Benedict, Julius, 96
Benjamin, Henry M., 102, 103, 108, 144-145, 400 n. 62, n. 63, n. 64, 401 n. 71
Bensman, Sender, 318
Berger, Victor L., 65, 113, 114, 150, 217, 253, 259, 262, 275, 301, 389 n. 132, 421 n. 17, 426 n. 50
Berko, Rev. Jonas, 263
Beth Am Center, 317
Beth El (Temple), 213, 318, 322, 324, 325, 338, 348
Beth El Ner Tamid Synagogue, 318-319
Beth Hamedrosh Hagodel B'nai Sholom Synagogue, 317
Beth Hamidrosh Hagodol, 152, 192, 194, 195, 196, 206, 237, 263
Beth Hatfiloh Synagogue, 206
Beth Israel Synagogue, 206, 207, 211, 263, 266, 271, 315, 316, 322, 338, 419 n. 60
Beth Medrash Hagodol Anshe Sfard Synagogue, 207, 317, 338, 419 n. 60
Beutler, Dr. Alfred, 295

Billikopf, Jacob, 231
Bimberg, David, 121
Bitker, J. L., 165, 284
Black, John (Jacob), 104, 146
Blade, Aaron, 13
Blade, A., & Son, 100
Block, Moritz G., 113
Blumberg, 92
Blumenfeld, David (Watertown), 48
Blumenthal, Leon, 80, 83
B'nai B'rith, Independent Order of, 56-58, 91, 115, 116, 158, 269, 311, 329; cemetery, 199, 375 n. 145, n. 152, 392 n. 161, 393 n. 178; see also Anti-Defamation League
B'nai Israel Synagogue, 206, 207, 213, 263, 317, 416 n. 146
B'nai Israel Anshe Hungari, see B'nai Israel Synagogue
B'nai Moshe, Order of, 56
B'ne Jacob Synagogue (1884), 193
B'ne Jacob Synagogue, 207, 317
B'ne Jeshurun (Temple), 29, 39, 45, 50, 66, 172, 200, 201, 261, 276, 369 n. 48, 409 n. 20, 414 n. 108
   Amalgamation with Emanu-El (Temple), 204-205, 418 n. 40
   Attitude toward non-affiliated, 176, 203
   Cantors, 188;
   Dedications, 39, 40, 172, 175, 369 n. 56
   Description, 39-40, 172, 175
   Dissension, 50
   Finances, 175, 203, 409 n. 29, 417 n. 23
   Ladies auxiliaries, 176
   Lay leadership, 39, 172, 176-177, 369 n. 58
   Membership, 48, 49, 175, 203; 418 n. 27
   School, 426 n. 50, 428 n. 20

B'ny Abraham Synagogue, 208
Board of Jewish Education, 323, 325
Boas, Fred (Montreal), 81, 82
Bolis, Mathilda, 83
Bonns, Henry, 13, 145, 372 n. 91
Boston Store, 99, 298

Brachman, Bernard, 99
Brachman, Oscar, 298
Brandeis, Jacob, 113, 114, 122
Brandeis, Louis D., visits Milwaukee,
   241
Brandt, Joseph, 98
Braunstein, David, 81
Bremer, Joseph, 16
Breslauer, A., 145
Breslauer, Max, 229
B'rith Abraham, Independent Order
   of, 56, 117, 269
Broude, Bert C., 304, 312, 320, 341
Browne, Rabbi Edward B. M., 178,
   411 n. 51
Bruno, Julius, 59
Brynwood Country Club, 327
Buchanan, President James, 45
Bureau of Jewish Education, 325, 344
Burstein, A., 273

Caeronsky, H., 151
Camp Sidney Cohen, 338
Cantor, Rabbi Samuel, 197
Cantrovitz, Mrs. S. M., 146
Caro, Rabbi Victor, 90, 92, 129, 185-
   187, 194, 195, 201, 202, 216, 223,
   260, 263
Carpeles, Philip, 29, 76, 85, 102, 107,
   120, 148, 216, 221, 222, 386 n. 66
Cemeteries, 33, 34, 37, 198, 199, 366
   n. 12, 367 n. 14, 416 n. 165, n. 166
Central Conference of American
   Rabbis, 346
Chamber of Commerce, 79, 106
Chenes, A., 151
Chevra Bikur Cholim (Hebrew Be-
   nevolent Society), 54, 217, 374
   n. 131
Children's Outing Society, 225, 229,
   344
Chudisch, Joseph, 81
Churches, early, 31
Civil Service Reform Association,
   147
Civil War:
   Casualties, 27-28, 365 n. 148
   Effect on industries, 29, 366 n. 153
   Home front activities, 26-27

Children's Orphan Asylum (B'nai
   B'rith), 218, 225, 228
Clubs, 117-118
Cohen, Alexander, 104
Cohen, Rabbi Boaz, 211
Cohen, Rabbi G. M., 45
Cohen, Isidor, 273
Cohen, Jonas, 99, 103
Cohen, Levi, 193
Cohen, Marcus, 99, 384 n. 37
Cohn, Hugo, 114
Cohn, Louis, 122
Common Council (Milwaukee), 306,
   350
Community Chest, 313, 343
Concordia Club, 117
Conservative Judaism, 213-214, 290,
   314, 318
Conversions, to Christianity, 63
Cook, Abraham, 194
County Board of Supervisors, 351
Cultural activities, 12, 52, 59, 113, 114,
   116, 120, 121-125, 176, 209, 331-
   335

Daily American (Milwaukee), 25
Daughters of Eva, *see* Moses Monte-
   fiore Gemeinde
David Pinsky Women's Club, 346
Dearborn Independent, 302
Deborah, Die, 123
Deborah Ladies' Hebrew Benevolent
   Society, 35, 53
Degel Israel Anshe Roumania Syna-
   gogue, 207, 317, 418 n. 53
Department stores, 99, 298
Depression (1920's), 164, 232, 234;
   (1930's), 289, 296, 298, 324
Desertion, 232, 424 n. 88
Deutelbaum, Leopold, 92
De Wolf, John E., 229
Discrimination, anti-Negro, 105
Dubinsky, M., 255
Dudley, Rev. J. L., 174

East-European Jews, 63-64, 67, 69, 70,
   73-74, 80, 81, 83, 85, 86, 87, 88, 89-
   90, 109, 117, 119, 128, 136, 155,
   156, 157, 158, 160, 162-164, 166-

168, 212, 219, 223, 235, 250, 269, 309-310

Eckstein, Solomon, 113, 177

Economic conditions, 7, 8, 12, 18, 30, 65, 88-89, 94, 96, 98, 101, 108, 112, 134, 162, 164, 165, 194, 219, 223, 232, 295, 299, 303

Education, 52-53, 259, 261, 315, 321-326
  Hebrew, 263-265, 266, 267, 318, 322, 324, 325
  Religious, 52, 53, 227, 261, 262-263, 316, 322, 324
  Yiddish, 264, 266, 267, 322, 323, 324

Eisen, H. L., 99

Ellinger, Moritz, 72

Emanu-El (Temple), 51, 66, 172, 173, 174, 201, 204, 261, 276, 338, 417 n. 21
  Amalgamation with B'ne Jeshurun, 204-205
  Attitude toward unaffiliated, 176, 203
  Dedication, 173-174
  Finances, 175, 203, 409 n. 29
  Improvements, 174
  Ladies' auxiliaries, 176
  Membership, 49, 203
  Officers, 176-177
  Rabbis, 174, 178-185, 200-202
  Ritual, 51, 187-188, 414 n. 102, 417 n. 16
  School, 261-262, 427 n. 18, 428 n. 23
  Youth, 176

Emanu-El B'ne Jeshurun (Temple), 205, 319, 320, 348

Emigrant Aid Relief Association of Wisconsin, 82

Emigrant Relief Association, 74

Enzer, Dr. Norbert, 341

Eppstein, Rabbi Elias, 45-46, 50, 53, 113-114, 123, 172, 177-178

Esselin, Alter, 332, 435 n. 39

Ethnic groups, 64

Ettenheim, George P., 300

Ezer be Tzar (Help in Distress), 269, 270, 272, 284

Falk, Rabbi Samson, 29, 45, 46, 371 n. 78

Fallows, Bishop Samuel, 283

Federated Jewish Charities, 225, 229, 230, 265, 267, 303, 313, 323, 339, 424 n. 82

Fein, Joseph S., 232

Fein, Solomon, 91, 193, 194, 196, 197, 232

Fein, Solomon, Dental Clinic, 233

Feingold, Joseph, 92

Feldman, Peter R., 153, 277

Feldman, Rabbi Abraham, 195

Folk Institute, 324

Folk Shule, 266, 324, 325, 423 n. 74

"Forty-eighters," 10, 59

Frank, Louis, 16, 100

Franks, Jacob, 11, 359 n. 44

Fraternal Orders, 55, 56, 113

Free Sons of Israel, Independent Order of, 56, 116

Freie Gemeinde (Free Congregation), 47, 59

Freschl, Max, 229

Friedberg, Joseph, 103

Friedberger, Alfred, 97

Friedlander, Theodore, 298

Friedman, Albert T., 99

Friedman, Ign., 109

Friedmann, Charles, 258

Friend Brothers Clothing Co., 95

Friend, Charles, 229, 231, 258, 279

Friend, Edward Jr., 99

Friend, Elias, 14, 37, 71, 76, 78, 103, 107, 368 n. 39, 382 n. 8

Friend, Mrs. Elias (Rosa), 37

Friend, Emanuel, 95, 99, 145

Friend, Mrs. Emanuel, 148

Friend, Henry, 14, 95, 382 n. 6

Friend, Isaac, 145, 382 n. 8

Friend, Jacob E., 101, 103, 109, 147, 388 n. 121, 402 n. 100

Friend, Meyer, 14, 372 n. 91, 382 n. 8

Friend, Dr. Samuel H., 110

Frisch, A. P., 259

Gallin, Meyer, 325

Gemilath Chesed Society (Hebrew Free Loan Association), 218, 229

Gentile-Jewish relations, 136, 137, 138, 149, 283-284, 302, 306
Gerechter, Rabbi Emanuel, 92, 113, 178, 188, 192, 411 n. 48
German Jews, 56, 64, 86, 128, 156, 166, 241, 330, 339
Germania, 135
Germania Society, 59
Germanism, 12, 18, 64
German-Jewish press, 123-127
Gettelman, Bernhard, 153, 301, 404 n. 143
Gill, Norman N., 301, 312
Gimbel, Adam, 99
Gimbel Brothers, 99, 100, 109, 298, 384 n. 43
Glassberg, Benjamin, 301, 339
Glassman, Israel, 236, 237, 245
Glick, Jacob, 193
Glicksman, Nathan, 109
Glueck, Prof Sheldon, 293
Goetz, Millie, 119
Goldberg, Charles L., 300
Goldman, Ben, 312, 314
Goldman, Julius, 91
Goldsmith, Jonas, 27-28, 365 n. 145
Goldsmith, Sophia Heller, 3, 364 n. 137, 369 n. 56
Goldstein, Barnett, 236
Goodman, Harry B., 318
Goodman, I., 91
Goodman, N. N., 231
Gould, Nathan J., 334
Gratz, George, 311, 312, 314
Grobanski, A., 193
Gross, Bernhard, 16, 84, 91, 101, 112, 120, 145, 148, 221
Gruenberg, Philip, 99

Habonim, 349
Hachnosas Orchim, 157, 220, 229, 336
Hadassah, 346, 348
Hammel, Leopold, 91, 131, 146, 284
Harmonie Club, 60, 117
Harris, Leo, 151, 177
Hart, J. M., 15, 35, 372 n. 91
Hart, W. L., 15
Hartman, F. W., & Co., 100, 385 n. 51
Hashomer Hatzair, 349

Hazzanim, 45, 46, 212
Hebrah B'ne Israel, 194
Hebrah Ohabai Sholem (Society of Lovers of Peace), 193
Hebrah Sholem (Ladies' Society of Peace), 194
Hebraists, 91, 120, 332
Hebrew Benevolent Association, *see* Chevra Bikur Cholim
Hebrew Educational Society, 92, 263
Hebrew Emigrant Aid Society (N.Y.), 76-78
Hebrew Free School, 263-264, 428 n. 25
Hebrew Home for Consumptives (Denver), 225
Hebrew Imigrant Aid Society, 230
Hebrew Institute, 228
Hebrew Orphan Asylum (Cleveland), 57-58, 115, 229-230
Hebrew Protective Association, 196
Hebrew Relief Association, 53, 54, 85, 90, 91, 215, 216, 220-225, 229, 231, 232, 233, 313, 374 n. 133
Hebrew Relief Society, *see* Hebrew Relief Association
Hebrew Widows' and Orphans' Association, 54, 218, 223, 225, 374 n. 132
Hebros, 54
Hebra Kadisha, 211, 318
Hecht, Samuel, 98
Hecht, Rabbi Sigmund, 91, 92, 129, 130, 132, 135-136, 147, 151, 182-185, 194, 196, 202, 216, 223, 413 n. 73, n. 74, n. 80
Heder, 263
Heifetz, Louis, 332
Heiman, Leopold, 148
Heiman, Marcus, 19, 39, 45, 46, 221
Heimann, Joe, 101
Heimann, M., & Co., 98
Heller, Bernard, 3, 16, 358 n. 37
Heller, Simon, 177
Herald Citizen, 305
Herbst, Emma, first Jewish child born in Milwaukee, 11
Herbst, S. C., 100, 108
Herman, Henry, 104

Herold, Der, 33, 135, 305
Herzfeld, Carl, 99
Hess, Dr. Adolph, 243
Hess, Robert A., 254, 311, 347
Hexter, Maurice B., 231
Hirsch, Rabbi Emil G., 123
Hirsch, Joseph J., 154
Hirsch, Samuel, 126
Hirschberg, I. M., 177
Hirschberg, Rabbi Samuel, 201, 202, 204, 260, 284, 319, 320, 418 n. 37
Hirschman, Leola (Sure), 147
Home for the Aged, 207, 228, 338
Horwich, Bernard, 237
Horwitz, Charles, 121
Horwitz, Isaac, 145
Horwitz, Isidor, 284, 334
Horwitz, Phillip, 28-29, 98, 365 n. 147
Hovevey Zion, 237
Hurwitz, 88

Imanu-Al Synagogue, 34, 38-39, 48, 372 n. 91
Immigration:
  East-European Jews, 64, 69, 70, 71, 72, 73, 76-77, 79, 80, 81, 82, 83, 86, 88, 159, 330, 339
  German Jews, 3, 9, 10, 11, 59, 63, 72-73, 90, 155, 157, 159, 206, 233, 250, 293-294
Indians, 4, 11
Industrial Removal Office (I R O), 98, 116, 156, 157, 158, 405 n. 15
Intermarriage, 63, 179-180
Isaacs, I., 87
Isaacs, Sam, 149
Israelson, Rabbi Solomon, 195-196, 197, 416 n. 153

Jewish Bakers' Union, 165, 298
Jewish Children's Home, 228, 336, 337, 338, 344
Jewish Chronicle (New York), 3
Jewish Colonial Bank, 240
Jewish Community Center, 227, 330, 336, 338, 343
Jewish Consumptives Relief Society (Denver), 230

Jewish Family and Children's Service, 338, 344
Jewish Labor Committee, 311, 312
Jewish Legion, 277
Jewish National Credit Association, 165
Jewish National Fund, 240, 349
Jewish National Workers' Alliance (Farband), 244, 324, 329, 347
Jewish neighborhood, 87, 89, 90, 162-163, 197-198, 290, 423 n. 77
Jewish Painters' Club, 298
Jewish People's Committee, 306
Jewish Relief Day, 270
Jewish Social Service Association, 225, 233, 234, 338, 339, 344
Jewish Vocational Service, 294, 344
Jewish War Veterans, 312
Jewish Welfare Board, 278, 308
Jews, general interest in, 32-33
Joint Distribution Committee, 340, 341
Judell, Philip, 232
Juneau, Solomon, 4, 6, 357 n. 19
Junge Maenner Verbruederung, 56

Kadis, Isadore, 231
Kahn, R. Robert, 258
Kahn, Simon, 177
Kalamazoo Knitting Co., 99
Kalisch, Rabbi Isidor, 26, 39, 40, 42-44, 49, 50, 52-53, 369 n. 64, 370 n. 64, n. 70, 371 n. 73
Kallen, Prof. Horace, 272
Kander, Simon, 104, 146
Kander, Mrs. Simon (Lizzie Black), 119, 146, 227, 263, 330
Kaplan, A., 255
Karger, David, 298
Karger, Max, 298
Kashrut, 193, 318
Katz, Henry, 52, 149
Katz, Mrs. Henry (Elizabeth), 52
Katz, Jacob, 97, 108
Katz, Mrs. Rosa, 27
Keren Hayesod, 255, 340
Kesher Shel Barzel, Order of (Iron Knot), 56, 116
Kilbourn, Byron, 4, 7

Kleinman, Rabbi Philip, 318
Knights of Honor, 113
Knights of Zion, Order of, 237, 238, 240-241, 242, 256, 272
Knitters' Club, 107
Kohn, Rabbi Eugene, 318
Kohn, Julius, 100
Kovenock, Harry A., 312
Krasnowitz, Paul, 81, 236
Krass, Rabbi Nathan, 81
Krauskopf, Harry, 229
Kuryer Polski, 282

Labor Party, 149, 150
Labor relations, 108
Labor Zionists, 310
Ladies' Aid Society, 220
Ladies' Benevolent Society, 53
Ladies' Gemilas Chesed, 54
Ladies' Relief Sewing Society, 76, 80, 219, 225, 229, 232, 344
Ladoff, Isadore, 88, 91, 138, 223, 246
Ladoff, Miss, 92
La Follette, Robert M., 64
Lake Superior Navigation Company, 17
Landauer, Adolph, 97, 229, 230, 232
Landauer, Max, 97, 105, 107, 109, 120, 177, 185, 194, 229
Landauer & Co., 97
Lando, Julius, 101
Lando, Max N., 101, 146
Lapham Park Social Center, 227, 230, 423 n. 77
Larson, Laurence M., 259
Lasker, Raphael, 46
Lazoff, M., 273
League for Labor Palestine, 348
League of American Jews, 242
Lederer, I. M., 101
Leeser, Isaac, 49
Leiboen, H., 151
Leidersdorf, Bernard, 101, 122, 145, 401 n. 73
Leiser, Isidore, 149
Leopold, Aaron, 103, 221
Leopold, Henry F., 17, 361 n. 79
Leopold & Austrian, 17
Lerner, Joseph, 273

Levitan, Solomon, 301
Levi, Rabbi Charles S., 165, 200, 202, 205, 242, 271, 274, 279, 284
Levin, Dr. Shmarya, visits Milwaukee, 241
Levy, Isaac, 105, 111, 372 n. 91
Levy, Simon, 24, 35, 47, 372 n. 91
Levy, Sally, 99
Lilienthal, Rabbi Max, 173
Lipkind, Rabbi G., 201
Lisitzky, Ephraim E., 264, 265, 274, 279, 280, 332, 431 n. 42
Literary and Social Life Club, 120
Litt, I. J., 120
Litt, Jacob, 105, 113
Litvishe Shule, *see* Beth Israel Synagogue
Loeb, Stella (Mrs. Ralph A. Block), 226
Loebel, Dr. Morris, 110
Loevenberg, Levi M., 46
Lubavishe Shule, *see* Anshe Lubavich Synagogue

Machzikei HaDass, 211
Mack, Edward S., 96, 110
Mack, Herman S., 15, 20, 56, 96, 109, 357 n. 21
Mack, Hugo, 15, 96
Mack, Lewis S., 15, 19, 59, 362 n. 96, n. 97
Mack, Max, 15
Mack & Co., 96
Mahler, Edward, 177
Mahler, Eugene H., 312
Mahler, Gustav, 27-28
Mahler, Jacob, 16, 19, 20, 29, 59
Malamut, Joseph L., 335
Mandel, Frieda, 274
Manesewitz, Rabbi Ben Zion, 317
Manhoff, M., 237
Mann, Louis, 259
Mansion House Committee (London), 76, 77
Manufacturers' Club, 107
Margalith, Haim, 323, 325
Margoles, Dr. Frank C., 300
Markham's Academy, 258
Markwell, J., 101

Markwell, M., 35, 47, 372 n. 91
Marquette University, 52, 300, 302, 326
Marshall, Sol, 153, 246
Mason, Maurice, 334
Masonic Order, 55, 56, 111-112
Matzot, 100
May Laws (1882), 69
Mc Arthur, Judge Arthur, 24, 361 n. 84
Meissner, C. A., 122
Meissner, Harry V., 301
Melamdim, 263, 264, 267, 322
Mendel, H. M., 14, 15, 19, 59, 105, 107, 142, 145, 148, 149, 384 n. 44
Mendel, Dr. Jacob, 110, 147
Mendelssohn, Moritz, 112
Merchants' Association, 94, 107
Metzel, Alexander, 27-28
Mexican War, 26
Meyer, Rabbi Julius H., 146, 201-202
Meyers, Fred P., 301
Michelbacher, 97
Miller, Morris, 177, 224, 229, 298
Milwaukee, early history of, 6, 7, 8, 9, 10, 11, 20, 93
Milwaukee Army and Navy Committee, 308
Milwaukee Association of Commerce, 302
Milwaukee-Downer Seminary, 52
Milwaukee Greater Temple, 318
Milwaukee Immigrant Relief Association, 72, 73, 83, 85, 87
Milwaukee Industrial Exposition, 107
Milwaukee Jewish Alliance, 90-92
Milwaukee Jewish Council, 304, 306, 308, 311, 314, 344
Milwaukee Jewish Industrial Aid Society, 158
Milwaukee Jewish Mission, 119, 220, 226
Milwaukee Jewish Orphan Home, see Jewish Children's Home
Milwaukee Jewish War Sufferers' Relief Committee, 271
Milwaukee Journal, 351, 352
Milwaukee Literary Society, 58
Milwaukee Municipal League, 148

Milwaukee Musical Society, 58-59, 122
Milwaukee Operatic and Dramatic Club, 123
Milwaukee Public Library, 59, 93
Milwaukee Sentinel, 106
Milwaukee Talmud Torah, 207, 228-229, 264, 265, 267, 322, 323-324, 325, 329, 423 n. 74, 429 n. 35
Milwaukee Jewish Welfare Fund, 311, 313, 325, 341, 342
(Milwaukee) State Teachers College, 301
Milwauker Idishe Shtimme, 313, 335, 345
Milwauker Wochenblat, 275, 334
Minhag, 34, 35, 36, 39
Minhag America, 49, 187
Mintz, Rabbi Max, 315
Mizrachi, 346-347, 348
Mohelim, 46
Montefiore, Moses, Gemeinde, 193
Montefiore Home for the Aged (Cleveland), 230
Montefiore, Sir Moses, 54, 115
Morawetz, Jacob, 98, 122
Morawetz, M. S., 104
Mortara Case, 25-26
Moses, Rabbi Isaac S., 71, 73, 83, 120, 123, 124, 179-182, 189, 191, 411 n. 56, 412 n. 71
Moshav Zekanim, see Home for the Aged
Mount Sinai Hospital, 201, 227-228, 233, 300, 303, 336-337, 338, 343, 423 n. 78
Music, 58-59, 121-122
Mutual aid societies, 56, 234
Mutual loan societies, 234
Myerson (Meir), Golda (née Mabovitz), 255

Nahin, Dr. H. L., 247
National Council of Jewish Women, 119, 225, 228, 229, 329, 395 n. 200
National Farm School (Doylestown, Pa.), 230
National Jewish Hospital for Consumptives (Denver), 230

National Knitting Works, 99, 108, 109

Native Jews, 63-64, 66, 92, 121, 159-160, 169-170, 240, 273, 279, 309

Nazi Bund, 303

Neustadtl, Isaac, 10, 11, 16, 19, 20, 23, 33, 48, 52, 59, 129, 149, 217

Neustadtl, Nathan E., 27-28

Newbouer, Charles, 96, 365 n. 148

Newbouer, Edward, 96

Newbouer, Leopold, 96

Newbouer, Nathan, 96, 177

New Home Club, 295, 296

Newhouse, H., and Co., 13

Newhouse, Henry, 33

Newald, M. D., 229

Newman, J. H., 229

Nickel, U., 151

Nickoll, B. F., 341

Nordberg Manufacturing Co., 101

Northwestern Knitting Works, 96

Northwestern Worsted Mills, 99

Oberndorfer, E. M., 146

Oberndorfer, Henry M., 95

Occupations and professions:
Bakers, 164, 165
Banking, 16, 17, 102, 109
Building trades, 89, 164, 165
Butchers and meat packers, 16, 89, 100, 163
Cap makers, 15, 98, 165, 250
Cigar making, 13, 164
Clerical, 13, 89
Clothing, 13, 14, 95, 96, 97, 99, 296, 406 n. 41
Coal, 103
Dentistry, 110, 159, 163, 299, 300
Distilling, 100, 101
Dry goods, 15, 97
Florists, 102
Flour milling, 101
Grocers, 16, 98, 100, 163
Insurance, 16, 97, 104
Jewelry, 101
Law, 16, 17, 18, 96, 109, 146, 150, 163, 165, 231, 254, 277, 294, 299-300, 341
Liquor, 96, 100

Lumber, 102

Manufacturing, 9, 12, 18, 94, 98, 99, 101, 102, 108, 163, 164, 251

Medicine, 18, 89, 110, 159, 162-163, 243, 247, 294, 299, 300, 432-433 n. 16

Merchants, 95, 102, 162, 296, 297

Millinery, 98, 101

Mining, 102, 103

Morticians, 198-199

Music, 18, 60

Needle trades, 96, 99, 298

Opticians, 101, 110, 163

Peddling, 8, 12, 15, 16, 160-161

Pharmacy, 154

Real Estate, 97, 103, 104

Scrap metals, 161, 162, 164, 296, 306

Shoemakers, 89, 164

Tailoring, 13, 89, 163, 165, 236, 296

Tanners, 89

Teaching, 299

Theatre, 105

Tobacco, 17, 101

Transportation, 16-17

Women's wear, 16, 98, 298

Odd Fellows, Independent Order of, 55, 56, 112

Oer Chodosh (New Light) Society, 213

Oettinger, B., 35, 372 n. 91

Orthodox Judaism, 192, 193, 194, 195-197, 206, 207, 213, 290, 314, 317, 348

Ostraykher Kranken Untershtitsn Farayn (OKUV), 328

Otterbourg, Marcus, 22-23, 364 n. 122

Padway, Joseph A., 163, 253, 254, 282, 300

Palestine Labor Fund (Geverkshaften), 244, 340, 341

Palman, 244

Pale of Settlement, 69

Pastor, Rabbi Harry B., 320

Patek, Gottlieb, 100

Patek, Mark L., 258

Peiser, Kurt, 226, 231

Peiser, Dr. Simon, 231

Peixotto, Benjamin F., 30, 45, 57, 115
People's Party, 149
People's Relief Committee, 270
Perchonok, Louis, 243, 245, 273, 347, 425 n. 21
Pereles, James Madison, 91, 102, 104, 109, 146, 148, 149, 259, 402 n. 93, n. 95, 403 n. 122
Pereles, Mrs. J. M., 148, 403 n. 109
Pereles, Nathan, 16, 17, 19, 20, 28, 35, 39, 48, 102, 109, 142, 357 n. 21, 361 n. 84, 372 n. 91, 388 n. 119
Pereles, Nathan, Jr., 258
Pereles, Thomas Jefferson, 102, 109, 145, 146, 149, 259
Perhift Players, 334
Perlman, Z., 237
Pevsner, Bella, 242
Philanthropy, 53, 54, 57-58, 67, 74, 215-217, 218-222, 225, 228, 229-234, 313, 336-344
Phillips, Dorothy, 229
Phoenix Club, 117, 394 n. 190
Pinsel, Jack, 283
Pioneer Women, 347-348
Poale Zion, 165, 241, 242, 243, 245, 251, 256, 260, 272, 273, 310, 324, 338, 340, 346, 347-348
Podlasky, Capt. H. B., 282
Pogroms, Jewish reactions to, 281-282
Polacheck, Charles, 146
Polacheck, J. & S., 252
Political activities, 12, 19, 20, 21, 22, 128, 138-139, 140-146, 150-154, 401 n. 84
Population statistics, 7, 9, 10, 11, 12, 18, 30, 49, 63, 65-68, 69, 86, 87, 89, 93, 115, 122, 152, 156, 178, 190, 261, 268, 292, 307, 327, 357 n. 18, 366 n. 155, 375 n. 143, 376 n. 1, n. 5, 381 n. 78, n. 88, 382 n. 1, 431-432 n. 1
Posey, A., 335
Poss, Benjamin, 283, 300
Poss, Jacob, 146, 177
Post, Major Arthur L., 307-308
Previant, J., 237, 241
Primakow, 88

Progress Club, 118, 395 n. 195
Progressive Order of the West, 328
Progressive Rag Peddlers' Union, 162

Rabinovitch, Samuel, 231
Rappaport, Rabbi Julius, 213
Raskin, Max, 301, 312
Reform Judaism, 48-49, 170, 171, 186-191, 200, 202, 203, 290, 314, 319
Refugees, German (1930's), occupations, 294, 295
Refugees, German, post-1945, 295
Refugee and Migration Service, 294, 344
Reichmann, R., 221
Religious denominations in Milwaukee (1845), 31, 171
Rhodes, Irving G., 334
Rice, Abe M., 312
Rice, J. H., 109
Rich, Adolph W., 15, 91, 97, 107, 108, 116, 120, 122, 123, 146, 148, 158, 216, 217, 221, 260, 401 n. 84, 405 n. 12
Rich, Mrs. A. W., 219
Rich, A. W., Shoe Co., 98
Rich, Edith, 119
Rindskopf, Elias, 101
Rindskopf, Jacob, 101
Rindskopf, Loebl, 142, 399 n. 57
Rindskopf, Louis, 19, 145, 151, 172, 400 n. 61
Rindskopf, L., & Sons, 100
Rindskopf, Samuel, 27, 101, 103, 104, 139-144
Rindskopf, Max, 101
Rose, Mayor David, 238
Rose, Rev. H. T., 79
Rosenbaum, Arnold, 27-28
Rosenbaum, Stella B., 226
Rosenberg, I. J., 315, 419 n. 60
Rosenheimer, L., 142
Roth, Moses, 17
Roth, Solomon, 17, 101
Round Table of Christians and Jews, 304
Rubenstein, Rabbi Charles, 315, 317, 348

Rubin, Ben, 301
Rubin, Jacob H., 153, 165, 273
Rubin, S., 281
Rubin, William B., 150, 165, 254, 283, 284
Rubinstein, Isaac, 231
Rukeyser, M., 103
Rumanishe Shule, *see* Degel Israel Anshe Roumania Synagogue
Russian Immigrant Relief Society (New York), 72, 73, 78
Russian Protective Club, 87
Russo-American Extradition Treaty, 246

Sabbath Observance, 190, 197, 203, 206
Safer, 237
Saffro, Joseph, 232, 237, 273, 347, 425 n. 11
Saltzstein, A. L., 229, 231, 232, 320
Sand, Nathan, 269, 273, 279, 280, 311, 347
Sandburg, Carl, 241
Sarner, Rabbi Ferdinand Leopold, 44-45, 371 n. 76
Sayles, Sidney H., 312, 314
Schlomovitz, Herman, 151, 153, 193, 195, 263
Scheftels, 100, 109
Scheinfeld, Aaron, 259, 341
Scheinfeld, Amram, 293
Scheinfeld, Rabbi Solomon Isaac, 195, 197, 208-211, 238, 243, 265, 270, 273, 276, 284, 315, 316-317, 332
Schnell, 237
Schoenfeld, Henry, 121, 385 n. 51
Schoenfeld, Theodore, 18, 121
Schoenmann, Jonas, 34, 47, 48, 102, 372 n. 91
Schools, 52, 66, 93, 110, 132, 245, 257-258, 260, 389 n. 132, 390 n. 133, n. 134
  Bible reading in, 131-132
  Higher education, 259, 300, 301, 302, 305, 326
  Private, 51, 52, 66, 93, 257
  School Board, members of, 146
Schurz, Carl, 22

Schuster, Edward, 99
Schwab, S., 273
Schwartz, Julius, 126
Schwarzenberg, M. H., 19, 35, 47, 372 n. 91
Schram, Bernard, 3, 145
Schram, Charles B., 259
Schram, David, 318
Schram, D. L., & Co., 199
Schram, Joseph B., 16, 96, 102, 373 n. 117
Schram, Louis B., 76, 78, 79, 81, 109
Schulson, Rabbi Solomon, 326
Schwenger, S., 100
Schiewitz, Charles, 153
Seebote, defends kidnapping of Edgar Mortara, 26
Seidel, Mayor Emil, 241
Sekles, Simon, 190
Seligman, Moritz, 105
Seidelman, Hyman M., 312, 347, 349
Seidelman, Lt. Joseph, 282
Settlement Cook Book, 226, 227, 330, 423 n. 76
Settlement, The, 119, 220, 226, 229, 428 n. 24
Shakman, Louis A., 95, 96, 103, 108
Shakman, Mrs. Abraham (Maria Heller), 30
Shalom (Temple), 320
Shapiro, Rabbi David S., 317, 326
Shapiro, I. M., 237, 273
Shapiro, S., 324
Sholom Aleichem Circle, 327
Shoyer, Emanuel, 13
Shoyer, E. M., & Co., 13
Shoyer, Charles, 11
Shoyer, Dr. Charles C., 18
Shoyer, Emanuel, 11
Shoyer, Gabriel, 11, 13, 19, 357 n. 21, 358 n. 22, 359 n. 47, 362 n. 93, 372 n. 91
Shoyer, Myer, 11, 13
Shoyer, Samuel, 11, 13
Shoyer, William, 11, 13
Shulkin, 88
Shutkin, Arthur, 154, 273, 301
Siegel, Chaim, 348
Siegel, Louis, 198, 318

Silber, Effie, 199; Silber, Marcus, 131
Silber, Lewis, 78, 97, 99, 104, 108, 112, 383 n. 23
Silver, Rabbi Abba Hillel, 352
Silverman, Emanuel, 14, 95, 383 n. 12
Silverman, Lion, 21-22, 29, 363 n. 115, n. 118, n. 121
Simon, Julius, 99
Simon, Nic, 17, 59
Simon, Victor, 13
Sinai (Temple), 200
Sinaiko, 88
Singer & Benedict, 98
Singer, Jacob, 96, 147
Sisterhood of Personal Service, 119, 219-220, 223, 225, 229
Slimmer, Abraham, 201, 228
Socialism, 65, 128, 150, 153-154, 236, 251
Social Democratic Party, 65, 150, 242, 245, 246, 253, 272
Social Territorialists, 245
Social patterns, 12, 23, 55, 56, 57, 89-90, 111, 113, 114, 115, 117-119, 156, 160 191, 197, 206, 226-227, 310, 326-330, 331, 406 n. 40a
Social Workers Tuberculosis Sanitarium, 201, 232
Society for the Care of Dependent Jewish Children, 228
Society for the Relief of the Jewish Sick Poor, 220
Society of Friends, 295
Sokolow, Nahum, visits Milwaukee, 241
Sonnlander, Moritz, 145
Sons of Benjamin, 117
Sons of Hermann, 47, 55, 113
Soref, Samuel M., 301
Spanish-American War, 149, 274, 403 n. 127
Sphardishe Shule, see Anshe Sfard Synagogue
Spichenetzky, L., 151
Spiegel, Arthur, 335, 435 n. 40
Spitz, Rabbi Moritz, 174, 179, 217, 261, 411 n. 55
Standard Club, 118, 395 n. 197
Stein, Charles, 96, 98, 221

Stein, Marcus, 15
Stein, Nathan M., 311, 341, 349
Steinhardt, Jacob, 14, 362 n. 93
Stern, Bernhard, 101, 109, 122, 139
Stern, H., Jr., & Bros. Co., 97
Stern, Helena, 226, 227
Stern, Henry, 4, 8, 9, 15, 27, 48, 360 n. 66
Stern, Herman, 15, 145
Stern, Morris, 146, 231, 260, 274
Stoler, Max, 236
Stone, Nat (Nathan), 99, 229, 284, 298
Stowell, John M., 76, 79, 85
Strauss, S., 35, 46
Strelzin, Alfred, 293
Strelzin, Morris, 277, 430-431 n. 35
Strikes, 107-108, 165-166, 236, 250-251
Sunday Closing Laws, 130-131
Swichkow, Rabbi Louis J., 312, 349, 350, 353, 375 n. 152, 393 n. 178, 437 n. 1
Swiss Treaty, protest, 25, 364 n. 131

Tax, Sol, 293
Thal, F. W., 149
Thal, S., 103
Tobias, L., 91
Tuchman, I., 347
Tucker, Sara, 349
Turnverein, 55, 114
Twerski, Rabbi Jacob, 316, 318, 434 n. 7
True Sisters, Benevolent Society of (Die Treue Schwestern), 43, 53, 218, 225, 370 n. 70, 374 n. 129, n. 130

Union Bank, 165
Union of American Hebrew Congregations, 346
Union Prayer Book, 187
Unionism, 101, 107, 165, 236, 245, 250, 252, 297
United Hebrew Charities, 223, 422 n. 58
United Hebrew School, 325
United Jewish Appeal, 340, 341, 343
United Palestine Appeal, 340

United Synagogue B'ne Sholom, 317
United Synagogue of America, 346
United Workmen, Ancient Order of, 113
University of Wisconsin, 300, 302, 305, 326

Vaad HaKashruth, 306
Verein Freie Männer (Society of Free Men), 47
Voorsanger, Rabbi Elkan C., 314, 341

Wachsner, Leon, 123
Walnut Street, 327
Weil, Baruch (Bernard) Schleisinger, 20-21, 146, 217, 362 n. 102, n. 103, n. 104, 363 n. 109, 402 n. 97, n. 98
Weil, Benjamin M., 76, 78, 91, 104, 107, 108, 109, 120, 123, 148, 222, 261
Weil, David, 105, 113
Weil, Dr. Herman, 295
Weil, Morris, 104
Weil, Moses, 11
Weil, Theodore, 104
Weingrod, Morris, 312, 347, 349
Weinshel, Howard, 334
Weisfeld, Israel, 193
Weizmann, Dr. Chaim, visits Milwaukee, 328
Welfare, 53-54
Welitzky, A. B., 237
Wendt, C. E., 16
Western Star, Independent Order of, 117
Wiley, Senator Alexander, 352
Wilitzkin, 92
Wisconsin Jewish Chronicle, The, 334-335, 345
Wisconsin *Nahalah* (landholding), 349
Wisconsin Territory, 4
Wise, Dr. Isaac Mayer, 18, 37-38, 40-41, 48, 49, 57, 126-127, 172, 178, 180-181, 368 n. 41, 400 n. 63

Wise, Dr. Stephen S., 254, 268, 328, 342
Women's League for Jewish Education, 325
Woodmen of the World, Camp Barbanel, 117
Woodmount Club, 327
Workmen's Circle, 244, 246, 247-250, 251, 253, 269, 272, 273, 276, 279, 325, 328, 338, 346
Workmen's Circle School, 266, 267, 324
World War I, 268, 273, 275-276, 285;
Casualties, 276, 430 n. 30
Citations, 276
Homefront, 274, 276, 277, 278
World War II:
Casualties, 307
Citations, 276
Homefront, 330-331
Lawyers and physicians in service, 307
German Jewish refugees in armed forces, 307

Yiddish, 347, 348, 350
Yiddish Drama League, 334
Yiddish press, 313, 334, 335
Young, Brigham, 100
Young Literary and Dramatic Society, 334
Young Men's Hebrew Association, 120
Young Men's Hebrew Literary Society, 91, 120
Youth, 321

Zeitgeist, Der, 72, 123-127, 182, 334, 397 n. 238
Zellner, Benjamin, 13
Zimmerman, Isaac, 81
Zionism, 65, 202, 235, 237-245, 254, 256, 308, 310, 313, 320, 326, 335, 346, 347, 349, 350, 351, 353

The Jacob R. Schiff Library
Of Jewish Contributions to American Civilization

1. **Jacob R. Marcus**
   EARLY AMERICAN JEWRY (2 Volumes)
2. **Jeanette W. Rosenbaum**
   MYER MYERS, GOLDSMITH
3. **Robert D. Abrahams**
   THE COMMODORE
4. **Norman Bentwich**
   FOR ZION'S SAKE
5. **S. N. Carvalho** (Bertram W. Korn, editor)
   INCIDENTS OF TRAVEL AND ADVENTURE IN THE FAR WEST
6. **Bernard Postal and Lionel Koppman**
   A JEWISH TOURIST'S GUIDE TO THE UNITED STATES
7. **Jacob R. Marcus**
   MEMOIRS OF AMERICAN JEWS (3 Volumes)
8. **Benjamin II** (Charles Reznikoff, translator)
   THREE YEARS IN AMERICA (2 Volumes)
9. **Rachel Wischnitzer**
   SYNAGOGUE ARCHITECTURE IN THE UNITED STATES
10. **Edwin Wold, 2d, and Maxwell Whiteman**
    THE HISTORY OF THE JEWS OF PHILADELPHIA
11. **Charles Reznikoff** (editor)
    LOUIS MARSHALL (2 Volumes)
12. **Alexandra Lee Levin**
    THE SZOLDS OF LOMBARD STREET
13. **Selig Adler and Thomas E. Connolly**
    FROM ARARAT TO SUBURBIA
14. **Harry L. Lurie**
    A HERITAGE AFFIRMED
15. **Moshe Davis**
    THE EMERGENCE OF CONSERVATIVE JUDAISM
16. **Louis J. Swichkow and Lloyd P. Gartner**
    THE HISTORY OF THE JEWS OF MILWAUKEE